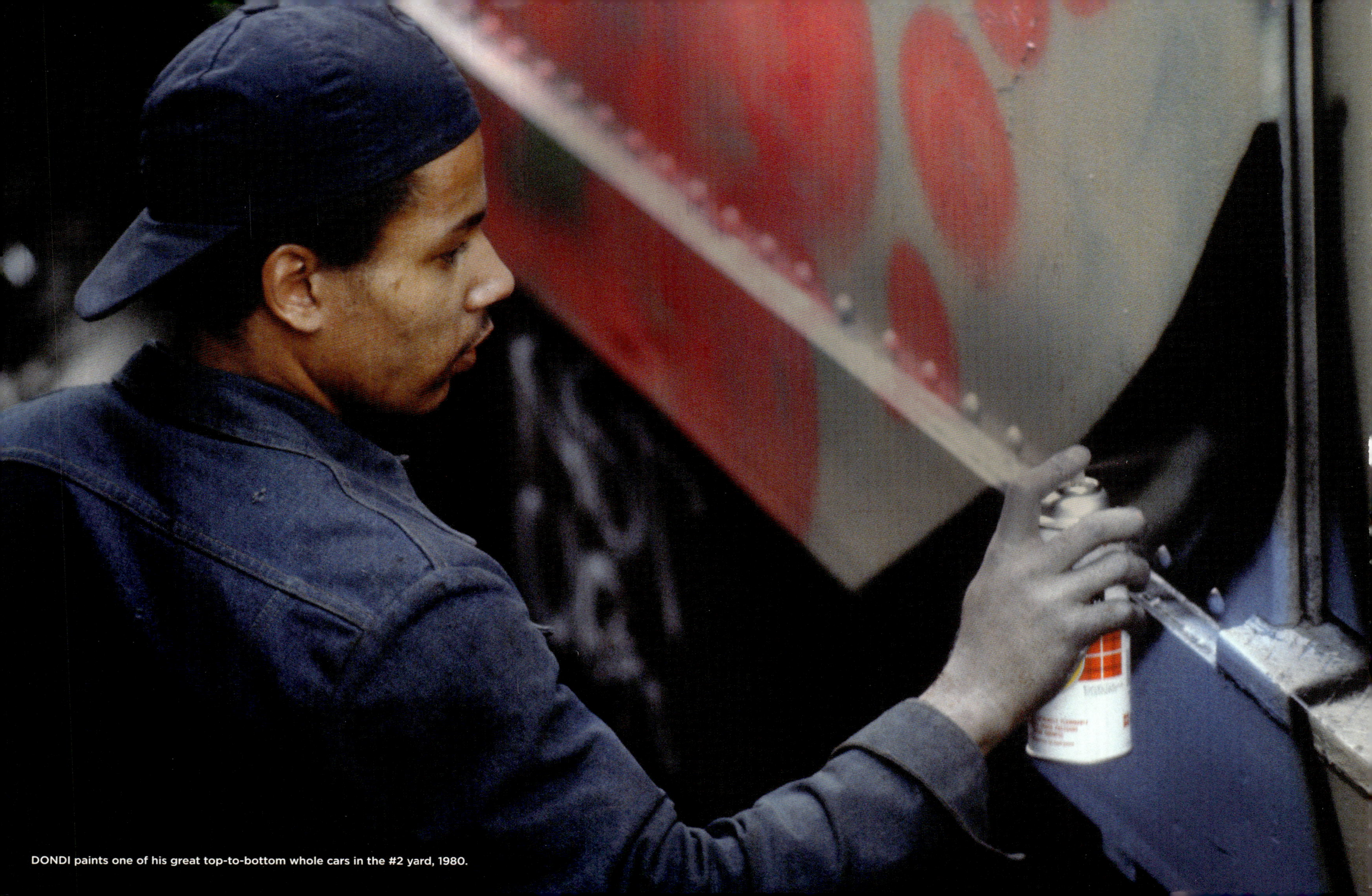

DONDI paints one of his great top-to-bottom whole cars in the #2 yard, 1980.

SPRAY NATION

1980s NYC GRAFFITI PHOTOGRAPHS

MARTHA COOPER

Prestel
Munich · London · New York

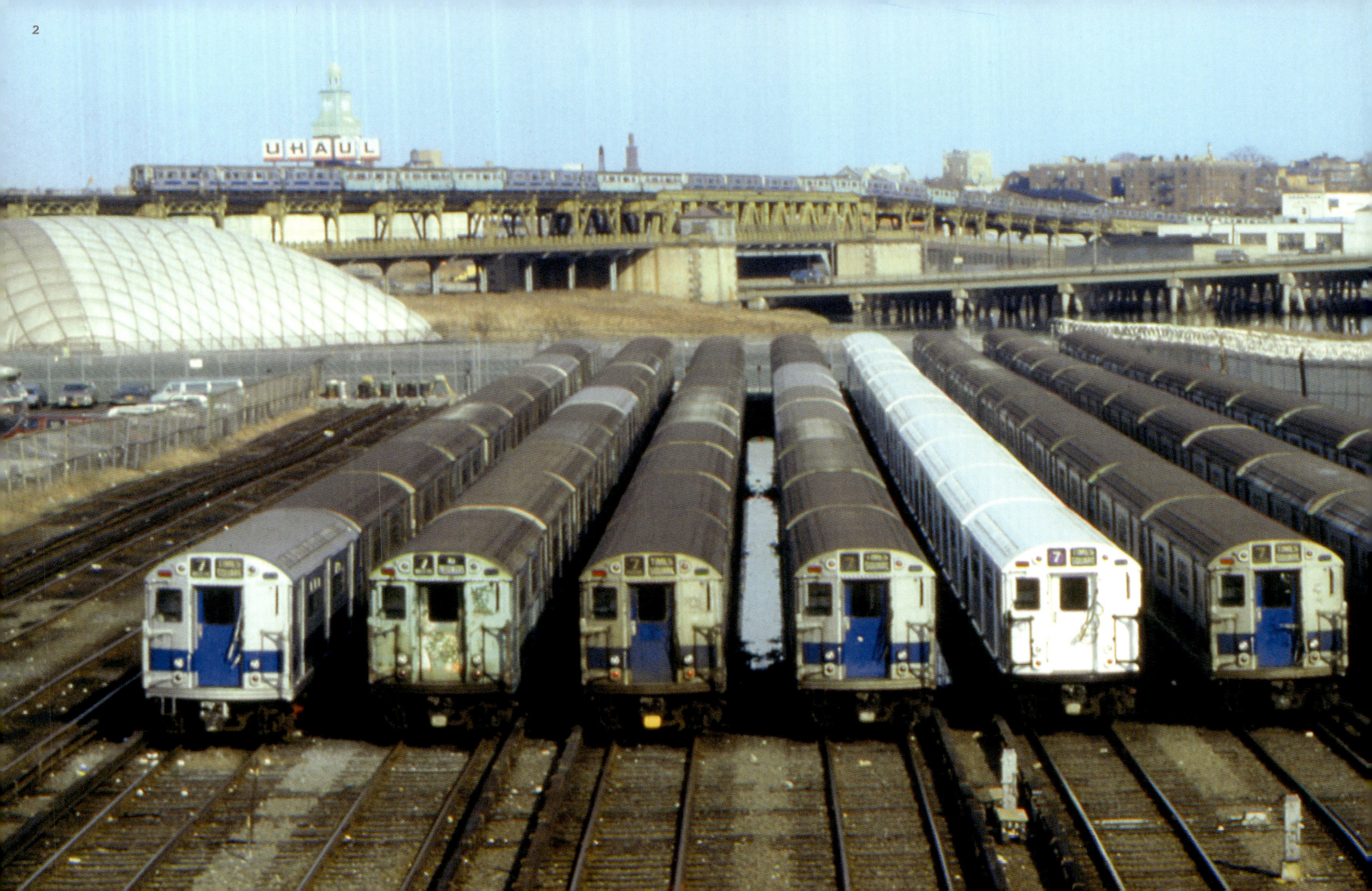
U-HAUL
7
7
7
7
7
7

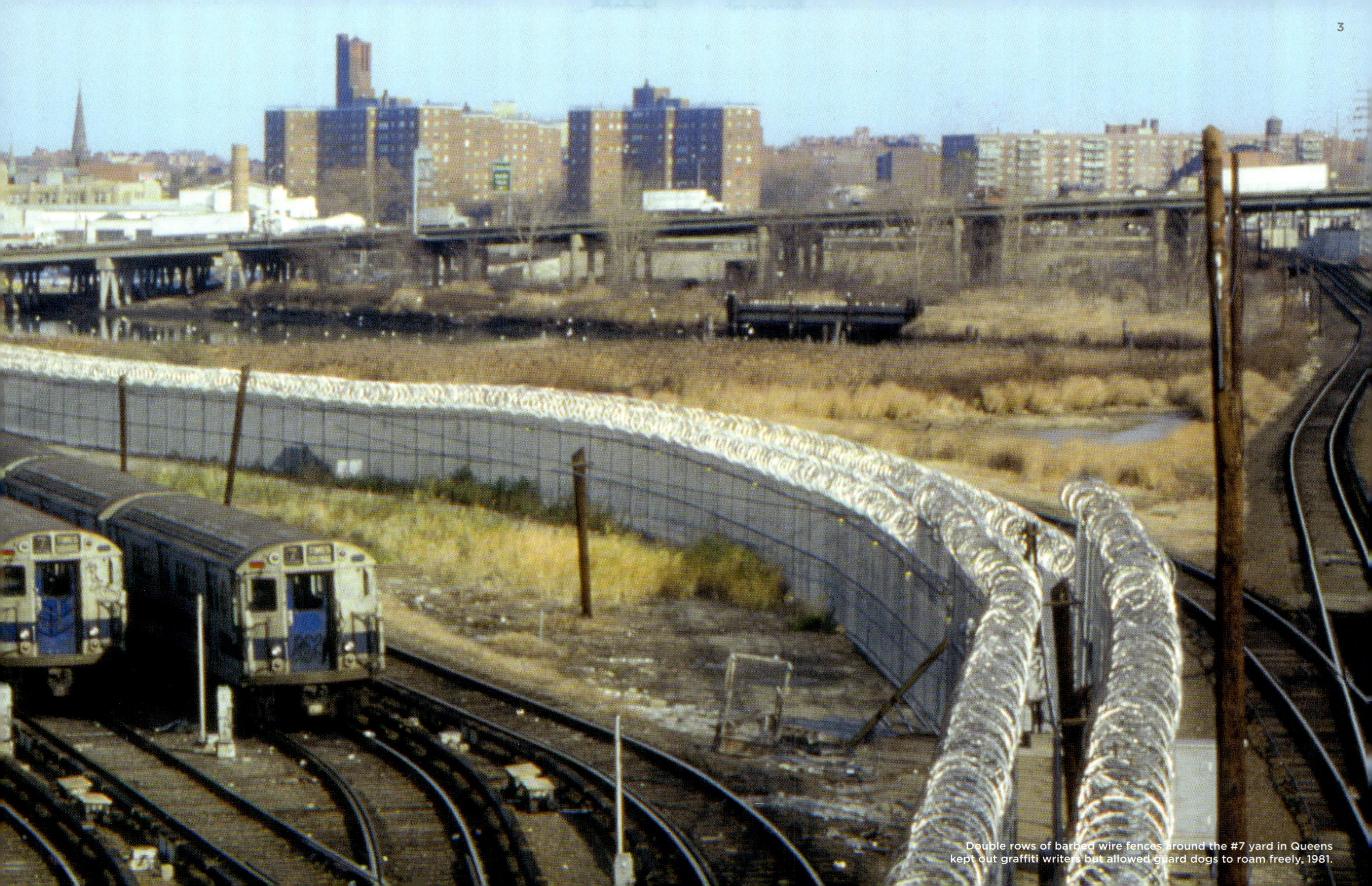
Double rows of barbed wire fences around the #7 yard in Queens kept out graffiti writers but allowed guard dogs to roam freely, 1981.

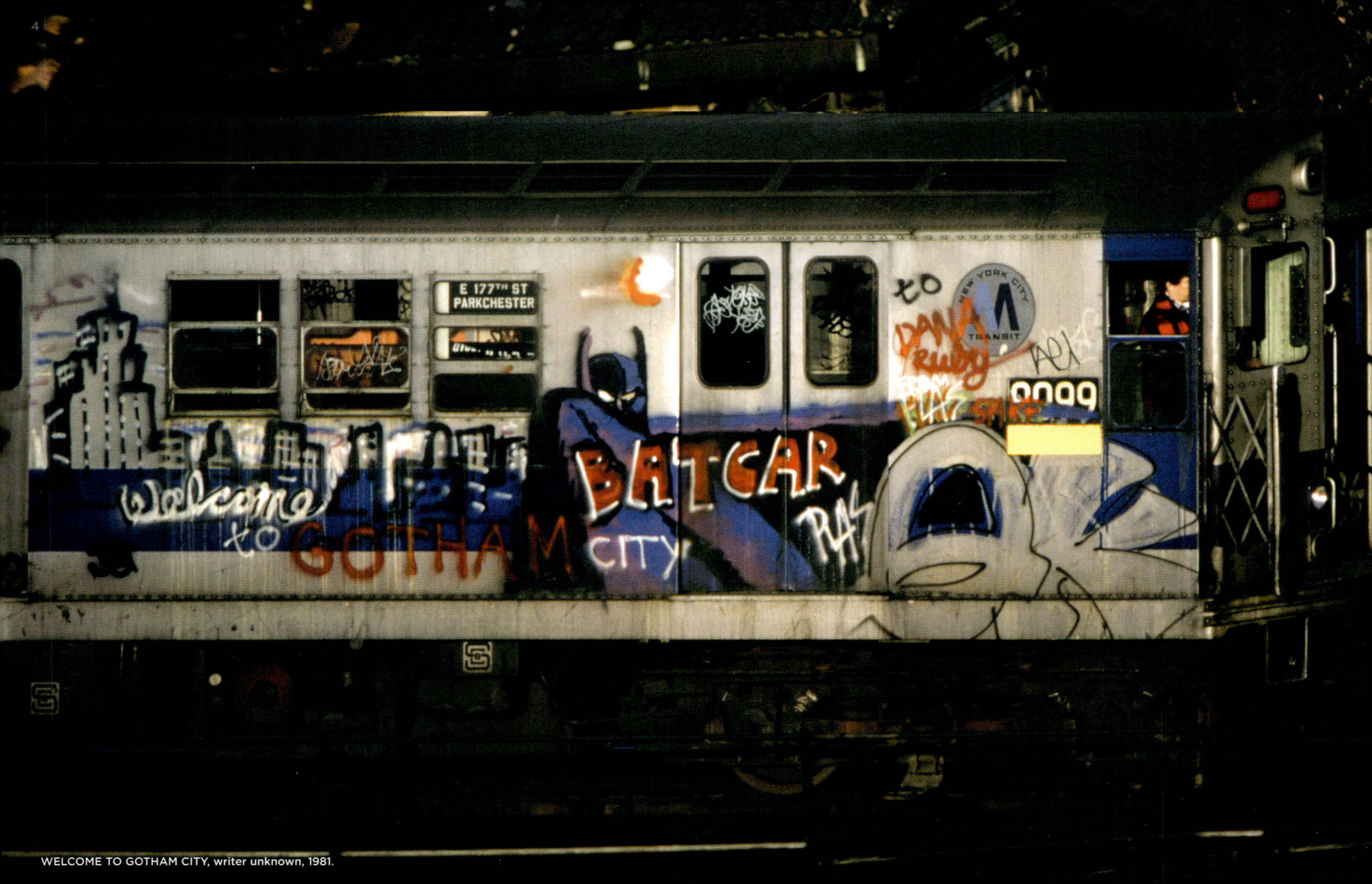

WELCOME TO GOTHAM CITY, writer unknown, 1981.

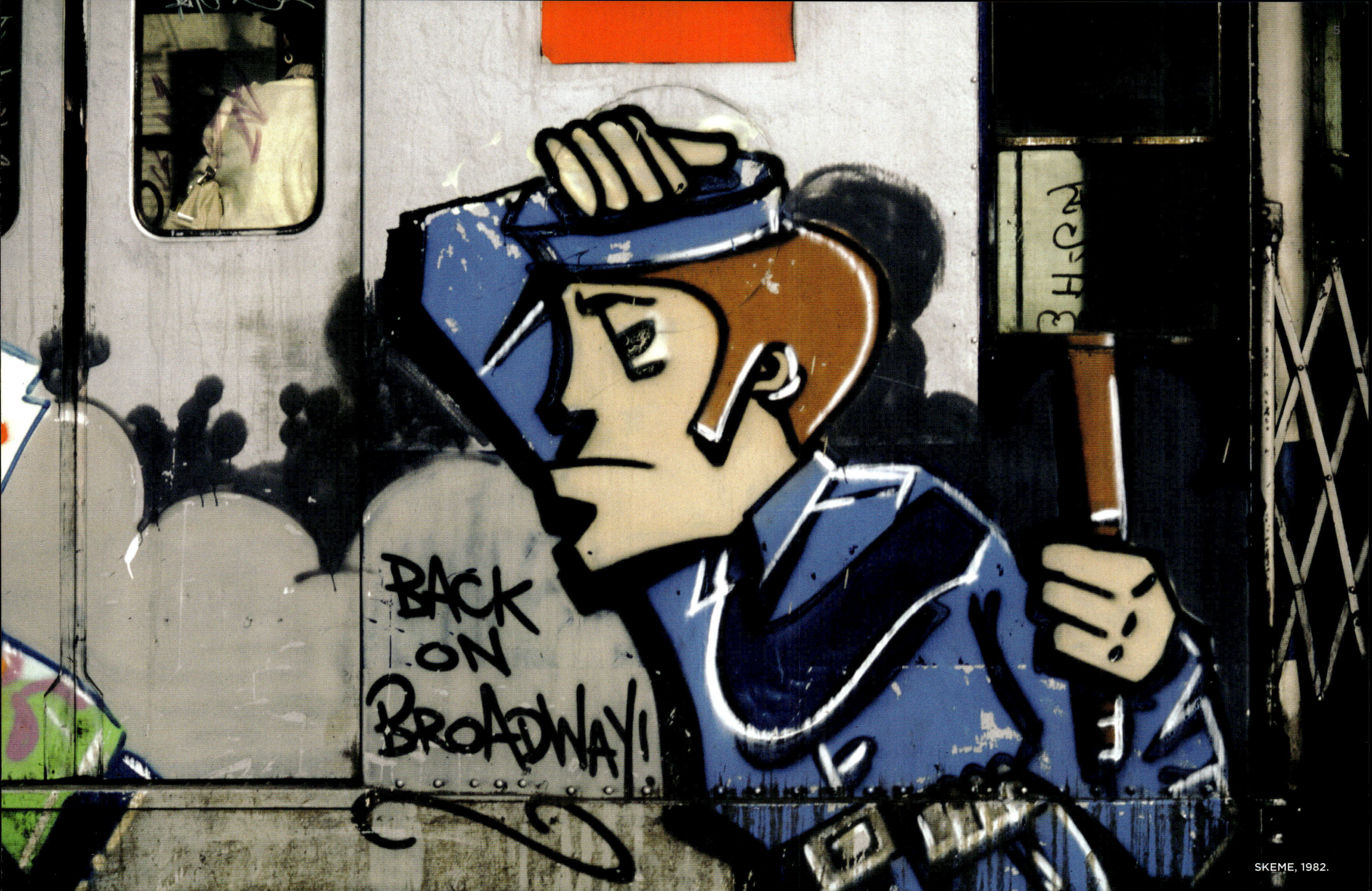

SKEME, 1982.

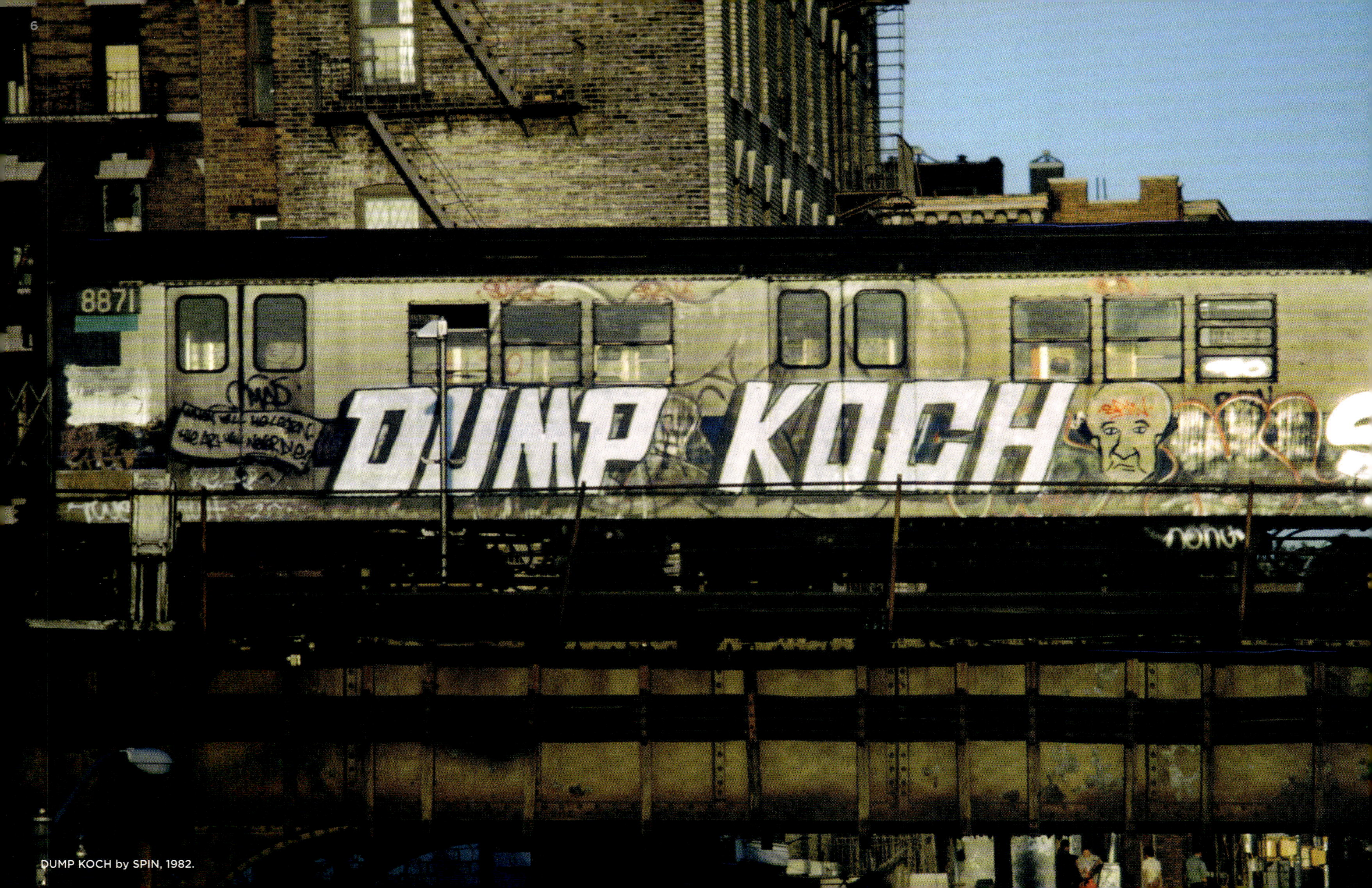

DUMP KOCH by SPIN, 1982.

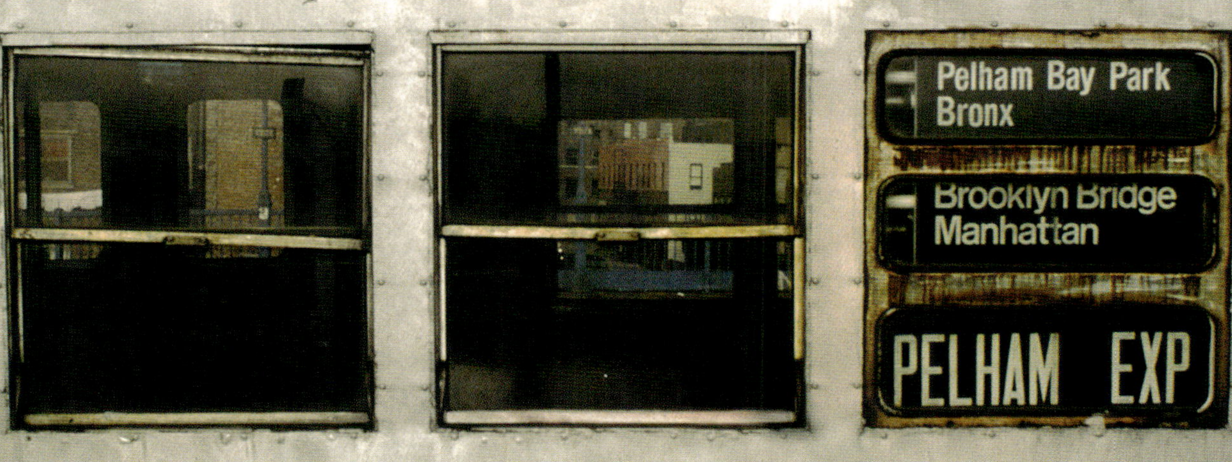

1,000 CANS REWARD for New York City mayor Ed Koch, 1982.

TABLE OF CONTENTS

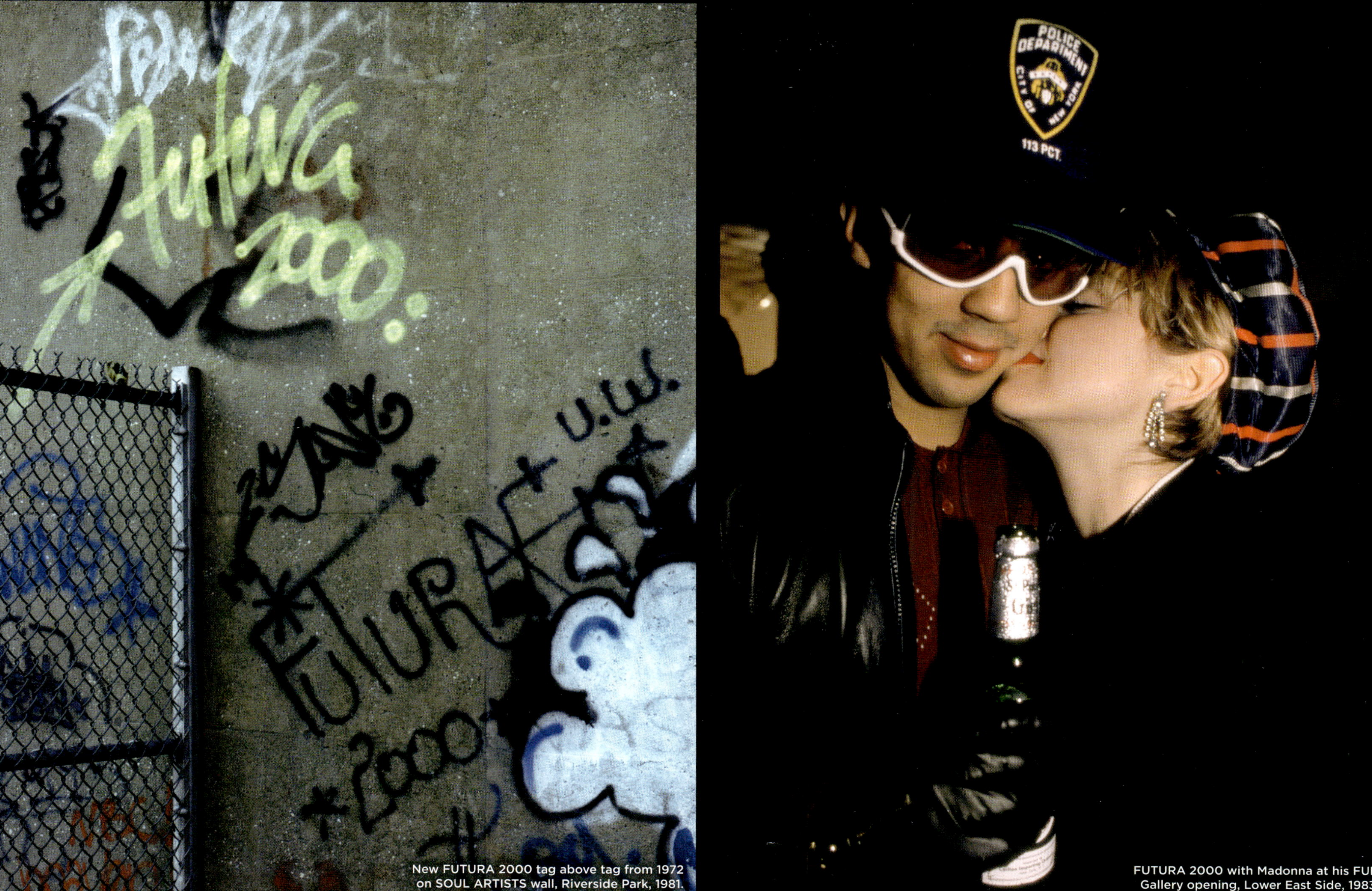

New FUTURA 2000 tag above tag from 1972
on SOUL ARTISTS wall, Riverside Park, 1981.

FUTURA 2000 with Madonna at his FUN
Gallery opening, Lower East Side, 1983.

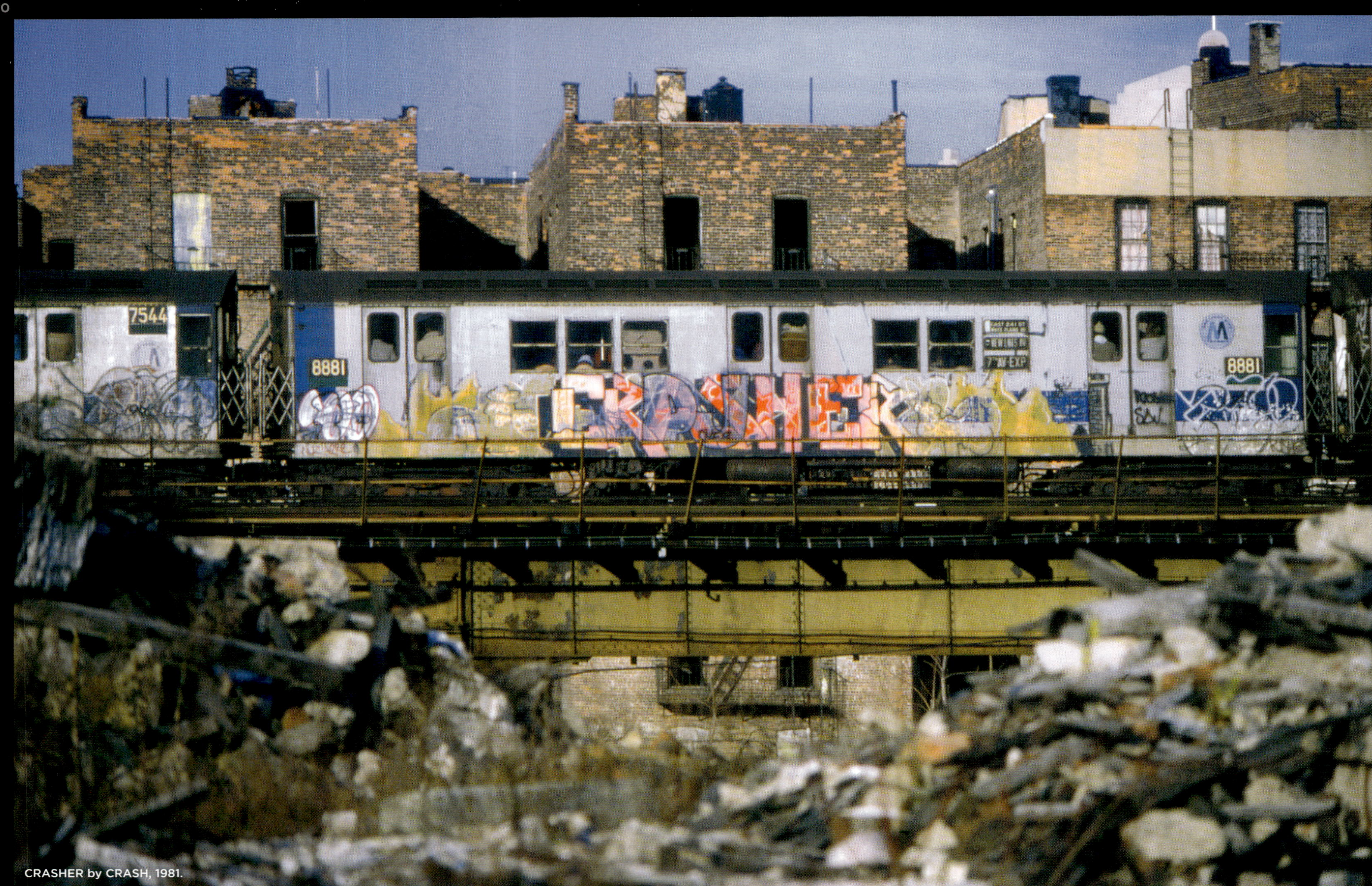

CRASHER by CRASH, 1981.

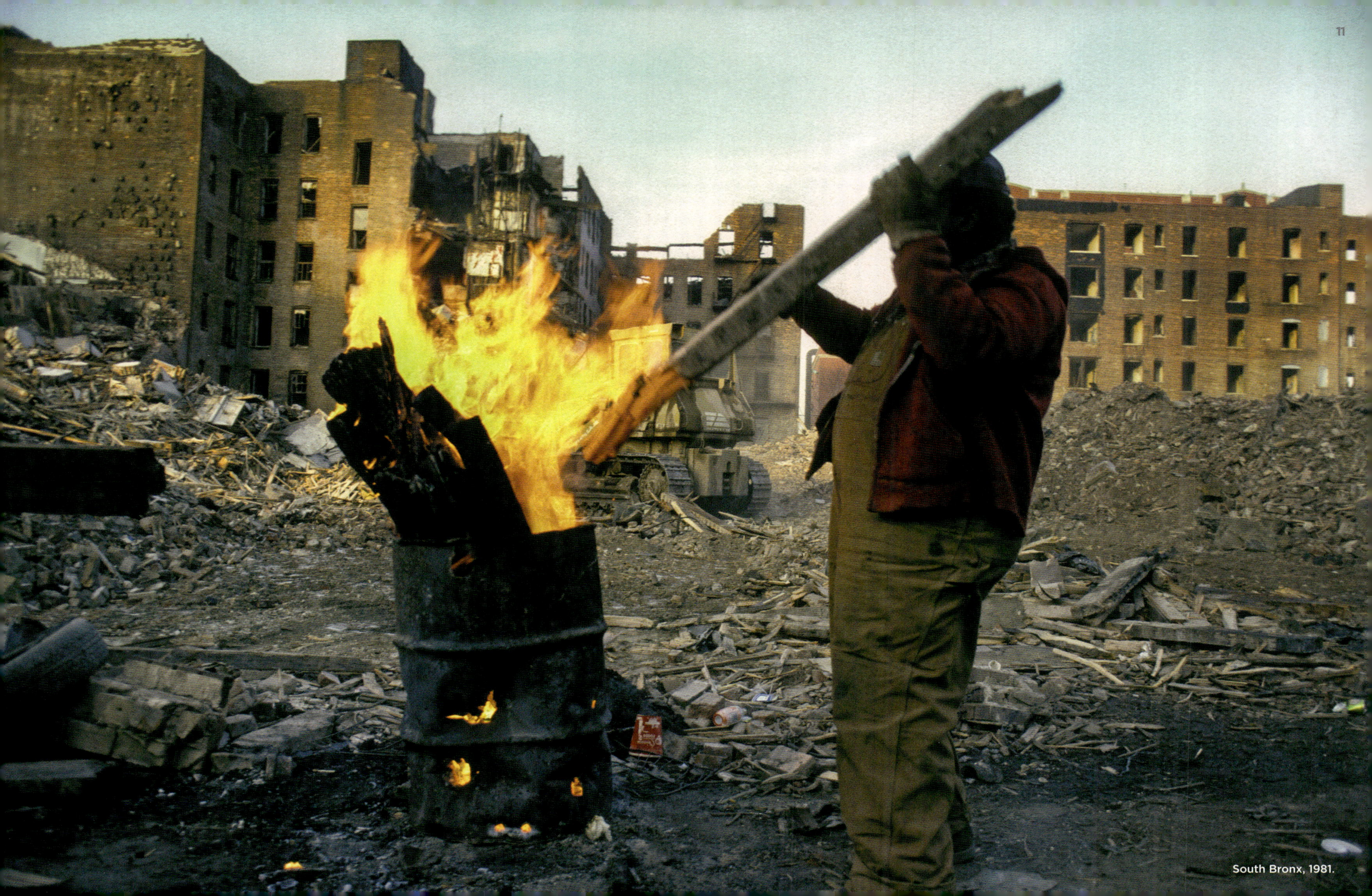

South Bronx, 1981.

FOREWORD

Roger Gastman

'90s, how I got into graffiti and found the book *Subway Art,* which impacted not only me but pretty much every graffiti writer ever. You can read about that later in the book. I don't need to tell you the history of Martha Cooper, how amazing she is and all of her traits and quirks. As I just said, you can read about that later on. What I do want to tell you about is how this book came to be — because everything needs an origin story.

Martha's photos have backed up graffiti writers' tall tales more times than I can count. They're like this crazy high school yearbook. As a result, Cooper is who every graffiti writer, fan, collector and researcher wants to come and see. Most of them have not had the privilege of going to her studio and seeing the great amount of work she has amassed over the years — it's truly awe inspiring. But every so often she pulls out yet another gem where we all scratch our heads and think, "Oh shit, what else is Martha holding?"

I was at her studio one evening in 2018 with my girlfriend Amanda and we were having a casual conversation about who knows what when I asked Martha if she had thought about doing one final graffiti-outtakes book of her early-'80s work. While she loves that body of work, she was both content with what was already out there and was — and still is — traveling the world shooting new photographs. It wasn't a long conversation, but there was an important takeaway: "yes," she had thought about it, but she wanted to know who was going to take the time and spend the energy going through thousands of slides, scanning, ID'ing, designing and all of the other things that go into making a book?

Of course I replied, "I'll do it." I knew her body of work, the context of the photos and was no stranger to packaging book projects. That very night Amanda and I began editing through her photos and stayed long after she went to sleep. We kept at it for a few days — including diving into the boxes of discarded shots she had not looked at since she first took them.

I thought I'd be able to fast-track the project and have it ready for several planned events in 2019. That didn't happen, but the project is better because of the extra time we spent on it. We've wrestled with many formats and even started over completely. In the end, there are hundreds of incredible photos — most that are being seen for the first time.

By no means do I think that this project is the last involving Martha's archives. Her files are just that deep. Just like a graffiti writer has his/her version of events, this is sorta like mine; a very specific vision of how I saw '80s graffiti through Martha Cooper's lens.

I'm happy this project was not always smooth. Martha and I set out to make a very particular book and then we decided to do something completely different. People toss around the word "collaboration" a lot. In this case, its usage is appropriate. I gave, Martha gave, and together we made something I'm very proud of.

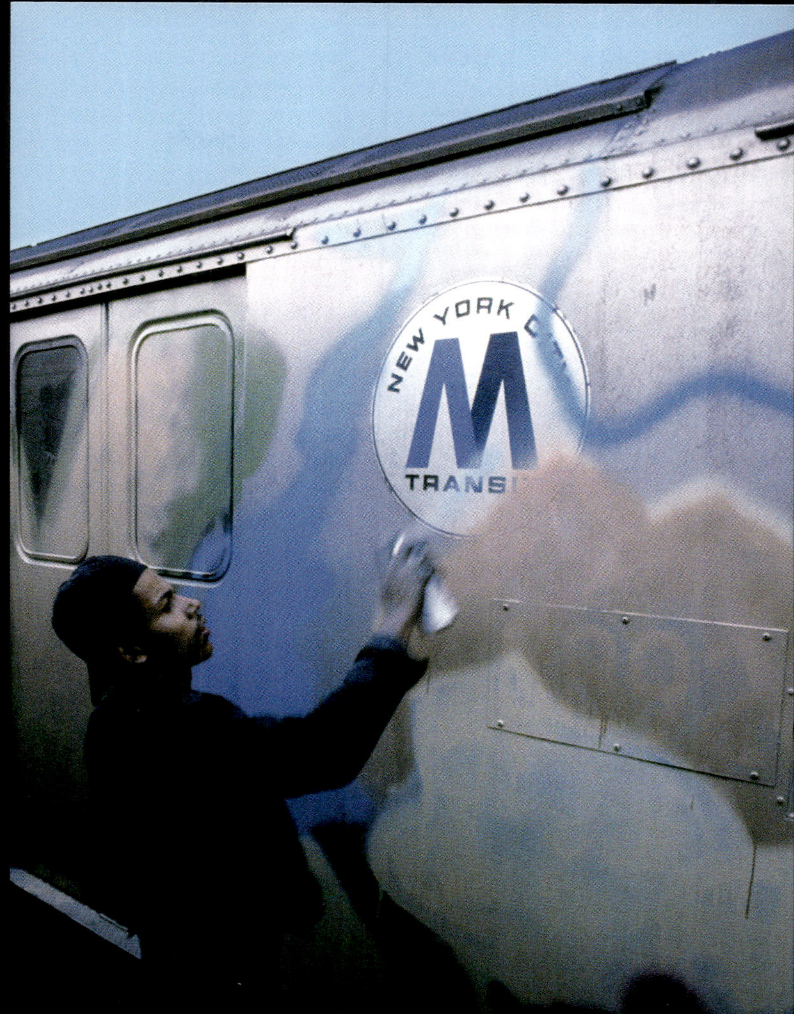

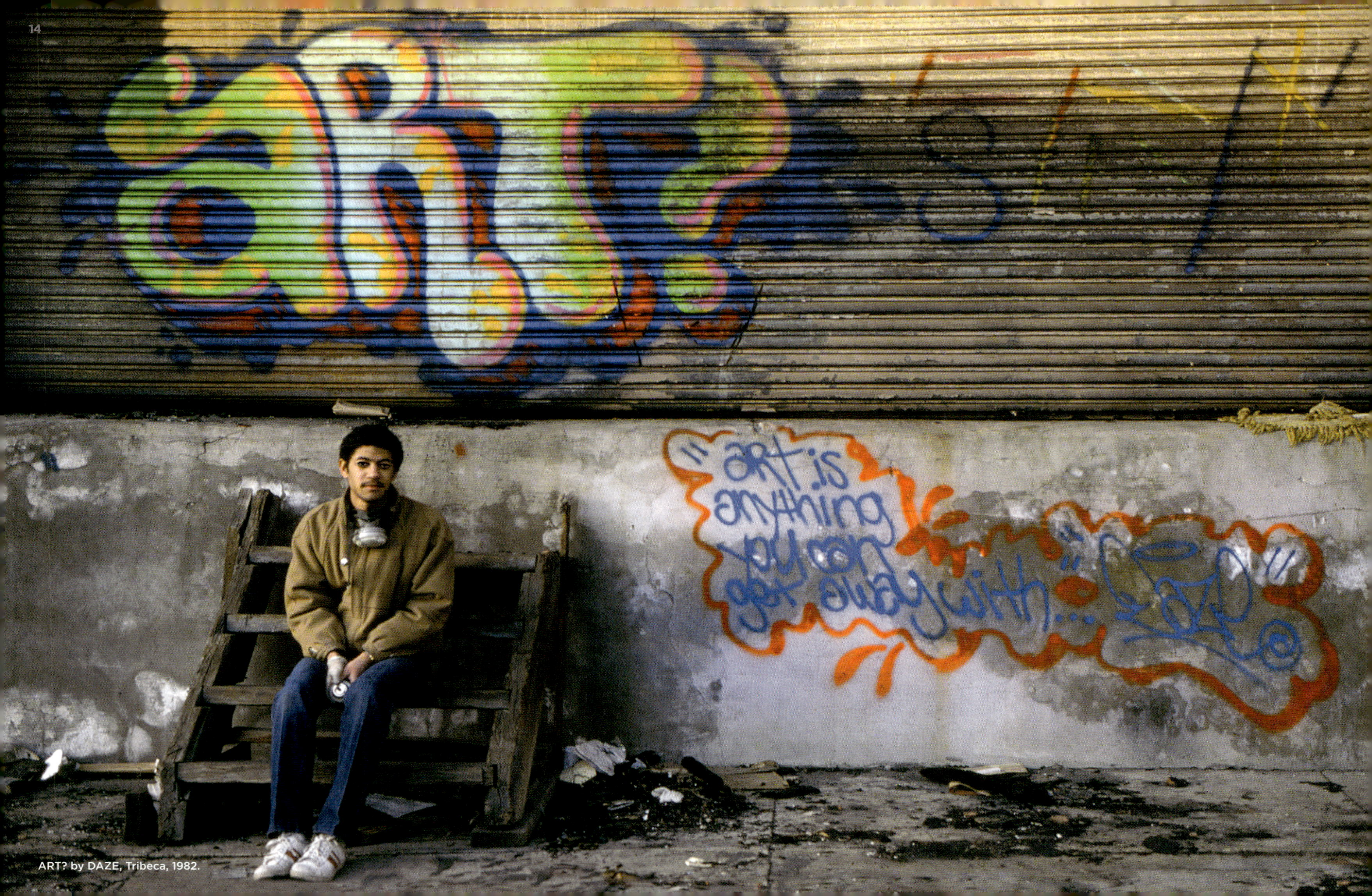

ART? by DAZE, Tribeca, 1982.

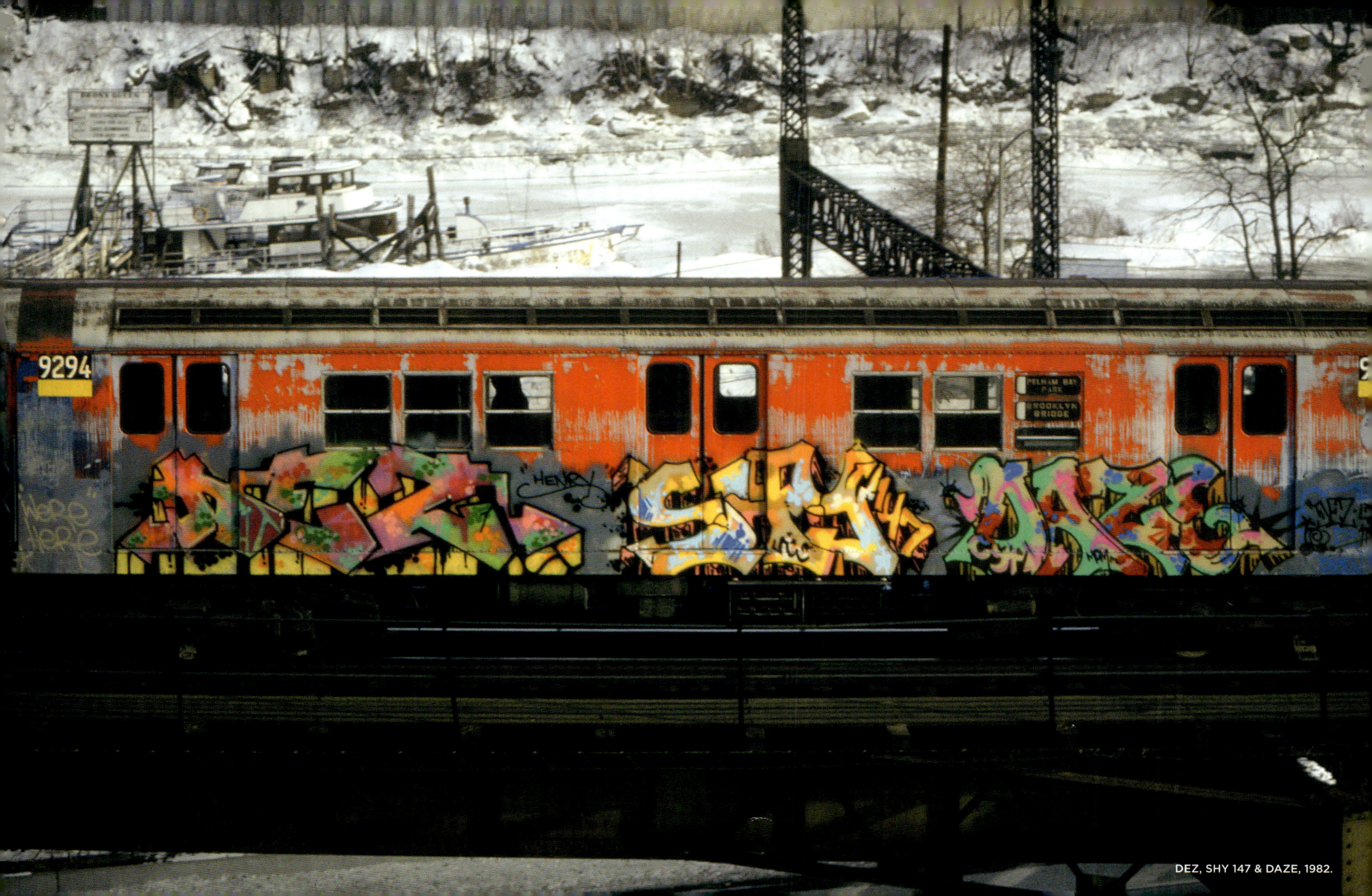

DEZ, SHY 147 & DAZE, 1982.

WHO
IS
MARTHA
COOPER?

Steven P. Harrington

"**I** always tried to give back pictures," Martha Cooper says about her days shooting graffiti writers on trains in New York's harrowing 1970s and 1980s. But she might as well be talking about her whole life.

Back then, few kids on NYC streets had access to a camera, and if they did it was usually a disposable one that produced blurry, poorly lit results, even in talented hands. The child of a Baltimore camera shop owner, Martha had been shooting with proper equipment for 30 years. When she met up with writers in abandoned lots or dicey train yards, they knew that she had the skills, but more importantly she had the curiosity, the reporter's instinct and the resolute disposition to push through a freshly cut hole in a rusty fence when necessary to get pictures of their pieces to give to them.

Decades later, in another economically bombed-out U.S. neighborhood, this one called Sowebo in Baltimore, Martha again made it her business to make friends first and broaden her circle through photography. In the more than 200 trips she made over 10 years from her home in Manhattan via the 3-hour bargain bus to "Charm City," she never showed up empty-handed.

She found a photo lab where she could buy 4-by-6-inch prints by the thousands, and she was determined to bring those birthdays, barbecues, parades, block parties, stoop-front stories and children's sidewalk games back to the people who were in them. She walked through potholed streets of boarded-up buildings and scattered crack vials with a sixth sense and camera in hand, ready for a reunion with a mother or an uncle who would call out to her, "Hey Picture Lady!"

Rifling quickly through envelopes that she'd prepared and labeled ahead of time, she would match the families with the photos, recalling names and relationships and stories told the last time she was there for a special occasion or just an everyday one. Actually somewhat shy, the photographer behind the lens found a conduit for a connection that brought special attention and preserved memories for a community.

This Baltimore adventure was just one of her many personal projects, "a self-given grant" as she puts it, combining her ▶

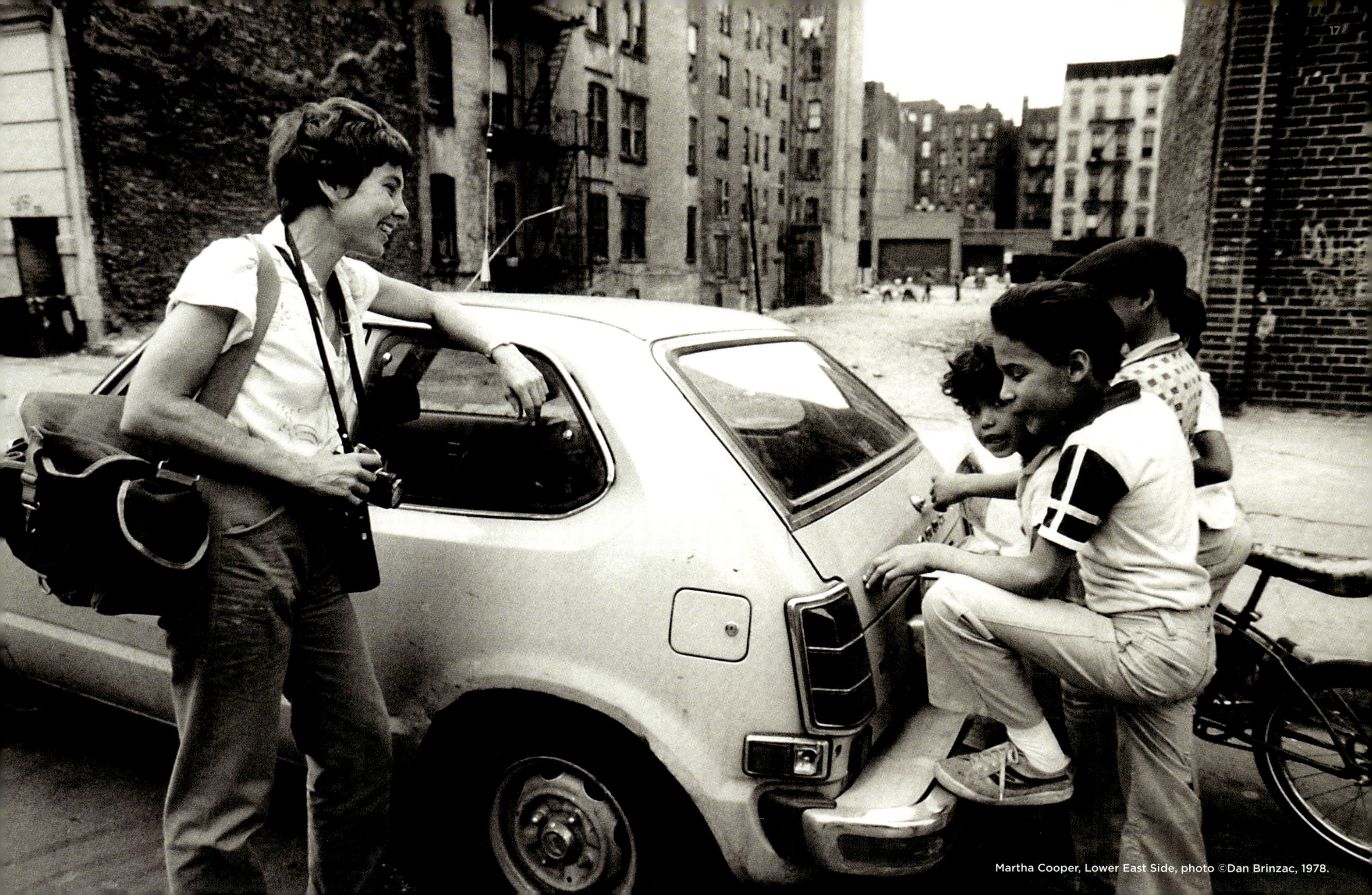

Martha Cooper, Lower East Side, photo ©Dan Brinzac, 1978.

interests in art and ethnography — always hoping to stumble upon an unknown treasure. With persistence as her motto, this is the Martha (Marty to her friends) you get to know just by being in her orbit through the years.

Some of those early graffiti writers may have thought she needed their permission as a woman to scale trains and jump the third rail. However, any permission or confidence that she may have needed to explore had already been given to her by her father when he took her out on "camera runs" as a girl in their hometown, both capturing city scenes and appreciating the historical and modern architecture of the built environment. Even then he must have seen the glint of excitement in her eyes when on an adventure. Without question the self-confident woman we know today is in no small way the product of that attentive education and the encouragement she received at home from both her father and her mother, who taught high school English and journalism. Indeed, their daughter graduated from high school early and received a degree in art from Grinnell College ahead of schedule.

Courage was already encoded in Martha's character by the time she ventured into the train yards to capture nighttime scenes of aerosol virtuosity. After teaching English with Kennedy's newly created Peace Corps in the early 1960s in Thailand, she had driven her motorcycle from Bangkok to England via Afghanistan, Iran, Russia and Europe. She'd received a graduate degree in ethnology from Oxford, worked at the Smithsonian and Yale University and interned at *National Geographic*. She wound up in 1977 with a gig as the first female photojournalist at the *New York Post* — by no means the last trail she would blaze.

A MATTER OF TIMING

"If you want to publish your work, you cannot be ahead of or behind your time," she says as she reflects on an impeccable sense for capturing the birth of scenes like graffiti, hip-hop and b-boying. "I was lucky to be at the right place and time." It is a modest statement that belies the hundreds of hours of waiting in empty lots for fresh graffiti pieces along the 1 and 2 train lines and the daily zigzagging through New York's decimated Lower East Side looking for pictures while on her job at the

New York Post. Back then she was looking for street scenes that interested her, not just her employer, to finish off her film rolls before taking them in to be developed.

Martha is heralded today for capturing those trains and scenes along with Henry Chalfant in the seminal graffiti holy book *Subway Art*, but few appreciate how painfully ahead of their time they really were at that point, unable to find a single publisher among over 50 they'd contacted who would agree to bring their work to a broader audience. After they did finally manage to publish, sales were lackluster. Shops kept the book in locked cases to prevent it from getting stolen, and school librarians hid it behind the counter, afraid to encourage an illegal activity.

"There were 20 years where almost nothing happened for me," she says of the book. It wasn't until she traveled to Europe for a promotional tour for her book *Hip Hop Files* in the 2000s that she realized that graffiti had taken root throughout the world, and *Subway Art* was highly revered. The fires of thousands of imaginations had been lit by the photos of New York train writers, and she was unaware of it.

Simultaneously, a nascent global street art scene with new aesthetics, different rules and wildly diverse participants had germinated and bloomed via the Internet on walls in the neglected margins of cities like New York, London, Paris, Barcelona, Berlin and, well, everywhere.

With renewed interest in graffiti and art in the streets in general, Ms. Cooper has been lifted and carried around the world again, traveling to multiple cities around the globe annually to street art festivals, exhibitions, museum openings, graffiti jams and a variety of academic symposia. You can walk alongside her on the streets through any of these cities, as I have many times, and you'll find awestruck fans in their teens or their 50s who walk up to her and tell her a personal story about the significant impact of *Subway Art* on their development as an artist.

They may ask for an autograph or a selfie, but the more pertinent exchange is the sincere thanks that they offer. Unendingly gracious in these instances, Martha flashes her megawatt effervescent smile, says thank you and invariably asks them about themselves or their art. There is a genuine sense of gratitude for the exchange, possibly because for many years she felt her own work had not made a meaningful impact despite all of her efforts, and now she never takes these compliments for granted.

A PROLIFIC COMPETITOR

By the way, if you are going to hang with Martha Cooper, be prepared to run.

An aesthetic urban-culture omnivore with a voracious appetite, Martha has an acute sense for things that are happening or are about to happen. And she is going to be there whether you keep pace with her or not.

First.

Many times I've been walking with her on the street and she is just ahead of me. I speed up to tell her something and out of the corner of her eye she sees me and moves just a little faster to stay ahead. It's a natural response honed from years of being a reporter, ready to catch the story before the competition, willing to sacrifice personal comfort to get it.

I've seen her hobbled by a twisted muscle in her back while walking up Broadway (probably from lugging two cameras and multiple lenses around everywhere). With little ceremony, she places her backpack on the sidewalk, and I watch her jerk her back in two or three directions with the force of a welterweight to straighten herself out. No trips to the masseuse for Ms. Cooper.

Similarly, she will refuse your offer of water on the mind-warpingly hottest day, or hot cocoa on the bitterest one, if she's tracking an artist who is painting a wall. Consuming liquids might prompt a trip to the restroom, and she might miss a critical moment. It may be learned behavior by a photographer who waited hours outside of courthouses for a verdict — or one who waited five hours in an empty Bronx lot for a top-to-bottom whole car on the number 2 train. Don't let the call of nature make you miss the story. As her dear friend Susan Welchman — who edited her photos at the *Post* and whom Martha helped get a job as photo editor at *National Geographic* — would tell you, if you want to be

a successful photographer, the shot must be your top priority. Martha embodies this credo.

Aside from her more famous projects, she has published a number of books on other areas that interest her, a long list that includes: Japanese paper making (her first book ever); a traditional Japanese tattoo practice called *irezumi*; the burgeoning global b-girl movement in the early 2000s (with photographer Nika Kramer); a sister-city examination of the street-cultural similarities between Sowebo in Baltimore and Soweto in South Africa; handmade postal-sticker art; New York's 9/11 memorials; and the significance of memorial murals to urban communities, with folklorist Joseph Sciorra.

She also has many photo archives loaned as a repository to City Lore, a nonprofit arts organization dedicated to New York City's vibrant ethnic cultures. A recent Martha Cooper exhibition featured photos of Brooklyn's rich Italian American traditions. For every book published, there are probably one or two potential ones on a shelf, wholly conceptualized, neatly collated and laid out in detail from start to finish.

PERSONAL PHILOSOPHY

Every experience, good and bad, has led her to this point in her life and career, and she trusts the wisdom of this stepping-stone approach. Case in point: On a vacation trip to Haiti in 1978, she saw children making their own toys from recycled materials on the street. It was that discovery that made her see New York's Lower East Side through this lens and led her to Edwin, the boy who wrote HE3 in his piece book and on the wall. It was a conversation with him that led her to drive out to Brooklyn to meet "the King," DONDI. It was meeting DONDI that led her to snap photos of trains and to discover the entire global graffiti community. These interconnections repeat throughout her life, and if she likes the work you are doing, she is likely to help connect you with someone or something else, because she quite naturally shares in that way.▶

WHO IS MARTHA?

In the applied sciences, the formula used to arrive at a result is as important as the outcome itself. When calculating the question of who a person is, one should consider their environment, their innate qualities and aspirations, their collected experiences, the tools available to them, the social, political and economic dynamics at play and the evolutionary effect of their life path on their core personality.

This is an inexact science, but as prone to error as my assessments have at times proven when applying this complex formulation for taking the measure of a person, I'm confident when I offer this: Martha is a brave, fearless, rebellious fighter who questions authority, dares you to prove your hypothesis, has a higher threshold for risk and discomfort than 95 percent of people I've met and is fiercely committed to getting the right picture in its context.

She's an intellectually curious ethnographer, a student of people, culture, tools and techniques who would rather experience things than read a book about them, and preferably right now. She's a true feminist who prizes the contributions of her sisters at whatever their station, and she has used her talents, personal network and industry to open doors and provide a stage for them to succeed. She listens to your stories, and if you say you learned a lesson, she asks you what you learned. Martha is a doubtful optimist, a playful pragmatist and an occasionally adorable profane witticist who can laugh so hard she cries.

KID AT HEART

Martha loves kids, and she is a kid.

She is a childlike explorer, a player of games, a solver of puzzles, a competitive rival, a collector of points who will lord her winnings over you boastfully and who likes to end any outing with a visit to the ice cream shop, regardless of time or location. Among the objects she collects are children's hand-crafted toys. Games in general capture her imagination, and you are as likely to find her scanning the streets for graffiti tags as you are seeing her marching with her eyes glued to her phone hanging on a lanyard around her neck in hot pursuit of a Pokémon. The Pokémon GO app is perfect for her because it combines escapism, adventure, discovery and the urban environment. One valid reason she has offered for her to travel to Australia is that Kangaskhan is a Pokémon that you can only capture on that continent.

Along with her cousin Sally, a lifelong confidante and science teacher with a great sense of humor, Martha has climbed over hills and through wooded areas around the world in search of hidden Letterboxes. This multiplayer participatory outdoor game of art and sleuthing rewards you with individualized stamps and shared experiences entered in a journal.

Sally's laid-back personality pairs perfectly with the hard-driving Martha, and seven decades of friendship have molded their dynamic of traveling together. As Martha is invited throughout the world to graffiti jams and street art festivals, Sally often discovers a new city with her — getting up very early, immediately hitting the streets on foot, meeting with artists to appreciate aesthetics and technique. After Sally returns to her home in Maryland and Martha to Manhattan, they'll call each other on the phone to relate family matters or discuss the latest episode of *Shark Tank*.

THE HARDCORE ADVENTURER

"Mademoiselle, this is the last time I'm telling you," bellowed the flight attendant on an Air Tahiti flight from Raiatea to Bora Bora a couple of years ago. "Please remain seated!" Photographer Jaime Rojo laughs as he repeats this story about Martha discovering that the "good" shot out the window at the upcoming island was frustratingly located on the opposite side of the aisle from where she was sitting. The PA-system tongue lashing had come after the attendant had told her twice in person that she could not move from her seat during landing. For Martha, the word "forbidden" is only a suggestion, especially if it gets between her and a good shot.

Lest we overlook the obvious, Martha has also traveled underground and in the margins of major cities around the world, chasing the shot with graffiti writers and street artists — the surreptitious and illegal painting of trains and walls that are

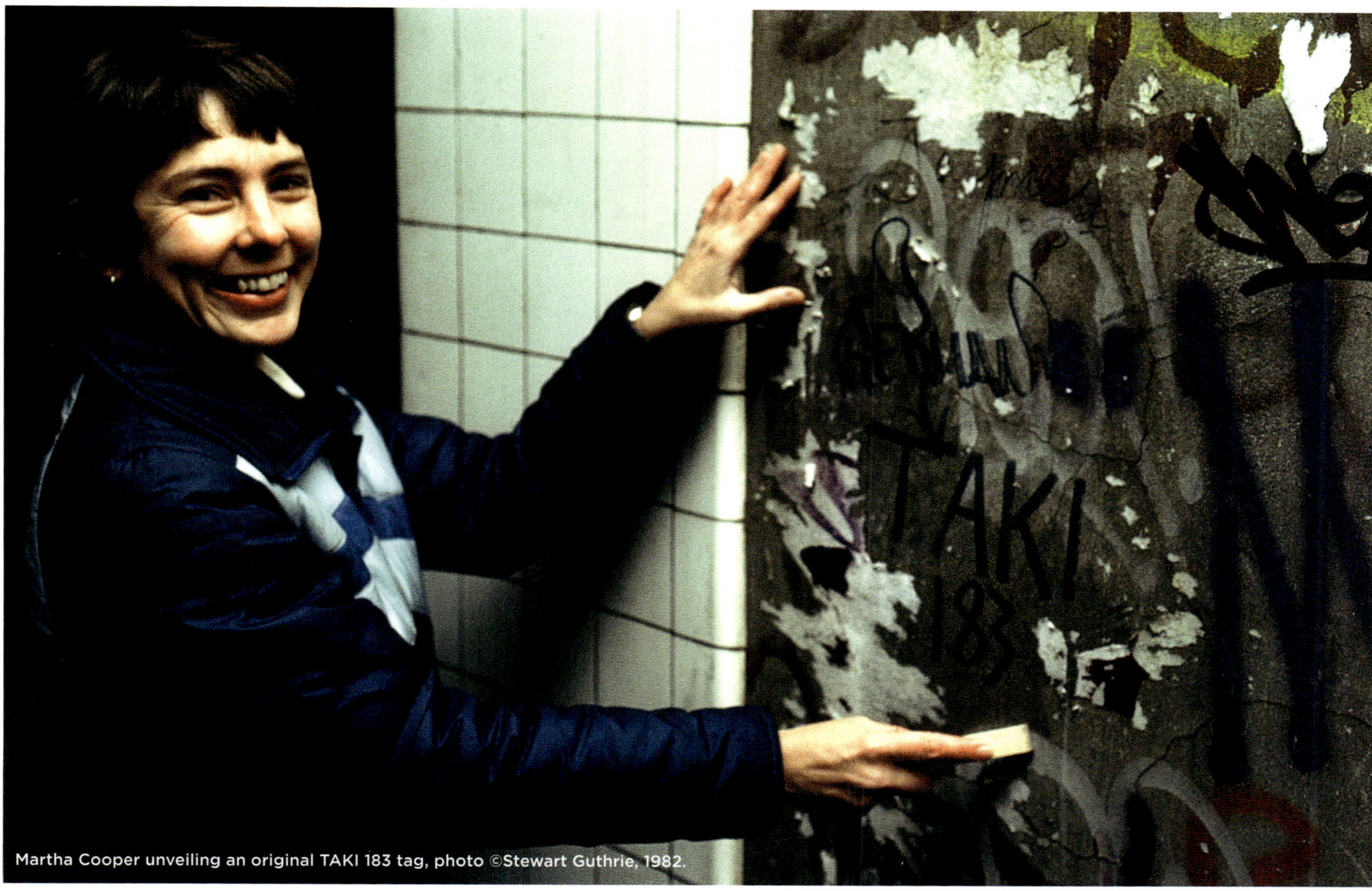

Martha Cooper unveiling an original TAKI 183 tag, photo ©Stewart Guthrie, 1982.

only gained access to via potholes, tunnels or holes in fences, through tall, overgrown brush or over intimidating, sometimes crumbling walls.

These are missions amid clouds of soot and aerosol and silent signaling in silhouette, carefully negotiating unpredictable terrain on foot, knees and bended back carrying heavy camera equipment. Sometimes a long night garners only a ripped pair of pants and a dusting of paint from head to foot. Other times it's a bruised leg, a bloodied hand or a pulled muscle in her

back from falling over an unseen obstacle or a sudden drop in the darkness while in a hurry.

Nothing fully describes the tenacity required and the electricity of raw fear that charges through the mind as one calculates the risk and payoff of following a crew of vandals who may exhibit various levels of regard for your work, your gender, your safety and your right to be there. A well-educated person with sincere curiosity, athletic comportment and a professional work ethic can make missions like these pay off academically, but only one ▶

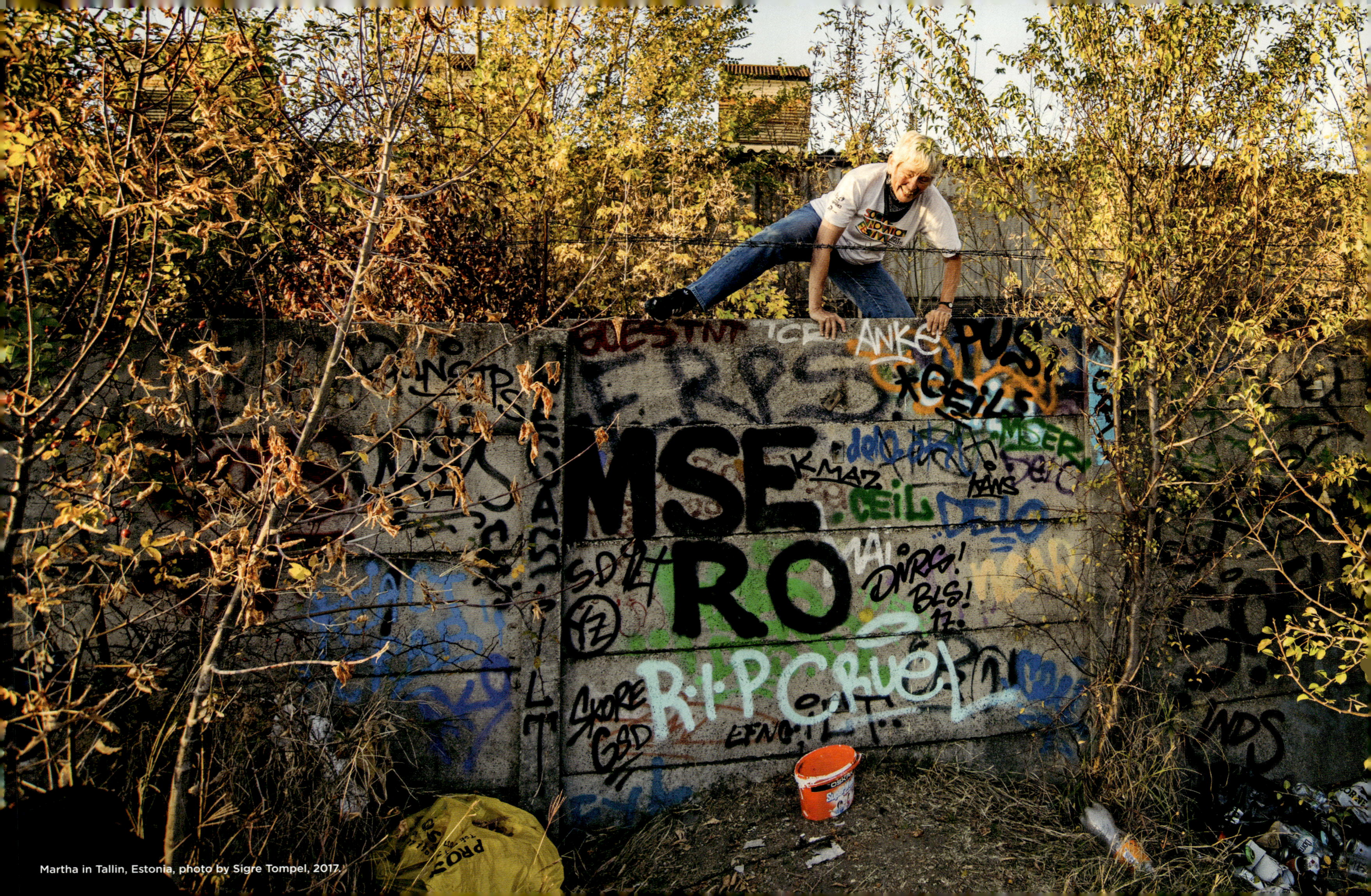

Martha in Tallin, Estonia, photo by Sigre Tompel, 2017.

with a studied diplomacy and teamlike disposition will earn respect from so many in the process.

Then again, this is a photographer who also traveled for days as the only woman with Surinamese ex-rebel leader Ronnie Brunswijk and his band of jungle commandos while on assignment with the German magazine *Geo* in the 1980s. In addition to hiking through rainforests and visiting the Saamaka Maroon village of Asindoopo, Martha brought back rolls of film and hand-carved calabash bowls in her backpack as physical evidence of her research into traditional artisan techniques and practices.

One great irony of her multiple photographic forays over seven decades is that much of this work and sacrifice has gone unrewarded or overlooked professionally. Regardless, Martha has persisted, because she sees her work as a form of historic preservation and feels that her photos will be more valuable in the future when the subject matter in them is no longer around.

BEYOND LUCK AND VISION

In the end, one should view this picture through a lens called context.

It is easy to frame the contribution of a photographer like Martha Cooper as that of a documentarian who was lucky at some juncture with her timing to capture important players and pieces in the birth of graffiti, the birth of b-boying and hip-hop culture and the emergence of street art as a global phenomenon.

But that analysis overlooks Martha's dogged determination to follow a lead and her eye for spotting subtle, innate qualities. It also entirely misses a sixth sense that can see the intrinsic value of a cultural contribution and a respect for the raw creative spirit at a time when something is being dismissed, derided, even demonized by the dominant culture. At the time she was recording these practices, being interested in graffiti and studying it with any seriousness meant following your instinct through a phalanx of social and political hostility, so unpopular had it become on news programs and in stump speeches. It was only her intuition and her intellectual curiosity that led

Martha to go there, because her employer and peers couldn't appreciate it, saw little value in it, perhaps even scolded her for it. But she persisted.

Martha could see something much greater happening, and it electrified her. She was fascinated by kids who were creating drawings in a piece book and translating them to entire subway cars; who fashioned art tools out of household items; who made toys out of other people's garbage. Her mind jumped with excitement when she discovered youth who created dance routines from athletic moves practiced on flattened cardboard boxes; who hand-made hundreds of stickers at a kitchen table; who composed spoken lyrics over prerecorded music on hand-engineered custom equipment. This ability to see something more led her to recognize the fundamental DNA of a culture while it was still coalescing as a subculture — and to document it.

The societal and legal debates about art, vandalism and criminality have necessarily followed this scene through its many decades, and Martha herself acknowledges the gray areas, choosing to be honest about conflicting perspectives. As regards the documentation of creative phenomena that went on to spawn a global grassroots art movement, she has no question. Hers is a curiosity born of academic knowledge of art history, a fundamental respect for creativity and the thrill of discovery that comes from experimentation and pure ingenuity.

I'm always listening to Martha to learn about what she finds next. Hopefully, she will show me the picture.

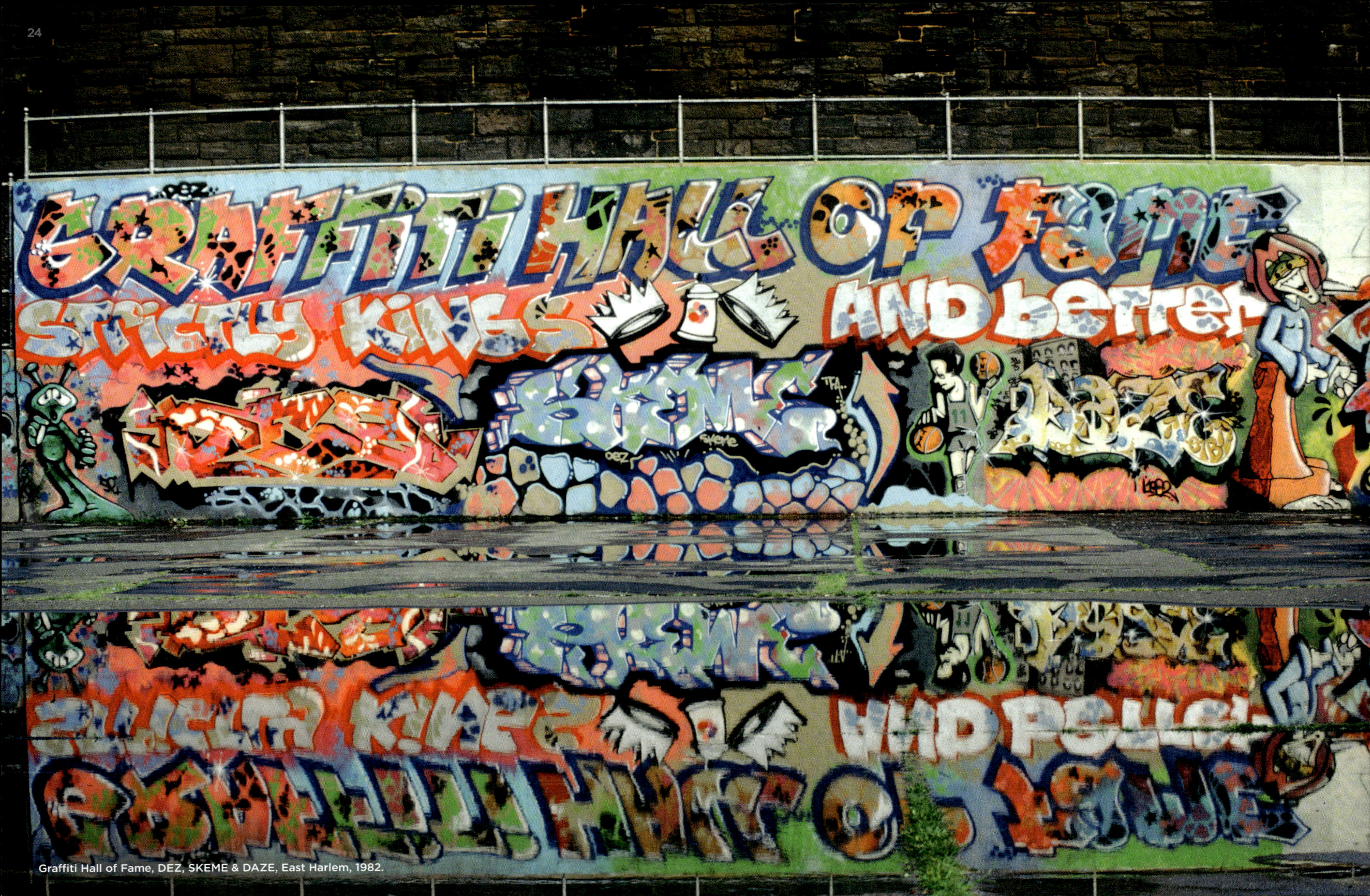

Graffiti Hall of Fame, DEZ, SKEME & DAZE, East Harlem, 1982.

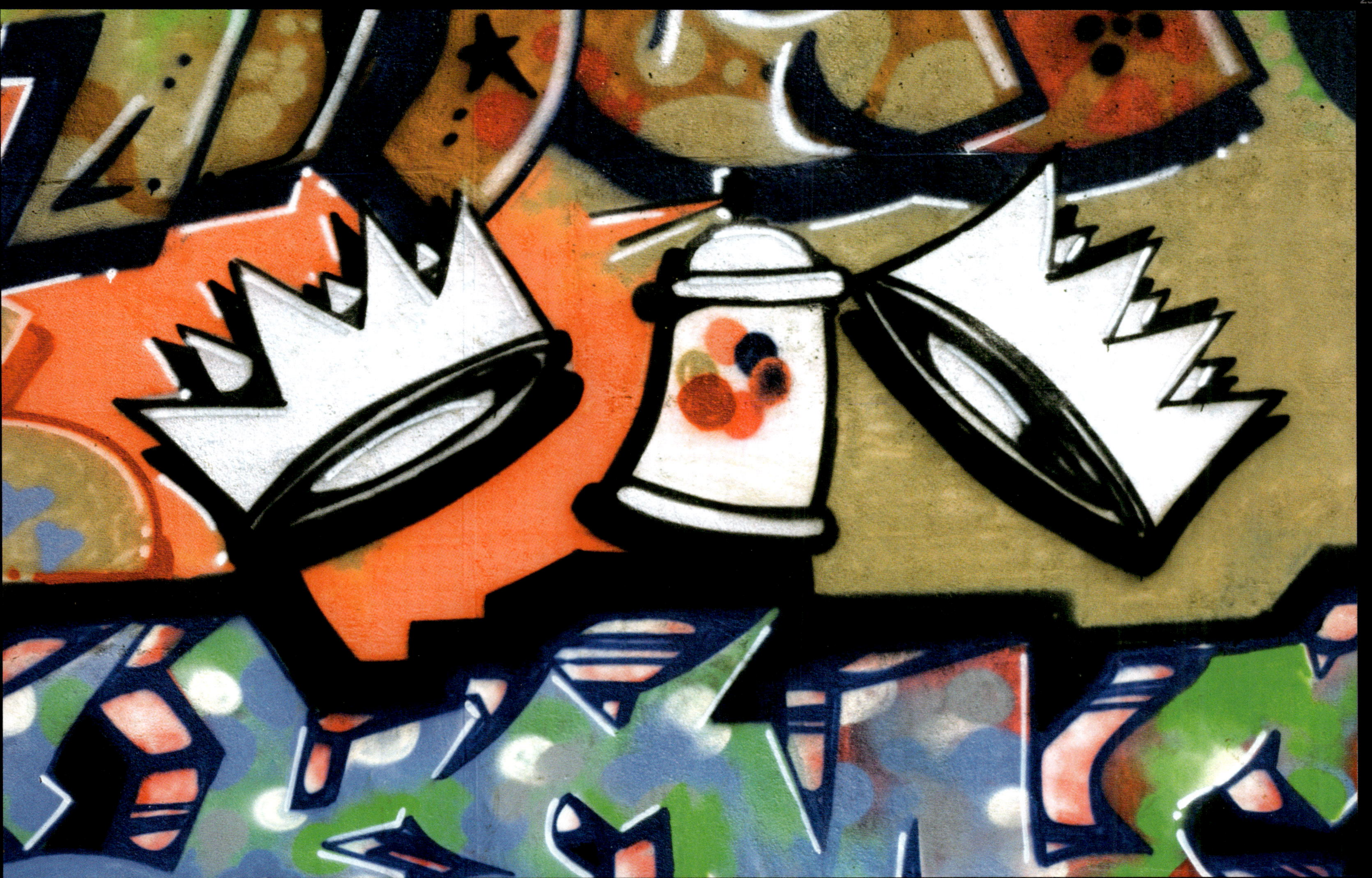

BETTER LIVING THROUGH GRAFFITI

Miss Rosen

With a single snap of the shutter, Martha Cooper captured the searing rush of seeing a whole car make its debut on the line after being painted all night. You can all but hear the train thunder along the tracks and feel the ground rumble beneath your feet while a gust of wind hits your face. Is that the smell of spray paint? In a Martha Cooper photograph, seeing is more than believing — it's a high you can't find anywhere else.

It's the kind of energy that just might change your life. Take it from Cooper, who knows better than anyone else. In 1980, she had been working as a staff photographer for the *New York Post* for three years, zipping around the city in a beat-up Honda Civic. She had been hearing about new trains being painted up in the Bronx — but she had to go to work.

"I said, 'Fuck it, I just want to do this,'" she recalls. "I picked a very good time to quit the *Post*." With her newfound freedom, Cooper became an integral figure on the burgeoning graffiti scene, her passion for her subjects matched by her boundless energy, which continues to this very day after more than 70 years of making photographs.

Standing inside her New York studio, Cooper grabs a copy of the 2018 book *One Week with 1UP* and flips to a picture in which she can be seen scampering up a hill on the run from the police. She laughs happily and says, "You understand the thrill when you do it and you're afraid you might get caught. The illegal stuff is super exciting. Oh my goodness!"

You might just say Marty Cooper has not changed a bit. The thrill of adventure is in her blood. Just put a camera in her hands and she is ready to go.

"Marty is, and always has been, fearless," says SKEME. "I was amazed at how adeptly she entered the yard, with no fear of heights or arrest, crossing the tracks with 6,000 volts surging through the third rail and climbing in between cars like a spry teenager."

Though sporty and petite, with a pixie haircut, Cooper was a professional photographer in her 30s at the time, singularly focused on her goal. Now freelancing full-time, Cooper gave graffiti the *National Geographic* treatment: in-depth, long-▶

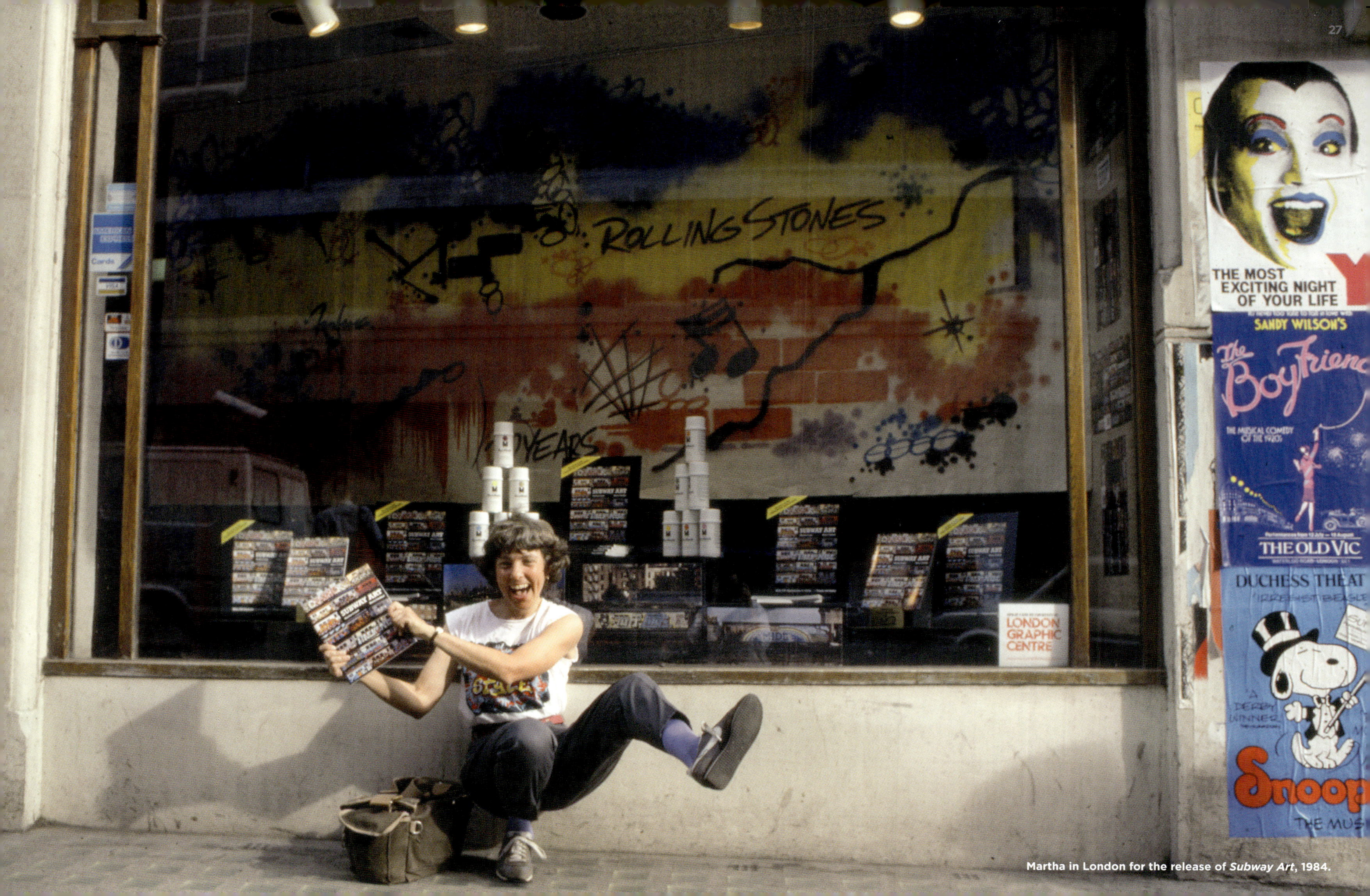

Martha in London for the release of *Subway Art*, 1984.

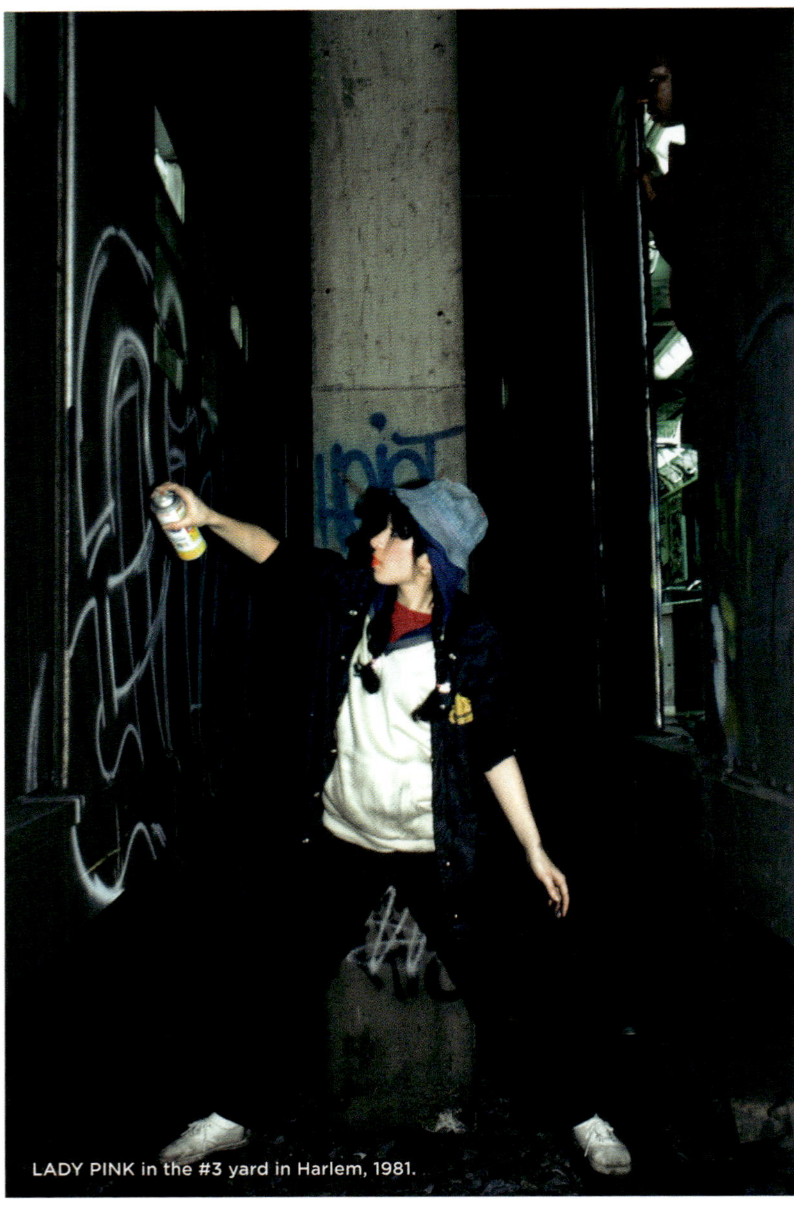

LADY PINK in the #3 yard in Harlem, 1981.

form, exquisitely detailed reportage — the best of which went into *Subway Art*, which she co-authored with Henry Chalfant in 1984.

Known as the "graffiti bible," *Subway Art* spread the word around the globe from Cleveland to Copenhagen, inspiring a new generation of writers to live the life. Kids got their start tracing styles from the book and then trying their hand at a piece with cans of freshly stolen spray paint. They penned letters in homeroom before the bell went off, thanking Cooper for the inspiration and inviting her to Chicago (or Kent, or Soweto) to photograph their work.

Today, the letters arrive by email, detailing the possibility of paid work documenting graff everywhere from Tahiti to Thailand, India to Portugal, in recognition of Cooper's influence and legacy. "Half the time I don't even know where I am going. Just put me on the plane," Cooper says with a laugh.

Cooper shares her love of adventure with the writers themselves, whether they are rappelling down the Manuel Gómez Morin Cultural Center in Mexico or sneaking into the #3 yard in Harlem during the dead of night. There, she documented a world few had ever seen, where Puma-shod writers moved like acrobats to paint masterpieces before the sun came up.

"Our shots were neither rehearsed nor coerced, neither directed nor suggested. Marty was there to capture the wild things in their natural habitat, and capture she did," SKEME reveals. "Most amazing is that she found value in what we were doing, her documentation a testimony possessing such extraordinary evidentiary value in the case against us just being poor, truant, rowdy vandals. I'm glad she came along."

Cey Adams agrees. "Martha was the first adult that really took notice of what we were doing," says the graff pioneer and founding creative director of Def Jam. "She documented all the early work and she never asked for anything. She just showed up and took photographs. She traveled to different parts of the city. At the time I was too young to appreciate what it meant to have someone documenting your career at such a young age. She really cared. It was one of the earliest creative relationships I had, and I didn't even know I was having it."

A natural collaborator, Cooper meets everyone where they are and quickly discerns the essence of the story in purely visual terms. "Marty does what great photographers do, which is to encompass all aspects of the scene in one image," filmmaker Charlie Ahearn says. "Marty is not just snapping a picture; she is thinking about all the ways in which this is going to work. She has total freedom and is managing to be in the exact right place for the photograph."

The perfect synthesis of music, style, fashion, art and attitude, Cooper's photograph of Frosty Freeze, FAB 5 FREDDY, LADY PINK and Patti Astor standing in front of the *Wild Style* mural has become "the" image of Ahearn's movie, even though it's not a scene from the film. "It's identified as this historical moment but it's made up," Ahearn says. "I wanted something that would carry to places like Brazil and Switzerland, and that's what Marty's photo did."

Despite the immediate impact of her work, it would be years before Cooper would discover the legacy of *Subway Art*. She describes the book's release as "a big disappointment. There was no hoopla. We didn't do any publicity. I don't remember having a release party. I don't remember anyone talking about the book. It just seemed like it came and went."

At the same time, the scene Cooper had been documenting was beginning to disappear. "The trains kind of died off right then. They had cracked down right at that moment," she remembers. "When the trains stopped, there was a lull. With FUN and all those galleries, there was a feeling something was happening but somehow it flatlined."

Suddenly, it seemed as though all that remained of graffiti's golden age were the photographs in *Subway Art*, a paperback book whose covers fell off if you cracked the spine once too often. But that didn't stop the book from becoming one of publishing's greatest sleepers to hit the shelves, selling more than half a million copies over the next 25 years.

Unbeknownst to Cooper, *Subway Art* went underground and traveled the globe, finding its way into the hands of the next generation of writers coming of age. While some stole copies, others, like OS GEMEOS, made do with a black-and-white photocopied version of the book.

Although Cooper stopped shooting graff in 1984, she continues to stay in touch with writers she has met through the exchange of letters, postcards, holiday cards, artwork, photographs, handmade gifts, custom-made objects, toys, emails and ephemera that she keeps neatly organized in her studio.

Cooper opens boxes and flat files, drawers and closet doors, revealing an amazing wealth of historic objects she has received over the years, including DONDI's whole-car sketch for "Children of the Grave, Part 2," vintage black books, handwritten letters from CAINE 1, STAY HIGH 149, LADY PINK and BLADE, and a special 70th-birthday card featuring a picture of the "MARTY" mural painted at the Houston Bowery Wall in 2013.

After searching, Cooper produces an envelope that contains a letter from SHY 147 dated May 12, 1983, along with a signed Polaroid taken in prison. "Martha thank you very much for the photos, they bring back memories of the good old times to me which are sometimes forgotten inside this prison," he writes. "Martha, the world I share now is a whole different prison society and I need all the outside contact I can get so I won't feel forgotten, and from what I see, you haven't forgotten me like a lot of people have done."

Not a chance. Cooper's memory is as long as her archive. She ain't forget . . . but for a long time it seemed as though the world had moved on. It wasn't until Cooper began working on the book *Hip Hop Files* in 2004, when she reconnected with the artists in *Subway Art*, that she saw what had come of the seeds planted two decades earlier.

Cooper traveled across Europe, launching her new book to the next generation of graff writers, b-boys and b-girls. "We did 22 cities in 18 days or some crazy number, and people would come. They really showed up — and talked about what *Subway Art* meant to them. It was amazing," she remembers.

After a 20-year detour, Cooper decided to jump back into the scene, her timing once again impeccable as her return to graffiti intersected with the rise of street art. With artists like Banksy spanning the divide between crime and commerce, everything was getting bigger — including the 25th-anniversary edition of *Subway Art*, which, now hardcover, measured nearly 12-by-17 inches. ▶

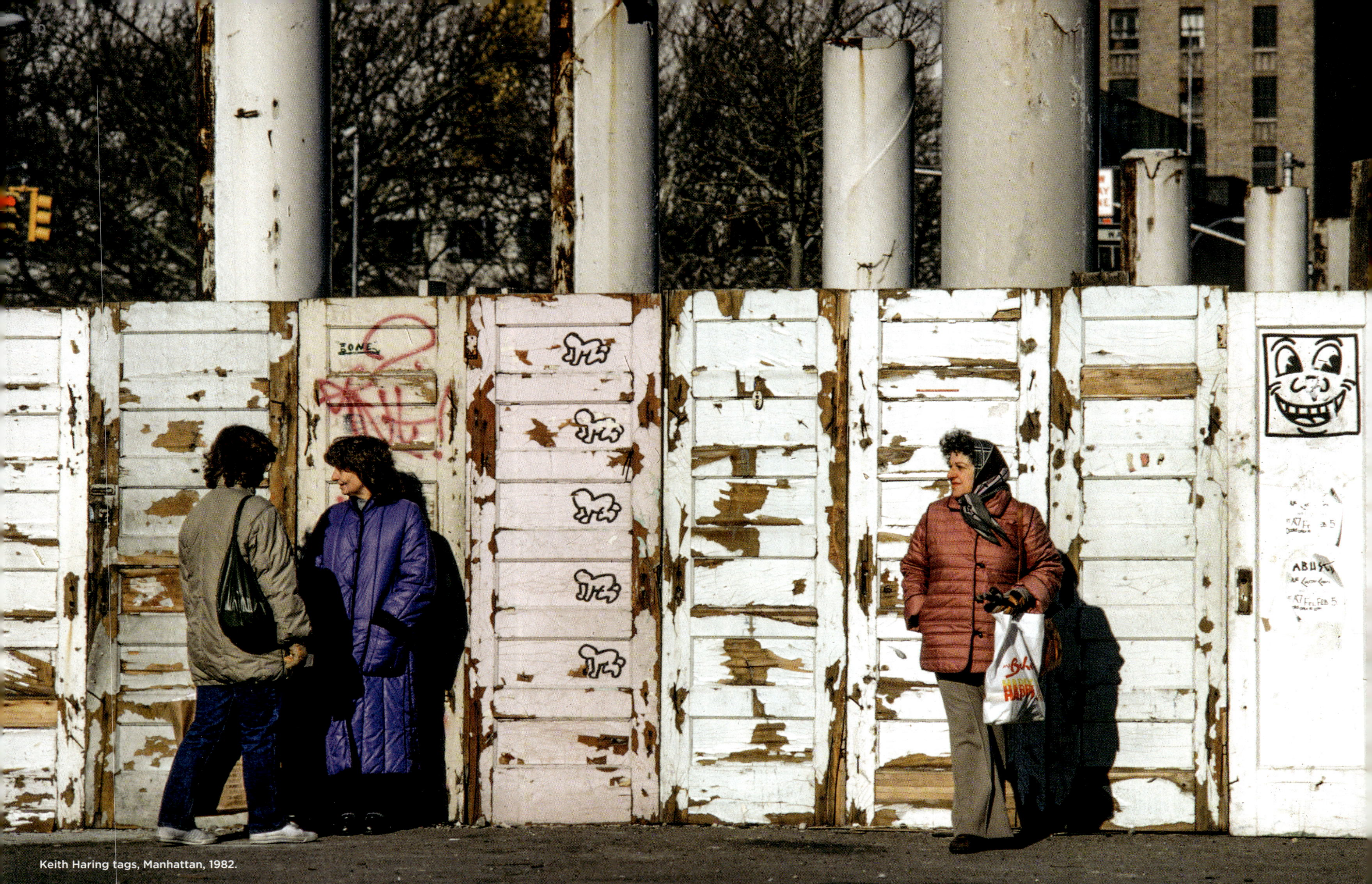

Keith Haring tags, Manhattan, 1982.

Cooper sent a copy of the very first hardcover edition of the book across the pond to Bansky. "Wow, it's a shame not all books can look like yours — they should have to be that size by law," he wrote in a thank-you card Cooper keeps filed away. "Thanks for turning a lot of kids onto a whole different path."

None of this was intentional and that's why it works. It is pure, unadulterated love and mutual respect for the art of getting over, its practitioners, and the communities in which it lives. You don't just look at a Martha Cooper photograph, you feel it. You want to be there only you can't, so you do it yourself.

Back in 2013, Dutch writer FURIOUS started remaking the pages of *Subway Art* on a lark. Like countless writers over the years, FURIOUS studied the hands of the masters, copying their techniques and adapting them in order to execute the perfect remix. Flicks were snapped and made the rounds on social media.

"Every now and then, it would reach the maker of the original piece. From their comments, I noticed how they appreciated that somebody on another continent was making an homage to the graffiti they made 40 years ago. That motivated me to keep on going," FURIOUS says, as he works toward completing the re-creation of every single piece in the book.

As *Subway Art* celebrates its 35th anniversary, a new reverence for the work has also found its way into the hallowed halls of academia. Edward Birzin has been working on "Subway Art(efact)," his PhD dissertation at Freie Universität in Berlin. In his examination of the growth of graffiti from child's play to an original art form, Birzin cites *Subway Art* as an integral text in the fixity and spread of graffiti to different lands and times.

"The universal appeal of graffiti might not be in the act of *writing* on walls and objects at all, but rather in its *playful performance*; walls and objects become a space on which young people can project their imaginations, dreams and aspirations," Birzin writes.

"Cooper's photographs told stories, showed the art moving and interacting with real and imagined dialogues, and captured the imagination of the graffiti writer. Her bird's-eye views and context-filled images offered a view of graffiti which few had seen before. She gave insight into how graffiti writers imagined the 'lives' of their creations."

Cooper's photos not only captured the glory and grandeur of graff — they made everyone feel like a star, whether you were in the picture or not. "Marty is the first in my book to capture the moment and essence of the human condition like I have never seen before," says legendary artist Lee Quiñones.

"She made the conscious decision to celebrate that New York minute. She captured that better than anyone as far as I am concerned. The heroic photograph that Martha has taken is one photograph — and that one photograph is to open the aperture of life to all of us and it can encompass anyone."

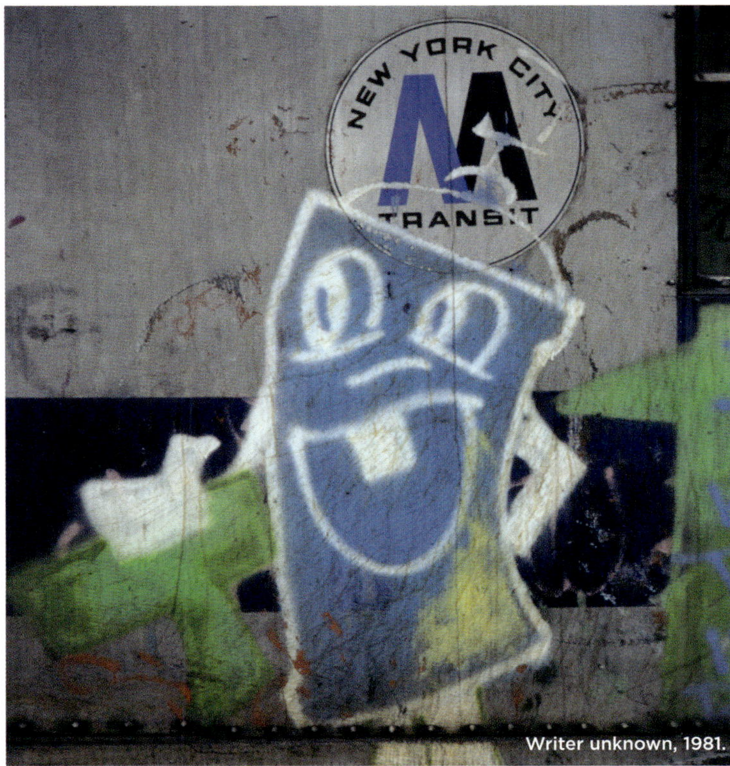

Writer unknown, 1981.

PETER PAN HAIRCUT

Jayson Edlin

Shortly after midnight in the winter of '82, I picked up CAP MPC and CABAN in the Morris Park section of the Bronx. Richie SEEN had told us to meet him down the block from his old alma mater, Lehman High School, in the Throggs Neck section of the Bronx, so that we could roll to Esplanade Tunnel together and pull off a whole car. SEEN was known as the King of the Six (#6 subway line); his ubiquity and artistic ability garnered respect accented with a smattering of awe from his peers. CAP MPC controlled the prestigious 2 and 5 lines, decimating the works of individuals and crews alike with thousands of throw-ups that turned the lay-up into his personal conveyor belt of destruction. CAP stood 6'4", dressed like a biker and struck fear in the hearts of most writers. He took shit from no one and rarely got tested.

I parked my weather-beaten blue '79 Monte Carlo after spotting SEEN across the street. He exited his van and then someone I couldn't recognize got out of a little compact car and accompanied him across the street. As they drew closer, I ID'd SEEN's accomplice as Martha Cooper, whom I knew casually from graffiti shows. Seeing her under these circumstances, however, cast SEEN in a suspicious light.

"Hey fellas, this is Martha Cooper. She's gonna come with us and photograph us doin' this."

How could this practically 40-year-old woman with the Peter Pan haircut care about us? I didn't really care about Martha's photographic abilities. My writing partner, AMMO, a great amateur photographer, had already been documenting our exploits with top Nikon gear.

"Yo, Jayson, I don't like this. I don't know her and I don't trust this set-up. If anything goes wrong it's on you," CAP warned me. "Relax pal, Martha's cool. Check out the outline." SEEN pulled a piece of paper from the pocket of his paint-splattered bomber jacket. Meticulous in his approach, SEEN often drew up pencil blueprints with a color schematic for his more elaborate pieces. He had drawn a Christmas-themed car, a J.SON and RICHIE with a Santa Claus holding a bag of toys. "Merry Christmas" would go between our names. I pulled the Jew card on SEEN and on religious grounds got him to change the greeting to Happy Holidays. Asking him to draw a menorah would have

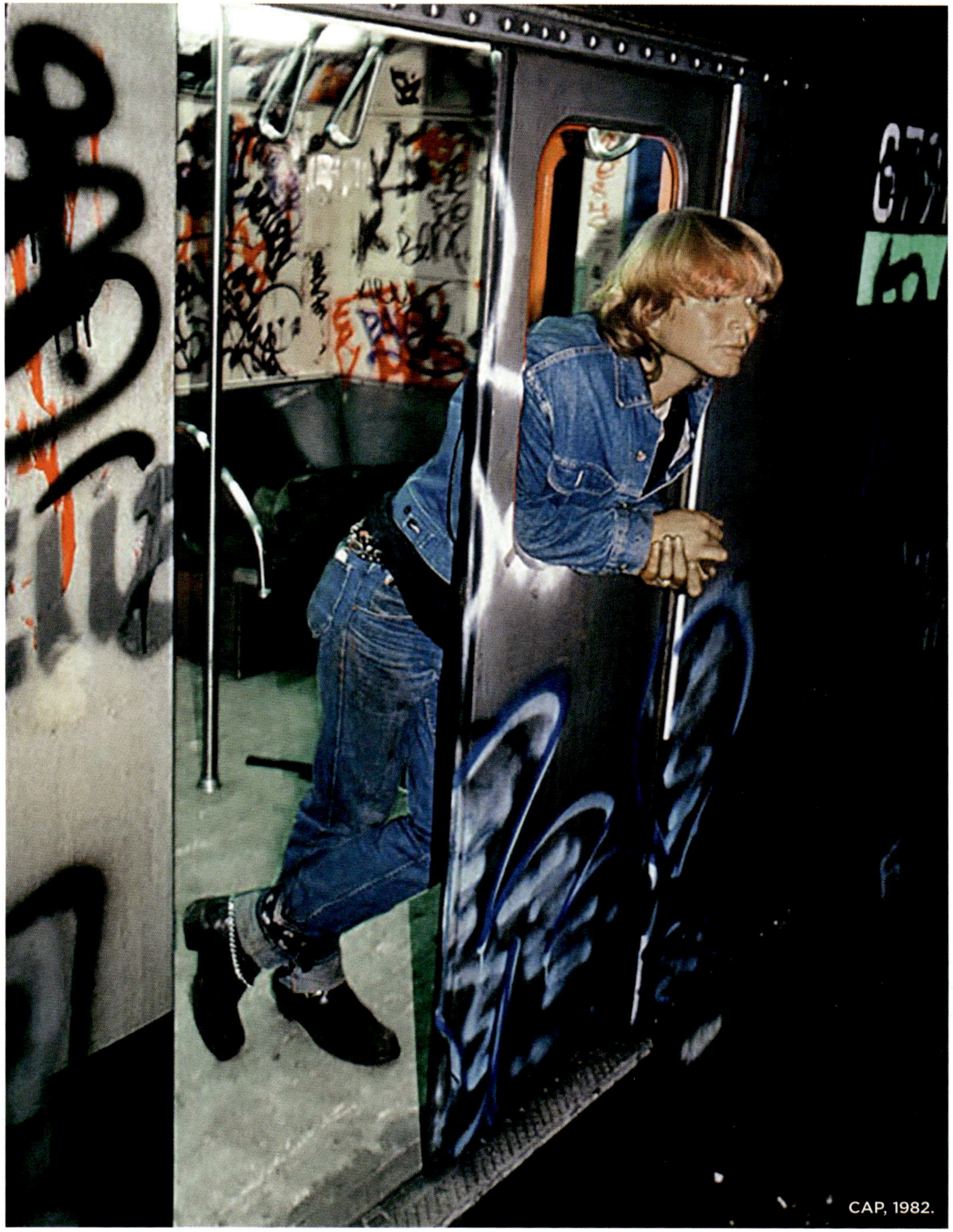

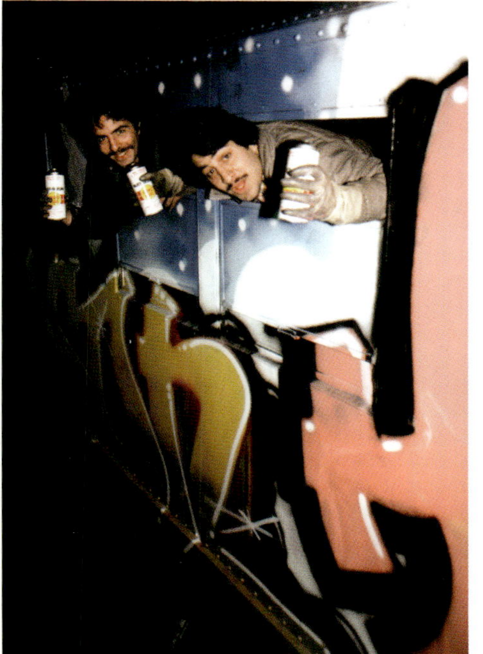

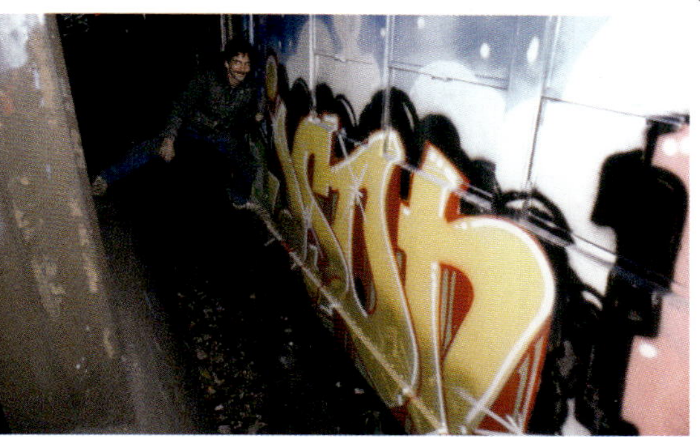

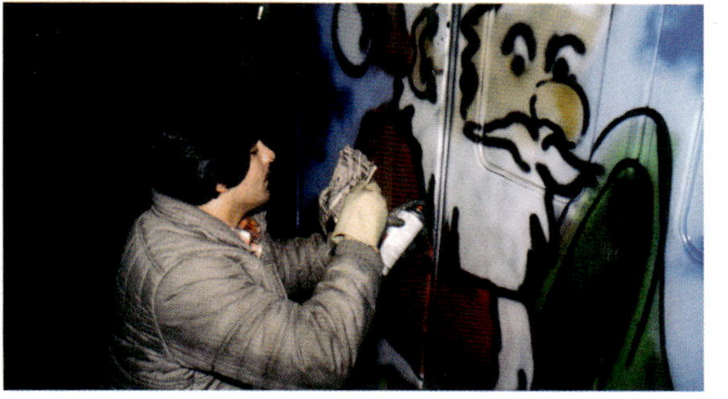

CAP, 1982.

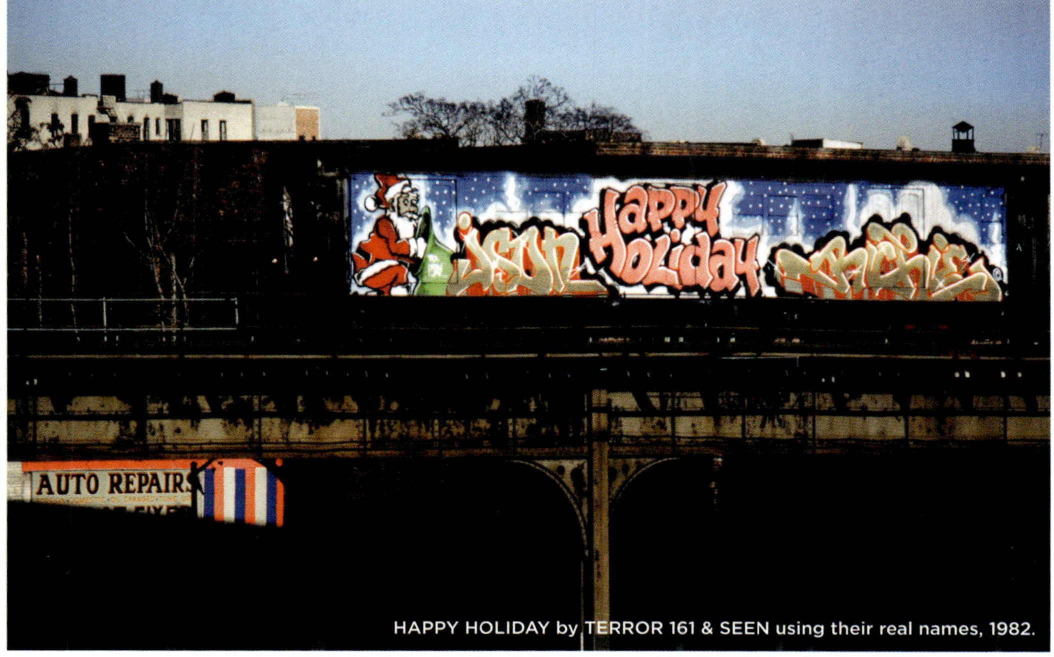

HAPPY HOLIDAY by TERROR 161 & SEEN using their real names, 1982.

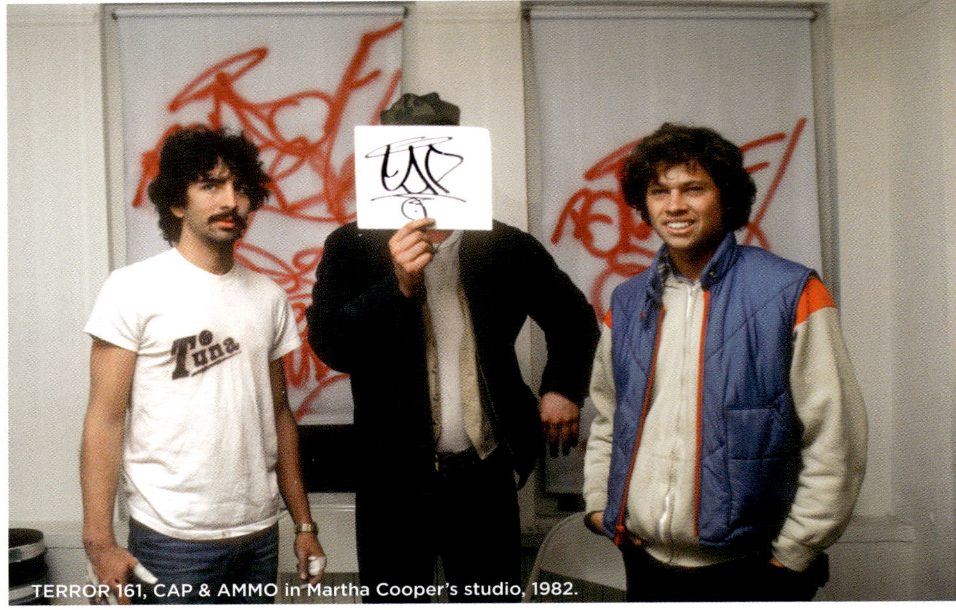

TERROR 161, CAP & AMMO in Martha Cooper's studio, 1982.

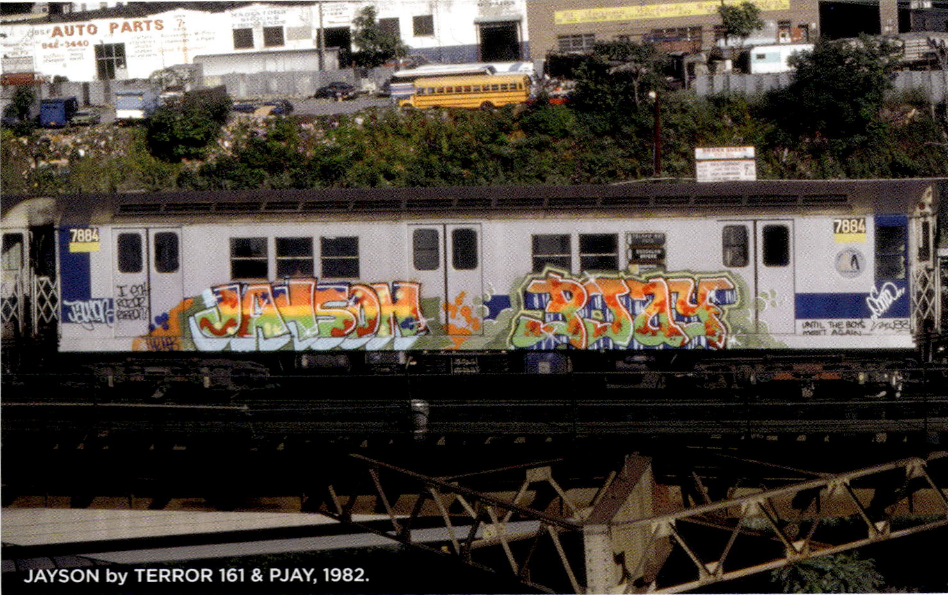

JAYSON by TERROR 161 & PJAY, 1982.

Martha kept her cool, jumping into my car without hesitation. Within 15 minutes the five of us walked into the tunnel, we with our bags of paint and Martha right in step lugging her camera gear. Before hitting the outsides we walked through a train with its lights on, allowing her to grab some candid shots of CAP inside the bombed-out car. She acclimated well, and her grace under pressure erased any prior misgivings regarding her presence.

"This looks like a good spot, Richie," CAP announced after we'd ventured halfway in. We lined up our cans on the bridges that separated the train lanes. Standing atop the bridges gave us the height to pull off top-to-bottoms. Martha began shooting in earnest. She caught every step of the process from first outlines to the final touches on the finished product. Her iconic photo of the car running across the South Bronx elevation would be taken days later in sunnier conditions.

Martha and I became friends that night, although she never came with us into the field again. The alliance forged behind battle lines gave us entrée to call her anytime we needed a Cooper photo of one of our productions. Validation from an adult professional photographer who made something ephemeral permanent with the snap of her shutter offered us a fast track to a wider, ultimately global audience none of us could envision. Martha's in situ shots of DONDI, SKEME, DEZ, DAZE and LADY PINK linked faces to their names. When Martha and Henry Chalfant's book *Subway Art* hit Europe, billions in collateral damage occurred when virgin subway systems were defiled.

The pursuit of fame, the unifying goal that drove graffiti writers to become CEOs of their own self-advertising agencies, enlisting NYC subway cars as billboards for vanity campaigns, remained constant throughout the '70s. But the Groundhog of Graff snuck a peek above ground in the '80s, smelled money and abandoned his subterranean haunts. Hip-hop, punk rock, graffiti, the emergence of street art, the crack epidemic, guns, clubs, drugs and women made NYC the epicenter of cultural debauchery. Cooper, a New York photographer, the daughter of a Baltimore camera shop owner, found herself in the right place at the right time. Training her lens on the madness of the period reminds us that a pulsating beat once existed in a city currently in the throes of a capitalistic catatonia. Fun City R.I.P.

By '83 the MTA started playing the opening notes of graffiti's swan song — B-boys, Blockbusters and Bodēs blown into oblivion by the white tornado handing us our own flag of surrender. Line by line, fences with razor ribbon forced writers to leave their comfort zones or retire completely. The crack epidemic wreaked havoc on the graff world as guns flooded the streets. Angel dust brought more white boys to Harlem than gentrification ever did. You couldn't walk down any block without seeing shattered car-window glass looking like urban crushed ice as the growing army of crackheads put Blaupunkt and Alpine radios atop the endangered species list.

One night, SEEN and I came out of Baychester lay-up after finishing a whole car and two of my tires had been stolen. Vandals as victims?

Danceteria, the Mudd Club, the Roxy, Area and the Fun House drew their clientele from the former patrons of Esplanade, Grant, New Lots and the 1 Tunnel. You could get a seat at the Writers Bench since the FUN Gallery, 51 X, G.P.I. and Sidney Janis paid big dividends to kids willing to trade steel for canvas. Hip-hop exploded and New York's subway graffiti vanished from the public eye. Martha took pictures of painted trains and b-boys because few bothered to at that time. Once people caught on, she considered her task completed.

Martha followed the paint trail as it rose above ground. QUIK and IZ on the streets with Scharf and Hambleton. Madonna clubbing with Basquiat, Patti Astor with DONDI and FAB 5 FREDDY. Subway graffiti gradually died, street art rising from its ashes. Disinterest, drugs and AIDS decimated NYC's cultural apex, its brightest stars perishing before their work hit the seven-figure mark — lives as ephemeral as our pieces on the train. These fleeting moments of births, peaks and deaths live in perpetuity thanks to the foresight of Martha Cooper and a handful of others who tracked cool's scent like underground bloodhounds. Nothing lasts forever. The media and art galleries fell in and out of love with graffiti during the '80s and Martha trained her lens elsewhere in pursuit of a livelihood.

In late 2009 I got a book deal and decided to contact Martha after a 25-year hiatus. Like most washed-up graffiti artists, I suffered from delusions of grandeur. I found her number on the net and dialed her up, assuming she'd be psyched to hear from me.

"Hello, Martha. How are you? It's Jayson," I began.

"Jayson who?" she asked without a scintilla of remembrance.

"You know, Jayson, AMMO's partner that used to bomb with CAP and SEEN," I reminded her, ego shattered.

"Oh shit, that Jayson! What have you been up to?"

"Well, I got a book deal and I'd like to get some photos from you. Can I come over?"

Although Martha retired from the subways decades earlier, she had come back after a long absence as the grand dame of street art photography, an occupation that kept her on foreign soil far more than domestic turf. She agreed to meet me in between jaunts to Moscow and Tahiti.

Martha welcomed me into her apartment and gave me complete access to whatever subway photos I needed. In addition she changed my view on street art, which I'd imagined as a sport for art school trustafarians using store-bought supplies which they dispatched their assistants to schlep back to the studio. It took a trip to Wynwood Walls with Martha and the well-respected Japanese street artist LADY AIKO to broaden my horizons. Martha became my key to the city — an all-access pass to an insular world.

The septuagenarian Energizer Bunny still hits 15 or 20 countries in a typical year and recently became the subject of Aussie filmmaker Selina Miles' documentary, *Martha: A Picture Story*. Martha continues to live her work. She recently turned down a six-figure offer for a DONDI drawing and refuses to sell her archive for a windfall, preferring a placement with the right museum. While Martha piled up photos, we commandeered trains, building intertwined legacies for the ages.

GRAFFITI AS THE PEOPLE'S ART FORM

Brian Wallis

Crackling with illicit spontaneity and overflowing with the exuberant, wild-style letters of the graffiti kings, Martha Cooper's subway photographs from the early 1980s record the brief phosphorescent activities of New York City's anarchic urban subculture. During a stretch between 1979 and 1984, when the city was still reeling from financial failure and much of the ruinous South Bronx was literally burning, Cooper almost single-handedly documented the ephemeral artistic activities of the youth who tagged and painted subway cars by night, then waited eagerly the next day to see their masterpieces rumbling through the stations. Each of Cooper's richly composed images captures this makeshift glory. The vivid colors, the cityscape backdrops and the you-were-there immediacy of her pictures impart a surprisingly innocent or romantic spin to what was, at the time, often regarded as a deeply antisocial, even criminal, activity.

The principal record of Cooper's photographic work is the now-classic paperback book *Subway Art*, co-authored with fellow photographer Henry Chalfant in 1984. Widely considered the magnum opus of the graffiti movement, *Subway Art* is also one of the decade's most innovative photobooks. Featuring hundreds of full-color photographs of extraordinary but by then already lost examples of subway graffiti, ranging from simple tags to elaborate and carefully planned whole-car paintings, *Subway Art* unfolds, visually and iconographically, like a deep dive into an alien way of life. While Chalfant meticulously recorded the individual cars as rolling artworks, Cooper carefully documented the subculture that produced them: the distinctive vocabulary, the taxonomy of tags, the black books of plans and sketches, the connoisseurship of the spray paint, the staging of their productions and the writer heroes themselves. Cooper's photographs are no mere documents; much of their impact lies not in what they represent but how they do so.

What sets Cooper's work apart from most documentary photography is what she refers to as her "own particular brand of photography — a combination of journalism and ethnography." This type of photographic investigation involves both a careful attention to the overlooked rituals and endangered productions of everyday life and the development of participant-observer techniques necessary to gather and analyze their documentation. In Cooper's case, the evolution of this approach ▶

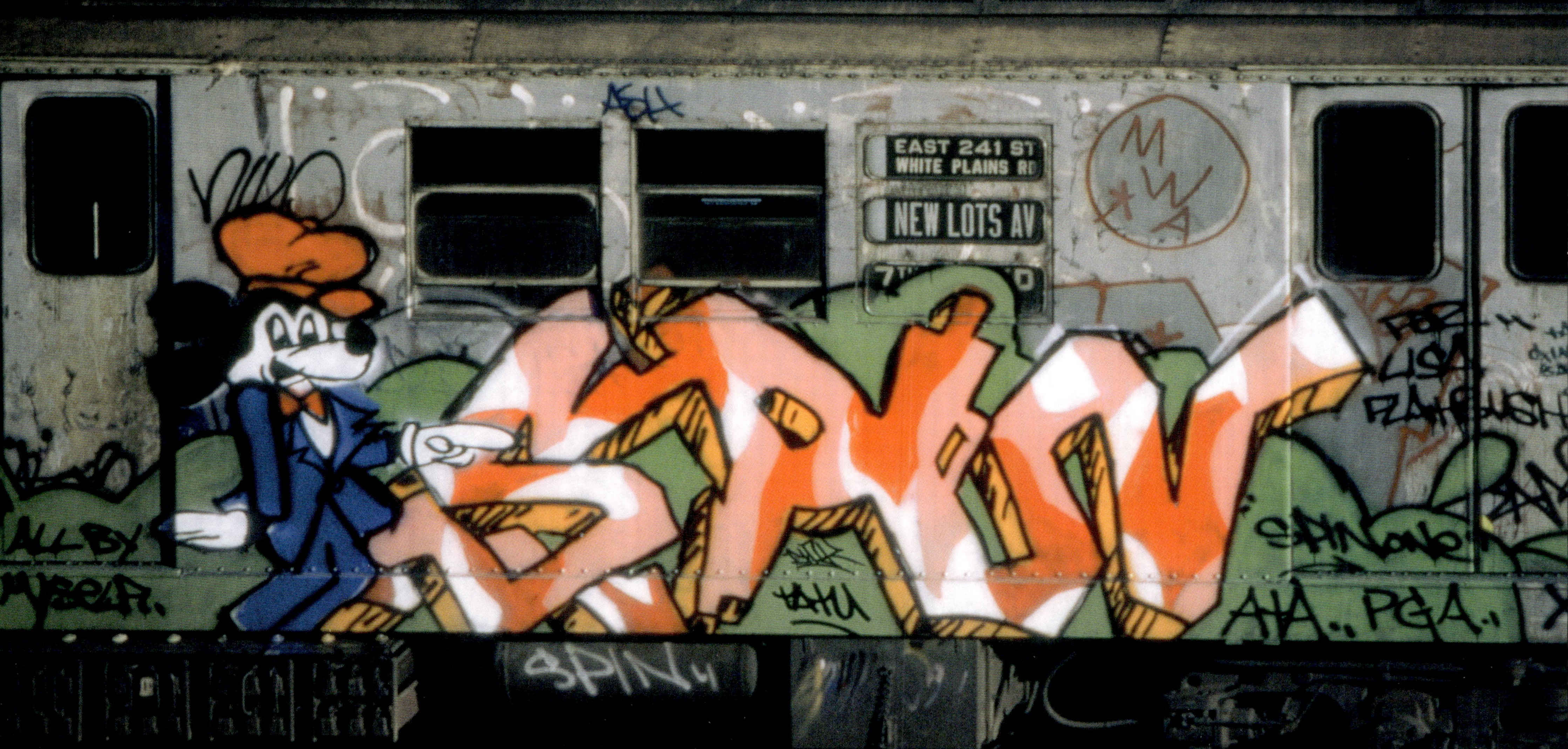
EAST 241 ST
WHITE PLAINS RD
NEW LOTS AV

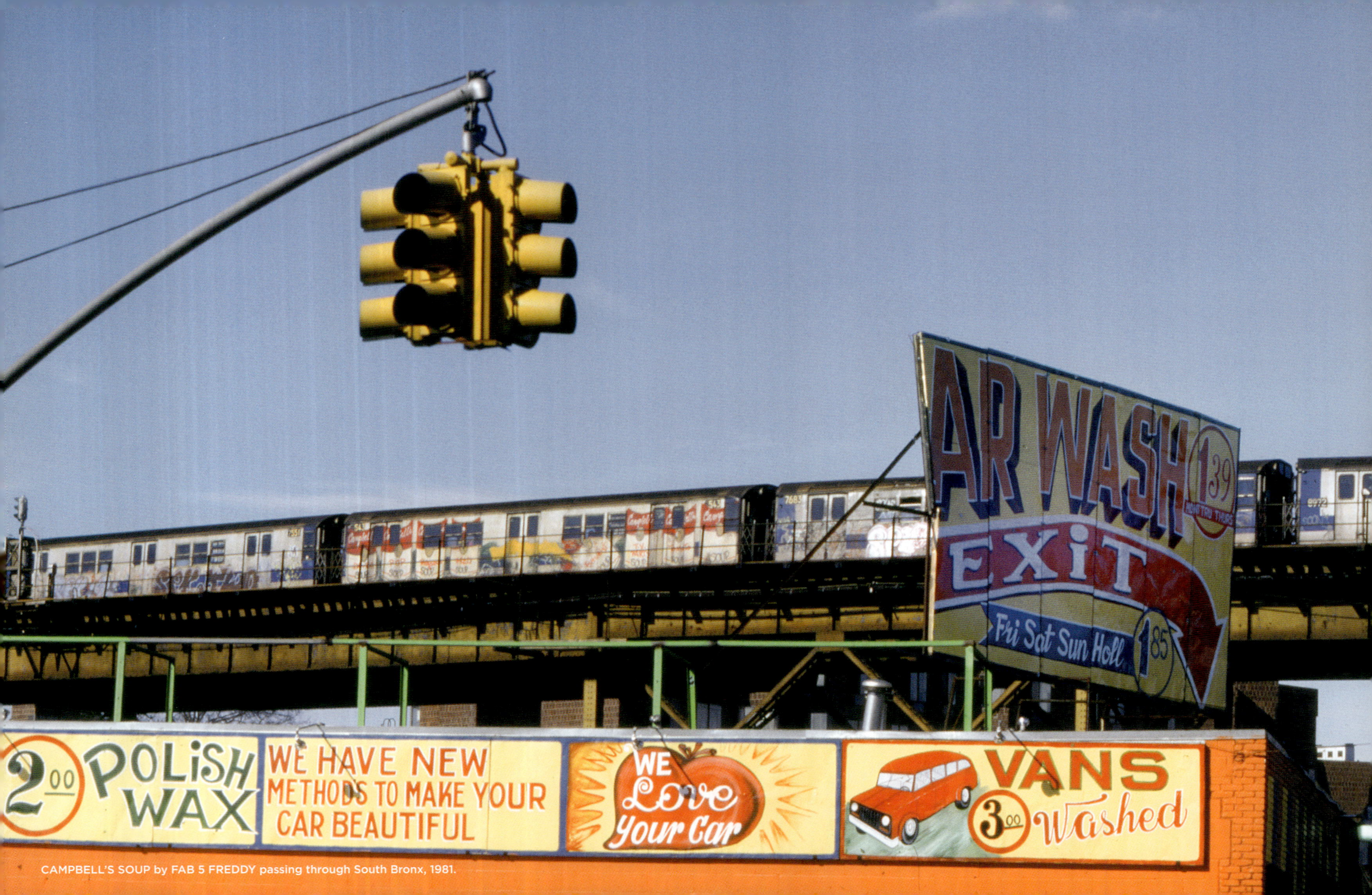

CAMPBELL'S SOUP by FAB 5 FREDDY passing through South Bronx, 1981.

was not a preplanned career path but was predicated on her own unusual life experiences. Growing up in a family dedicated to photography — her father and uncle were proprietors of the Camera Mart in Baltimore for 45 years — Cooper acquired her unfaltering photographic skills early. Then, having spent two years in the Peace Corps in Thailand, she realized her commitment was to interpreting the expressive creativity in various international communities. She studied anthropology at Oxford, worked in an ethnographic museum at Yale University and secured an internship and freelance work at *National Geographic*.

Cooper's photographic engagement with New York graffiti writers was born out of this unique documentary approach. Having witnessed children in Haiti making toys from scraps, Cooper began to look for similar street activities as she wandered the Lower East Side for her photojournalistic essays for the *New York Post*. Her empathetic black-and-white documentary photographs of street children (since collected as *Street Play* in 2006) show kids chalk-marking on pavements, building forts from scrap lumber, spraying water from fire hydrants. This self-assigned project led directly to her involvement with subway graffiti in 1979, when one of the street kids, a young writer named HE3, offered to tell her about the trains and to introduce her to legendary graffiti king DONDI.

Cooper's subsequent immersion in the graffiti subculture of the South Bronx allowed her intimate access at the very high point of the movement and has few precedents in the history of documentary photography. In a sense, Cooper's photography picks up on the New Documentary approach of the early 1970s, in which independent photographers such as Larry Clark, Susan Meiselas, Jill Freedman, Mary Ellen Mark and Danny Lyon recorded insider's views of various closed societies of outsiders, social groups and "others" shoved aside by postwar American society in thrall to consumerism. The alienated drug users, prisoners, bikers and prostitutes that those photographers lived among and depicted were largely invisible and had been further marginalized in America by class, race and gender prejudices. In a similar vein, Cooper sought to expose and to legitimize the young subway writers as earnest and mildly rebellious artists with a purpose and a rational aesthetic agenda, rather than as the lawless urban vandals the police and the media sought to represent. A keen observer of people and situations, Cooper offered an intimate view of the pulsing communalism of the subway artists, with their own language, rules, hierarchy and moral codes. Understanding and participating in that coterie was, for Cooper, crucial to documenting the imagery of the graffiti, with empathy and without judgment.

"Documentary is an engagement," says folklorist and photographer Bruce Jackson, "an engagement with a community, a process, a social issue and an audience; you are engaging that thing and you are part of it." All of Cooper's photographic work has, in this sense, followed this rule. Her photographic projects, including her subway pictures, have always sought to record — and to participate in — the popular expressions of distinct neighborhood cultures. An engaged folklorist, she co-organized the first serious demonstration of b-boying at the Bronx Folk Festival in 1981 and is today director of photography for City Lore, a nonprofit that documents urban folk culture. She has created an archive of photographs of improvised street memorials set up in New York City following the terrorist attacks of 9/11, and she has produced photographic books and exhibitions on such diverse cultural practices as vernacular photography, Japanese *irezumi* tattoos, New York name tagging, R.I.P. memorial street murals, postal-sticker graffiti, controversial casita dwellings and Long Island domestic architecture. For her 2018 exhibition "Italian Brooklyn" at the John D. Calandra Italian American Institute in Manhattan, Cooper drew from her vast file of photographs of yard shrines and sidewalk altars, the Sicilian marionette theater, the annual Giglio Festival in Williamsburg and other images of everyday life in Italian neighborhoods of New York City.

Like the best socially engaged documentary photography, Cooper's work offers crucial insight into such communities and their collective struggle for identity and visibility. And like the best ethnographies, her photography points to creative elements of everyday human behavior that might otherwise be overlooked, while preserving through her photographs aspects of culture in danger of disappearing. Celebrated b-boy Frosty Freeze put it best when he said, "If it wasn't for Martha Cooper, our culture would not have been captured in its purest form."

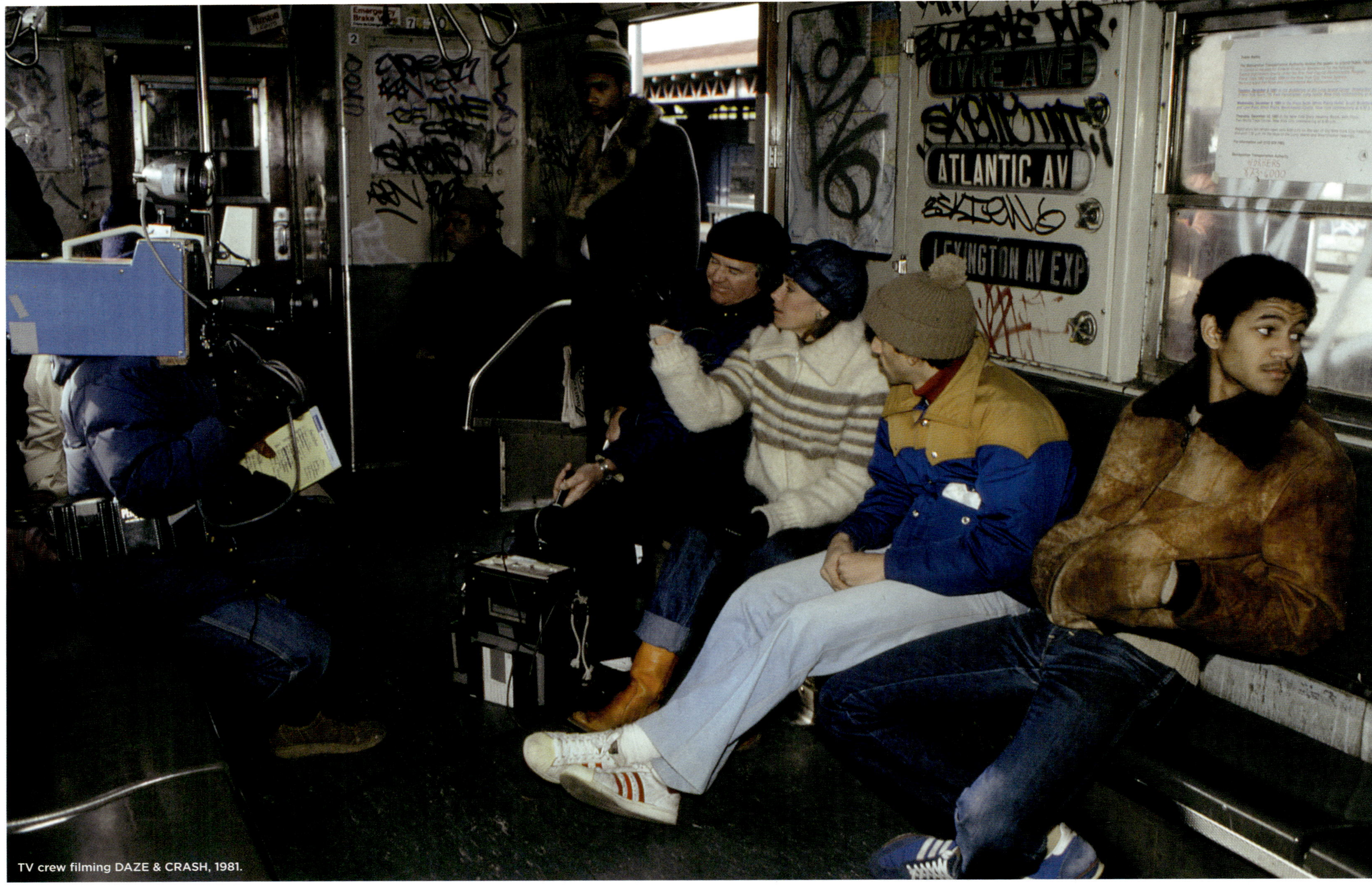

TV crew filming DAZE & CRASH, 1981.

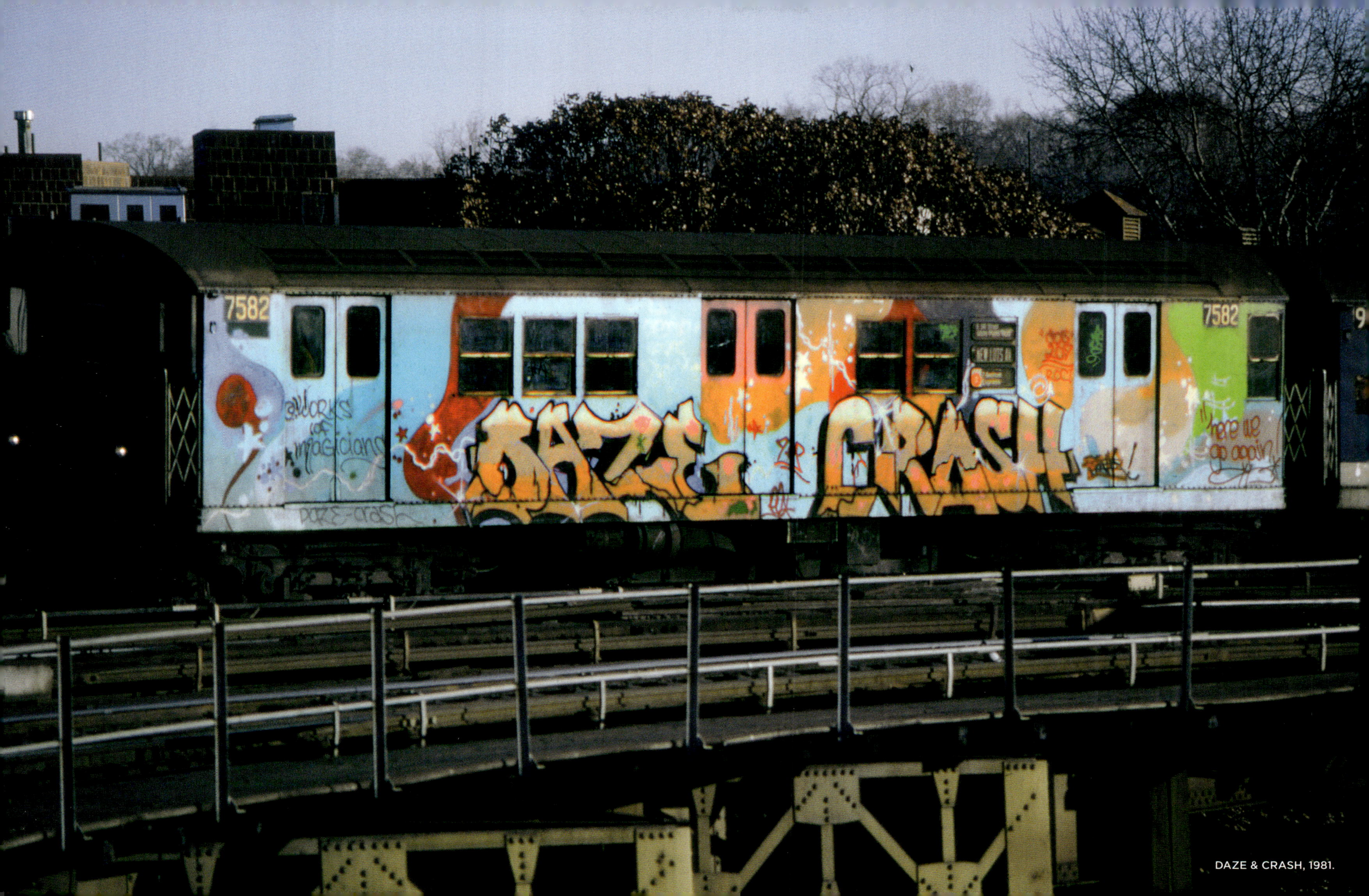

DAZE & CRASH, 1981.

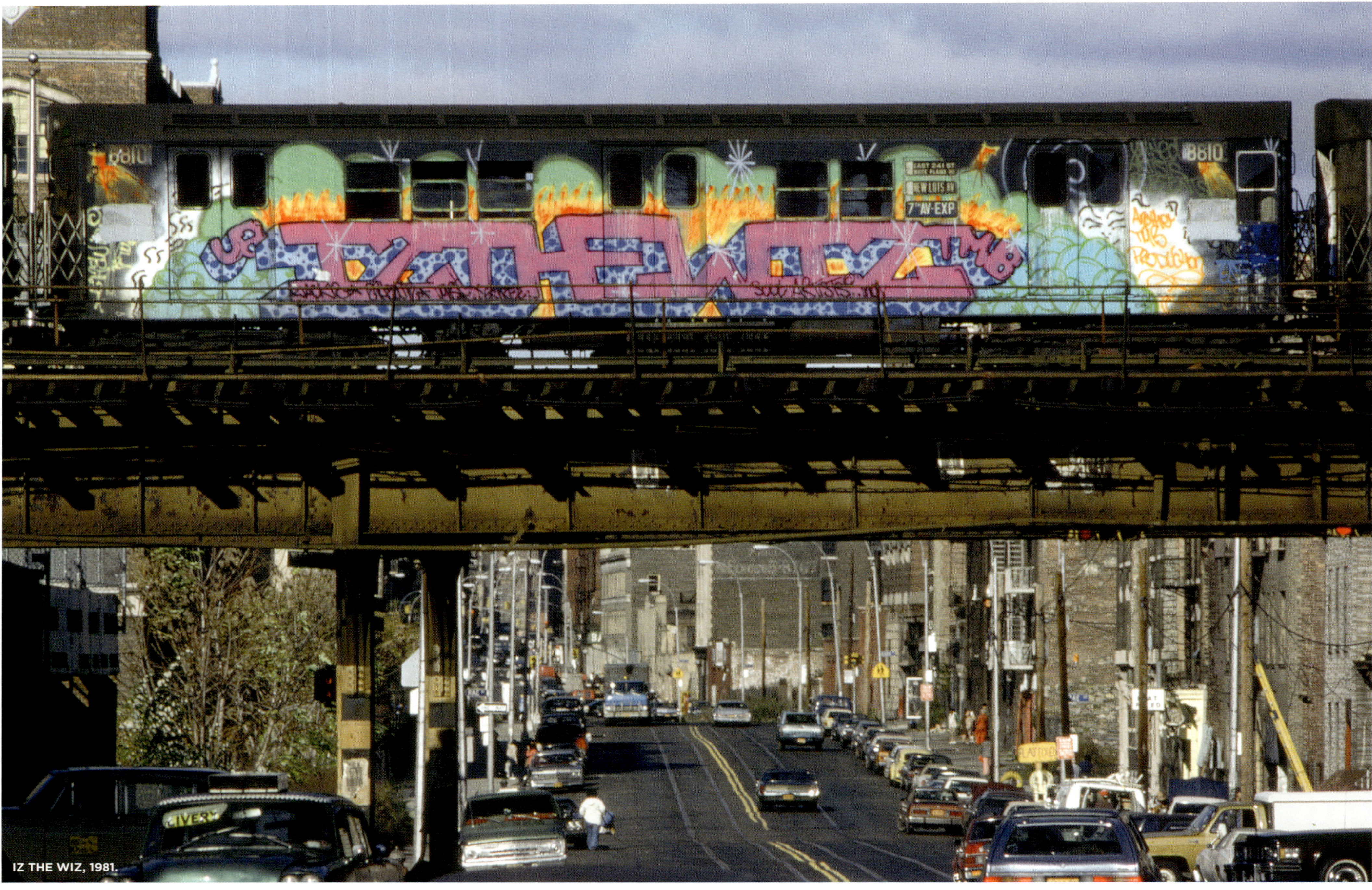

IZ THE WIZ, 1981.

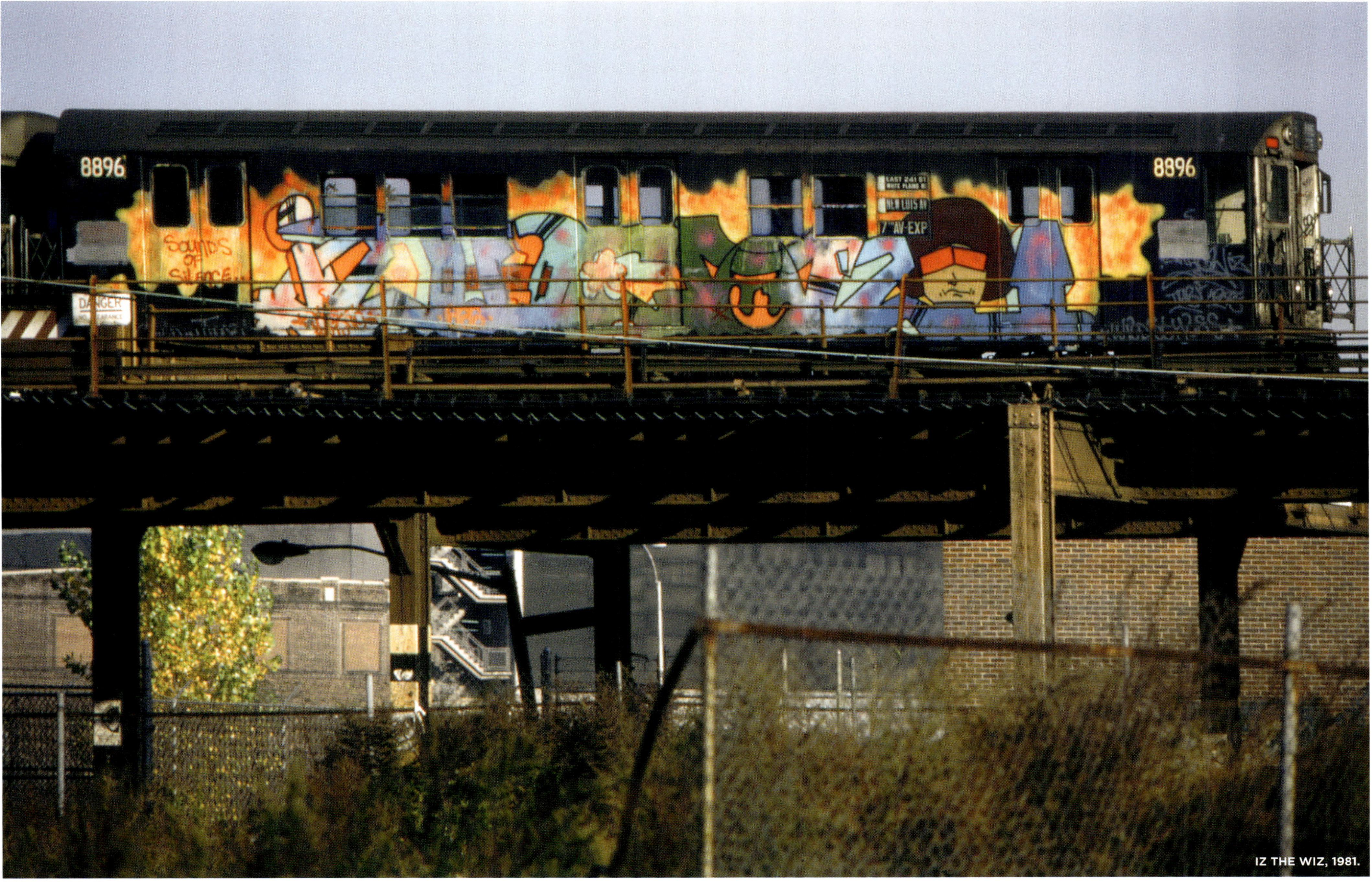

IZ THE WIZ, 1981.

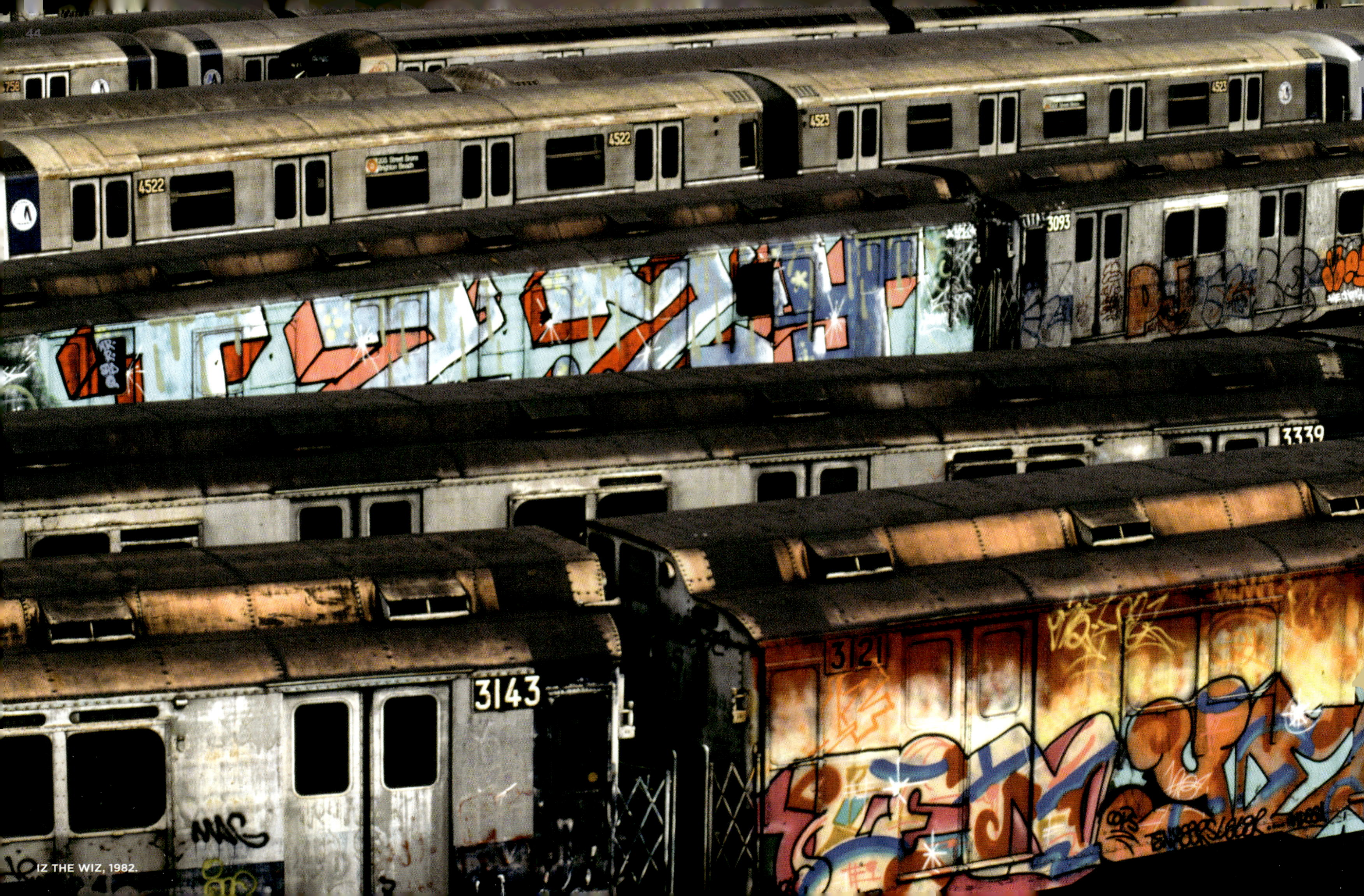

IZ THE WIZ, 1982.

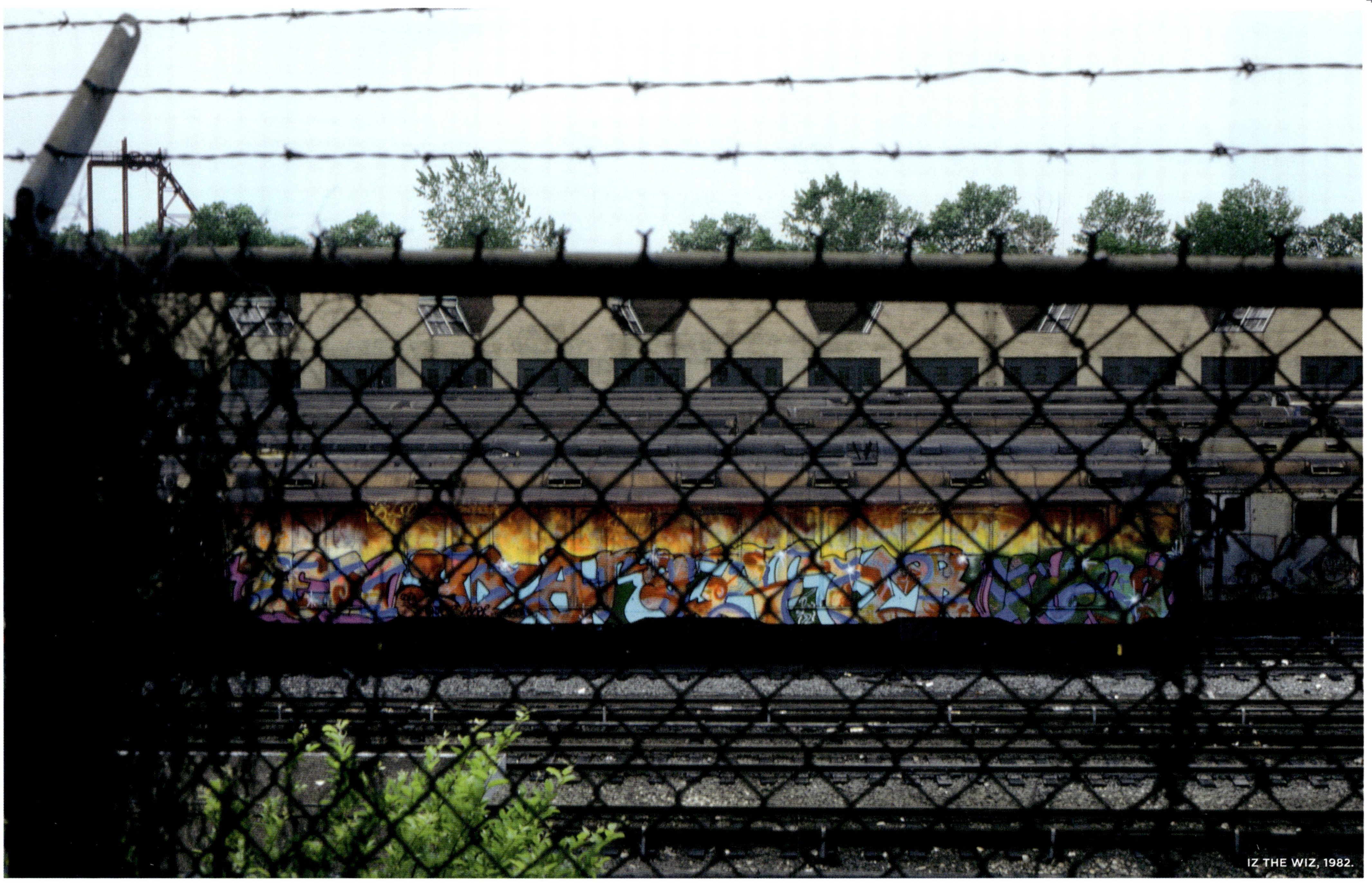

IZ THE WIZ, 1982.

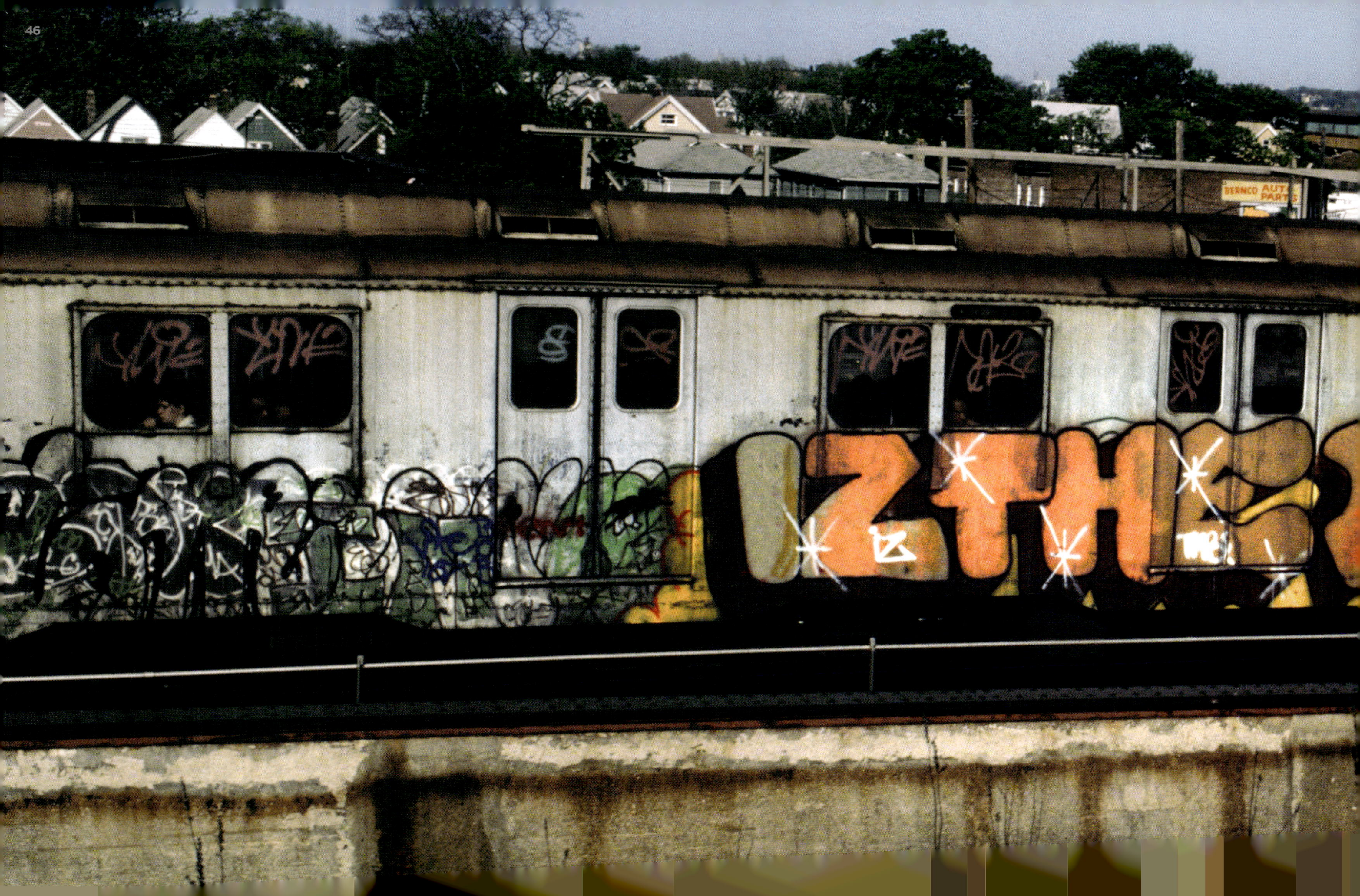

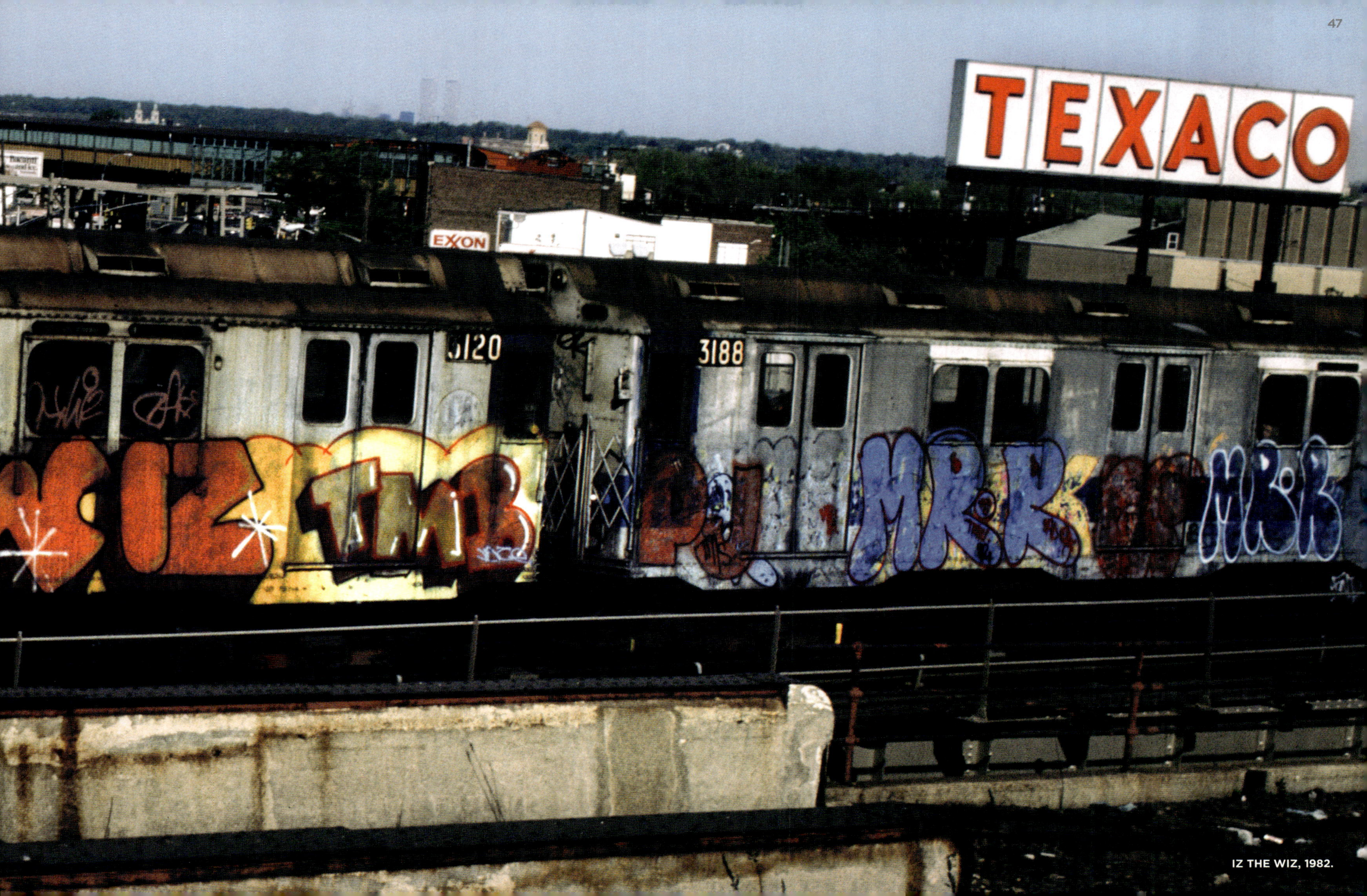

IZ THE WIZ, 1982.

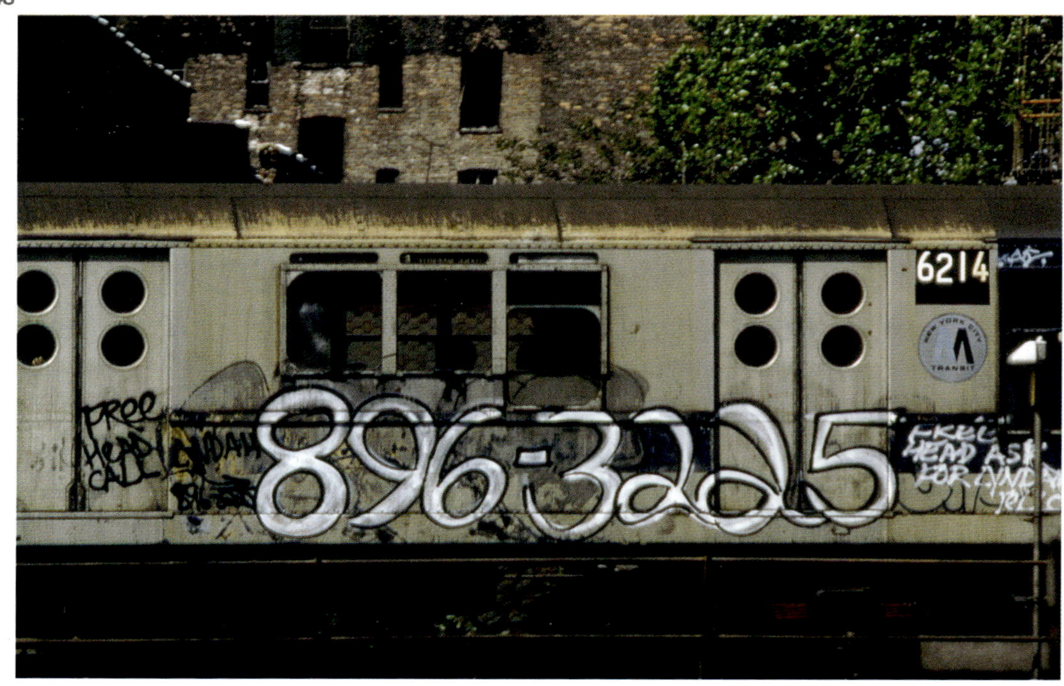

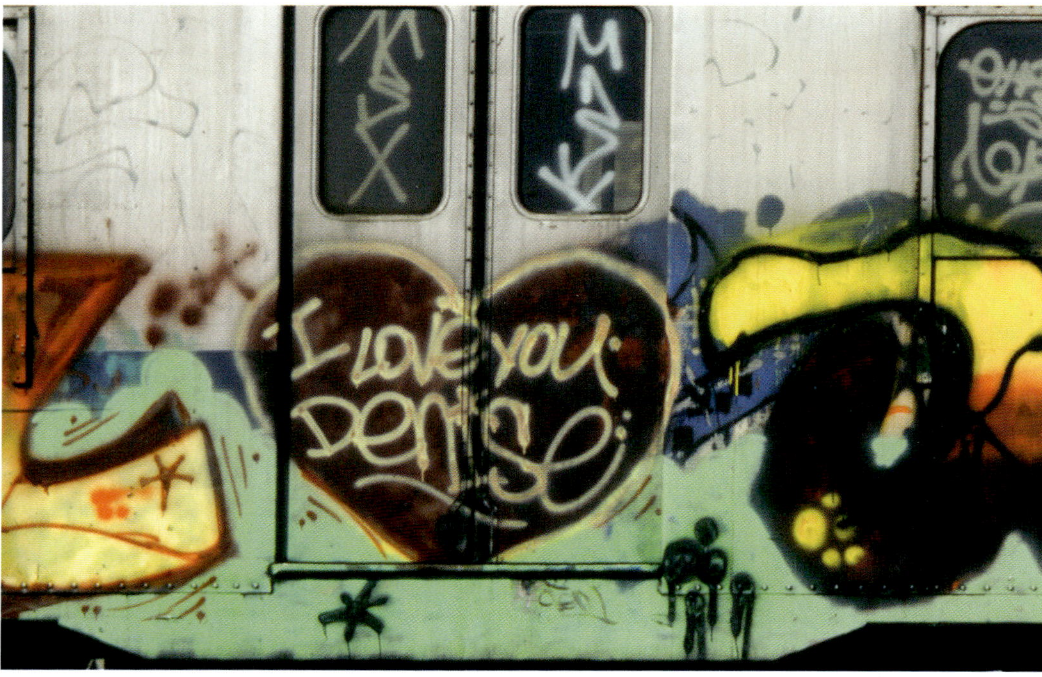

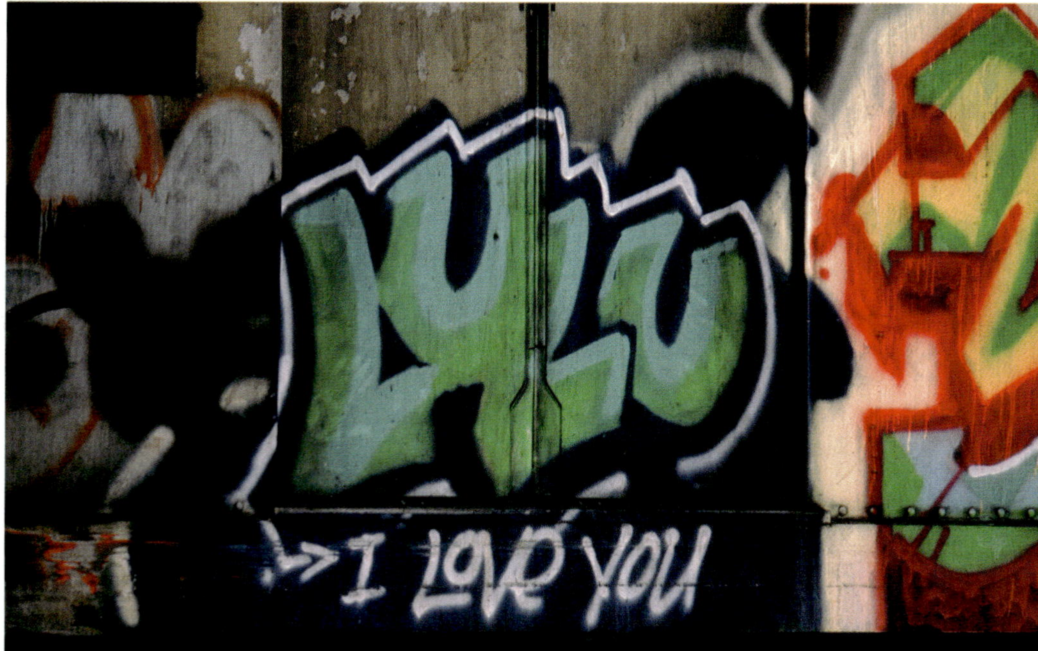

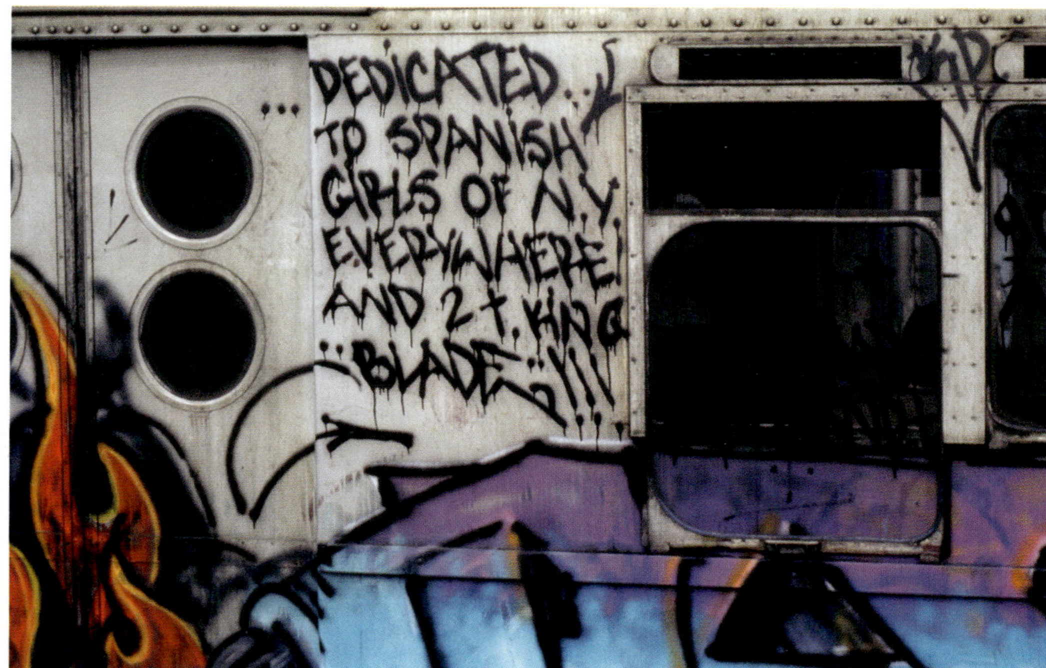

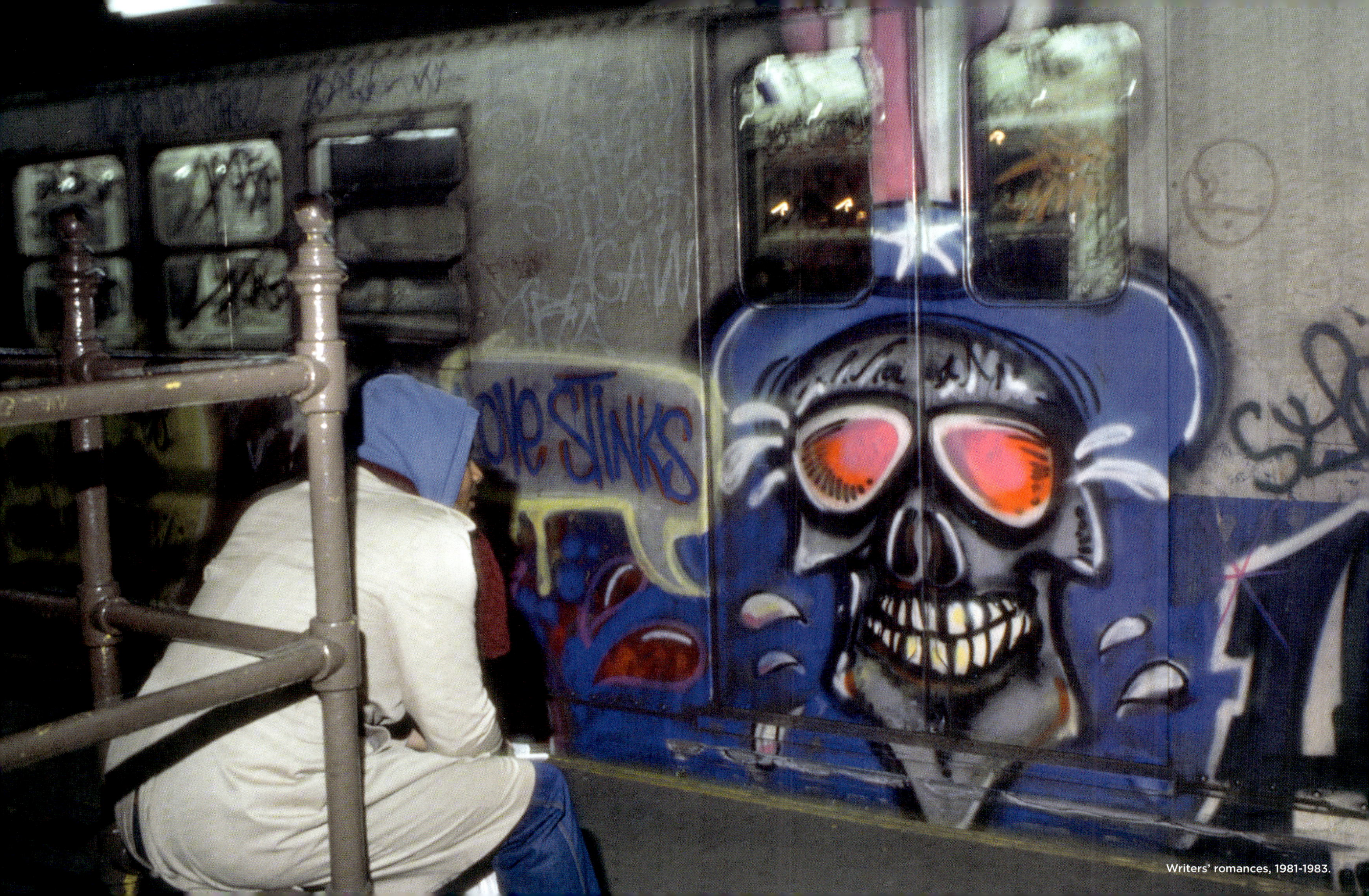

Writers' romances, 1981-1983.

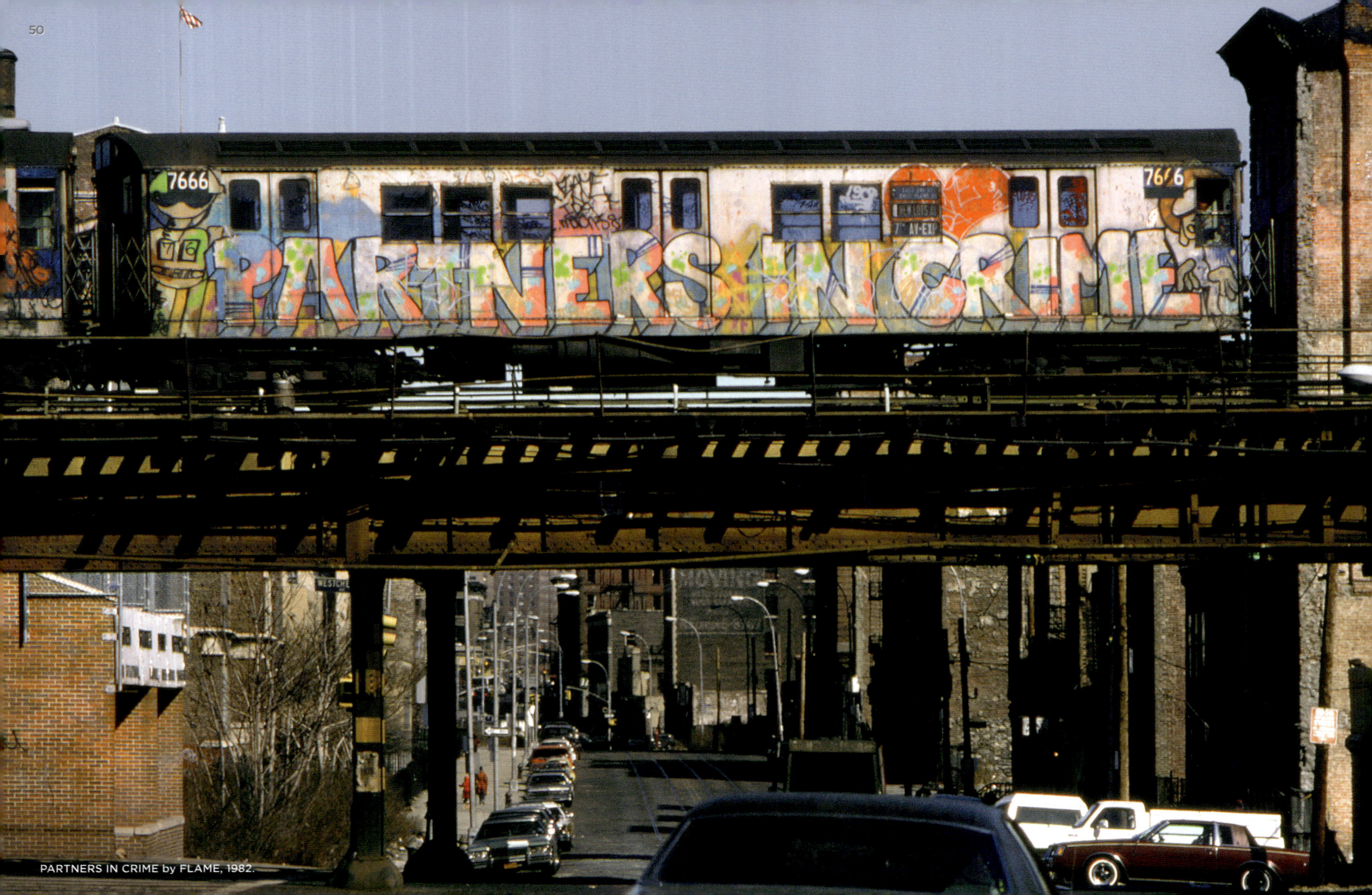

PARTNERS IN CRIME by FLAME, 1982.

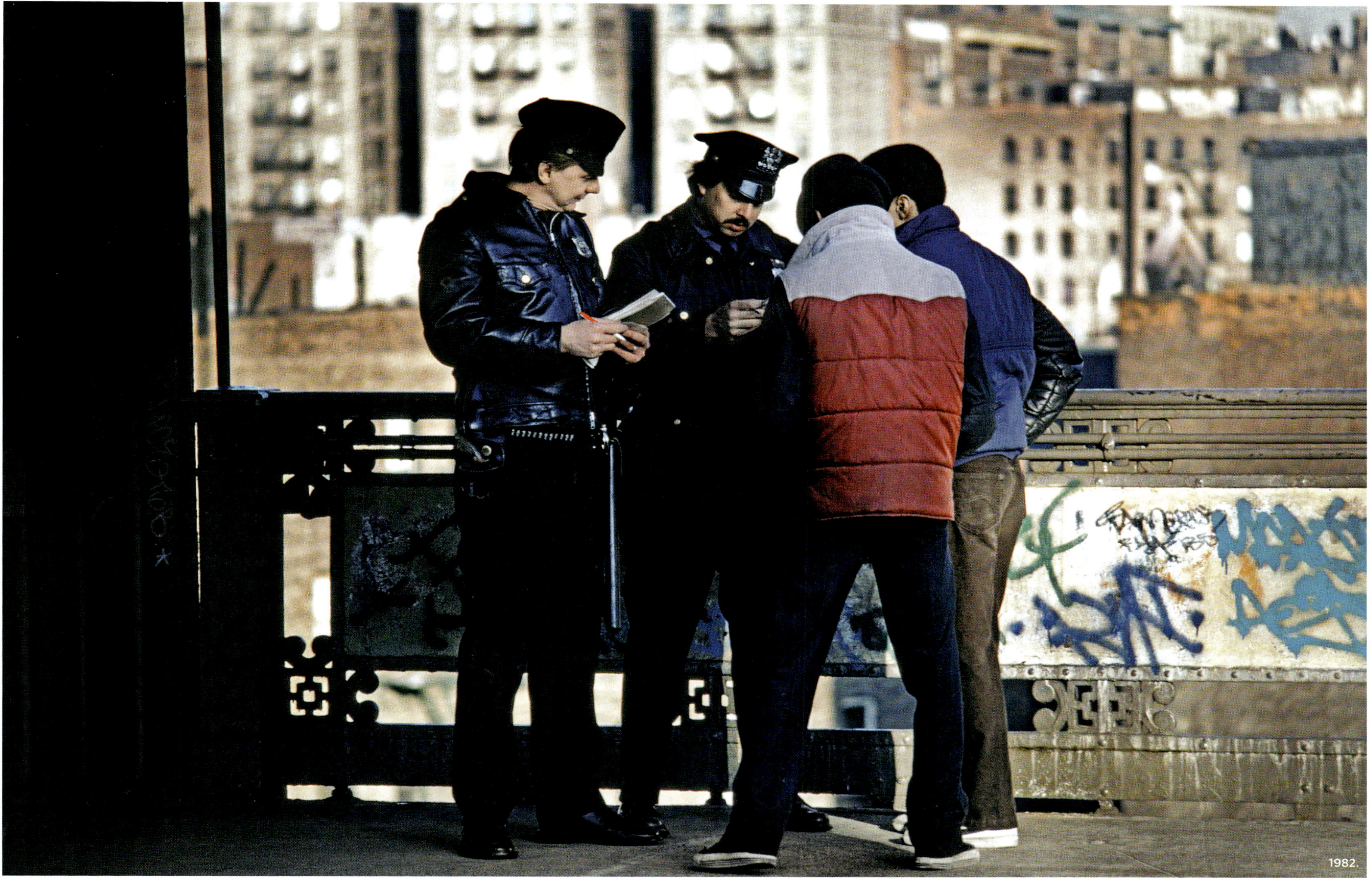

1982.

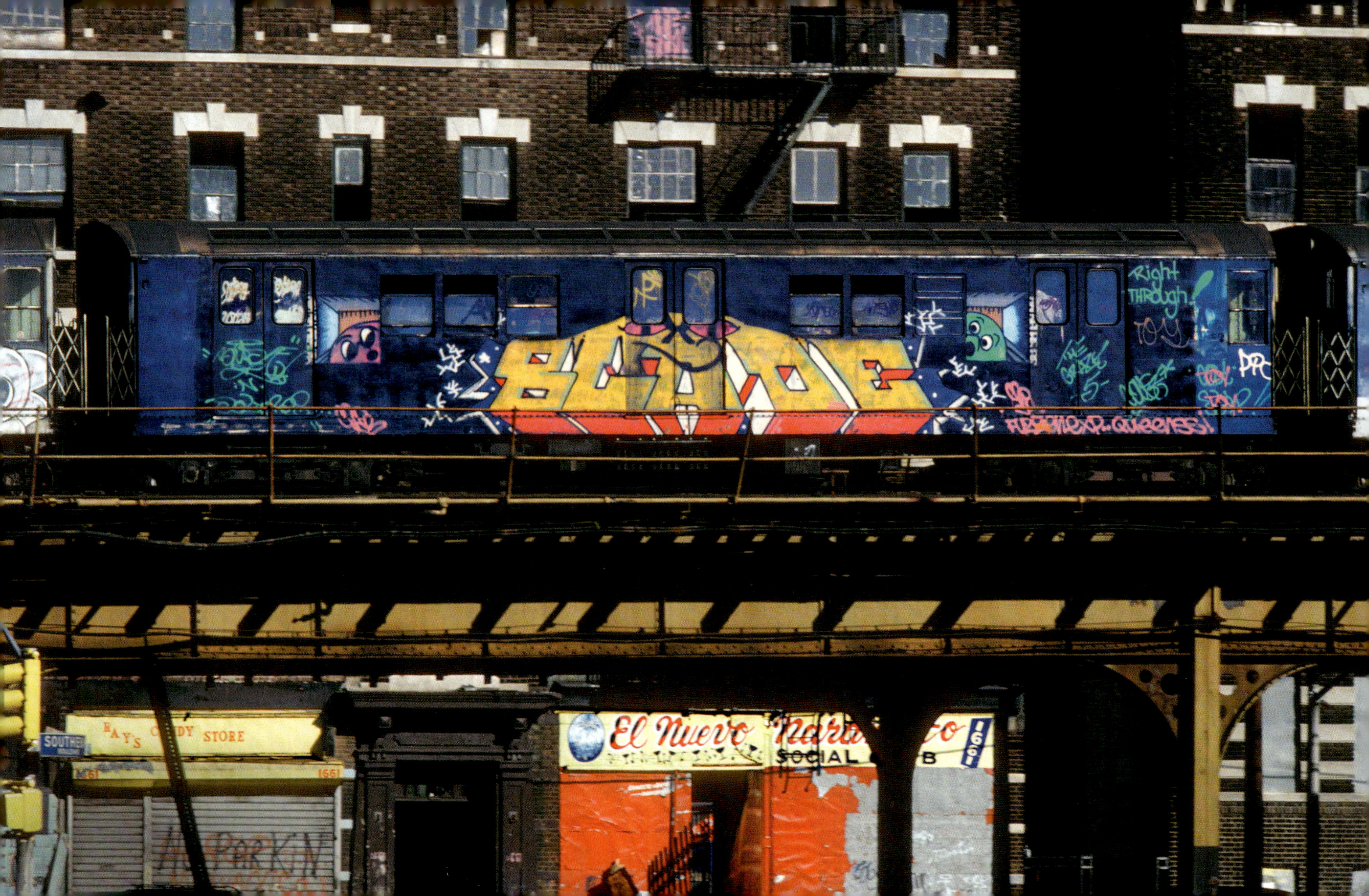

BLADE
Right THROUGH!
RAY'S CANDY STORE
El Nuevo Marabino
SOCIAL CLUB
1661

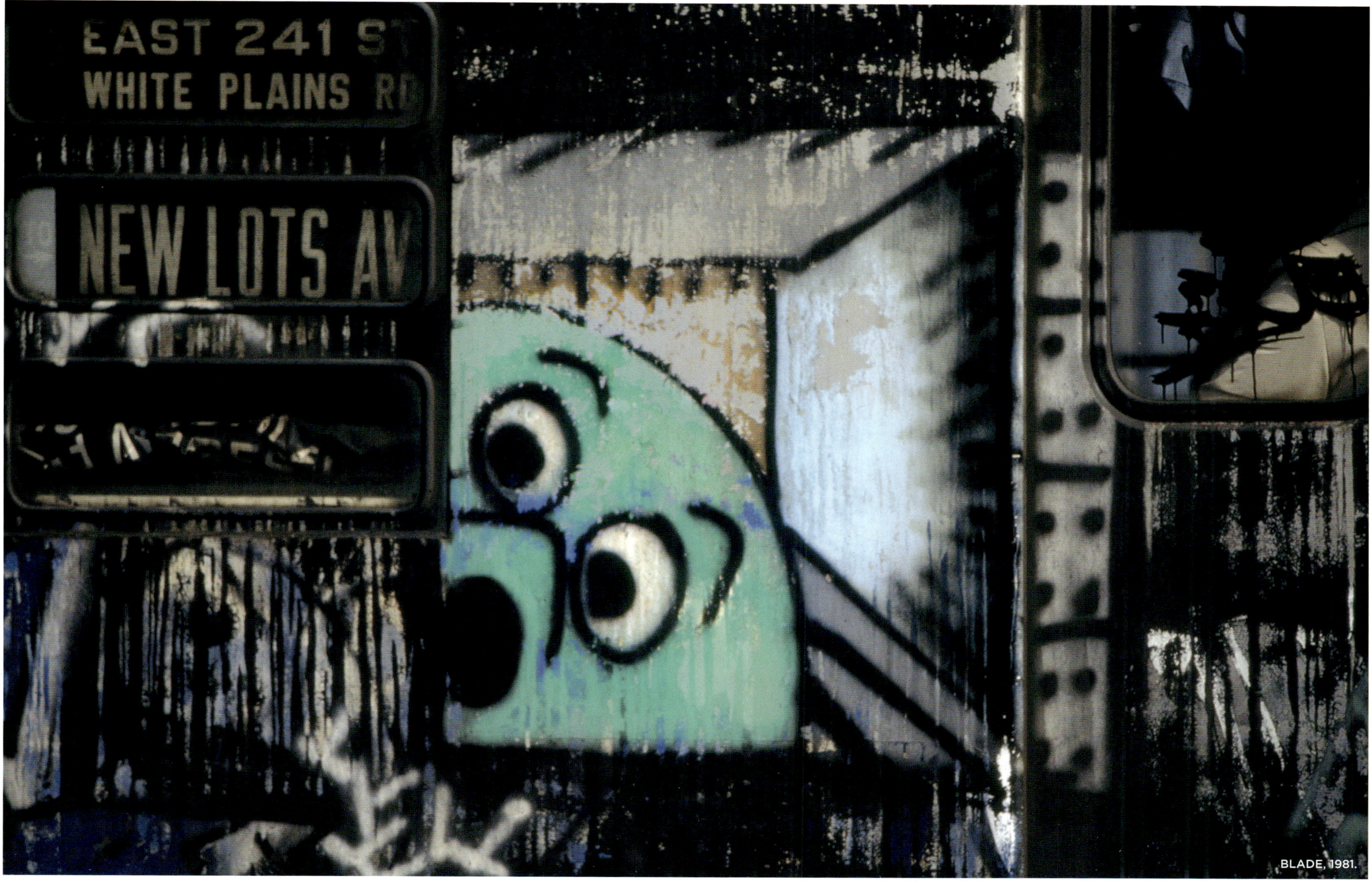

BLADE, 1981.

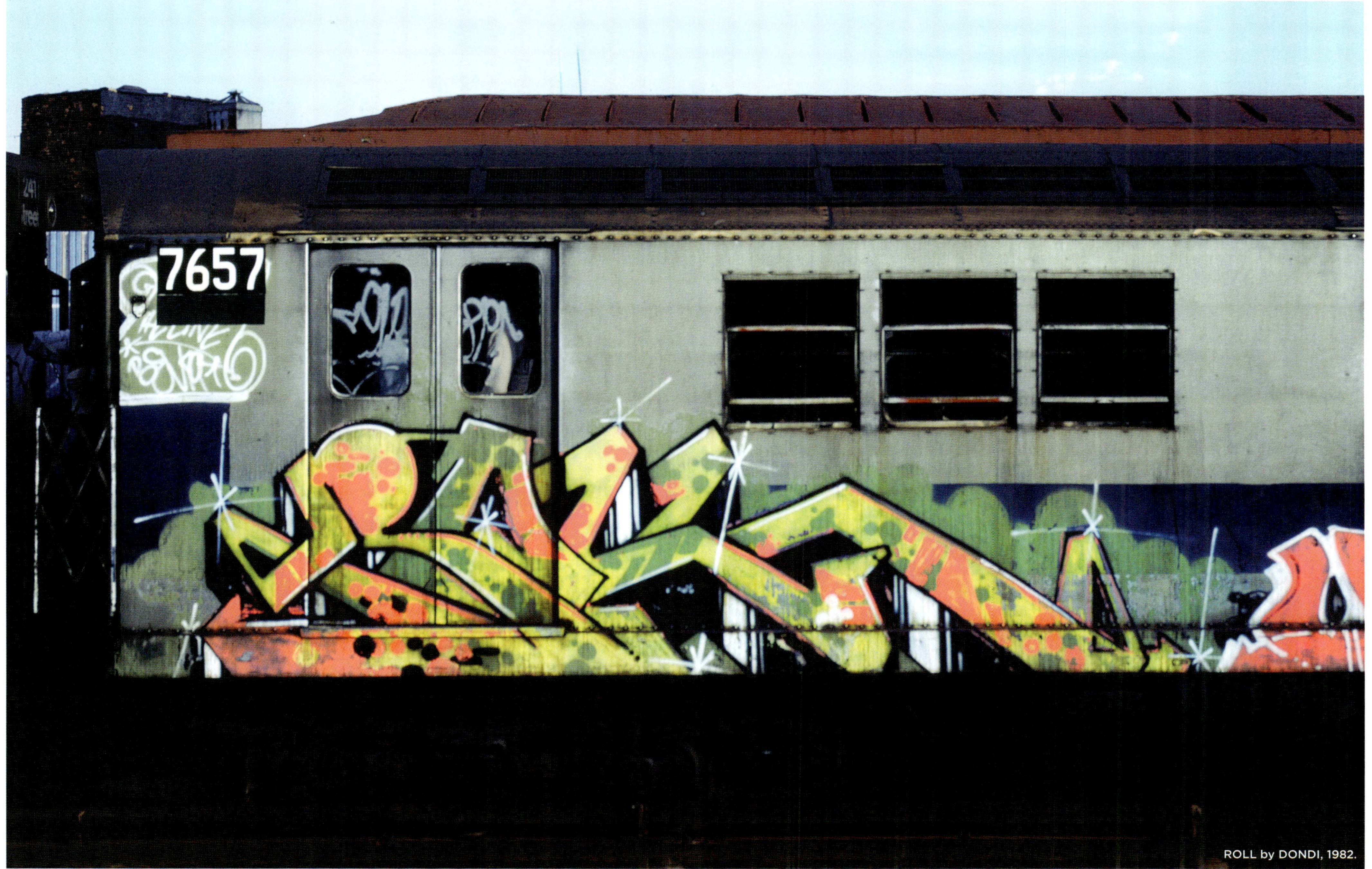

ROLL by DONDI, 1982.

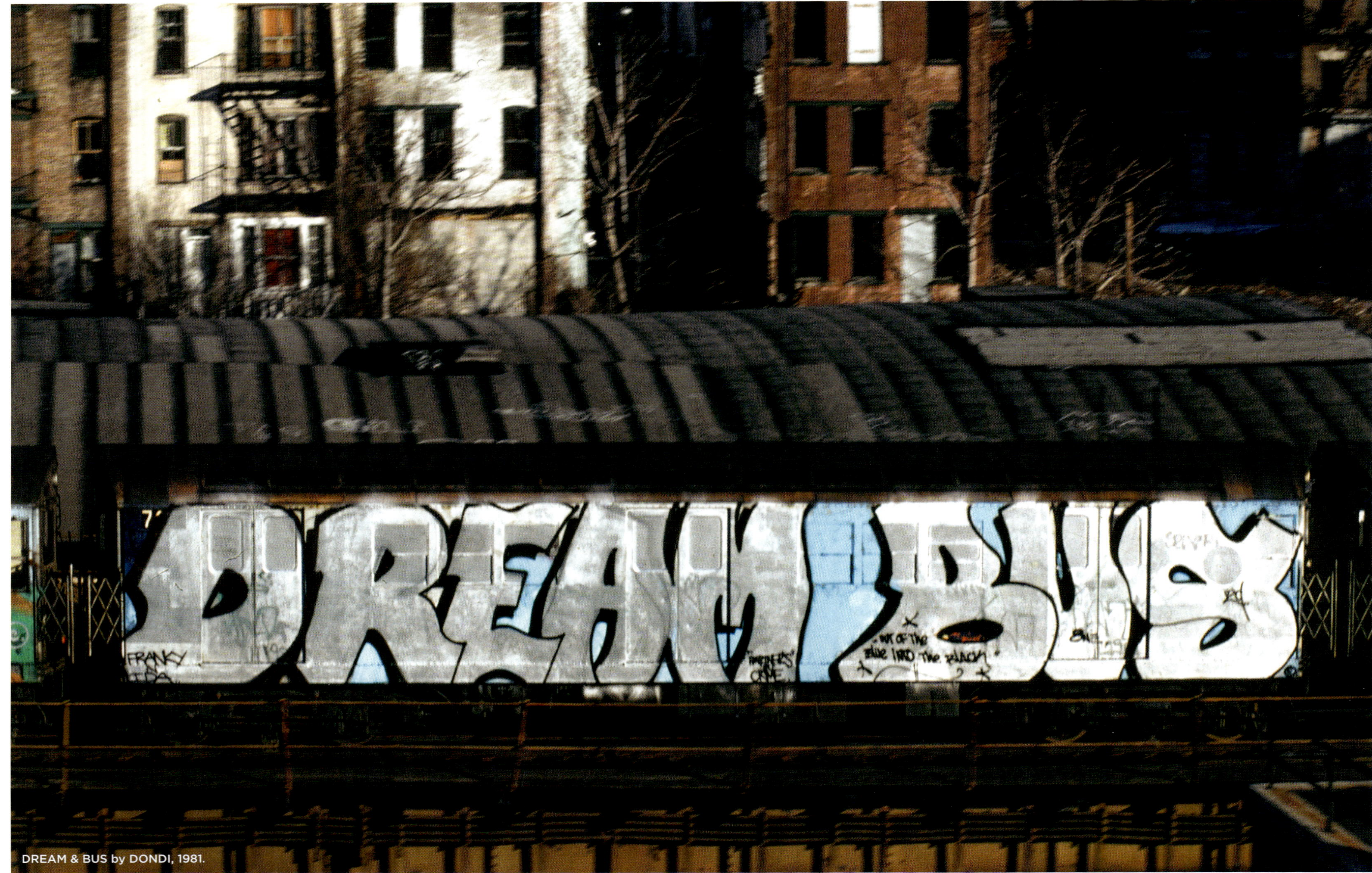

DREAM & BUS by DONDI, 1981.

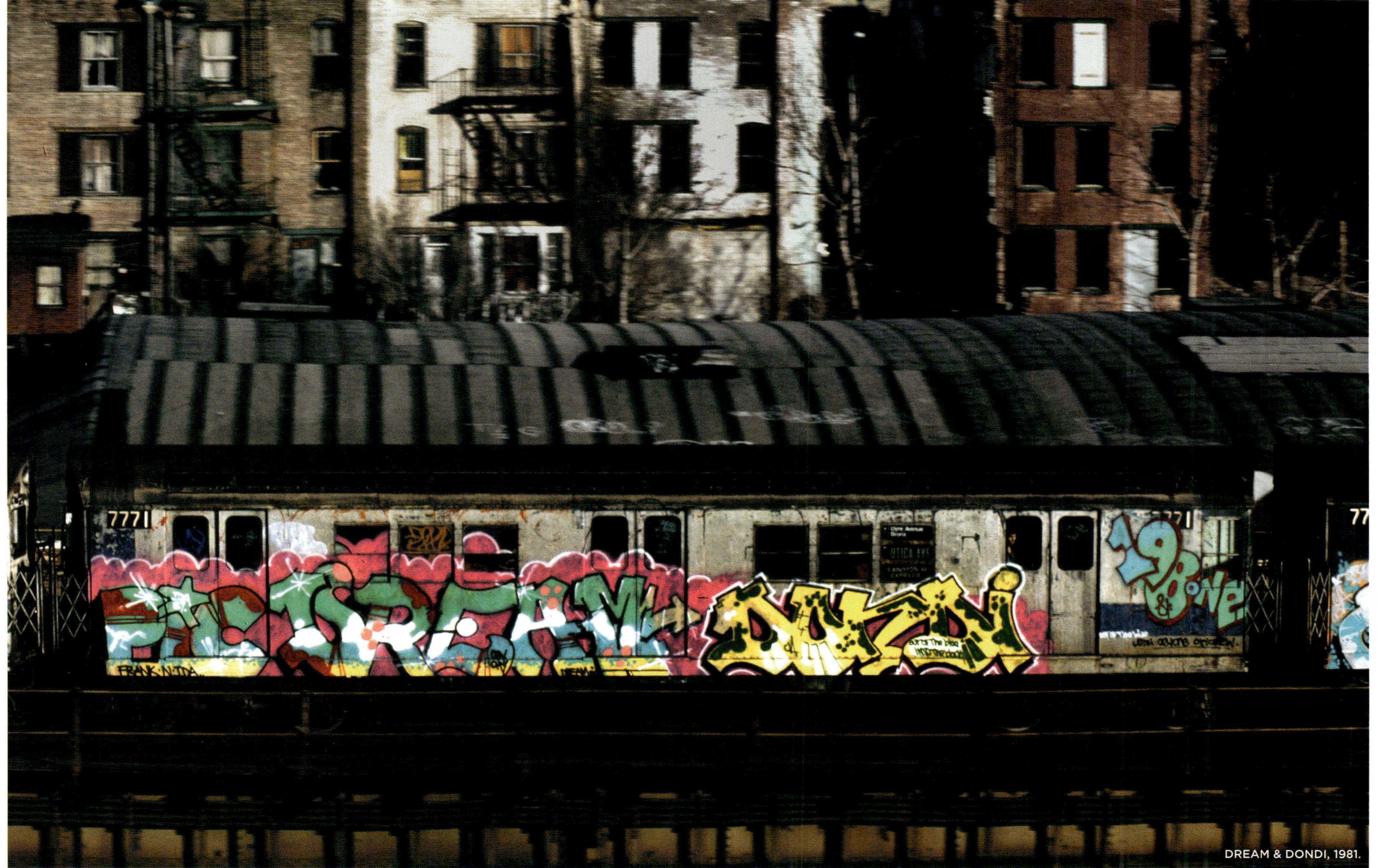

DREAM & DONDI, 1981.

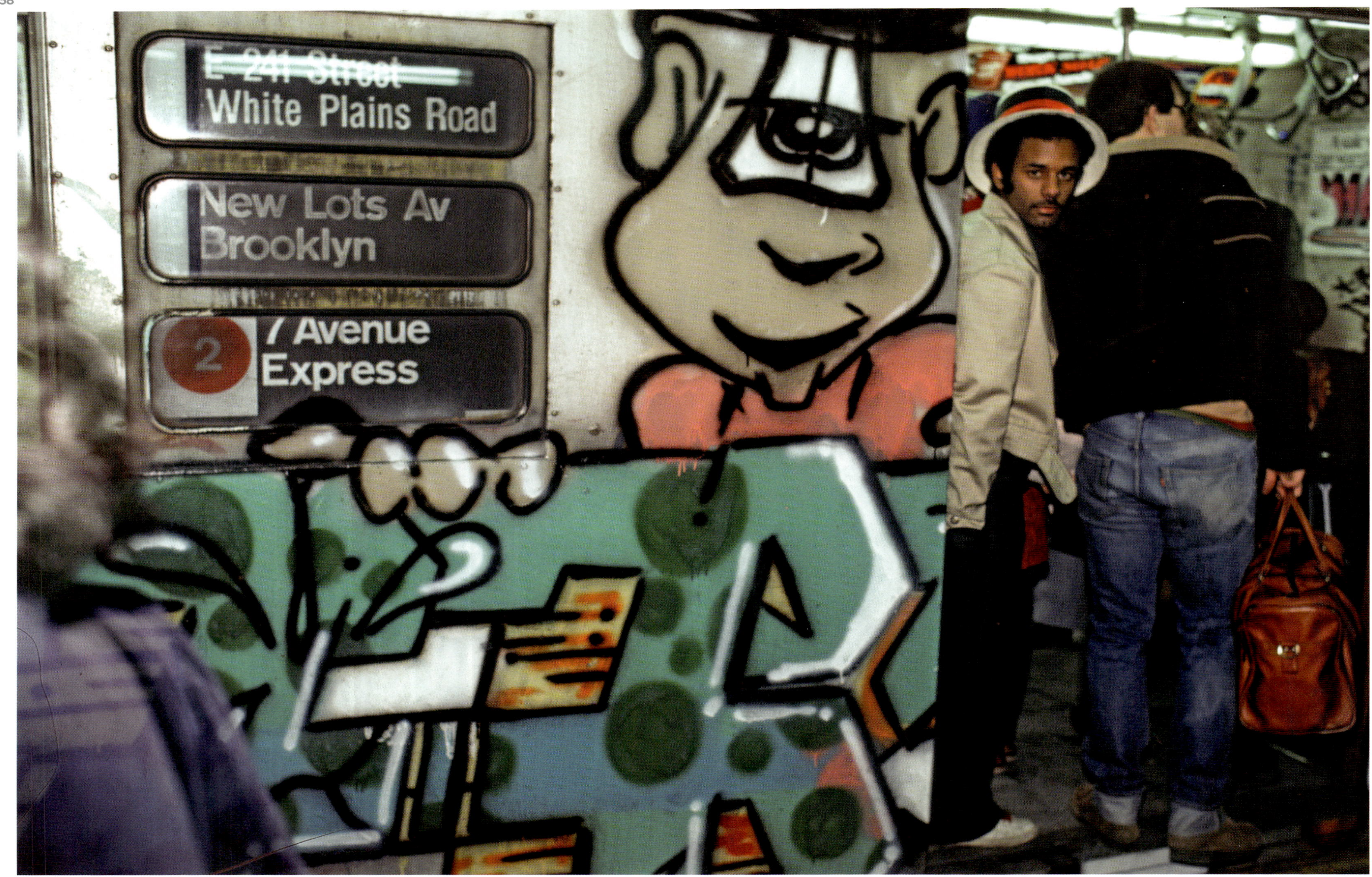
E 241 Street
White Plains Road
New Lots Av
Brooklyn
2
7 Avenue
Express

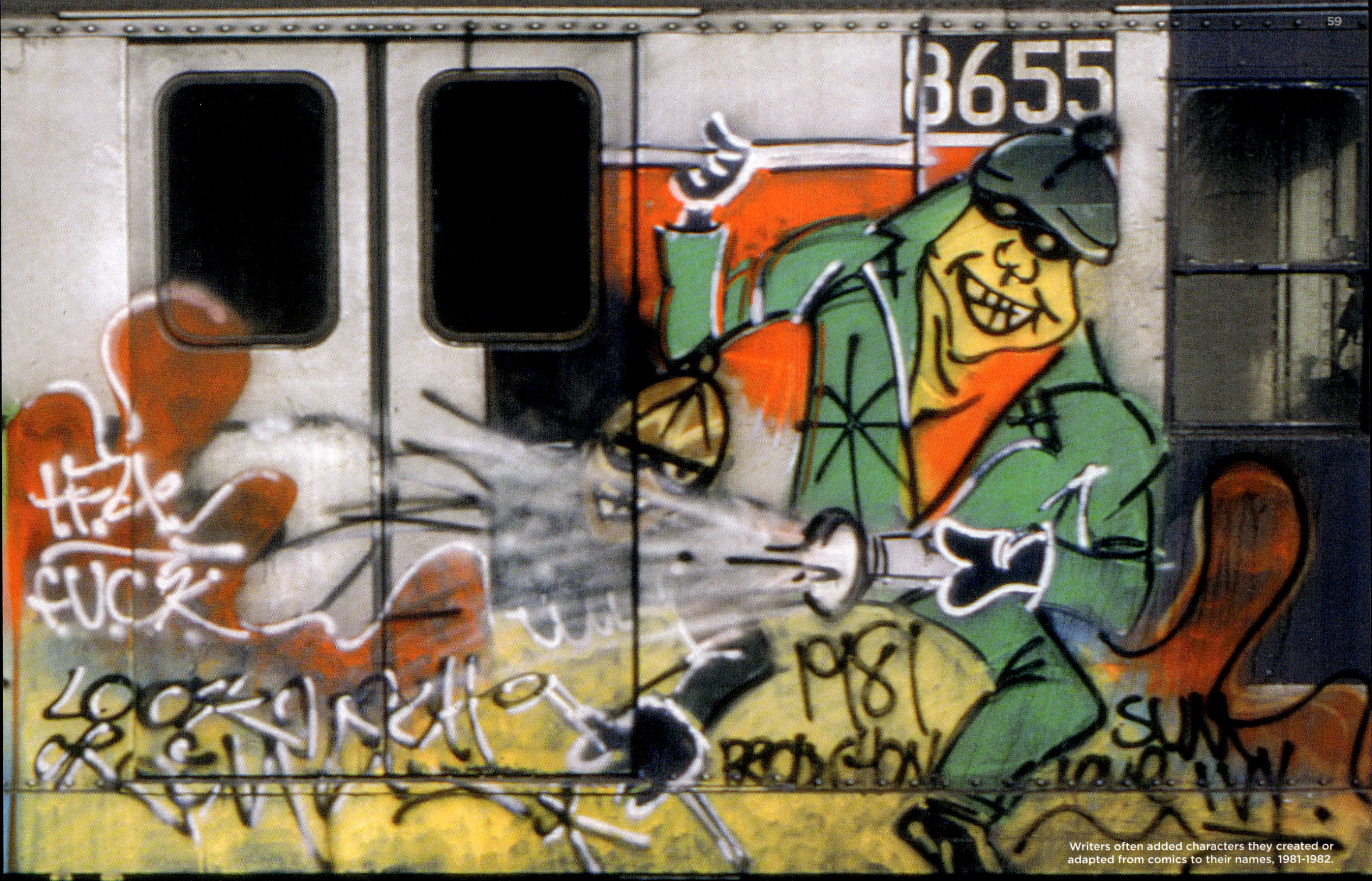

Writers often added characters they created or adapted from comics to their names, 1981-1982.

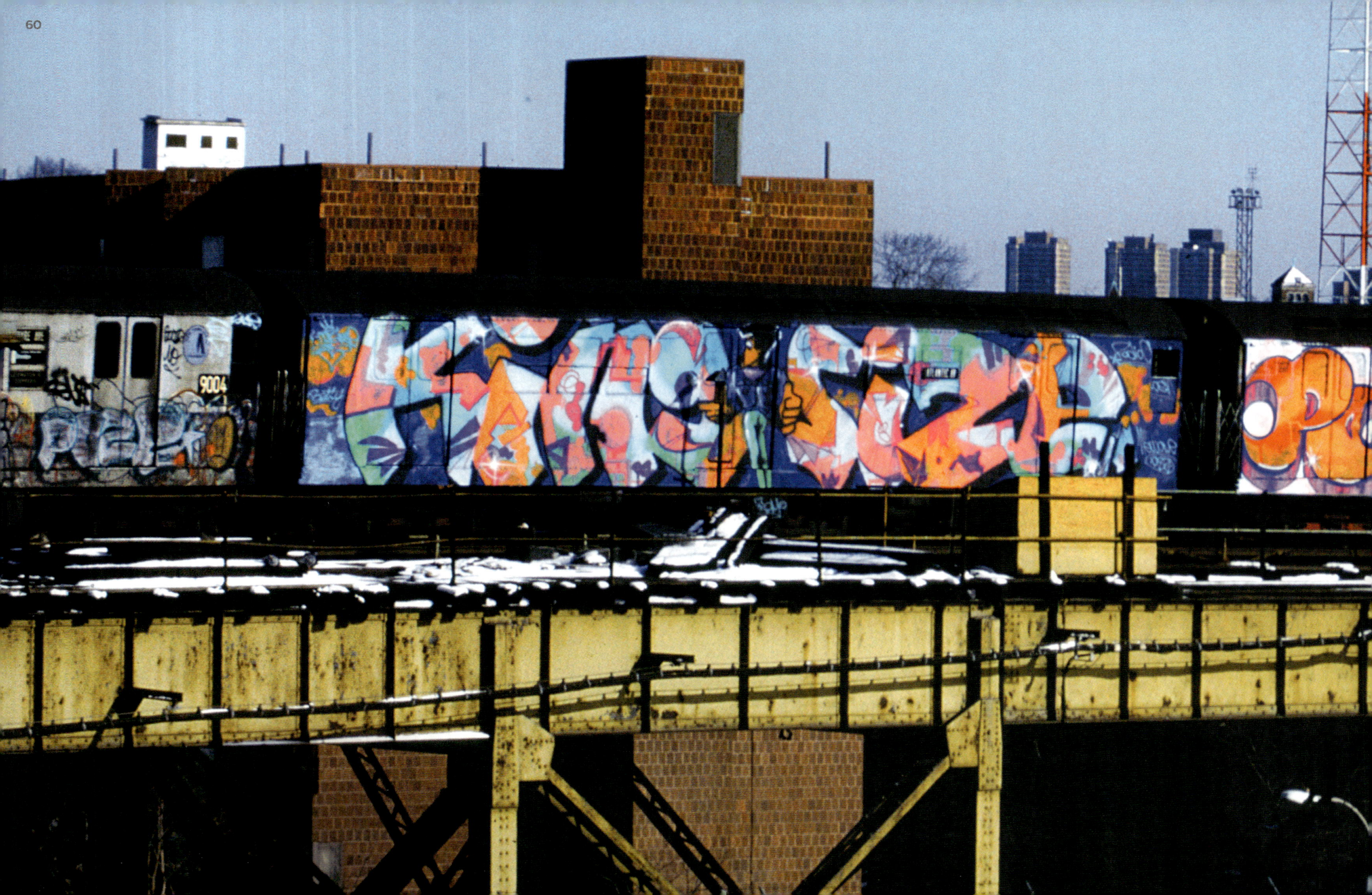

9004

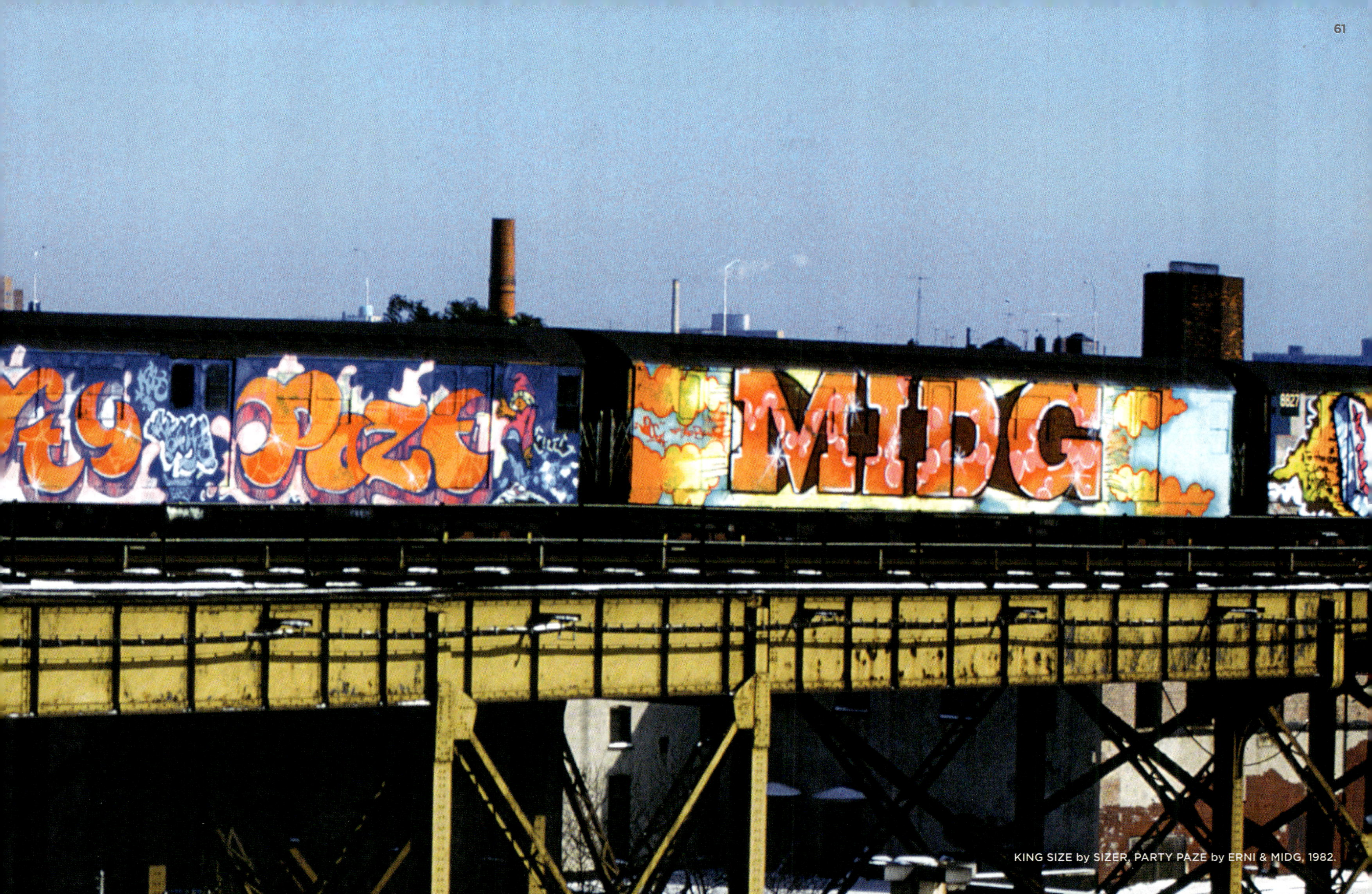

KING SIZE by SIZER, PARTY PAZE by ERNI & MIDG, 1982.

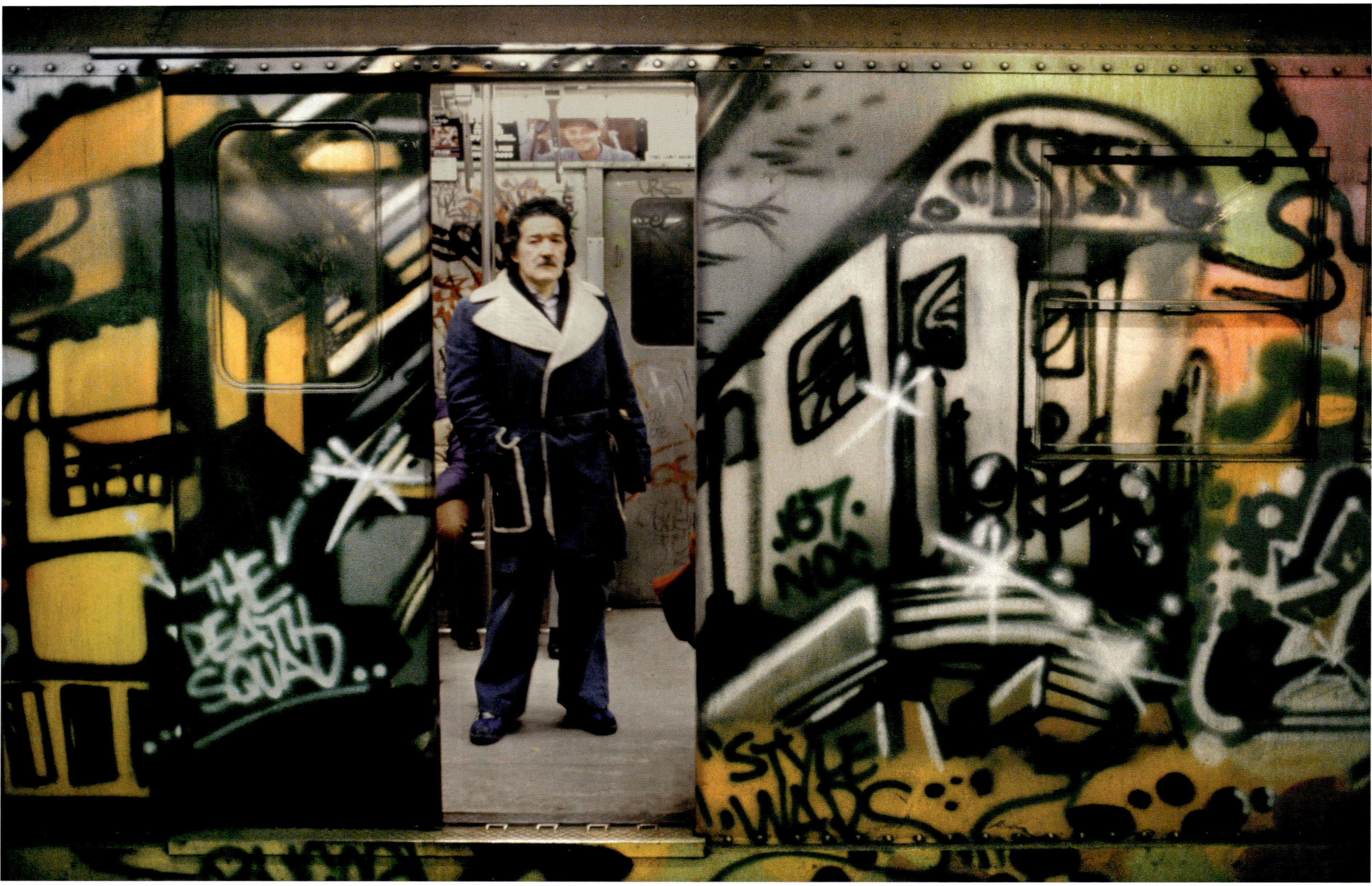
THE DEATH SQUAD
67 NO
STYLE WARS

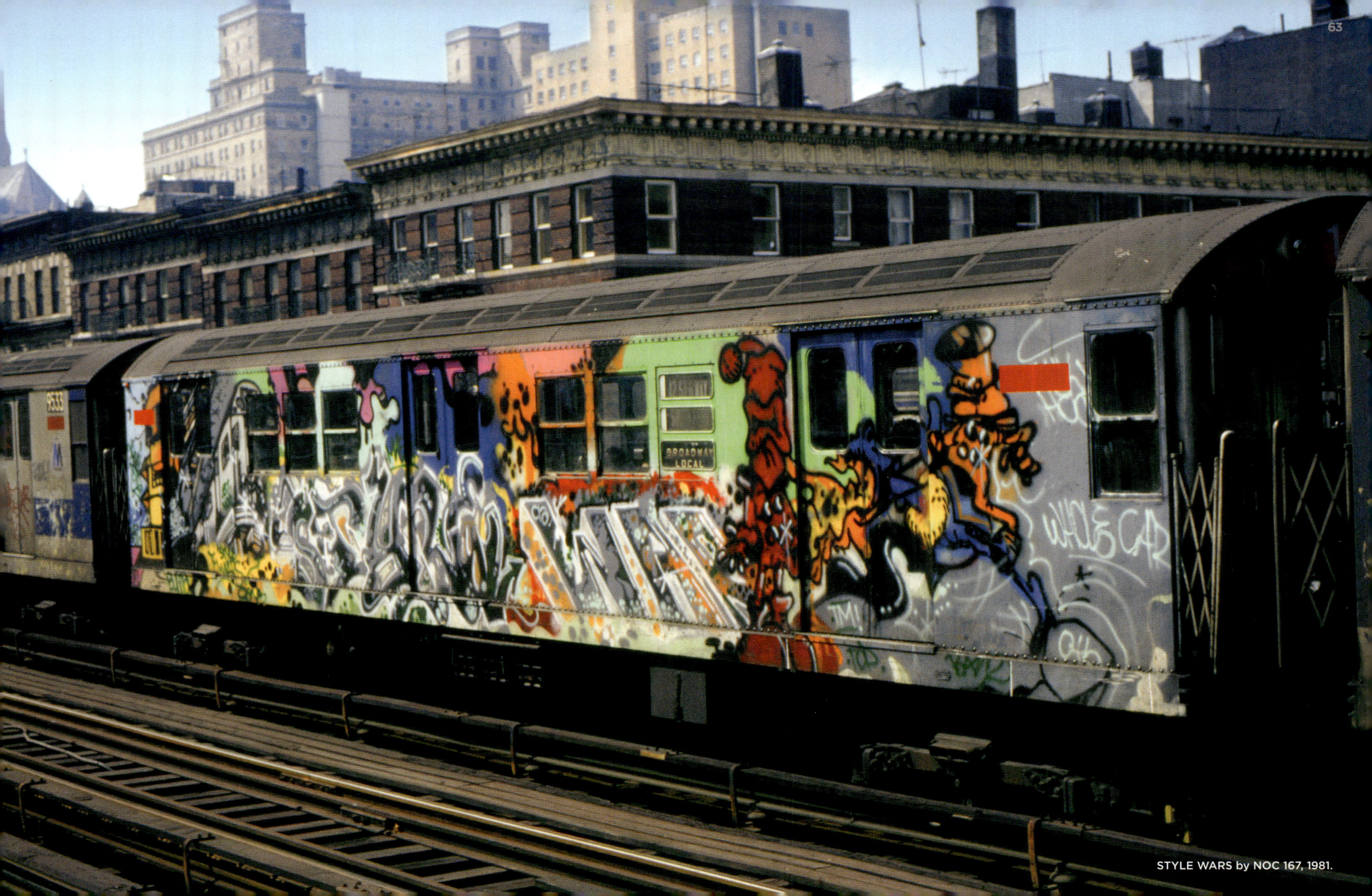

STYLE WARS by NOC 167, 1981.

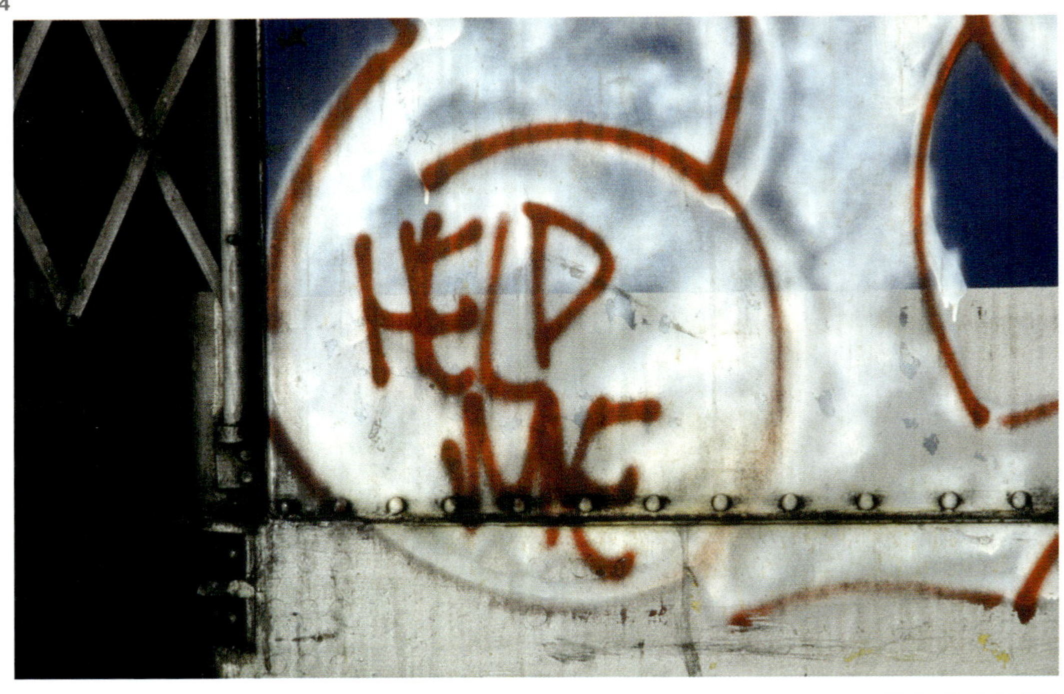
HELP
ME

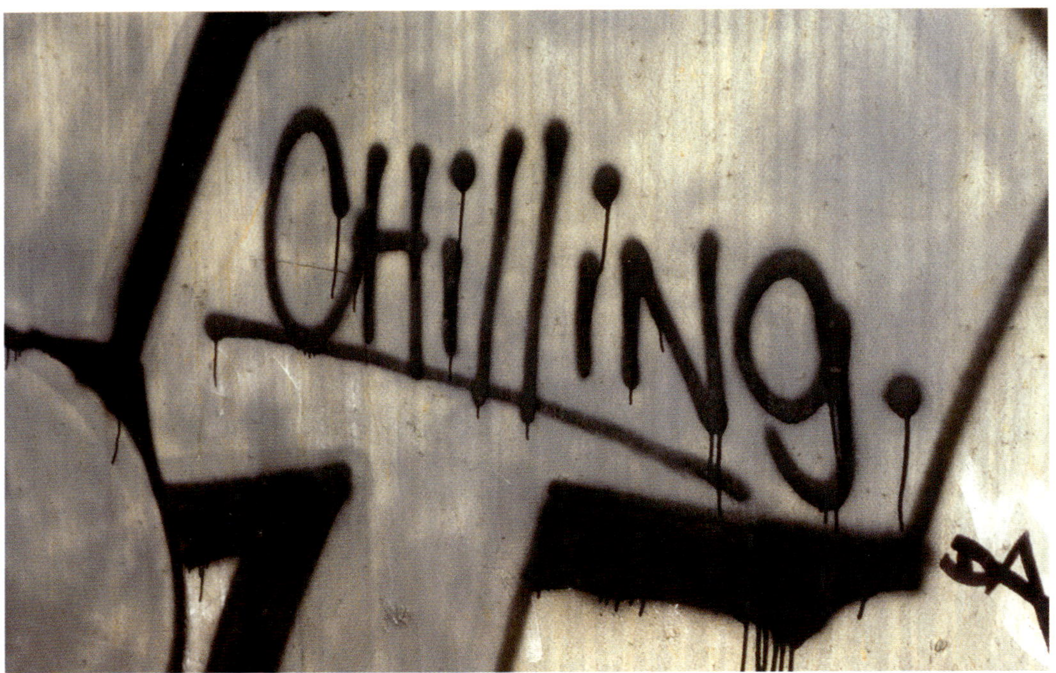
Chilling.

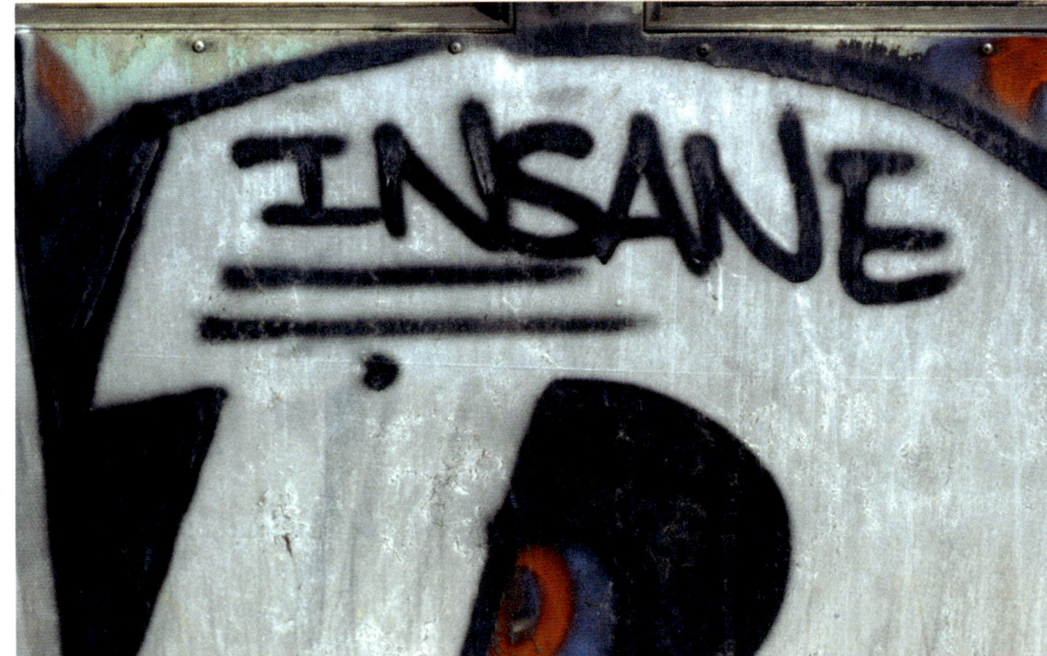
INSANE

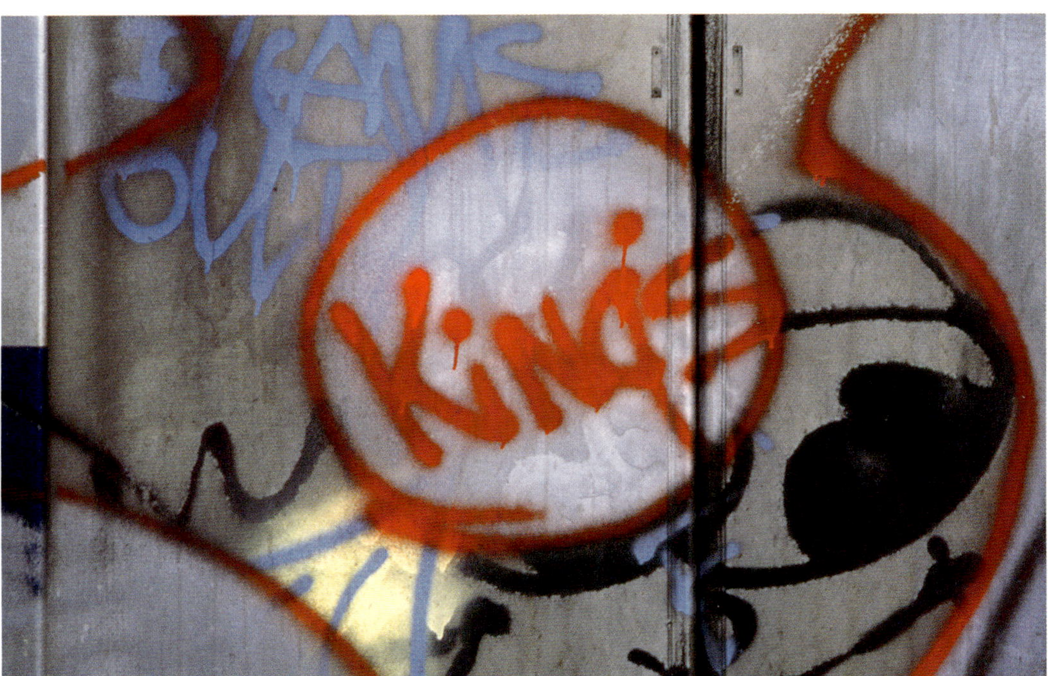
KINGS

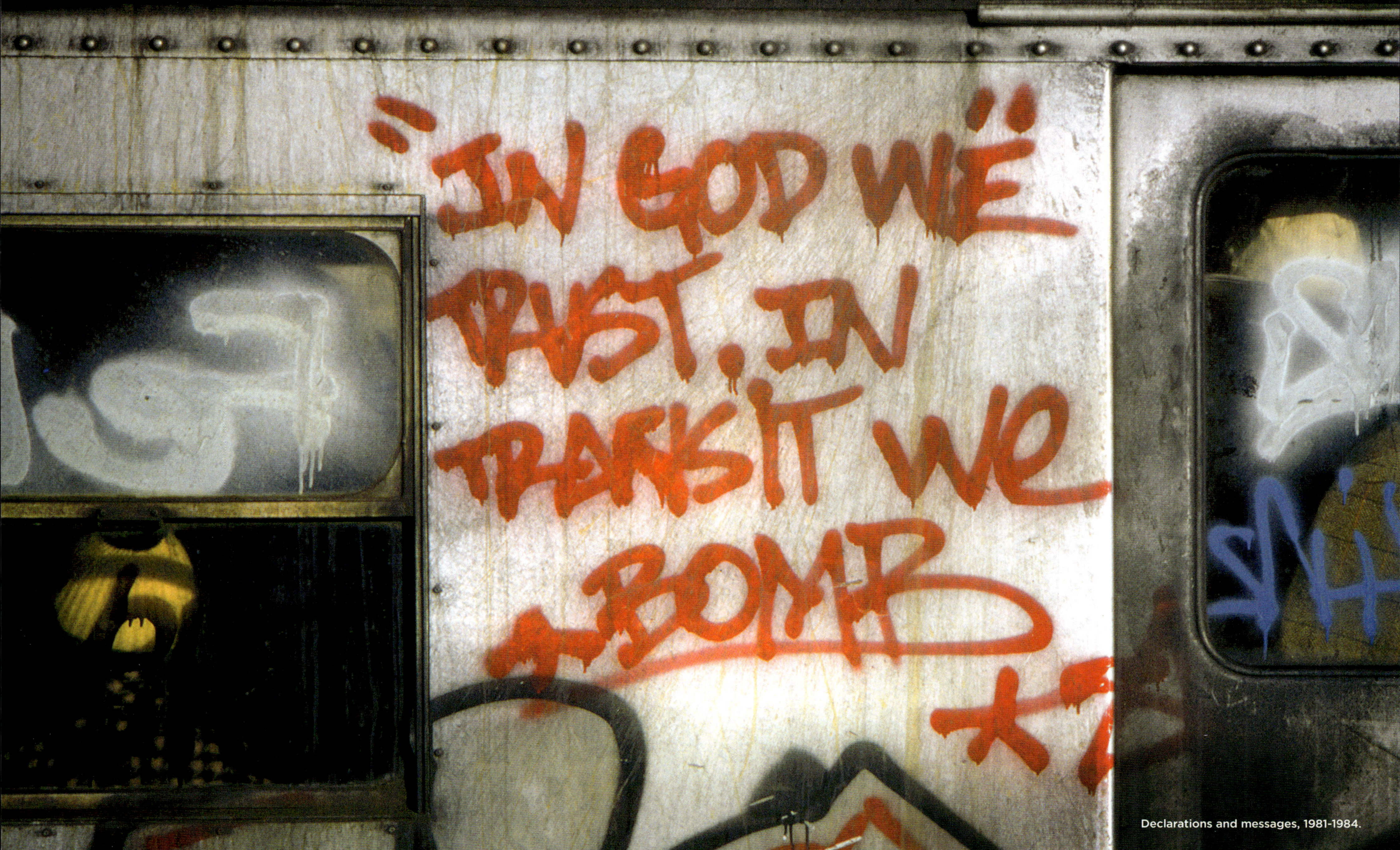

Declarations and messages, 1981-1984.

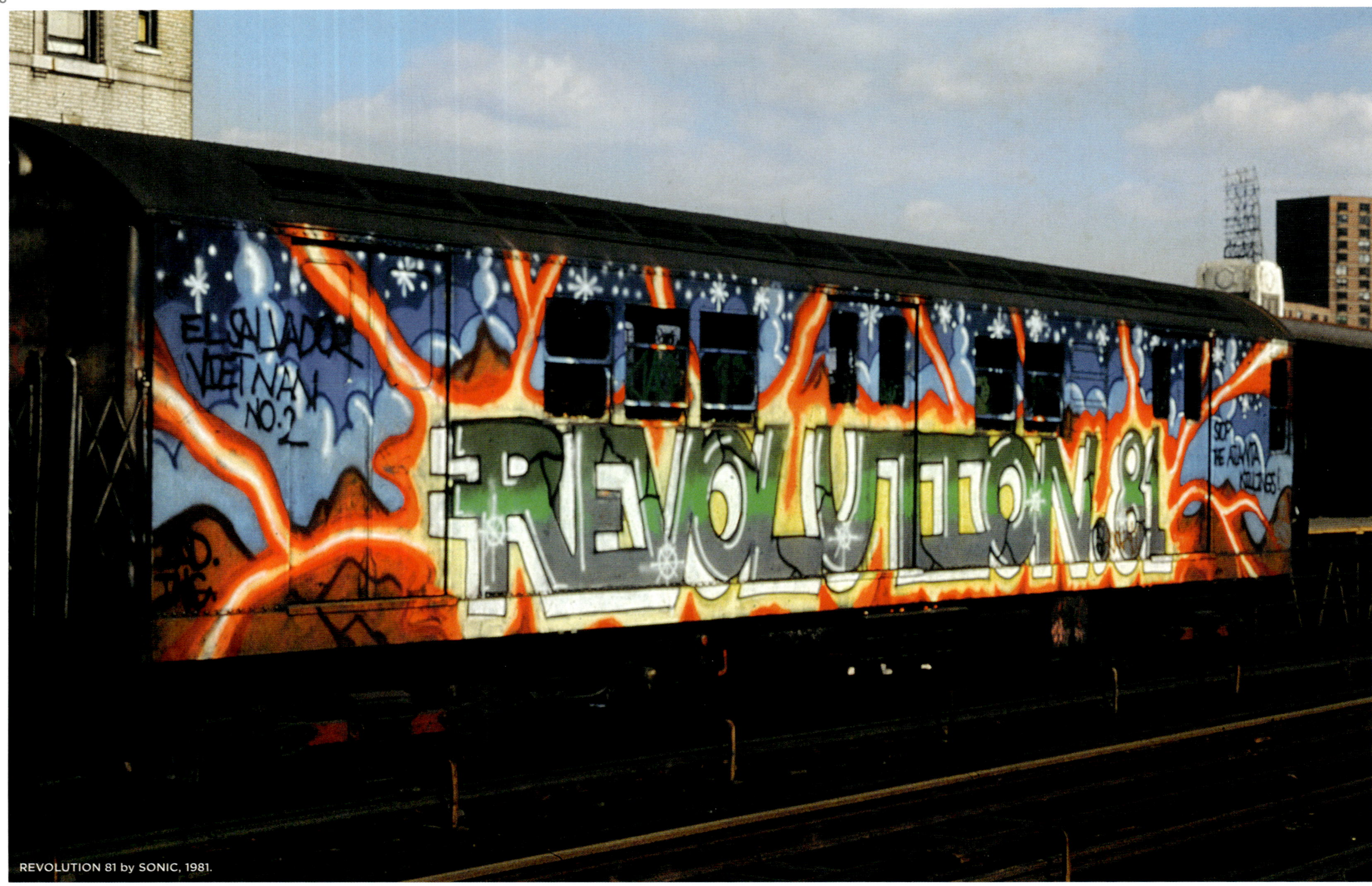

REVOLUTION 81 by SONIC, 1981.

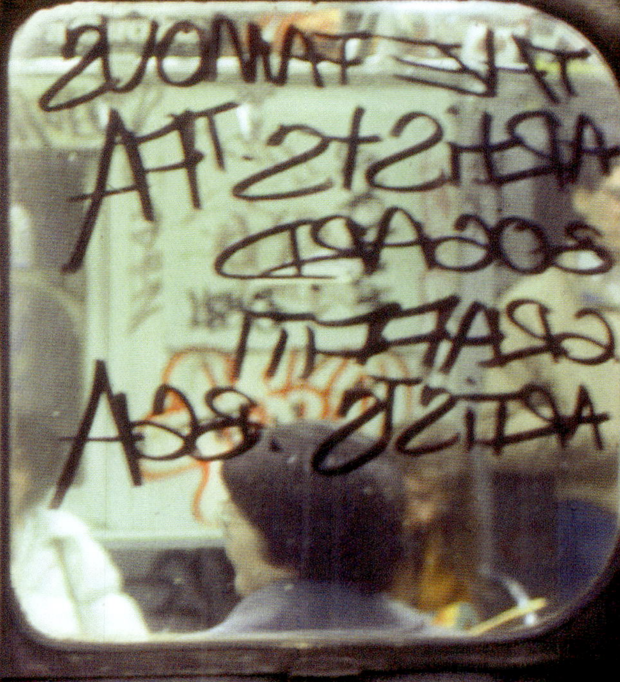

1980.

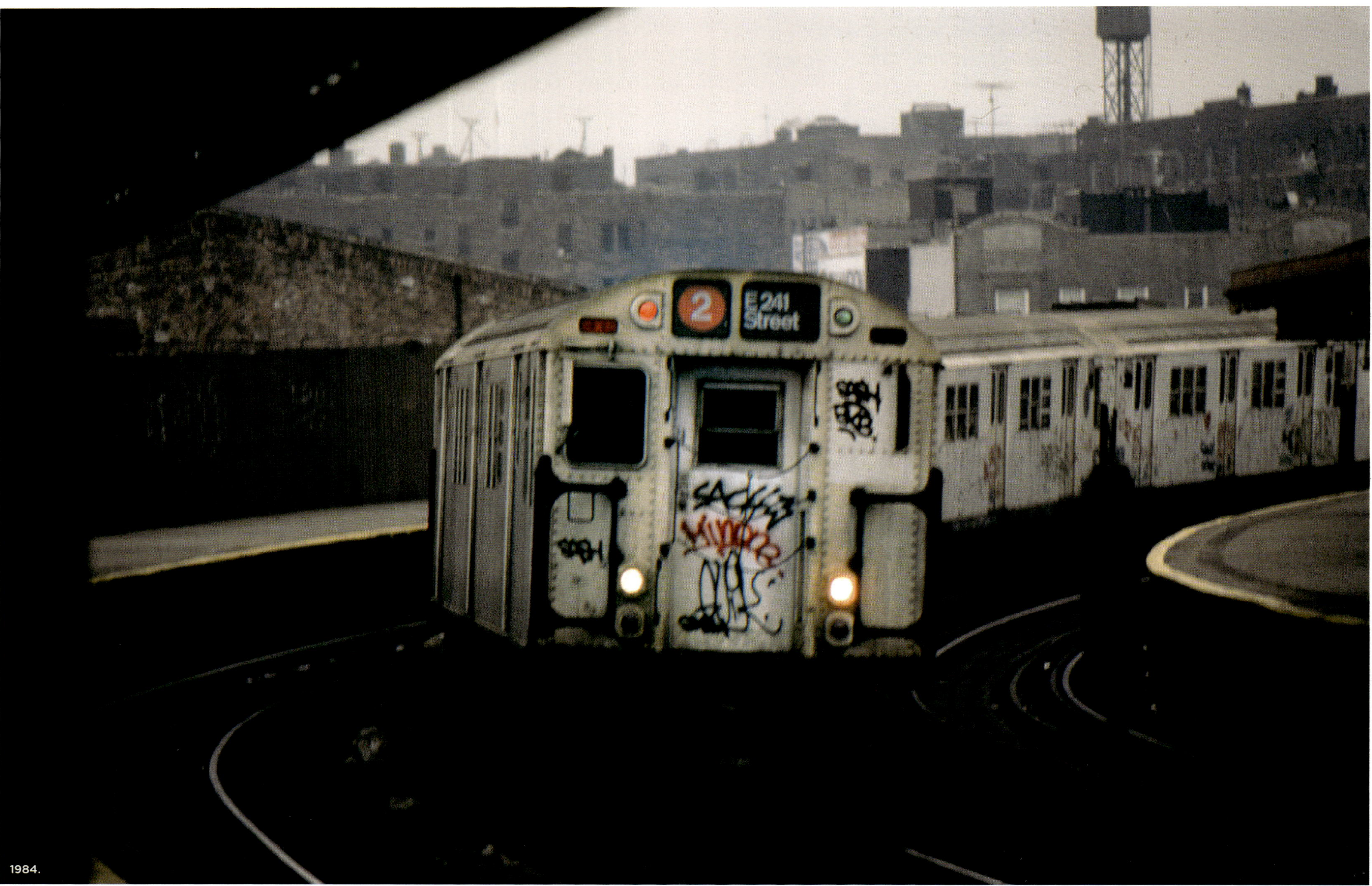

1984.

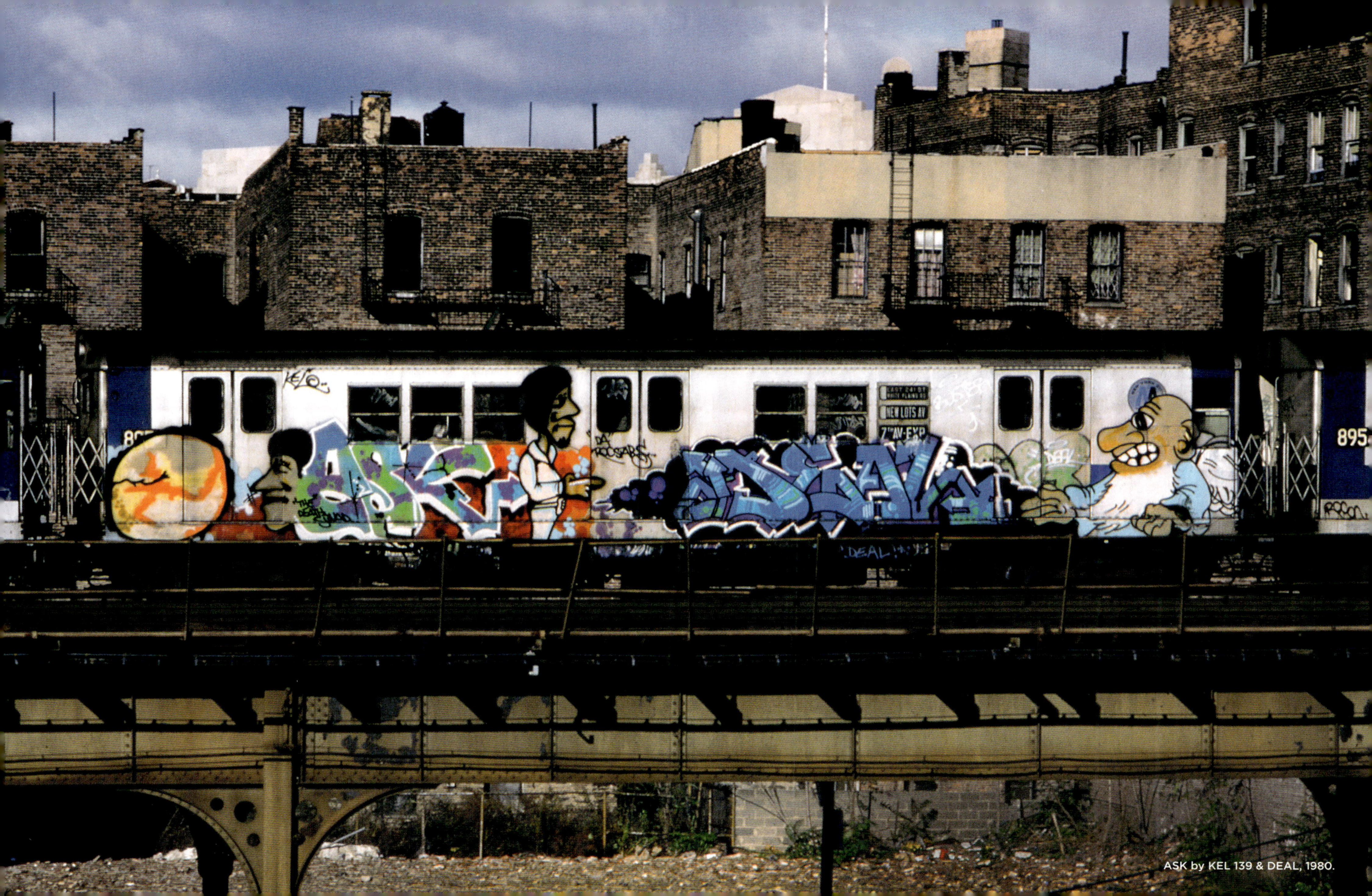

ASK by KEL 139 & DEAL, 1980.

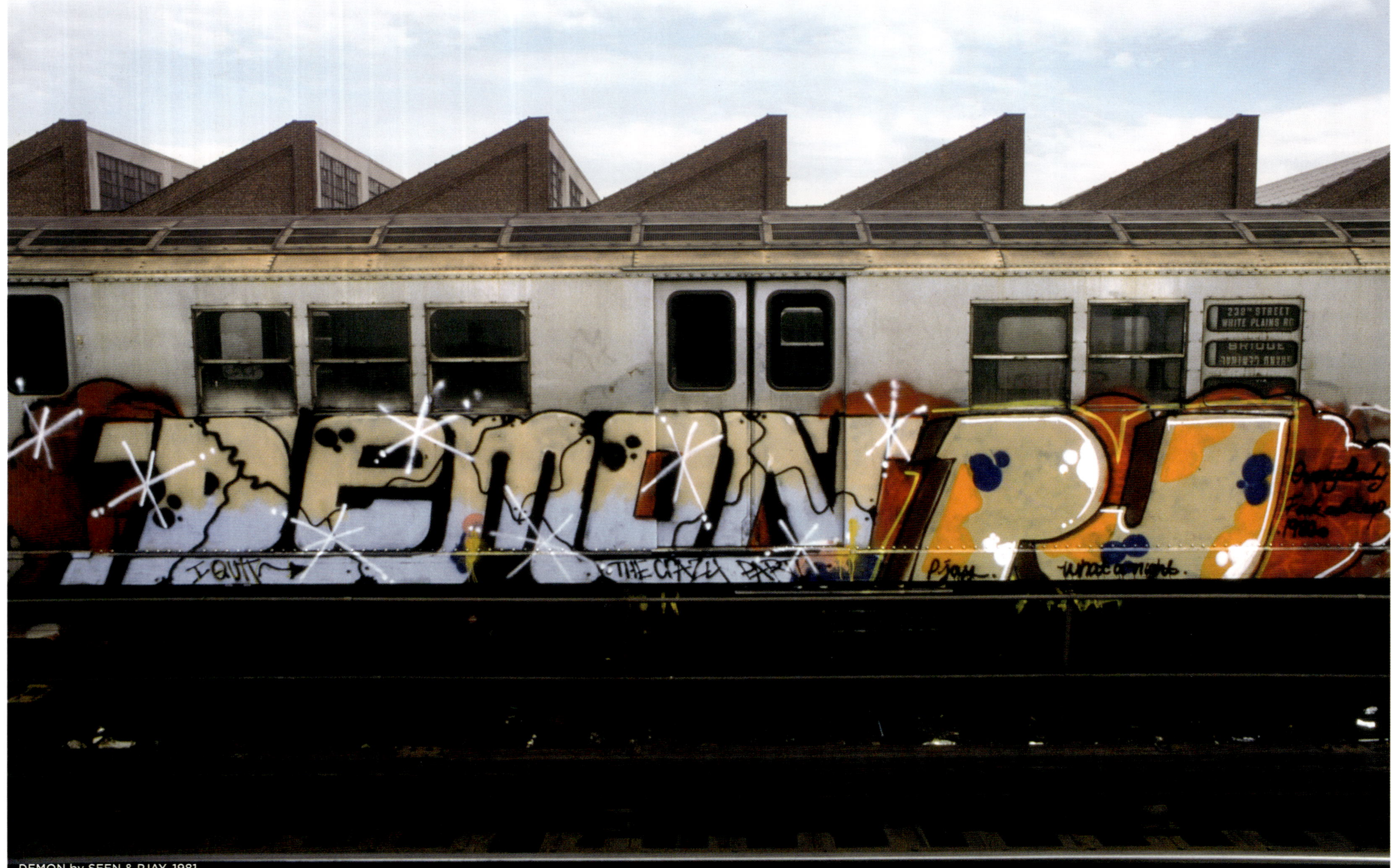

DEMON by SEEN & PJAY, 1981.

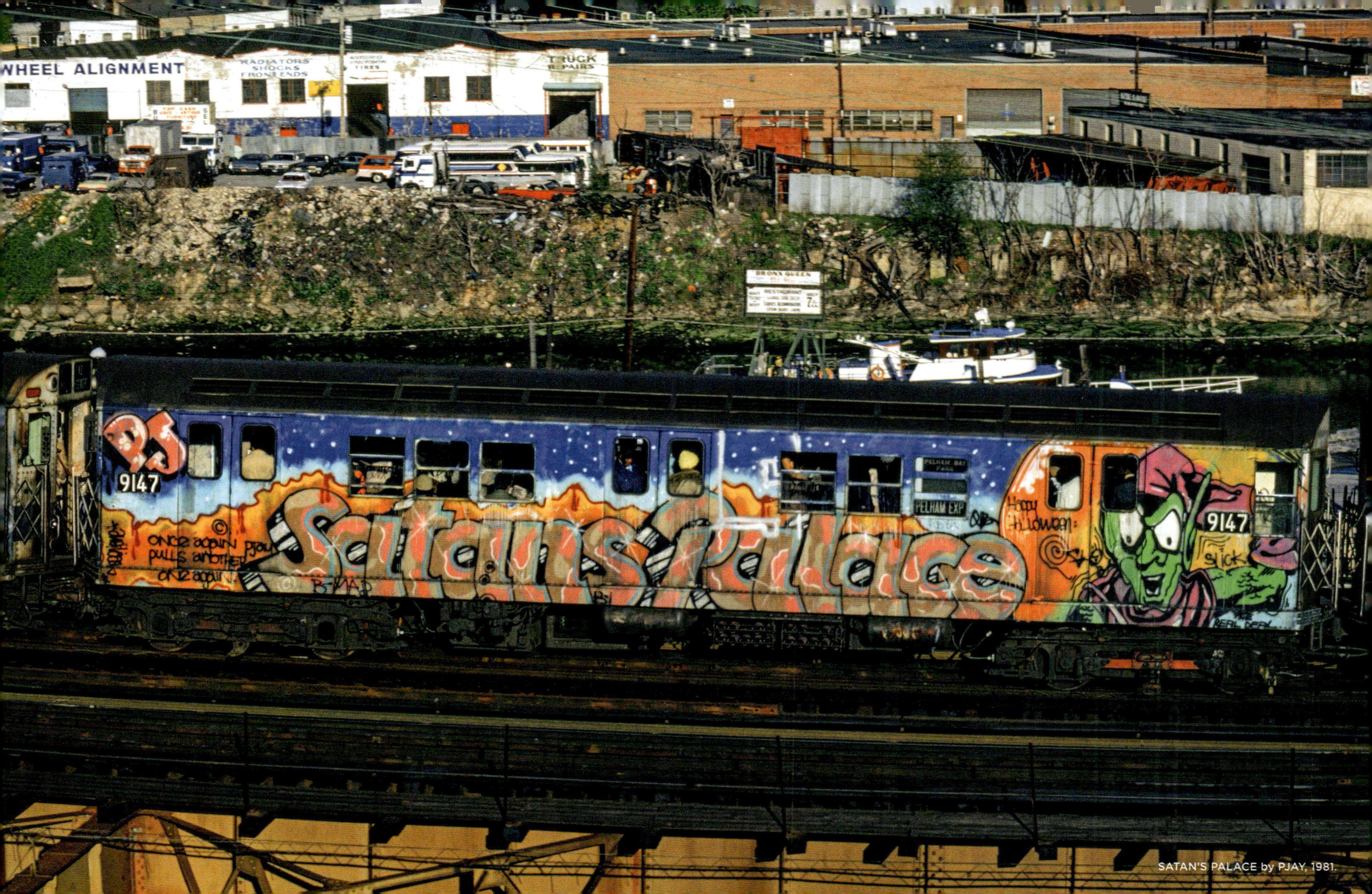

WHEEL ALIGNMENT
RADIATORS
SHOCKS
FRONT ENDS
TIRES
TRUCK
REPAIRS
PJ
9147
Satans Palace
once again pjay pulls another once again
Happy Halloween
9147
BRONX QUEEN
RESTAURANT
PELHAM EXP

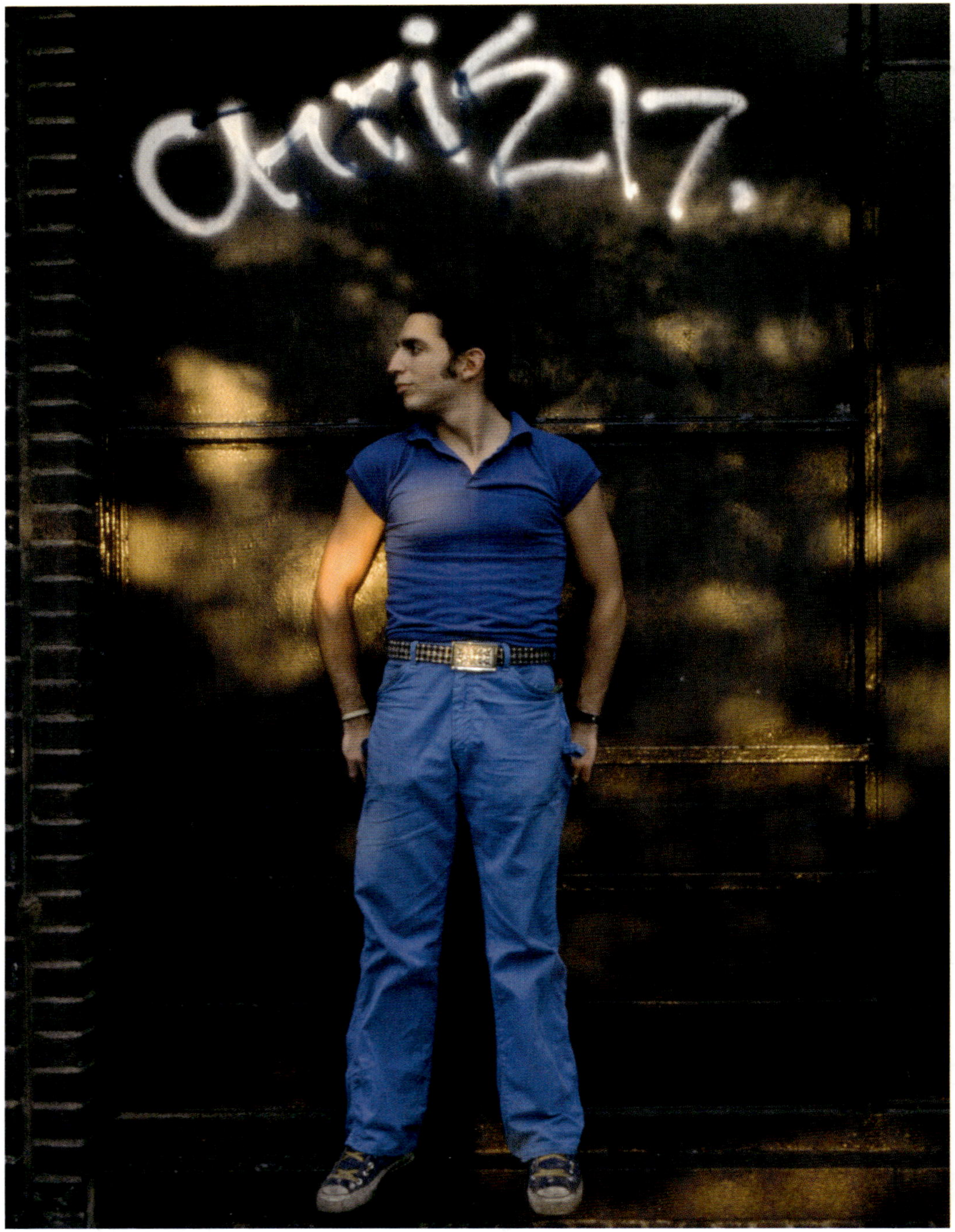

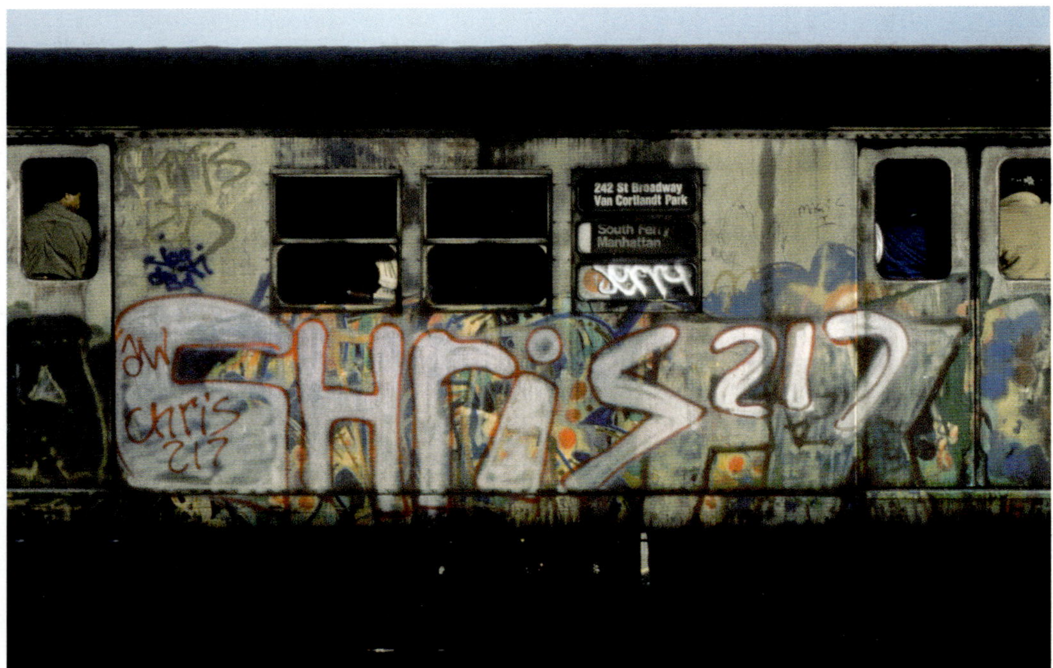

242 St Broadway
Van Cortlandt Park
South Ferry
Manhattan

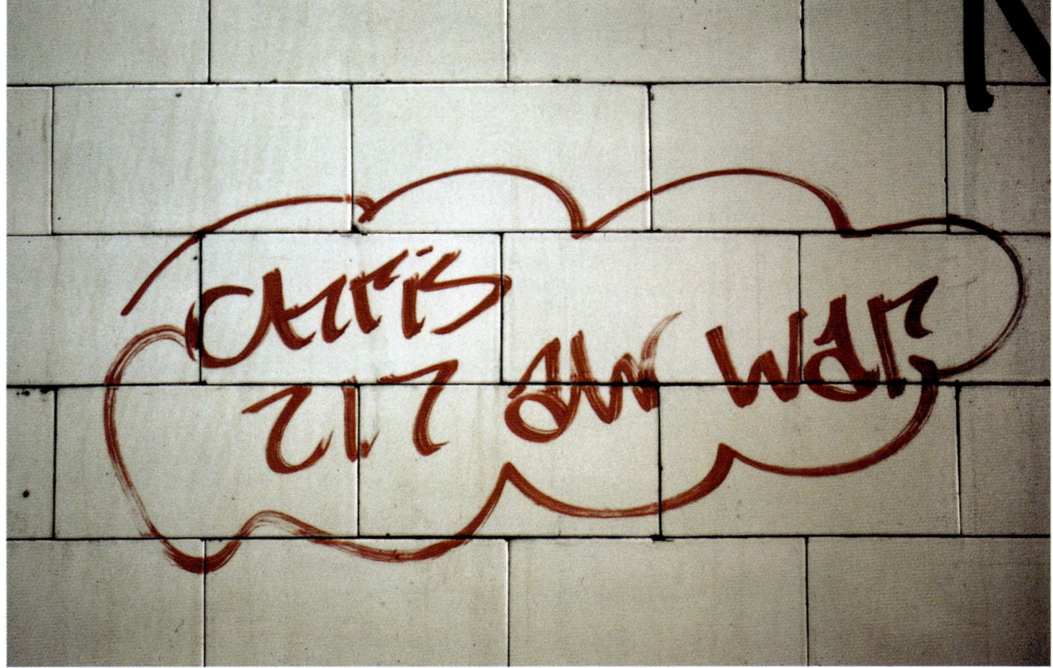

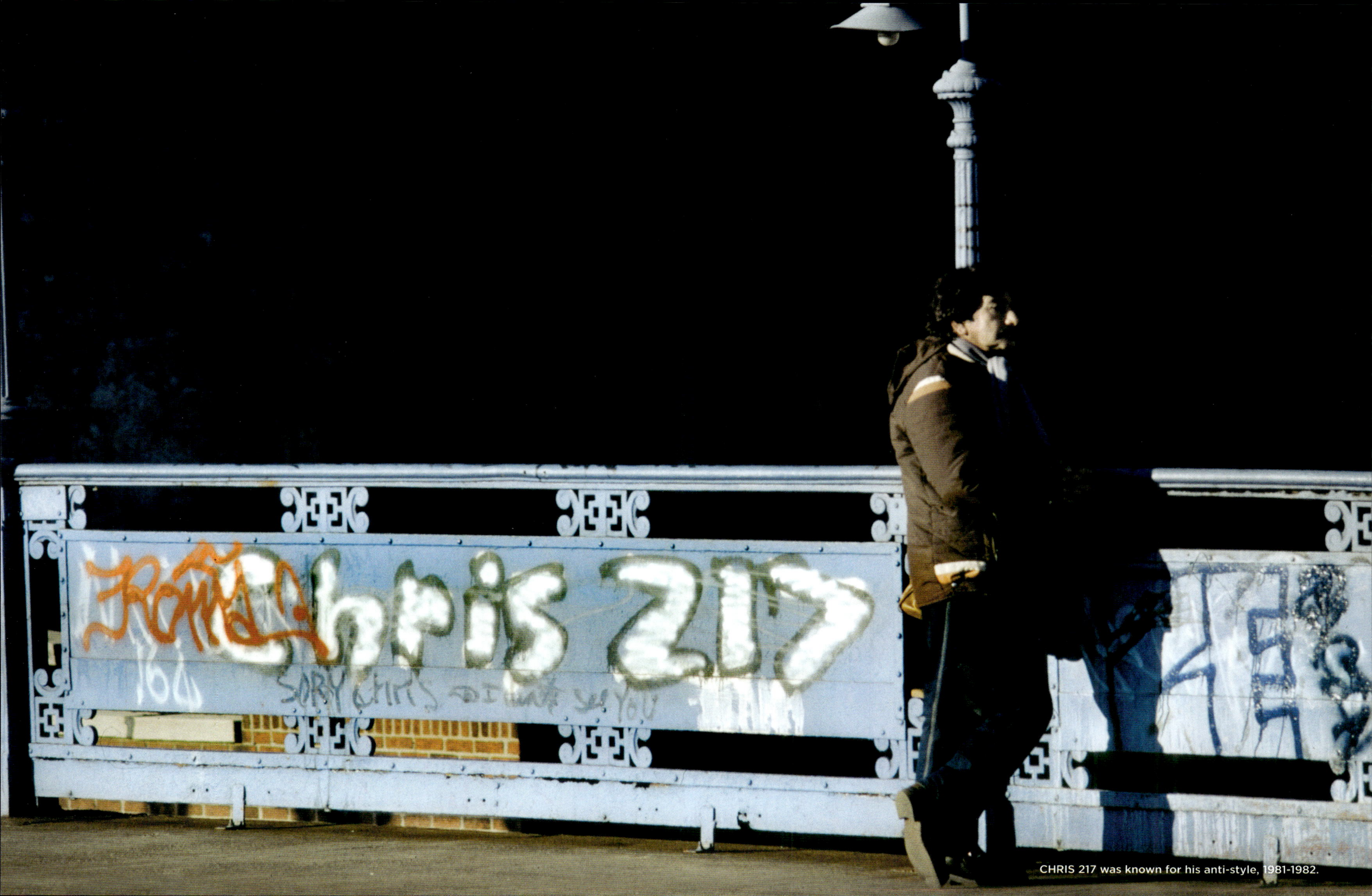

CHRIS 217 was known for his anti-style, 1981-1982.

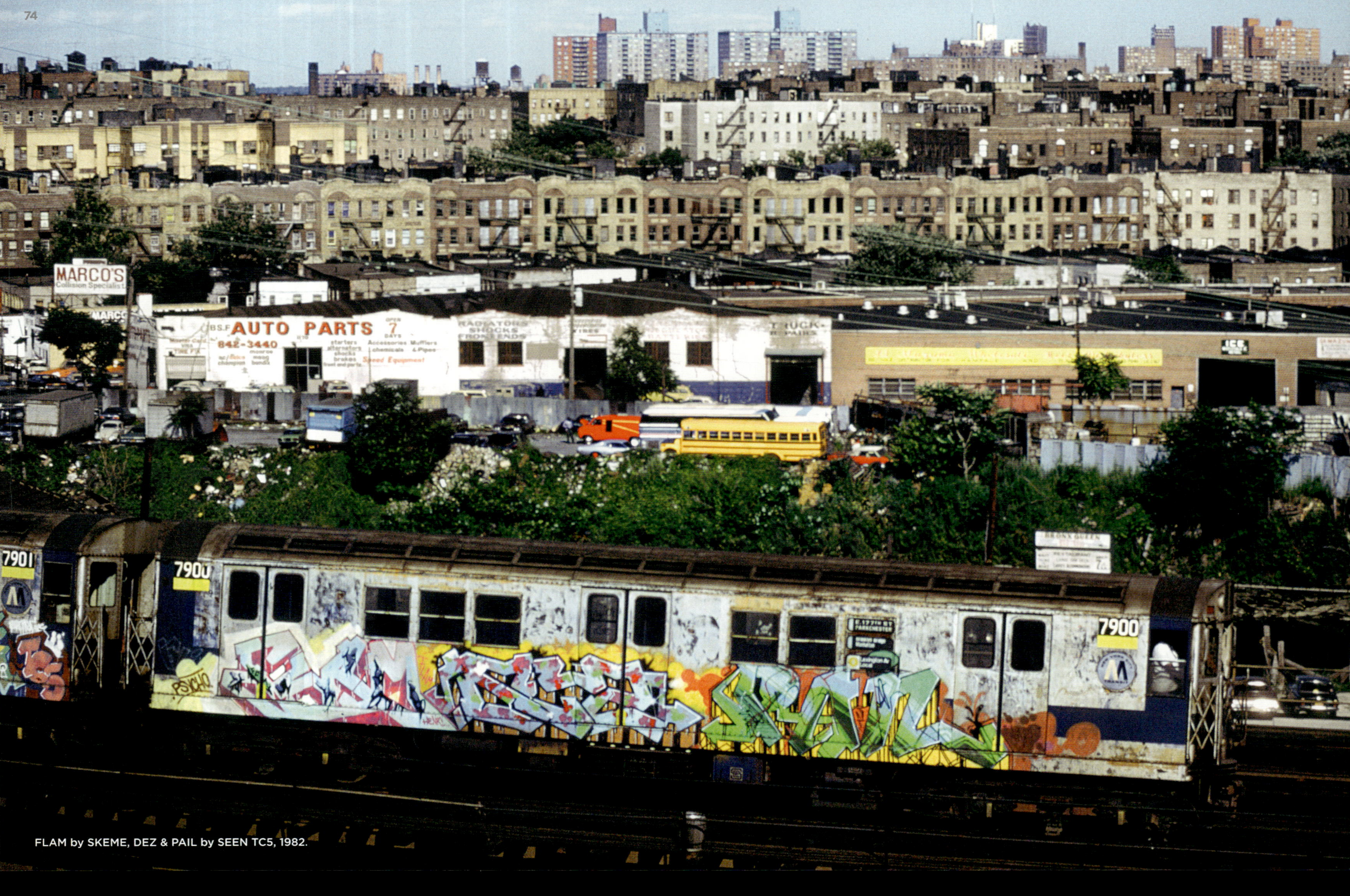

FLAM by SKEME, DEZ & PAIL by SEEN TC5, 1982.

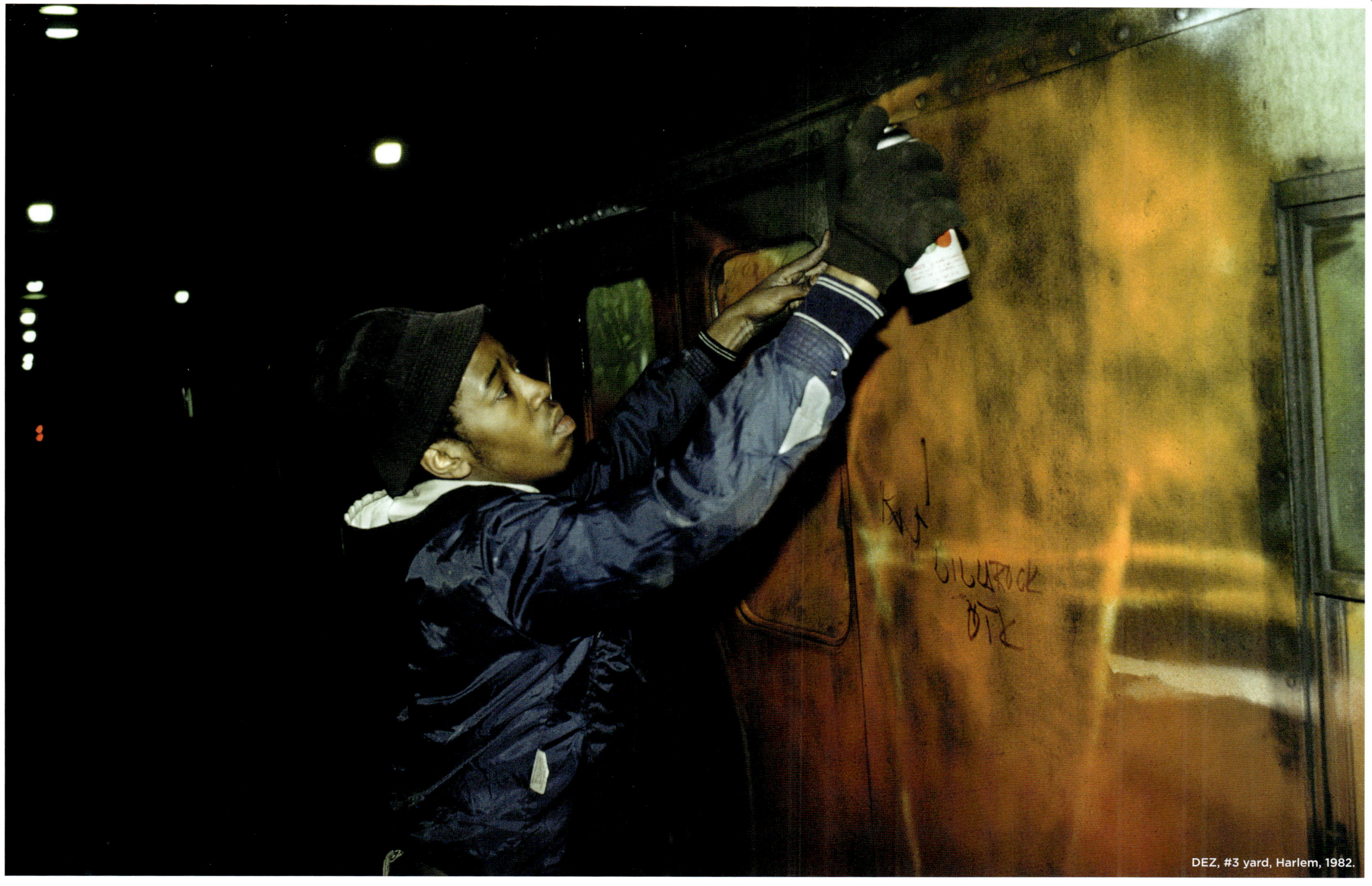

DEZ, #3 yard, Harlem, 1982.

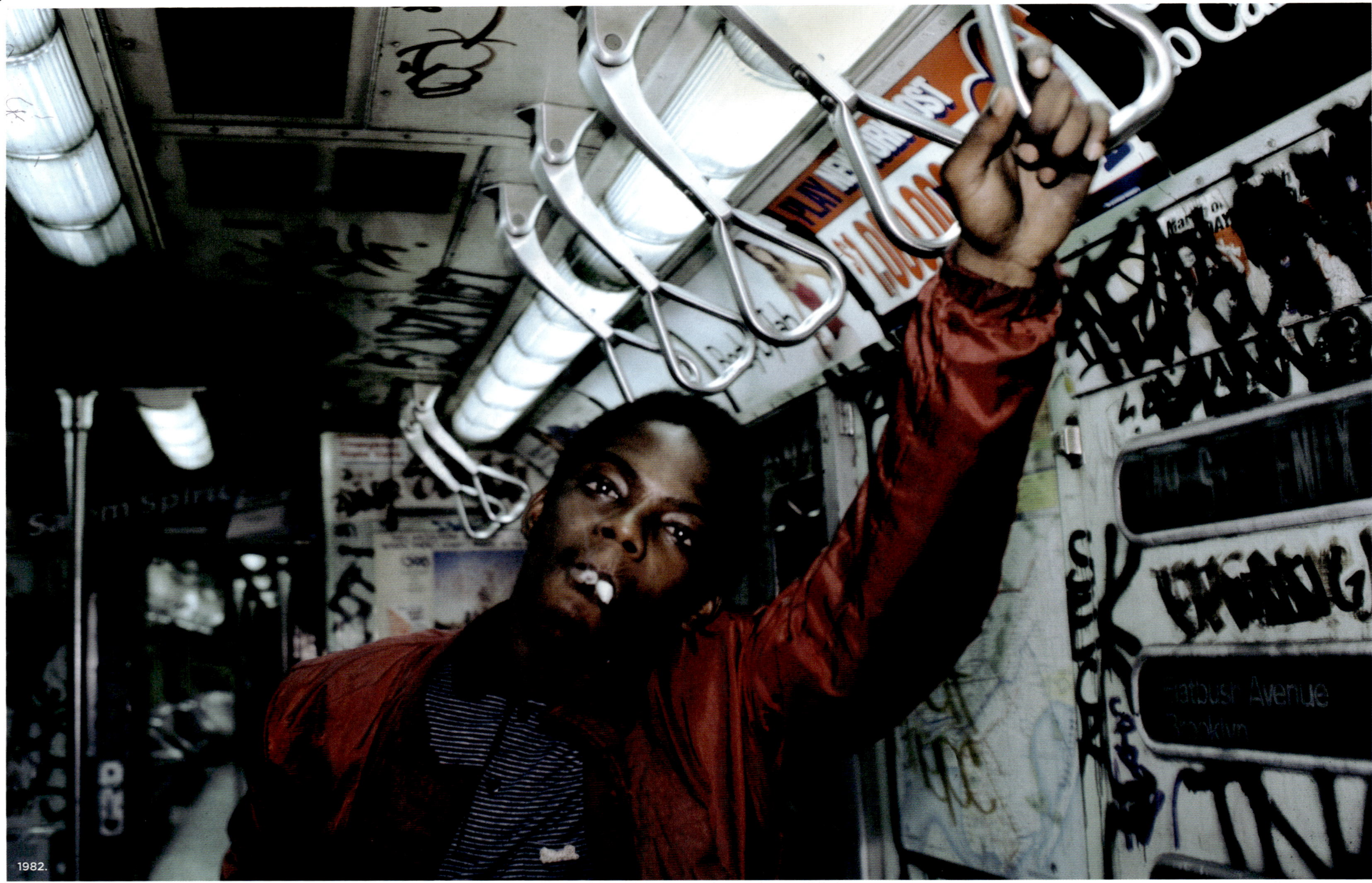

1982.

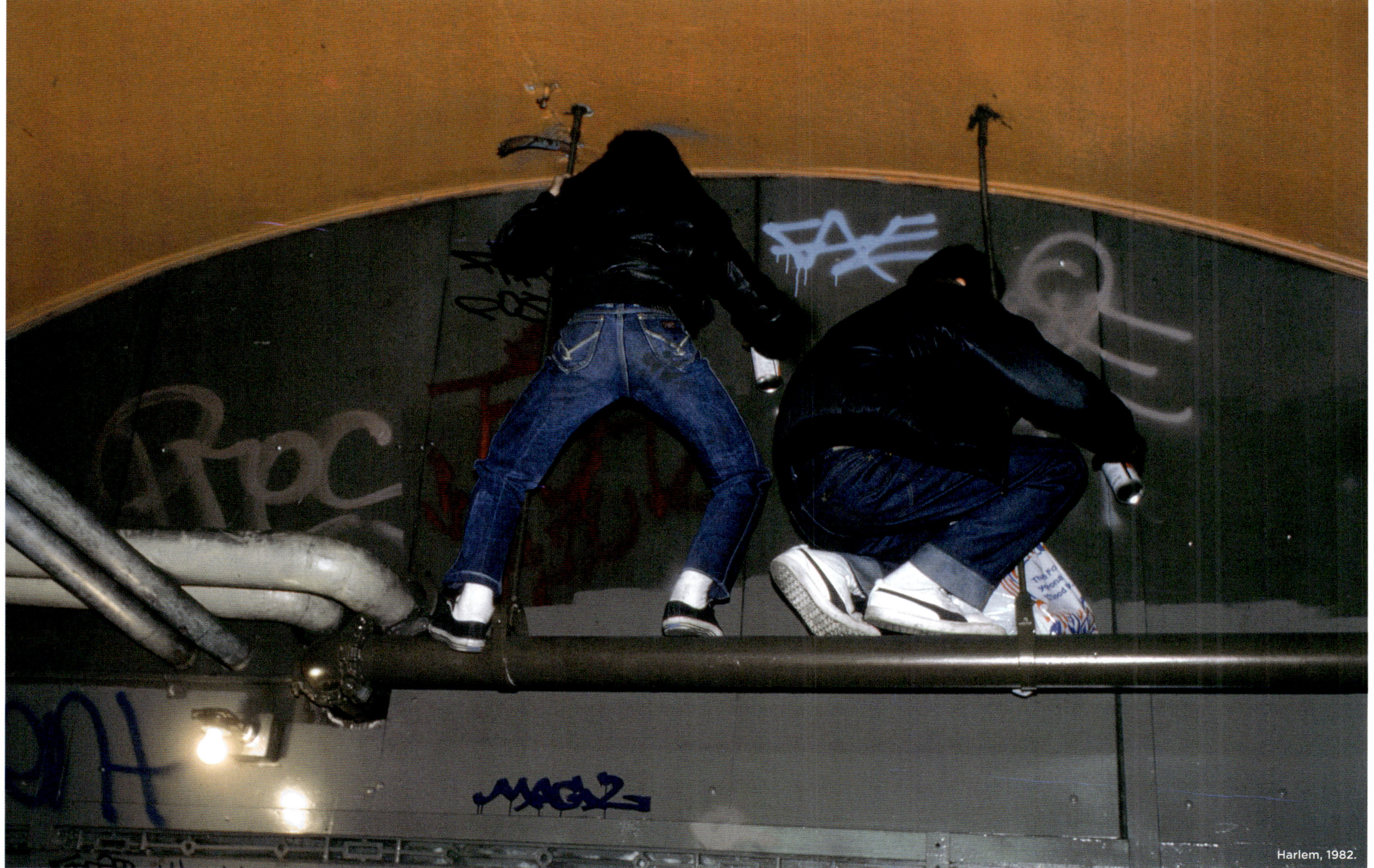

Harlem, 1982.

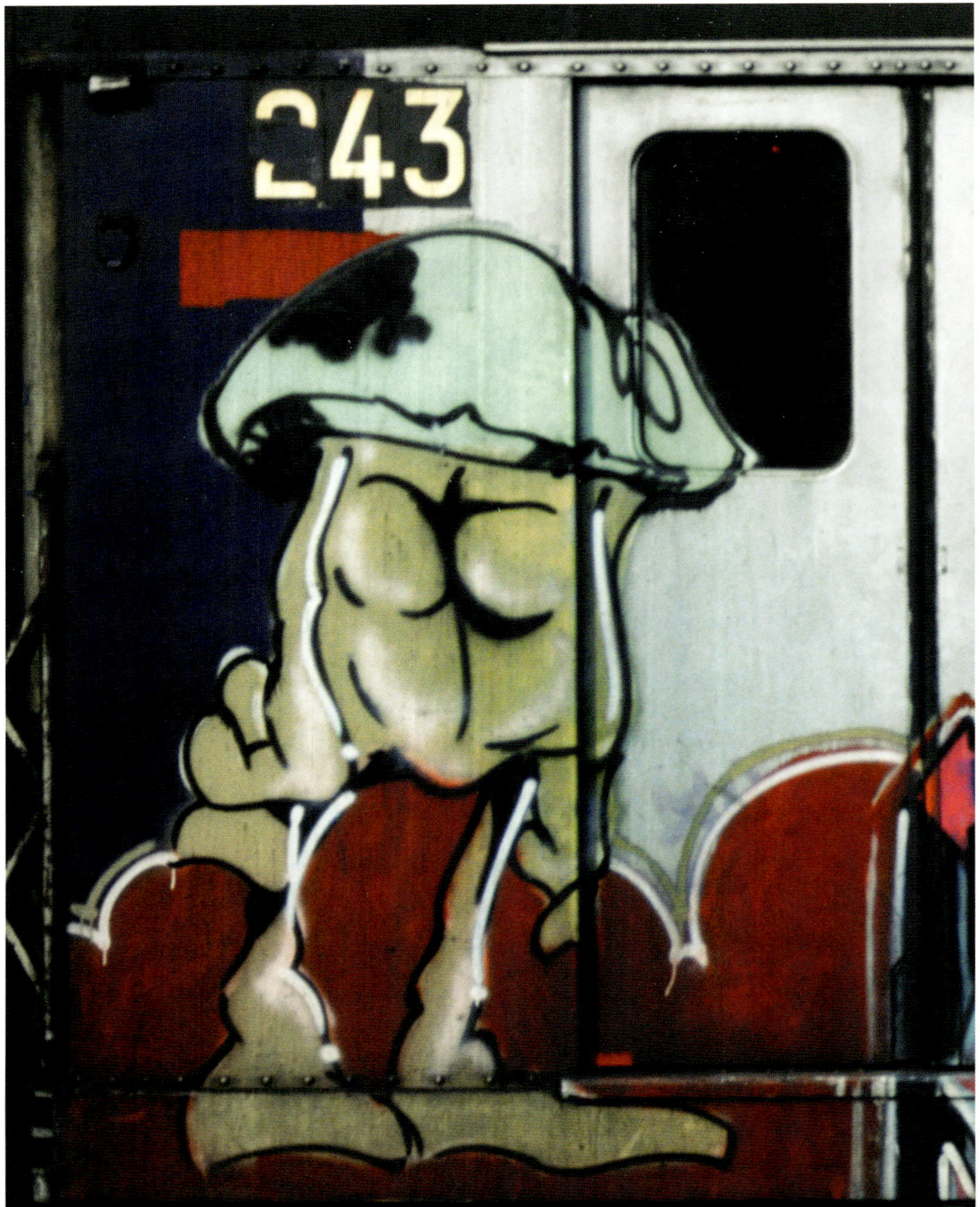

TACK, 1982.

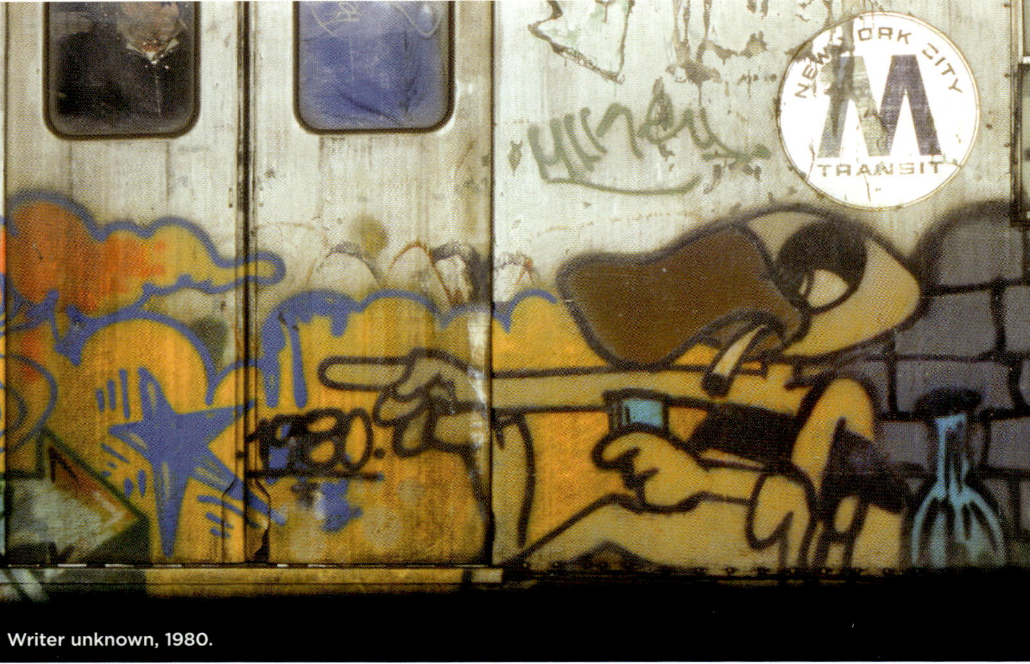

Writer unknown, 1980.

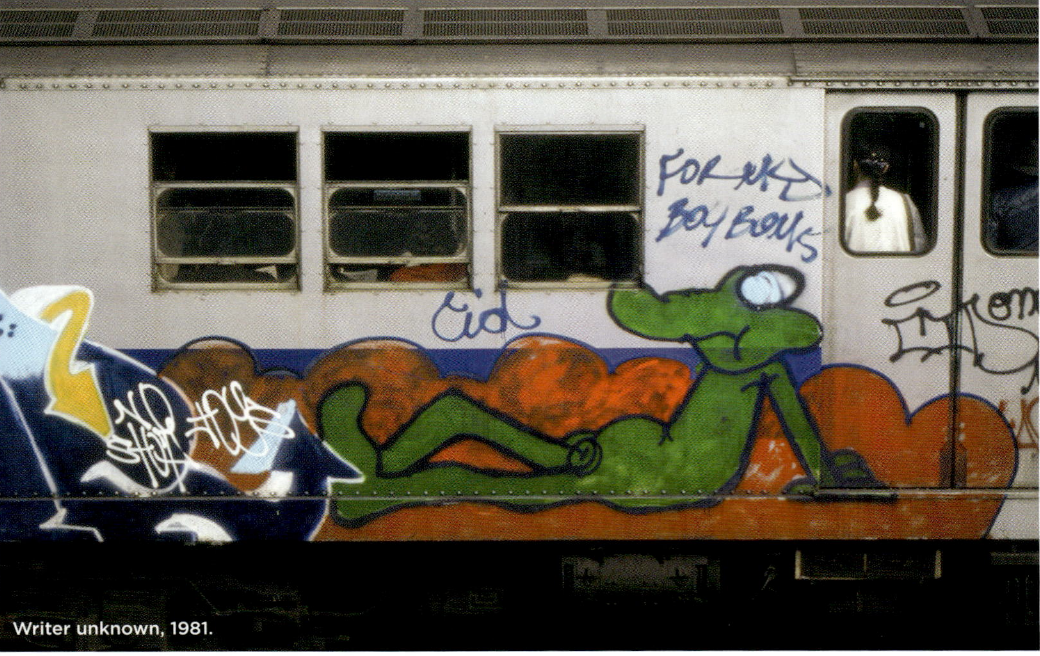

Writer unknown, 1981.

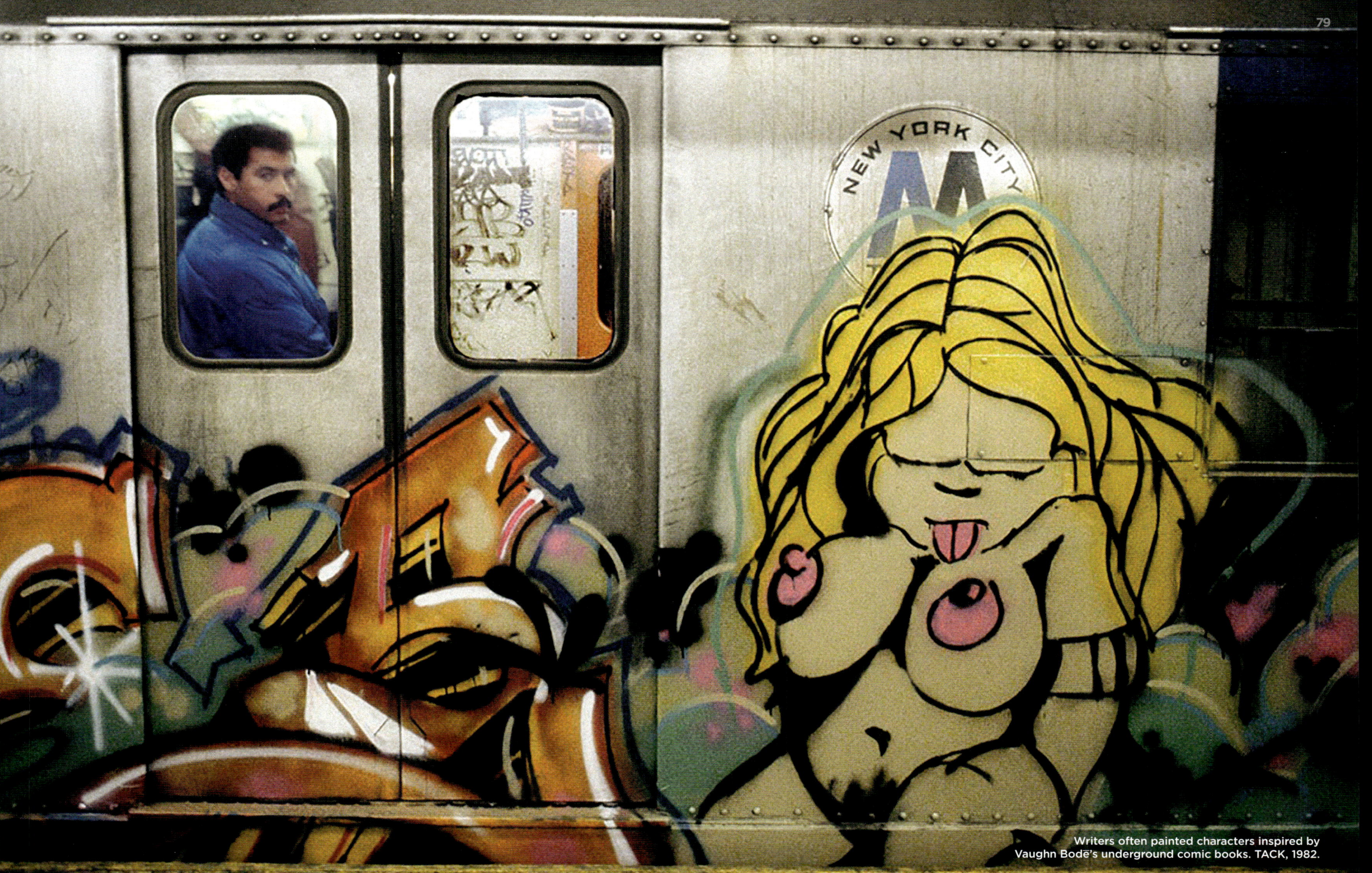

Writers often painted characters inspired by Vaughn Bodē's underground comic books. TACK, 1982.

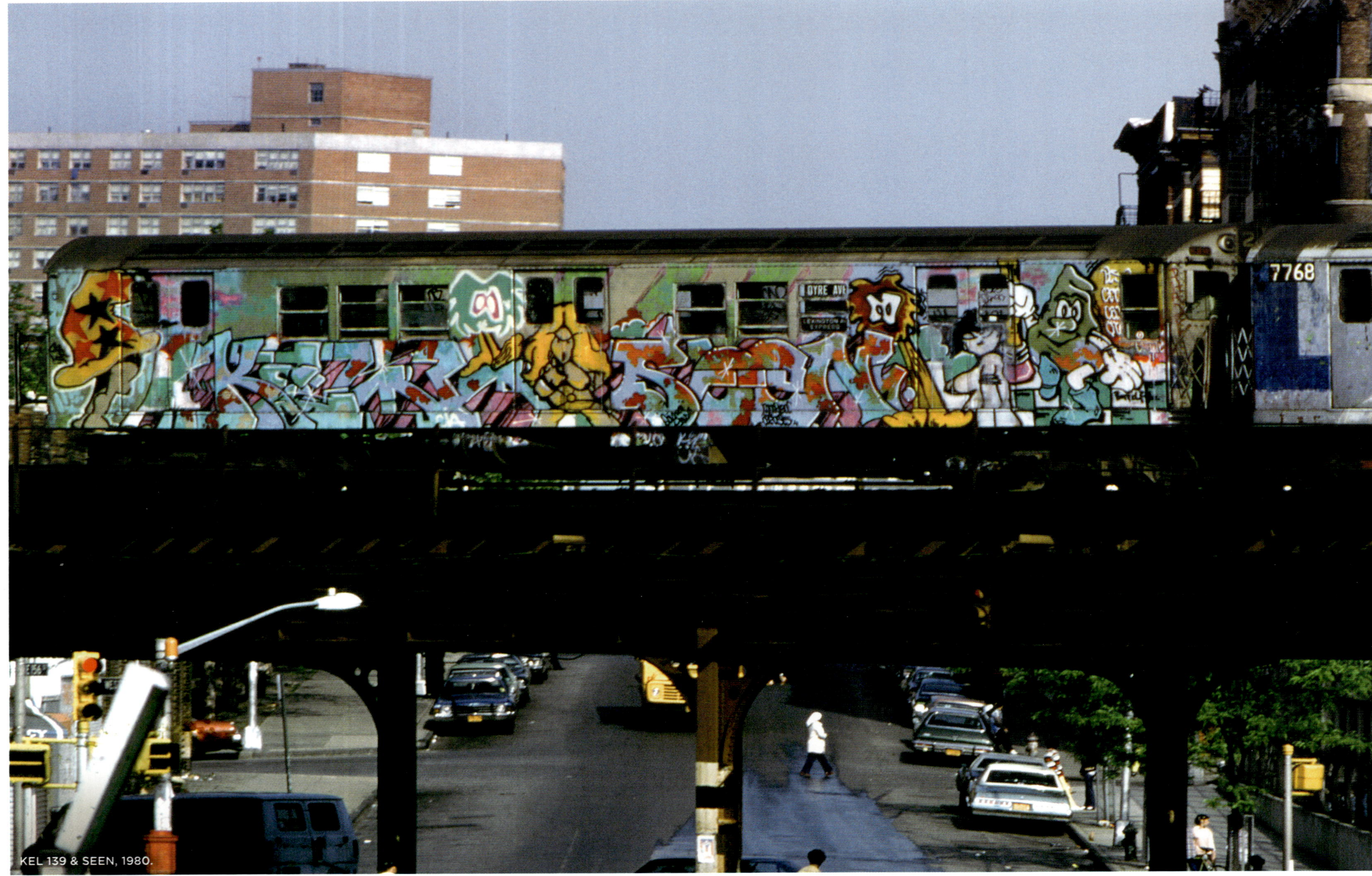

KEL 139 & SEEN, 1980.

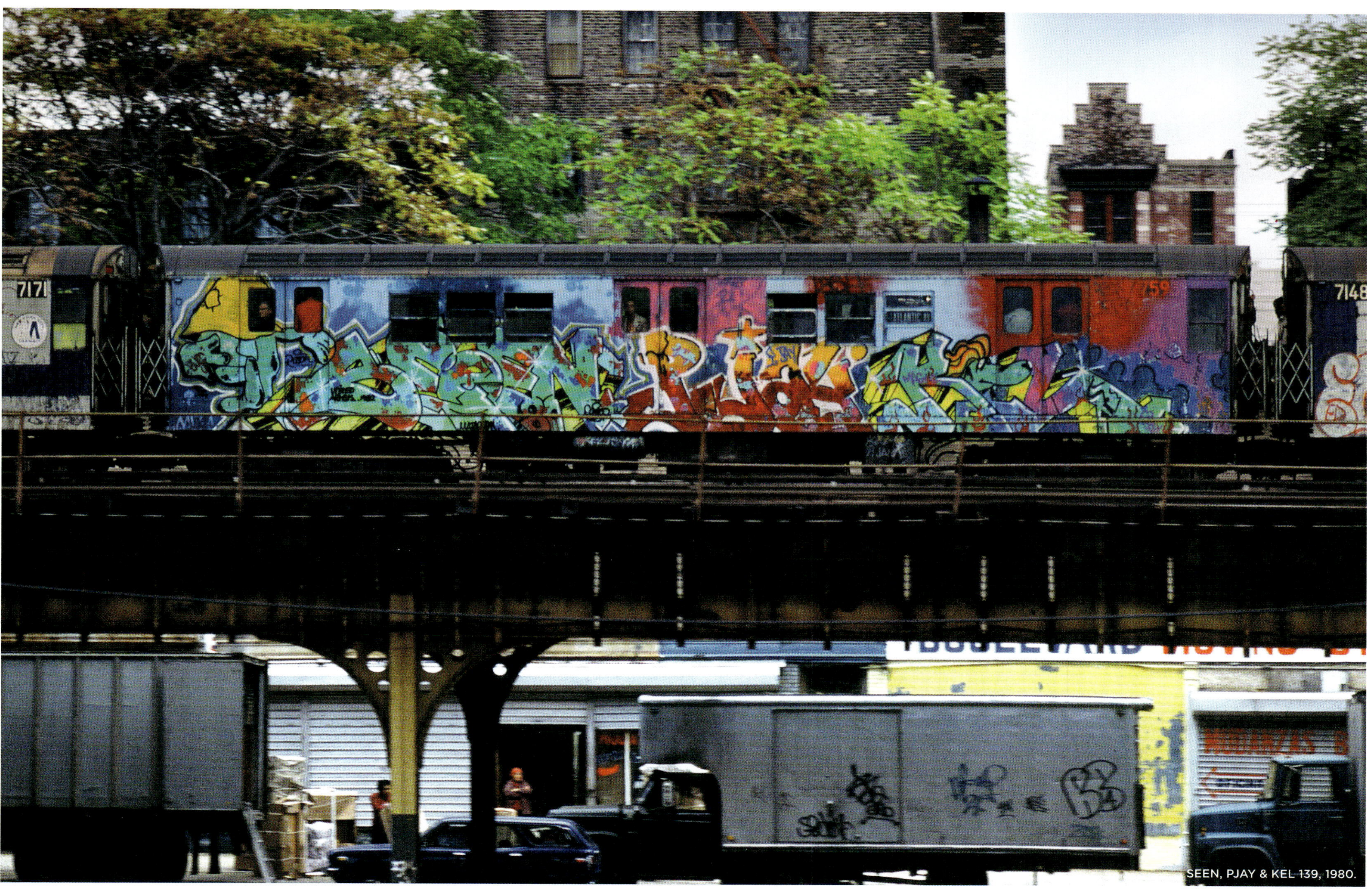

SEEN, PJAY & KEL 139, 1980.

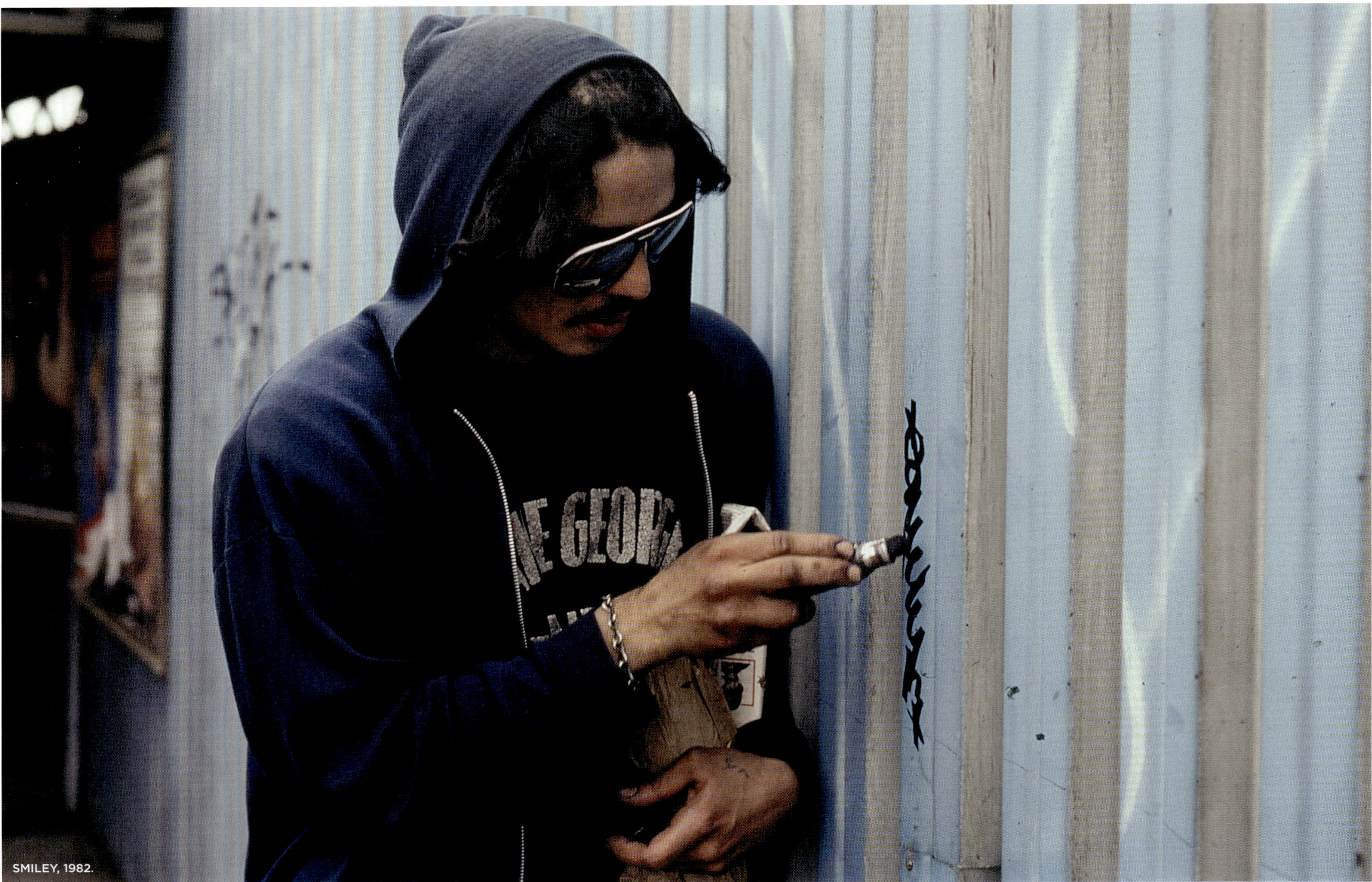

SMILEY, 1982.

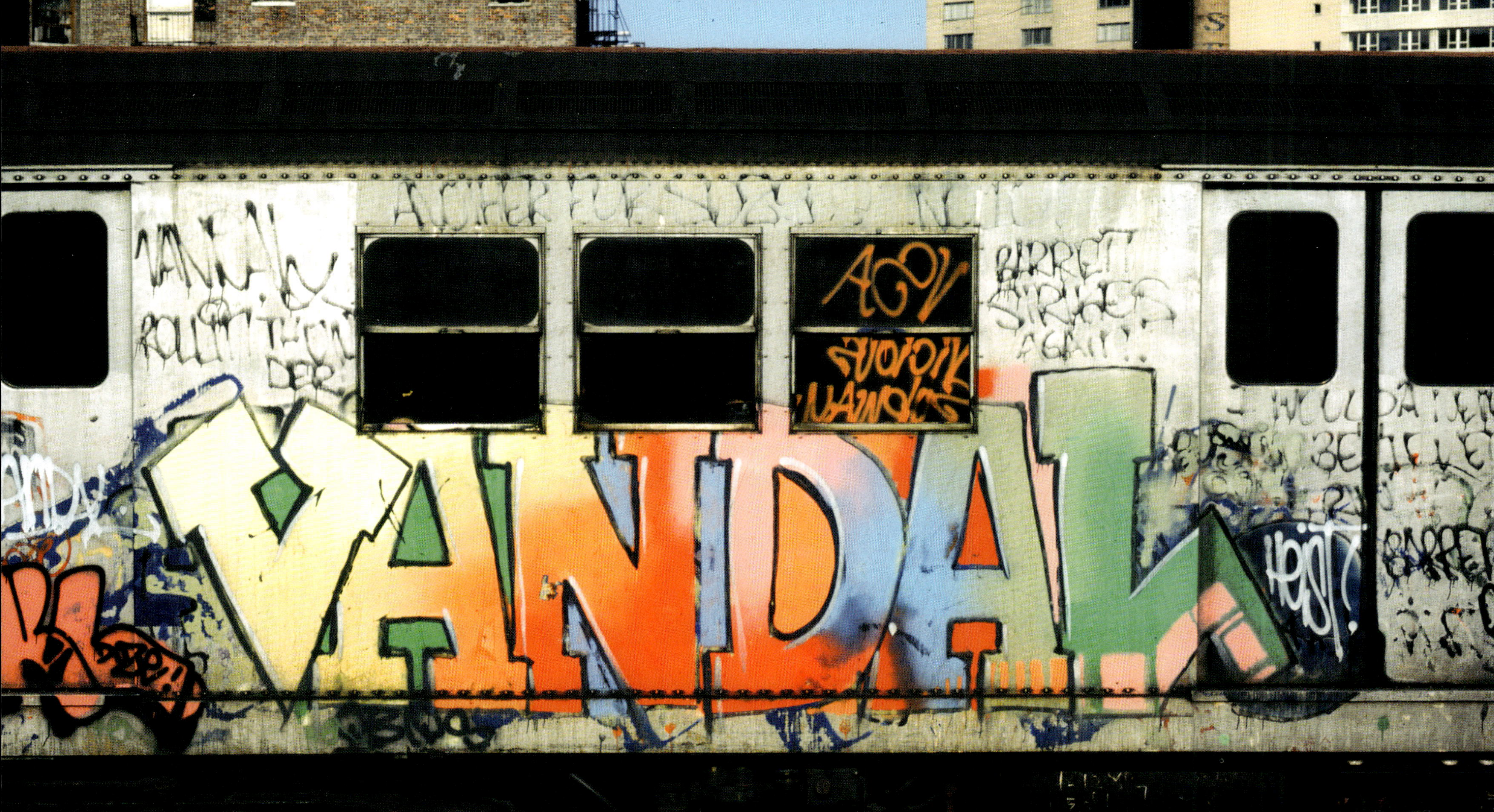

VANDAL
AGOV
BARRETT STRIKES AGAIN

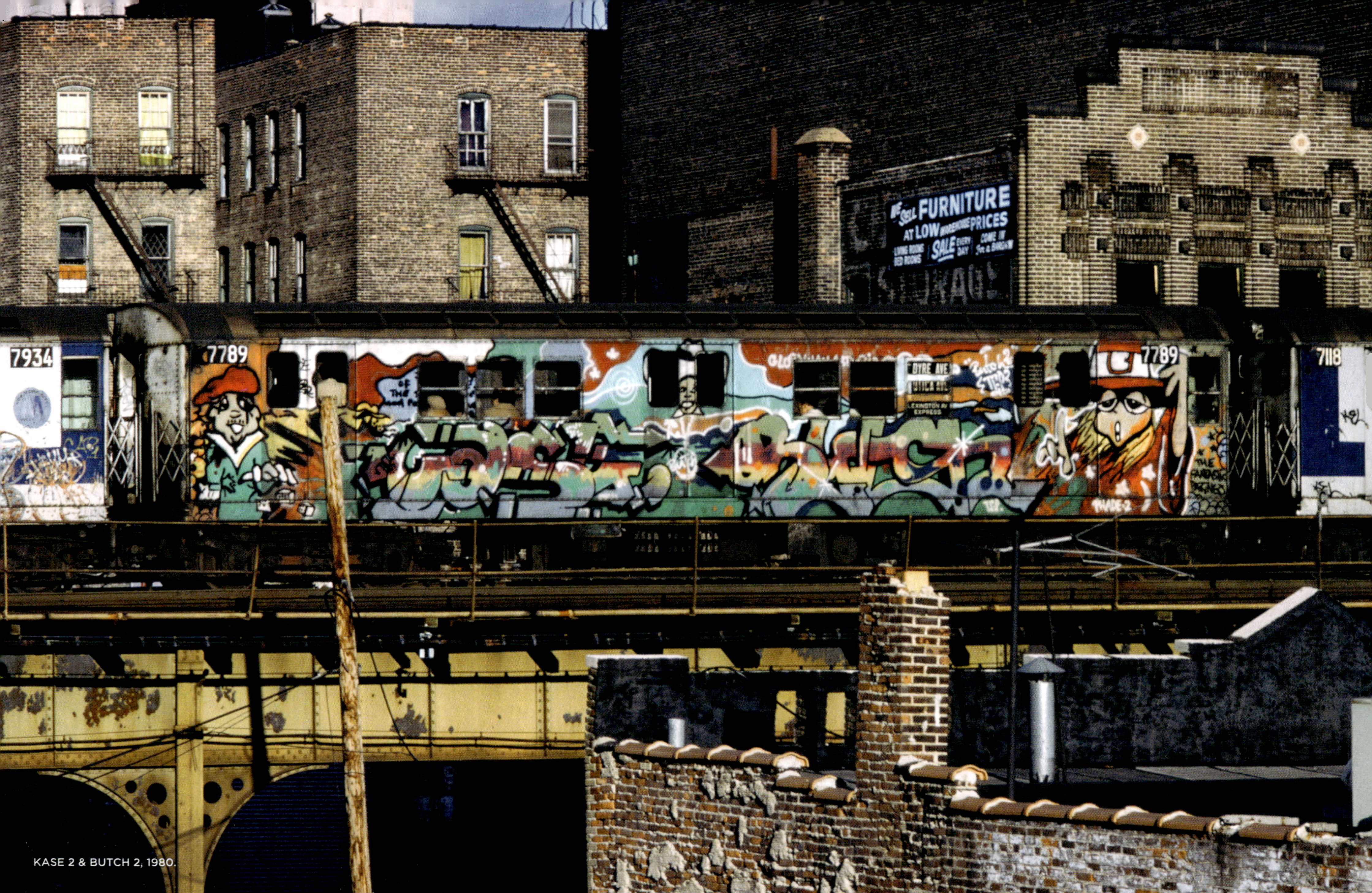

KASE 2 & BUTCH 2, 1980.

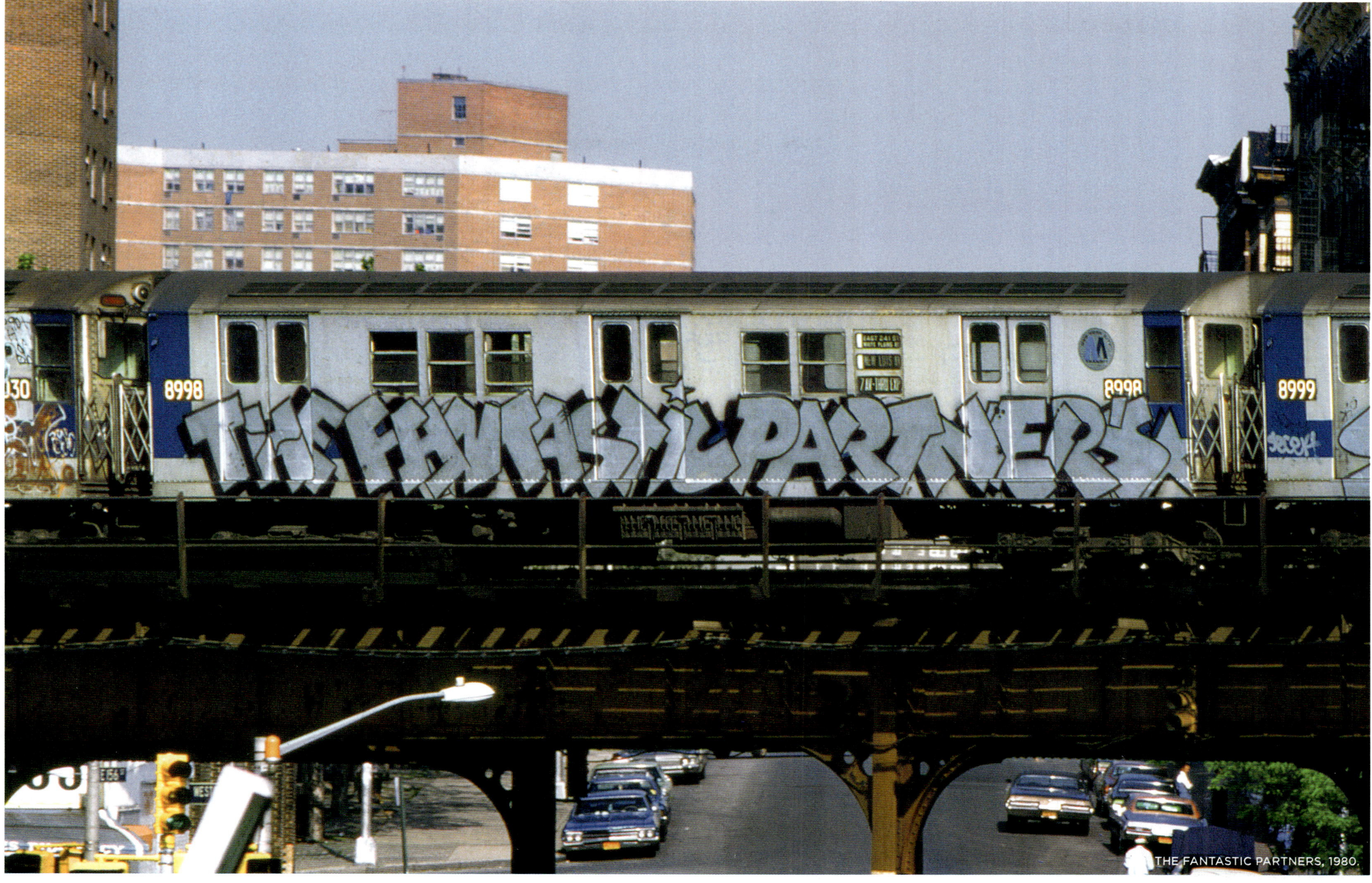

THE FANTASTIC PARTNERS, 1980.

DYRE AVE
ATLANTIC AV
5 Lexington Av Express
EVEN WITH HOUSE PAINT

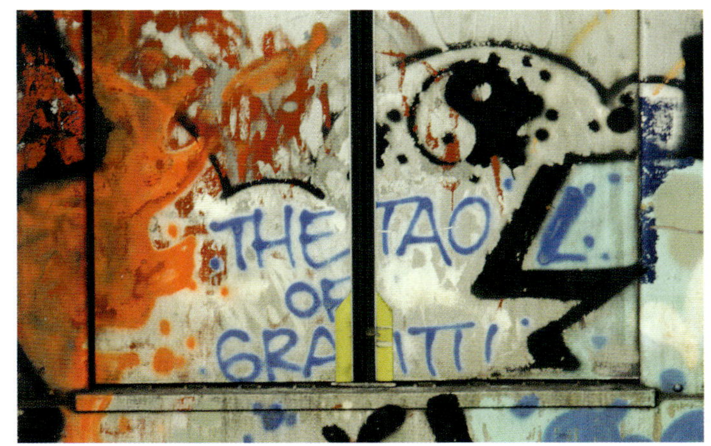

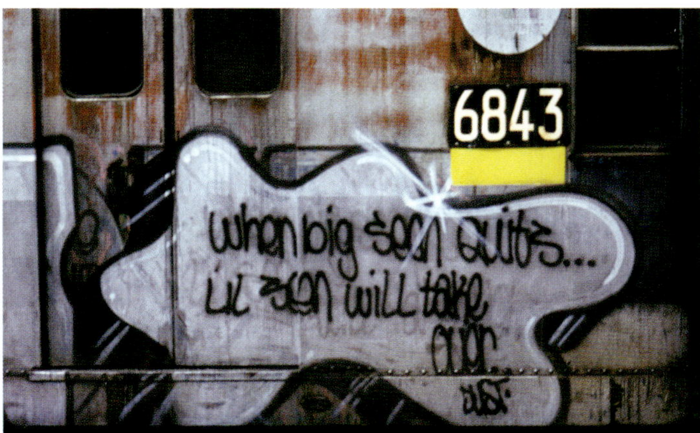

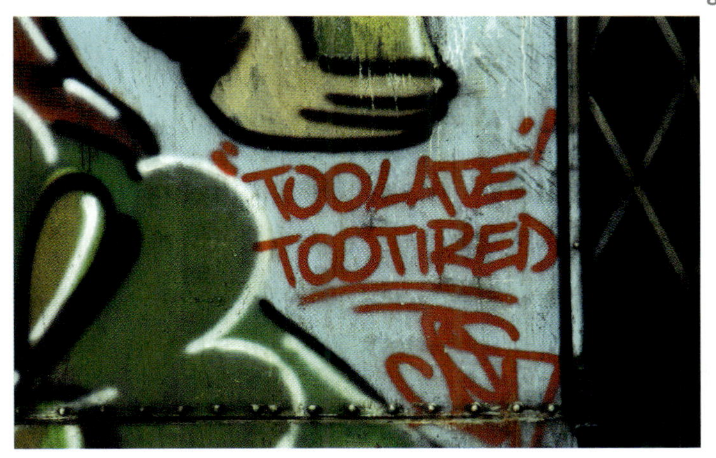

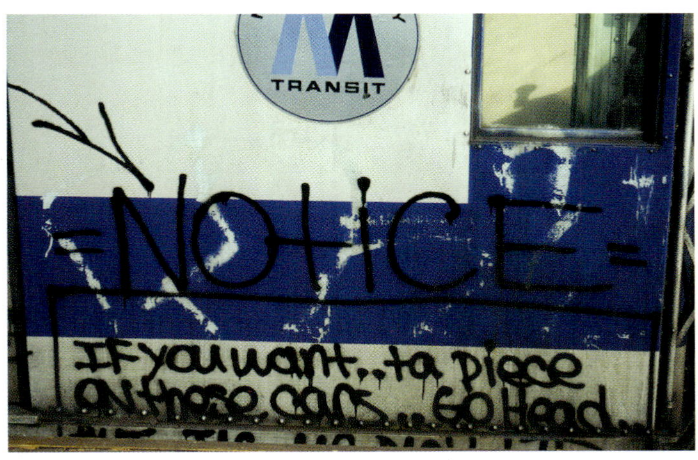

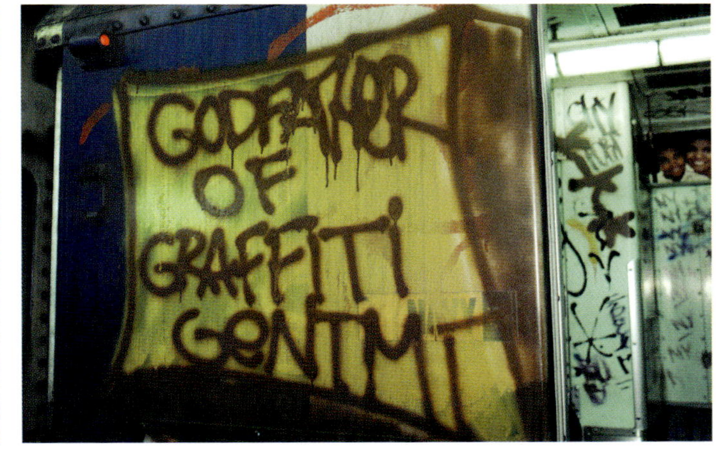

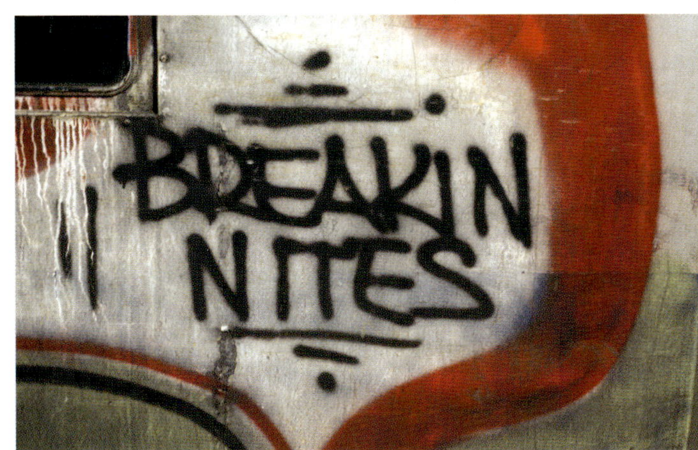

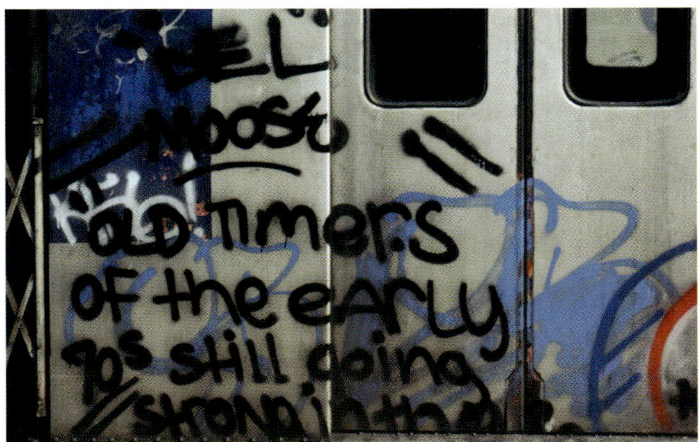

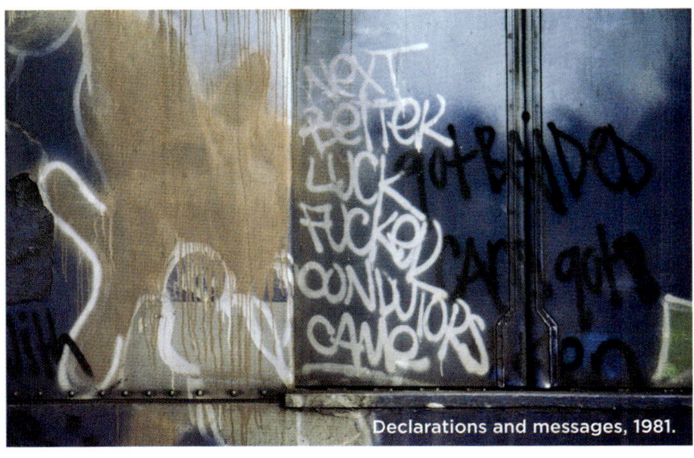

Declarations and messages, 1981.

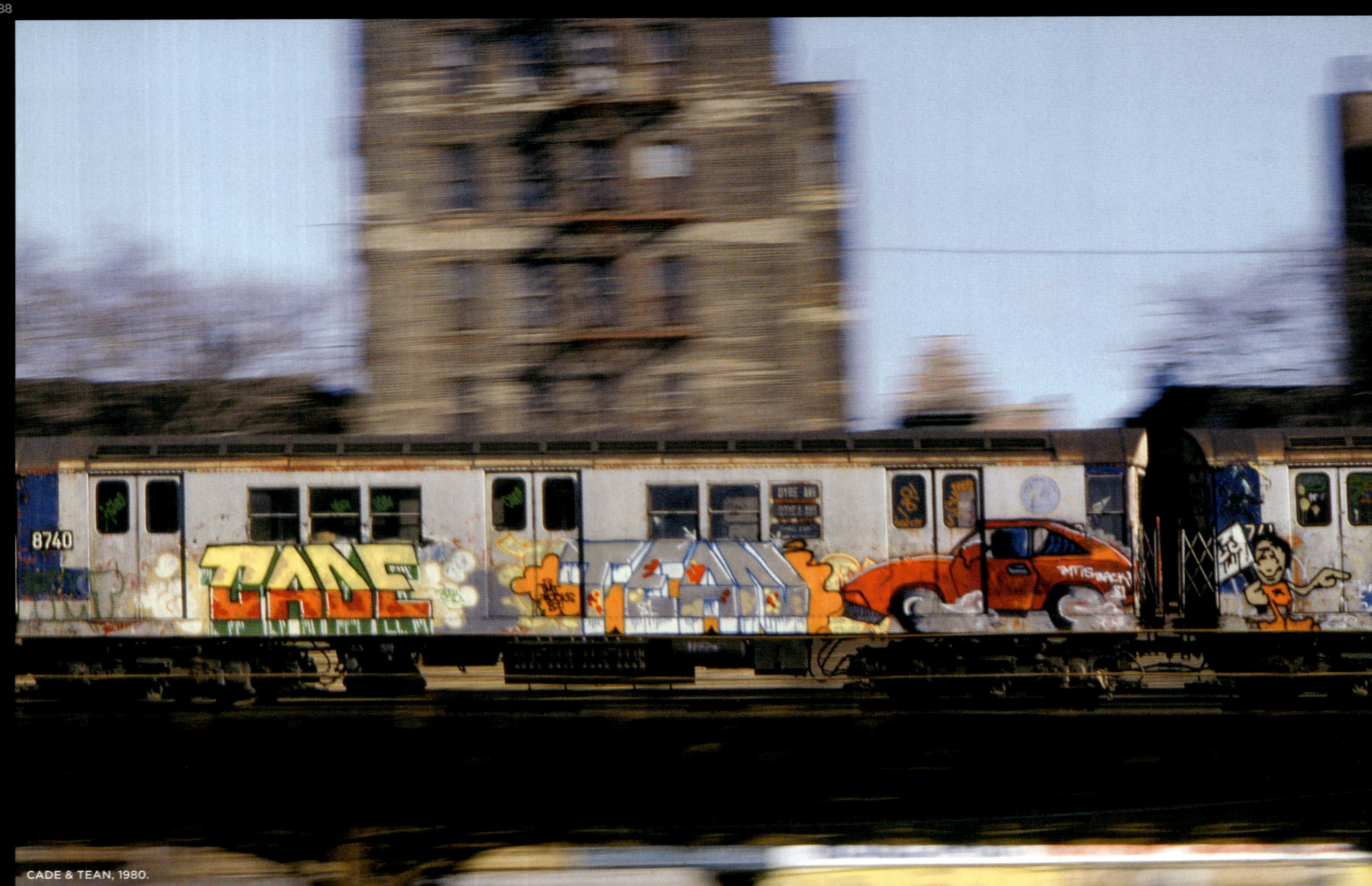

CADE & TEAN, 1980.

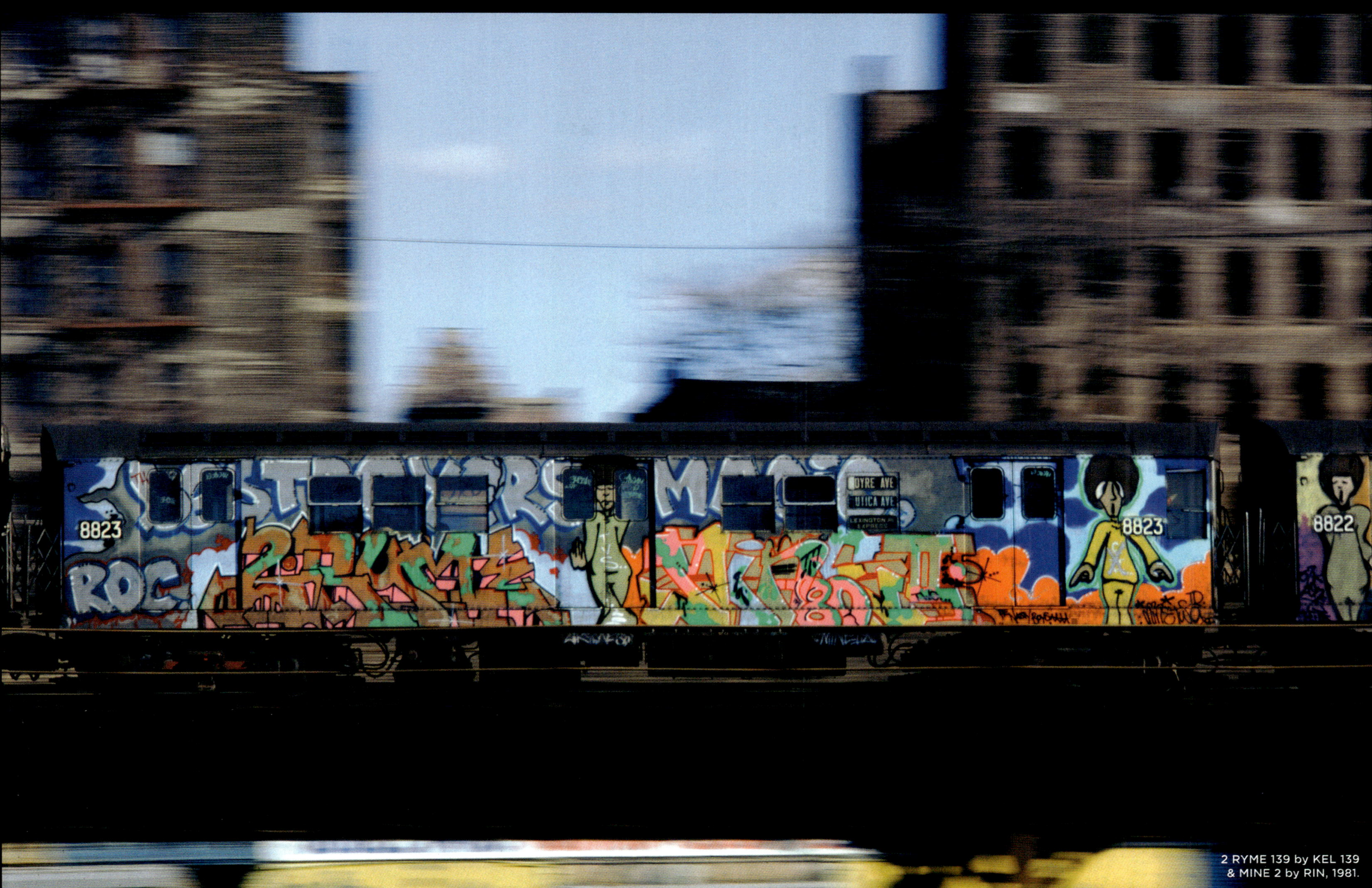

2 RYME 139 by KEL 139
& MINE 2 by RIN, 1981.

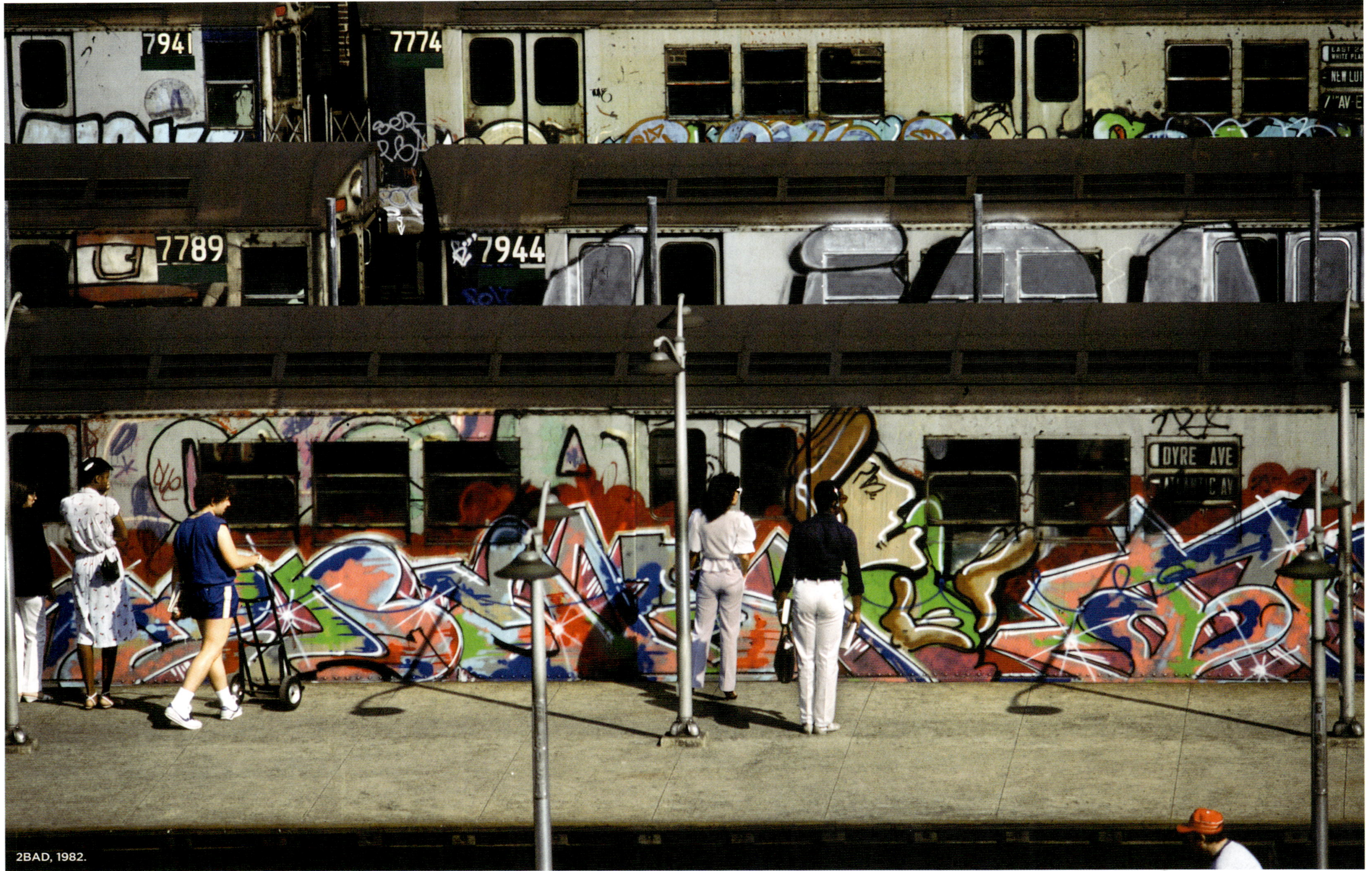

2BAD, 1982.

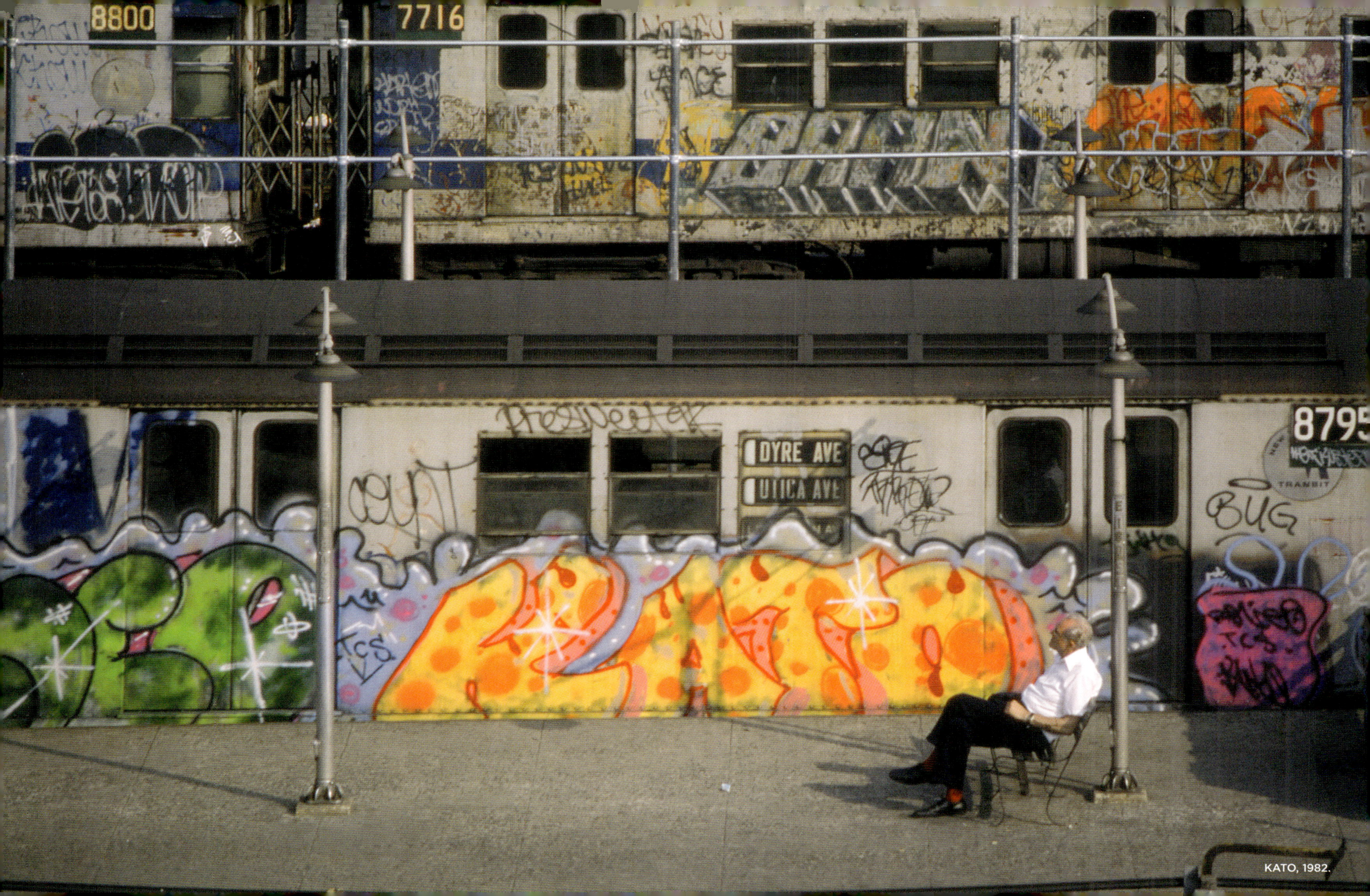

KATO, 1982.

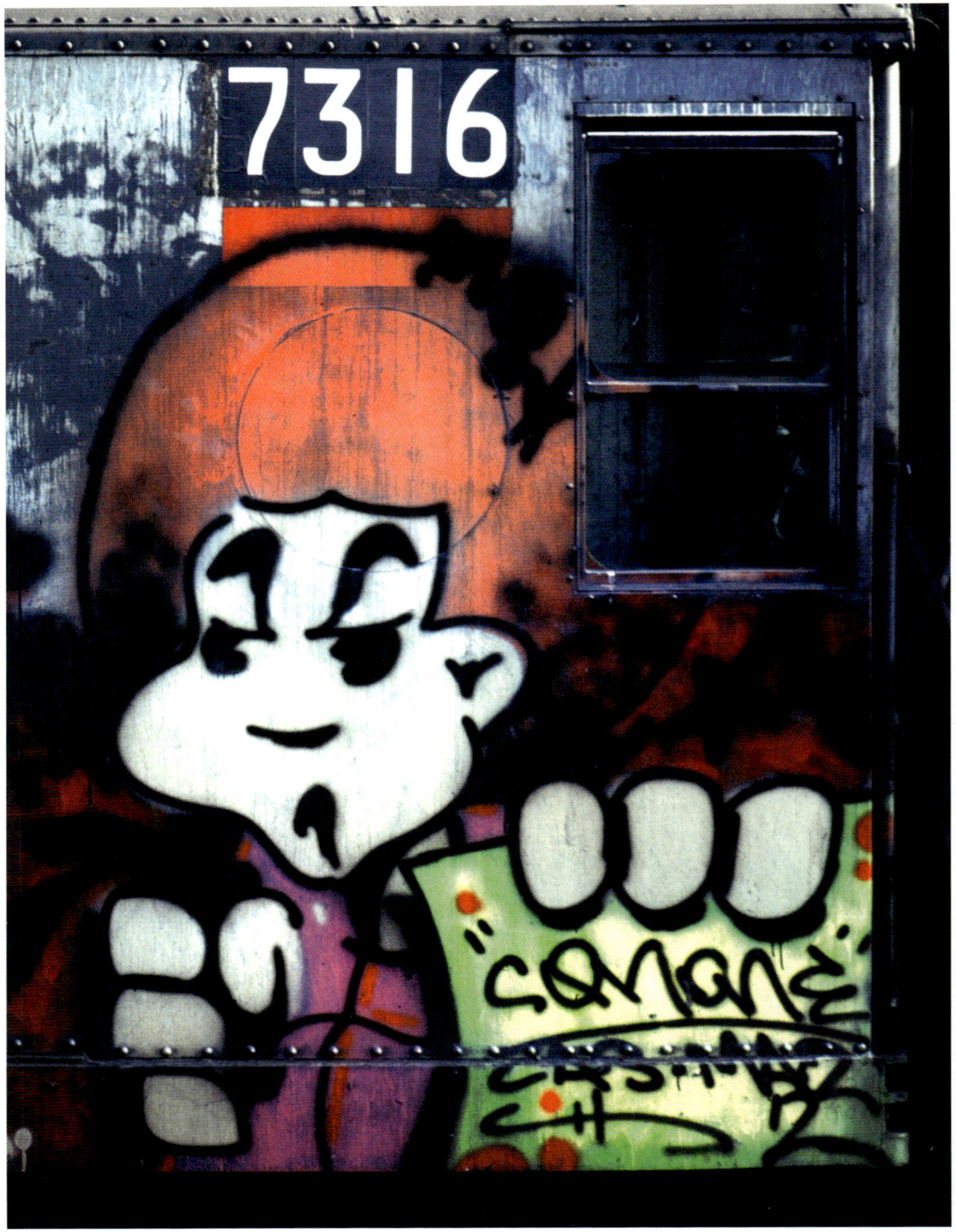

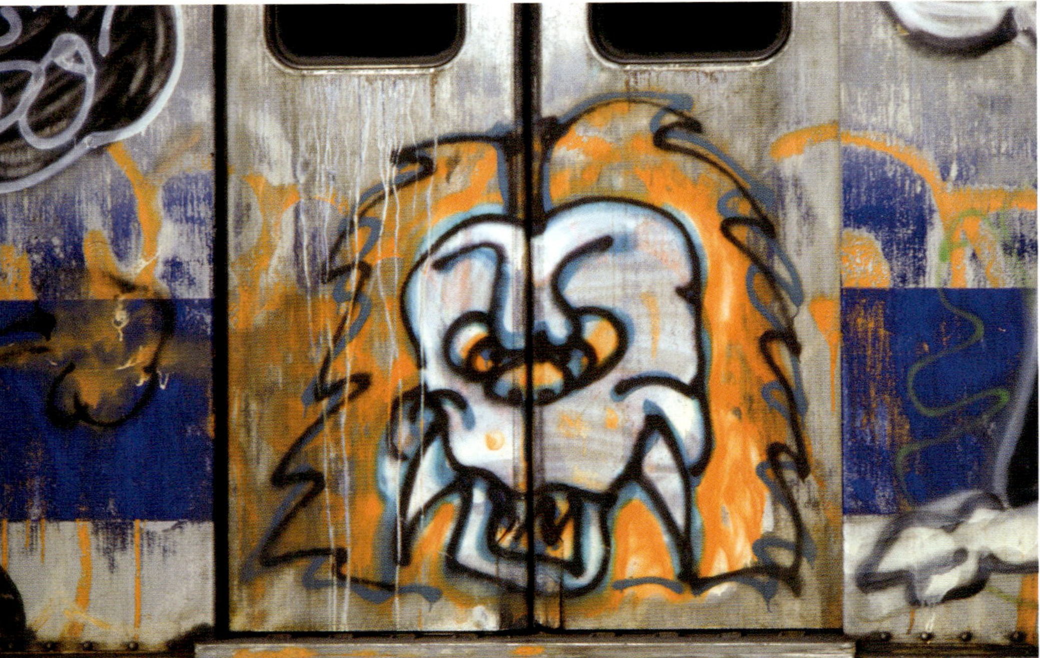

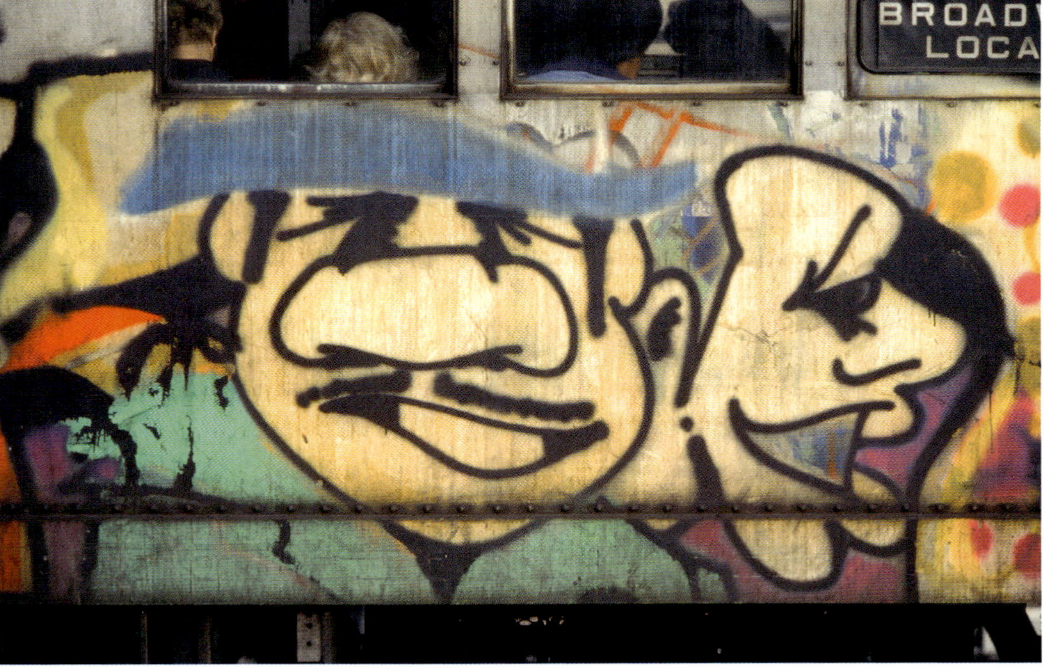

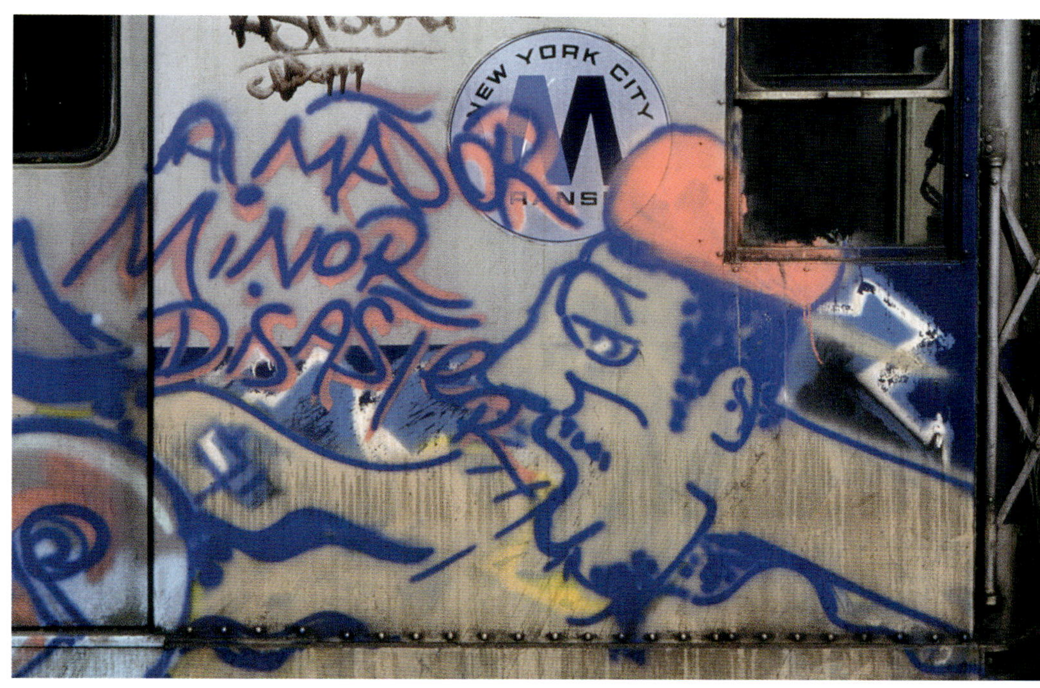

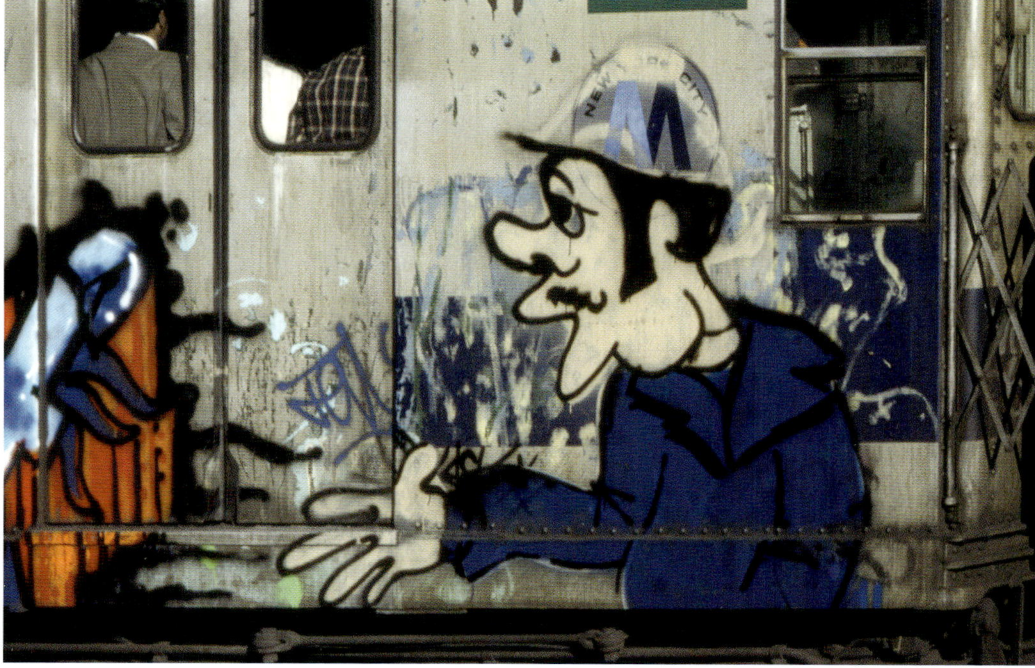

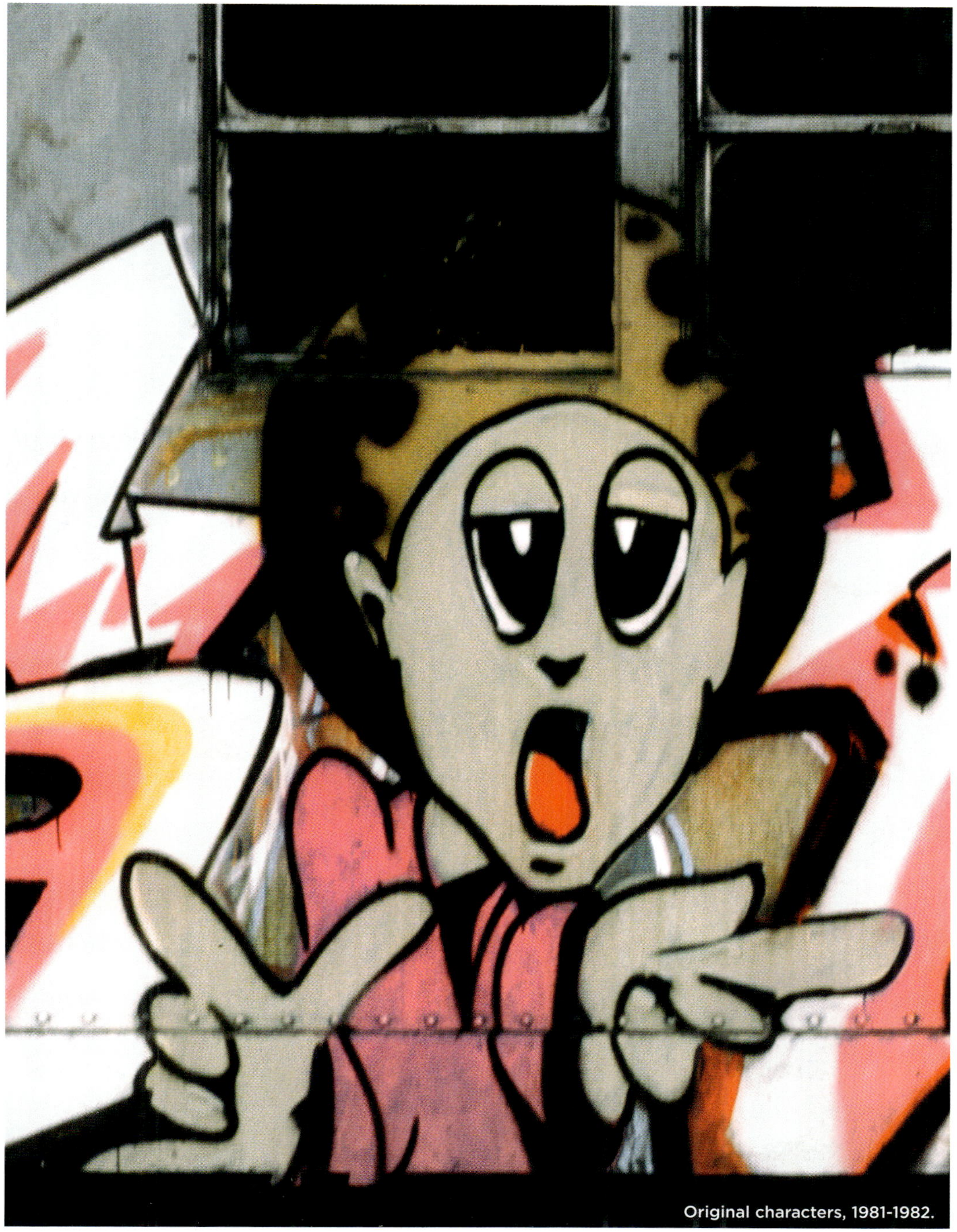

Original characters, 1981-1982.

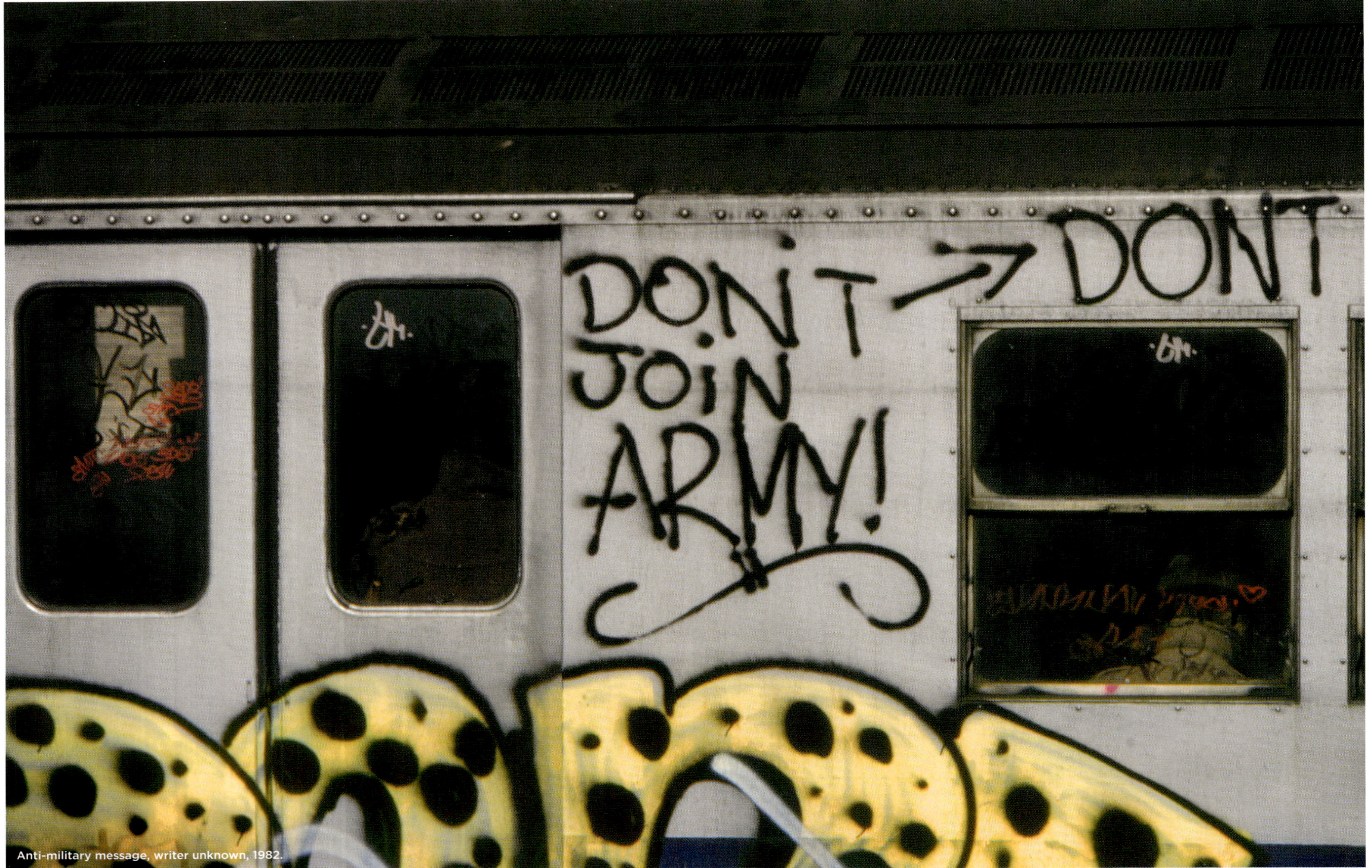

Anti-military message, writer unknown, 1982.

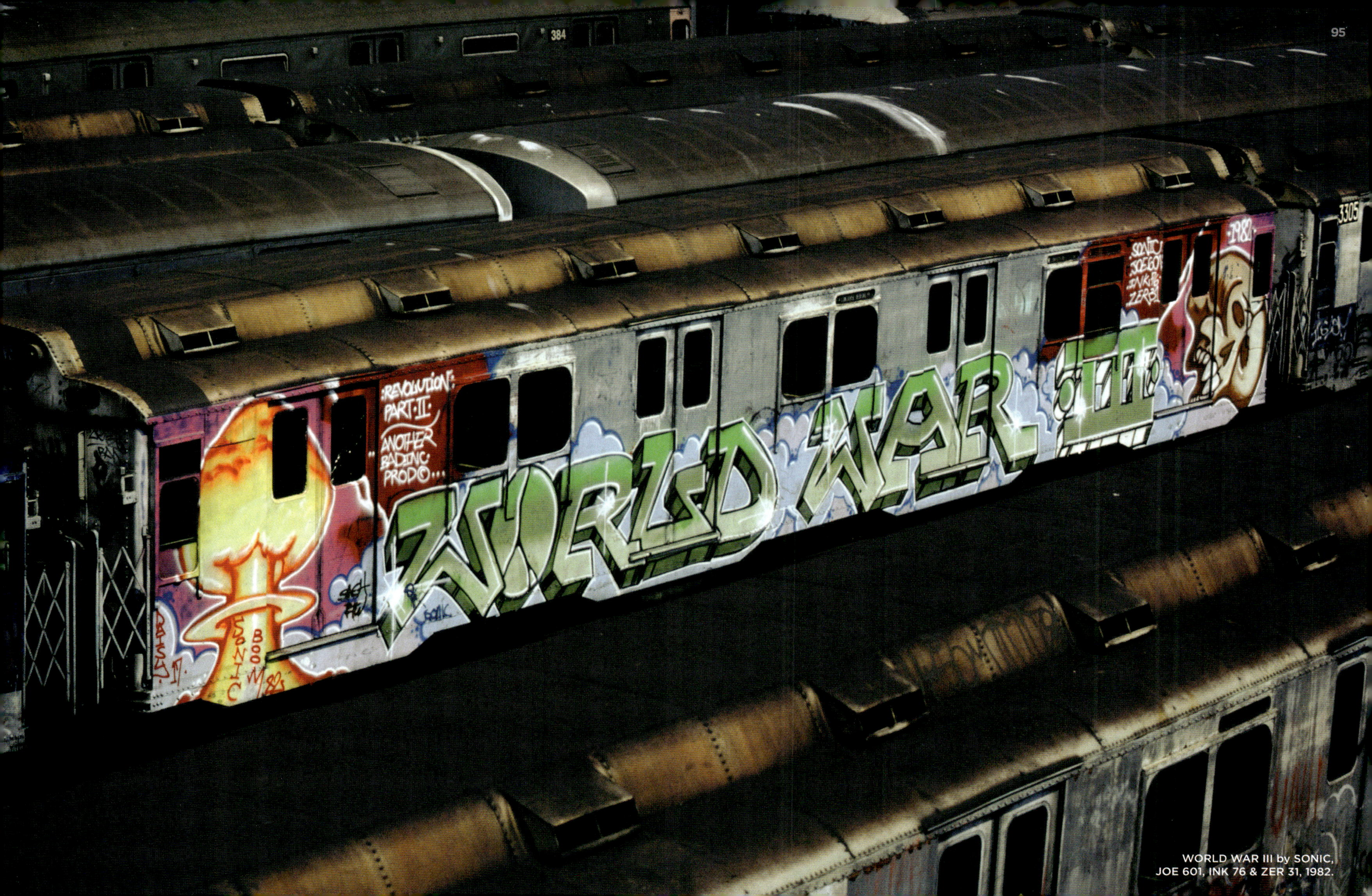

WORLD WAR III by SONIC,
JOE 601, INK 76 & ZER 31, 1982.

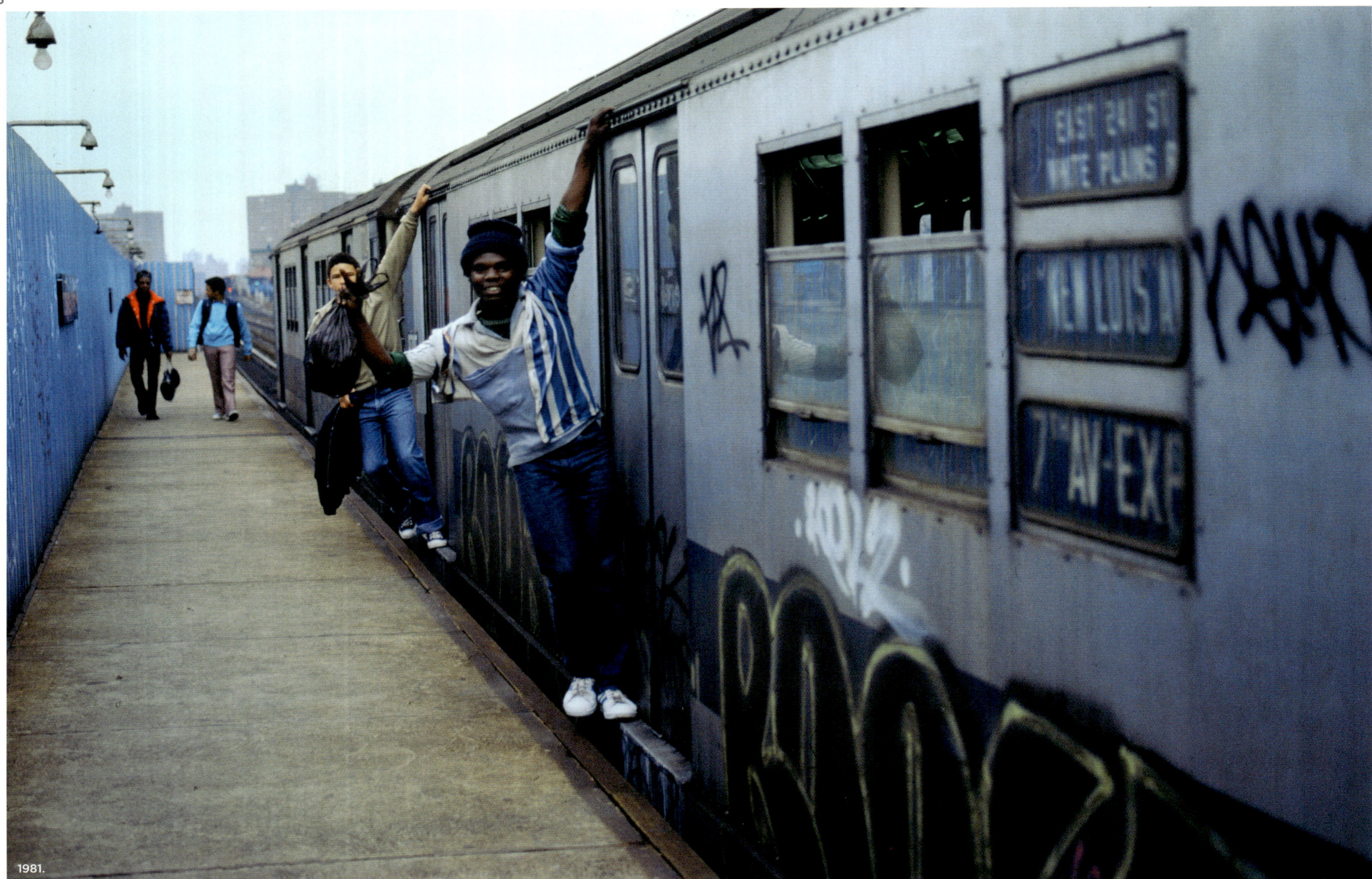

1981.

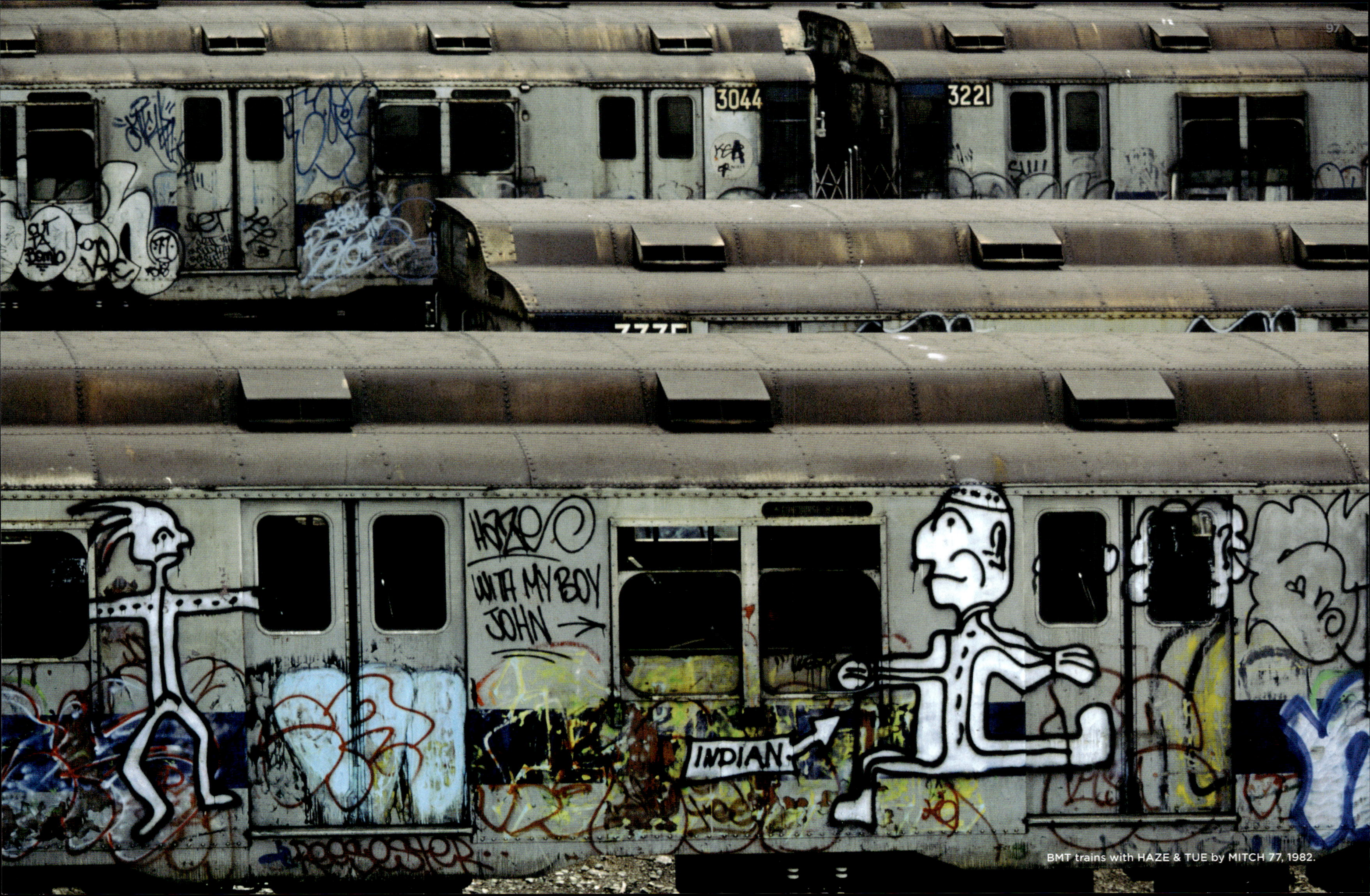

BMT trains with HAZE & TUE by MITCH 77, 1982.

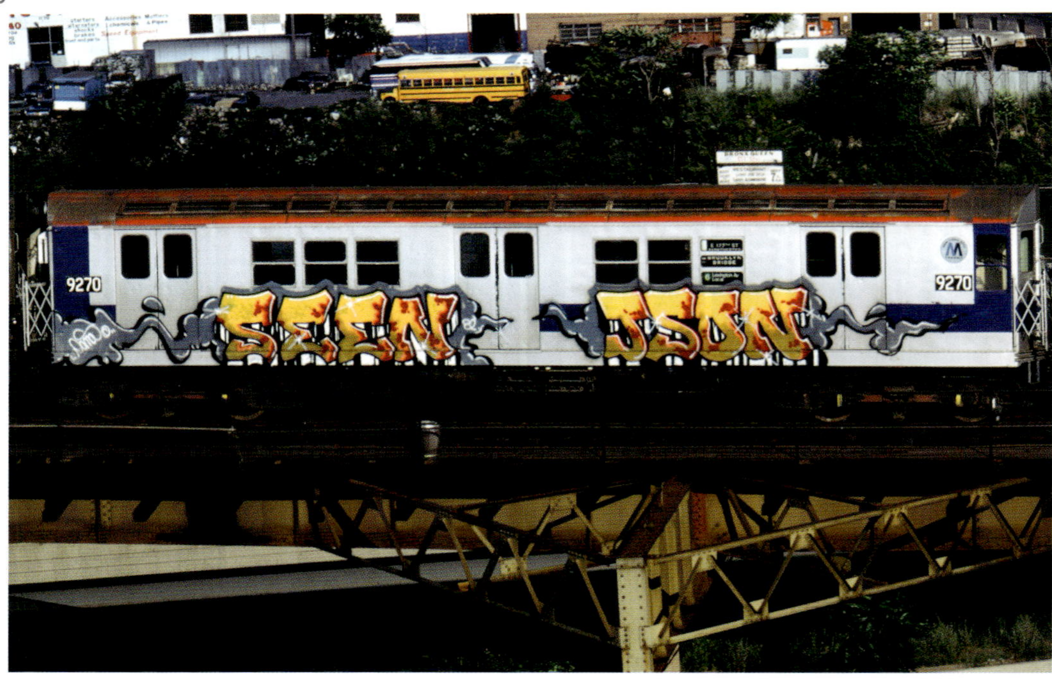
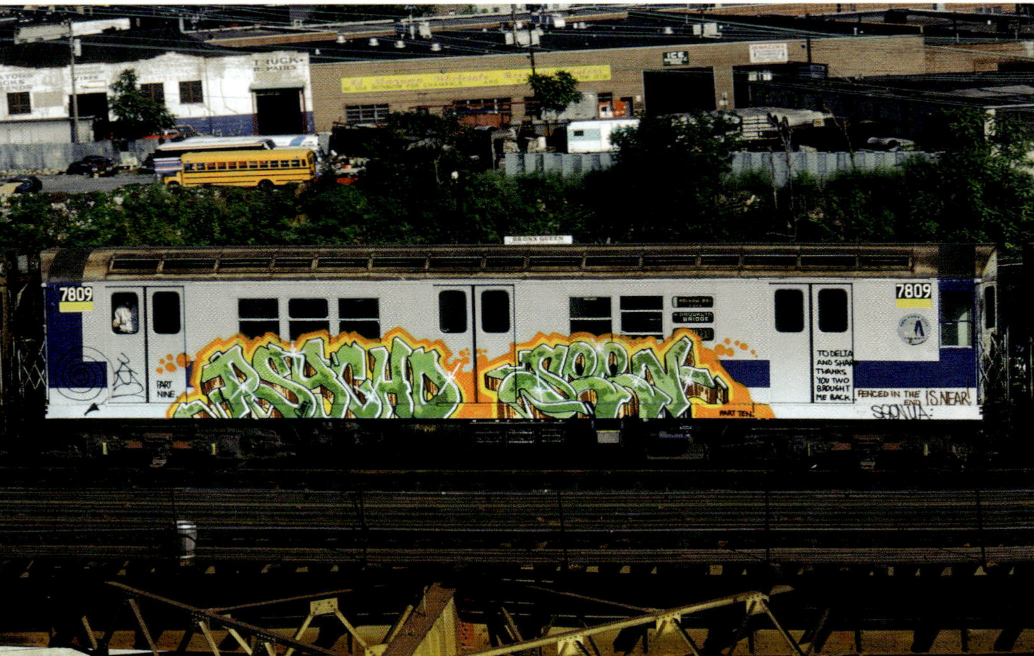
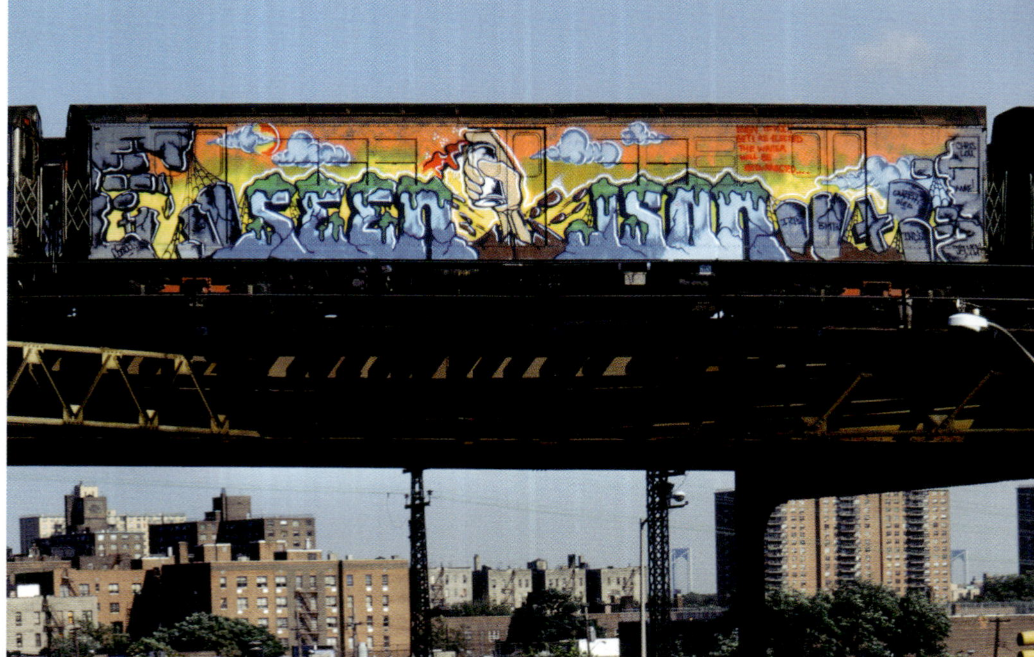
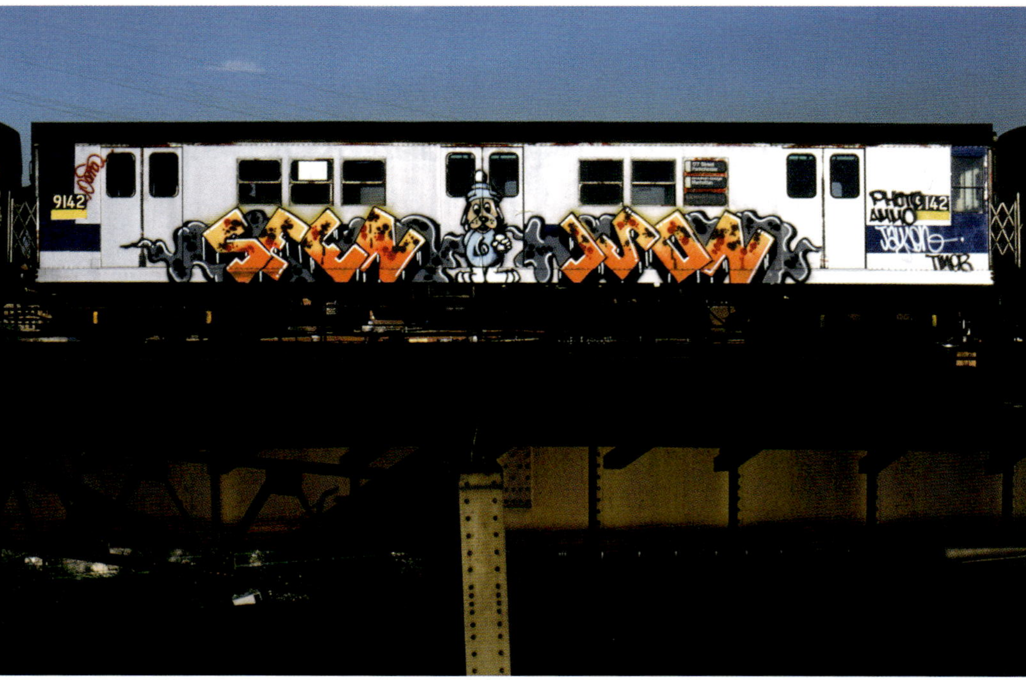

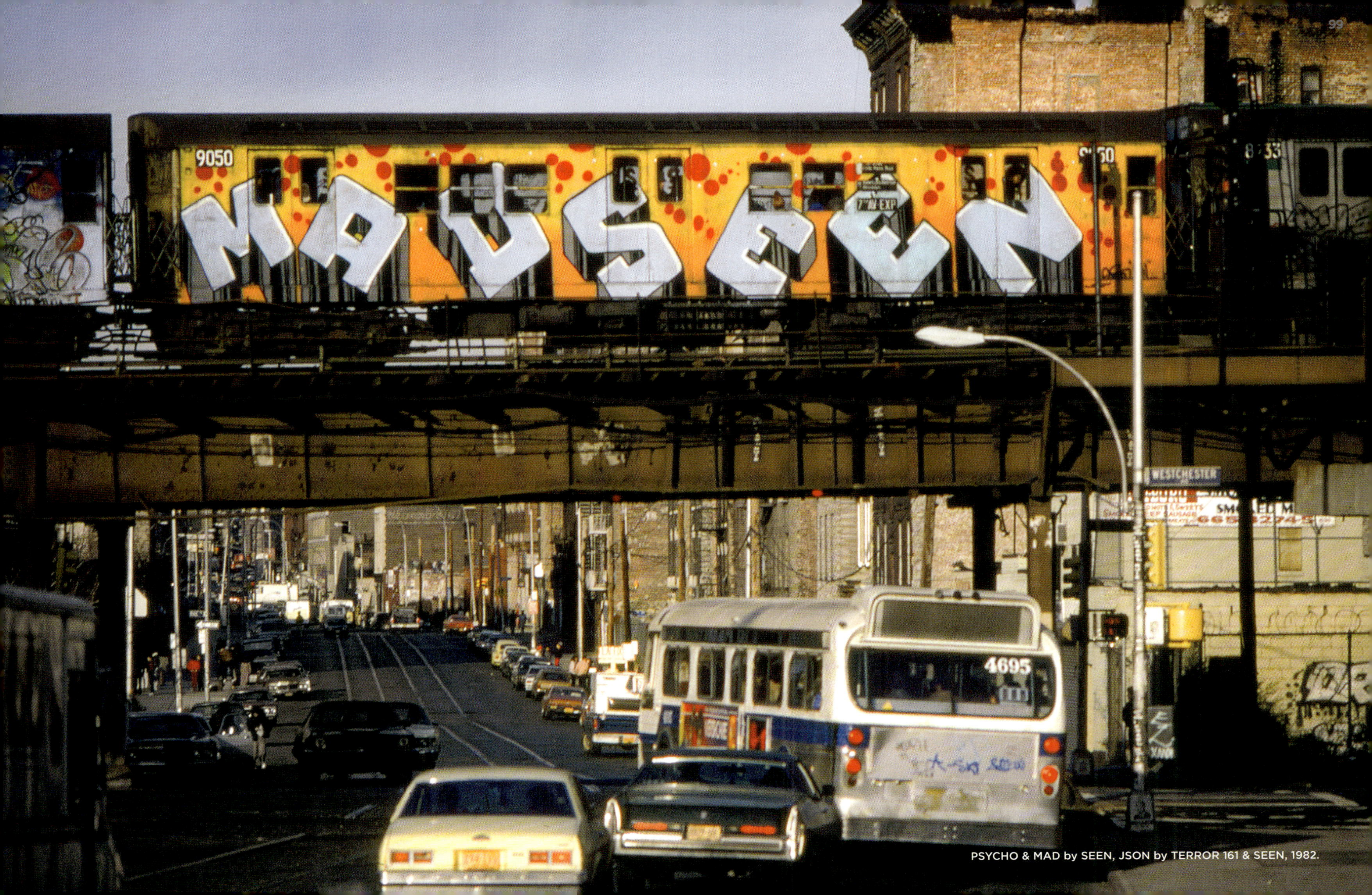

PSYCHO & MAD by SEEN, JSON by TERROR 161 & SEEN, 1982.

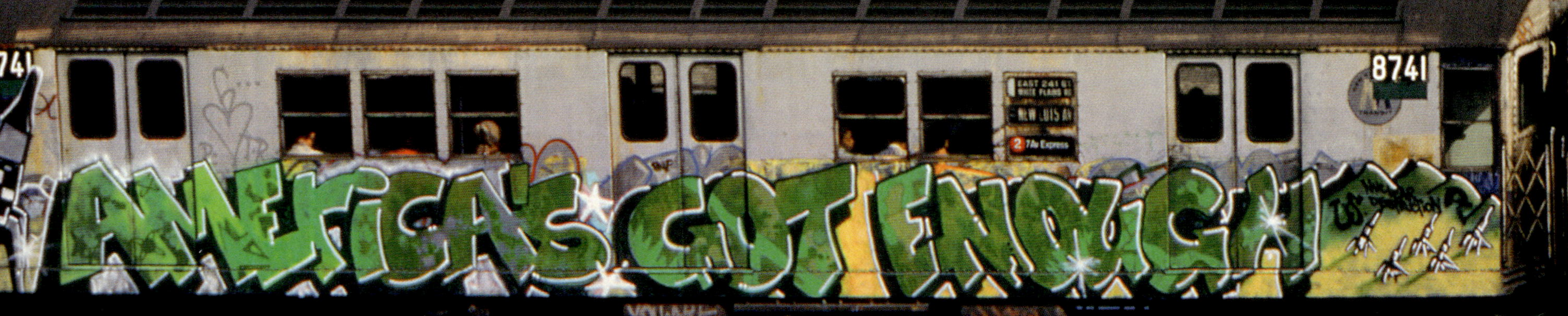
8741
EAST 241 ST
WHITE PLAINS RD
2 7Av Express
AMERICA'S GOT ENOUGH
8741

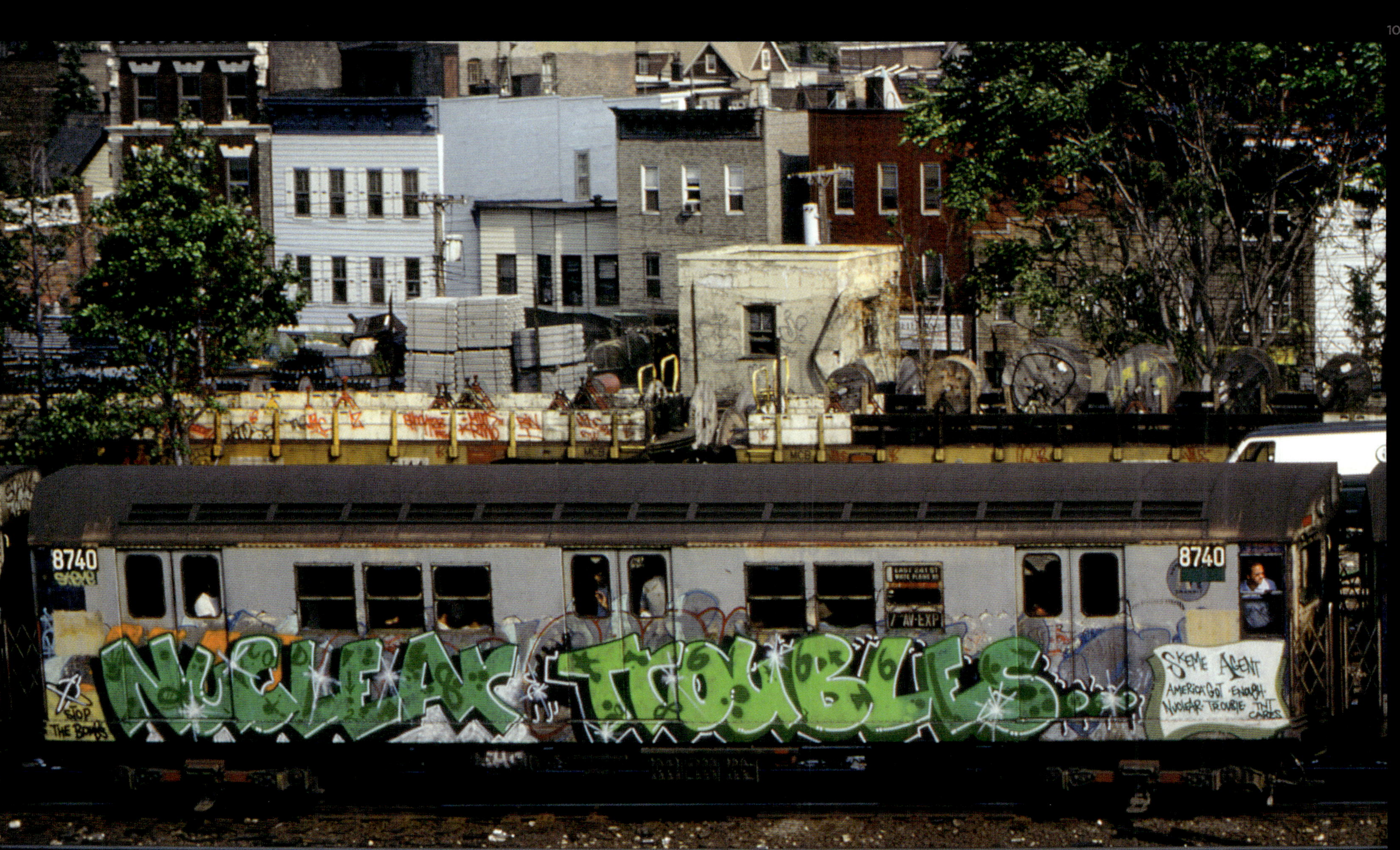

AMERICA'S GOT ENOUGH NUCLEAR TROUBLES by SKEME & AGENT, 1982.

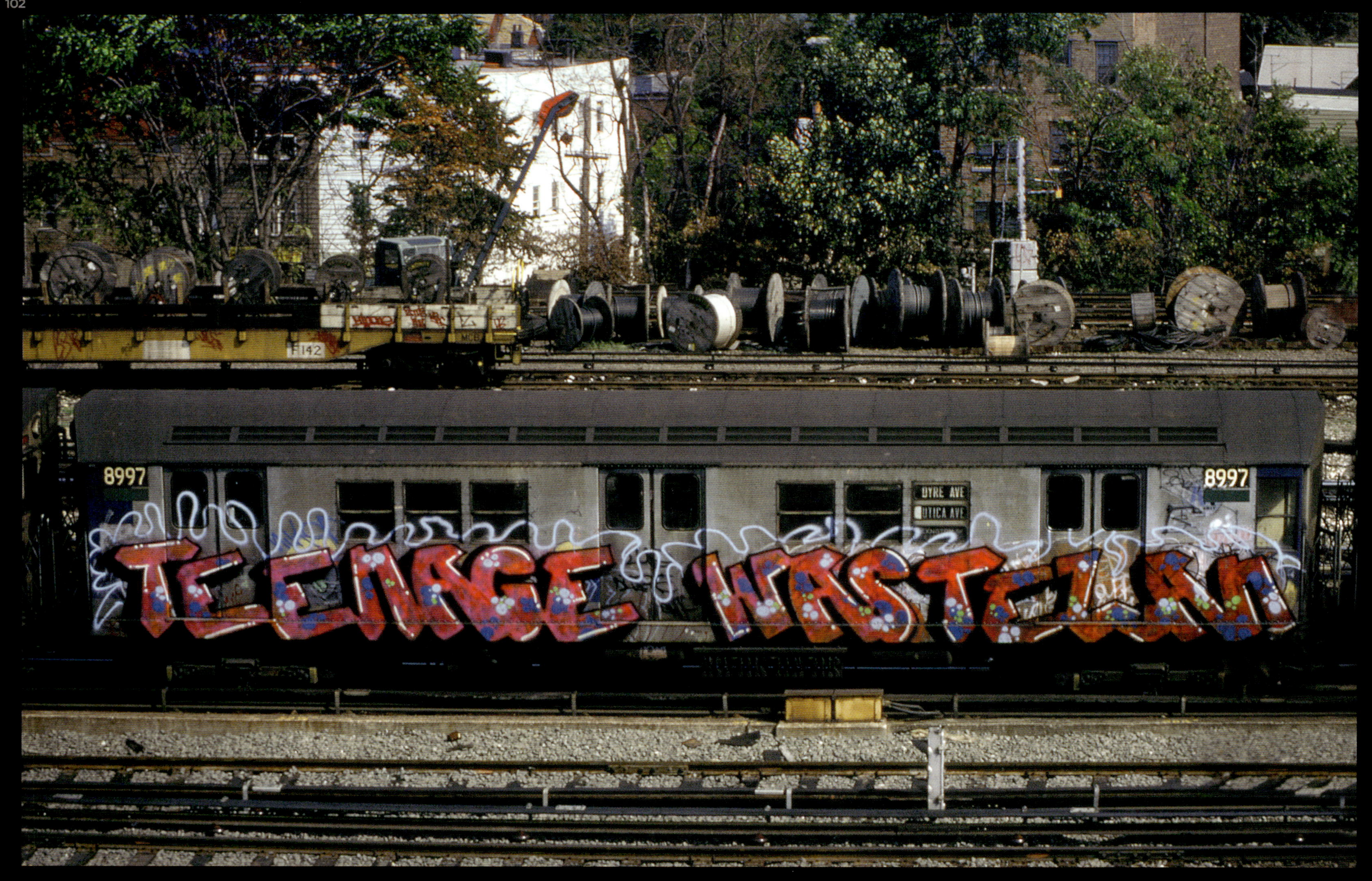

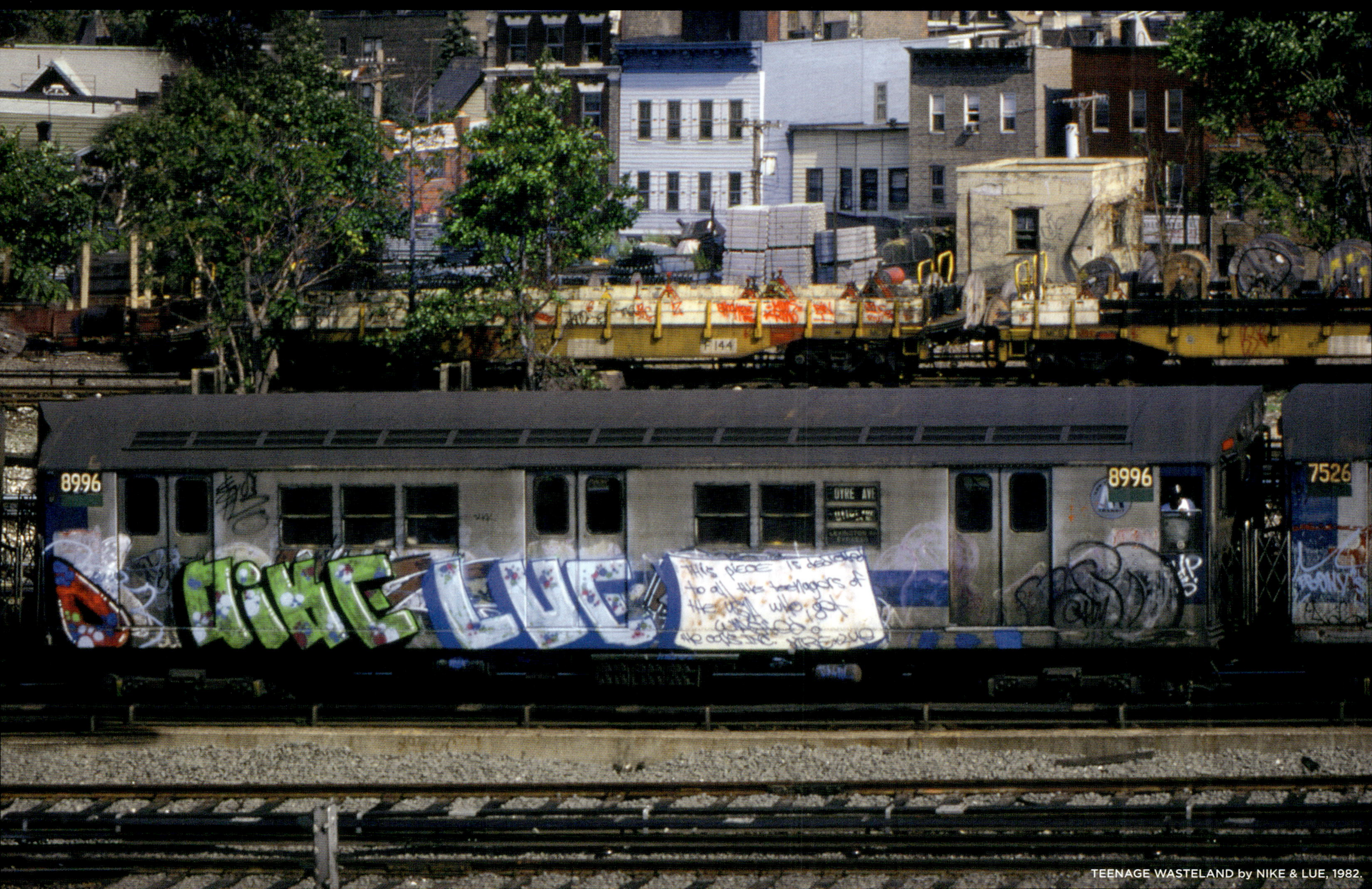

TEENAGE WASTELAND by NIKE & LUE, 1982.

PUT YOUR
NAME UP
IN LIGHTS

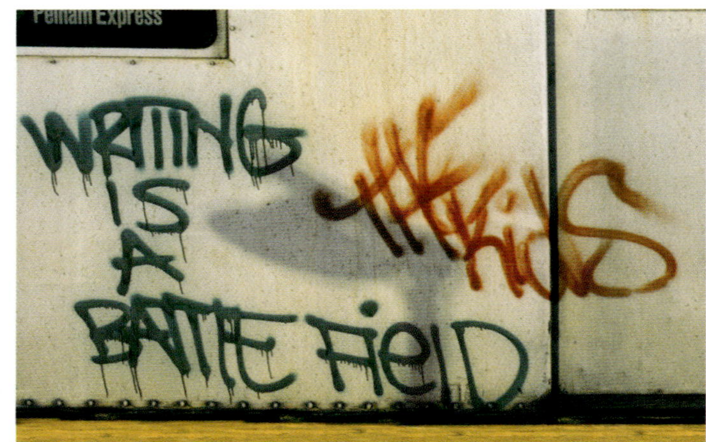
Pelham Express
WRITING
IS
A
BATTLE FIELD
KIDS

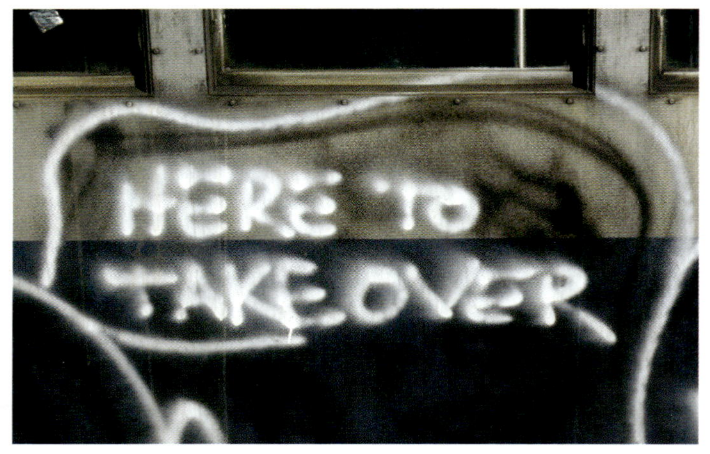
HERE TO
TAKE OVER

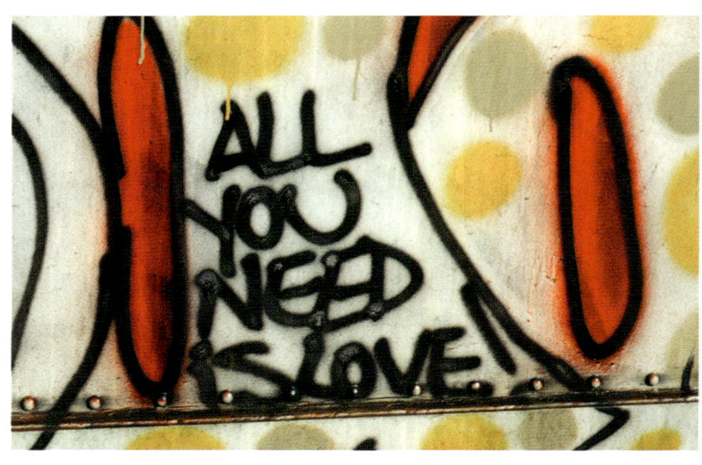
ALL
YOU
NEED
IS LOVE

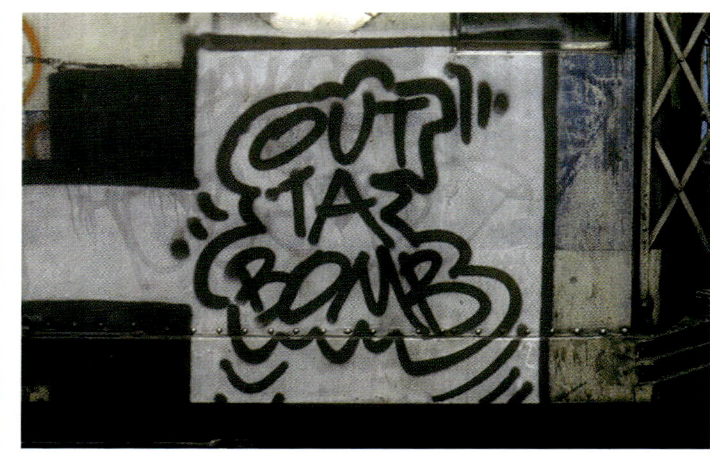
OUT
TA
BOMB

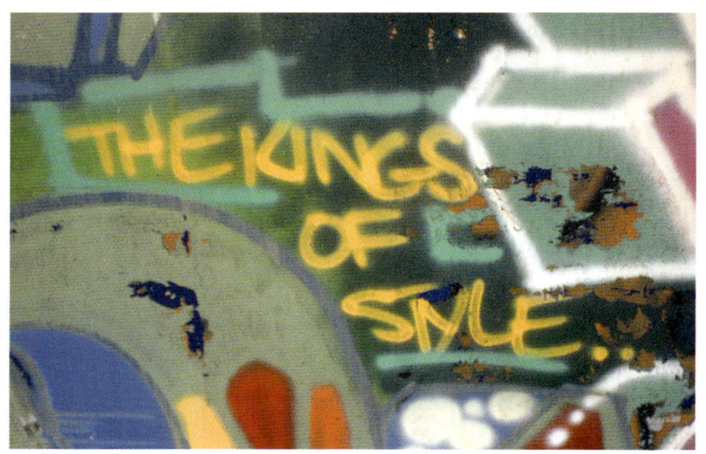
THE KINGS
OF
STYLE

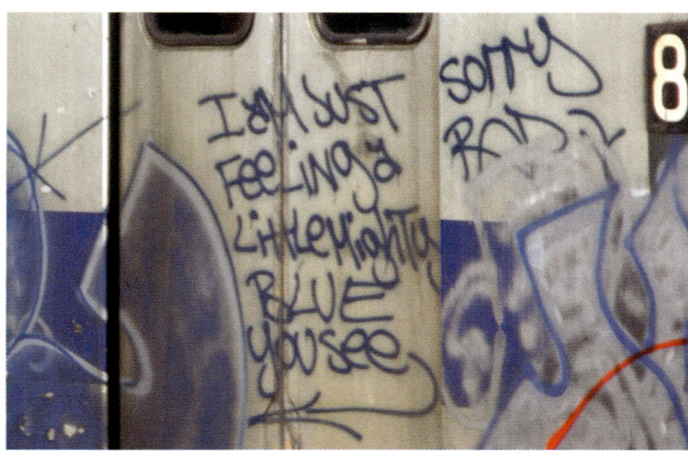
I am just
feeling a
Little mighty
Blue
you see
SORRY
ROD
8

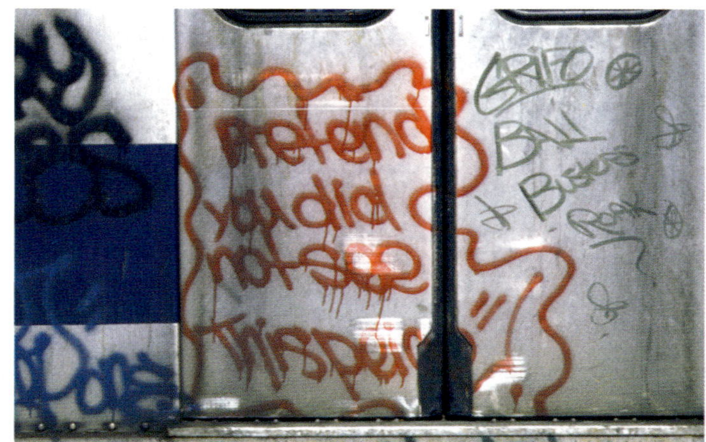
Pretend
you did
not see
Trespar
GRICO
BALL
+ Burros
ROAK

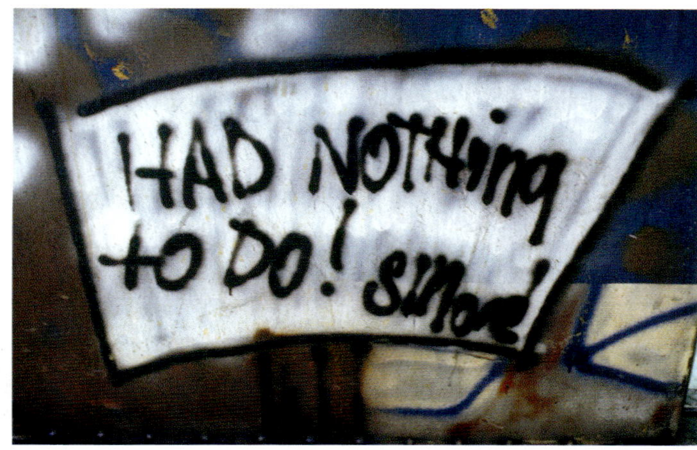
HAD NOTHING
to DO! SINER!

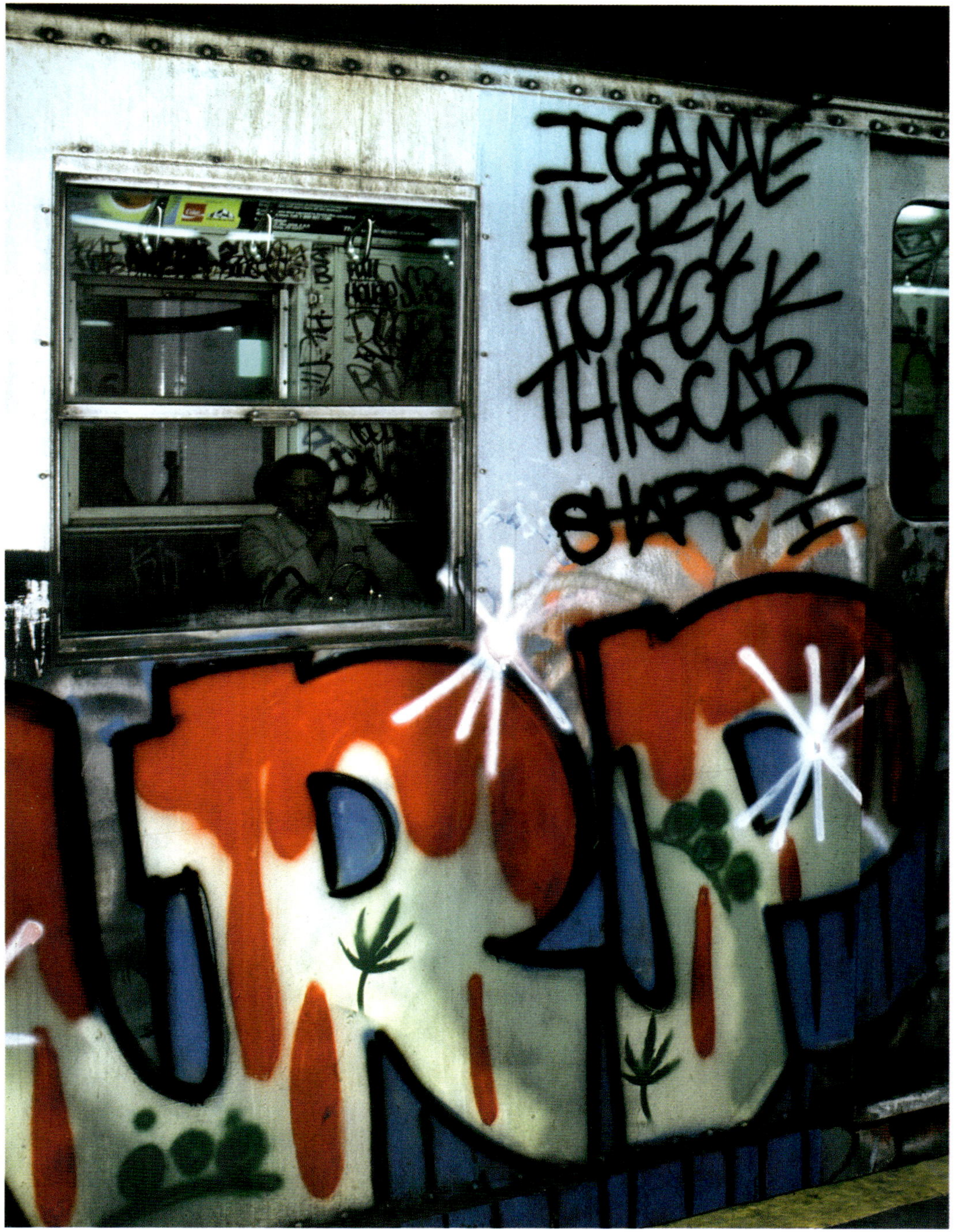

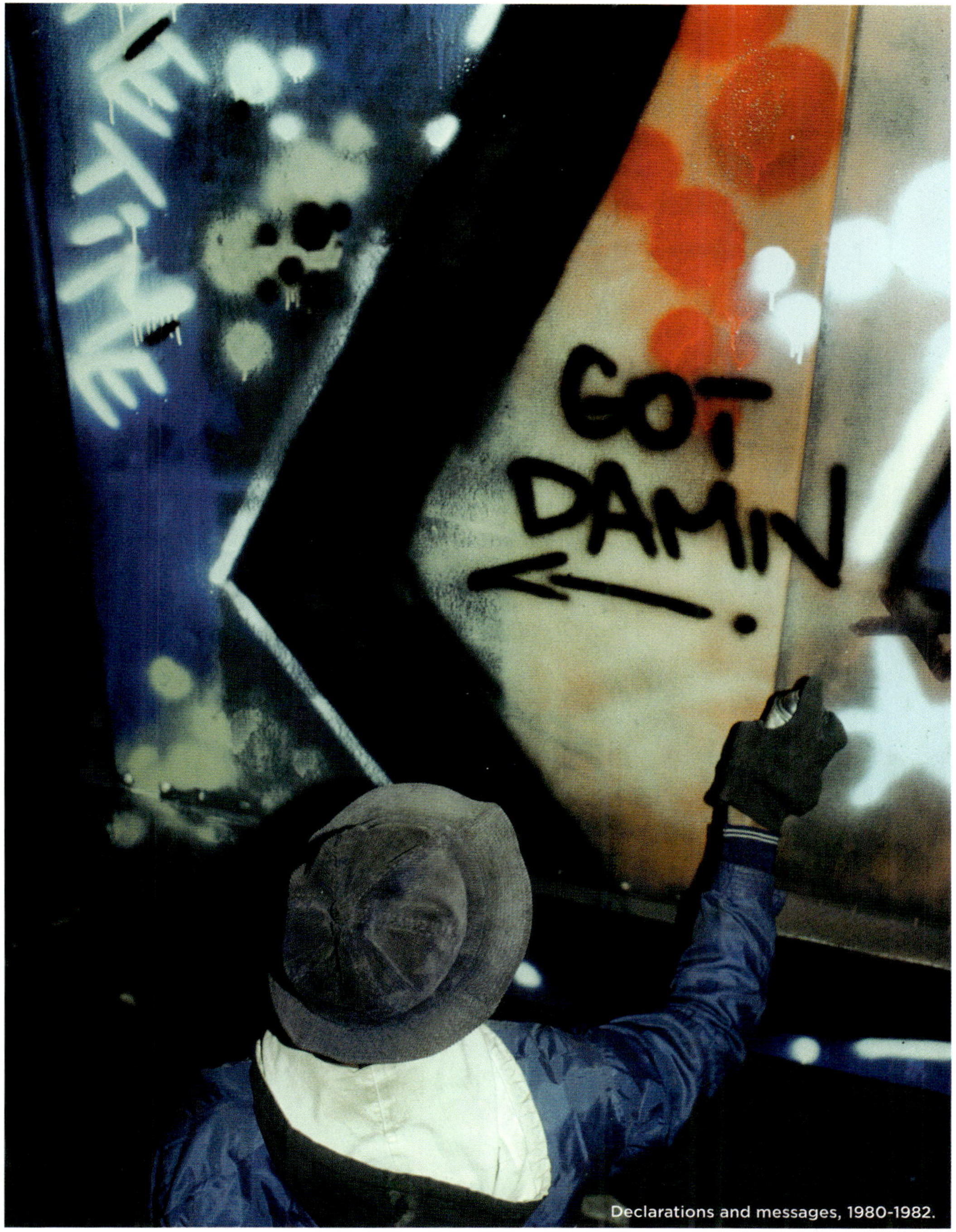

Declarations and messages, 1980-1982.

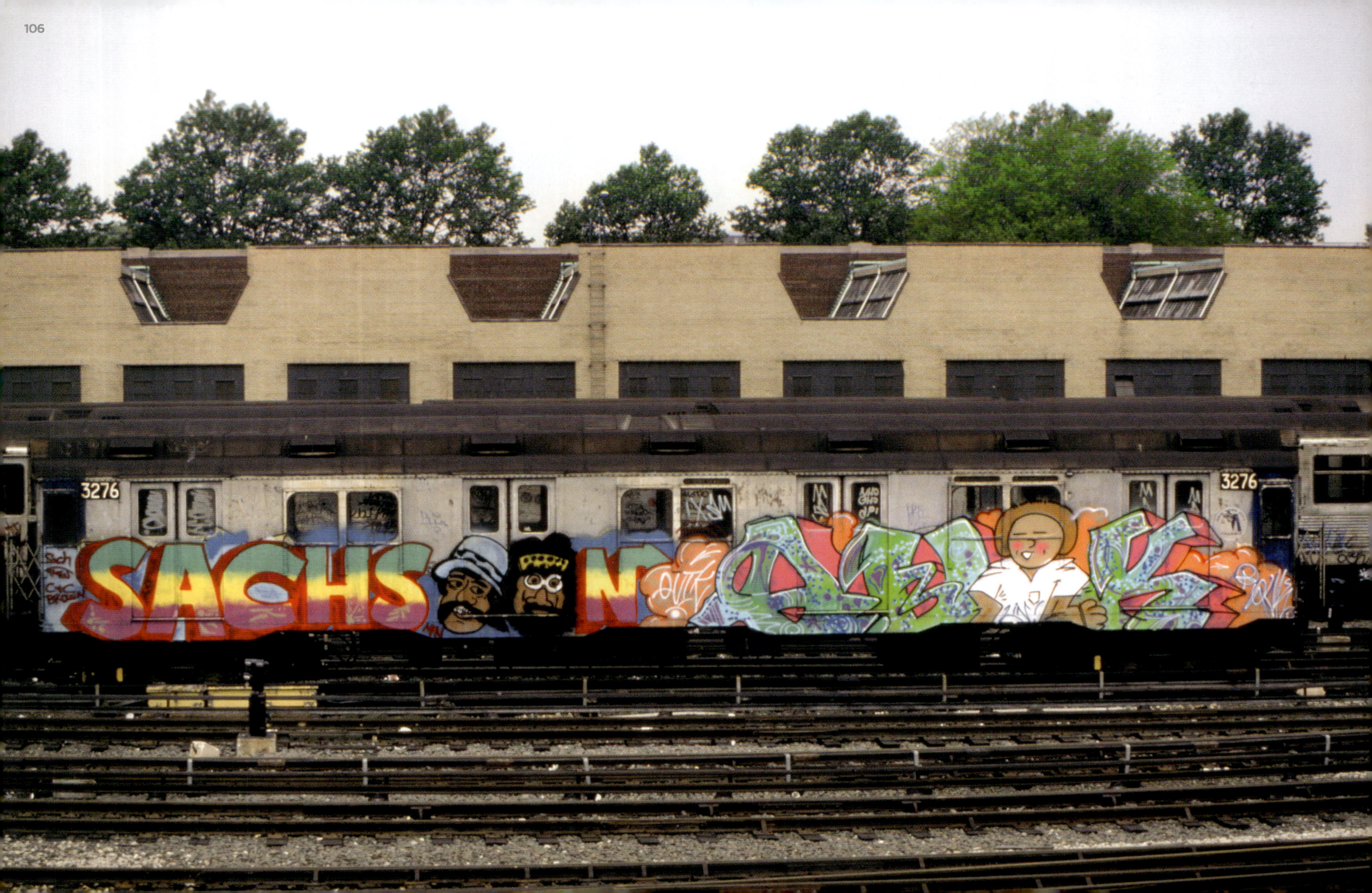

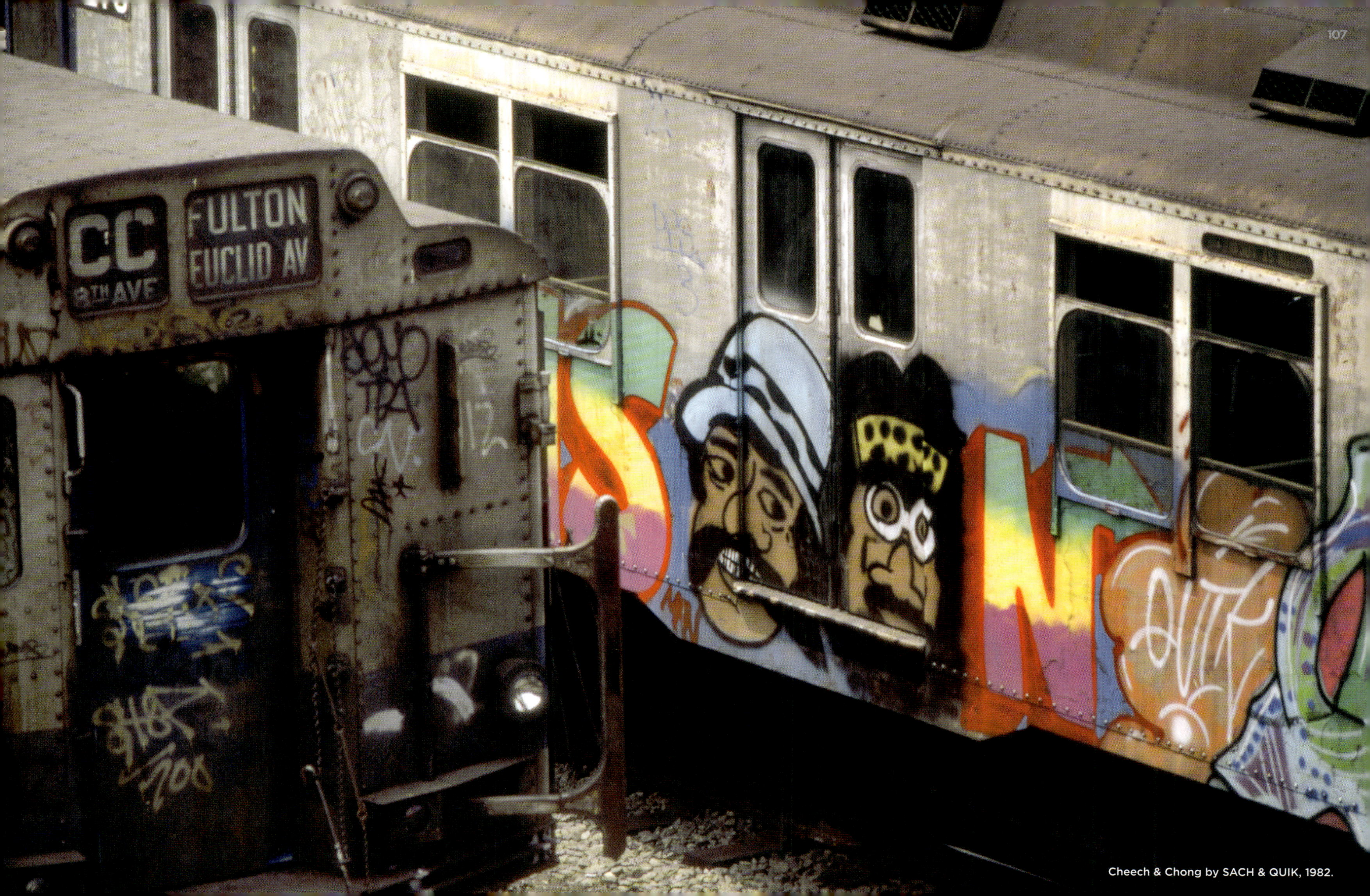

Cheech & Chong by SACH & QUIK, 1982.

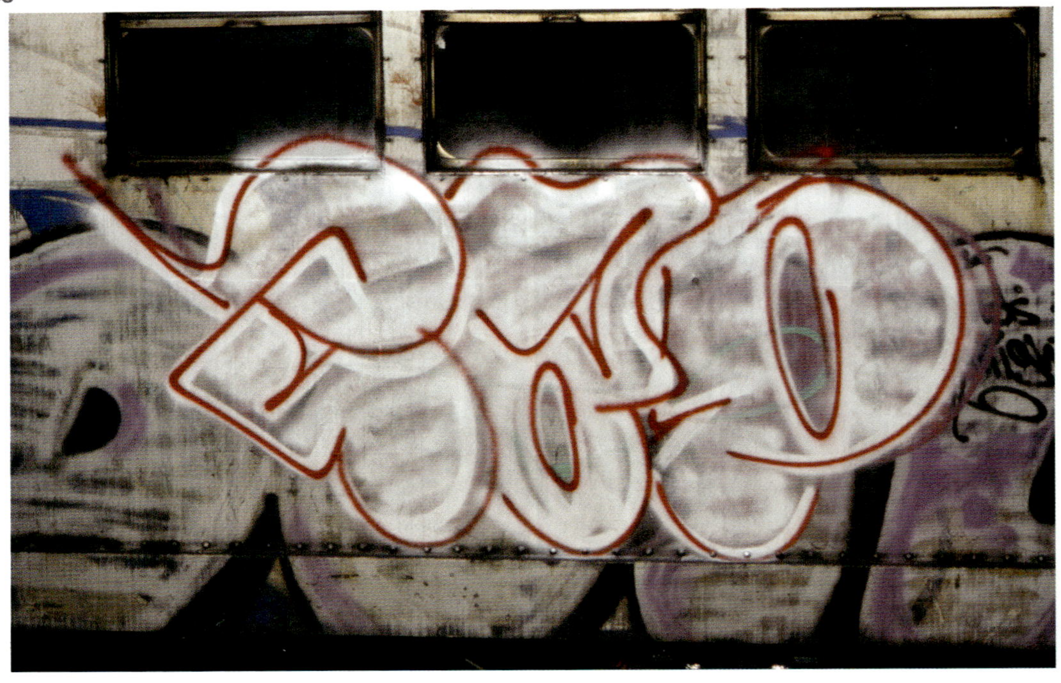

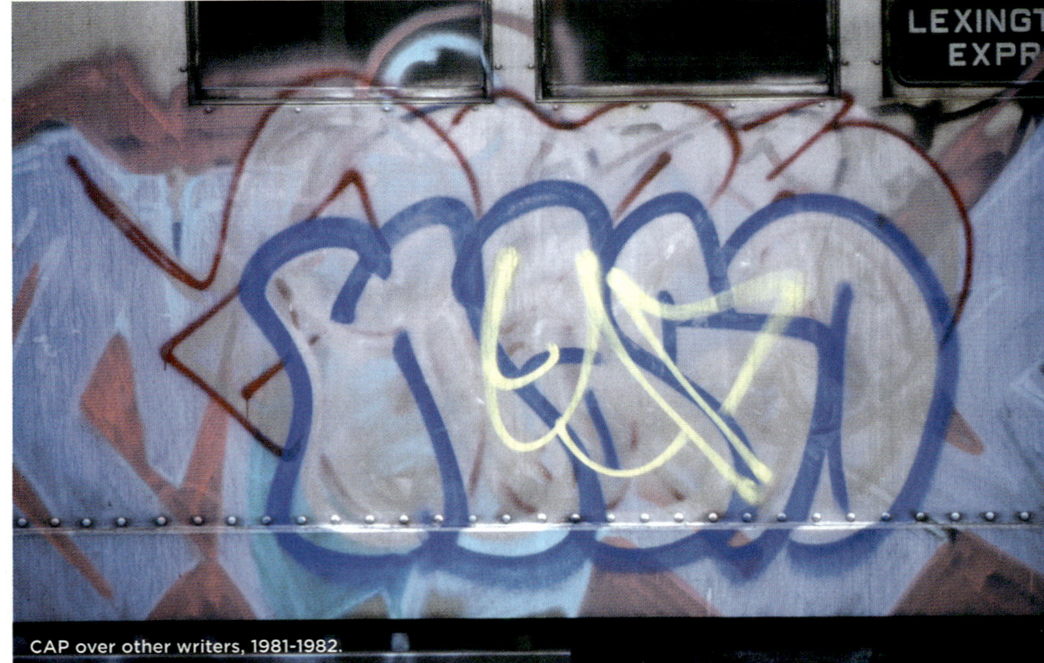

CAP over other writers, 1981-1982.

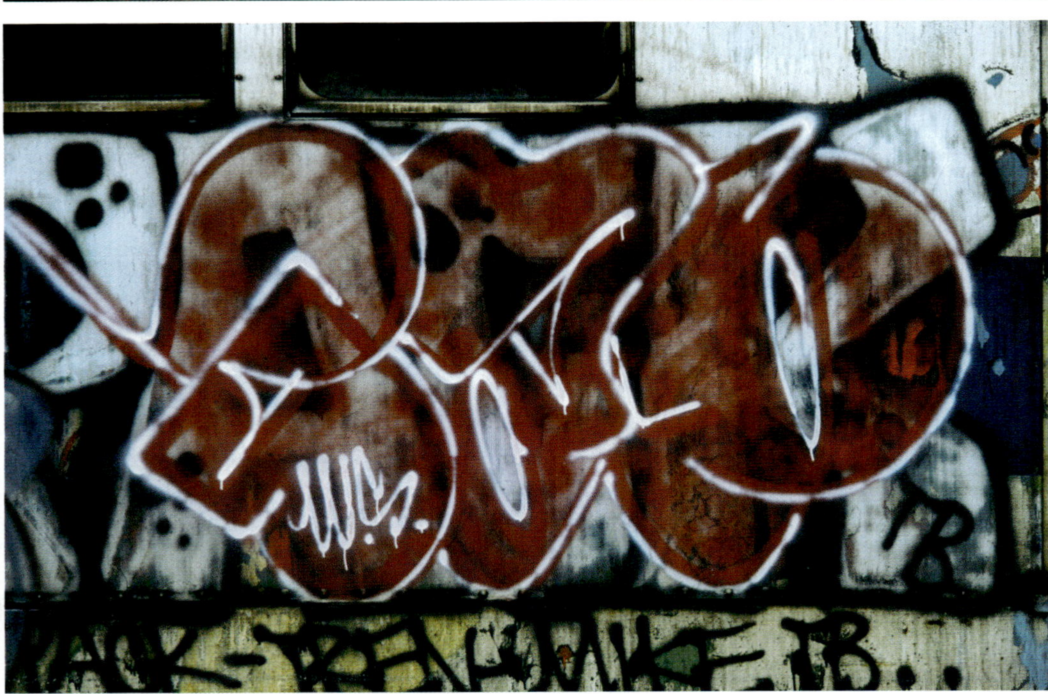

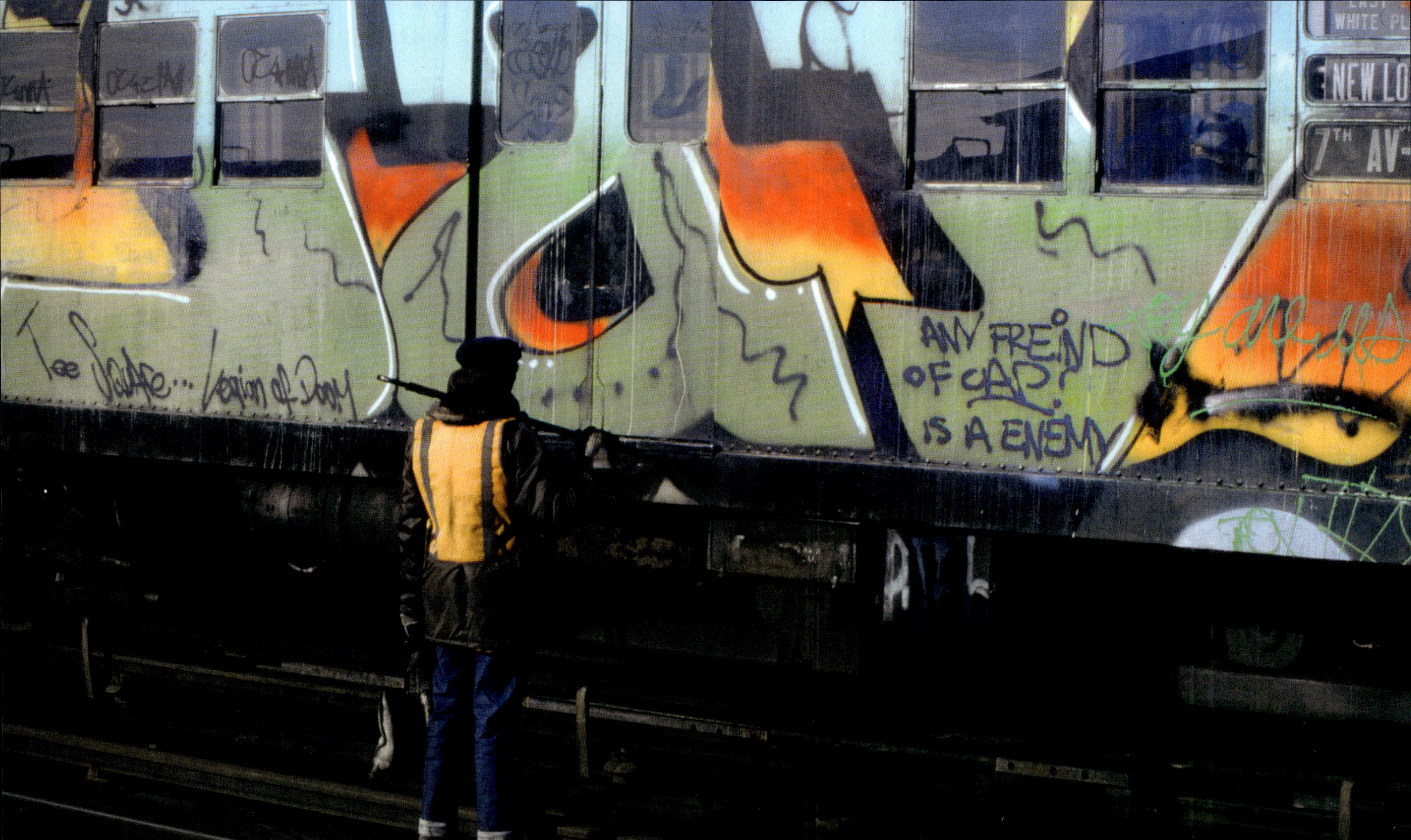

NEW LO
7TH AV-
ANY FREIND OF CAP? IS A ENEMY

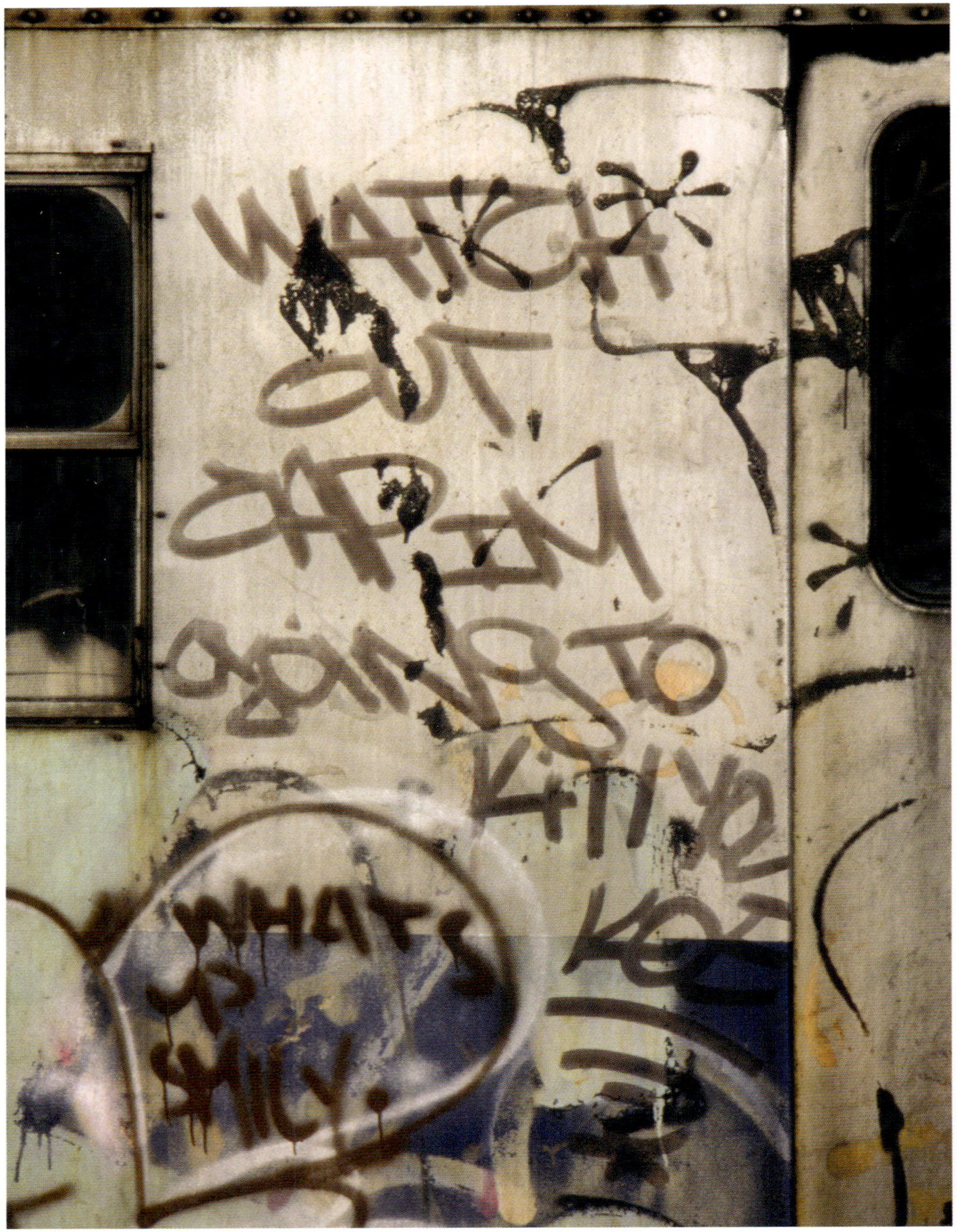

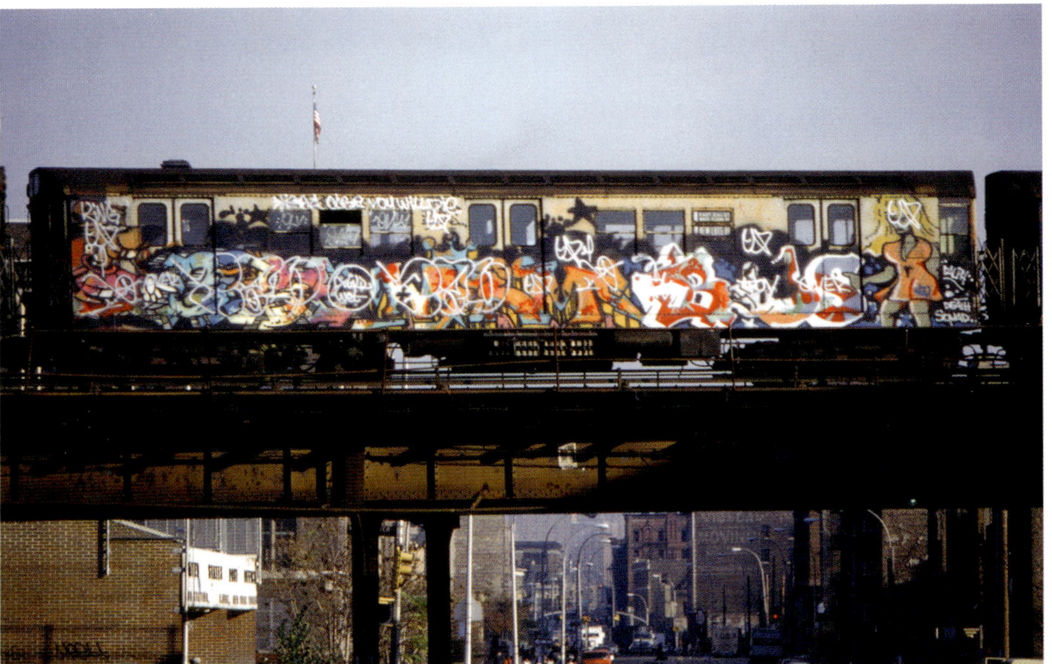

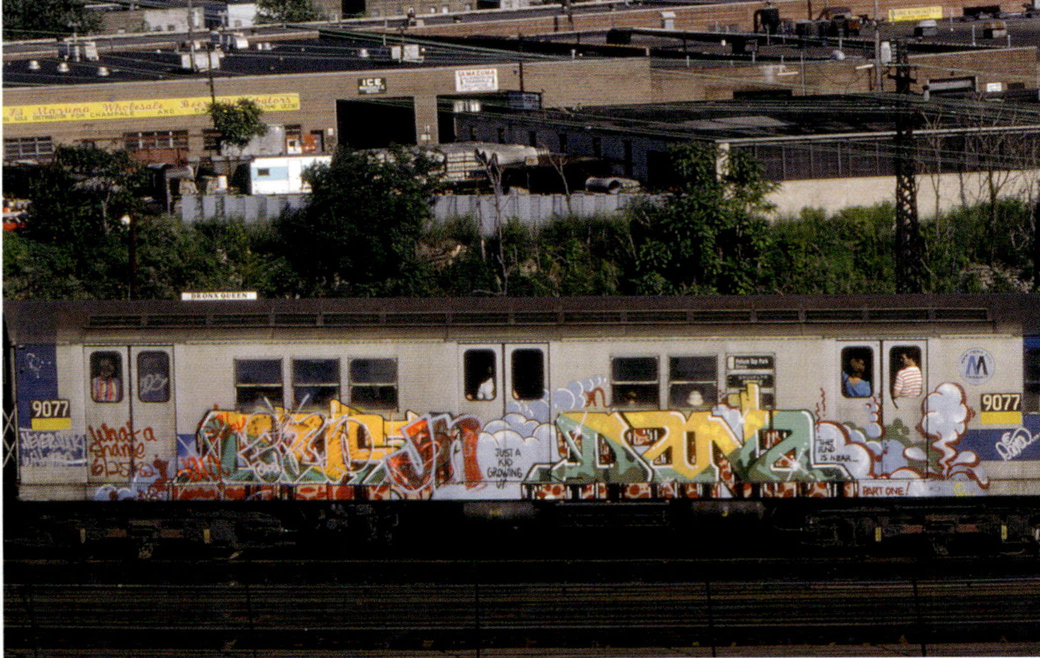

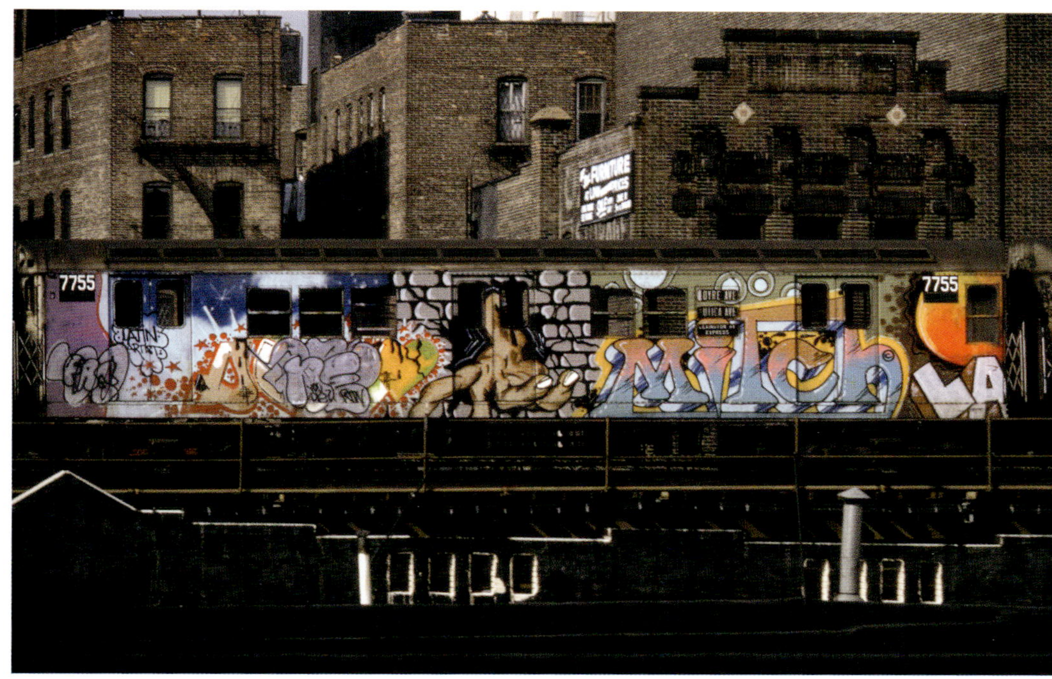

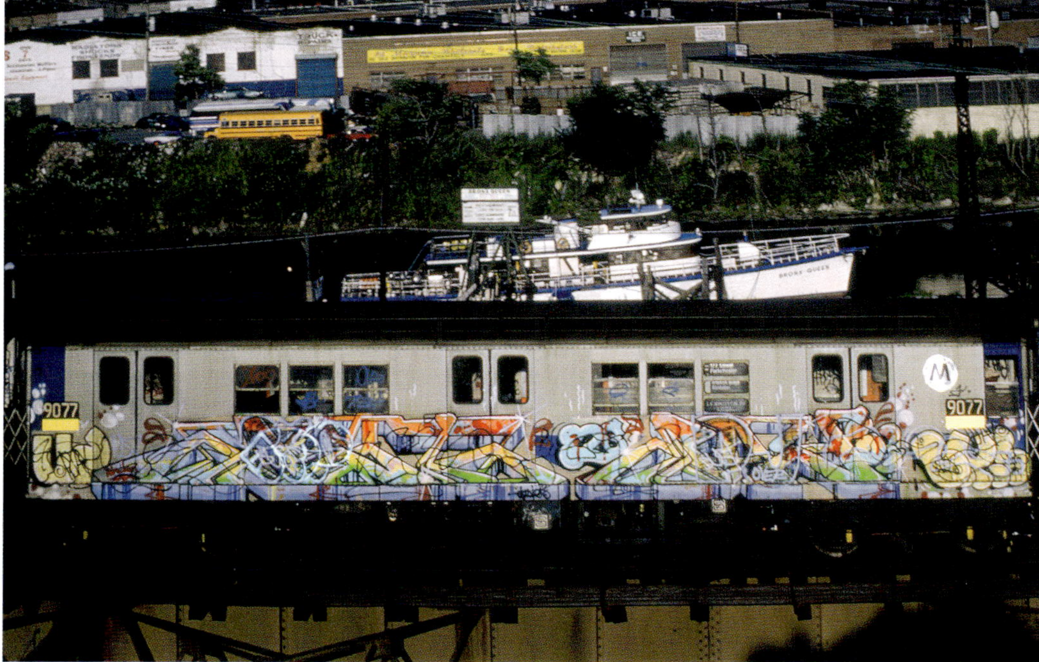

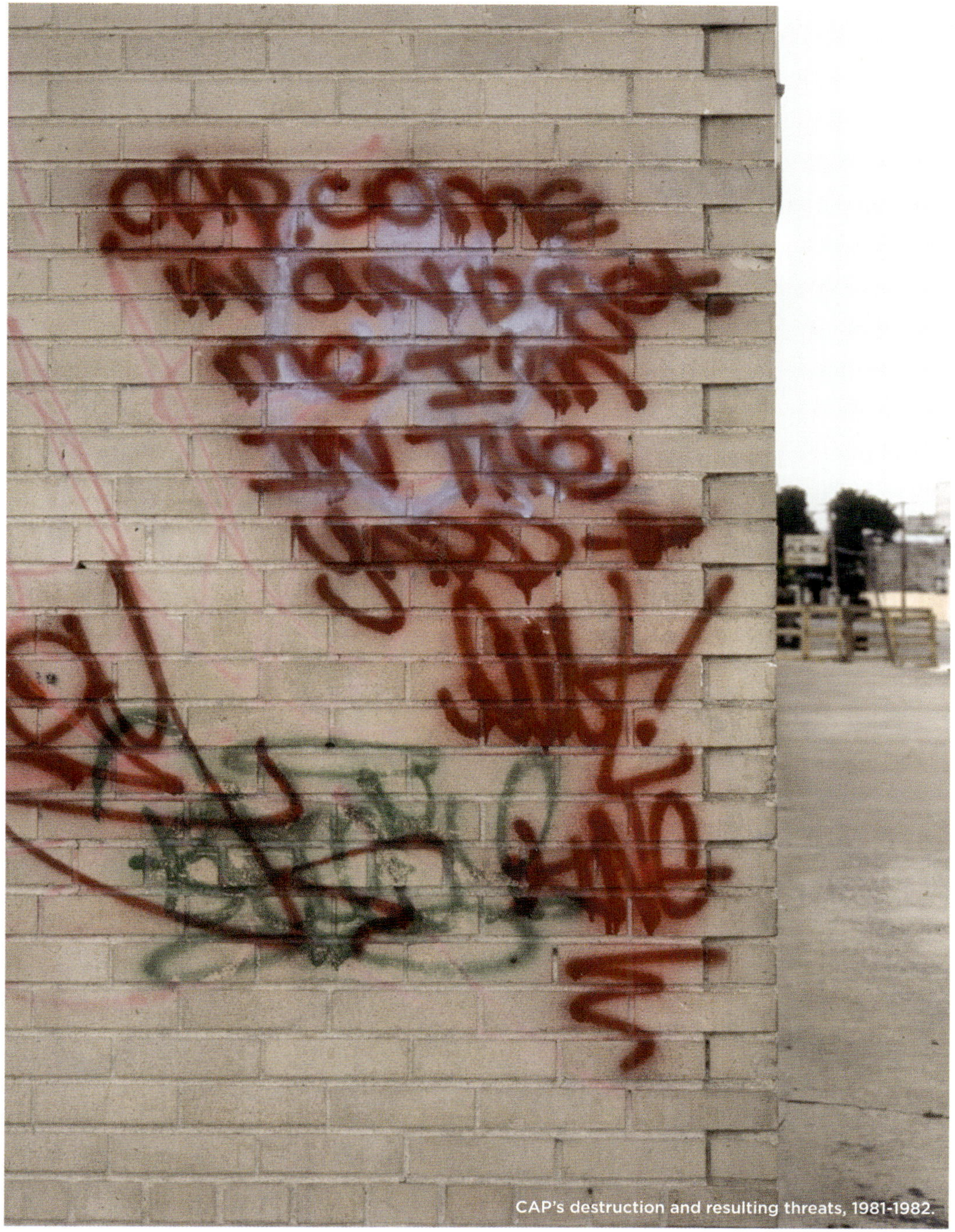

CAP's destruction and resulting threats, 1981-1982.

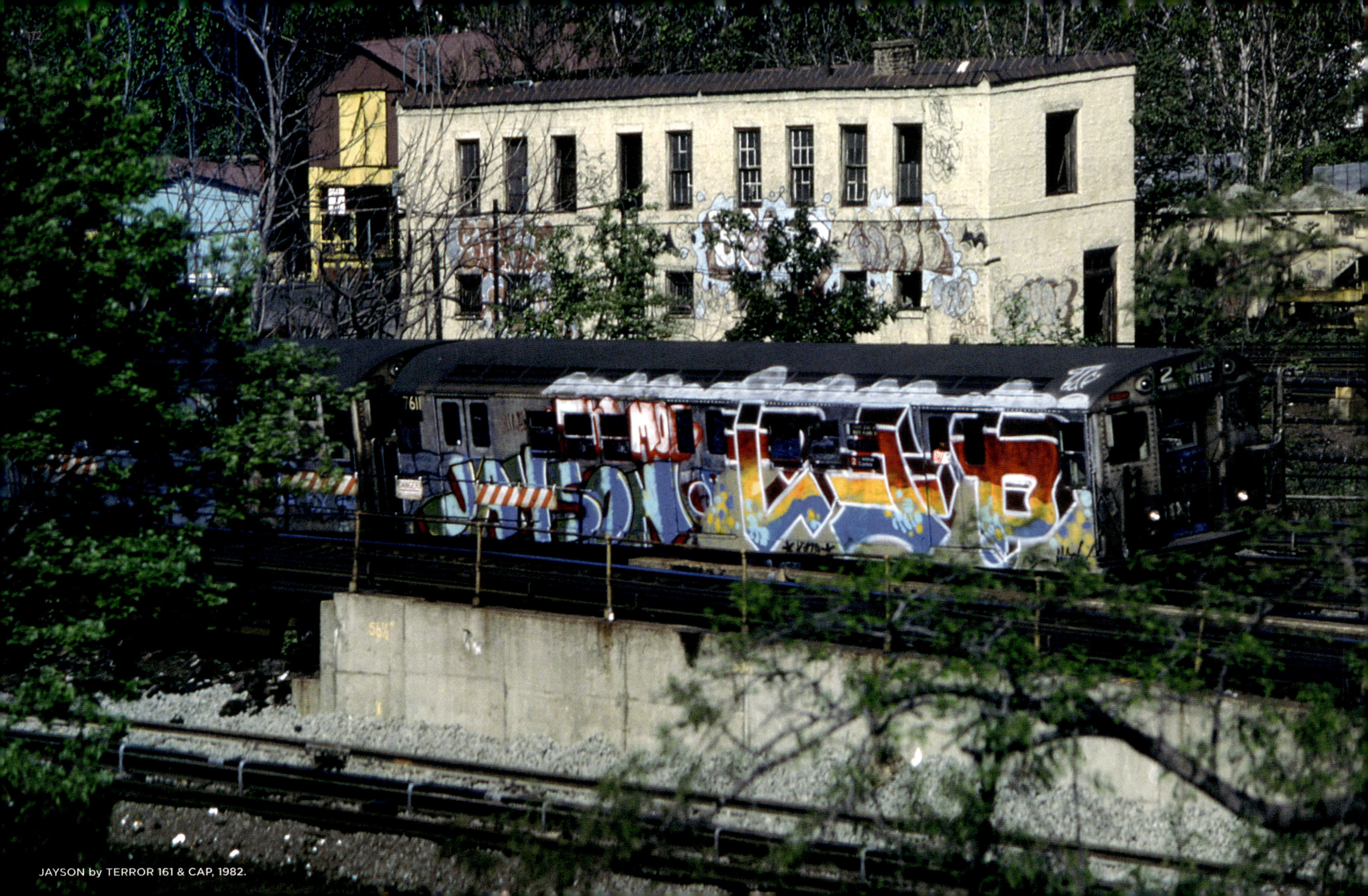

JAYSON by TERROR 161 & CAP, 1982.

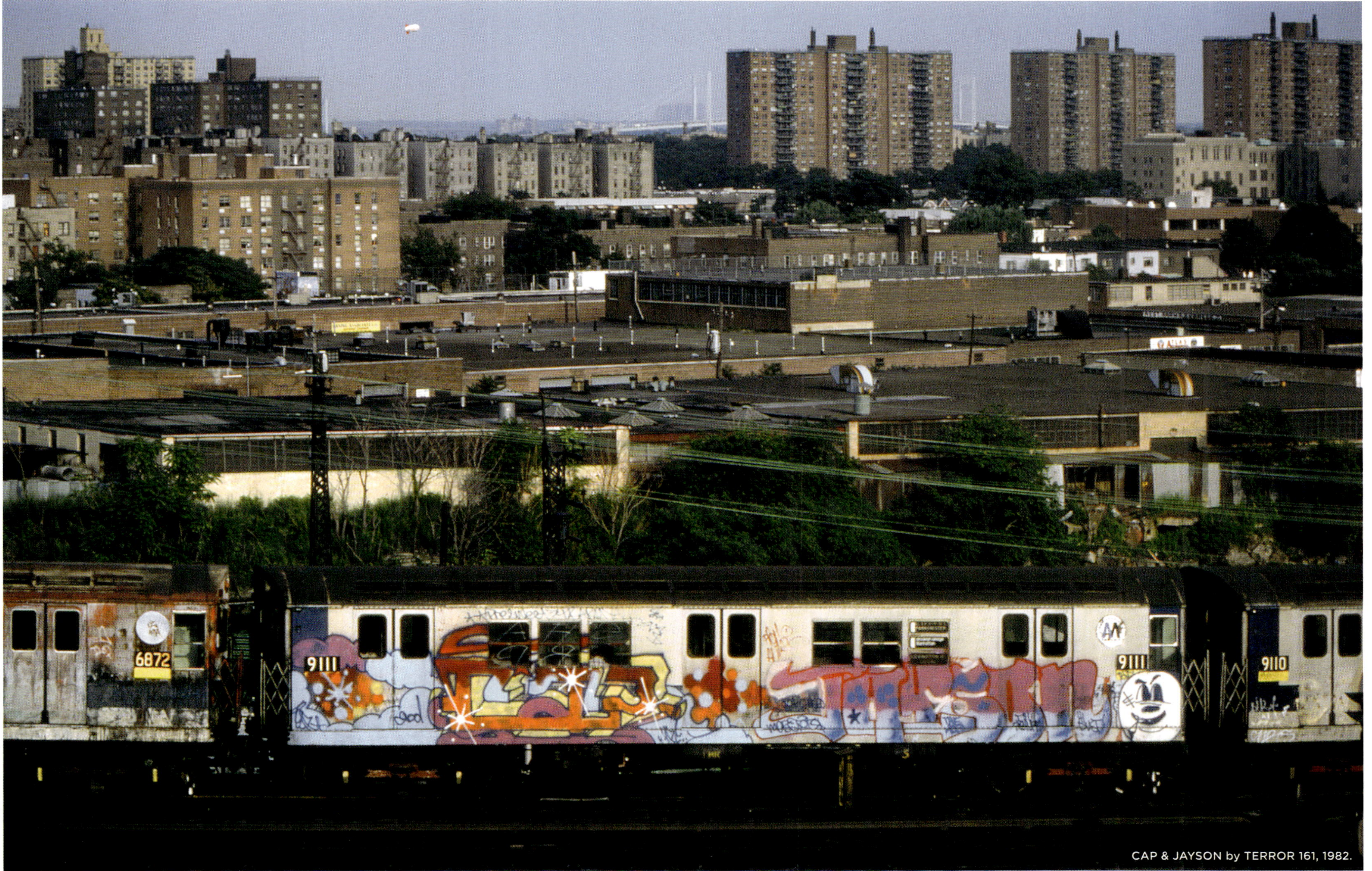

CAP & JAYSON by TERROR 161, 1982.

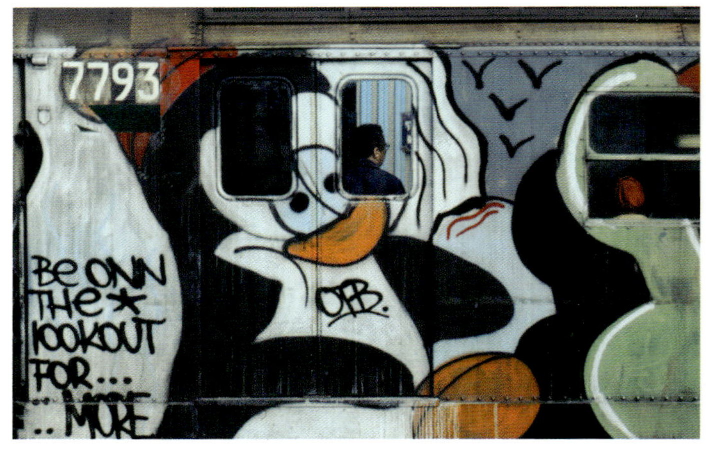
7793
BE ONN
THE
LOOKOUT
FOR...
.. MORE

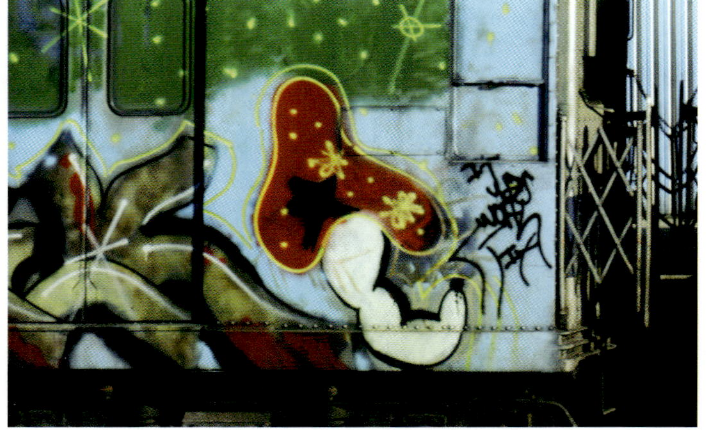

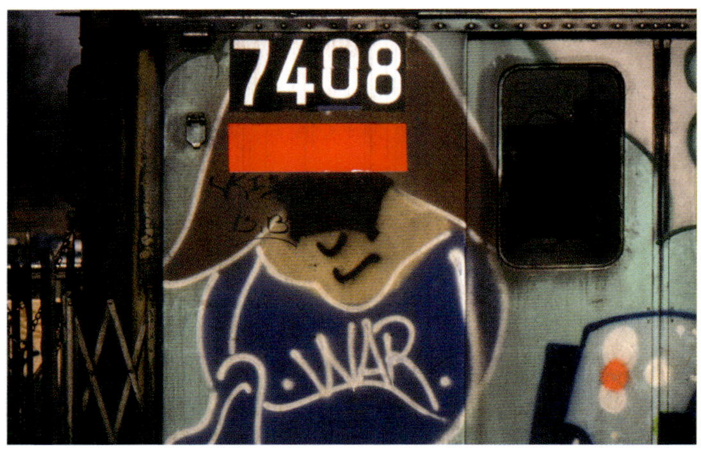
7408
WAR

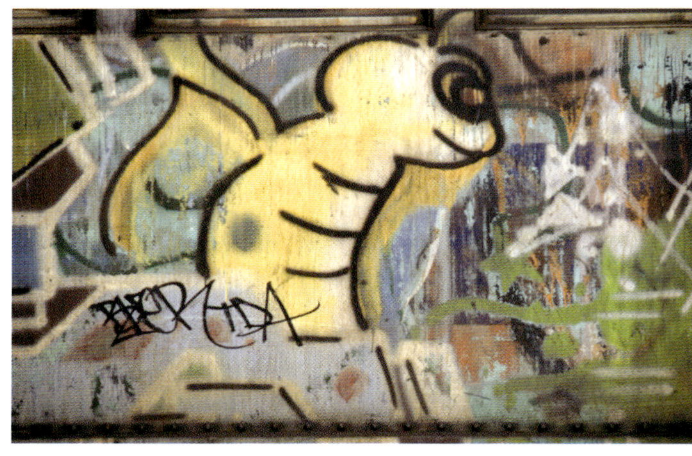

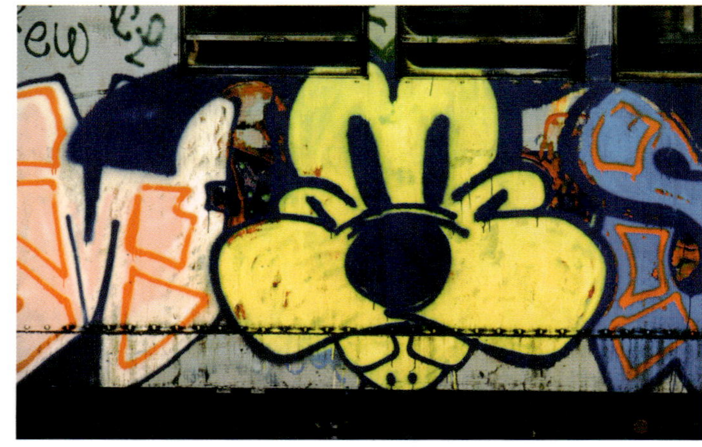

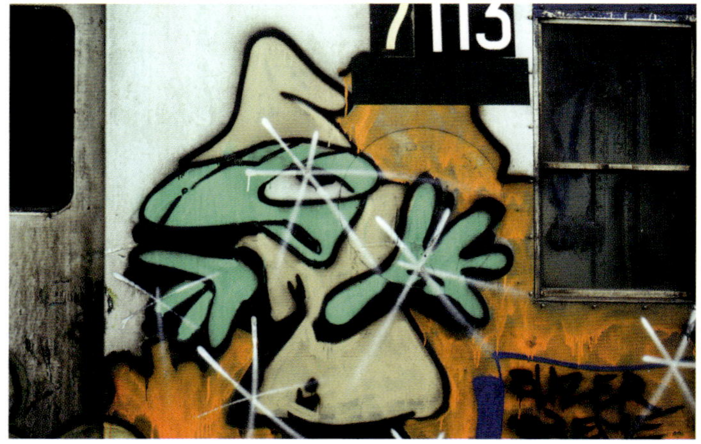
7113

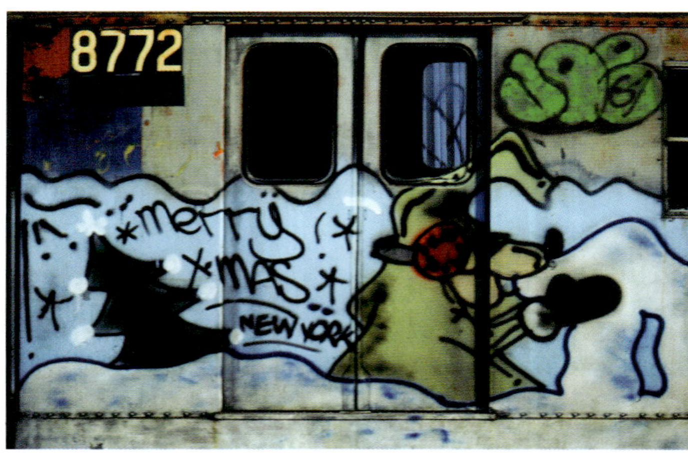
8772
merry
xmas
NEW YORK

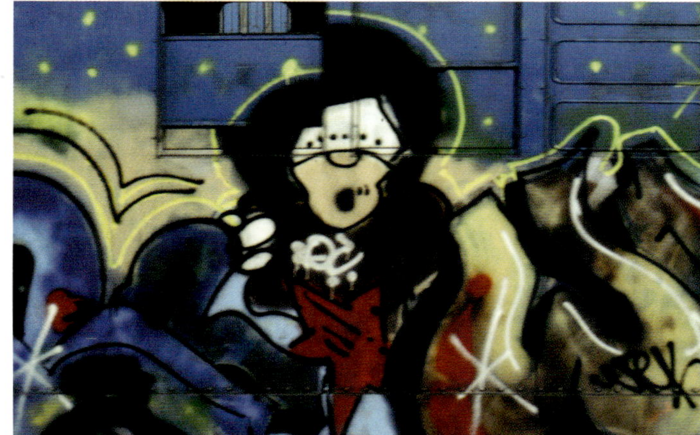

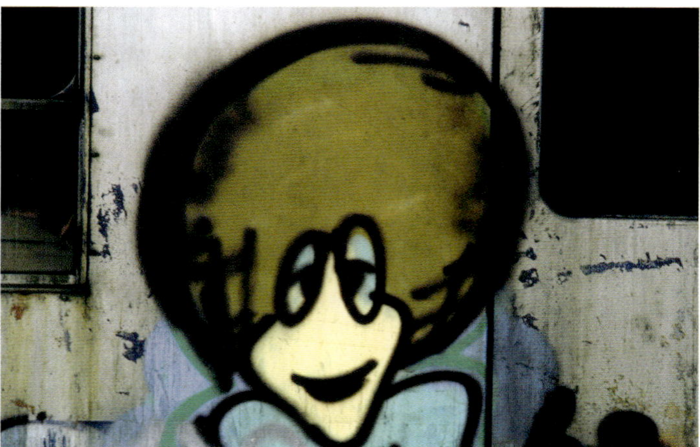

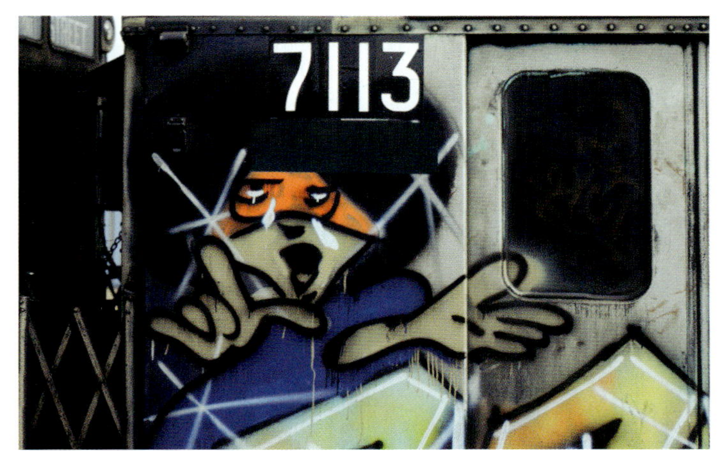
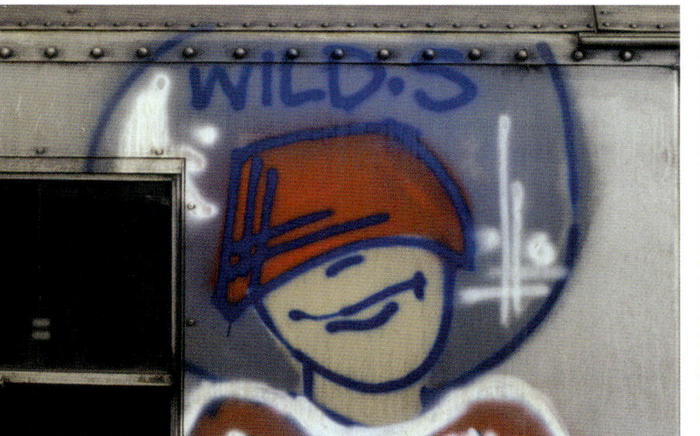
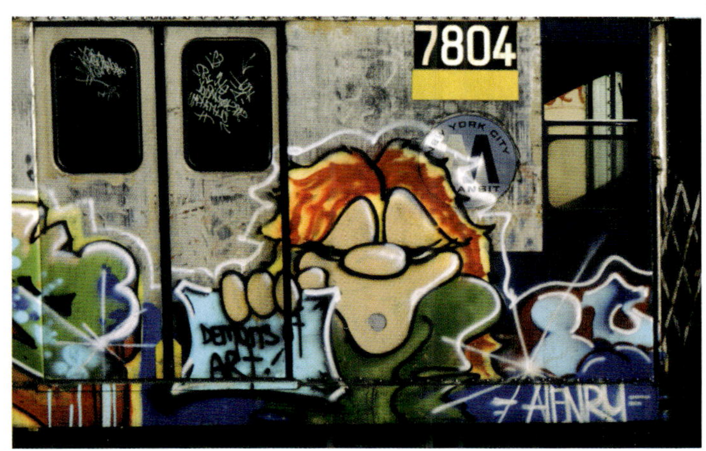
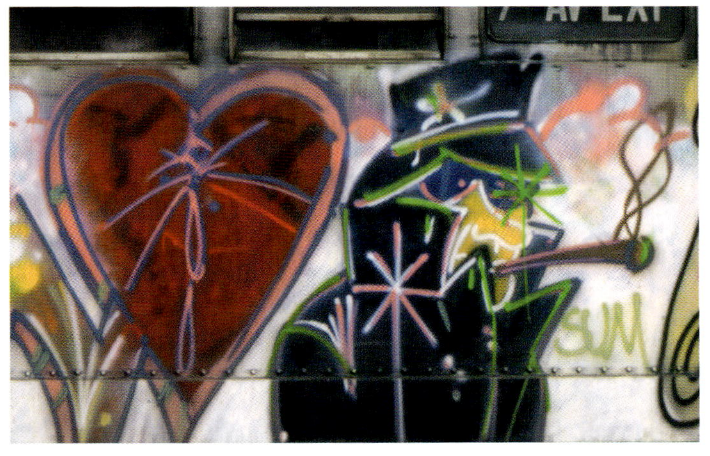
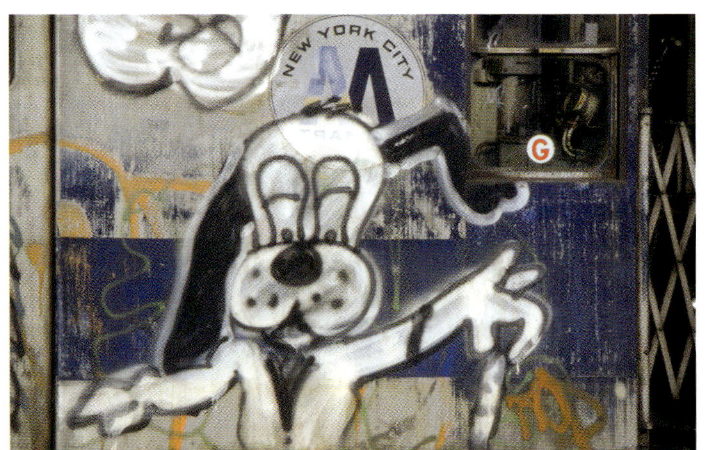
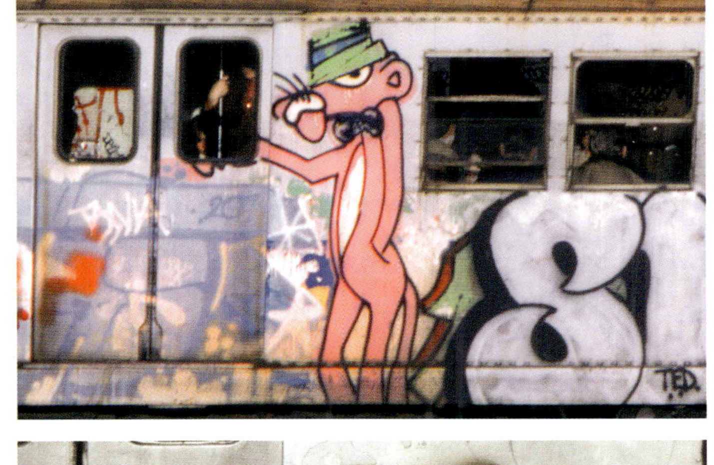
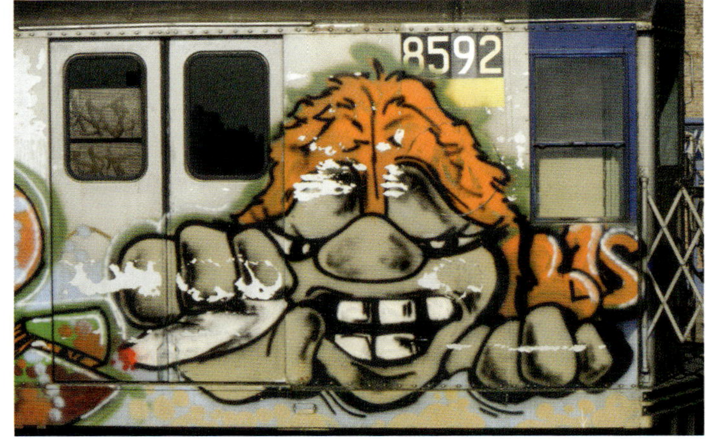
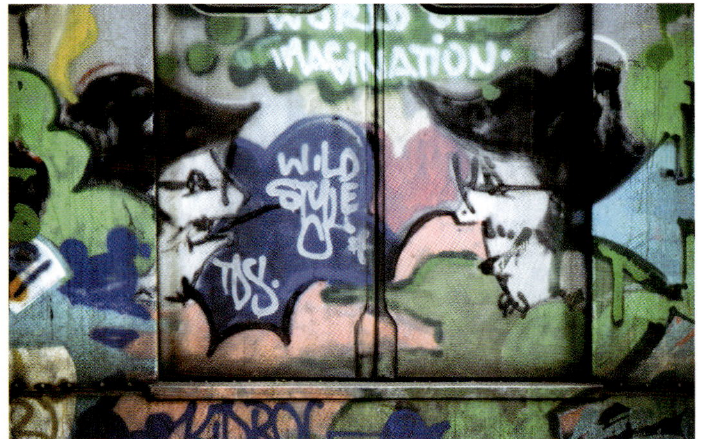
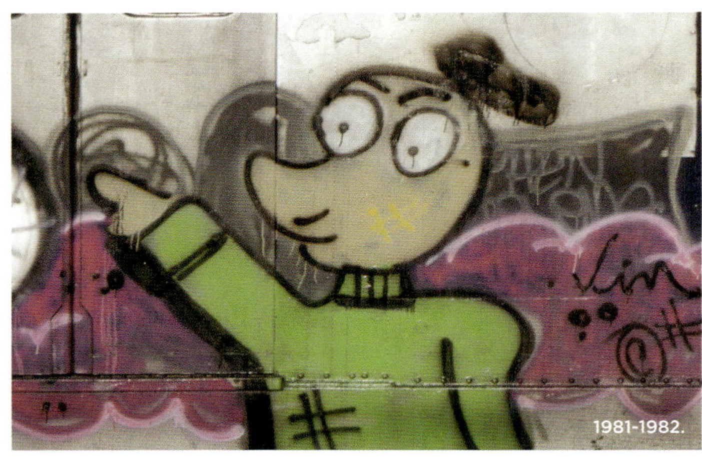

1981-1982.

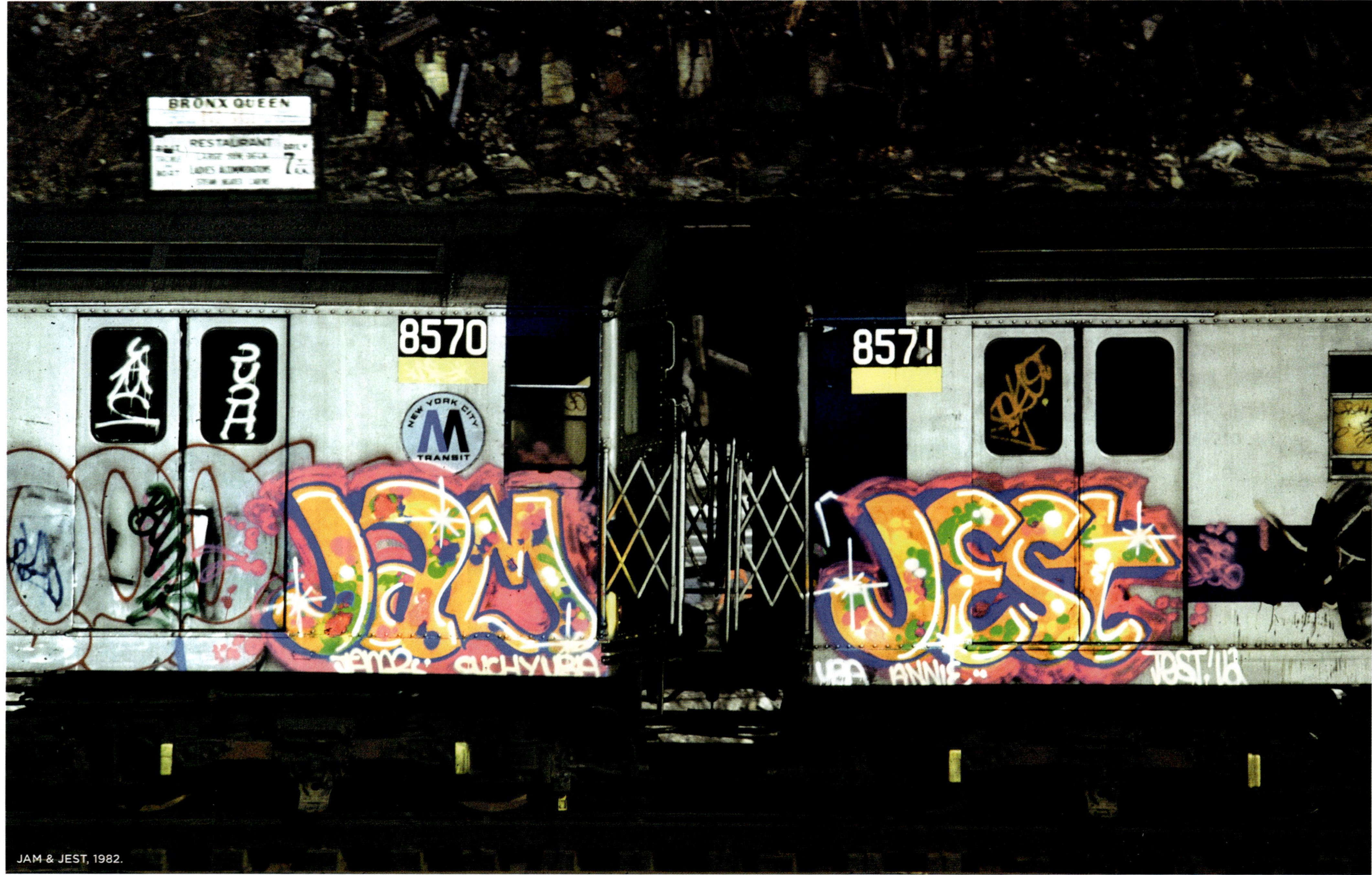

JAM & JEST, 1982.

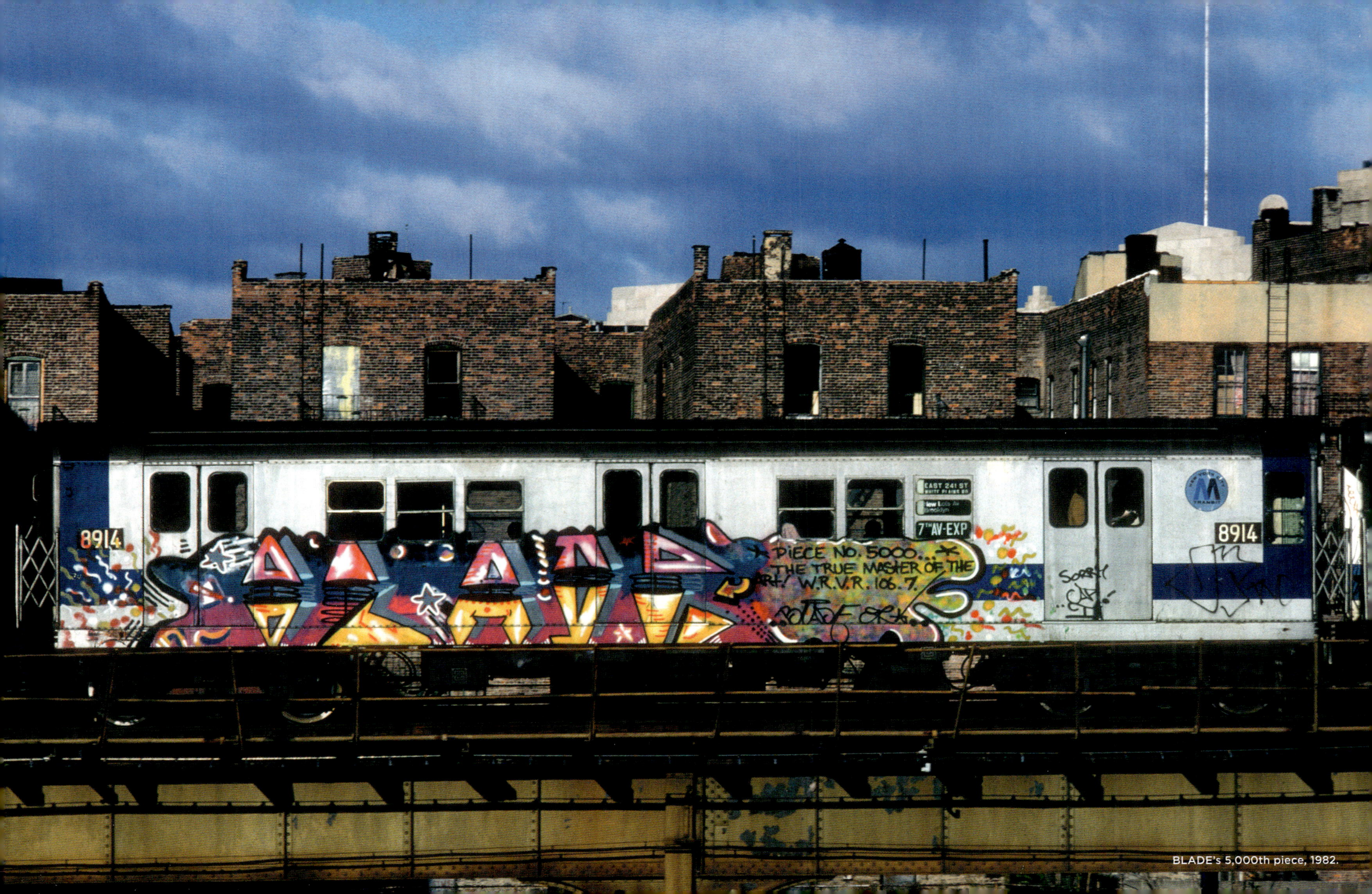

BLADE's 5,000th piece, 1982.

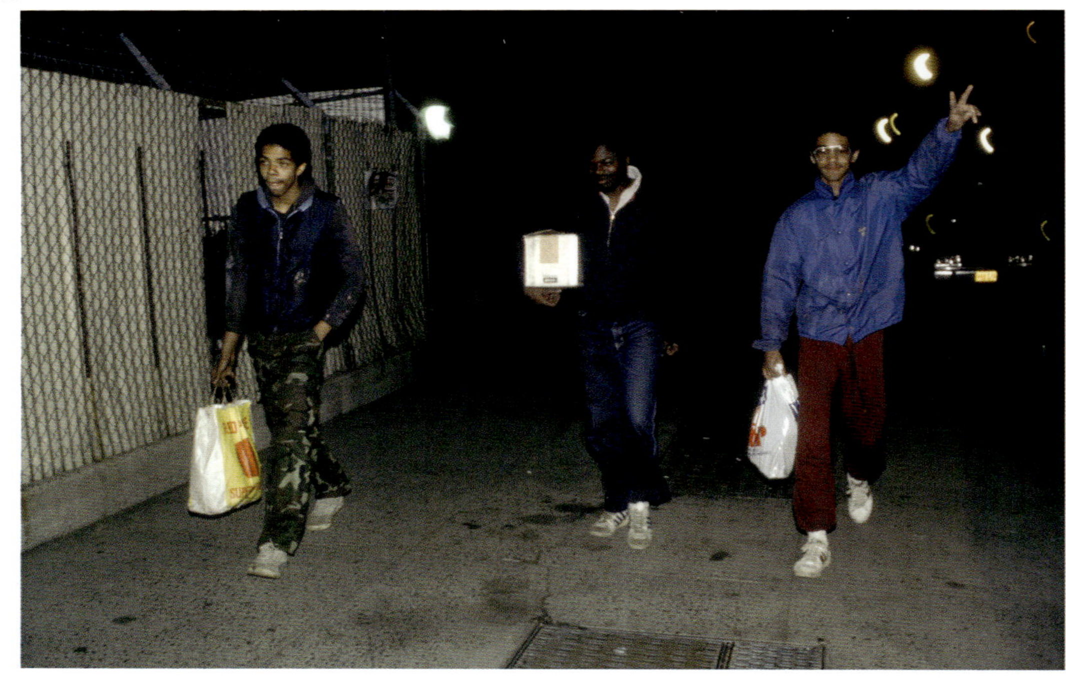

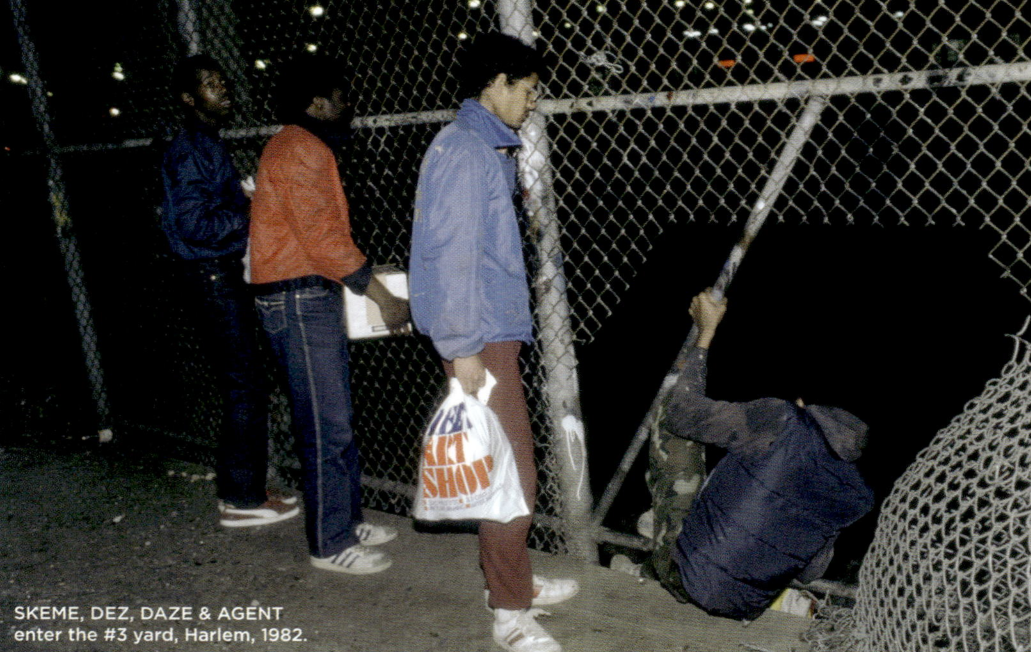

SKEME, DEZ, DAZE & AGENT
enter the #3 yard, Harlem, 1982.

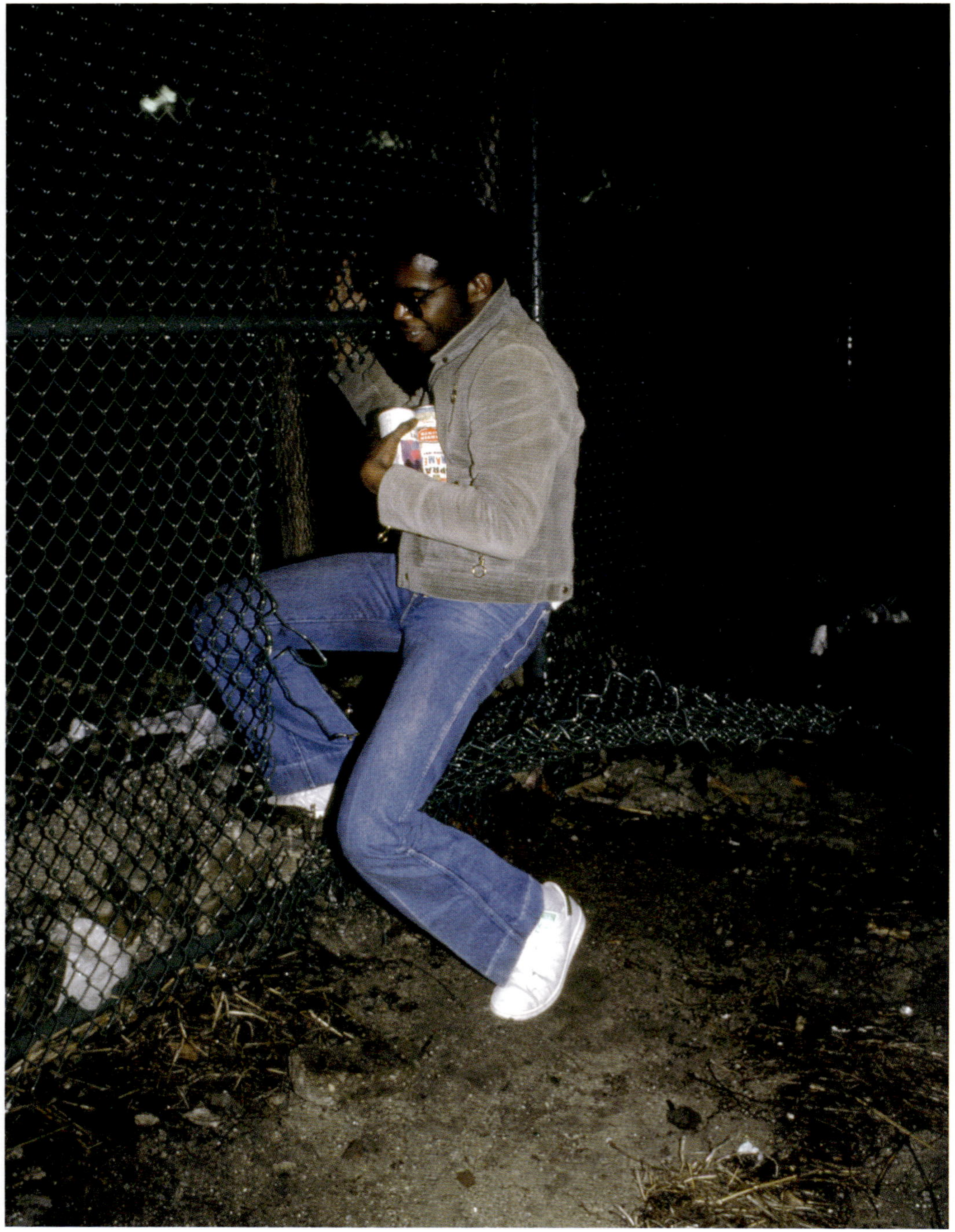

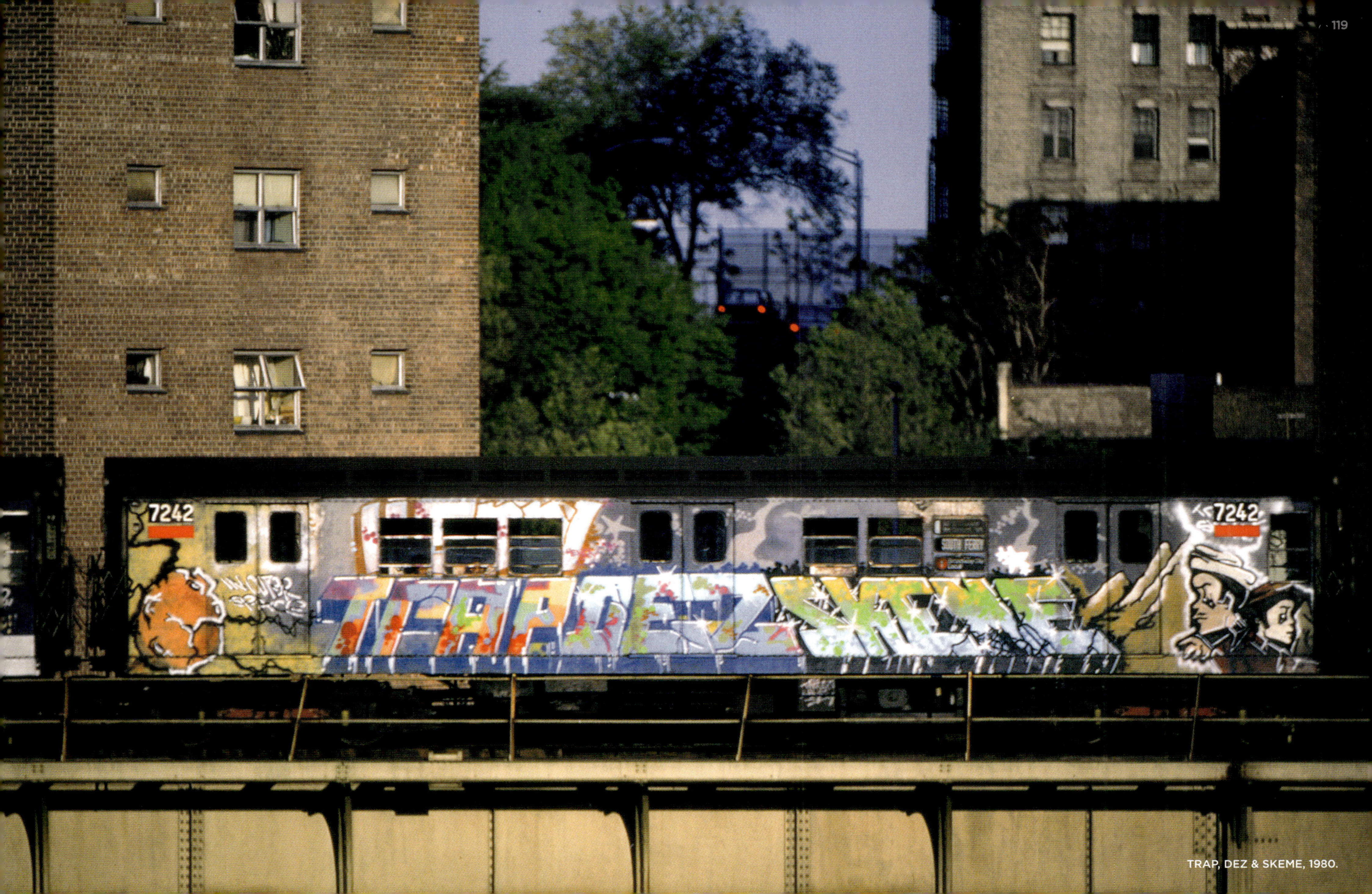

TRAP, DEZ & SKEME, 1980.

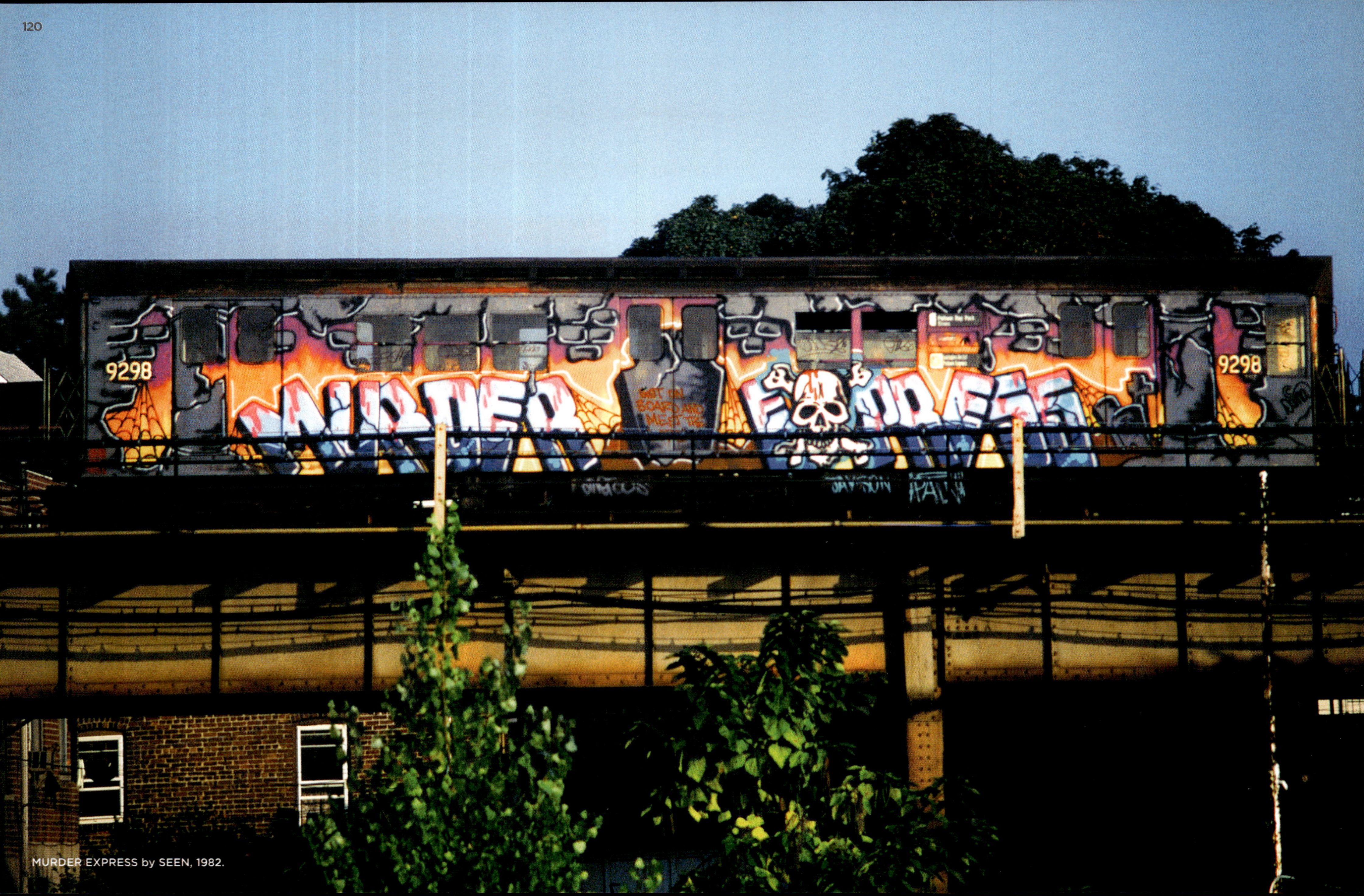

MURDER EXPRESS by SEEN, 1982.

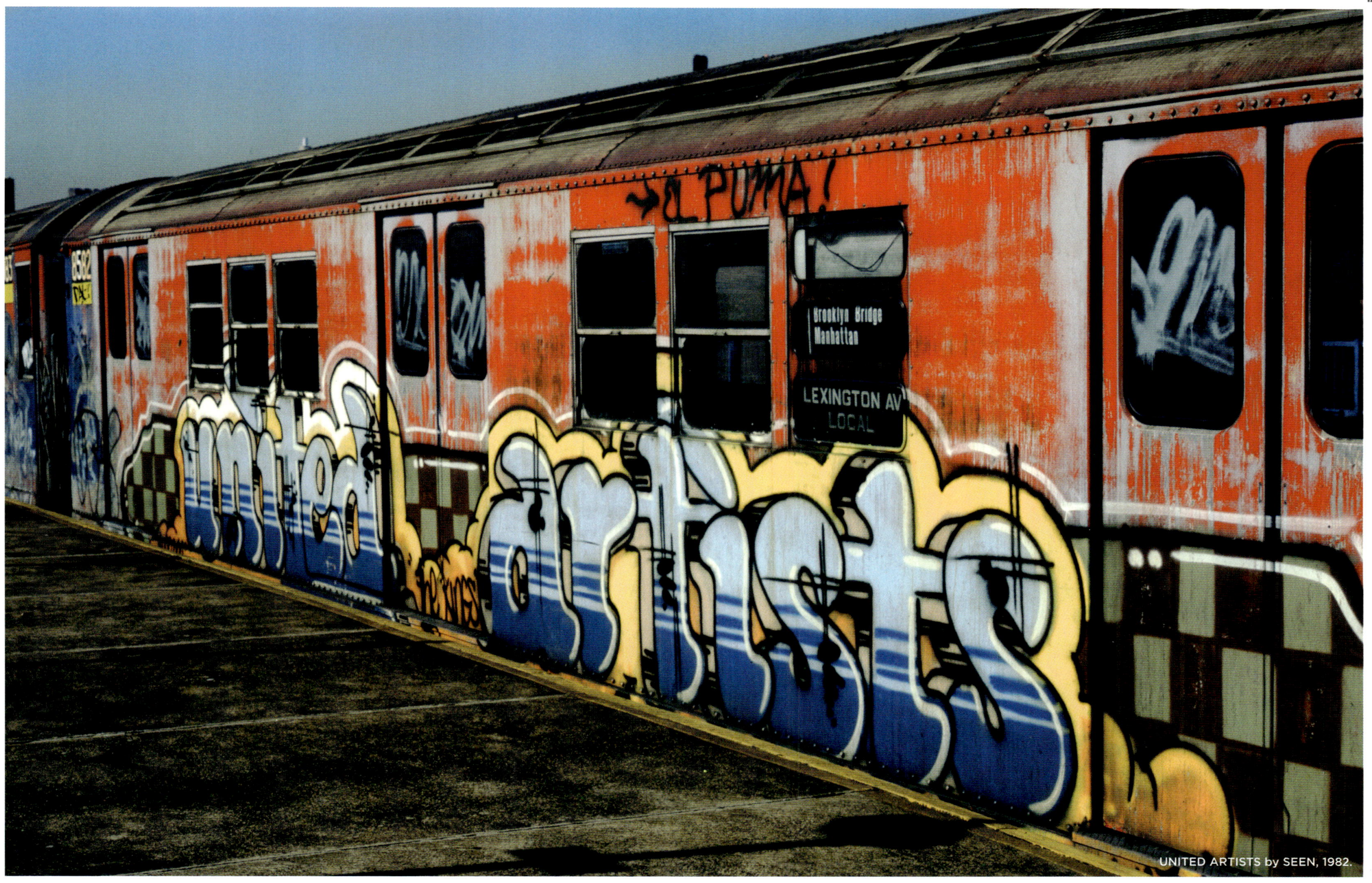

UNITED ARTISTS by SEEN, 1982.

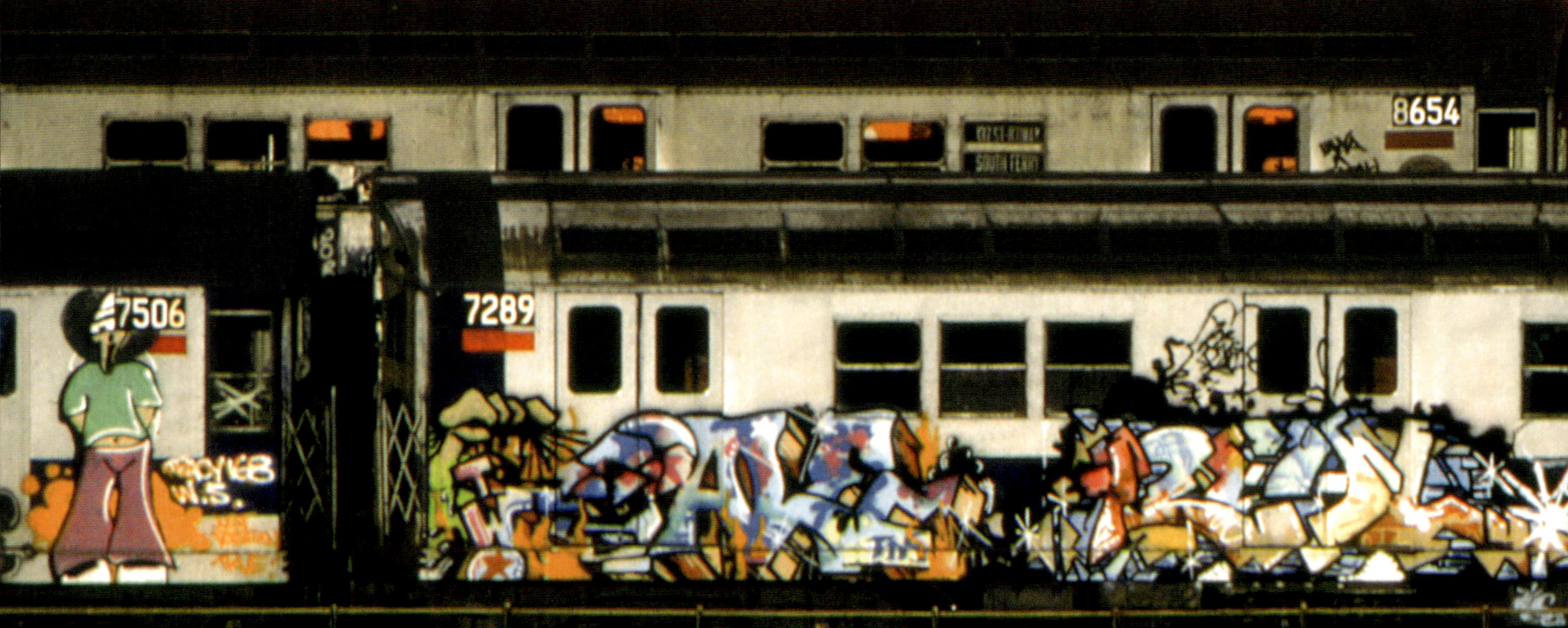

SELF -
8654
7506
7289

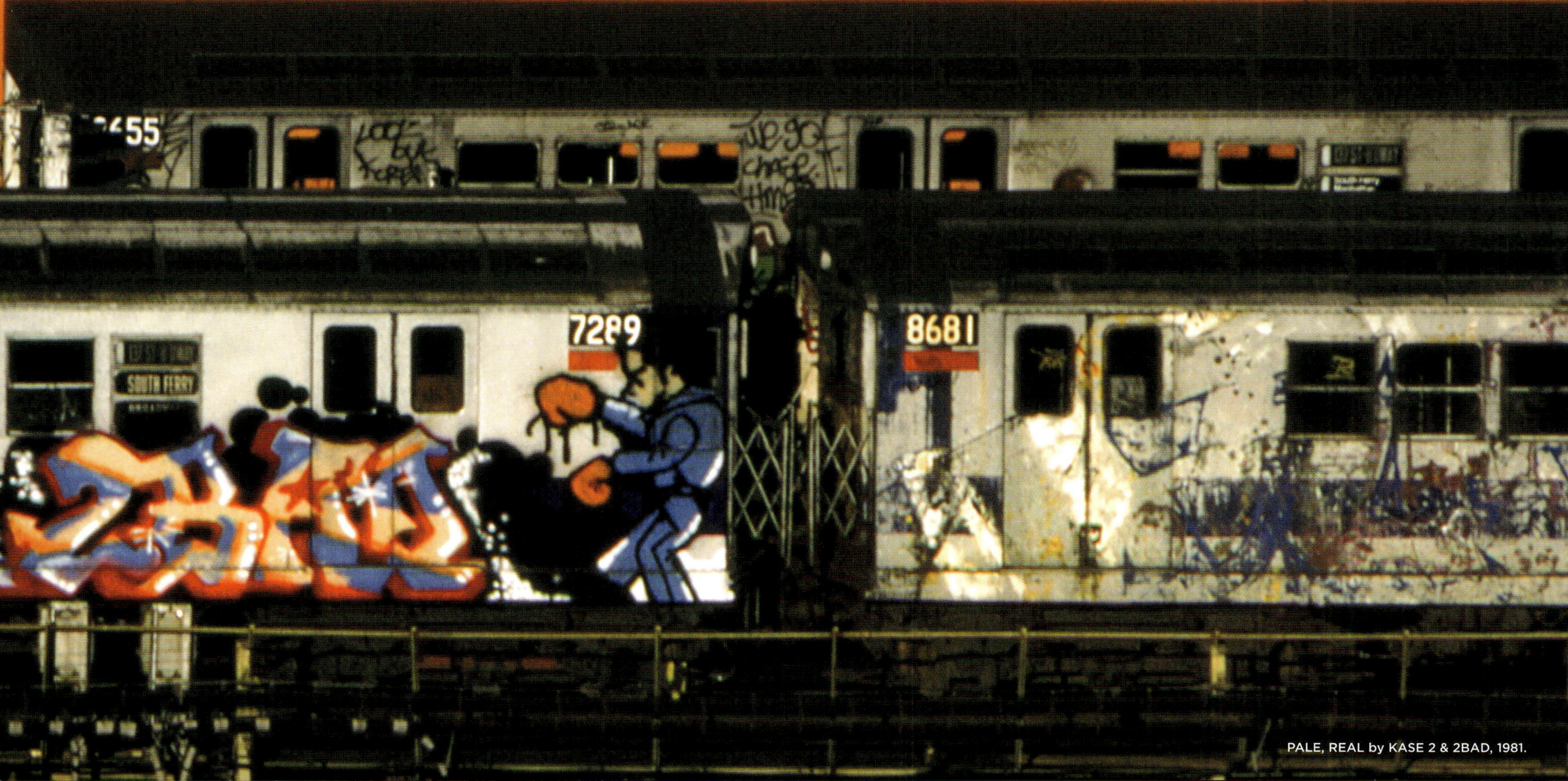

STORAGE RO
PALE, REAL by KASE 2 & 2BAD, 1981.

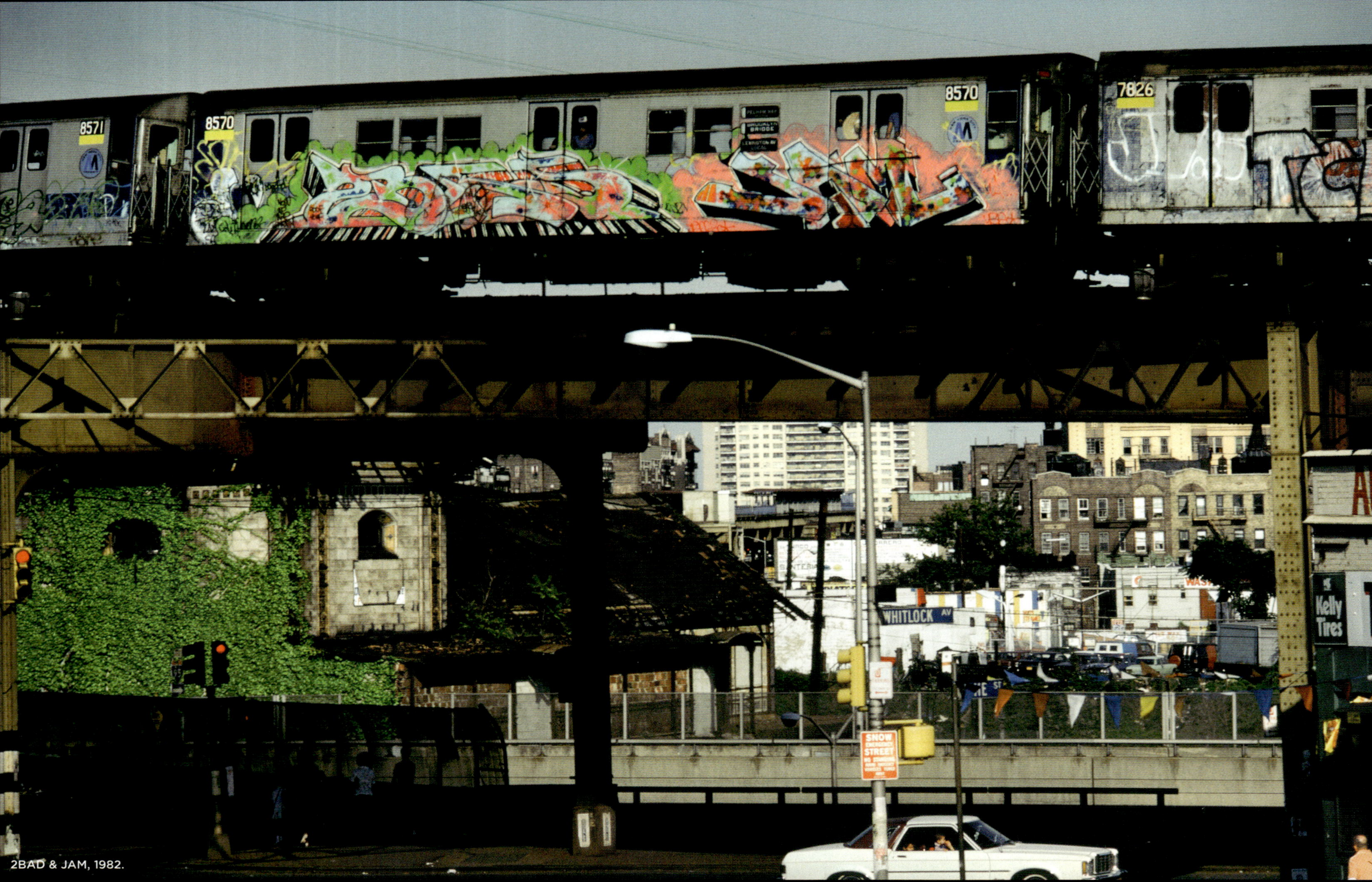

2BAD & JAM, 1982.

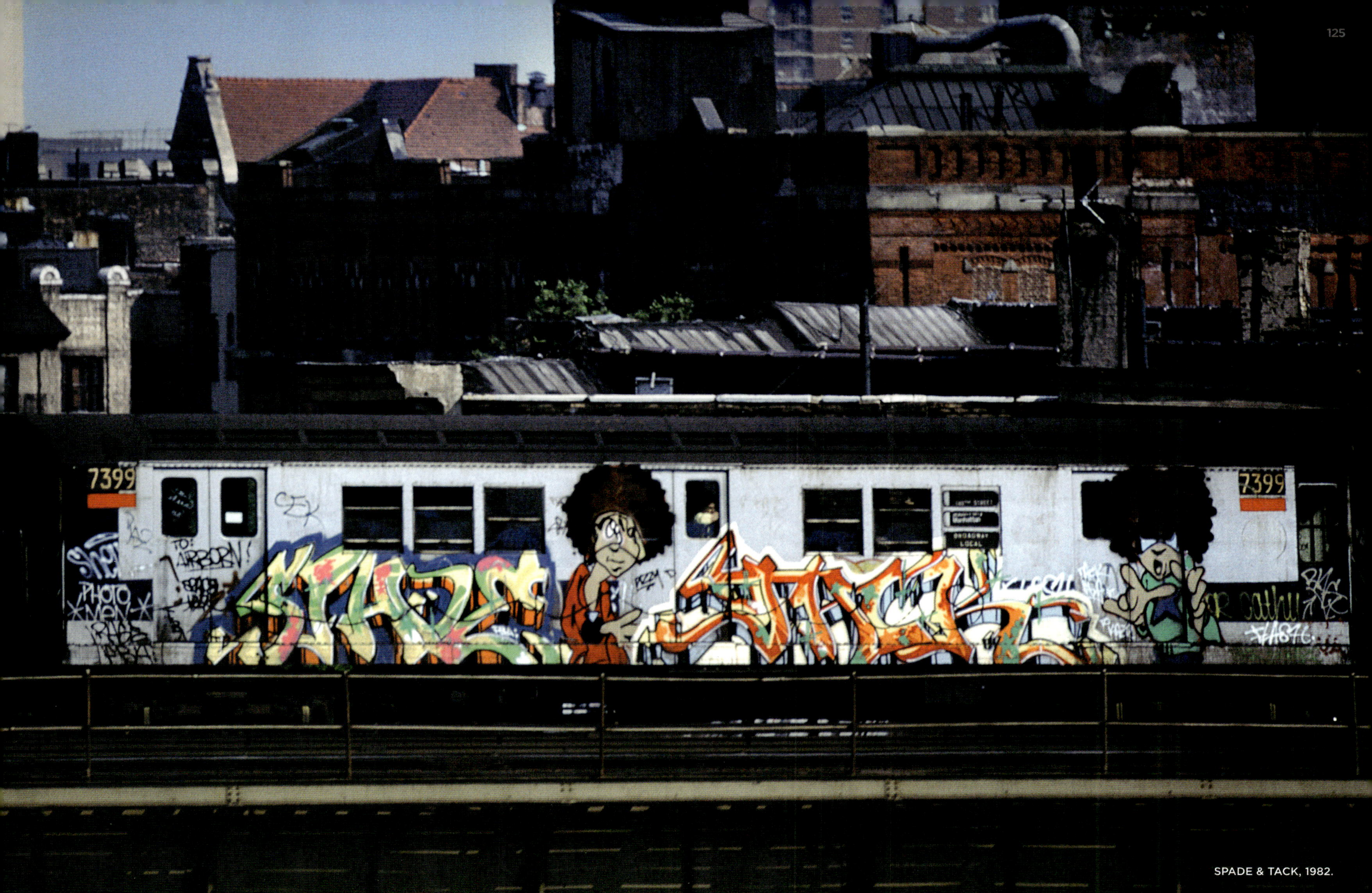

SPADE & TACK, 1982.

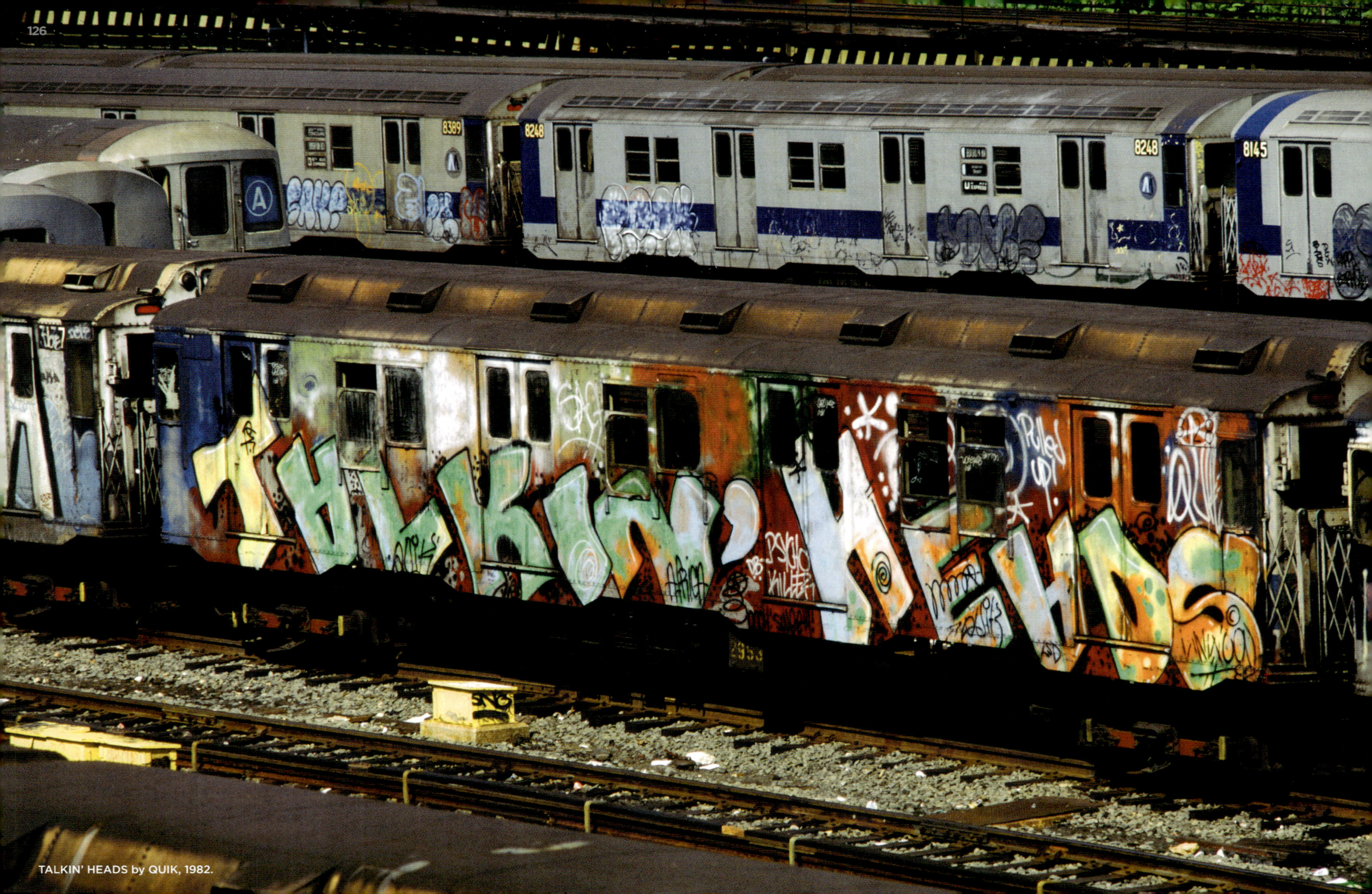

TALKIN' HEADS by QUIK, 1982.

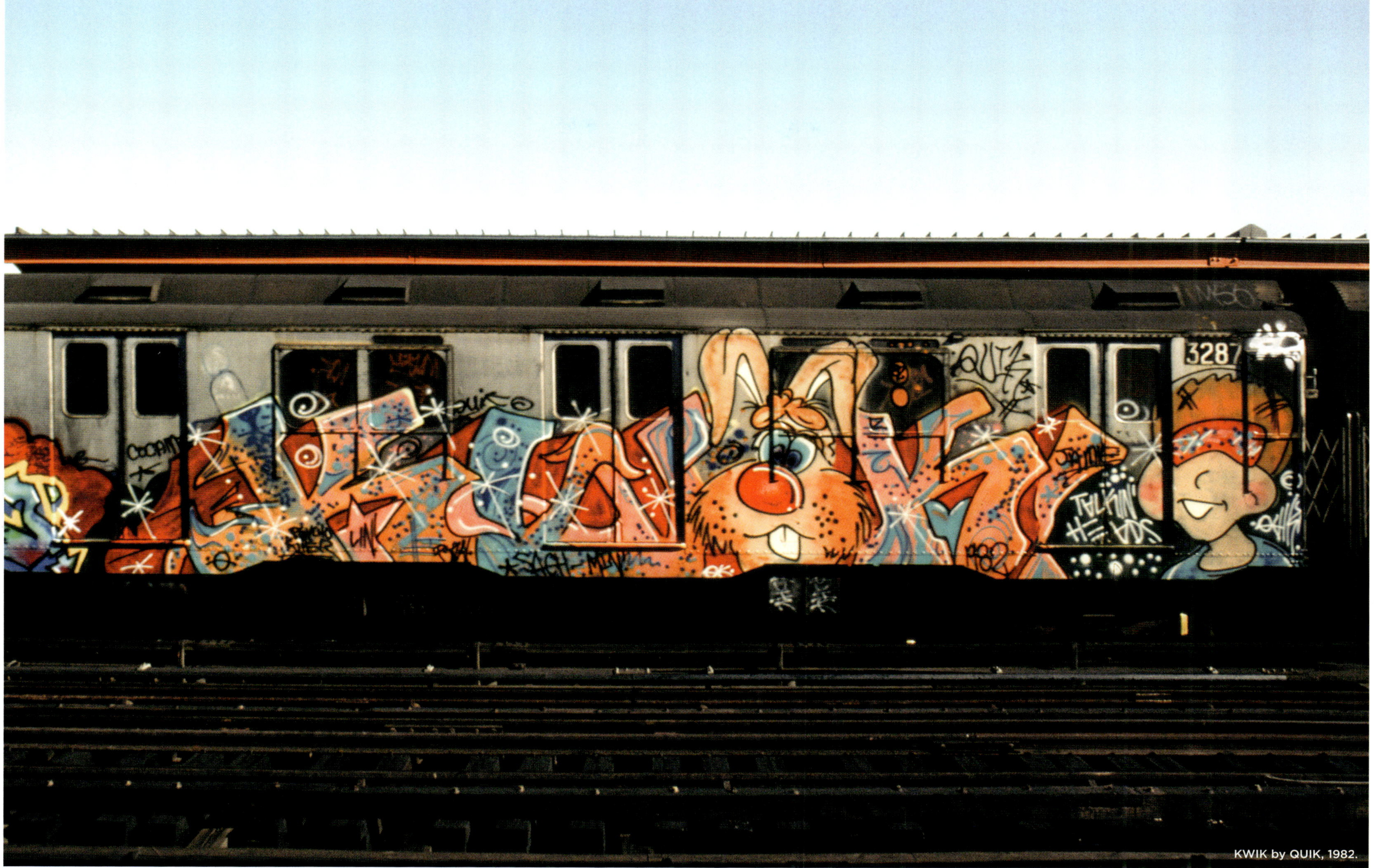

KWIK by QUIK, 1982.

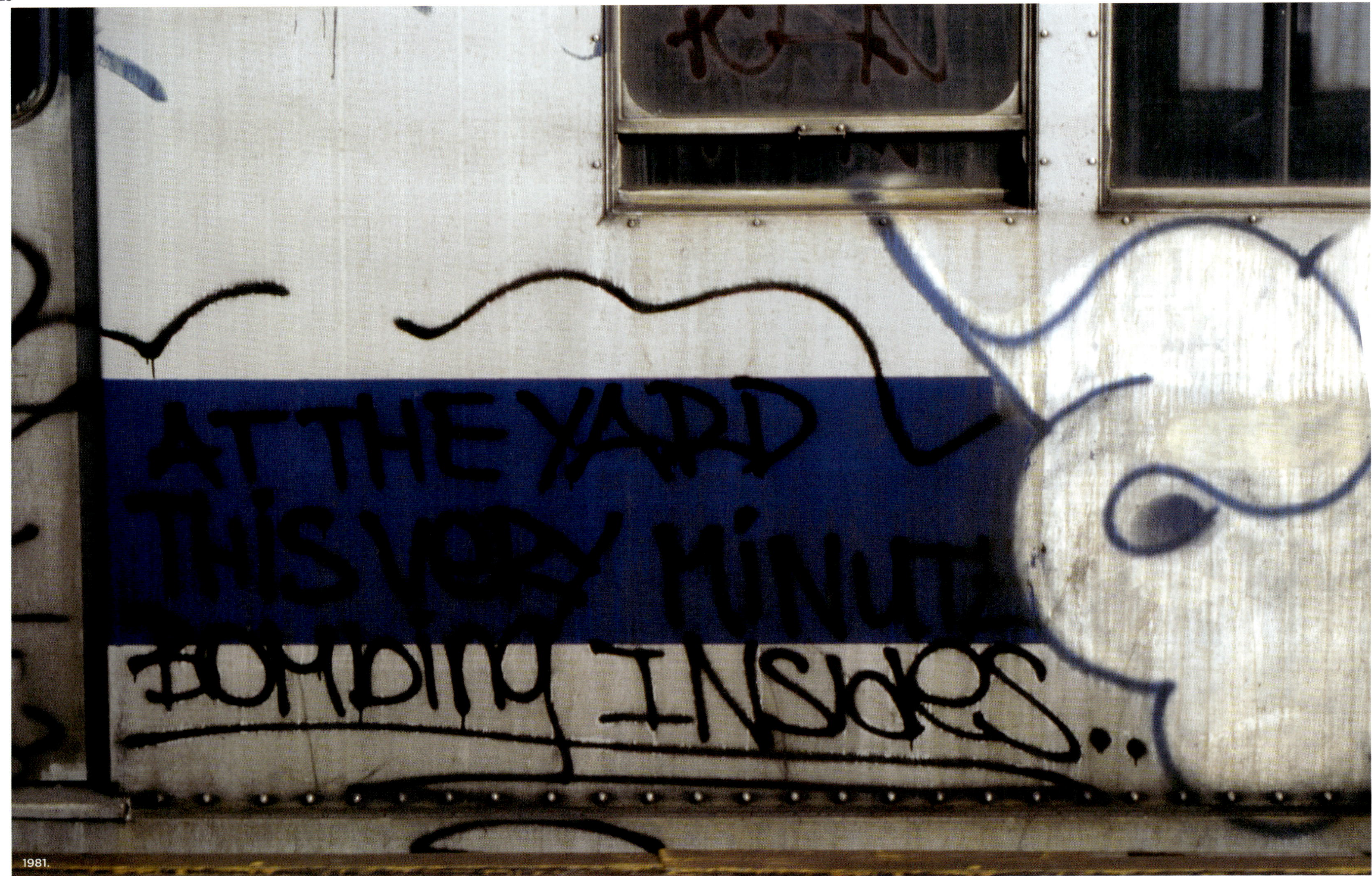

1981.

Emergency
Brake Valve
Freno de Emergencia valvula
ome home
to Carolina.
Please
NO
Radio
PACK
NINE

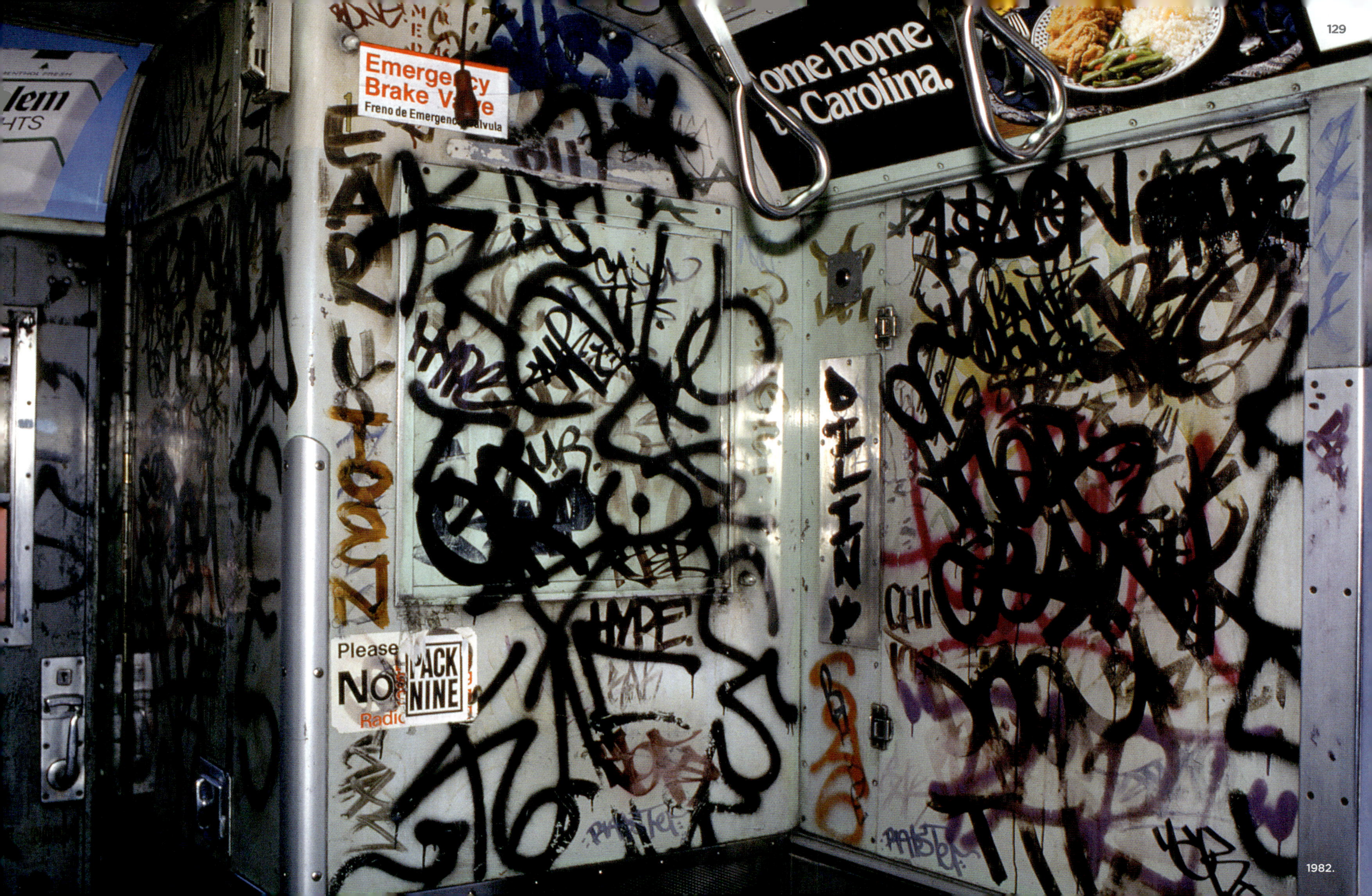

1982.

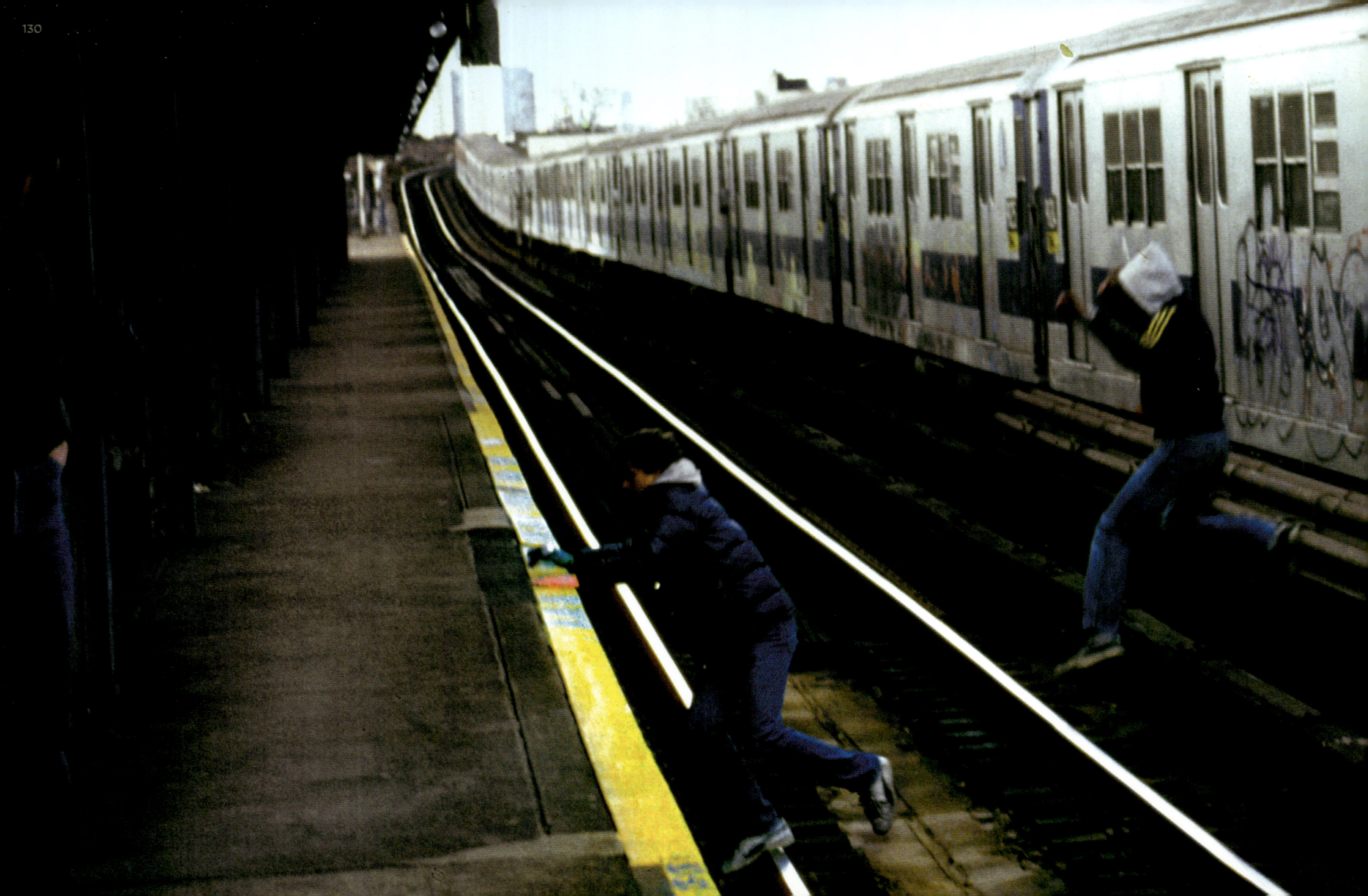

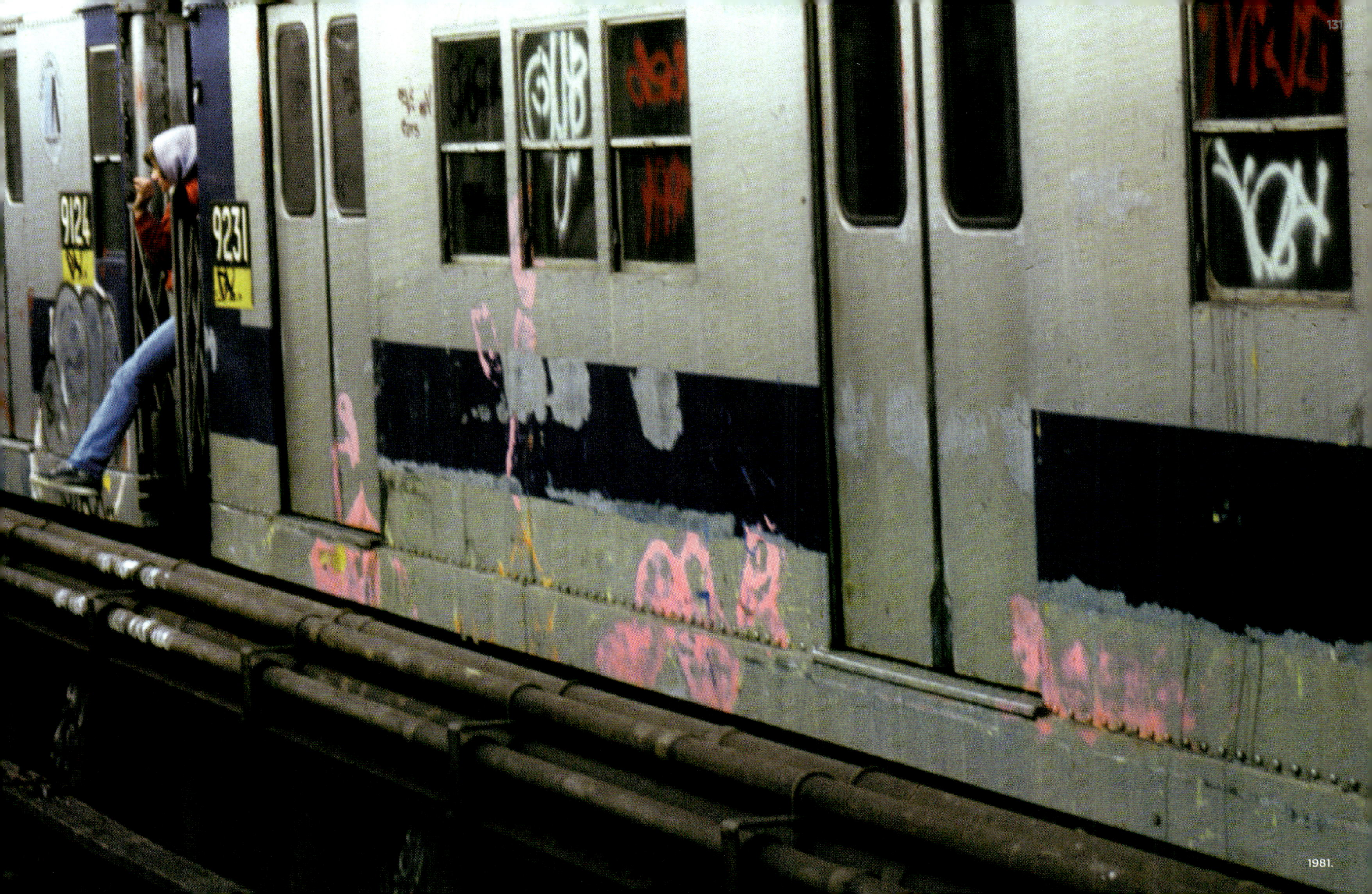

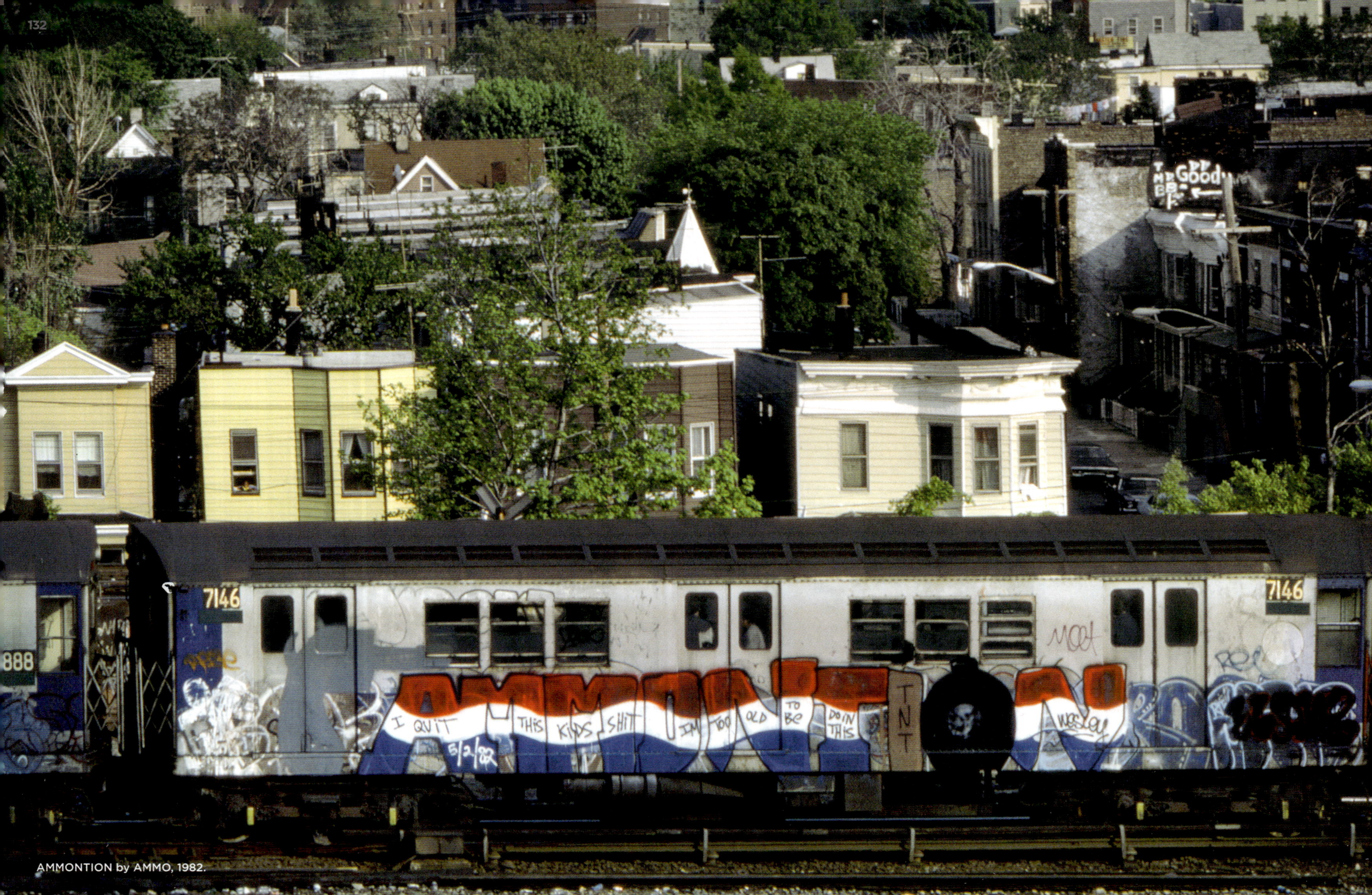

AMMONTION by AMMO, 1982.

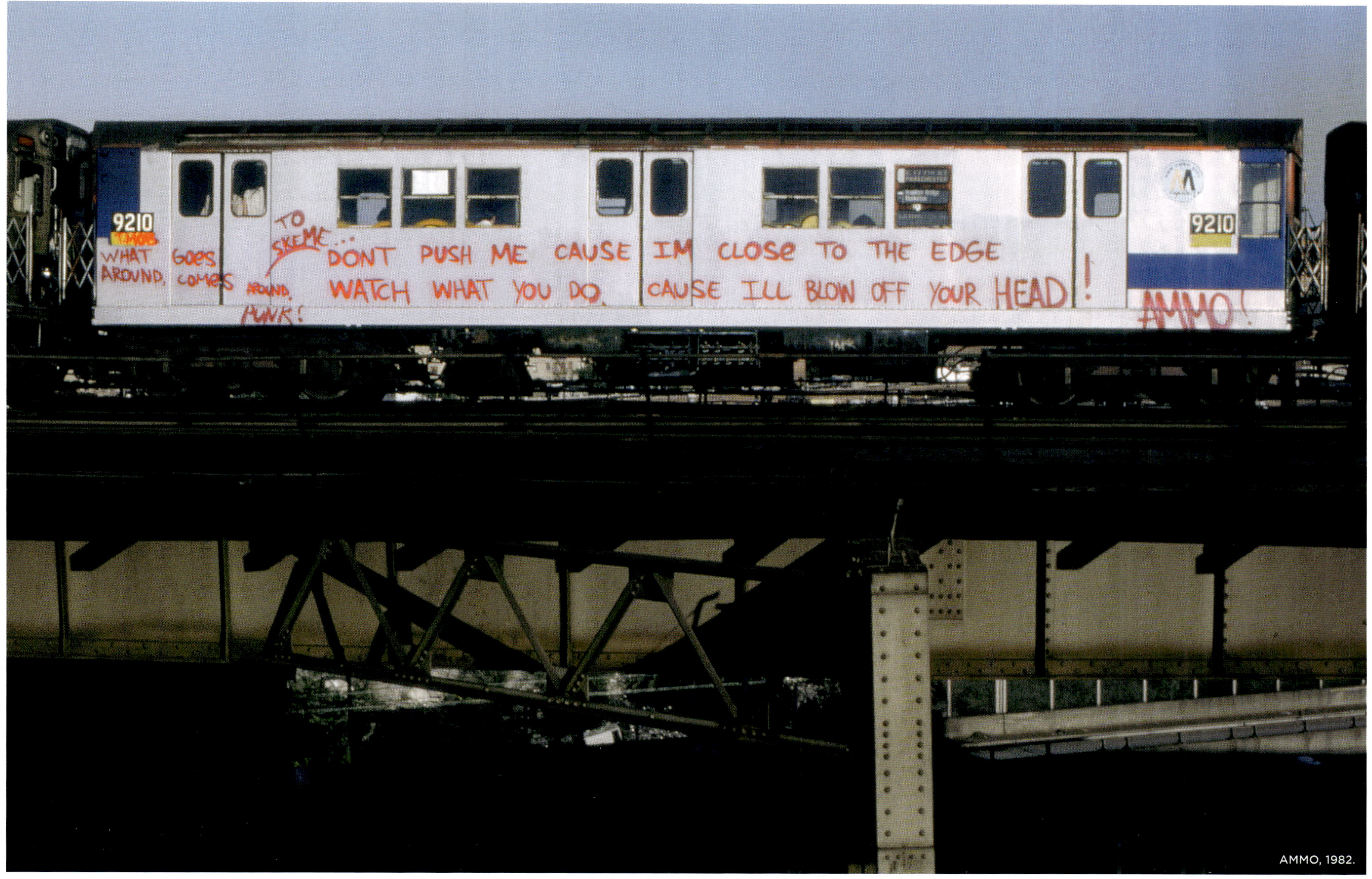
9210
9210
WHAT GOES
AROUND, COMES AROUND.
TO SKEME...
PUNK!
DONT PUSH ME CAUSE IM CLOSE TO THE EDGE
WATCH WHAT YOU DO. CAUSE ILL BLOW OFF YOUR HEAD !
AMMO!

AMMO, 1982.

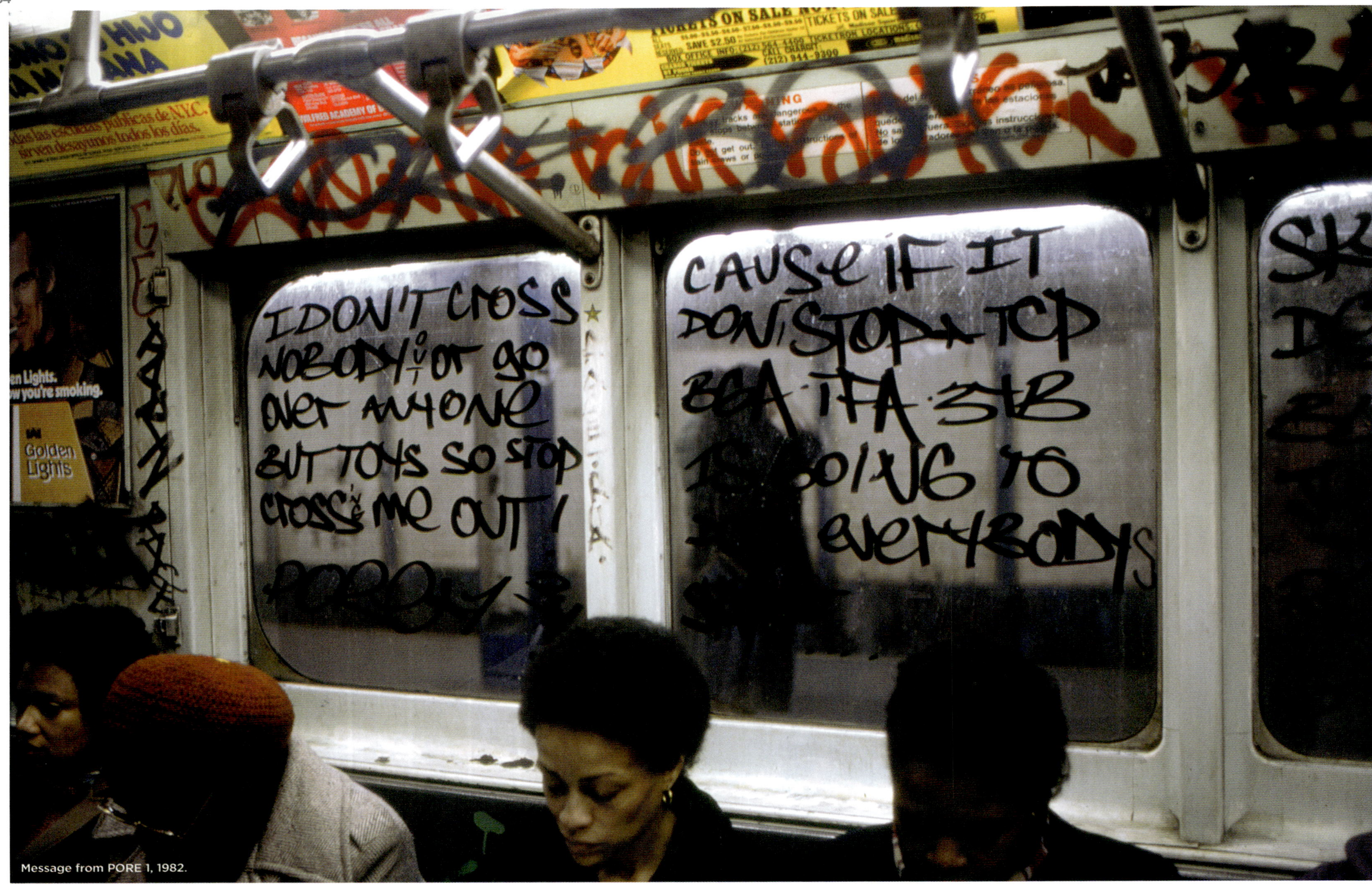

Message from PORE 1, 1982.

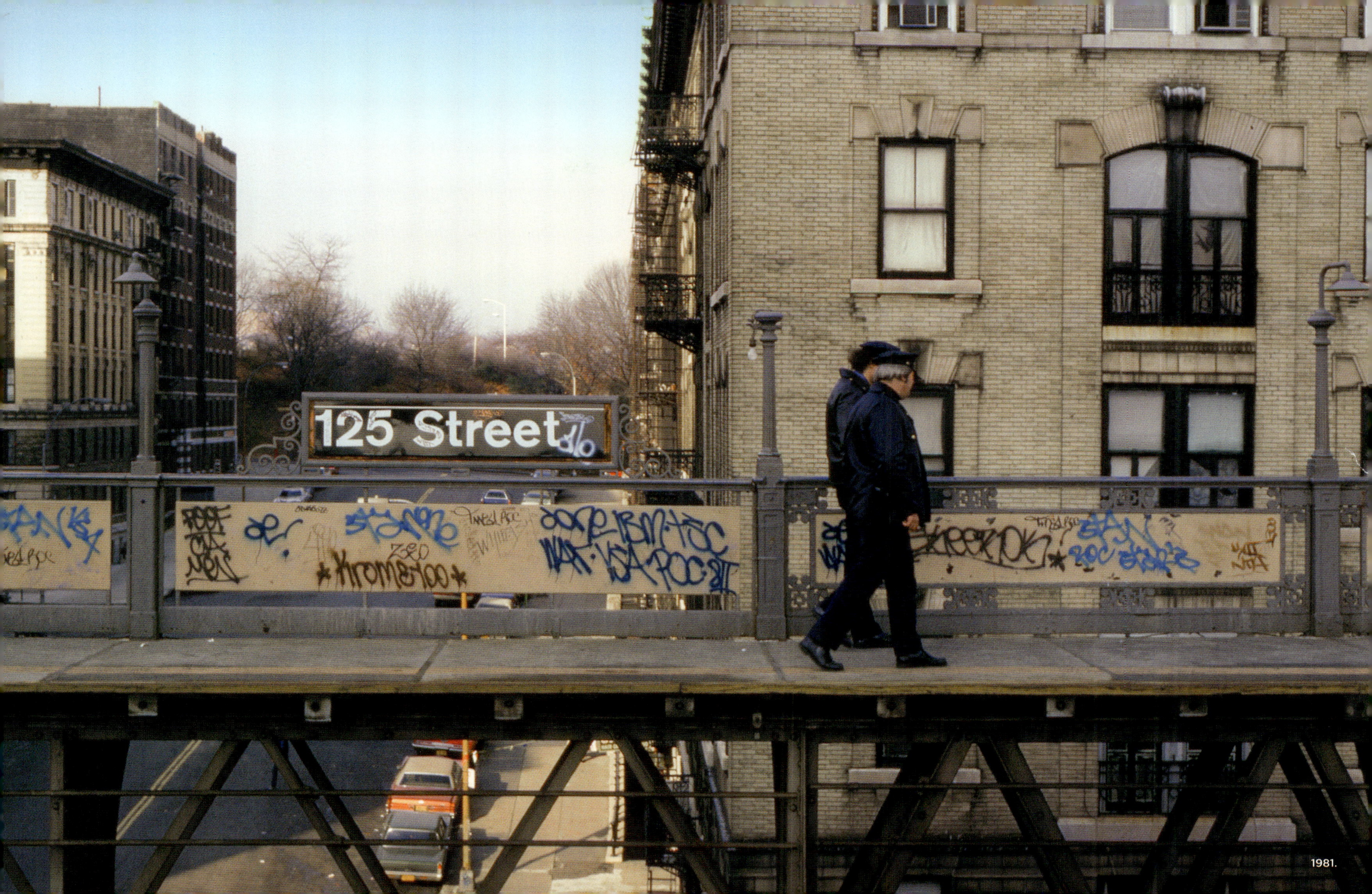
125 Street
1981.

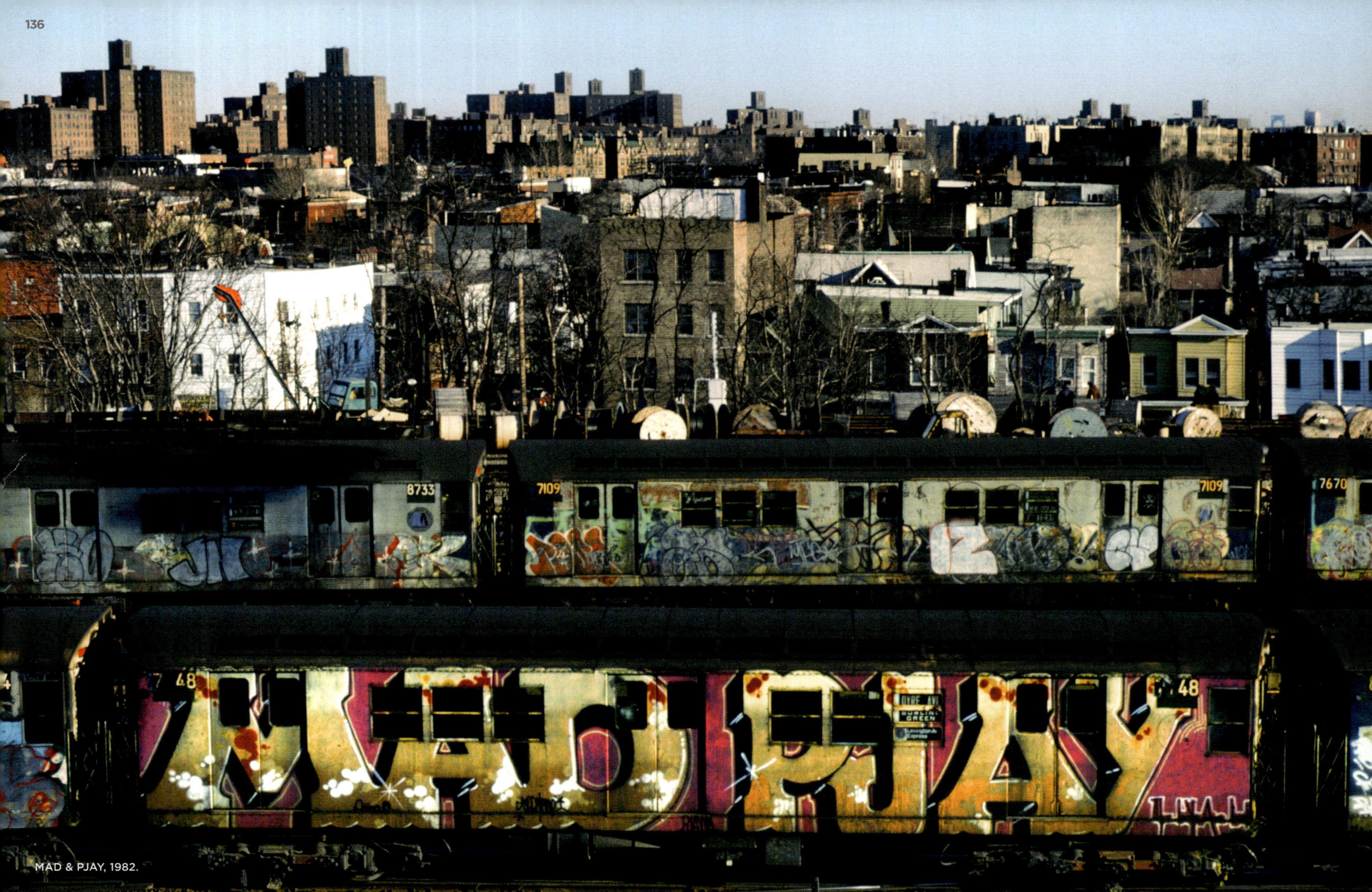

MAD & PJAY, 1982.

DYRE A
Utica Avenue
Brooklyn
Lexington
Express
NEW YORK CITY
TRANSIT
RACY'B
INSP. BY. 1-21-82

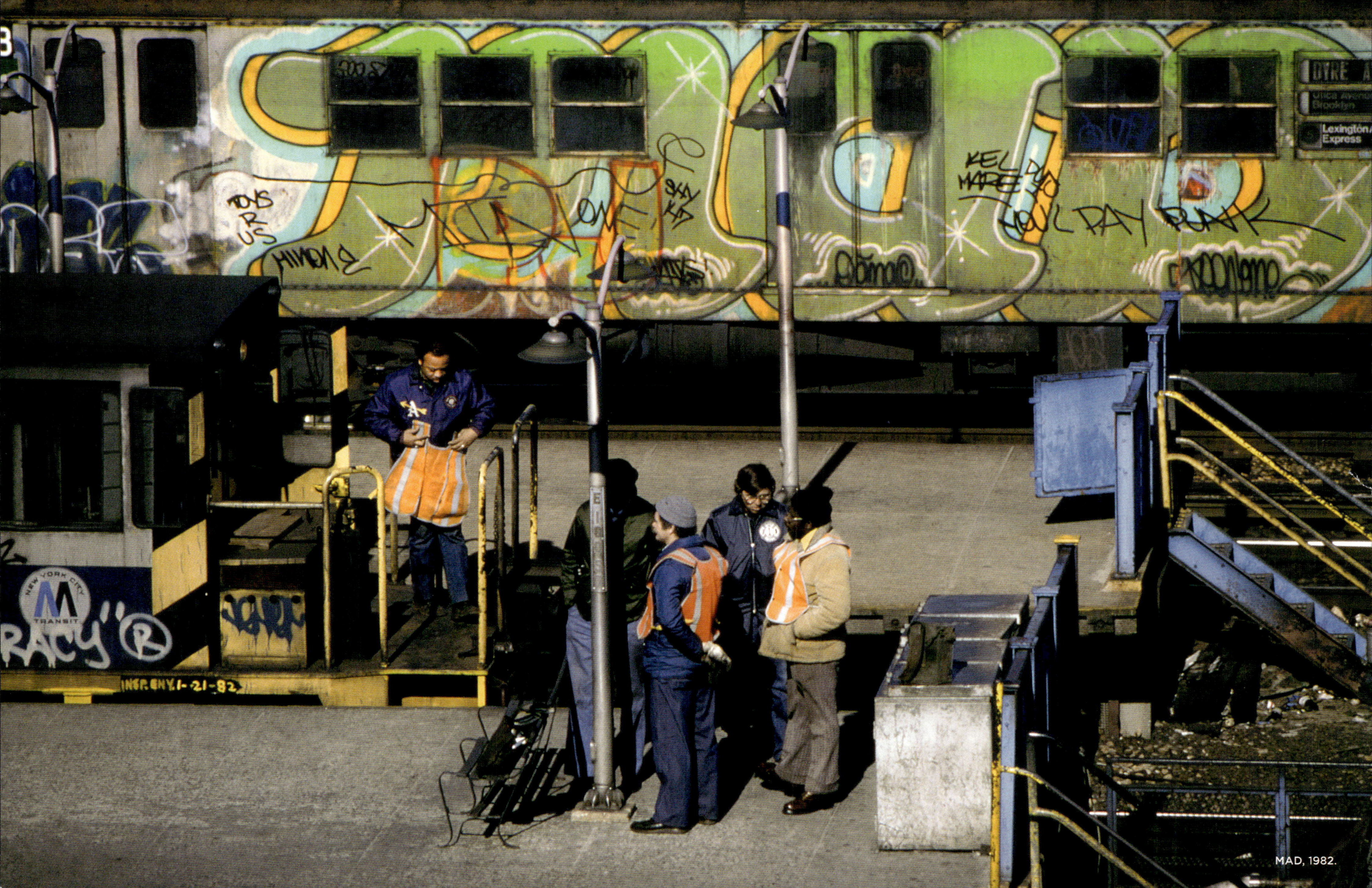

MAD, 1982.

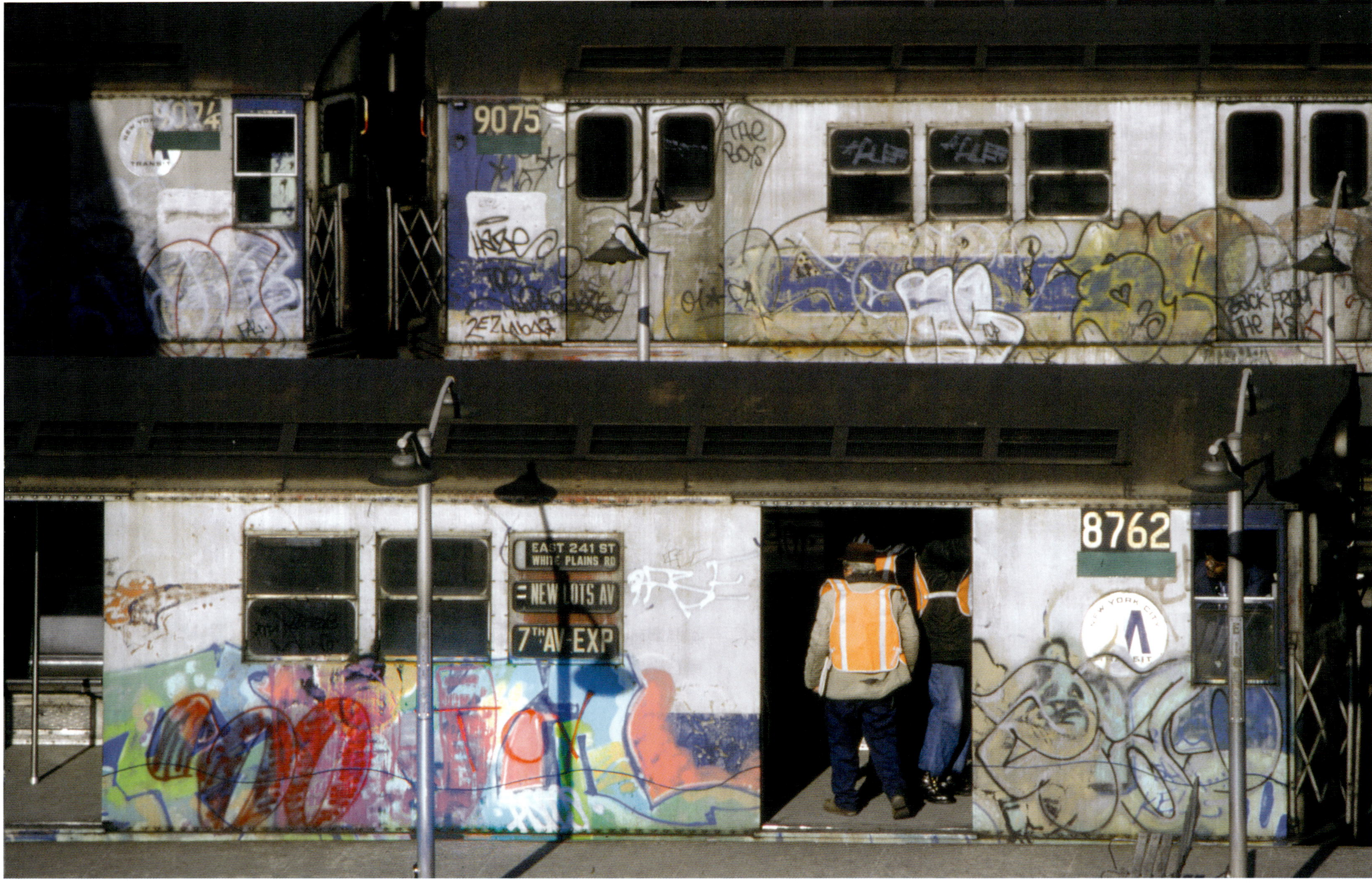
9074
9075
THE BOS
8762
EAST 241 ST
WHITE PLAINS RD
NEW LOTS AV
7TH AV EXP
NEW YORK CITY TRANSIT

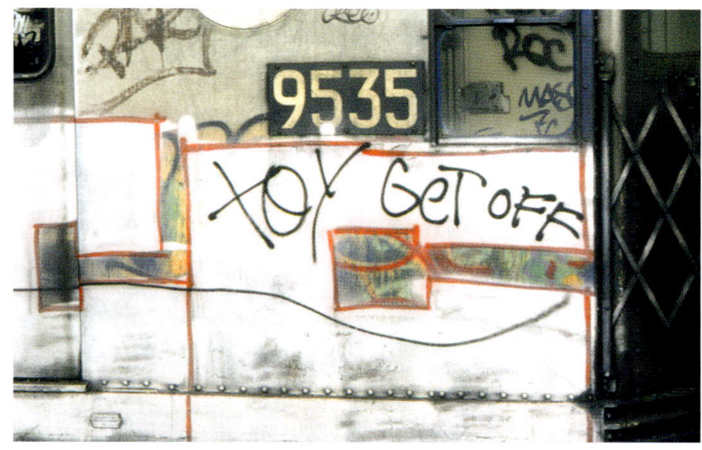

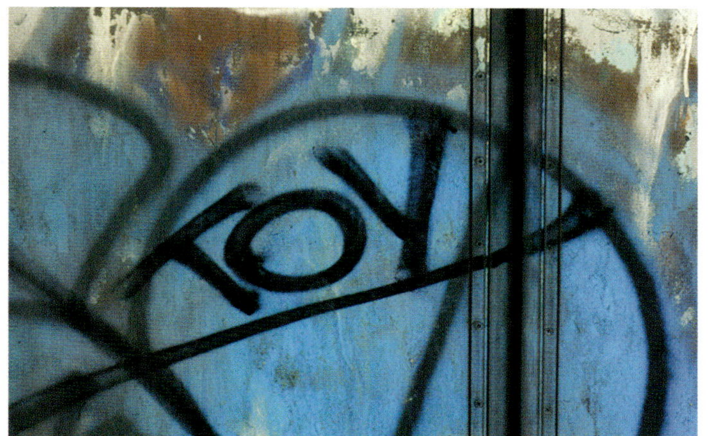

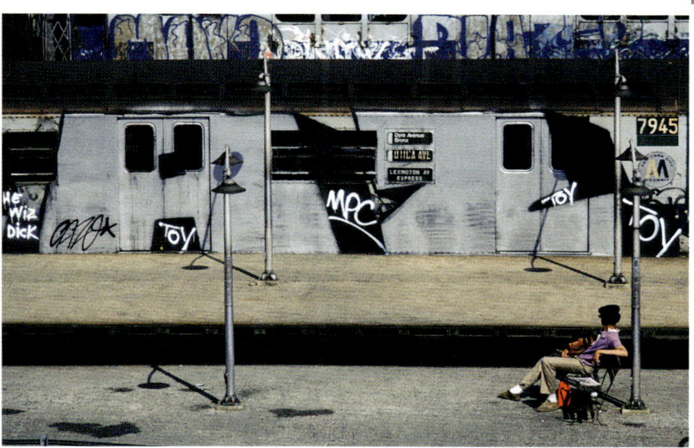

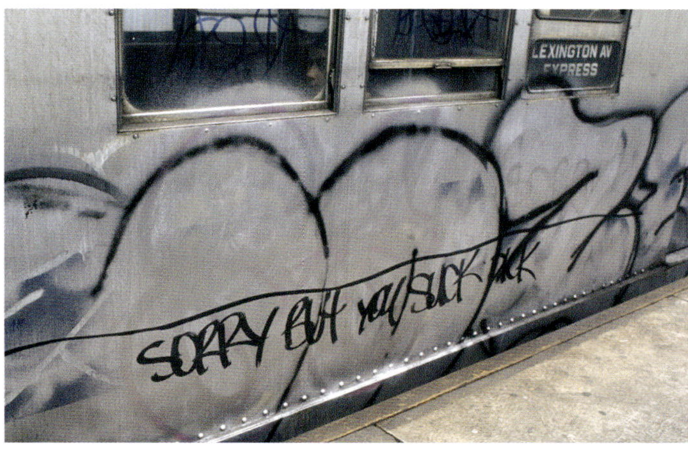

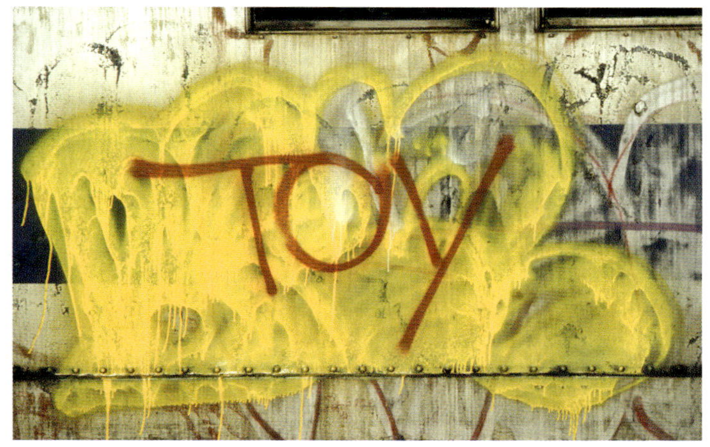

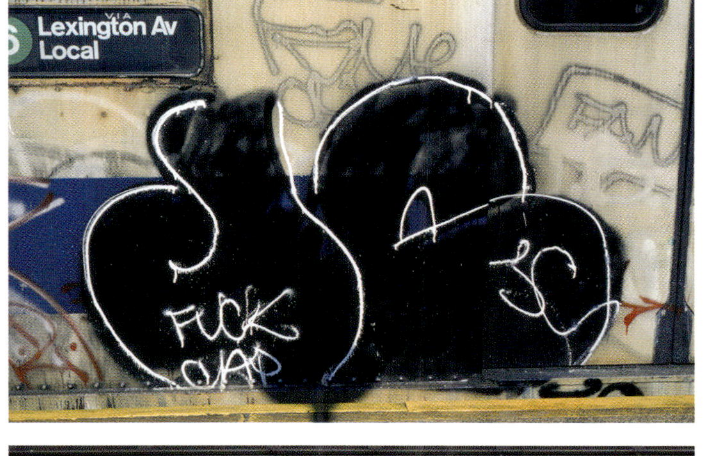

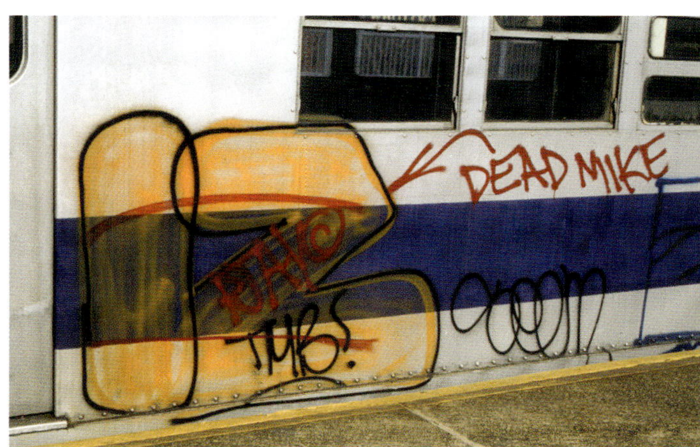

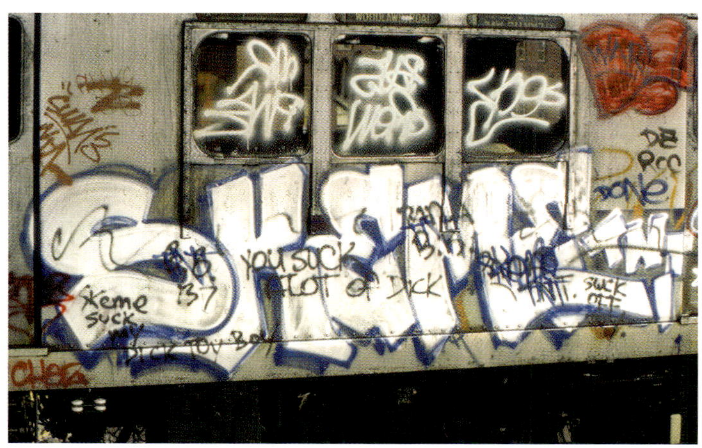

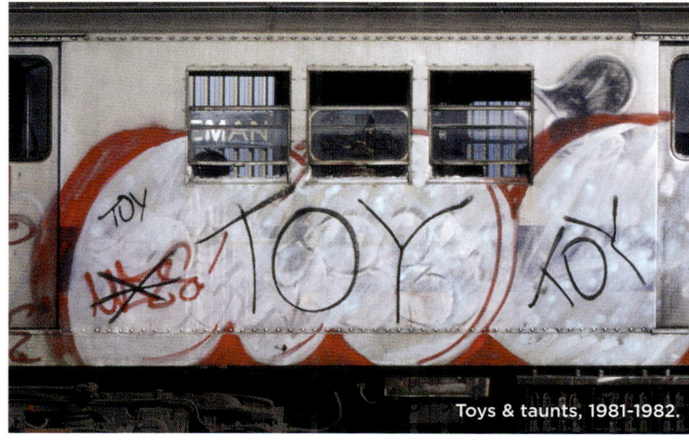

Toys & taunts, 1981-1982.

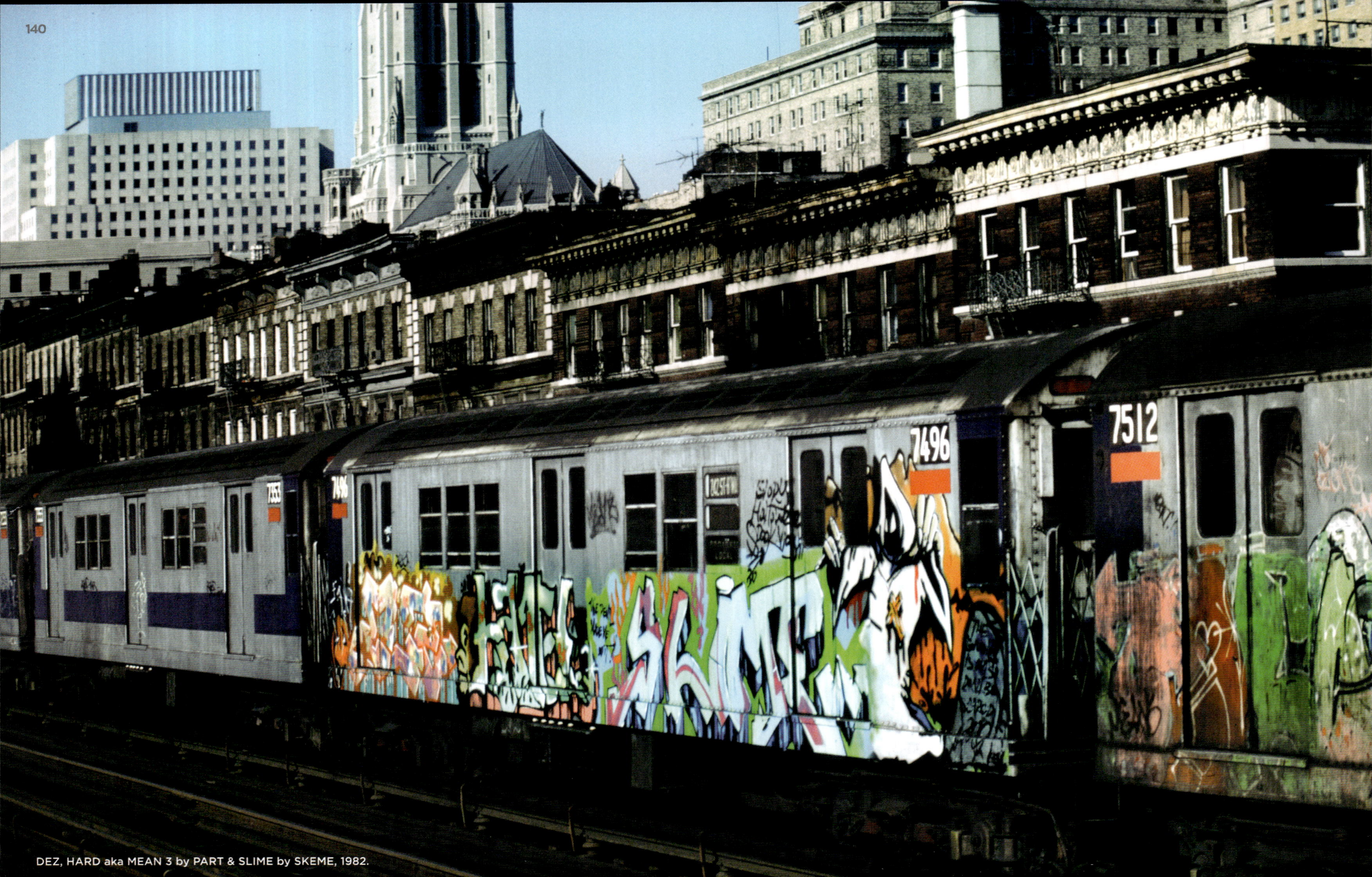

DEZ, HARD aka MEAN 3 by PART & SLIME by SKEME, 1982.

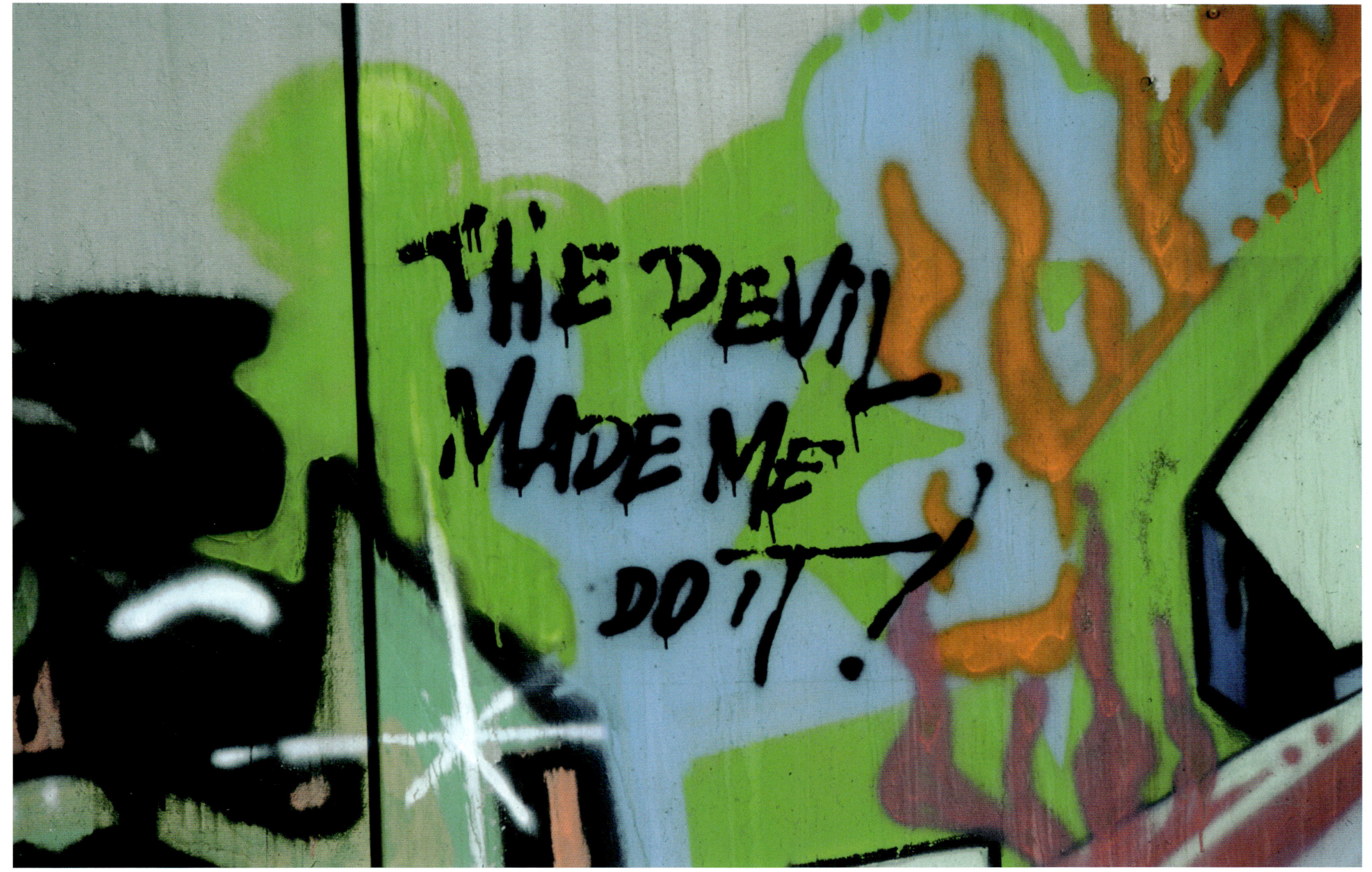
THE DEVIL
MADE ME
DO IT.

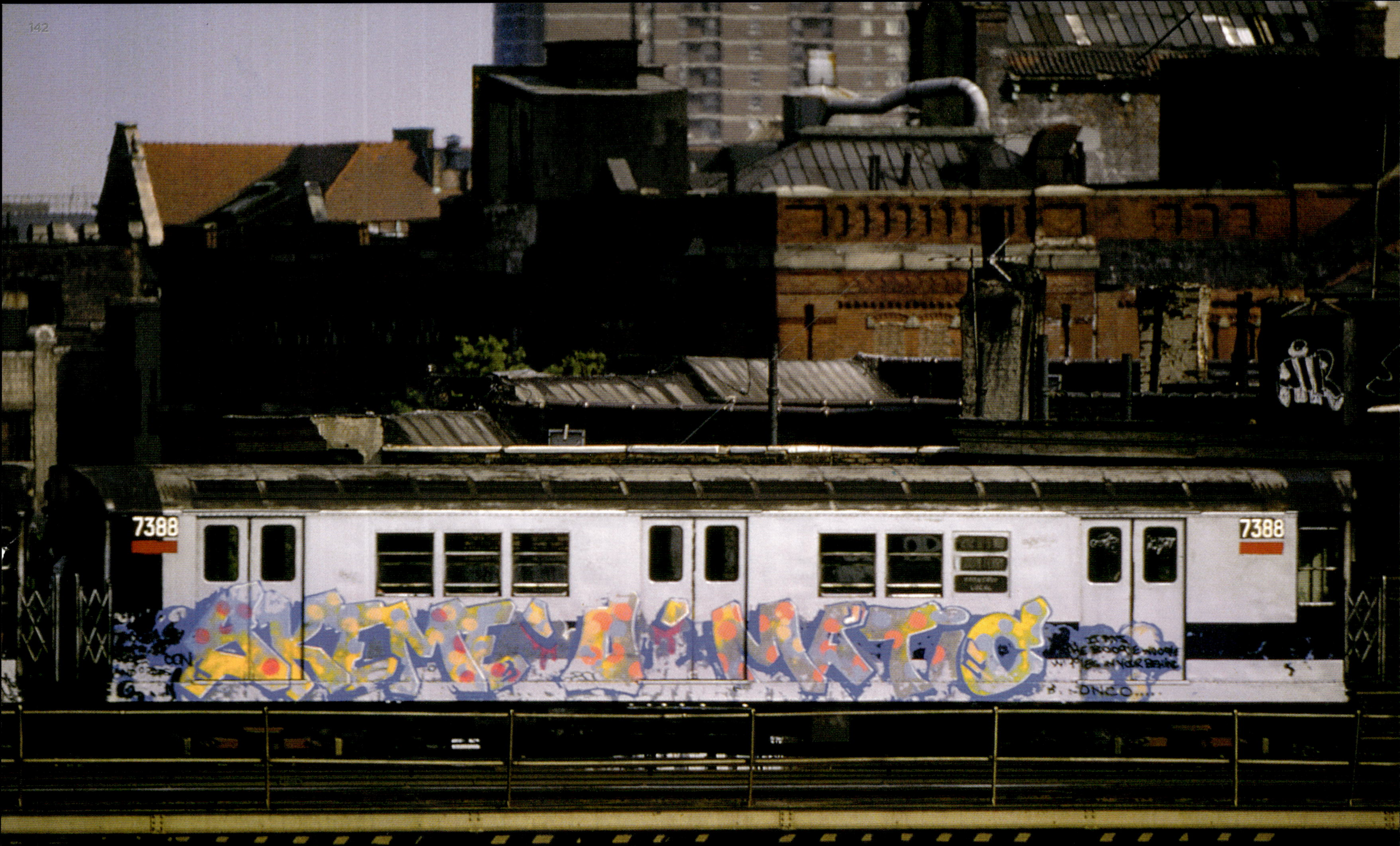

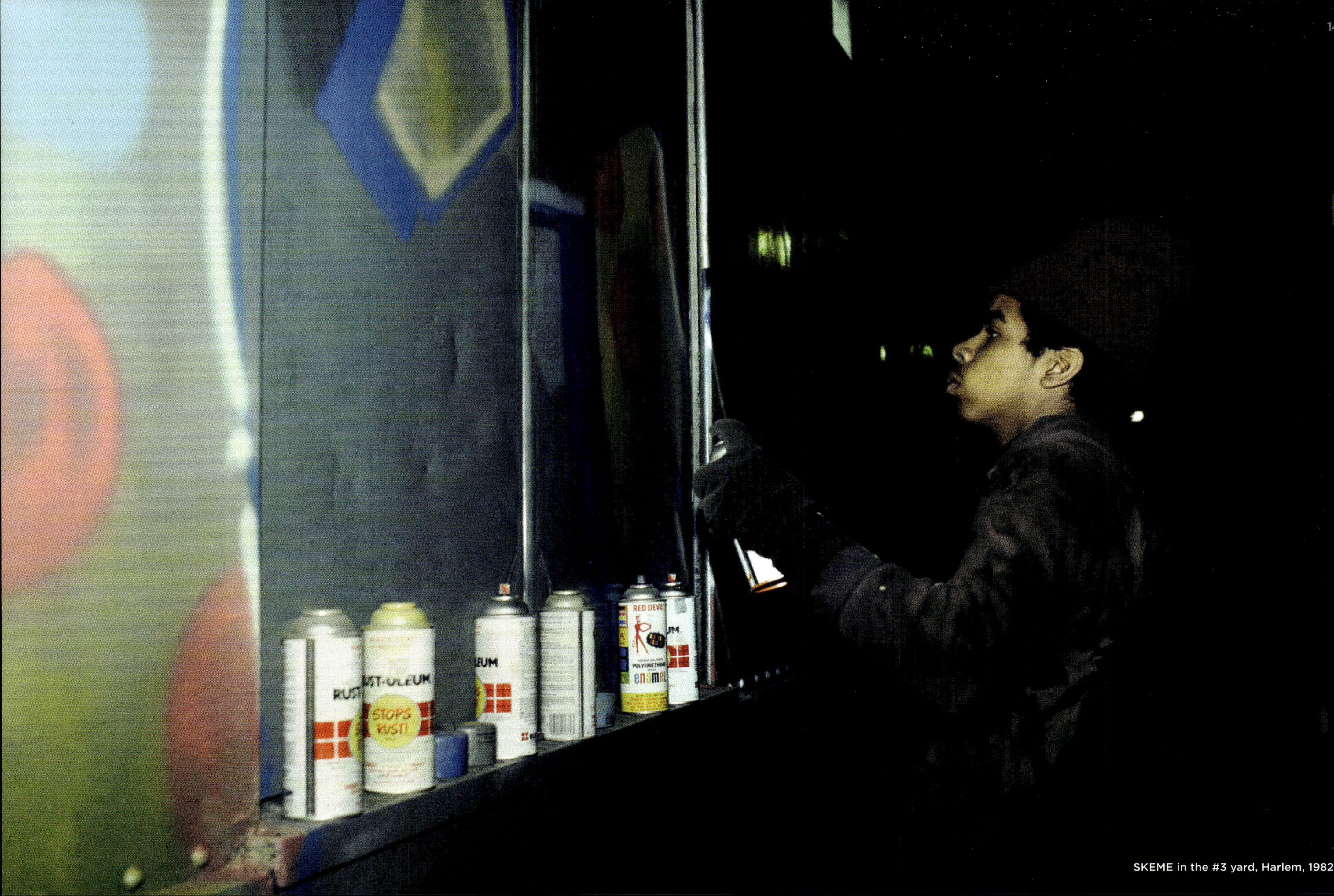

SKEME in the #3 yard, Harlem, 1982

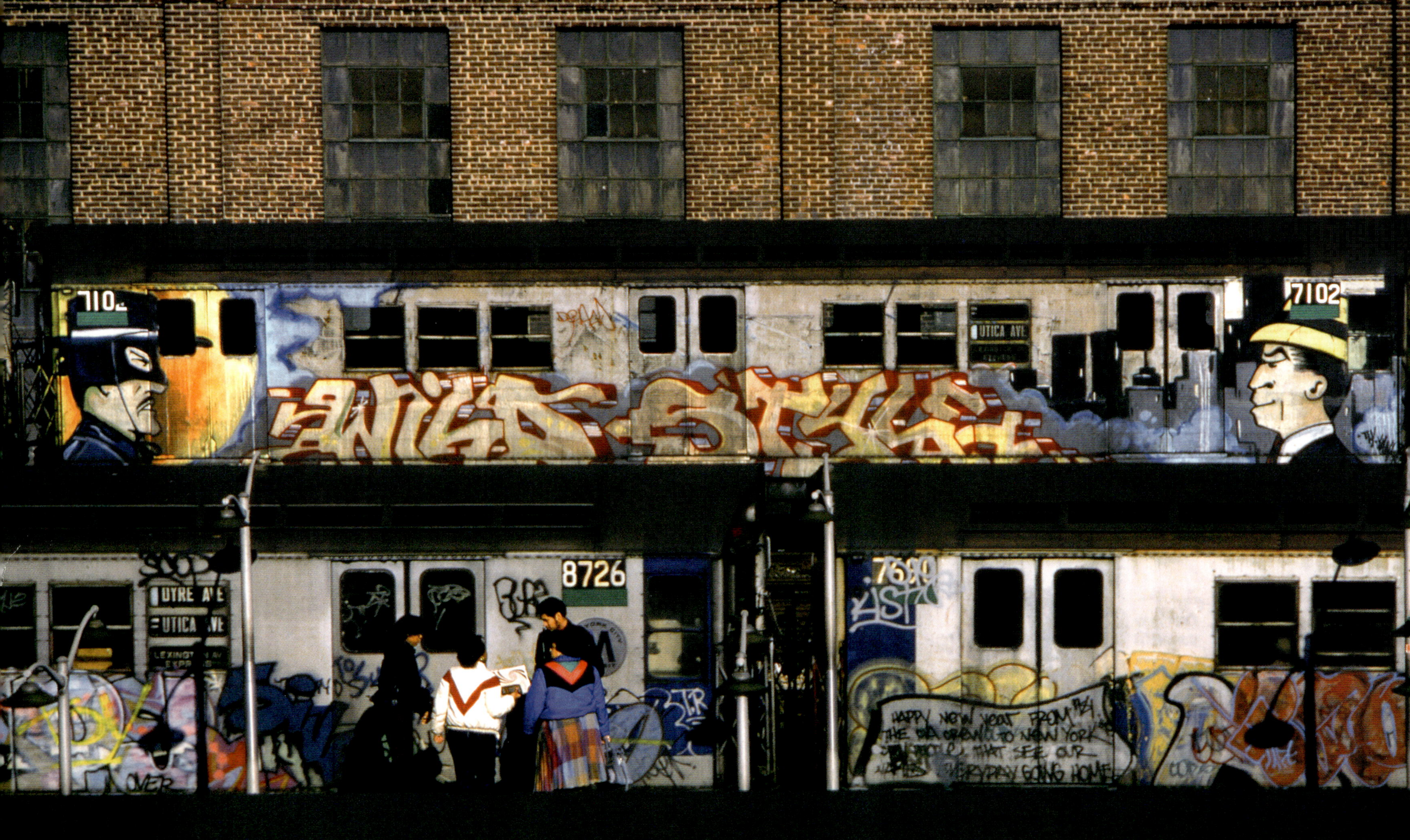

WILD STYLE by DONDI for Charlie Ahearn's film, 1982

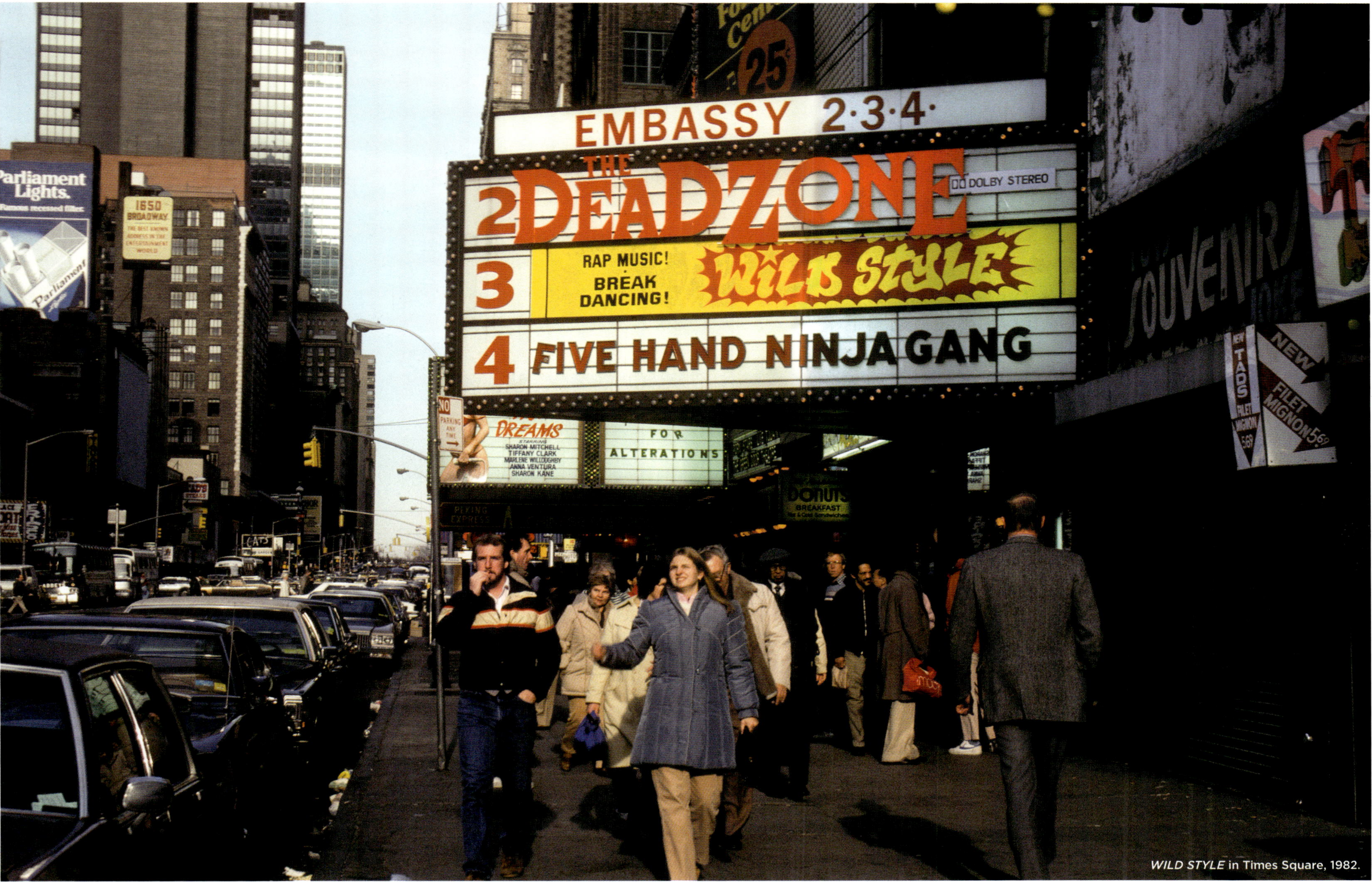

WILD STYLE in Times Square, 1982.

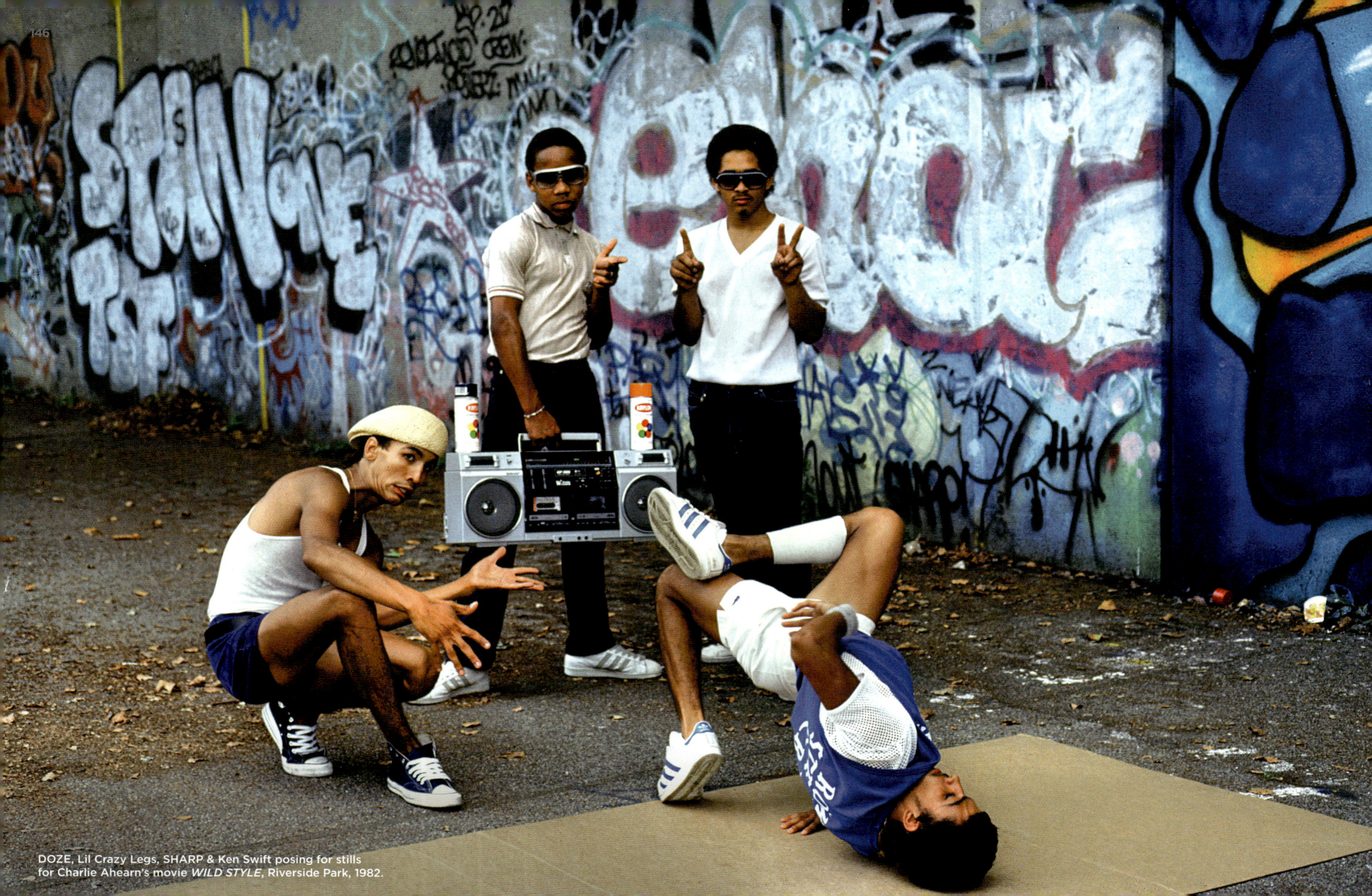

DOZE, Lil Crazy Legs, SHARP & Ken Swift posing for stills
for Charlie Ahearn's movie *WILD STYLE*, Riverside Park, 1982.

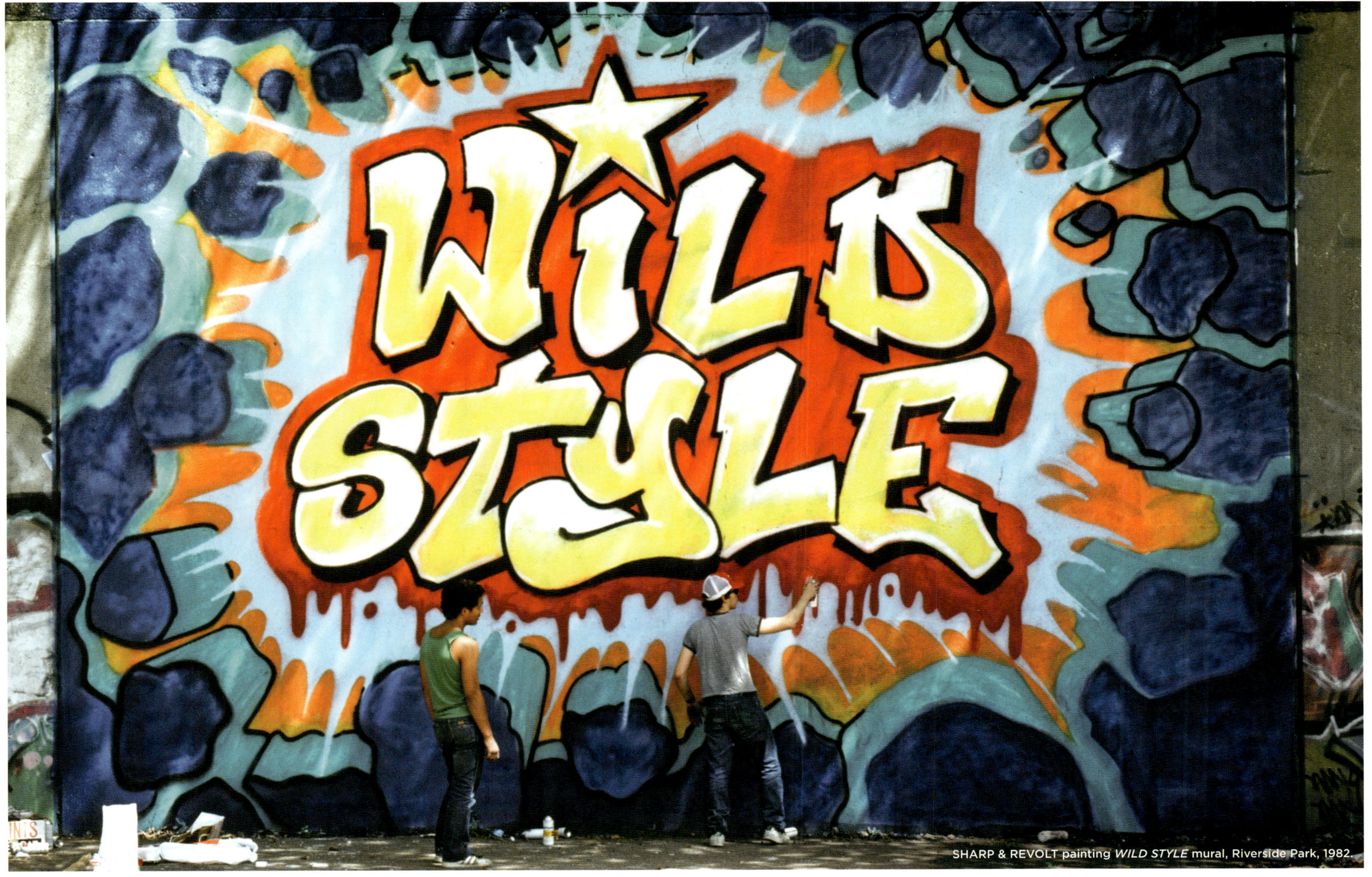

SHARP & REVOLT painting *WILD STYLE* mural, Riverside Park, 1982.

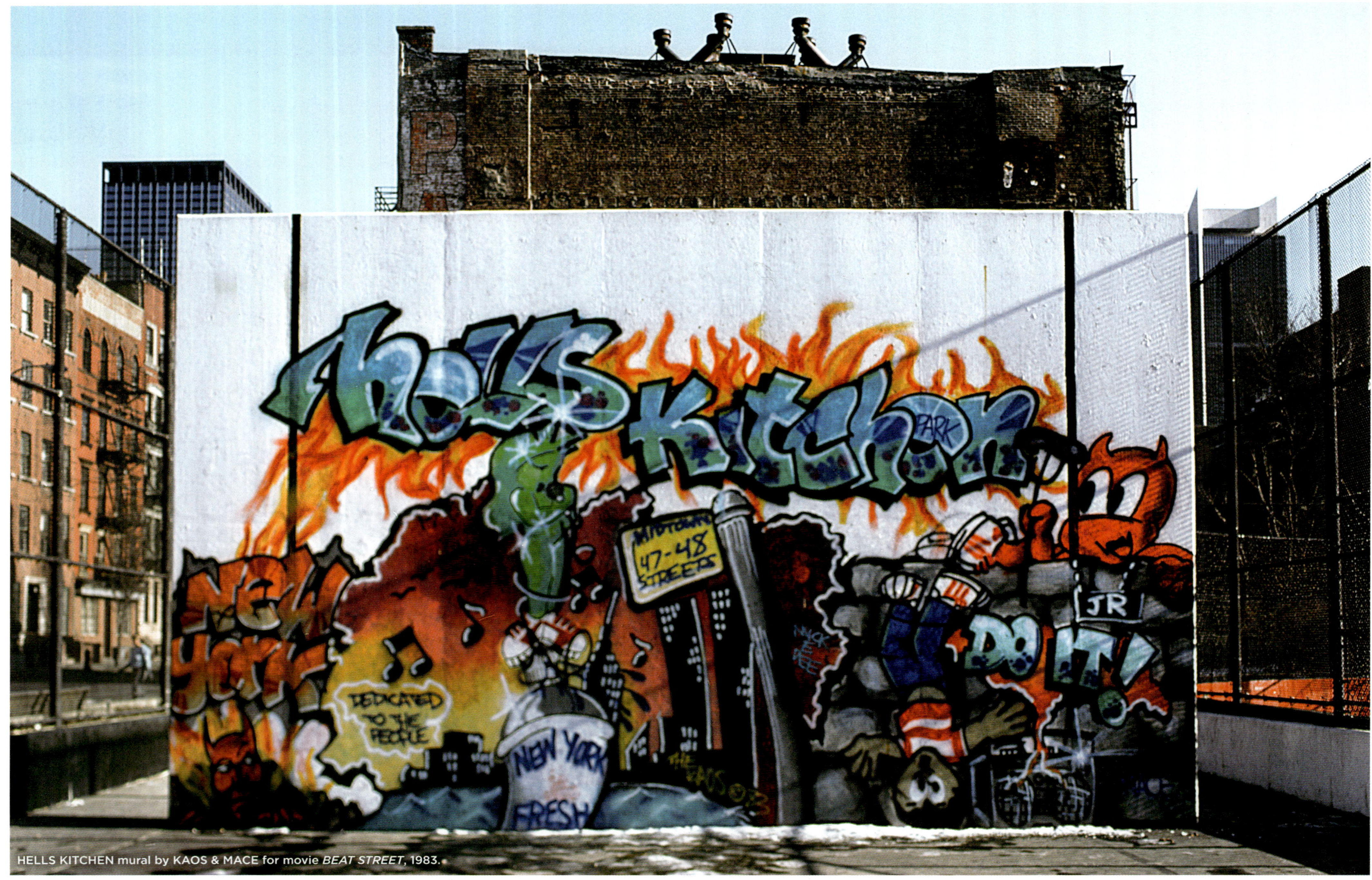

HELLS KITCHEN mural by KAOS & MACE for movie *BEAT STREET*, 1983.

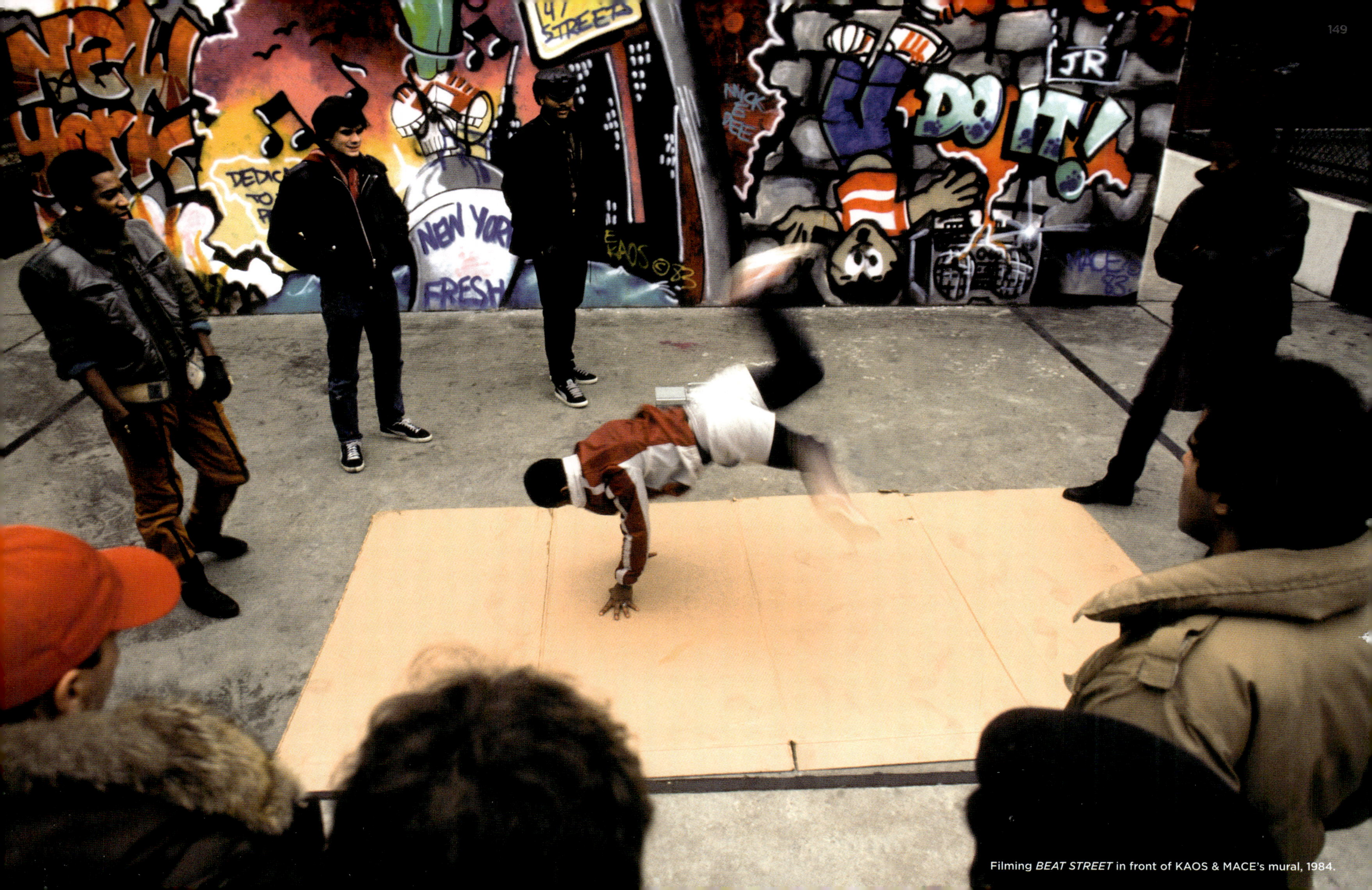

Filming *BEAT STREET* in front of KAOS & MACE's mural, 1984.

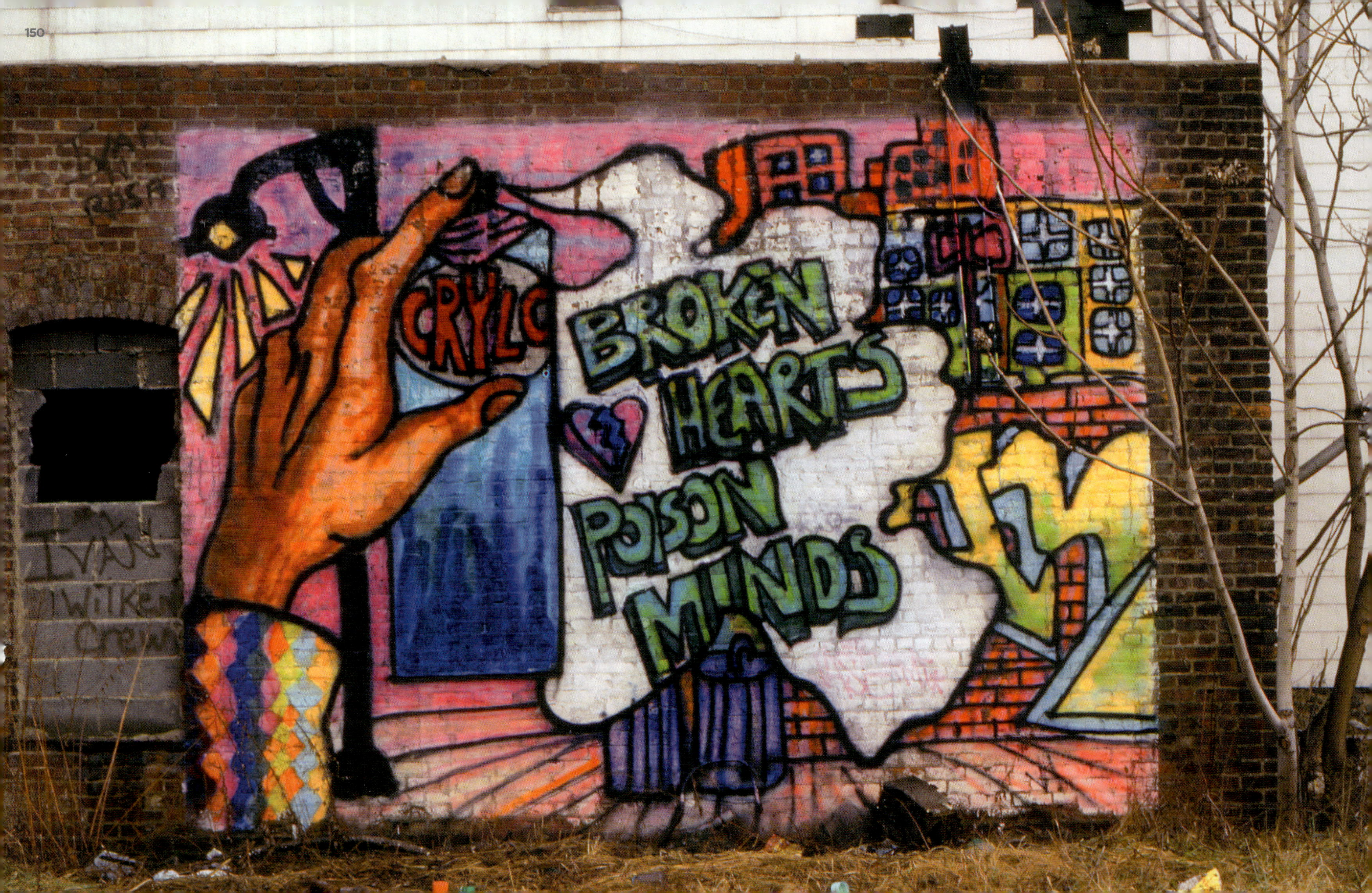
CRYLO
BROKEN
HEARTS
POISON
MINDS

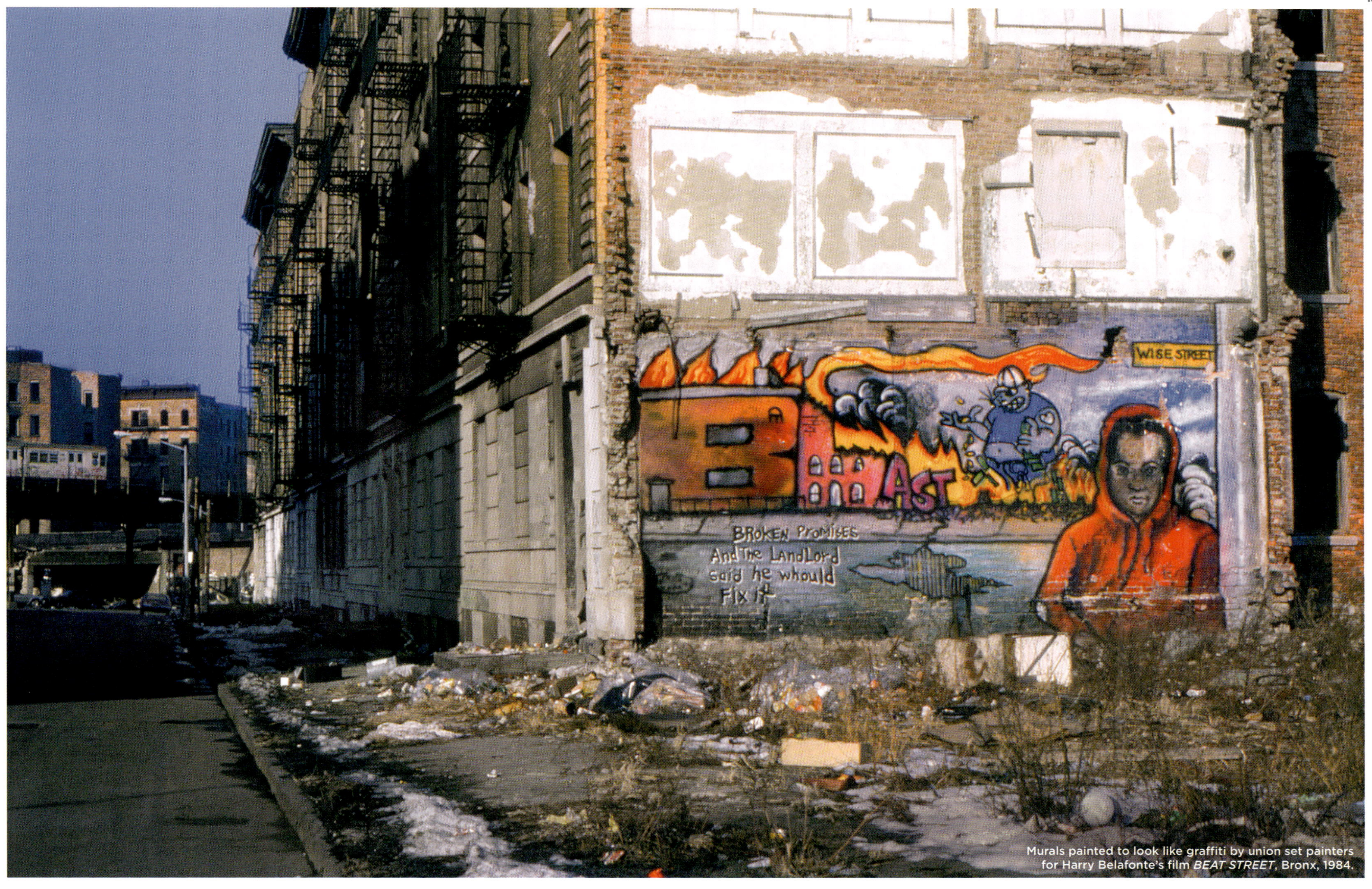

Murals painted to look like graffiti by union set painters for Harry Belafonte's film *BEAT STREET*, Bronx, 1984.

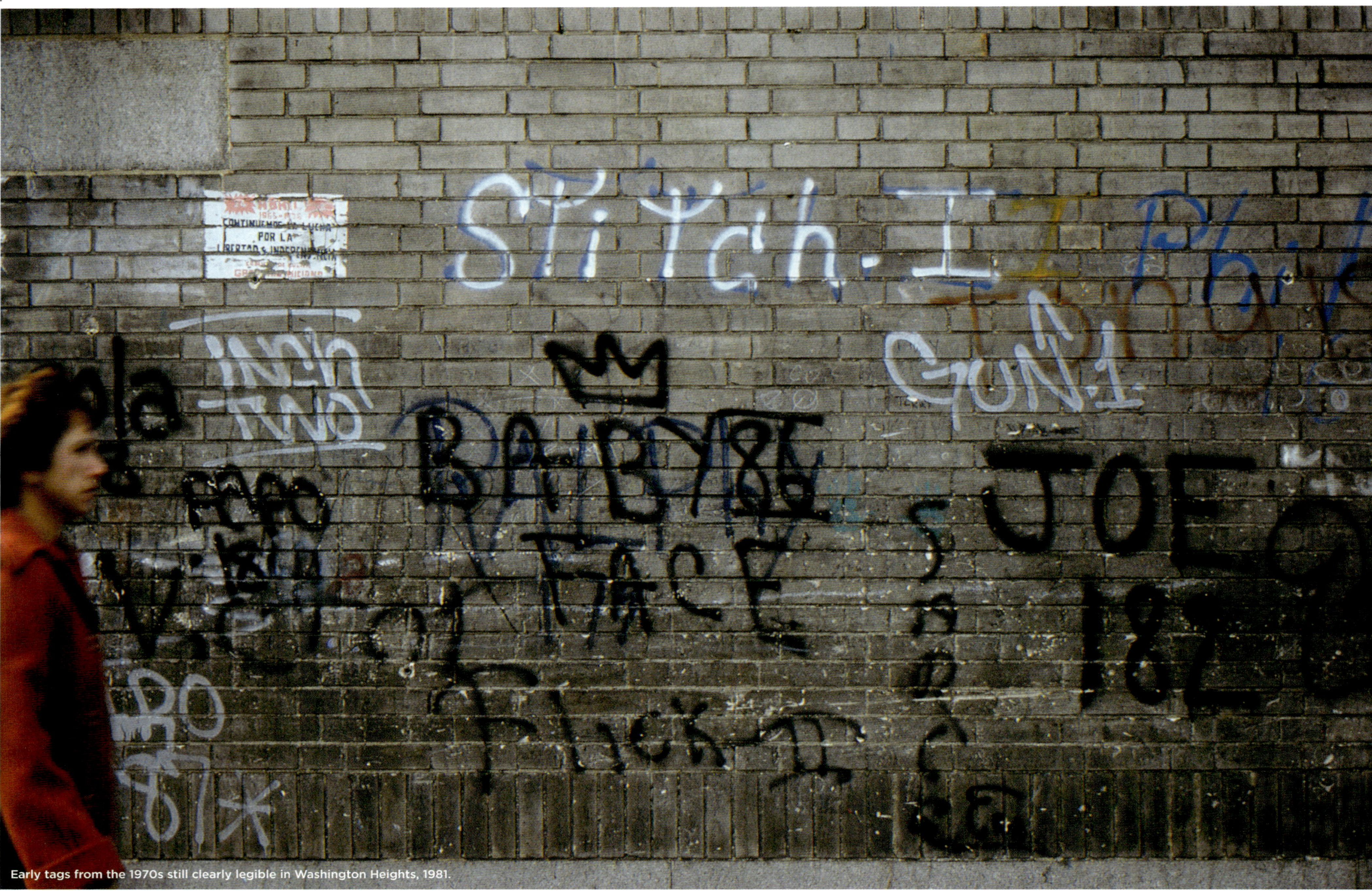

Early tags from the 1970s still clearly legible in Washington Heights, 1981.

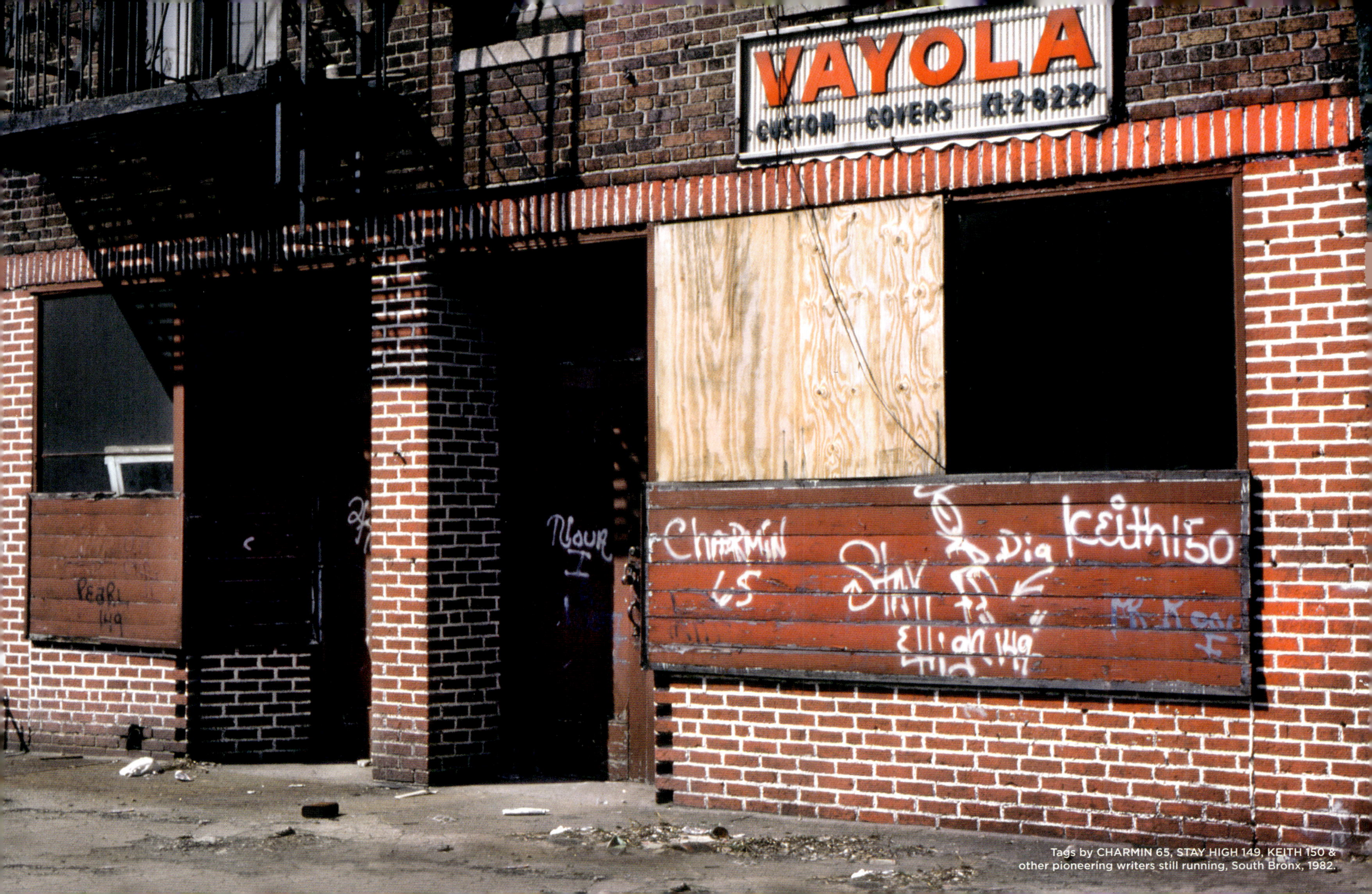

Tags by CHARMIN 65, STAY HIGH 149, KEITH 150 & other pioneering writers still running, South Bronx, 1982.

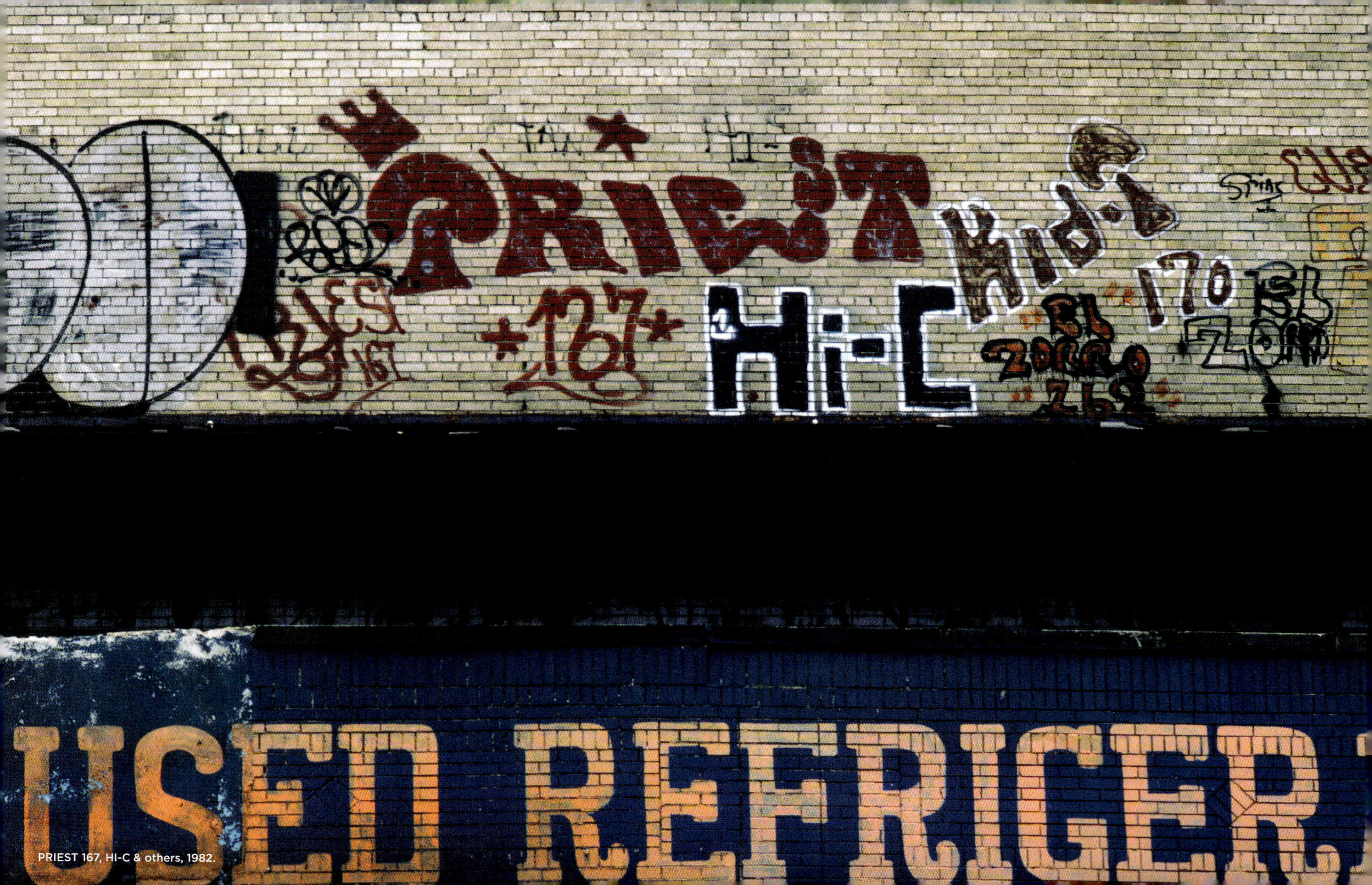

PRIEST 167, HI-C & others, 1982.

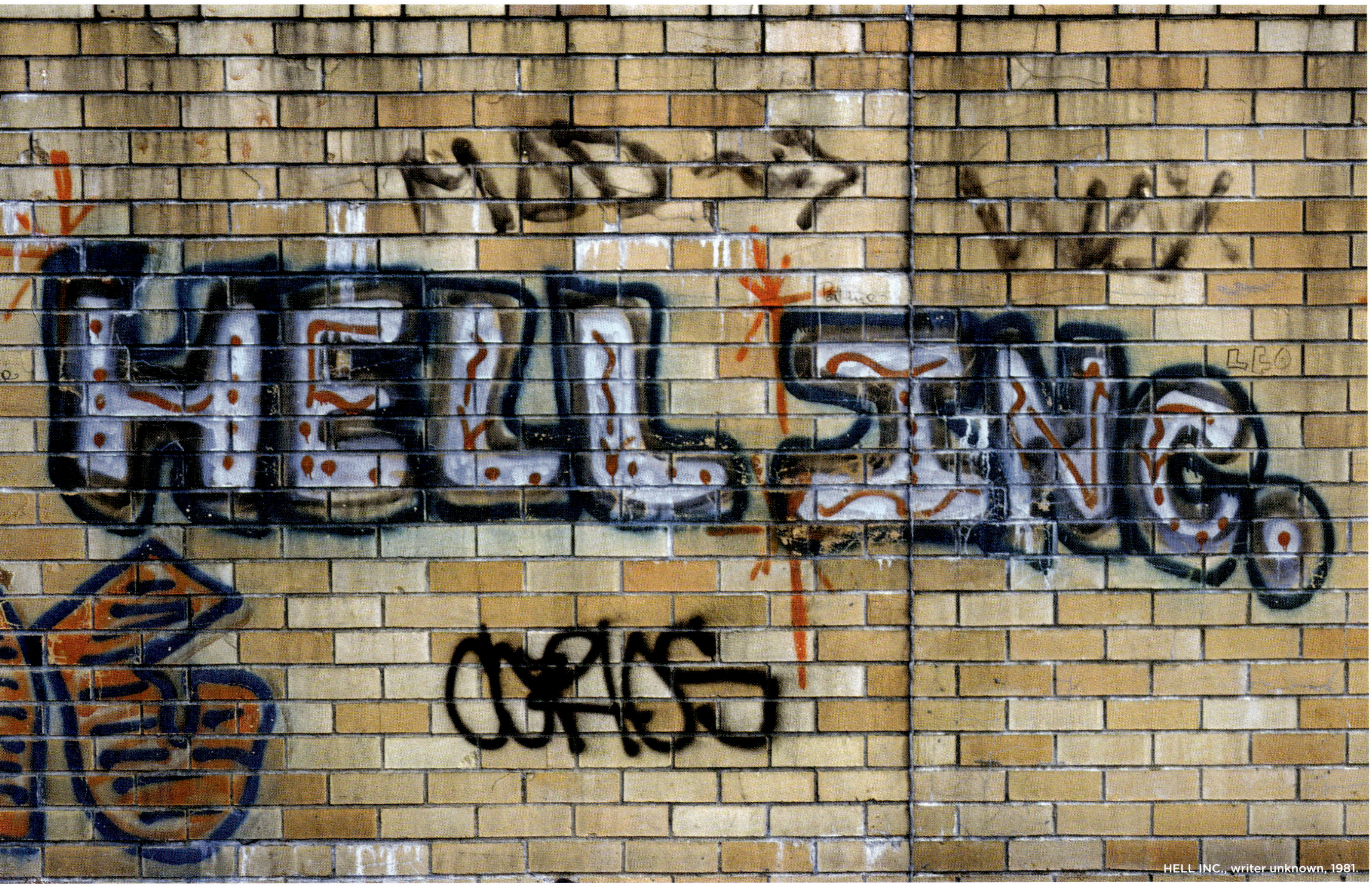

HELL INC., writer unknown, 1981.

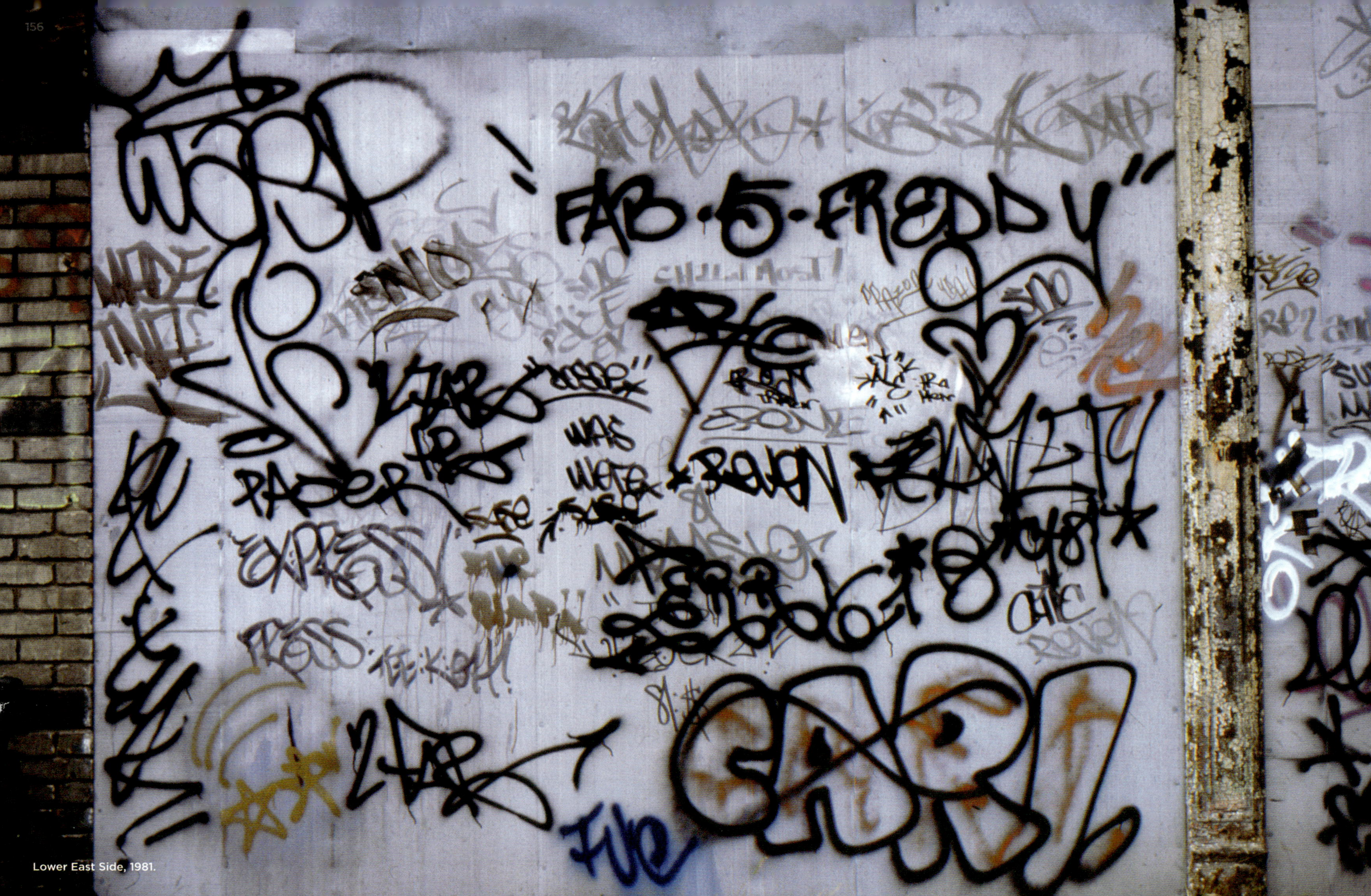

Lower East Side, 1981.

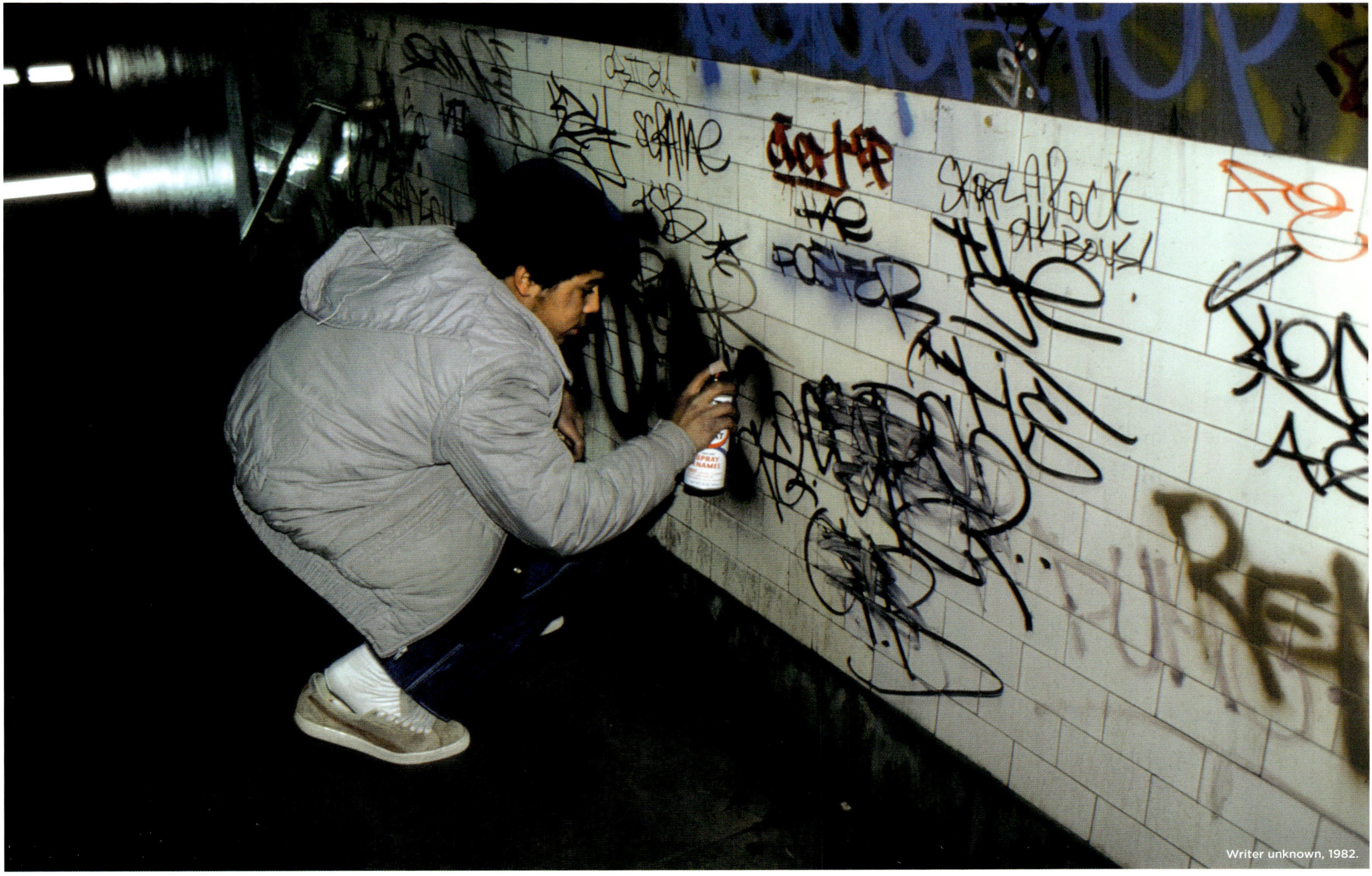

Writer unknown, 1982.

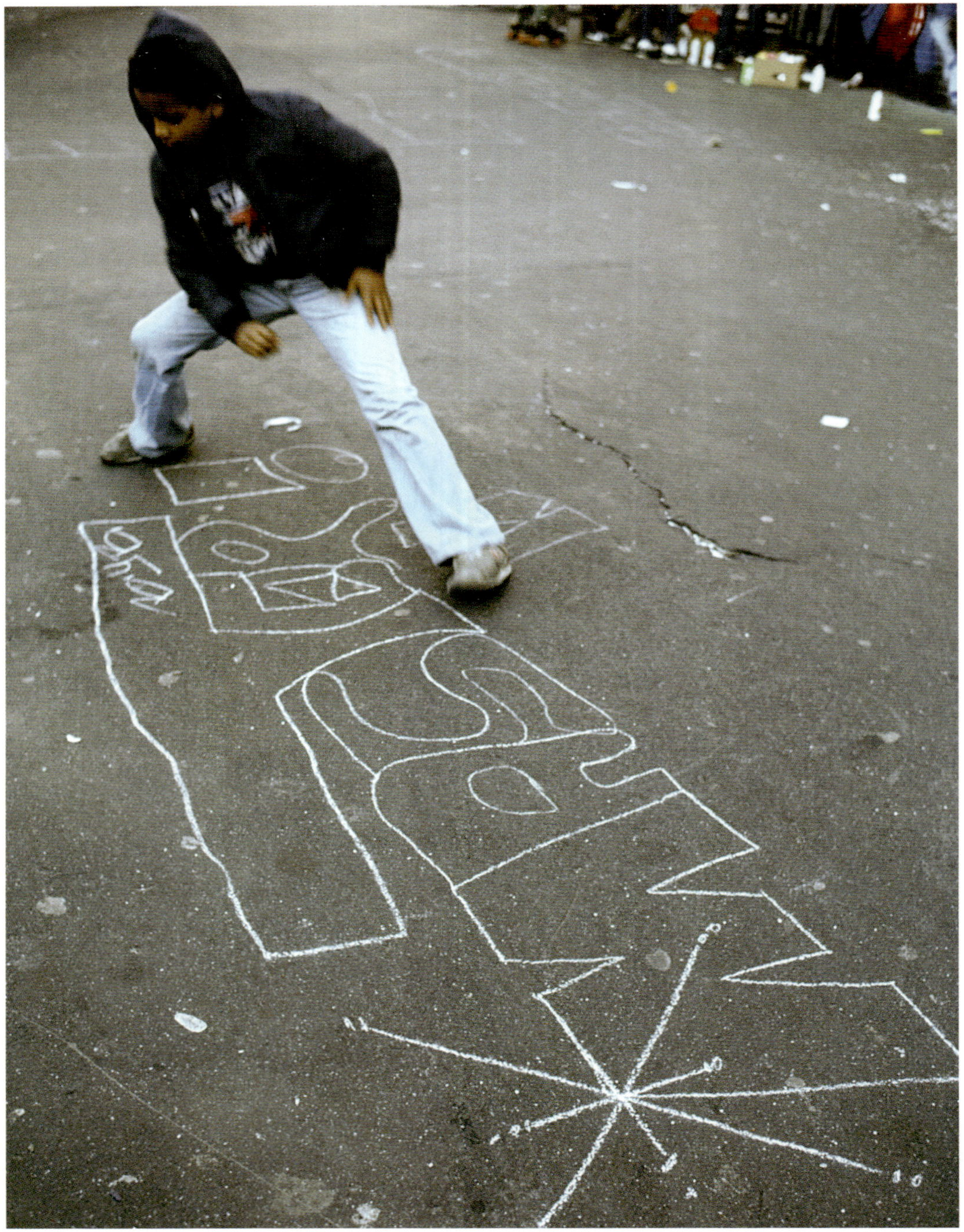

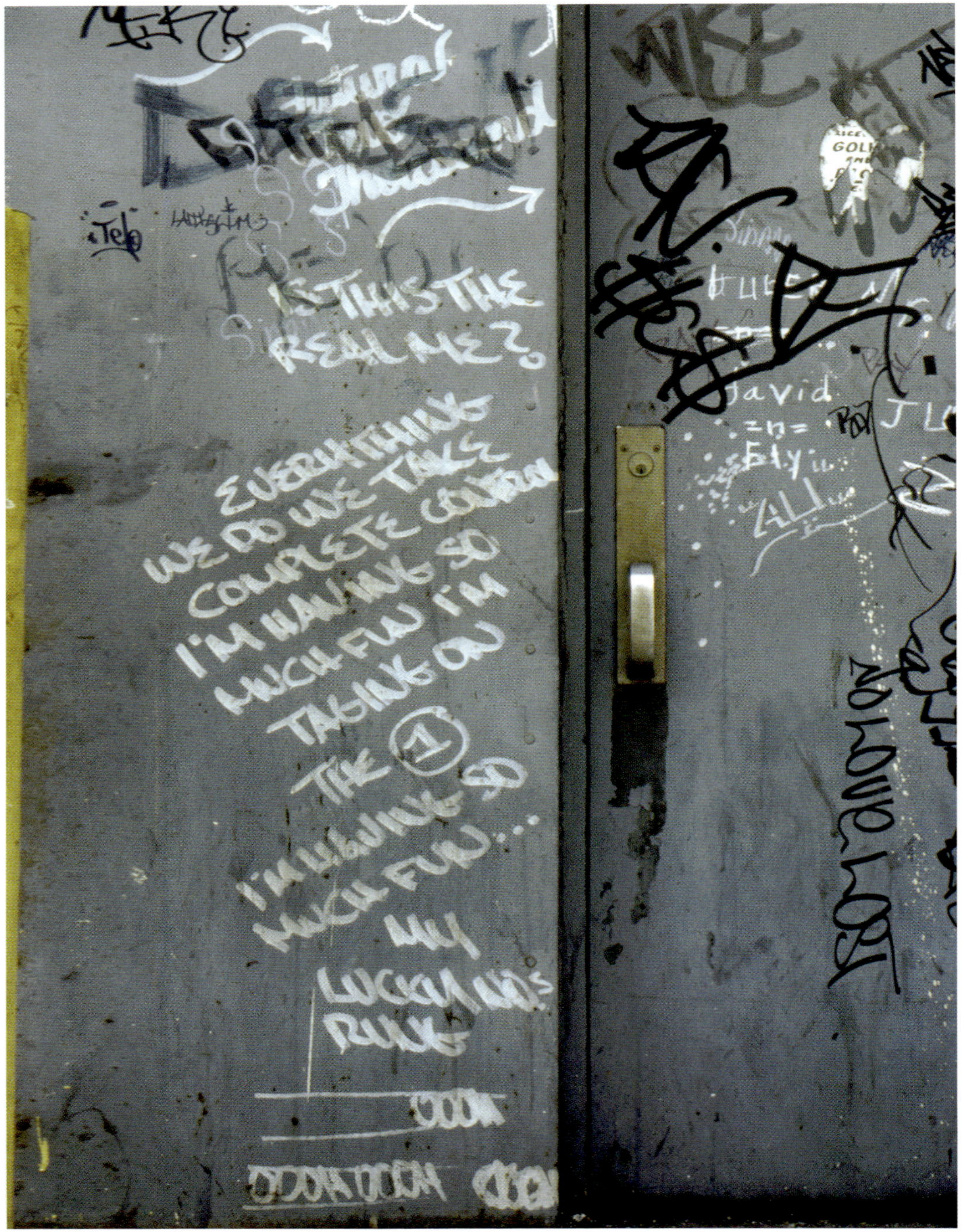
IS THIS THE REAL ME?
EVERYTHING WE DO WE TAKE COMPLETE CONTROL
David

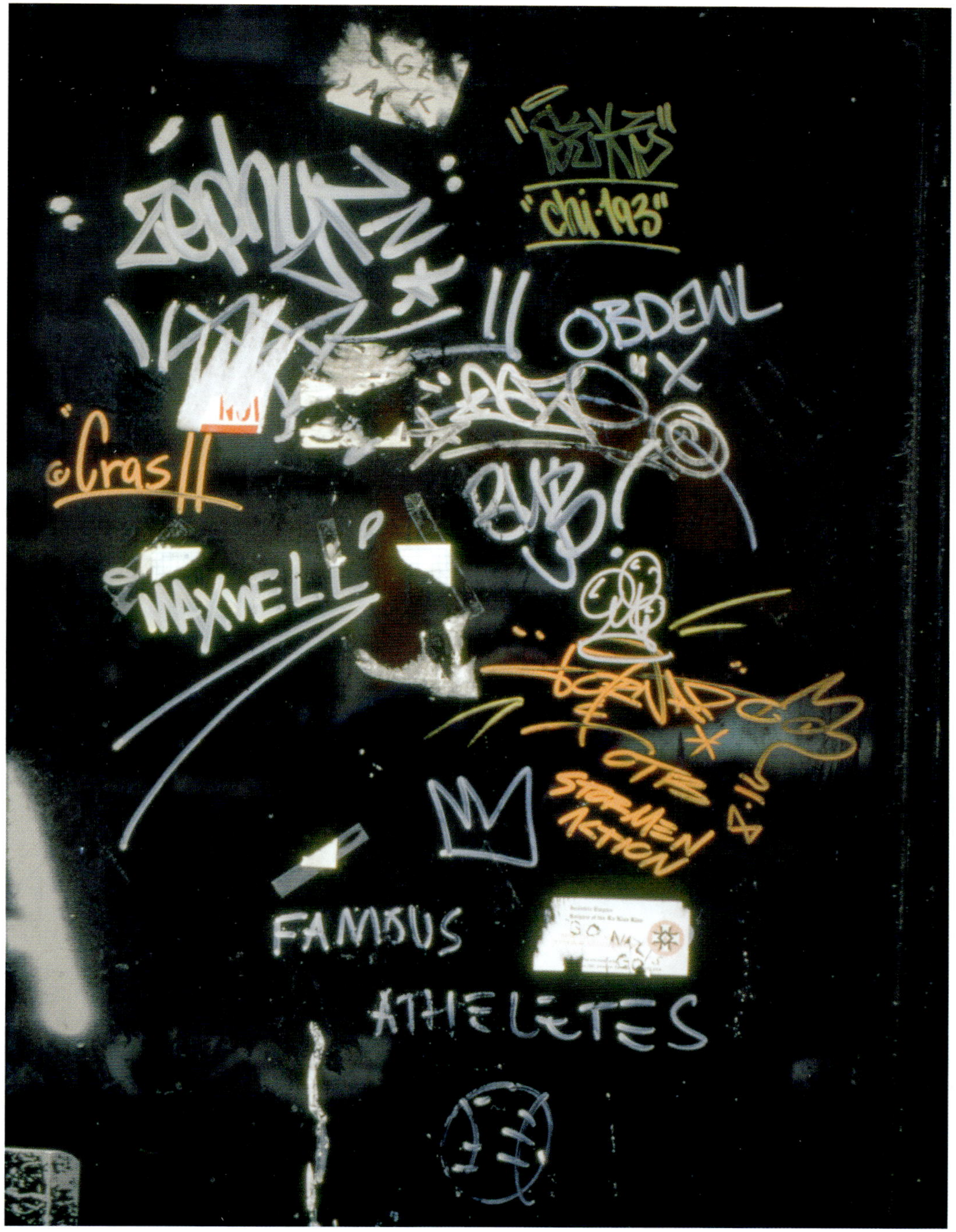

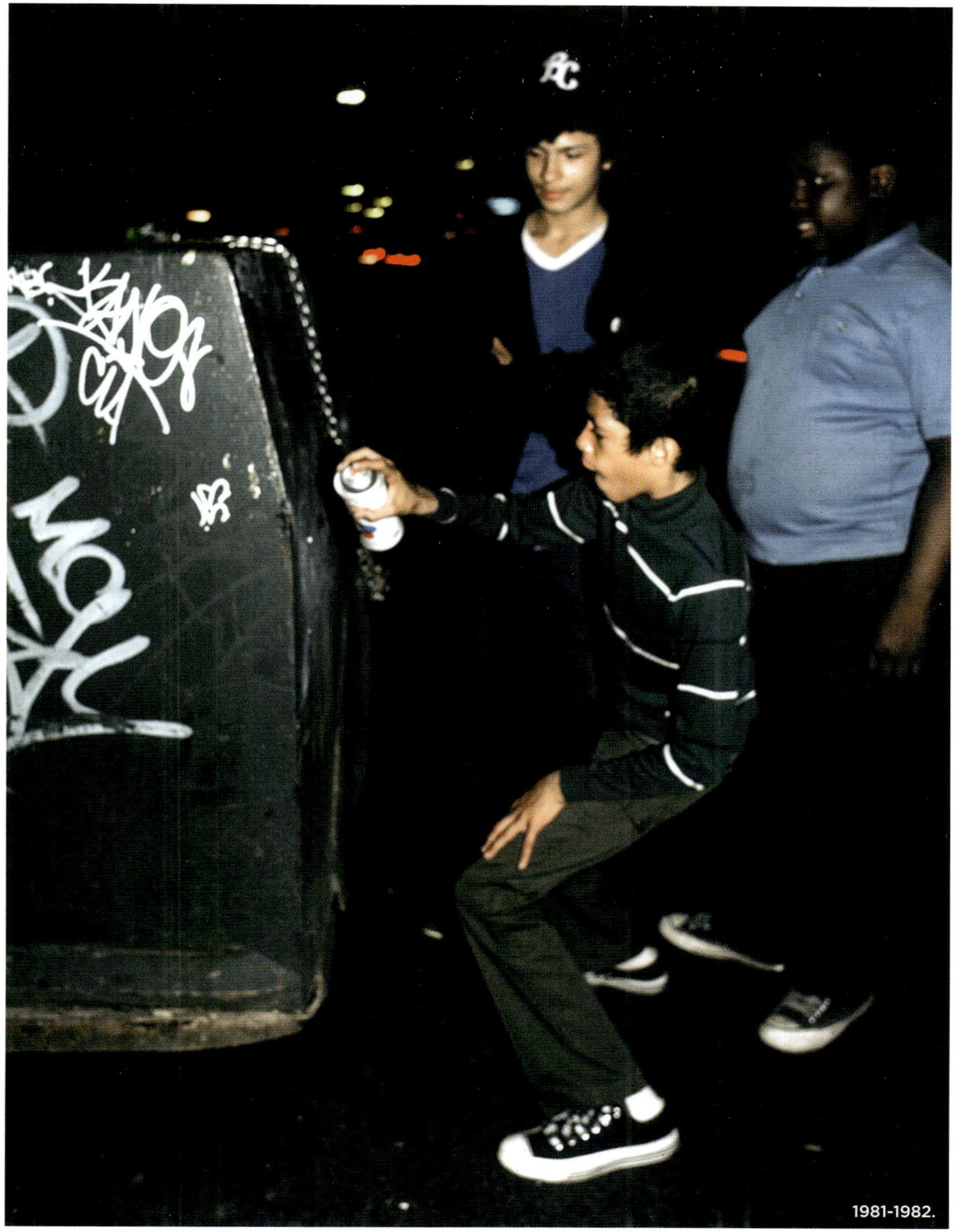

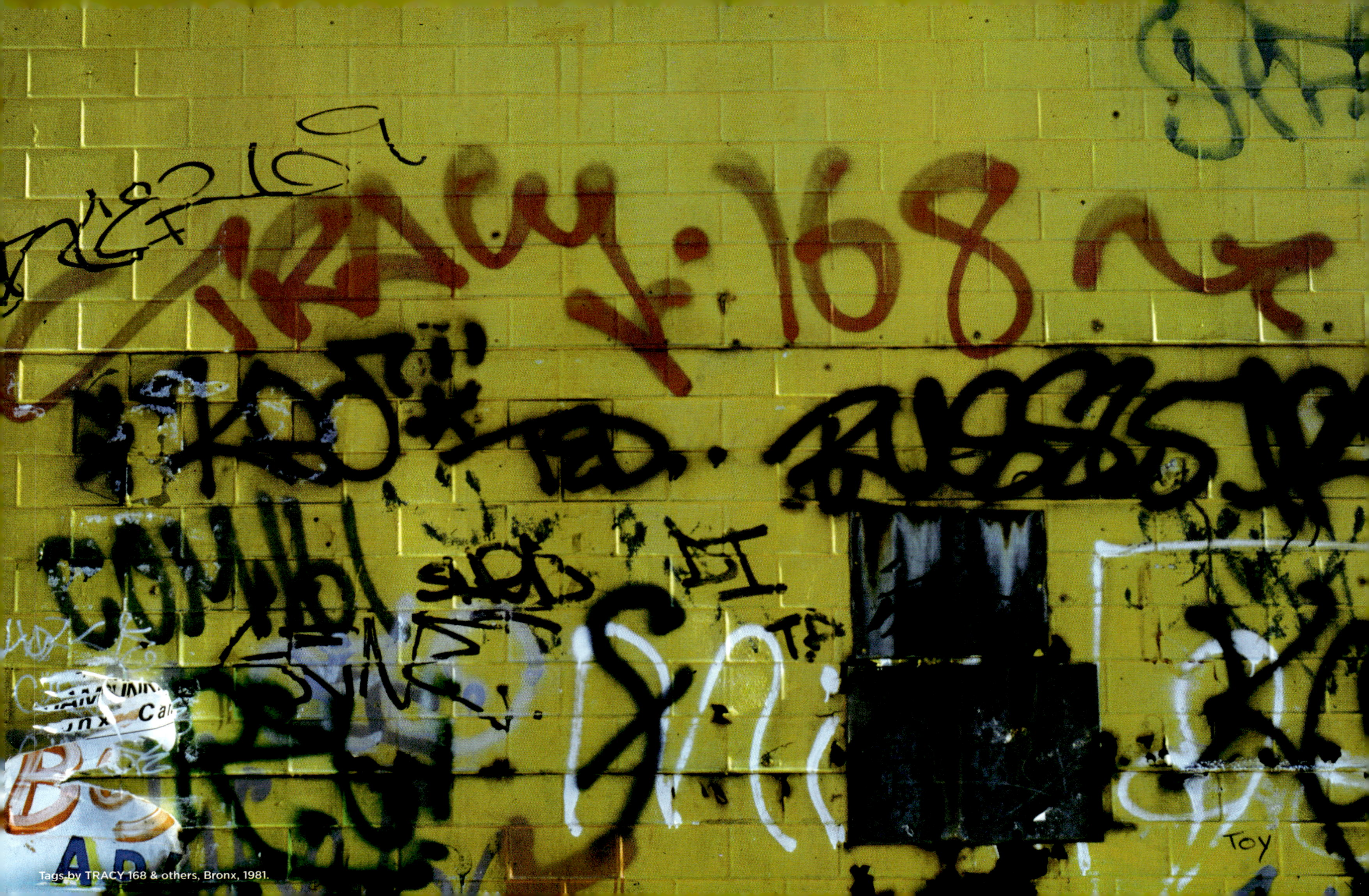

Tags by TRACY 168 & others, Bronx, 1981.

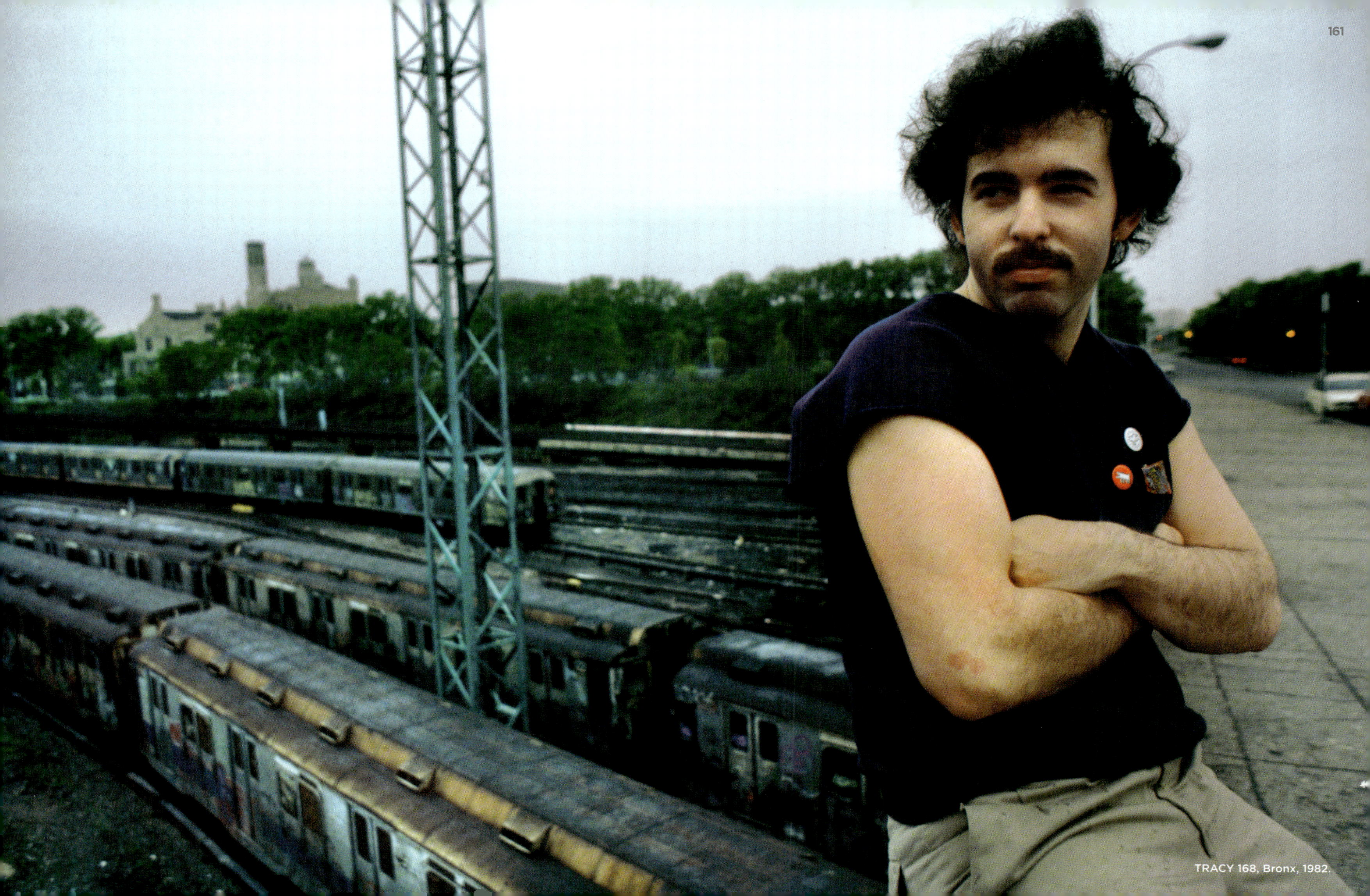

TRACY 168, Bronx, 1982.

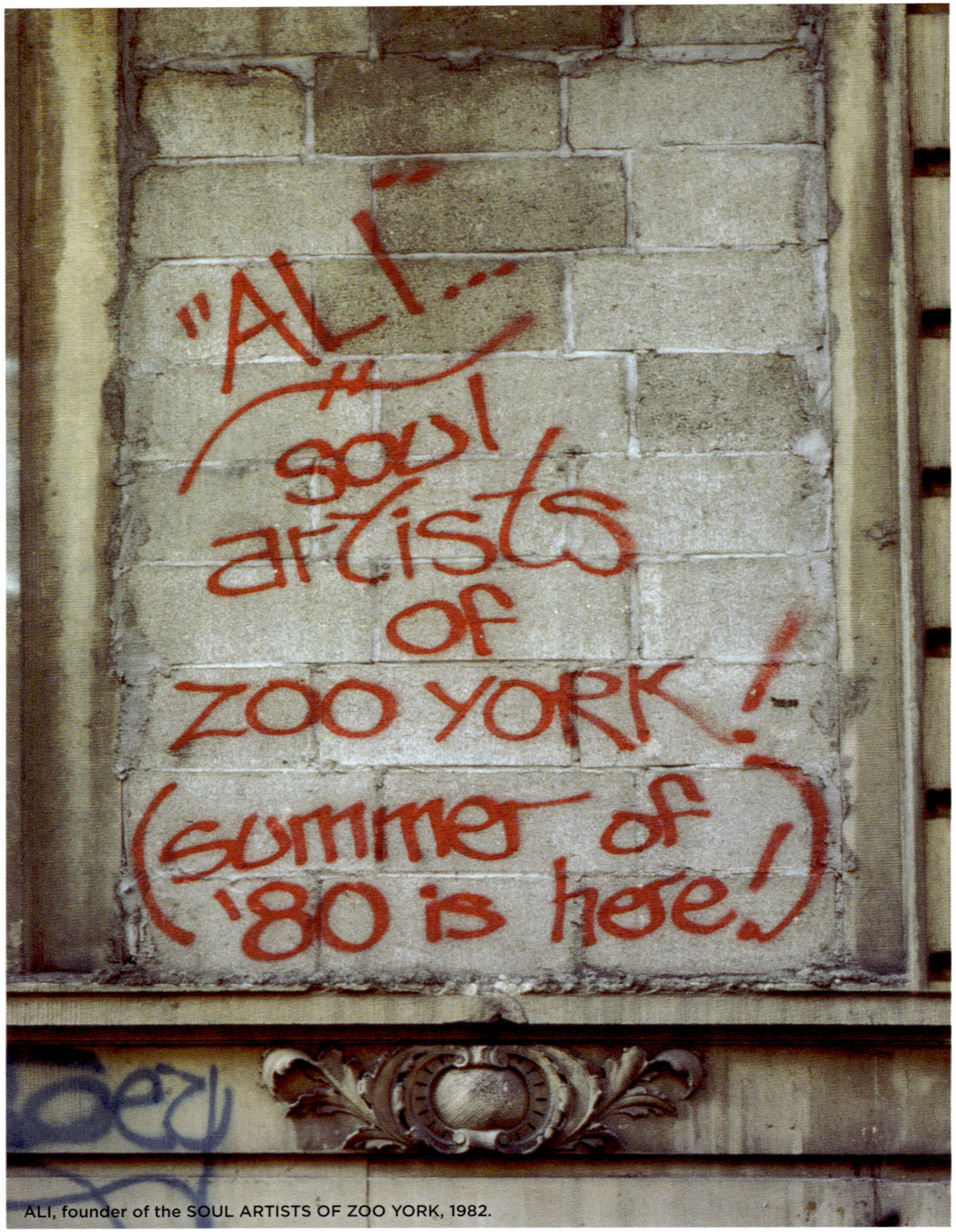

ALI, founder of the SOUL ARTISTS OF ZOO YORK, 1982.

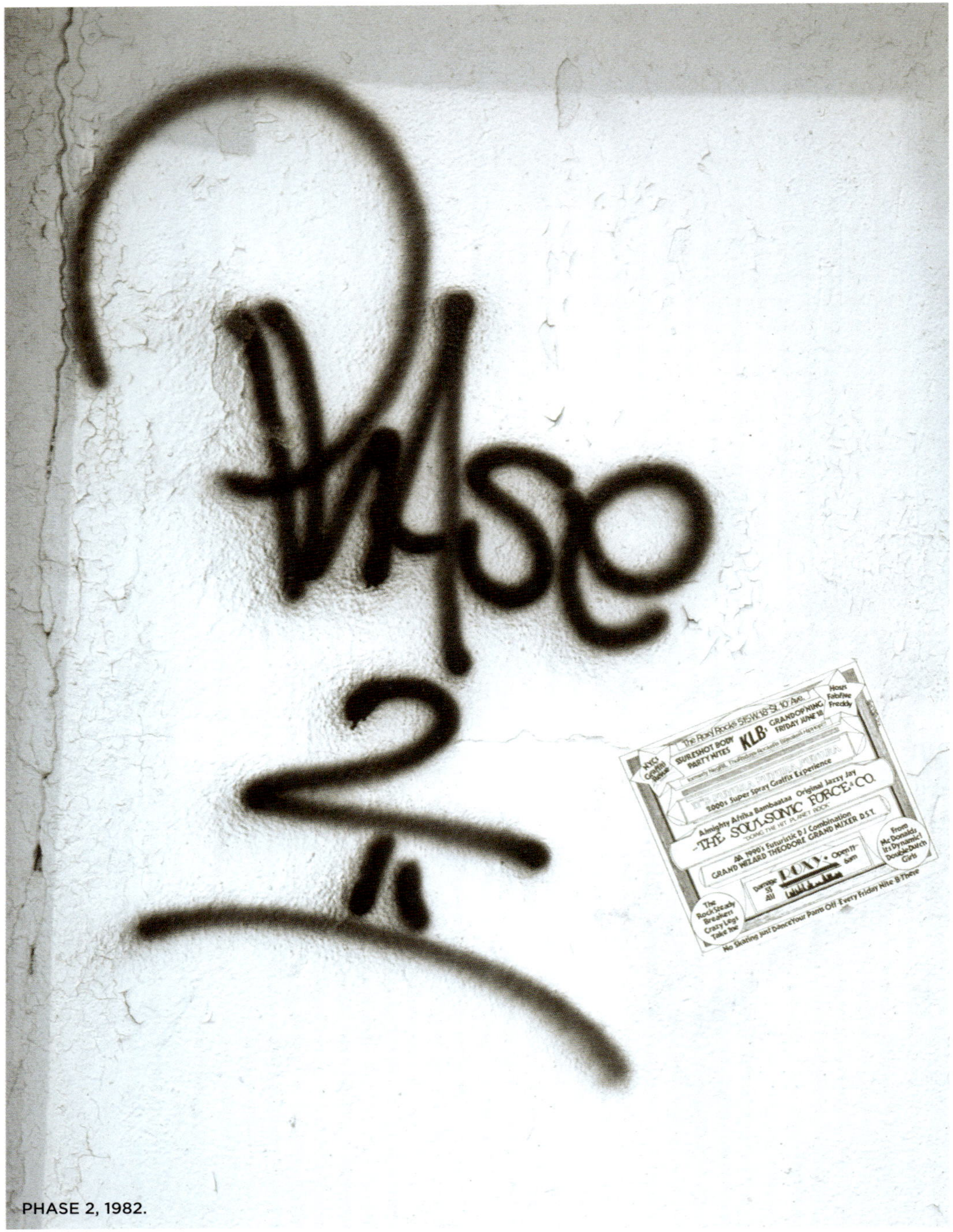

PHASE 2, 1982.

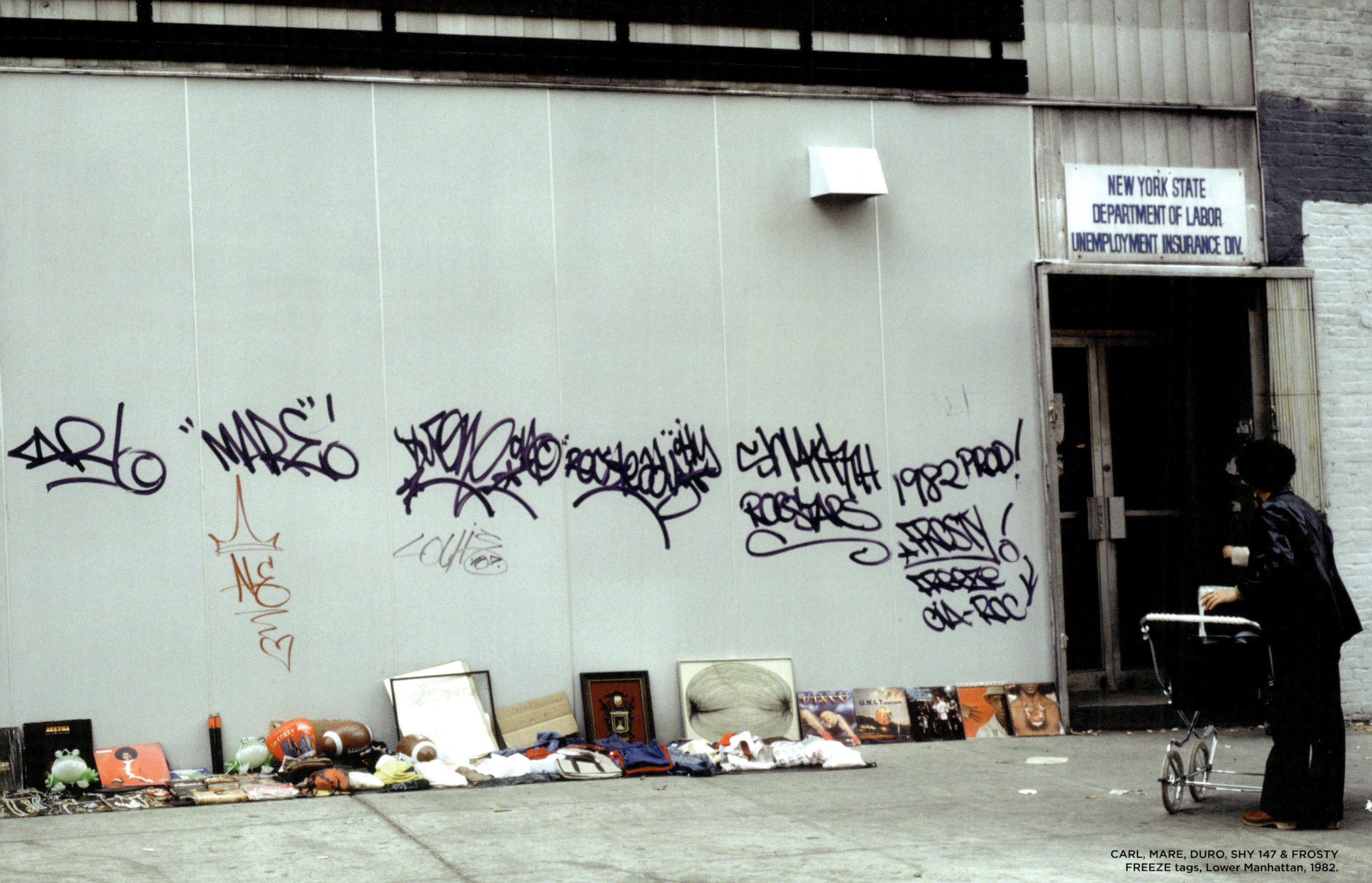

CARL, MARE, DURO, SHY 147 & FROSTY
FREEZE tags, Lower Manhattan, 1982.

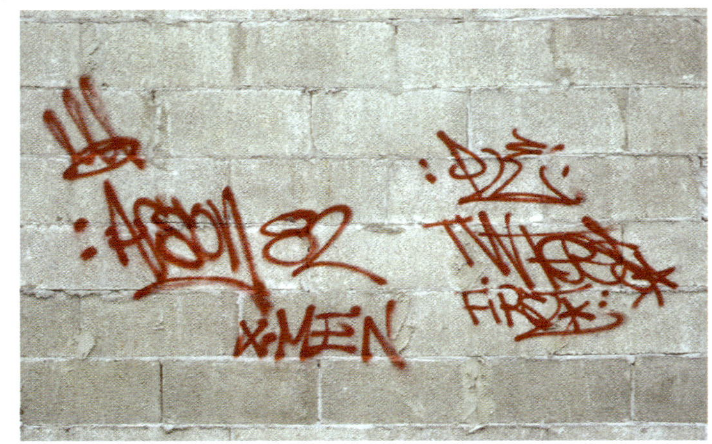
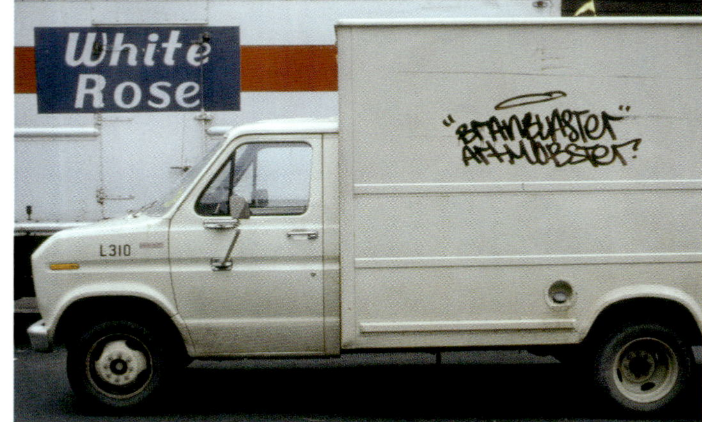
White
Rose
L310

U.S.MAIL
:II: BURNT.

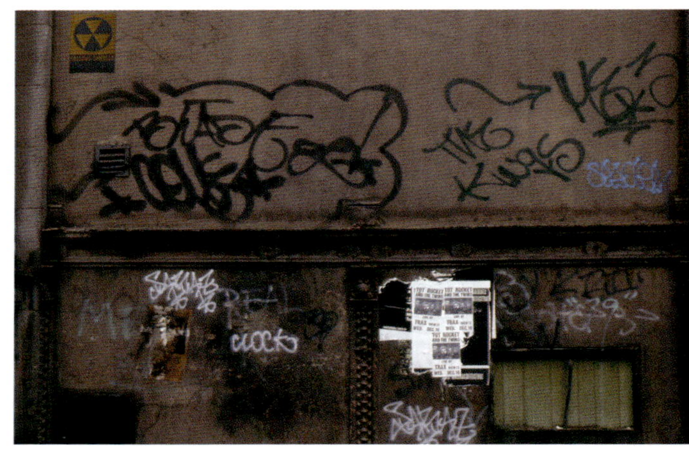
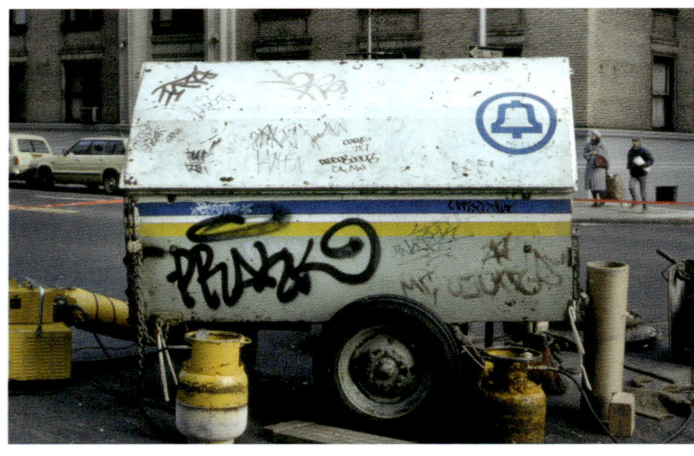
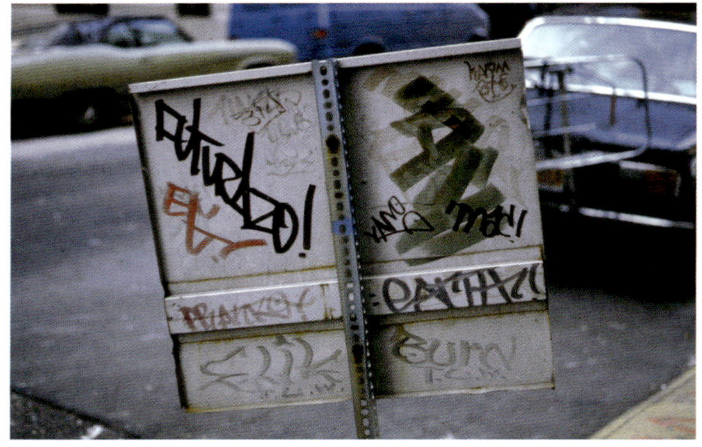

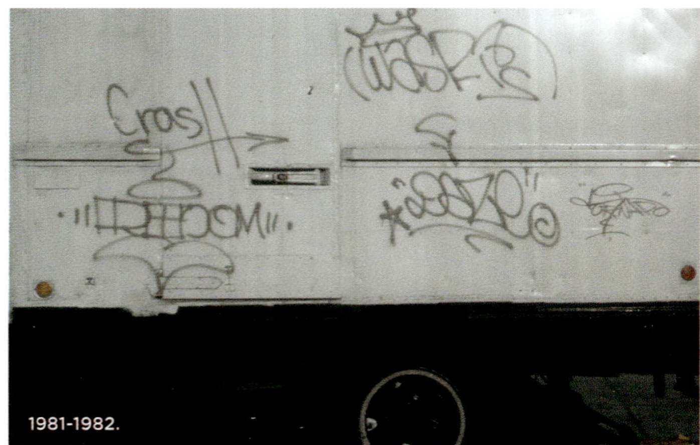
1981-1982.

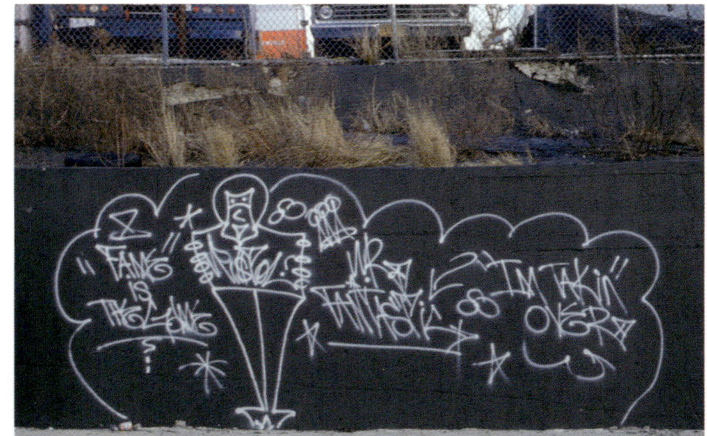
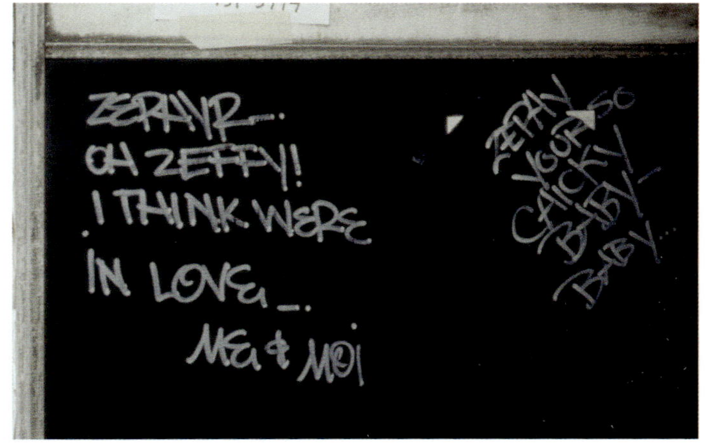
ZEPHYR..
OH ZEPHY!
.I THINK WERE
IN LOVE ..
MEG & MOI

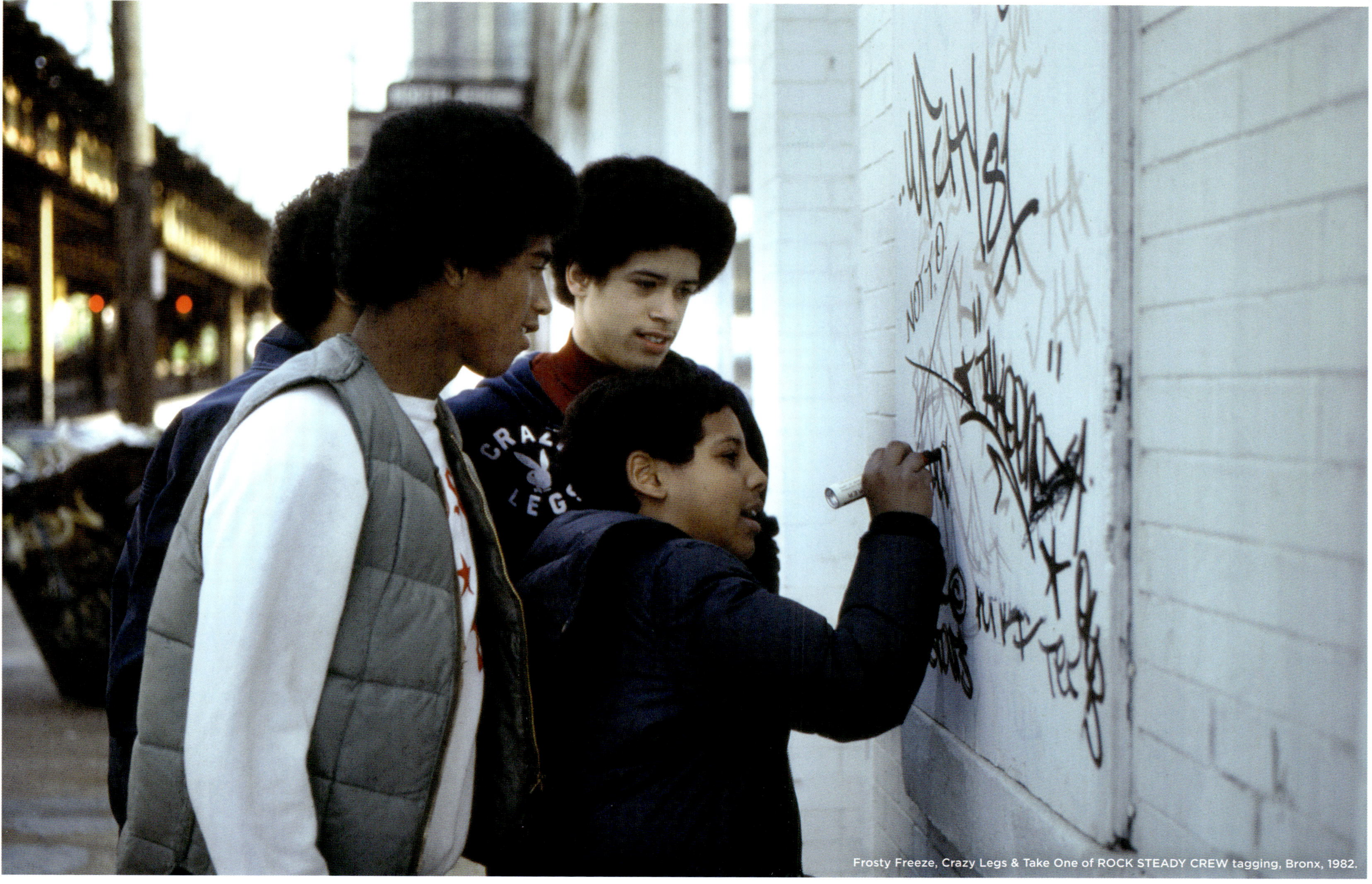

Frosty Freeze, Crazy Legs & Take One of ROCK STEADY CREW tagging, Bronx, 1982.

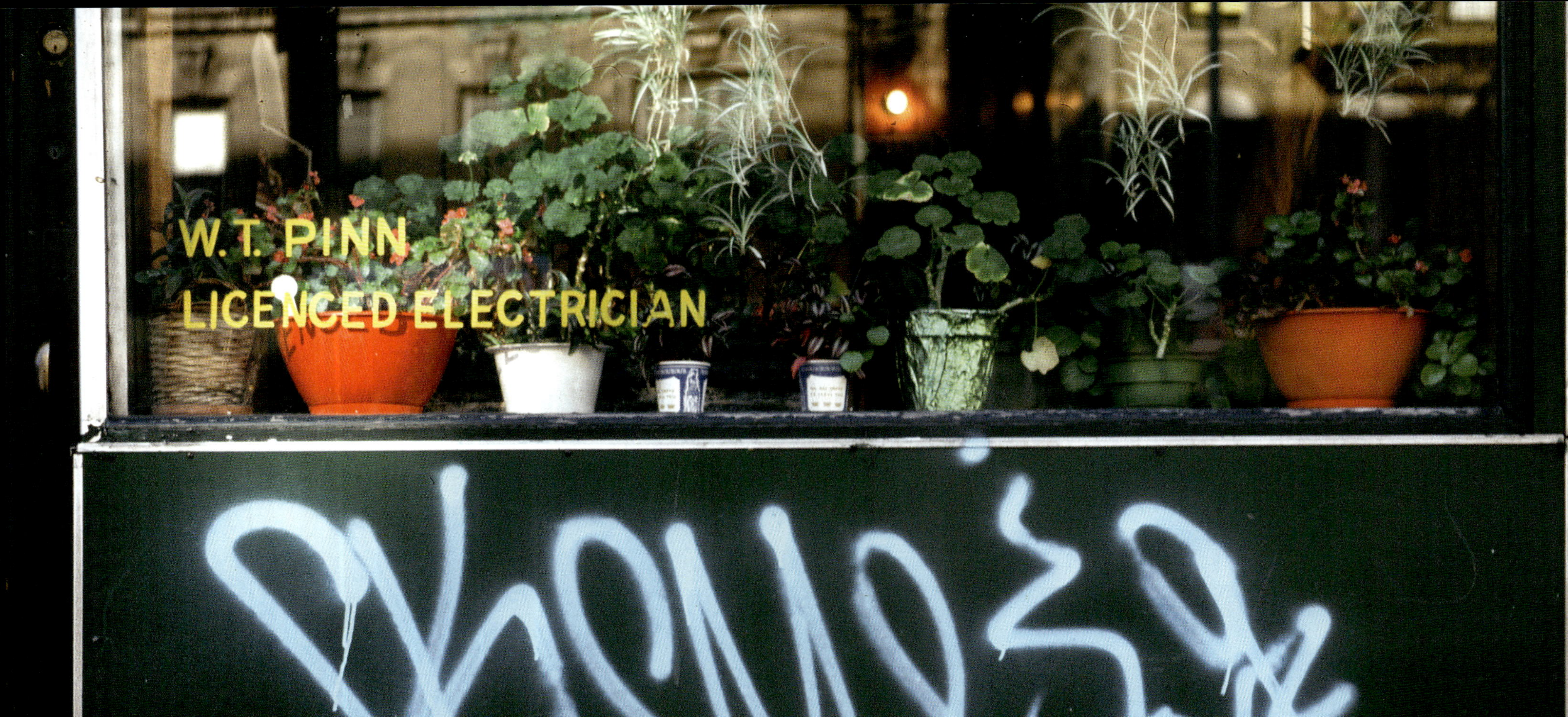

SKEME, 1982.

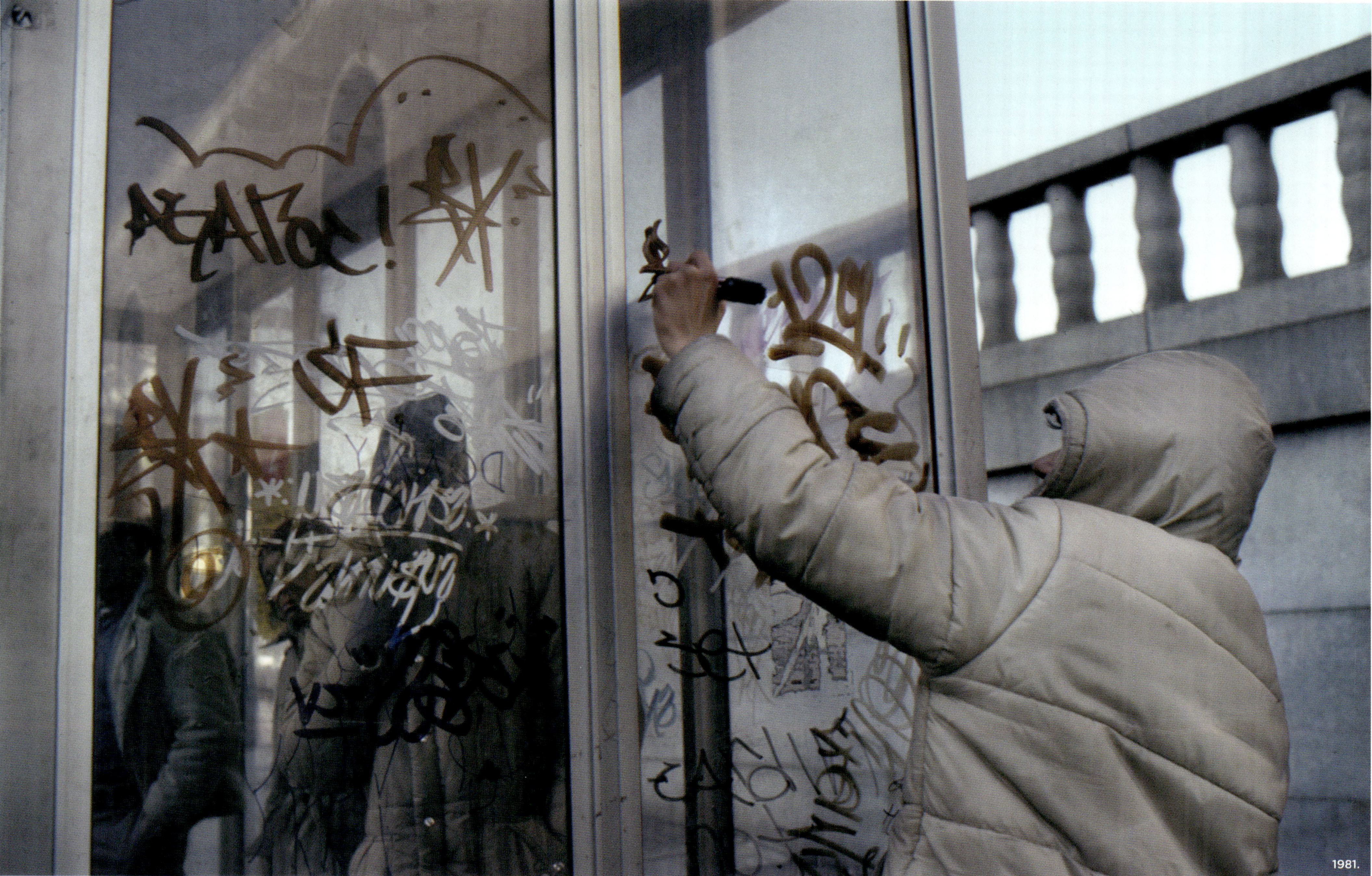

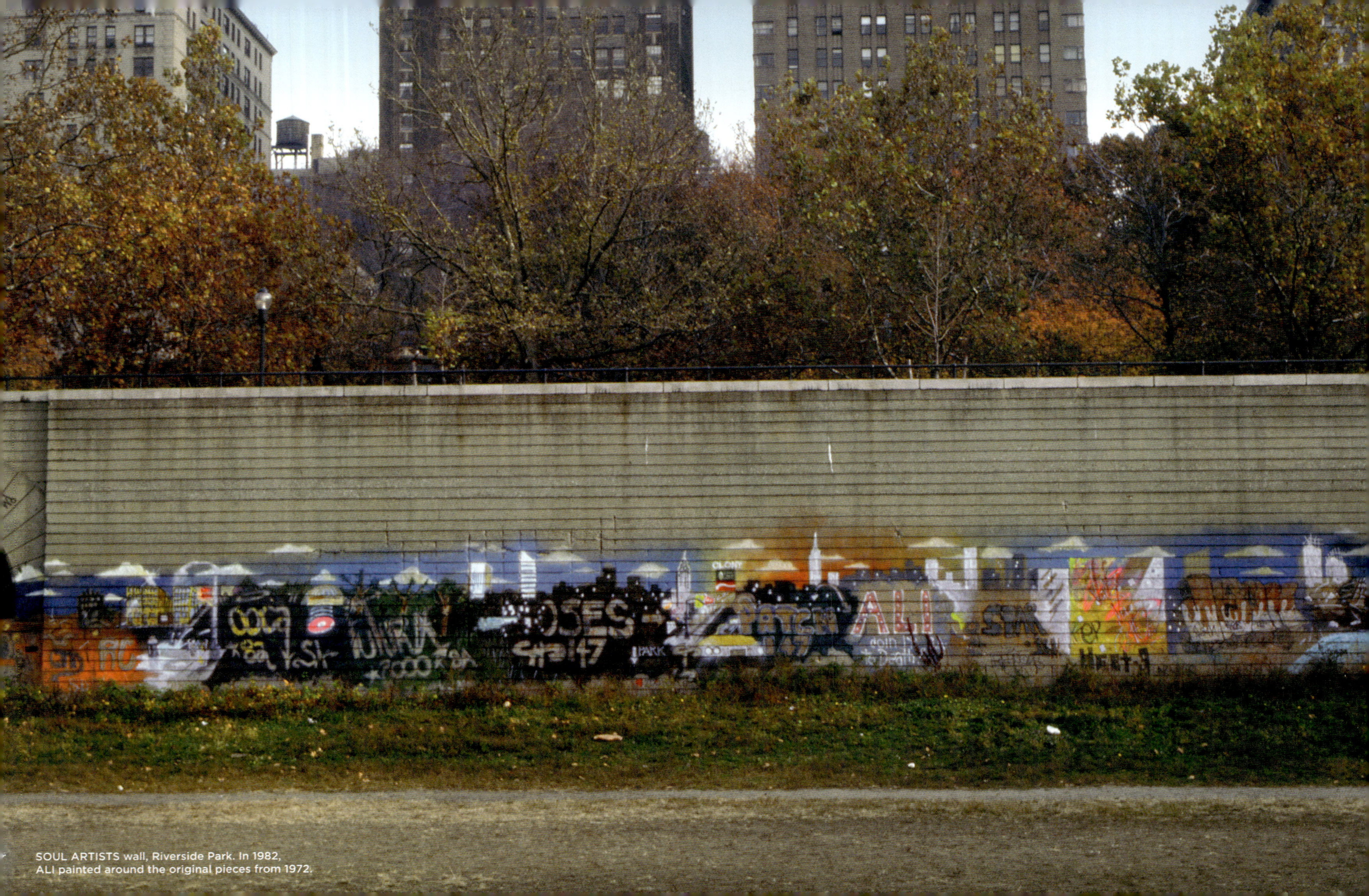

SOUL ARTISTS wall, Riverside Park. In 1982,
ALI painted around the original pieces from 1972.

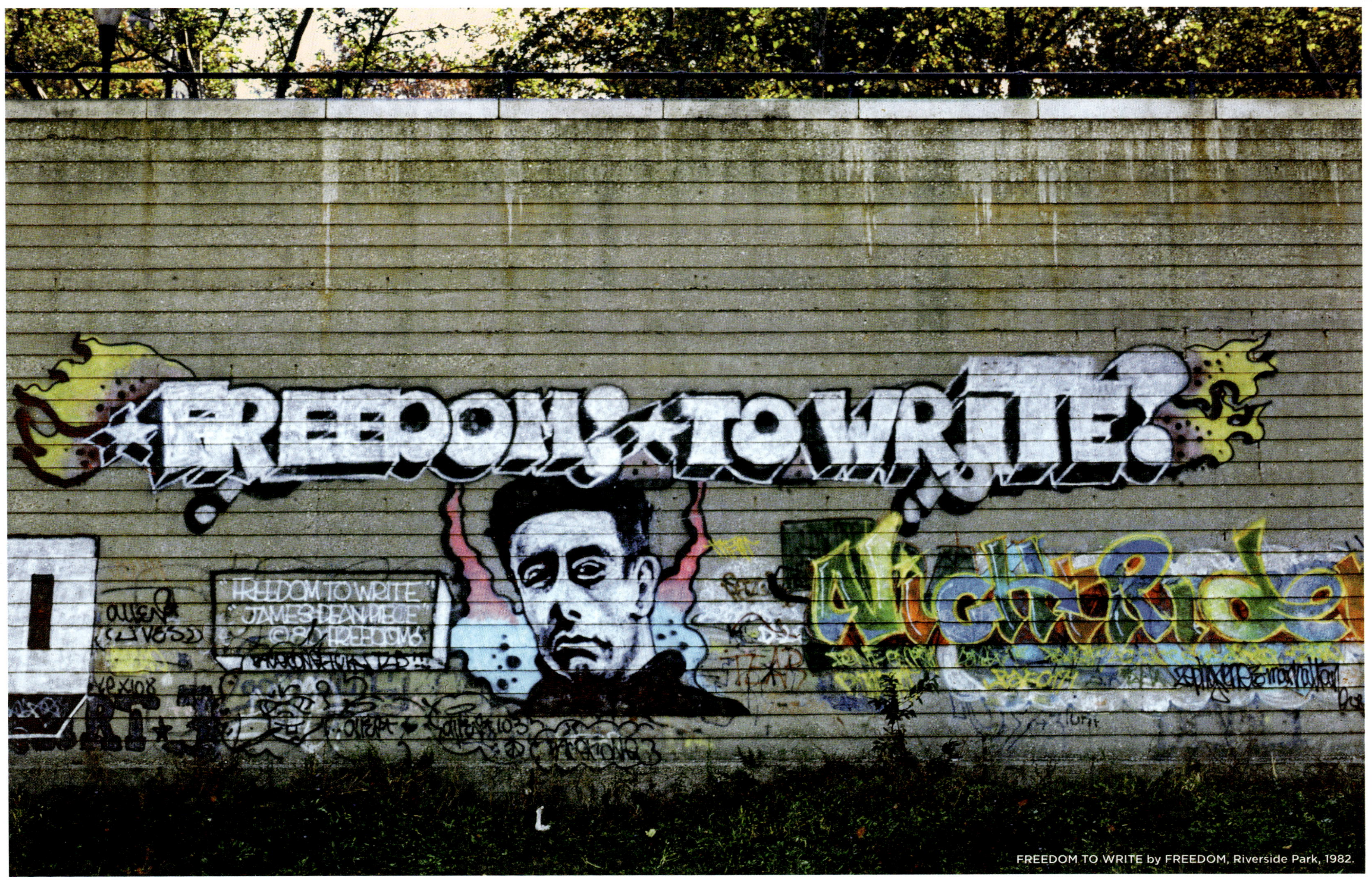

FREEDOM TO WRITE by FREEDOM, Riverside Park, 1982.

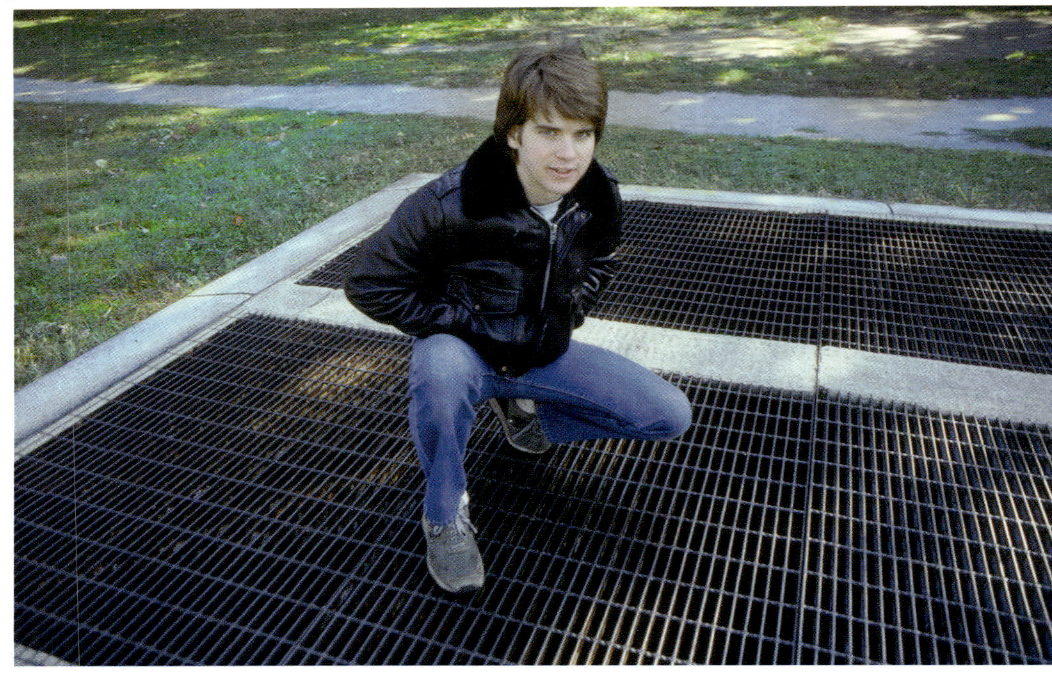

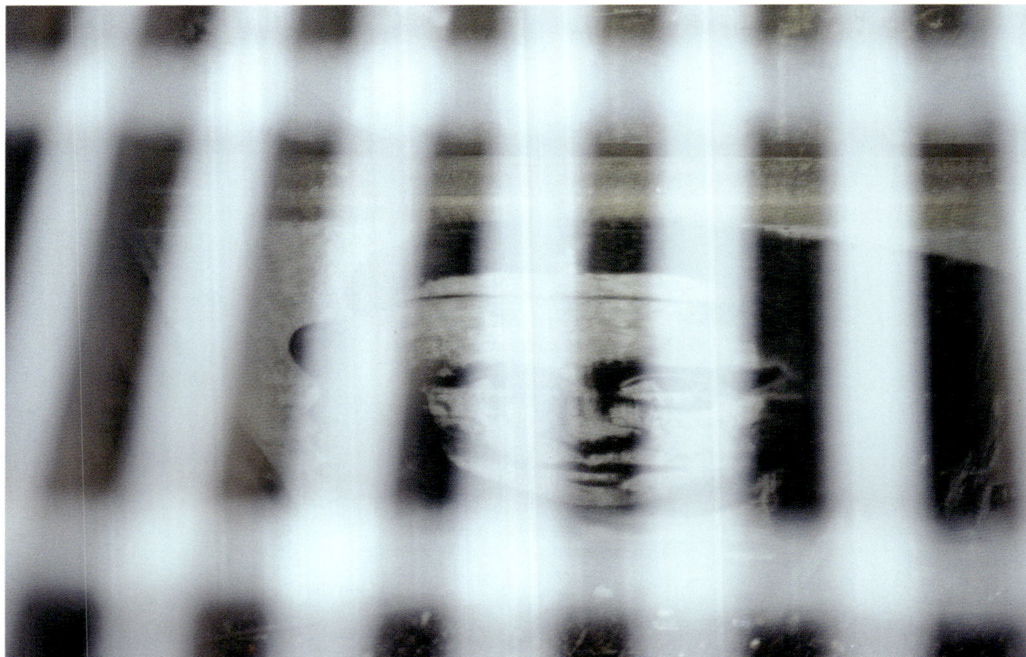

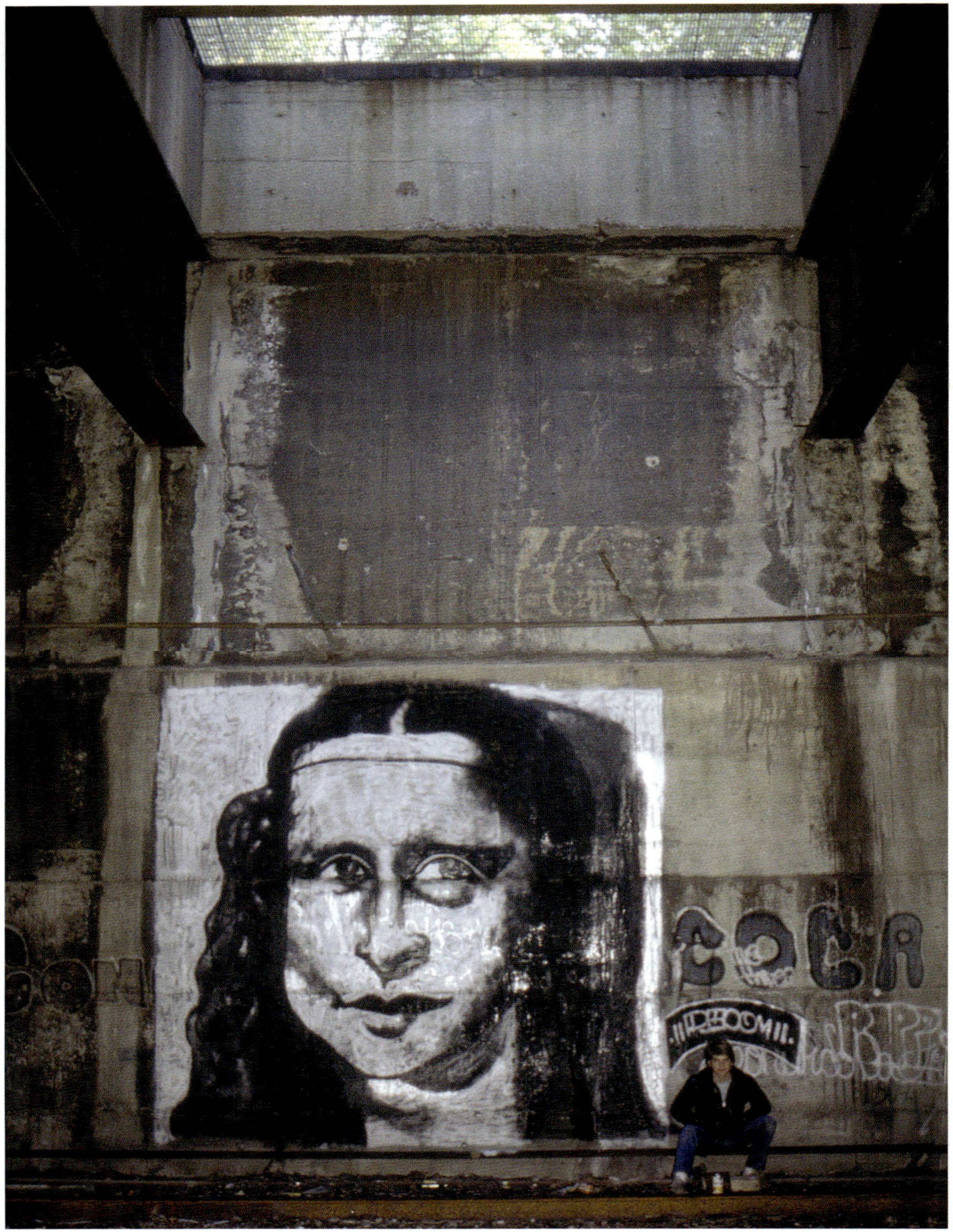

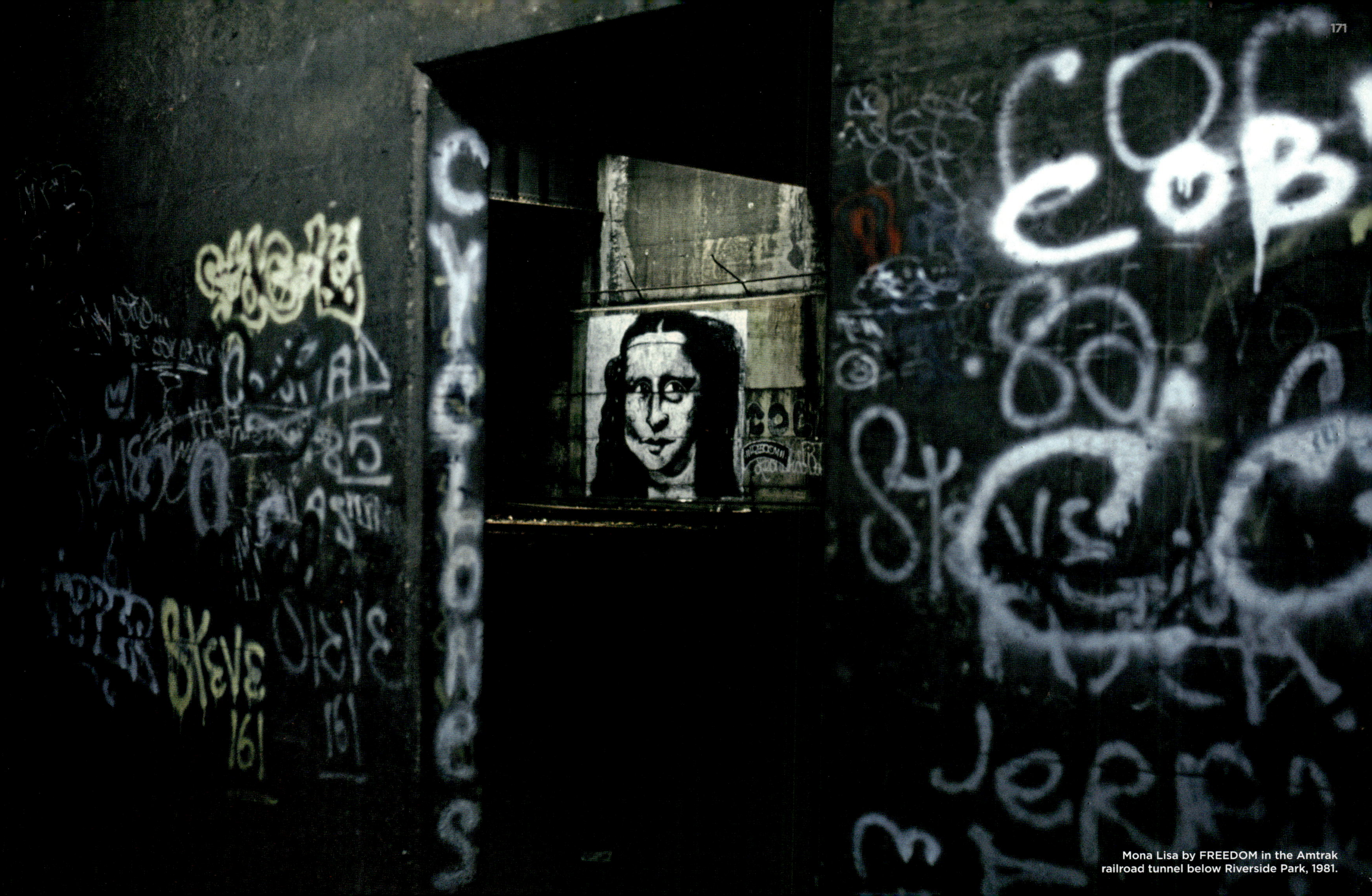

Mona Lisa by **FREEDOM** in the Amtrak railroad tunnel below Riverside Park, 1981.

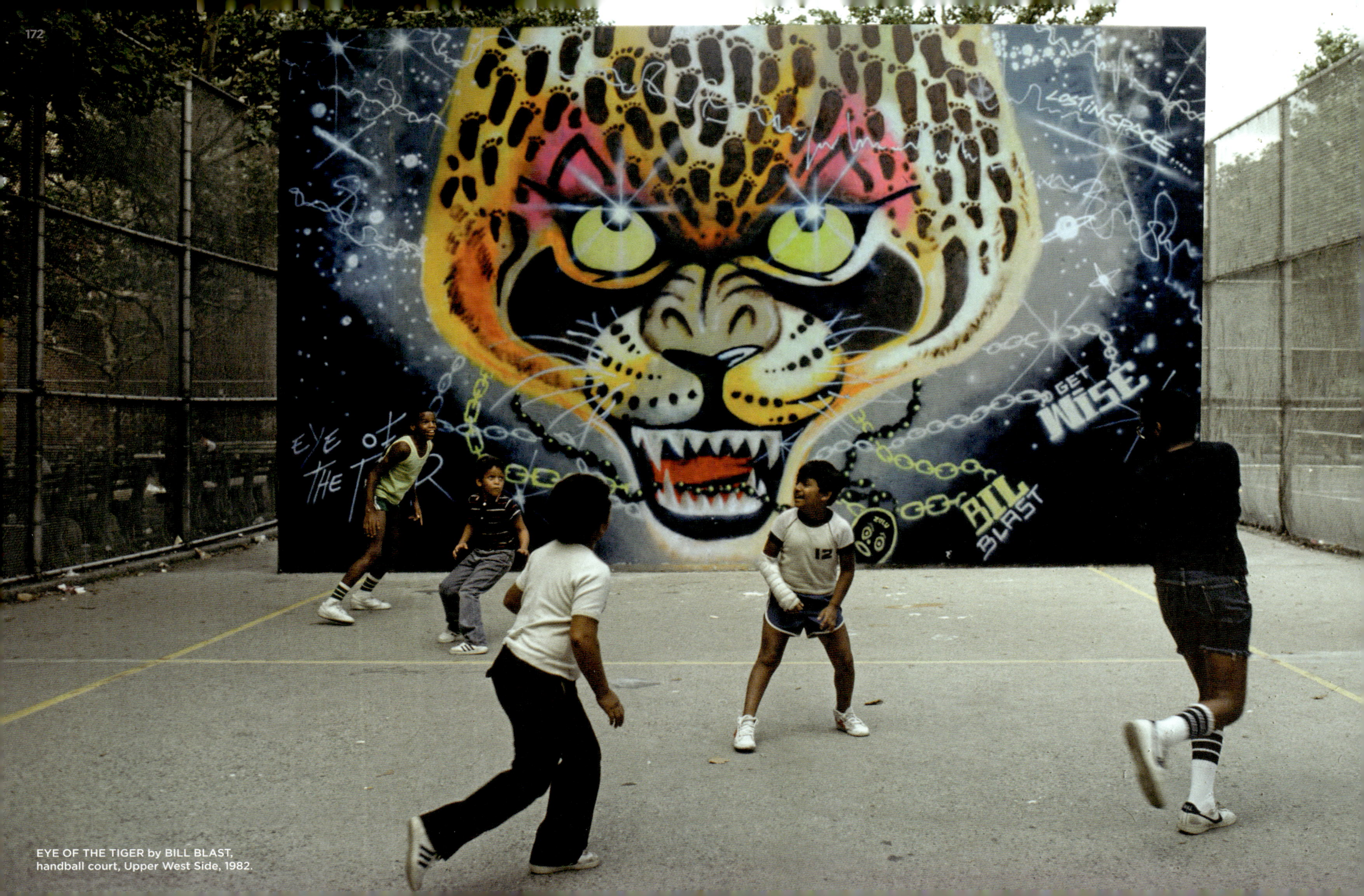

EYE OF THE TIGER by BILL BLAST,
handball court, Upper West Side, 1982.

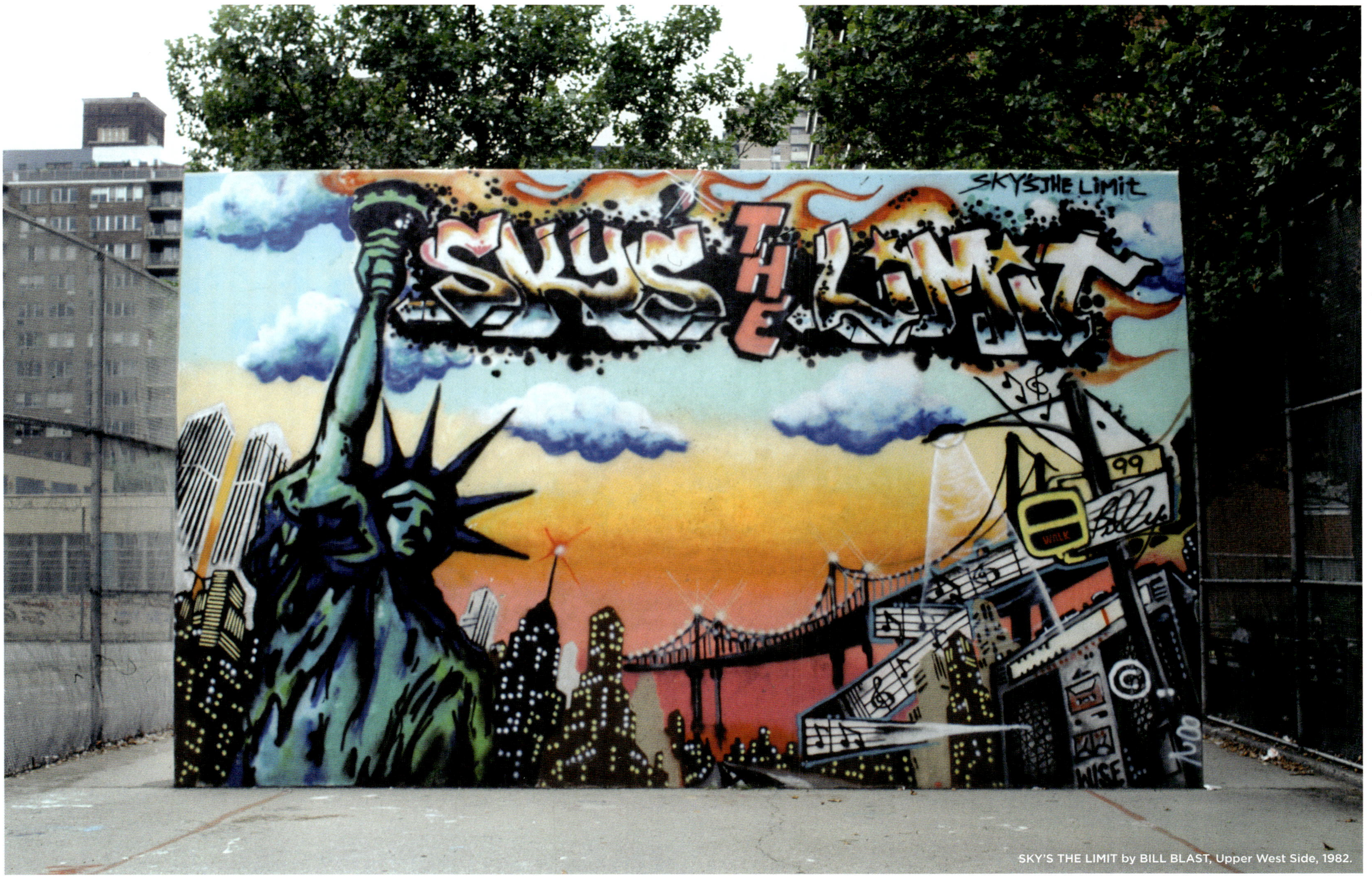

SKY'S THE LIMIT by BILL BLAST, Upper West Side, 1982.

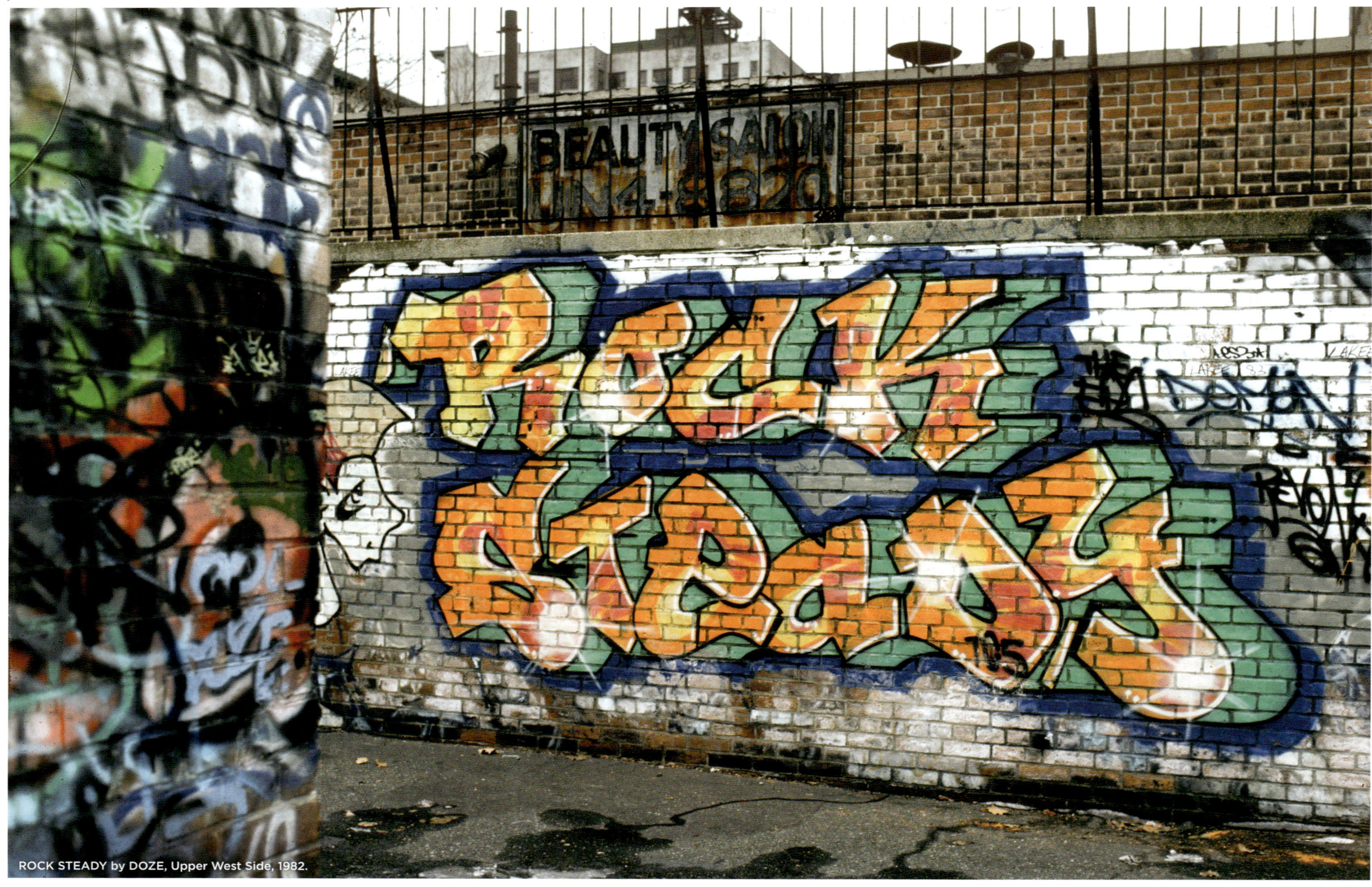

ROCK STEADY by DOZE, Upper West Side, 1982.

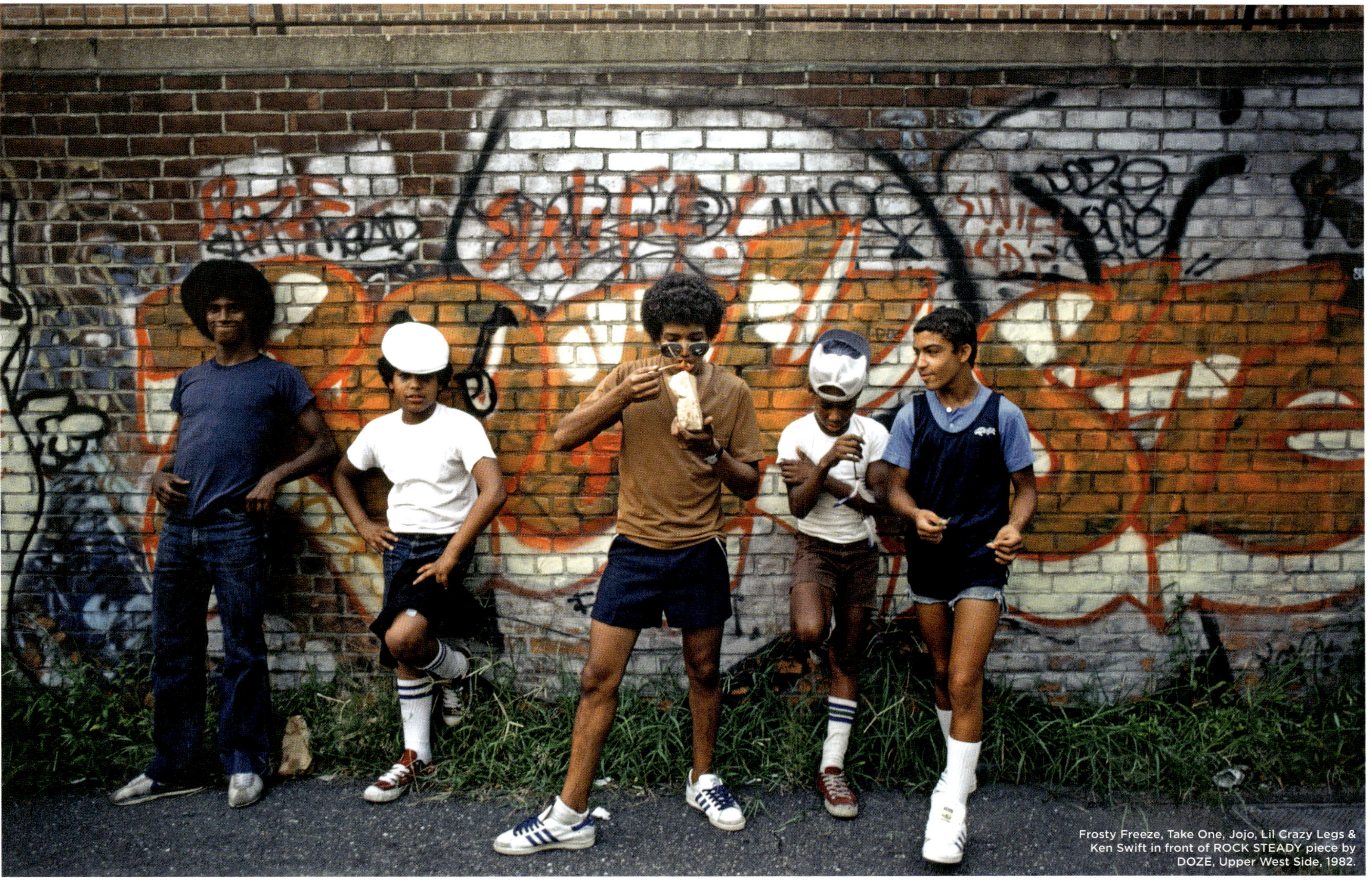

Frosty Freeze, Take One, Jojo, Lil Crazy Legs &
Ken Swift in front of ROCK STEADY piece by
DOZE, Upper West Side, 1982.

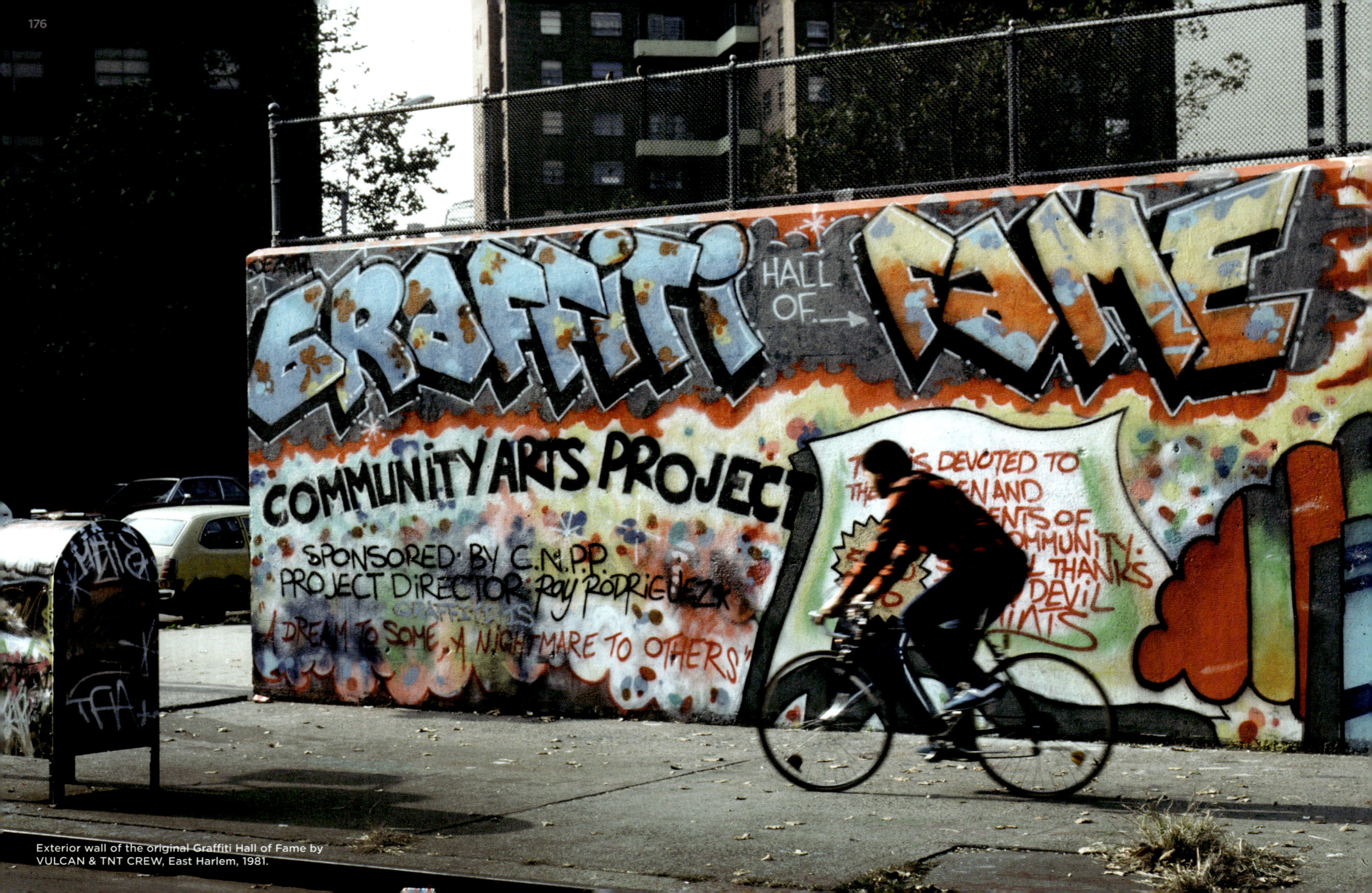

Exterior wall of the original Graffiti Hall of Fame by
VULCAN & TNT CREW, East Harlem, 1981.

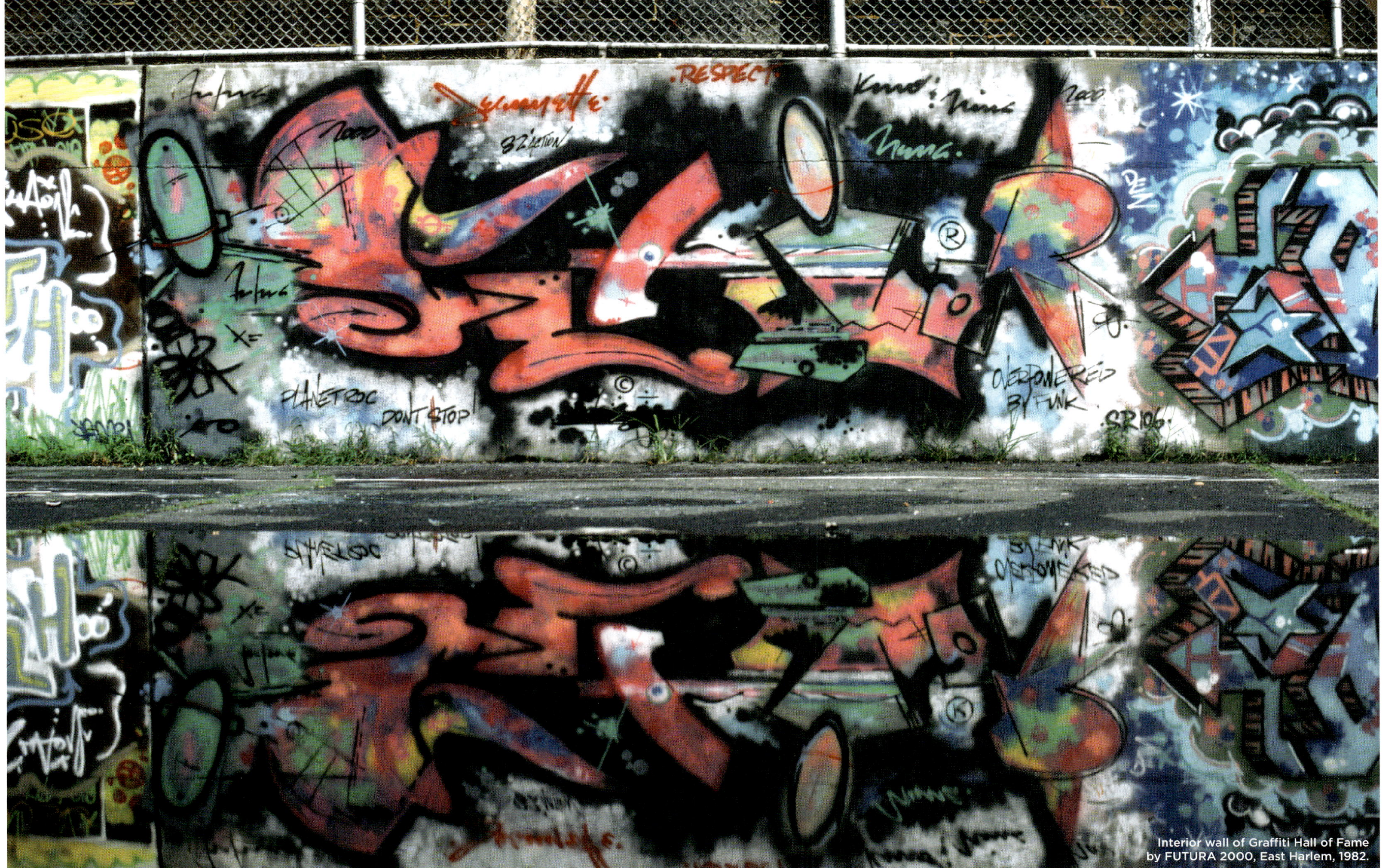

Interior wall of Graffiti Hall of Fame by FUTURA 2000, East Harlem, 1982.

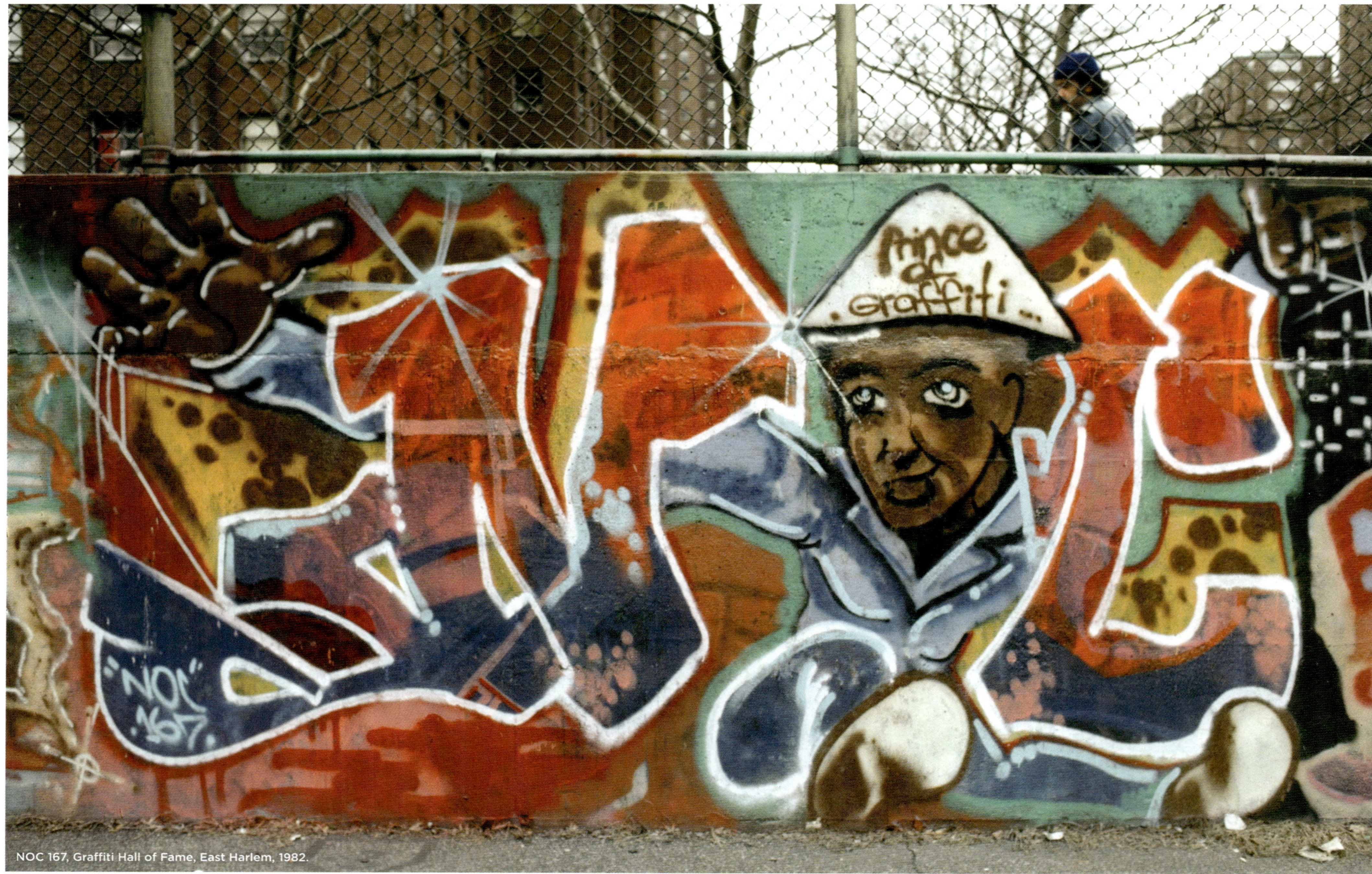

NOC 167, Graffiti Hall of Fame, East Harlem, 1982.

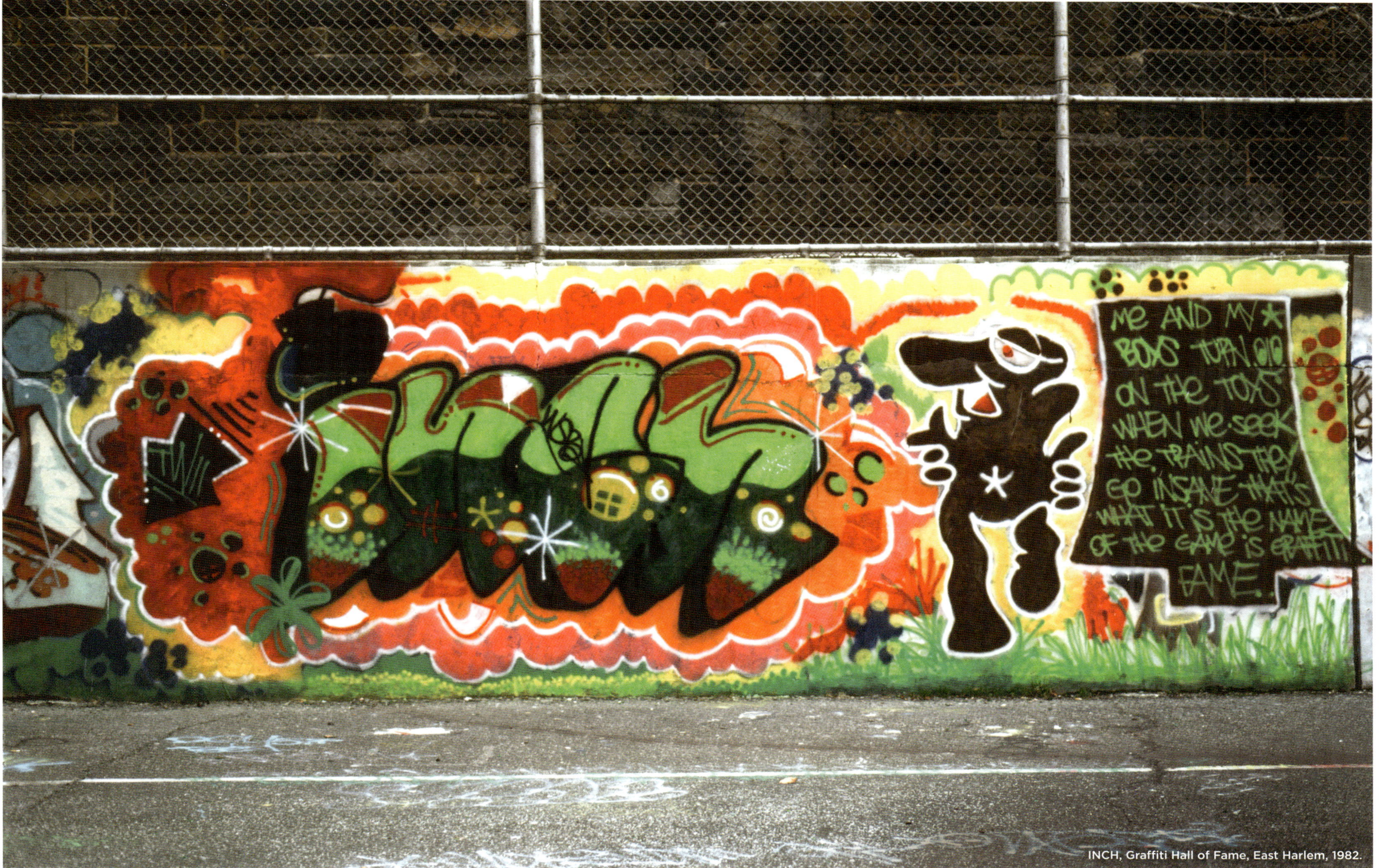

INCH, Graffiti Hall of Fame, East Harlem, 1982.

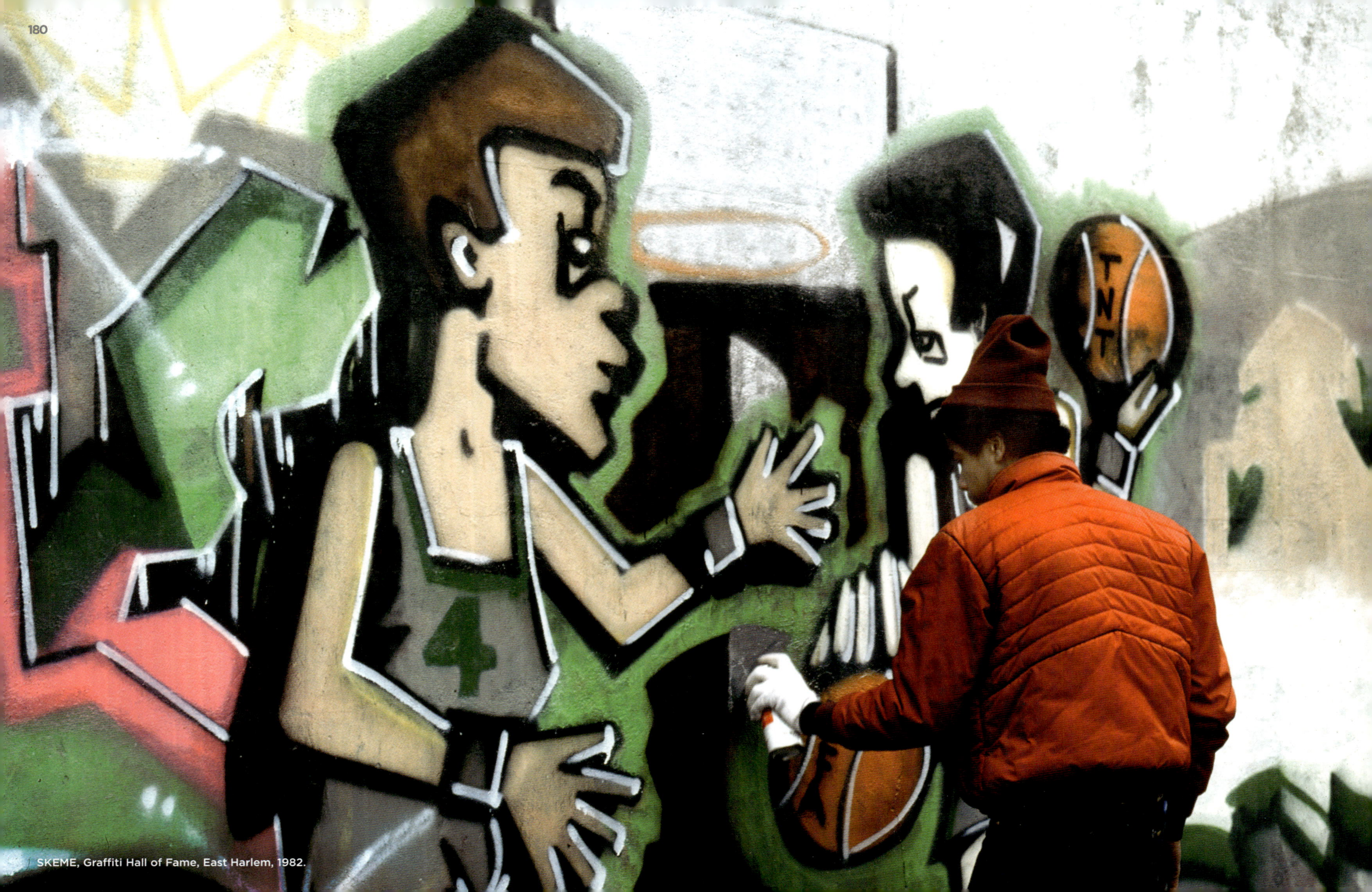

SKEME, Graffiti Hall of Fame, East Harlem, 1982.

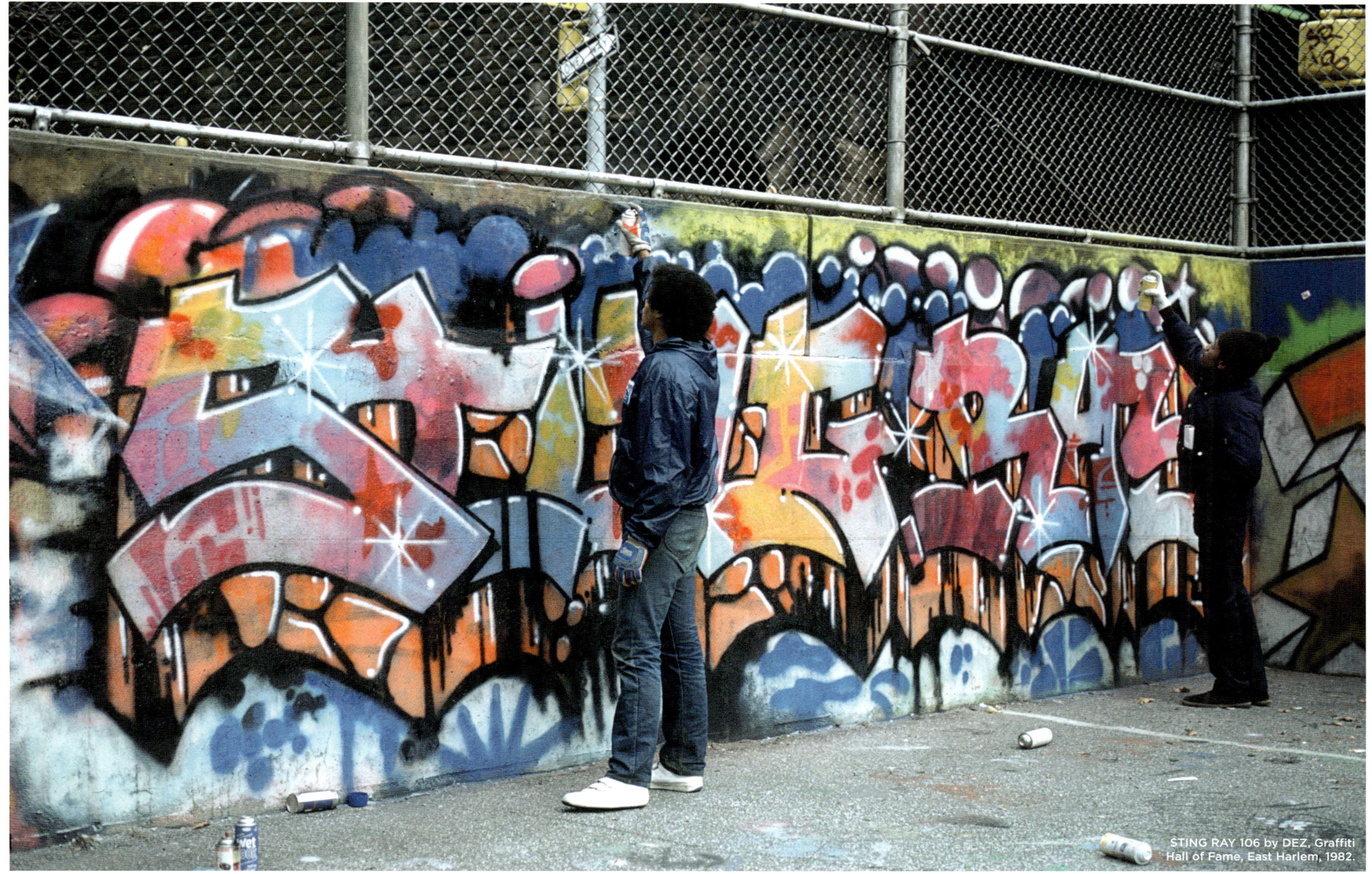

STING RAY 106 by DEZ, Graffiti Hall of Fame, East Harlem, 1982.

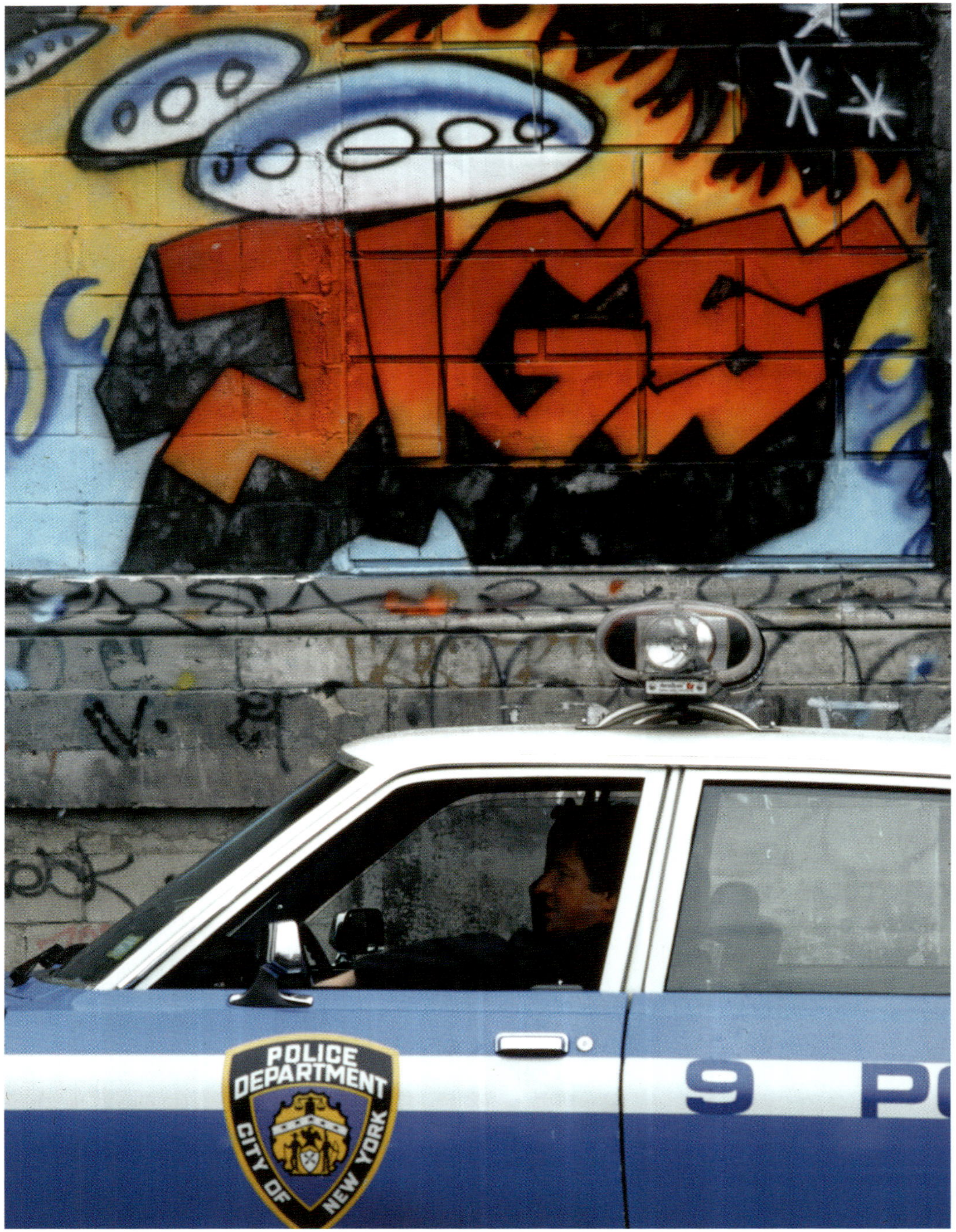
POLICE DEPARTMENT
CITY OF NEW YORK
9

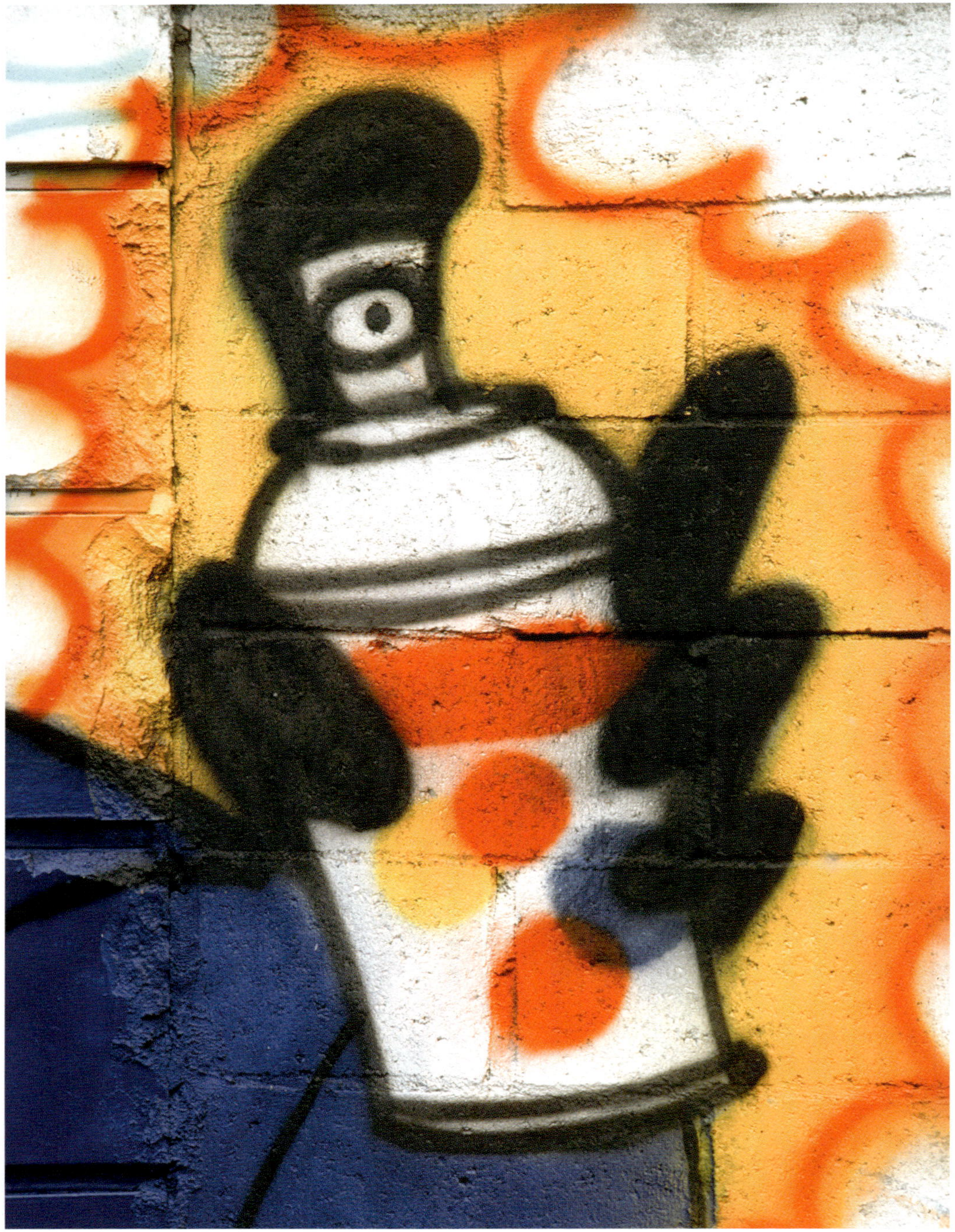

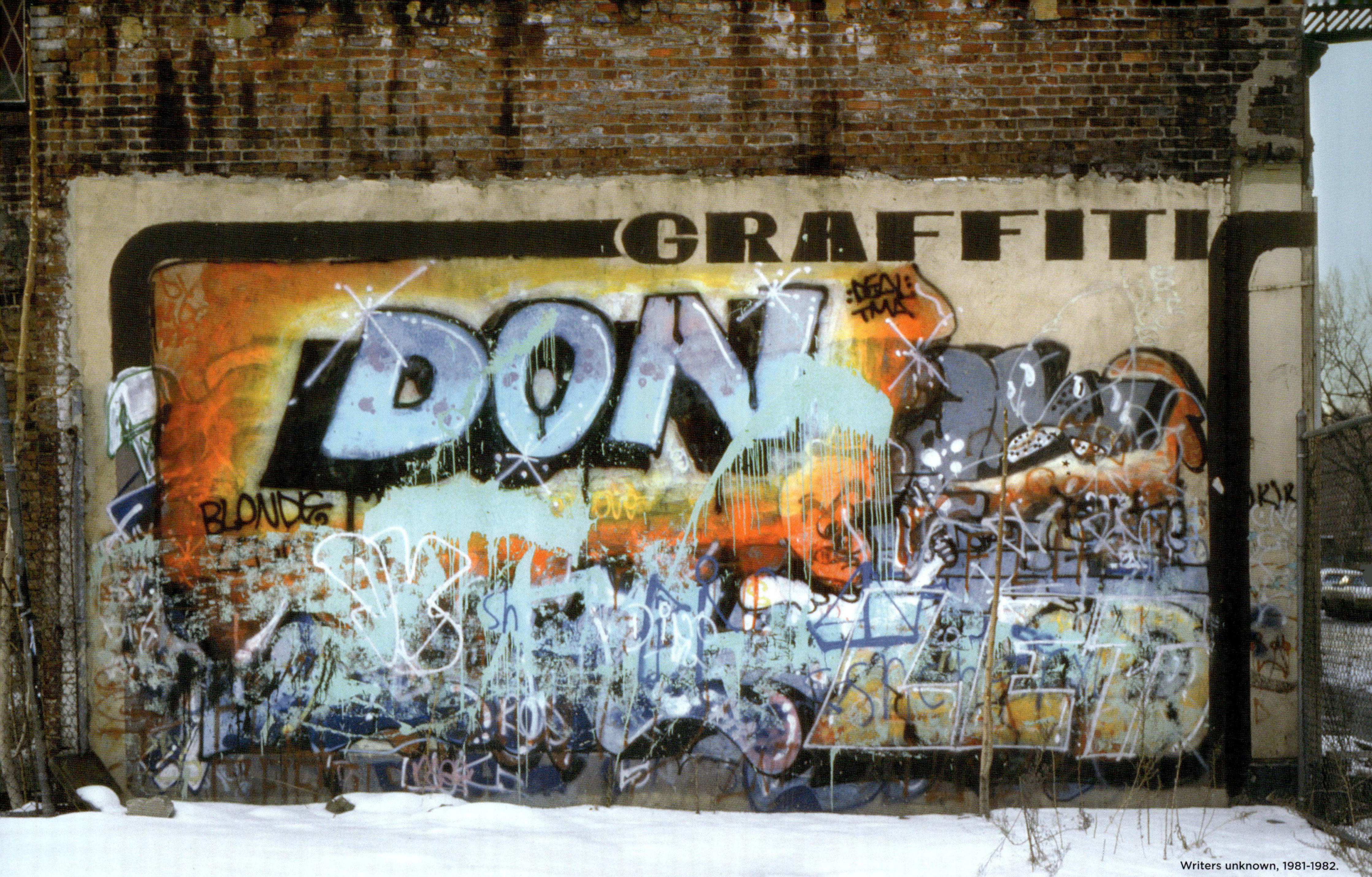

Writers unknown, 1981-1982.

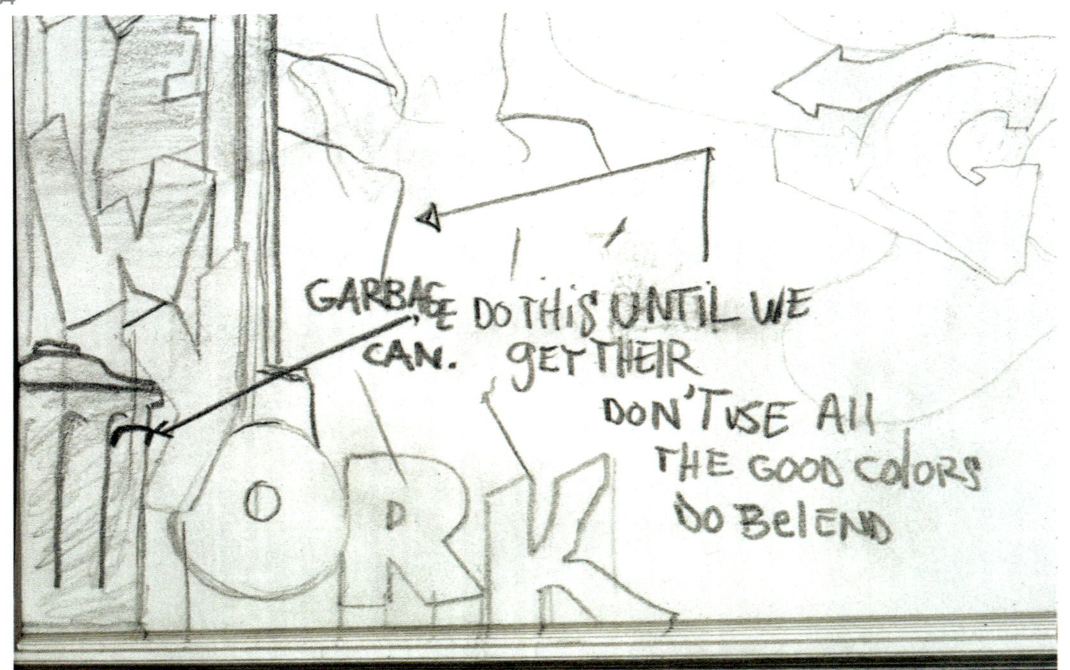
GARBAGE DO THIS UNTIL WE
CAN. GET THEIR
DON'T USE ALL
THE GOOD COLORS
DO BELEND
ORK

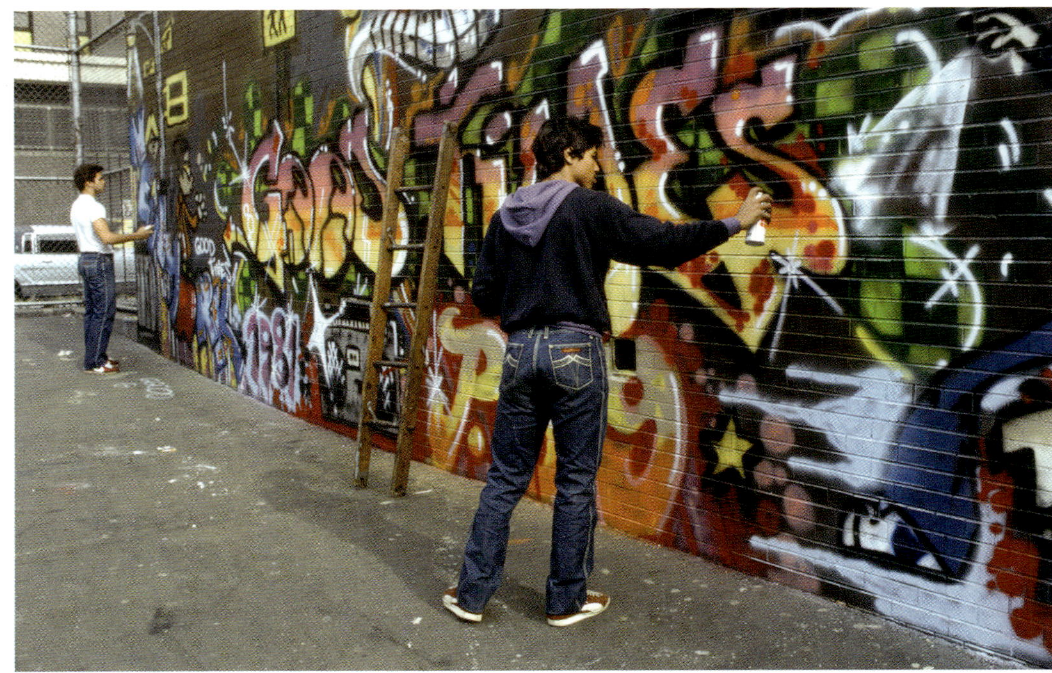

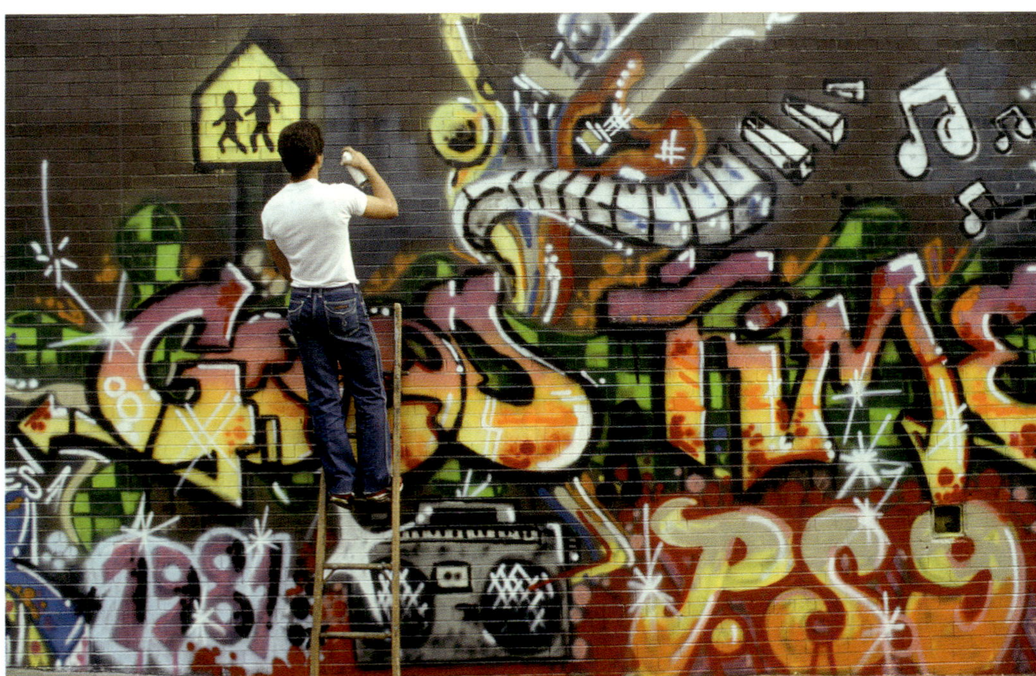

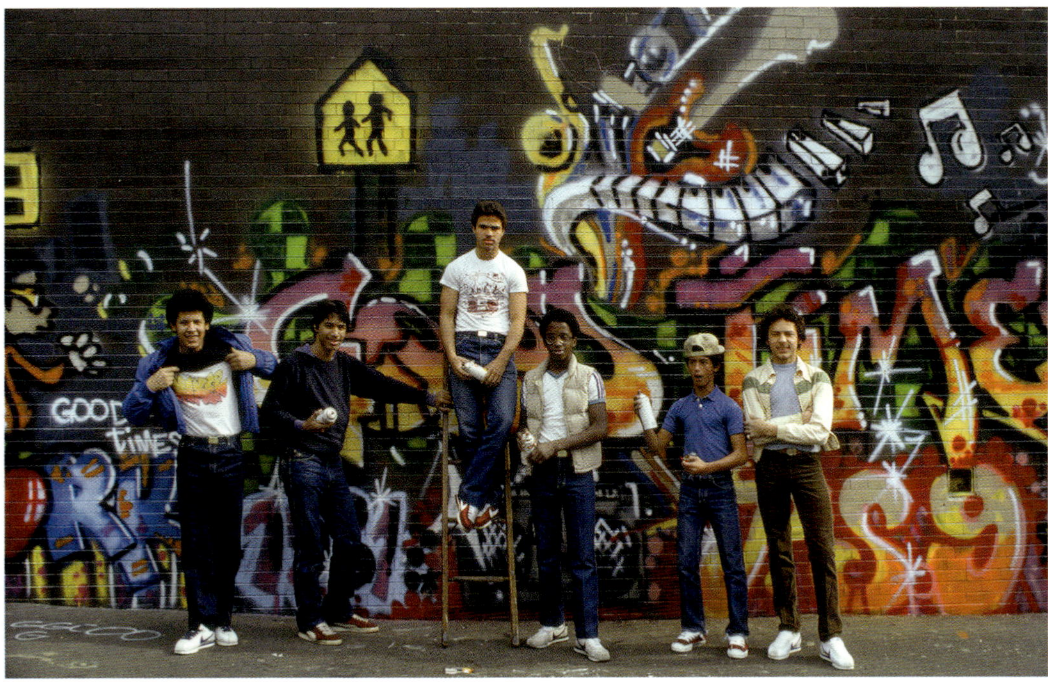

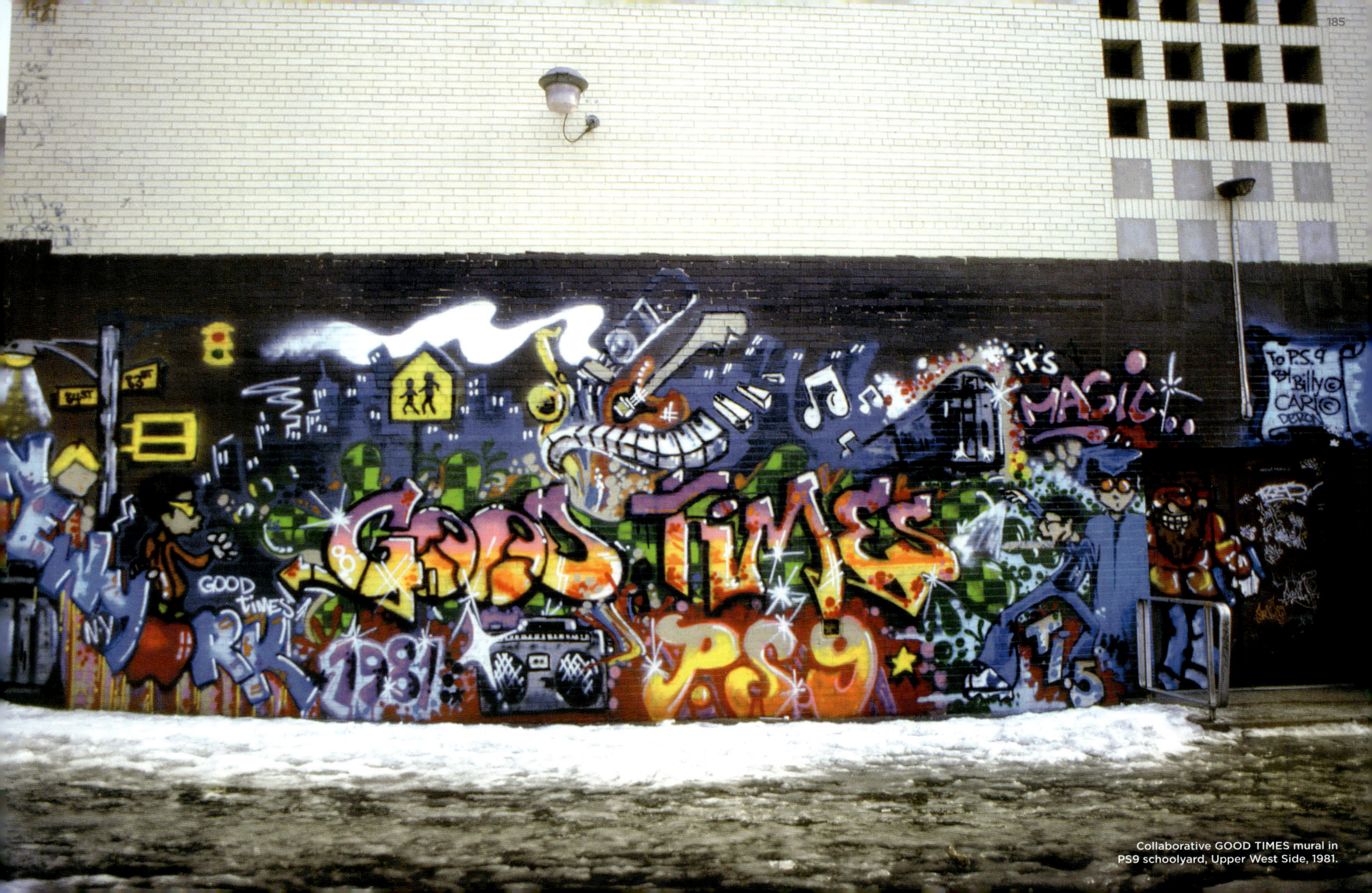

Collaborative GOOD TIMES mural in
PS9 schoolyard, Upper West Side, 1981.

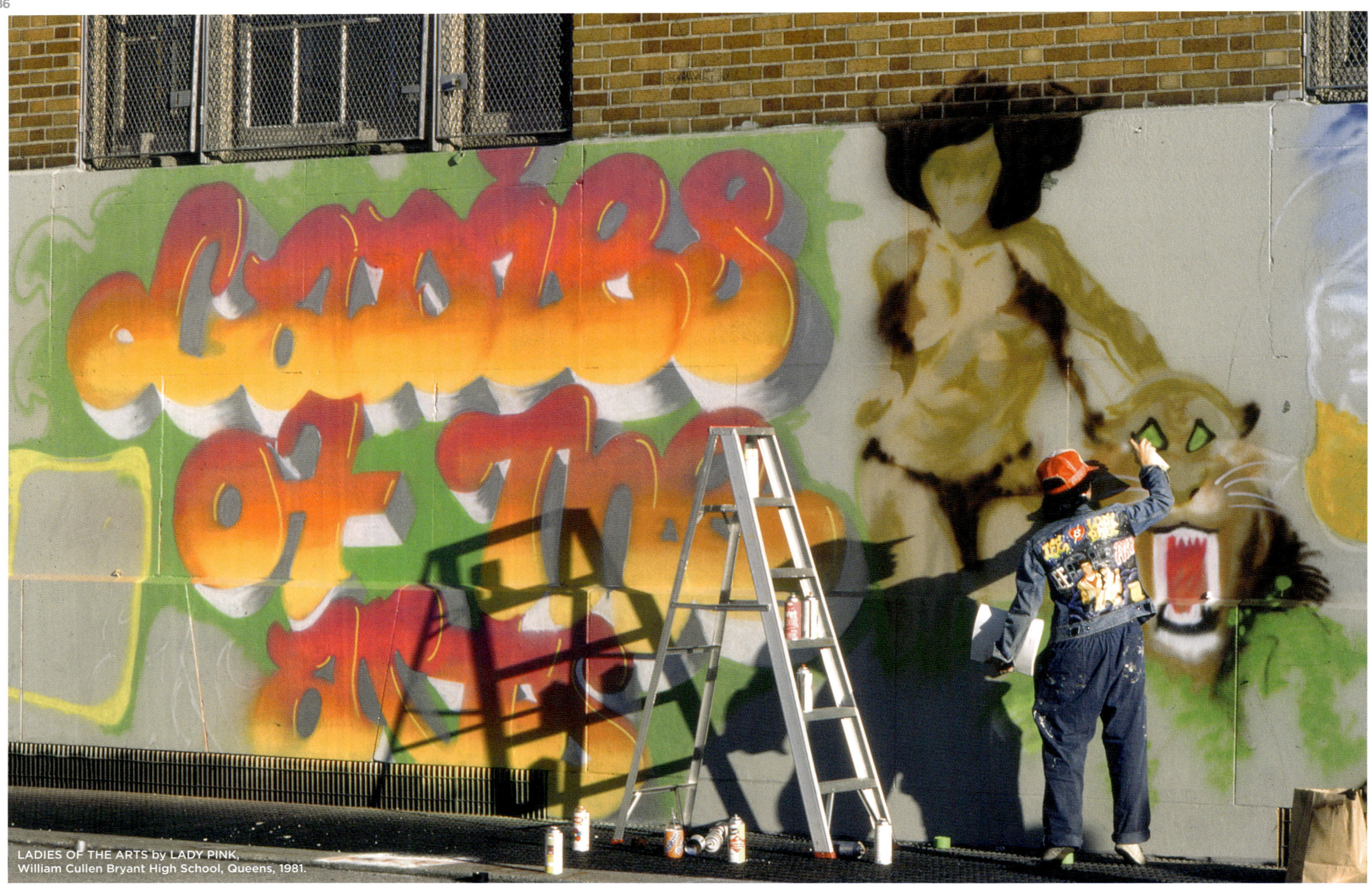

LADIES OF THE ARTS by LADY PINK,
William Cullen Bryant High School, Queens, 1981.

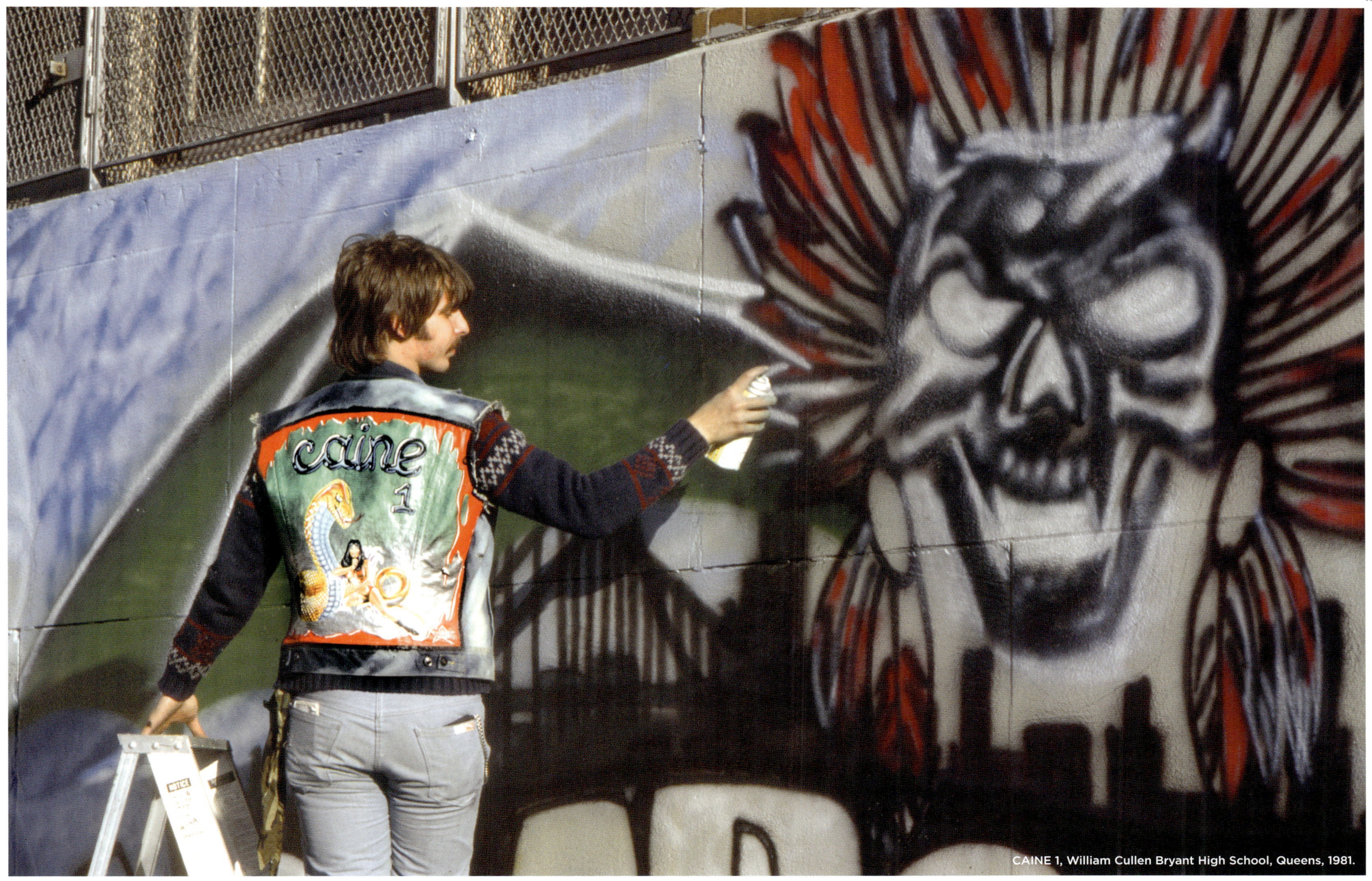

CAINE 1, William Cullen Bryant High School, Queens, 1981.

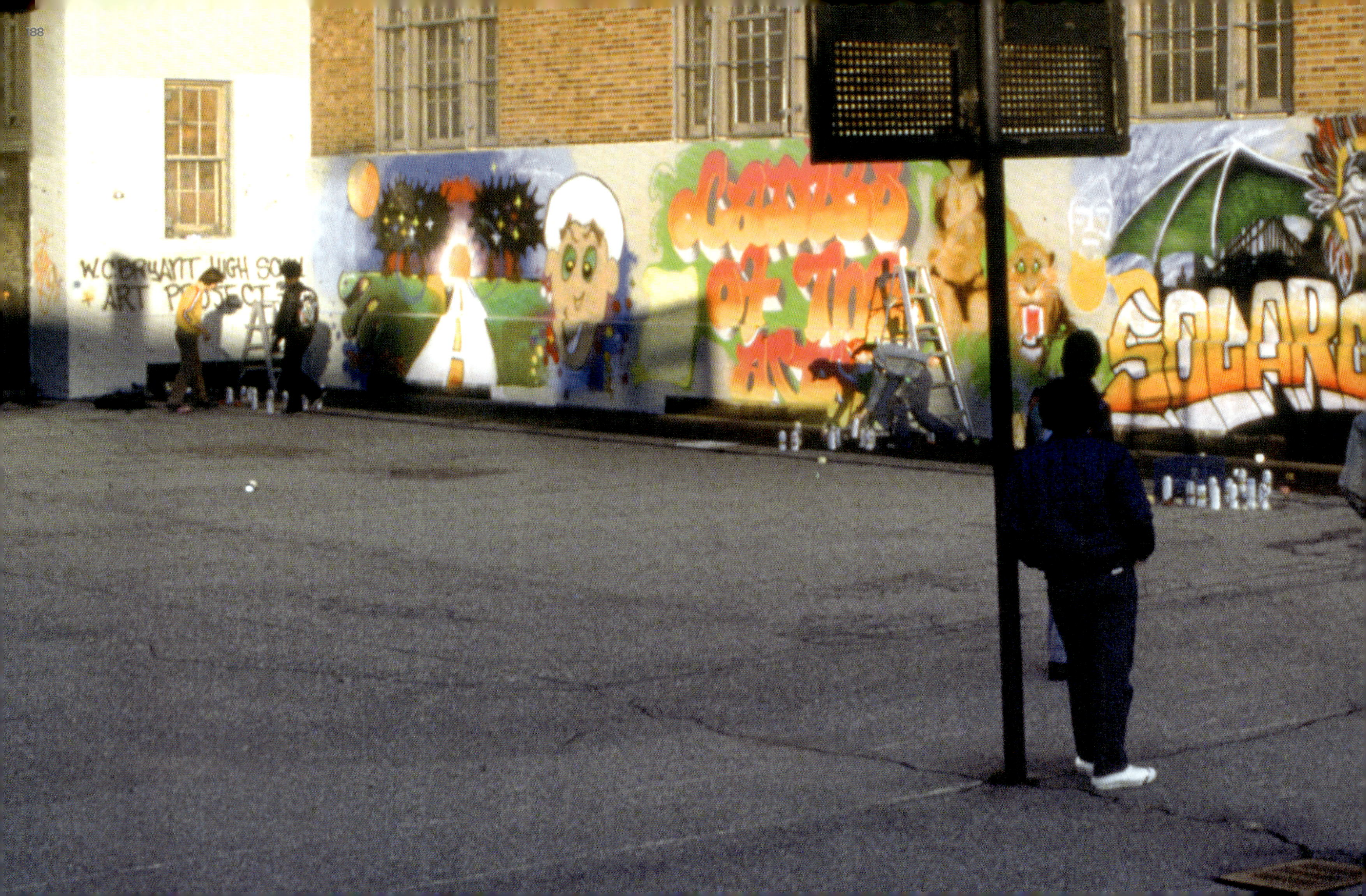

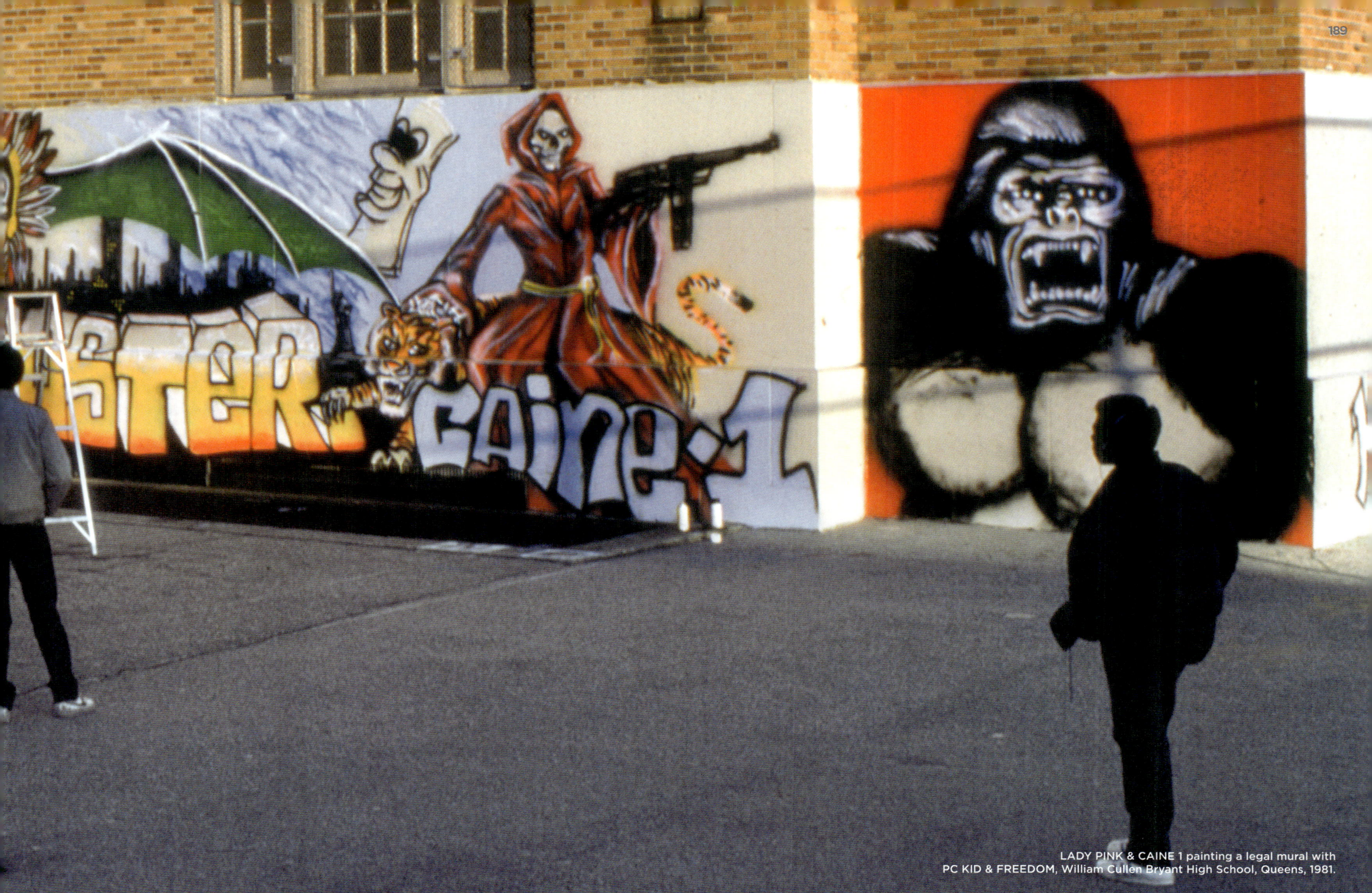

LADY PINK & CAINE 1 painting a legal mural with
PC KID & FREEDOM, William Cullen Bryant High School, Queens, 1981.

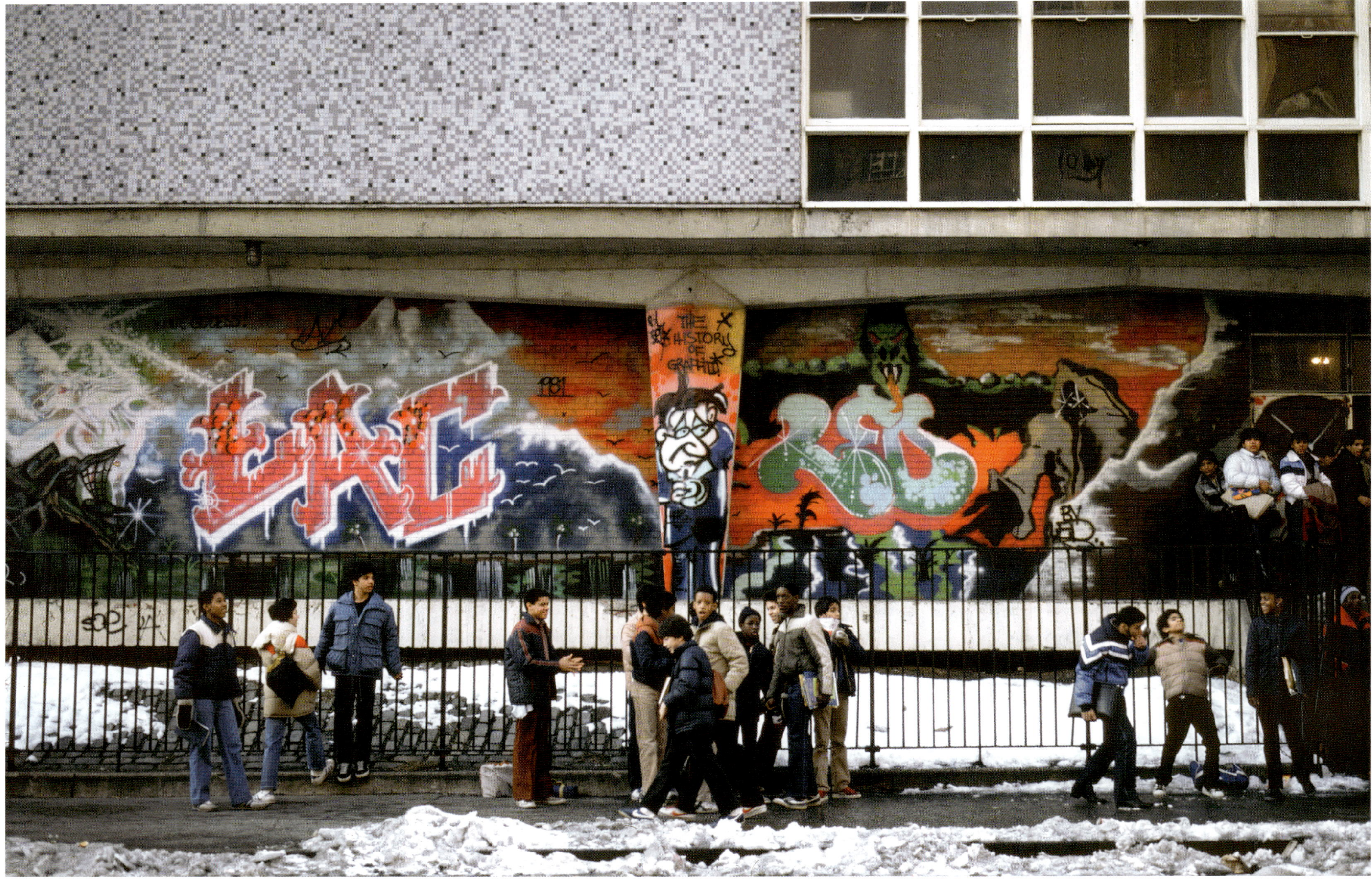

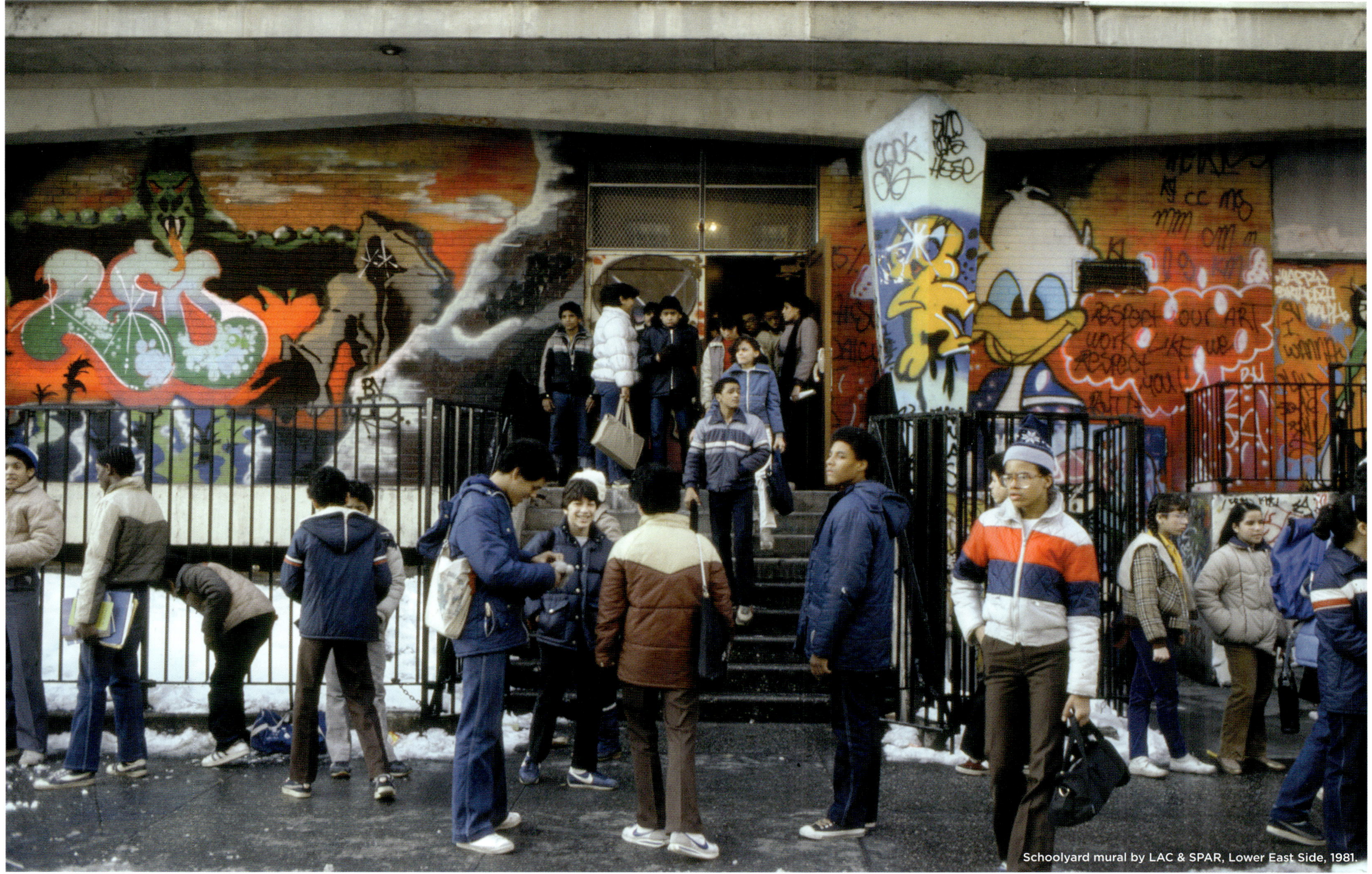

Schoolyard mural by LAC & SPAR, Lower East Side, 1981.

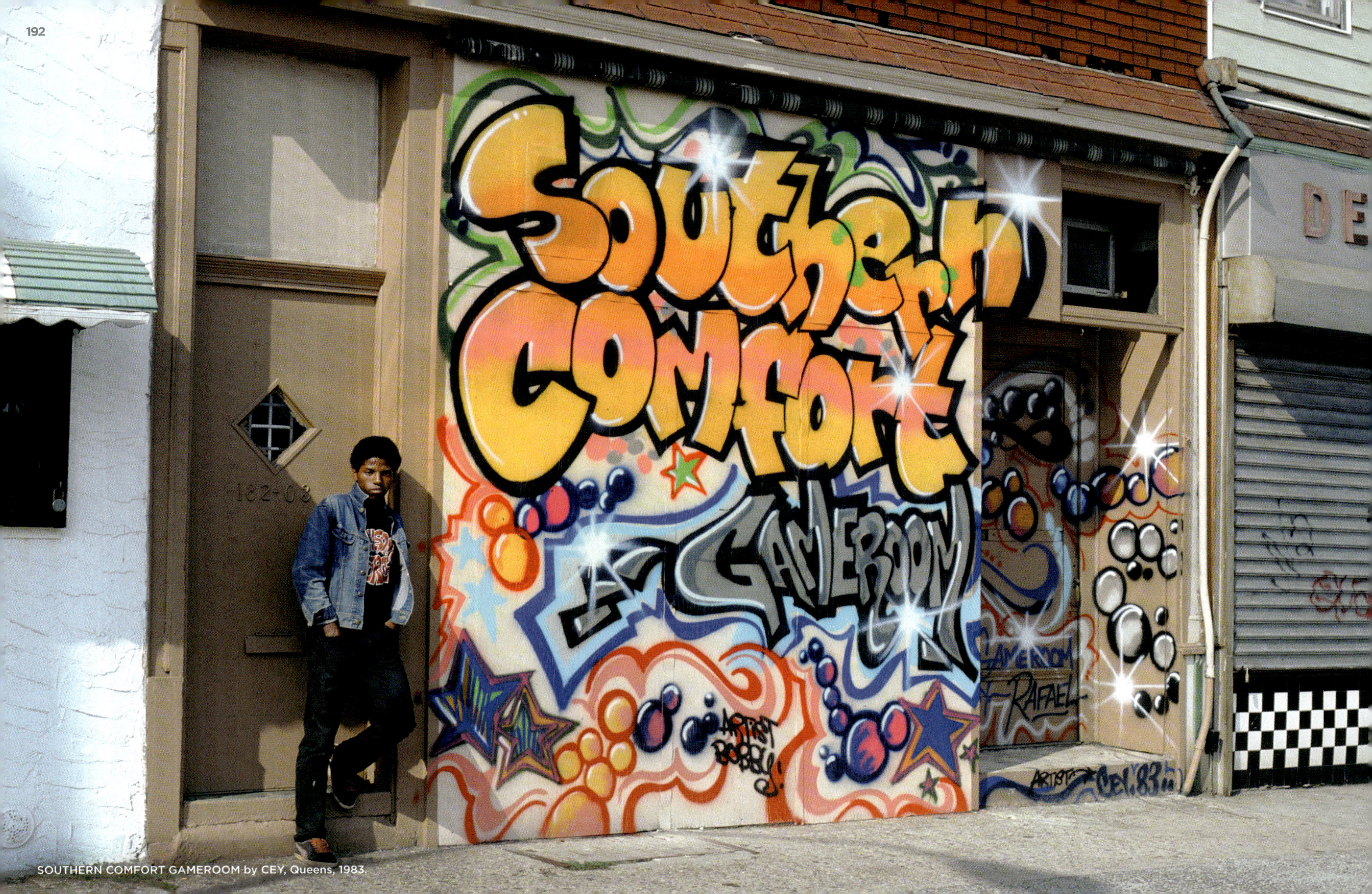

SOUTHERN COMFORT GAMEROOM by CEY, Queens, 1983.

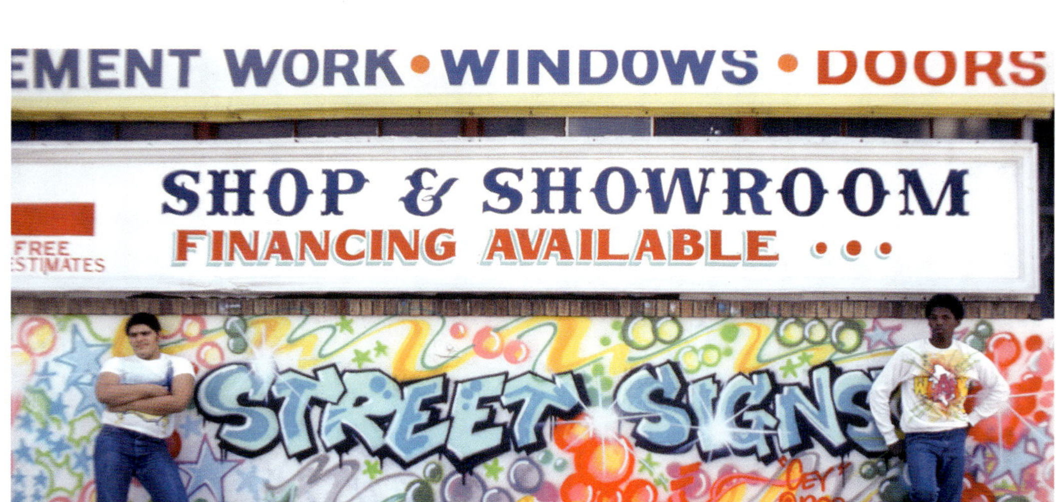

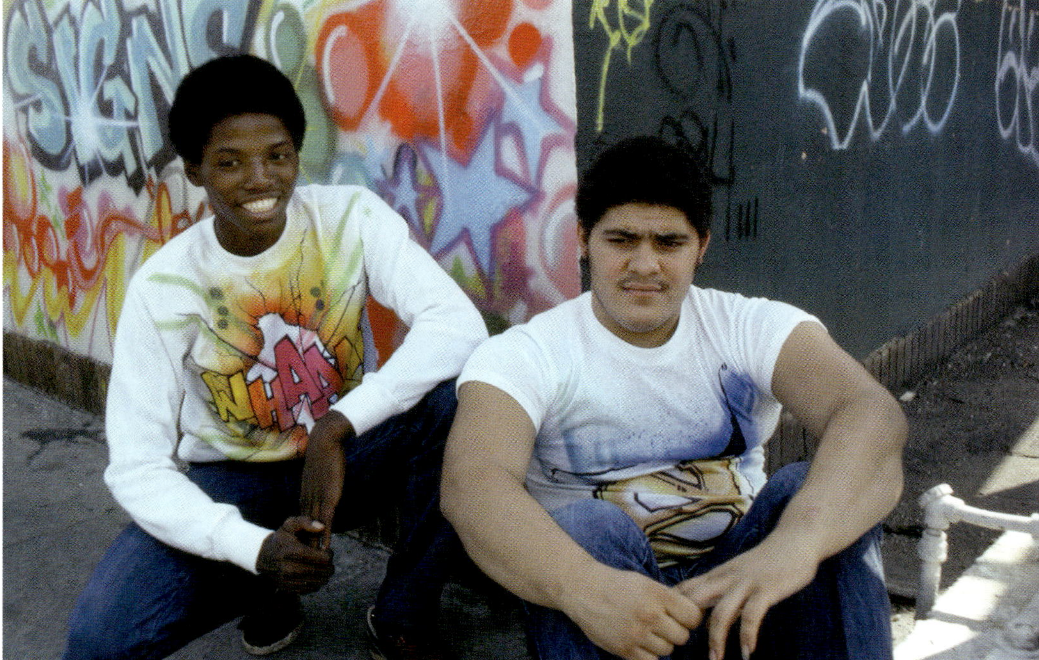

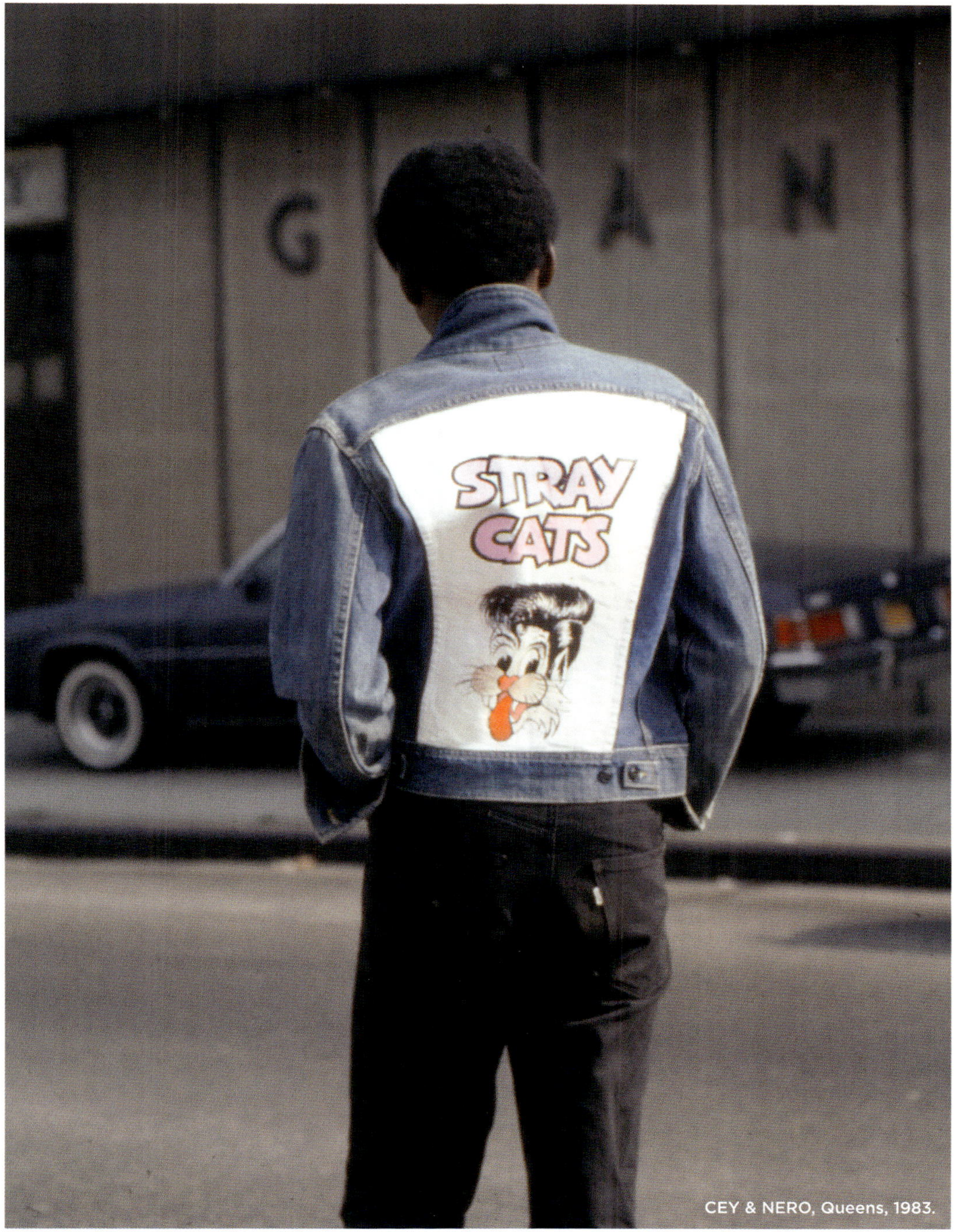

CEY & NERO, Queens, 1983.

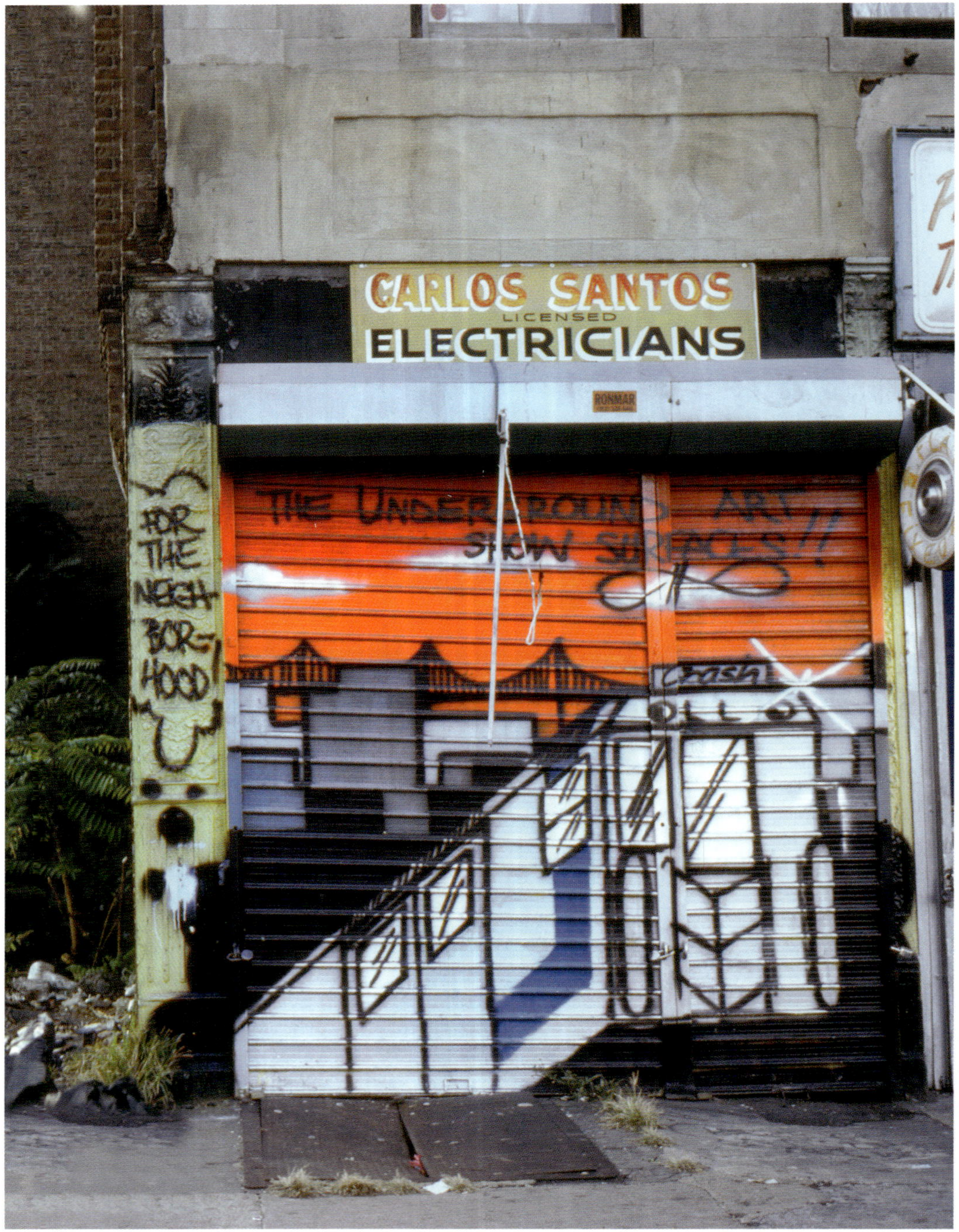

CARLOS SANTOS
LICENSED
ELECTRICIANS
RONMAR
THE UNDERGROUND ART
SHOW SUCCESS!!
FOR THE NEIGH BOR HOOD
Crash

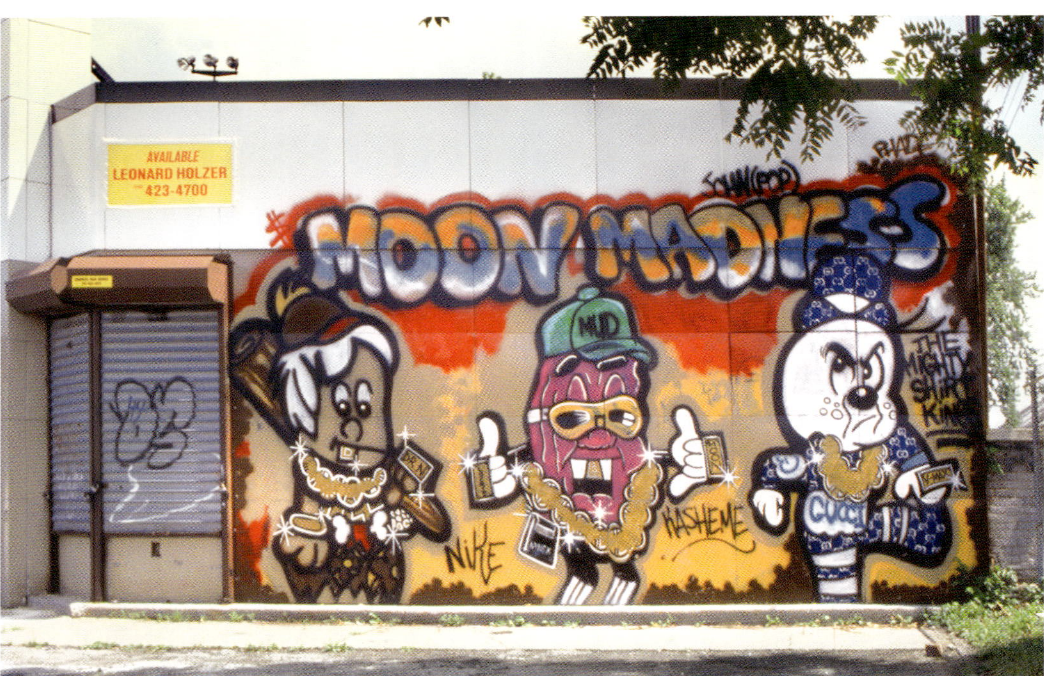

AVAILABLE
LEONARD HOLZER
423-4700
MOON MADNESS
MUD
NIKE
RASHEME
GUCCI

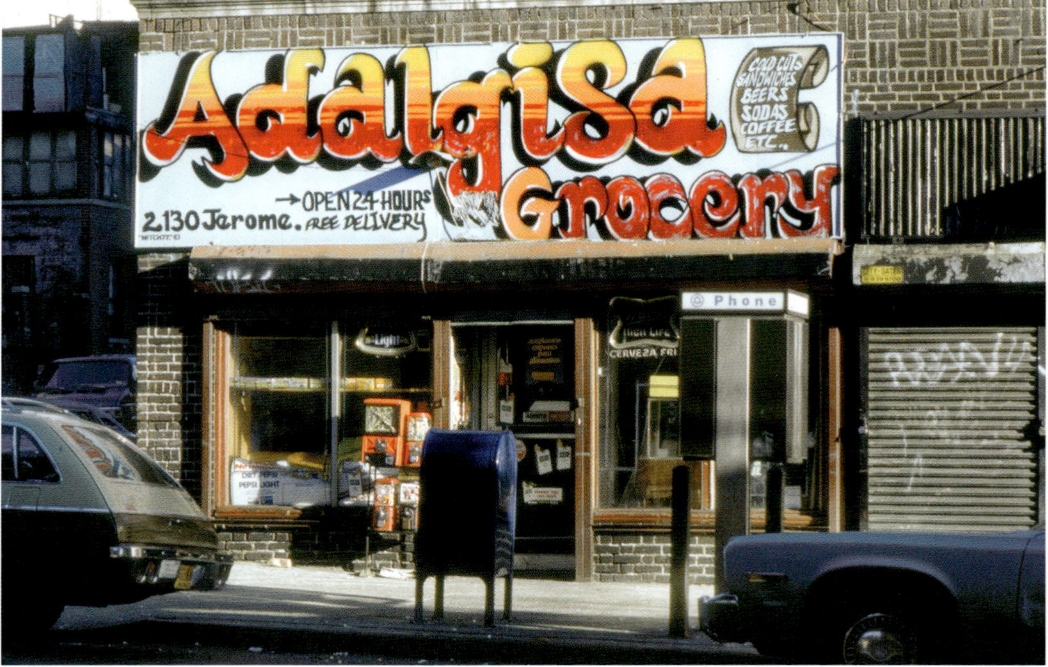

Adalgisa
Grocery
COLD CUTS
SANDWICHES
BEERS
SODAS
COFFEE
ETC.
2130 Jerome.
OPEN 24 HOURS
FREE DELIVERY
Phone

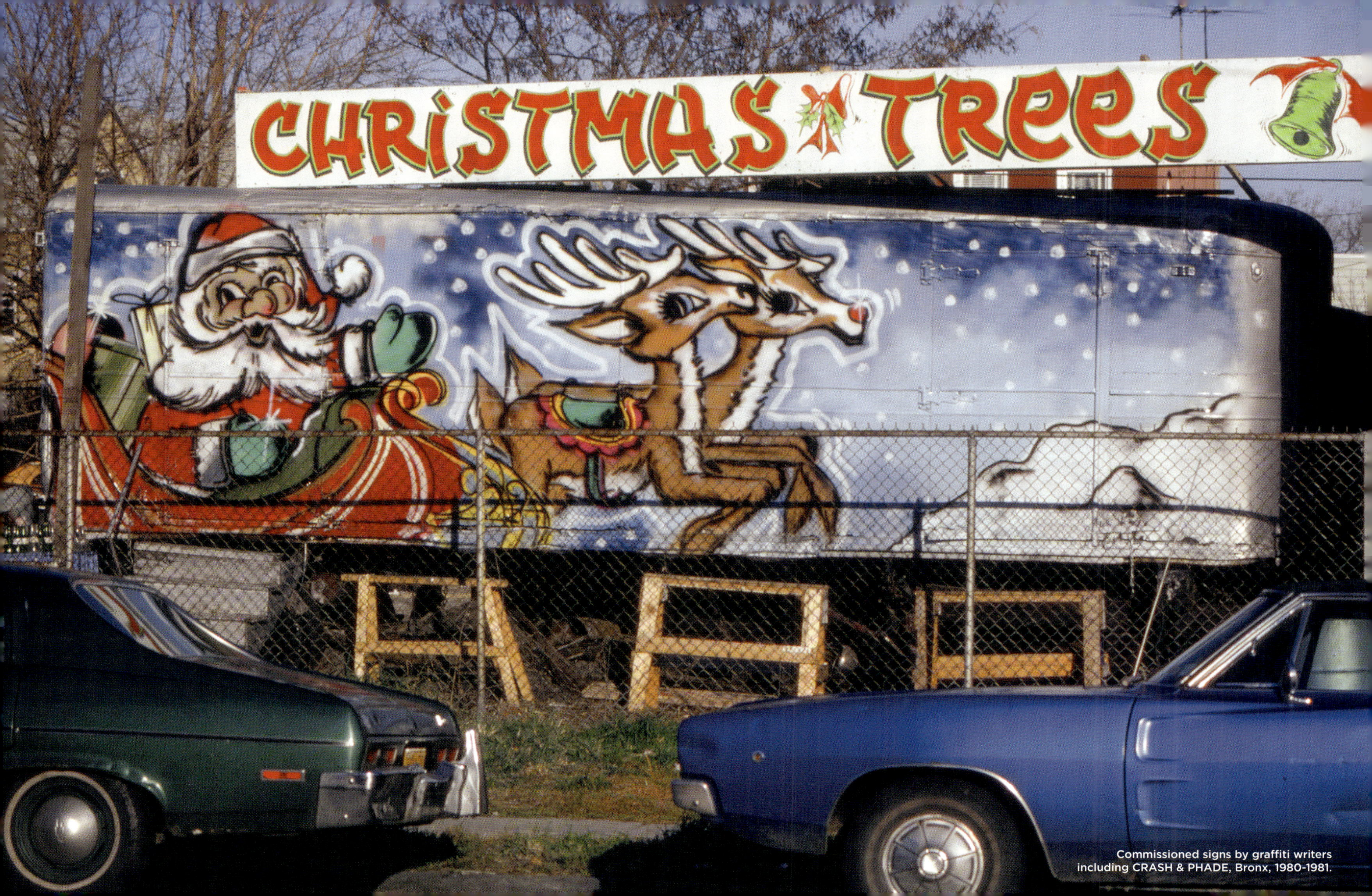

Commissioned signs by graffiti writers including CRASH & PHADE, Bronx, 1980-1981.

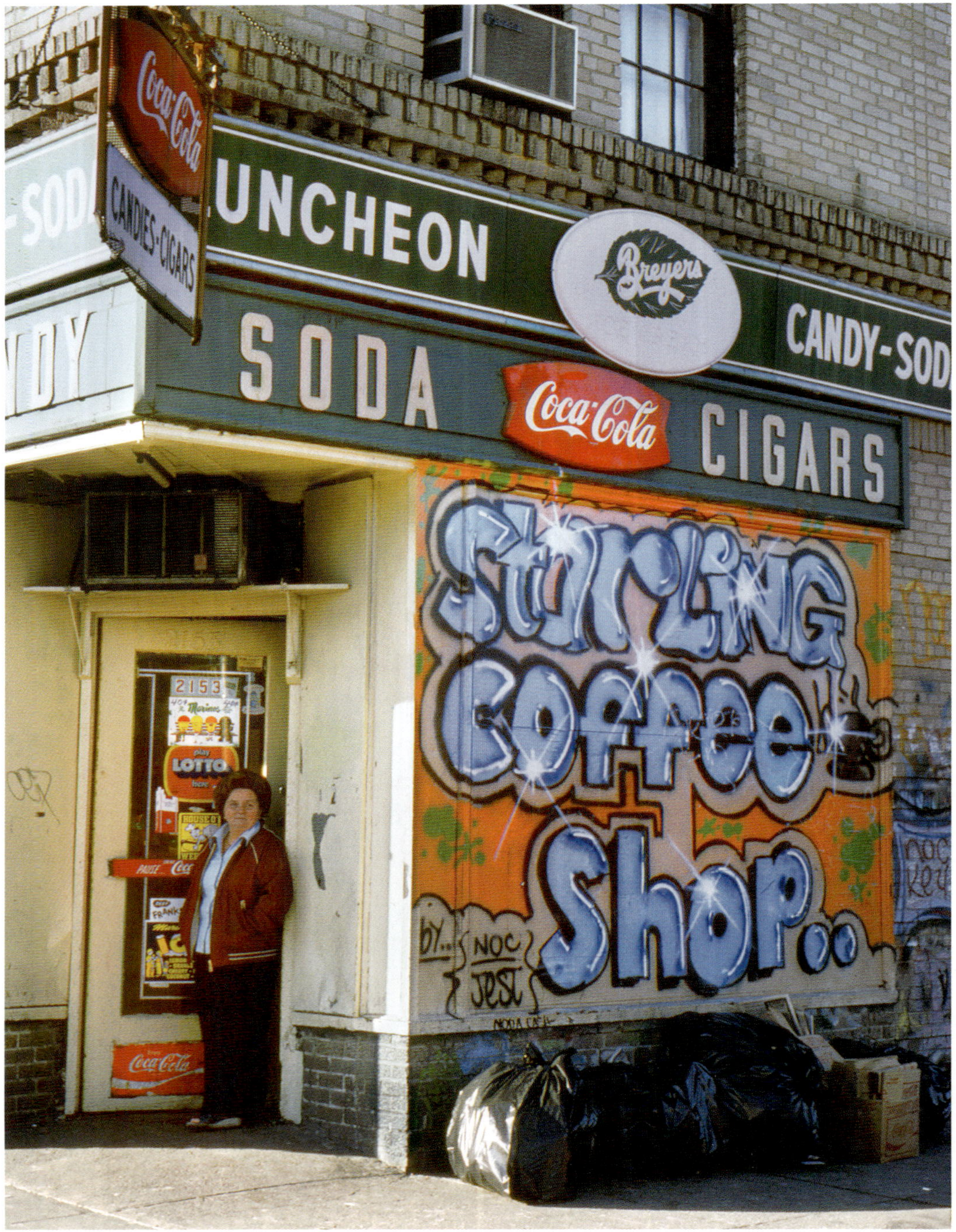

Coca-Cola
CANDIES-CIGARS
UNCHEON
Breyers
CANDY-SODA
SODA
Coca-Cola
CIGARS
2153
LOTTO
Starling Coffee Shop..
BY.. NOC JEST
Coca-Cola

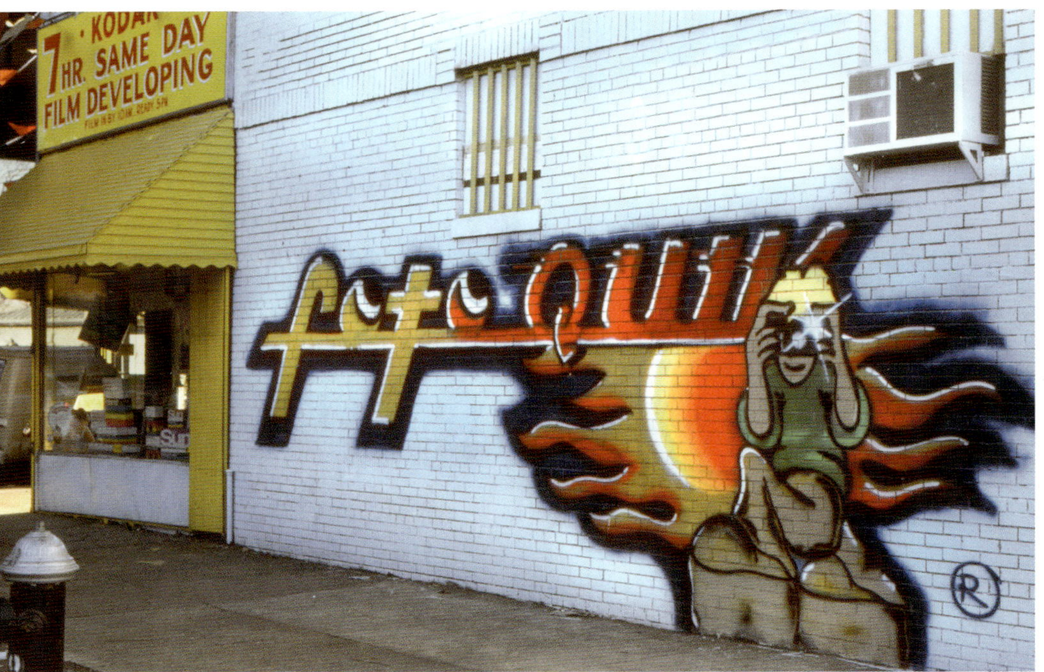
7 HR. SAME DAY FILM DEVELOPING
KODAK
foto Quik

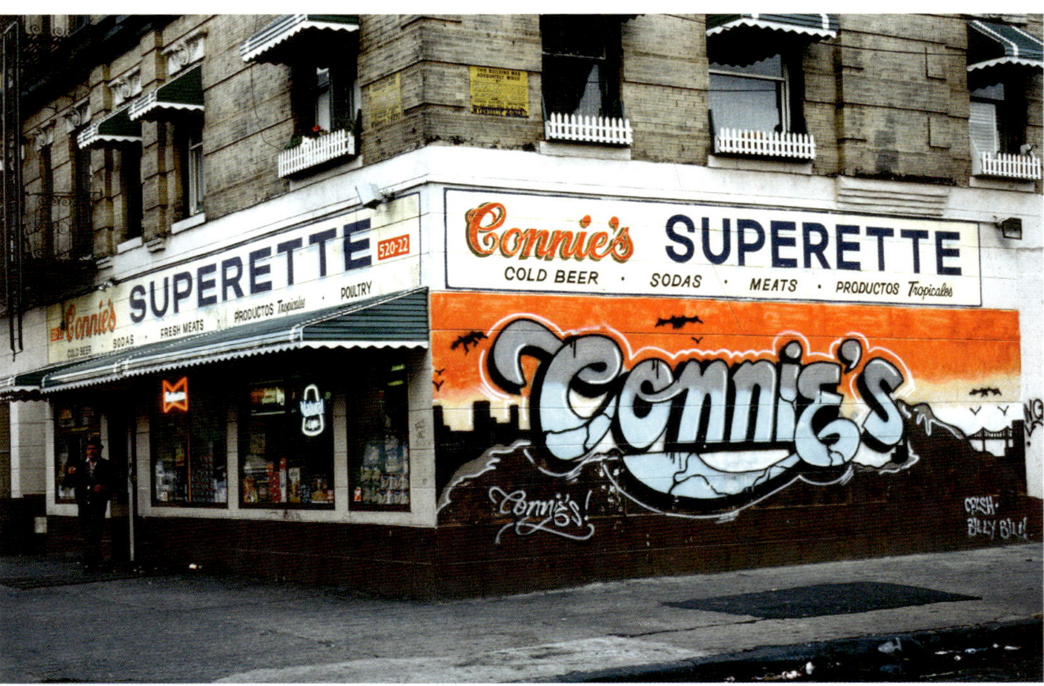
Connie's SUPERETTE
COLD BEER · SODAS · MEATS · PRODUCTOS Tropicales
SUPERETTE
Connie's
COLD BEER · SODAS · FRESH MEATS · PRODUCTOS Tropicales · POULTRY
520-22
Connie's
CE5H
BILLY BILL

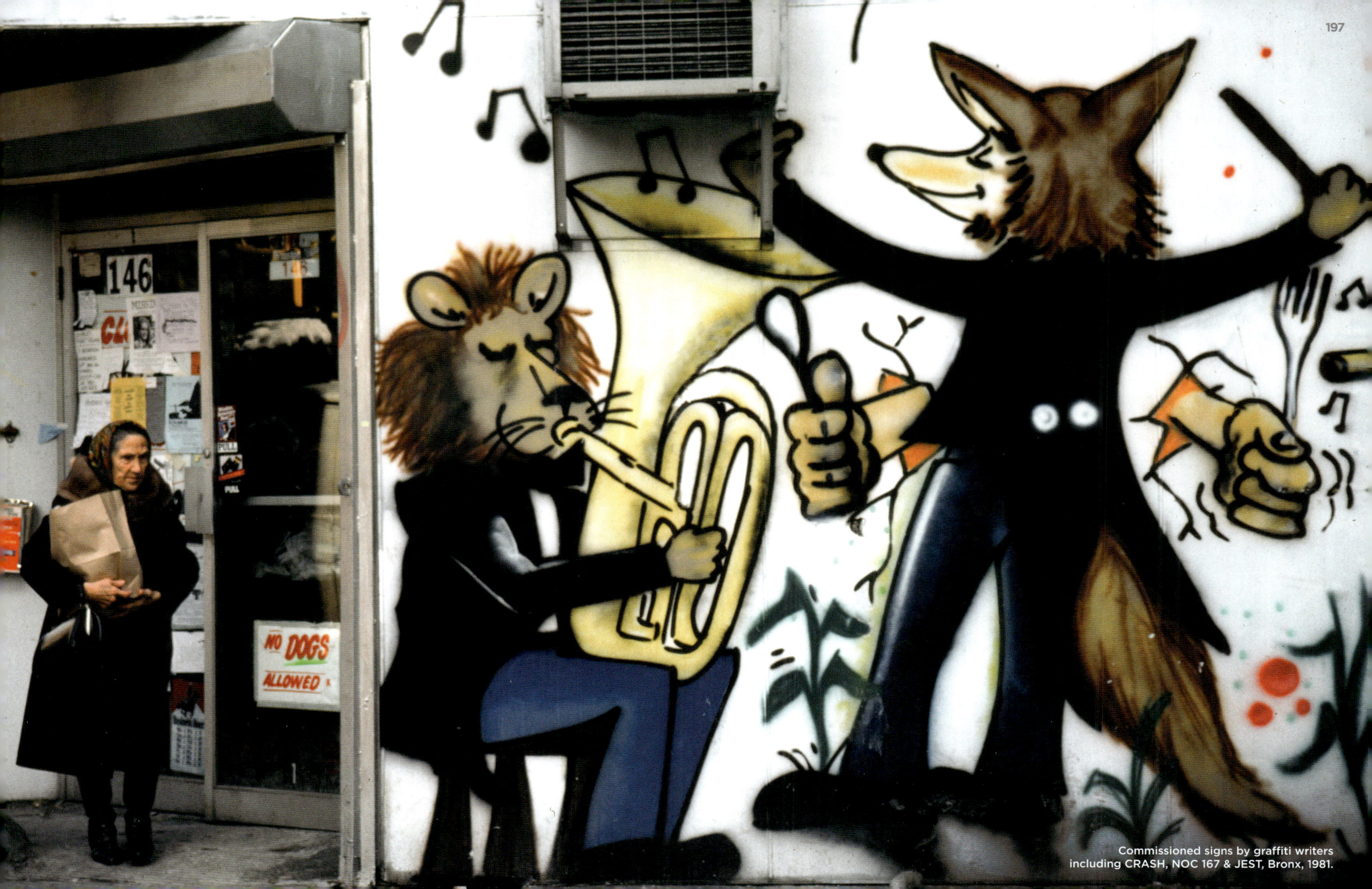

Commissioned signs by graffiti writers including CRASH, NOC 167 & JEST, Bronx, 1981.

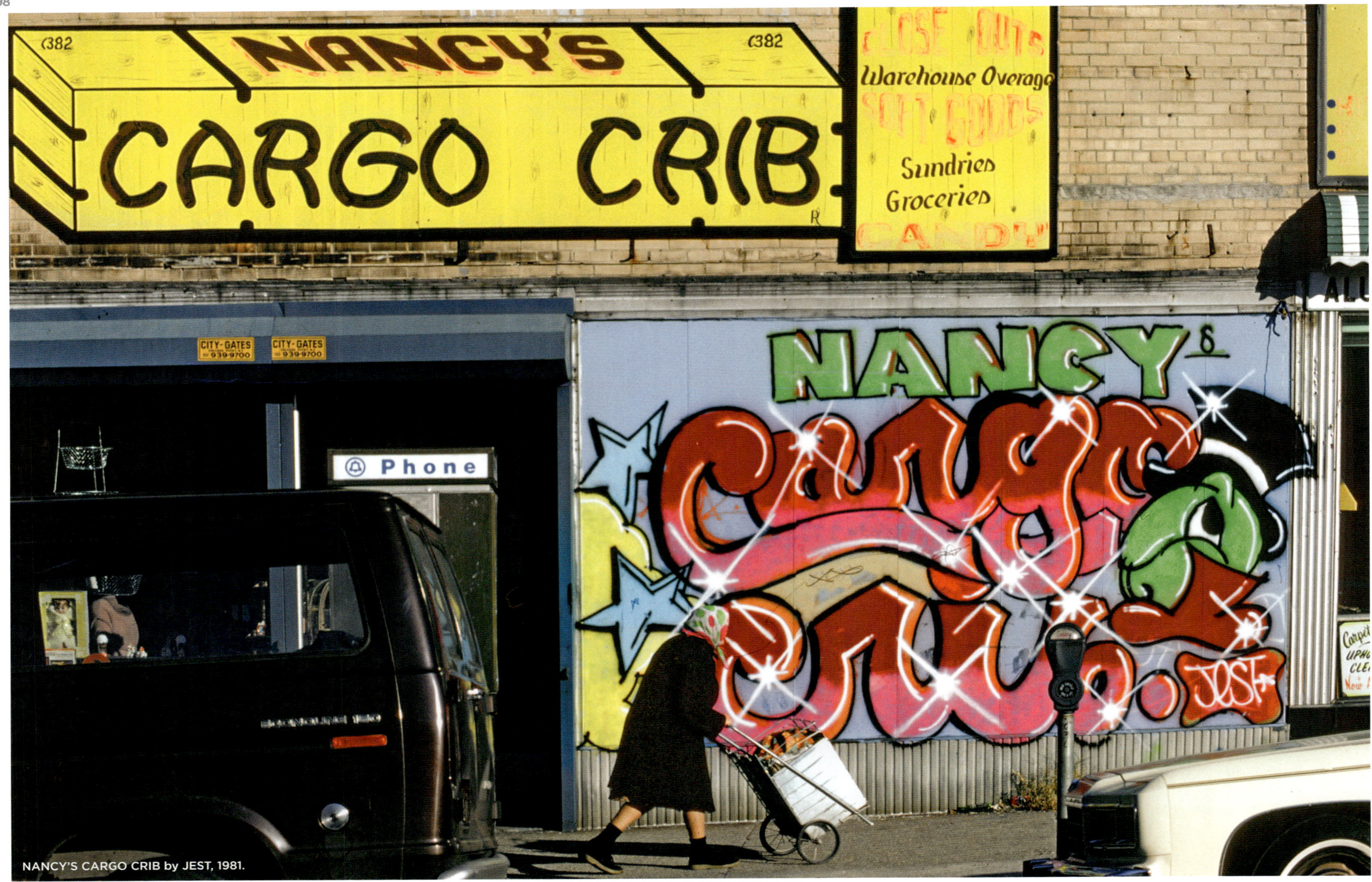

NANCY'S CARGO CRIB by JEST, 1981.

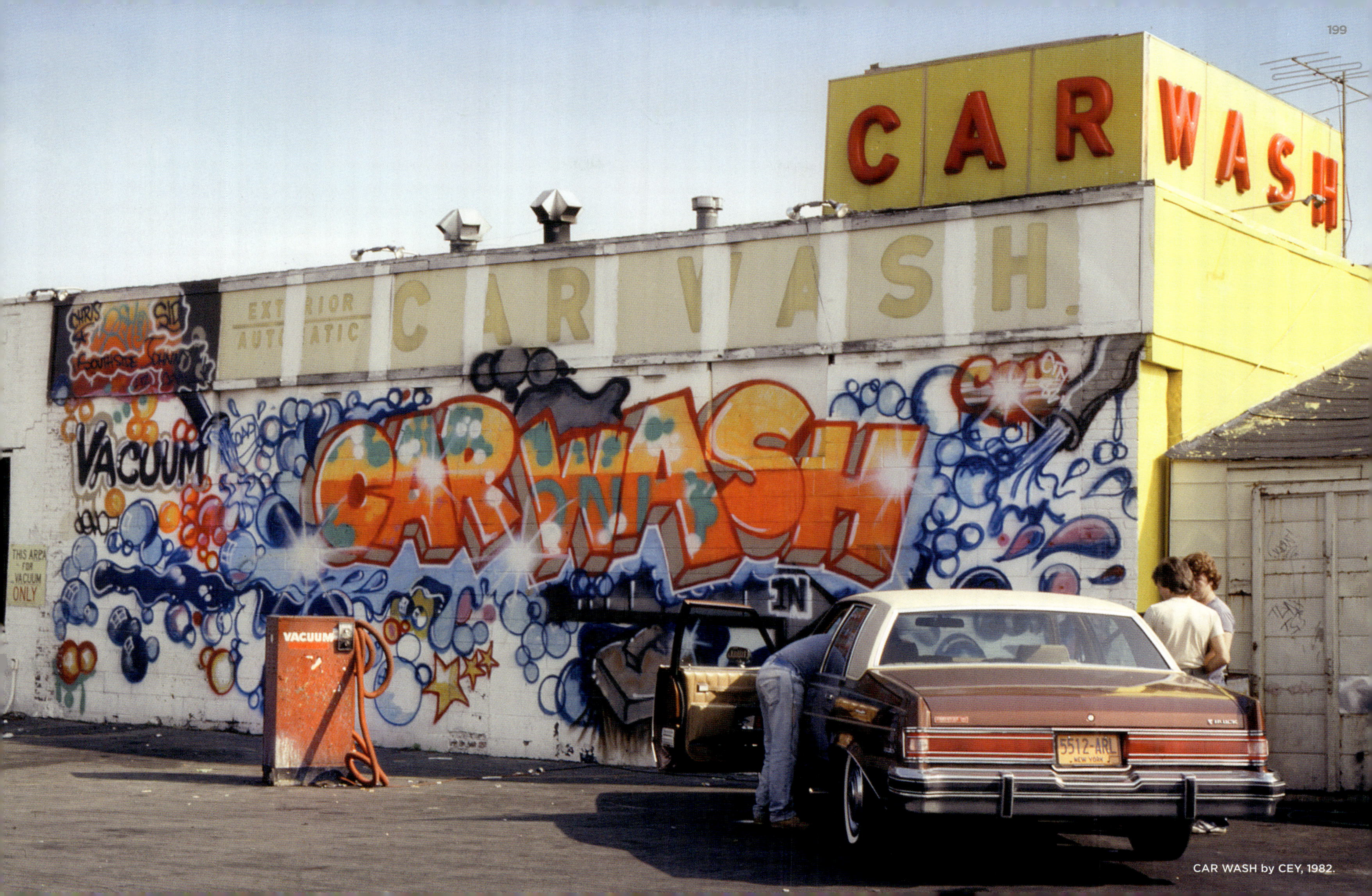

CAR WASH by CEY, 1982.

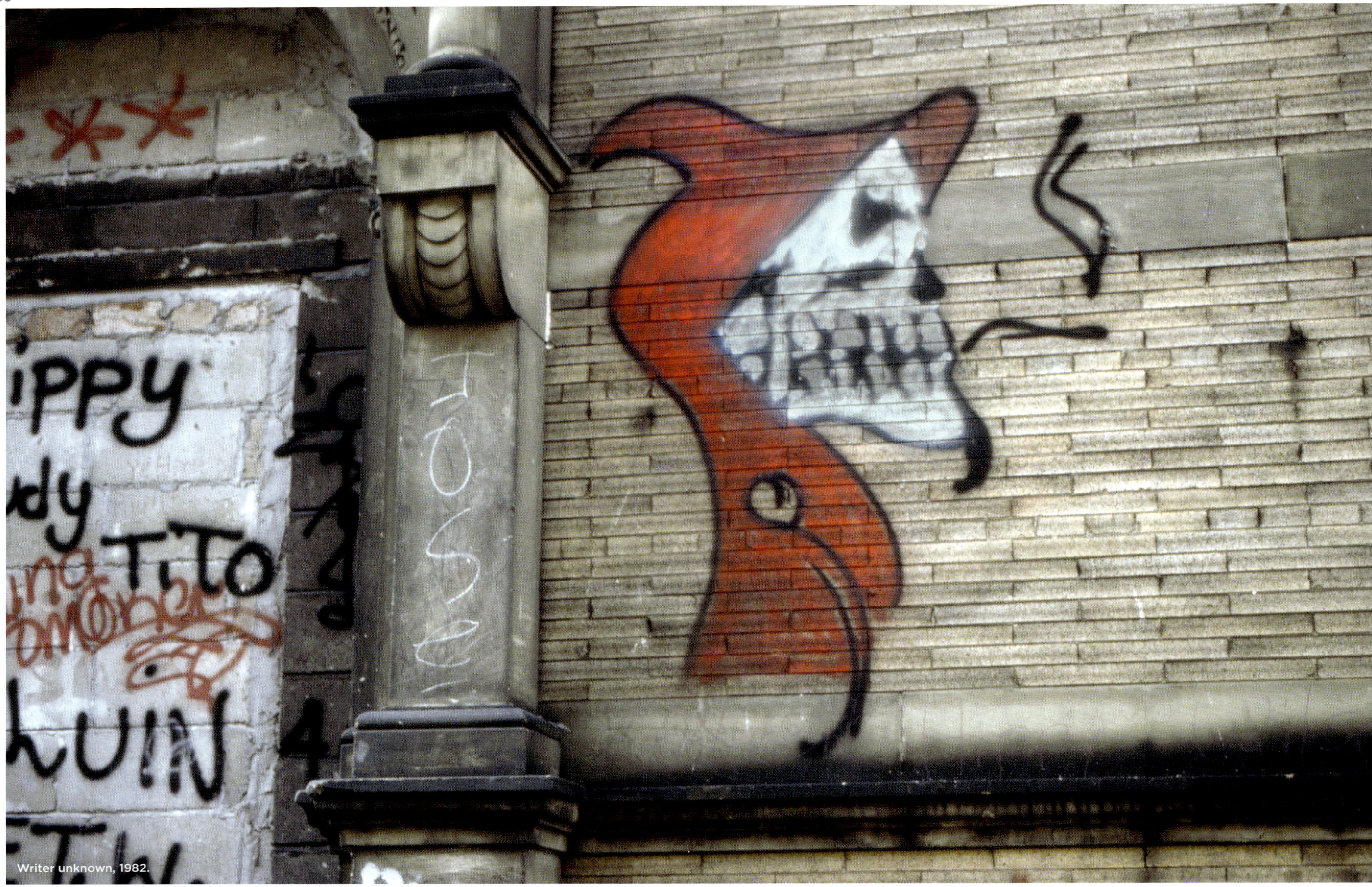

Writer unknown, 1982.

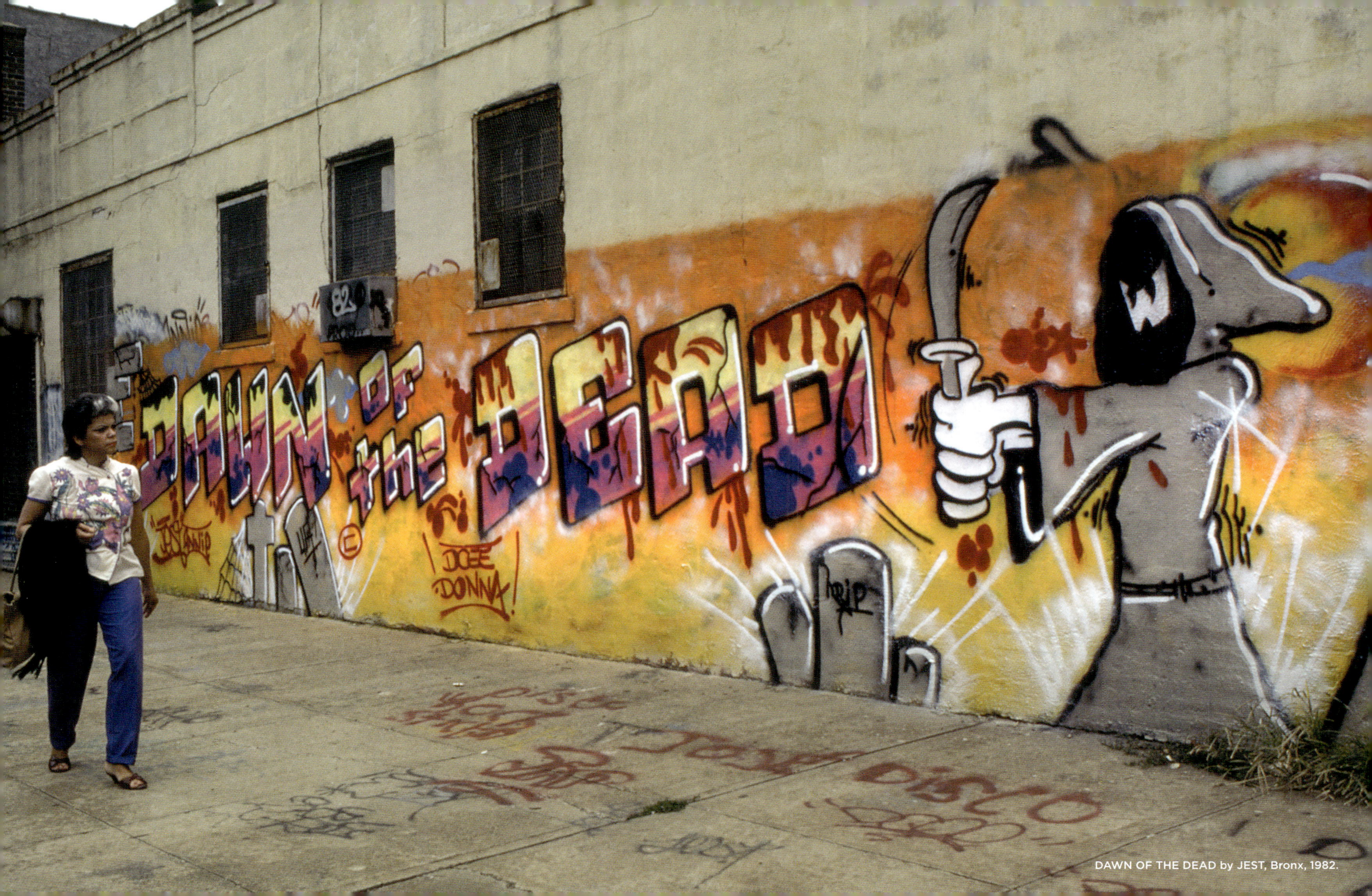

DAWN OF THE DEAD by JEST, Bronx, 1982.

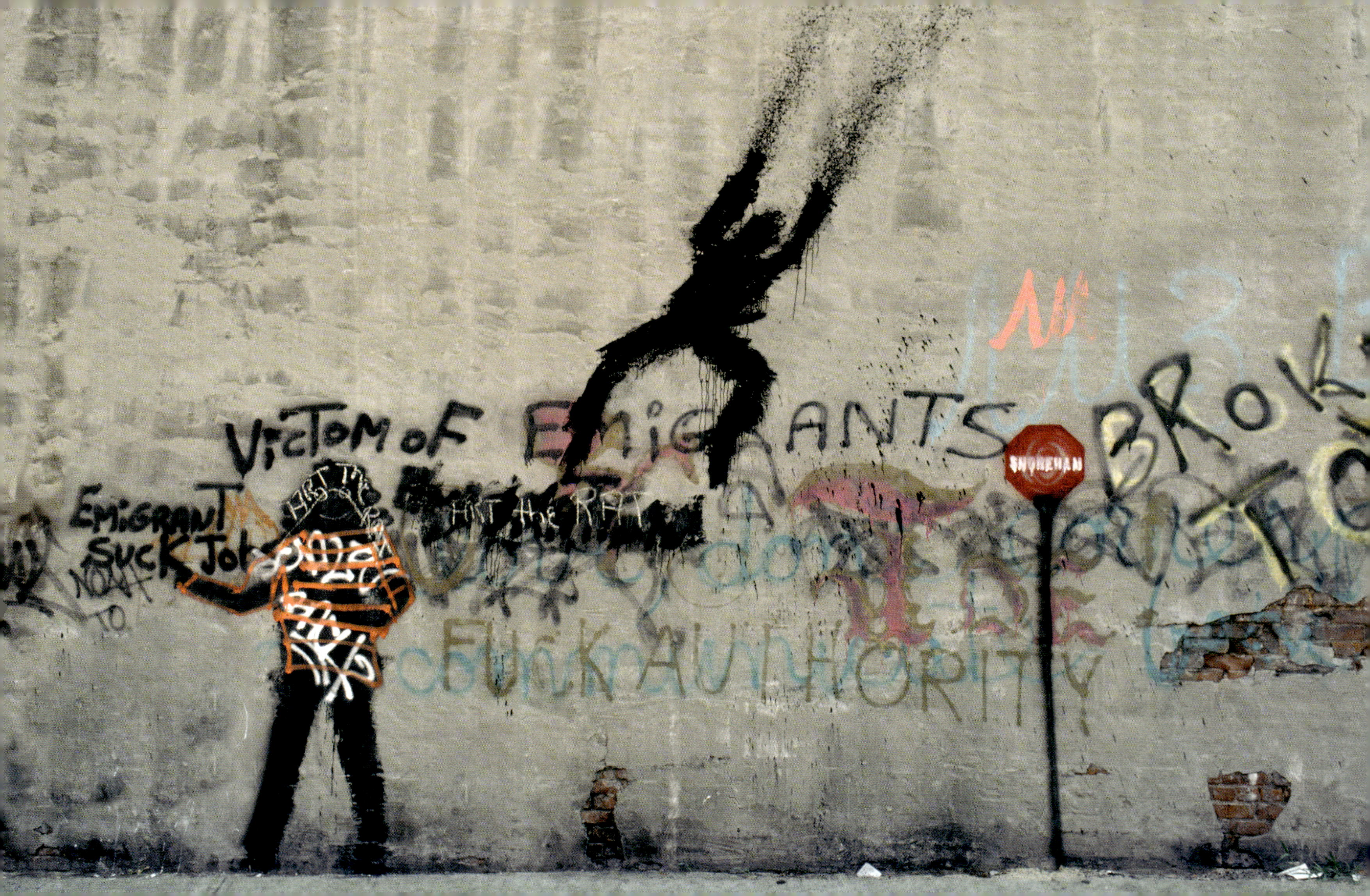

VICTOM OF EMIGRANTS BROK
EMIGRANT SUCK JOB
HNT THE RAT
SHOREHAM

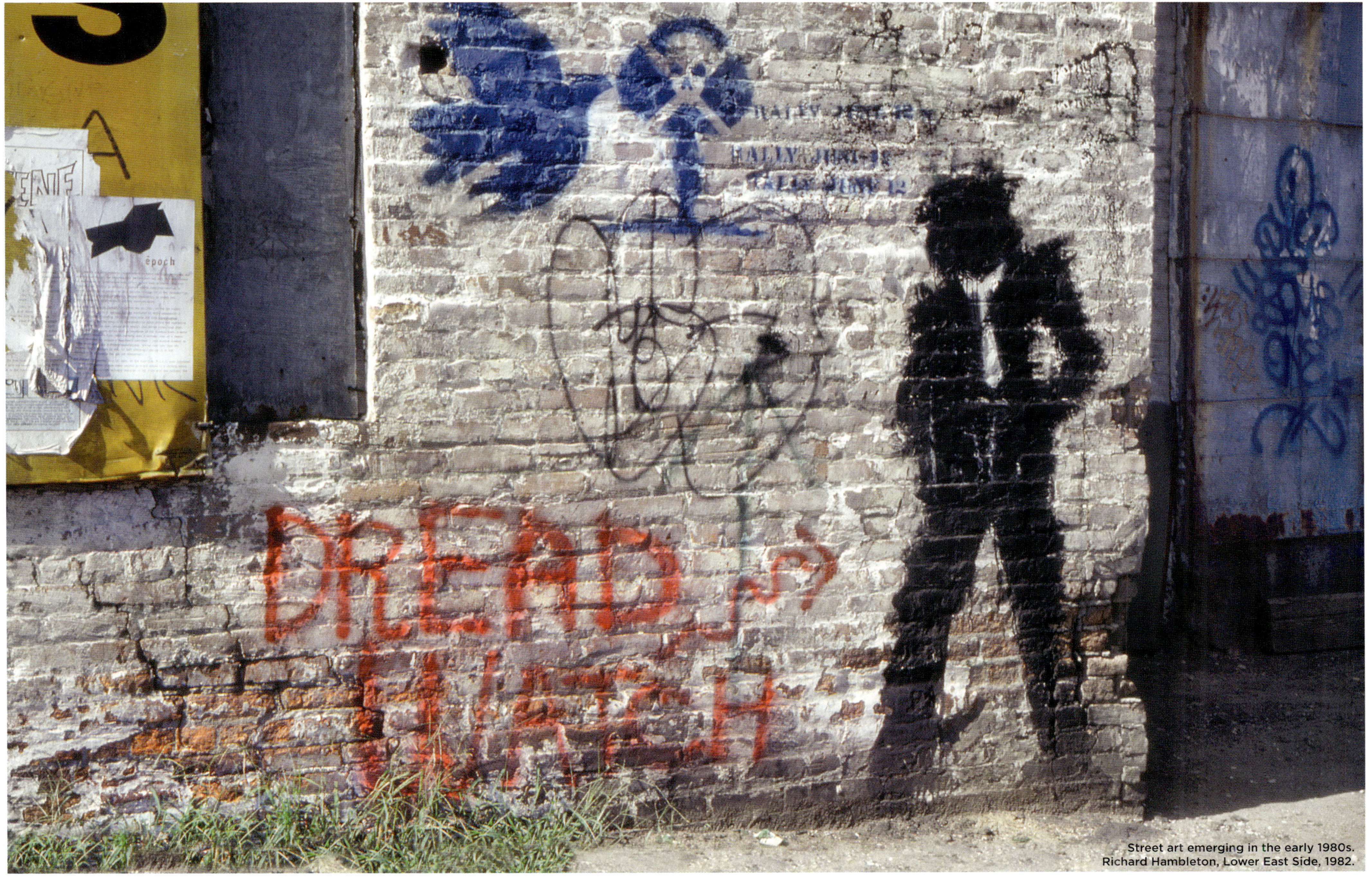

Street art emerging in the early 1980s.
Richard Hambleton, Lower East Side, 1982.

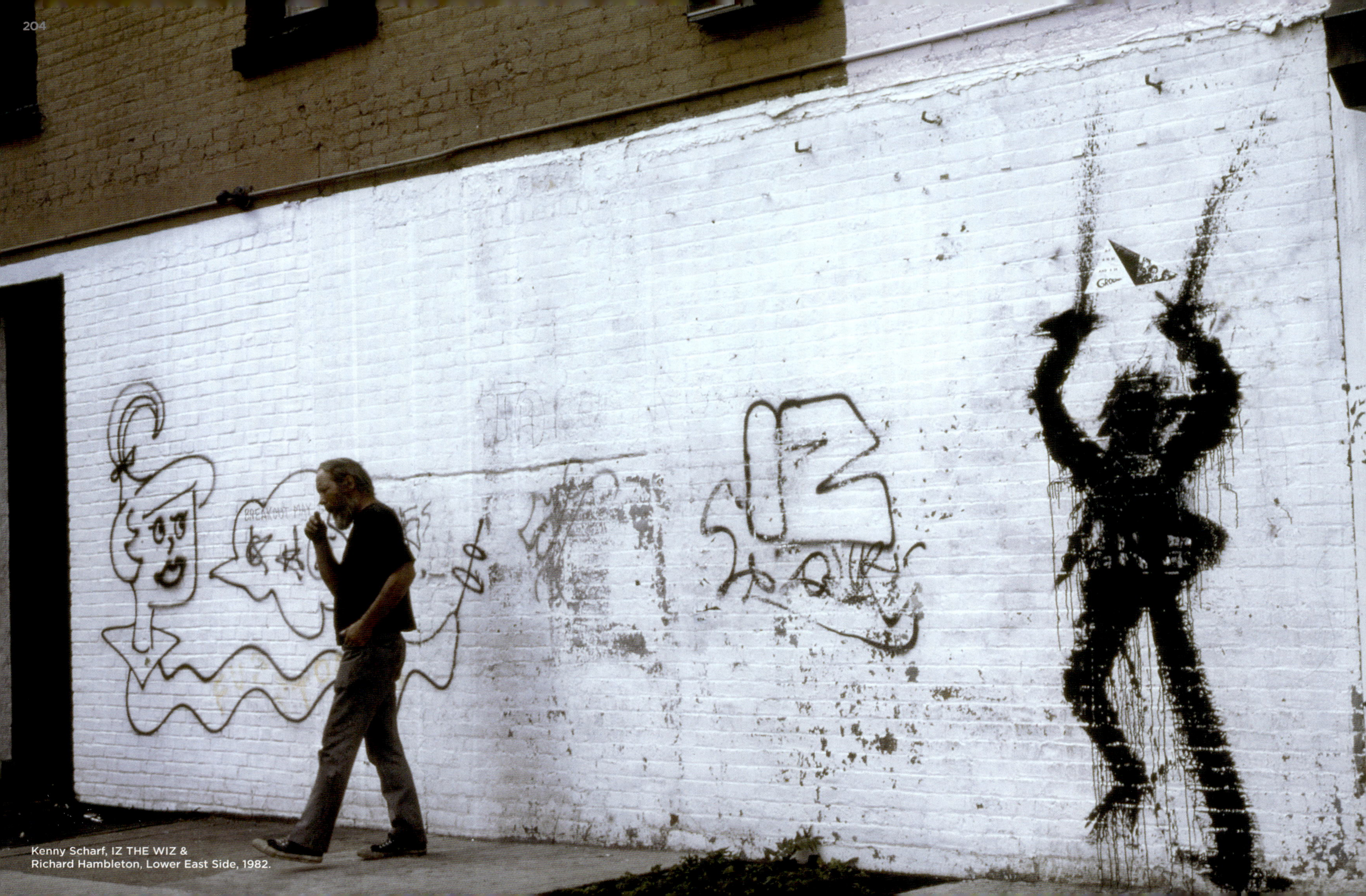

Kenny Scharf, IZ THE WIZ &
Richard Hambleton, Lower East Side, 1982.

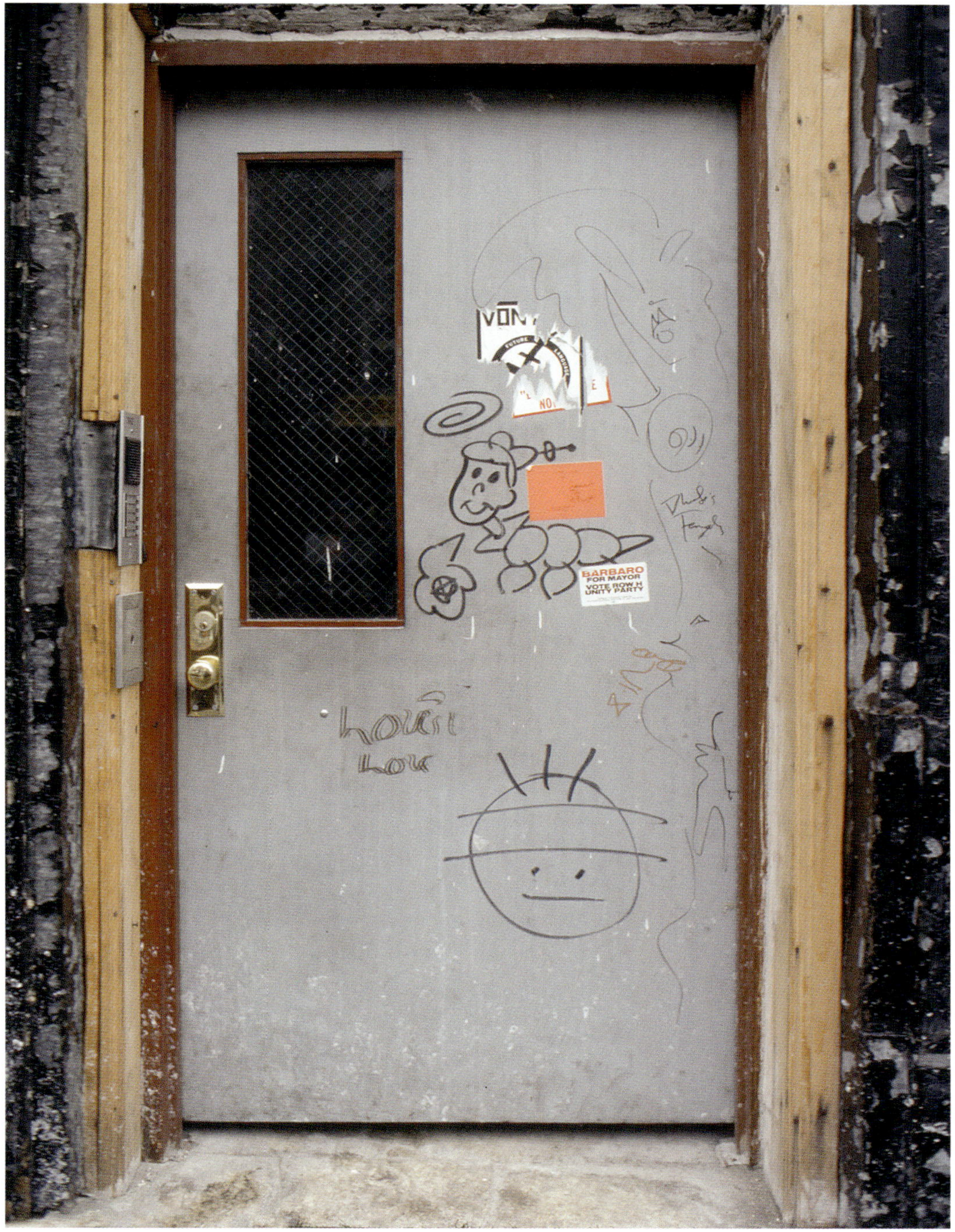

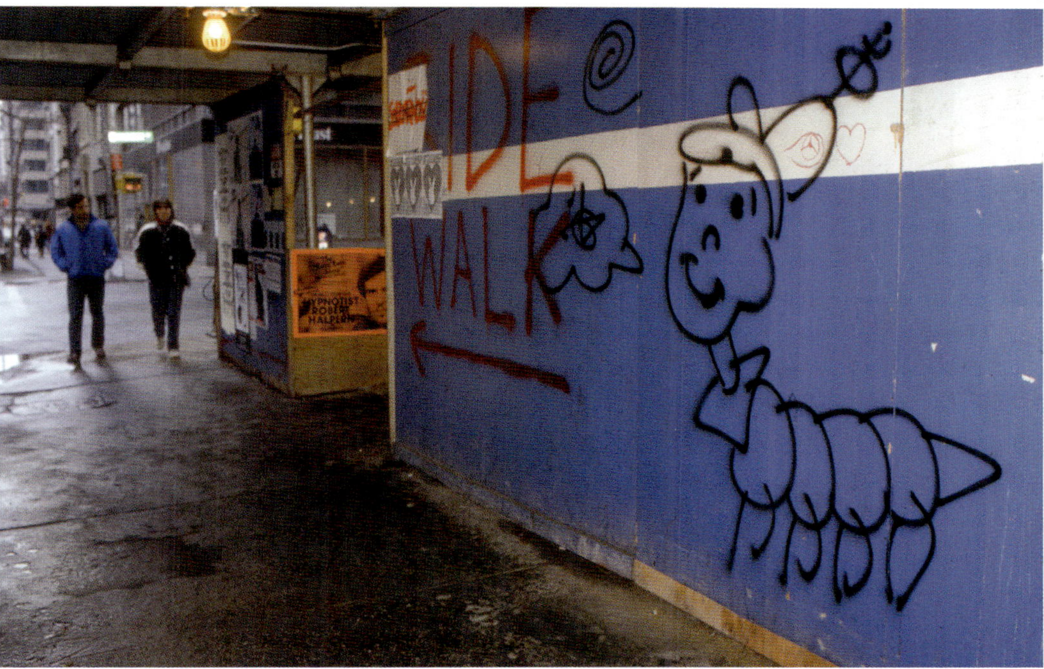

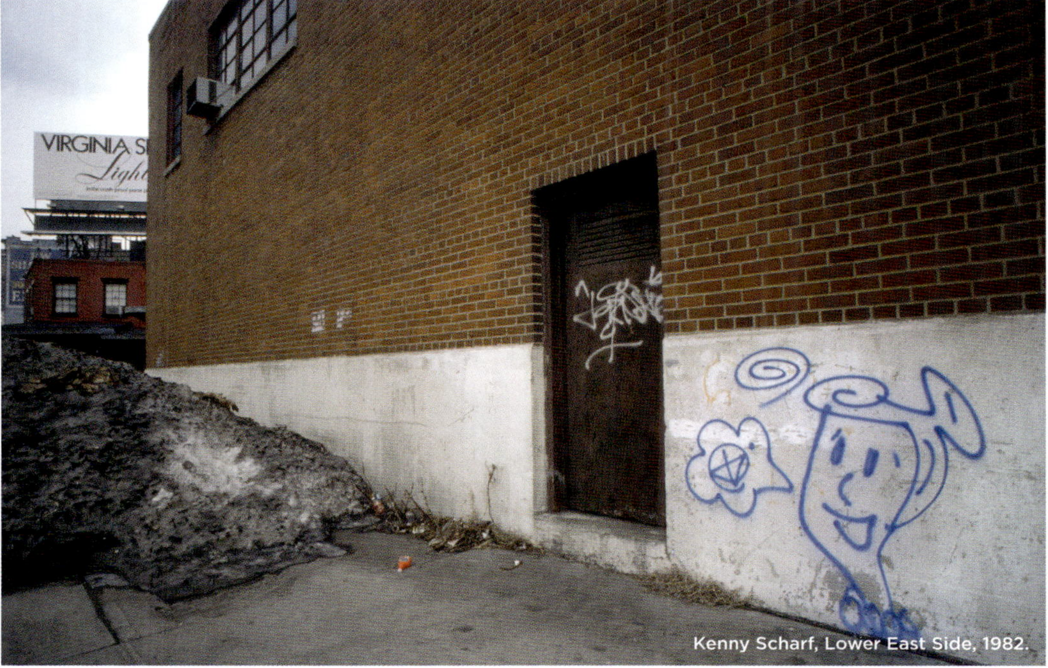

Kenny Scharf, Lower East Side, 1982.

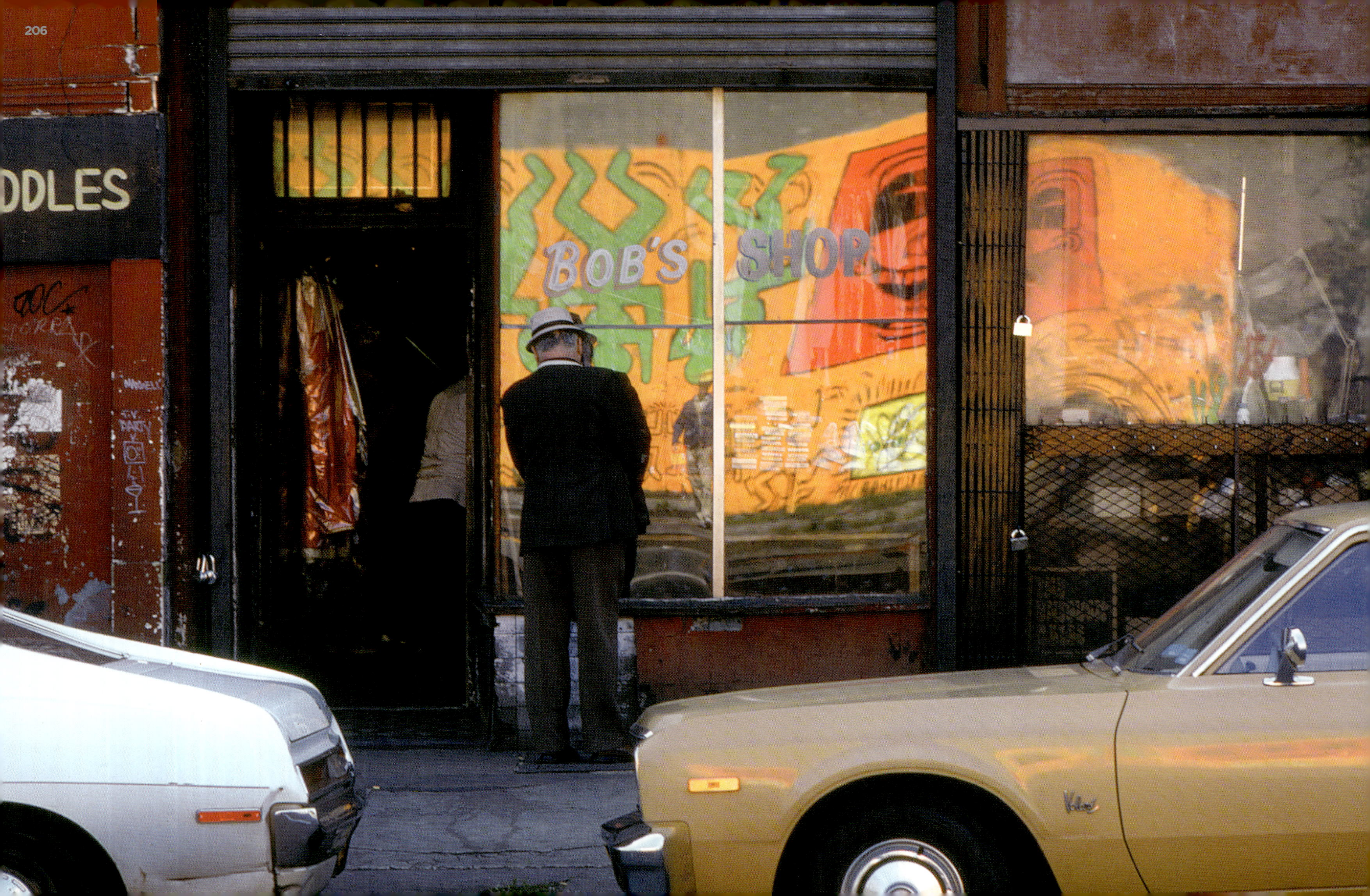
DDLES
BOB'S SHOP

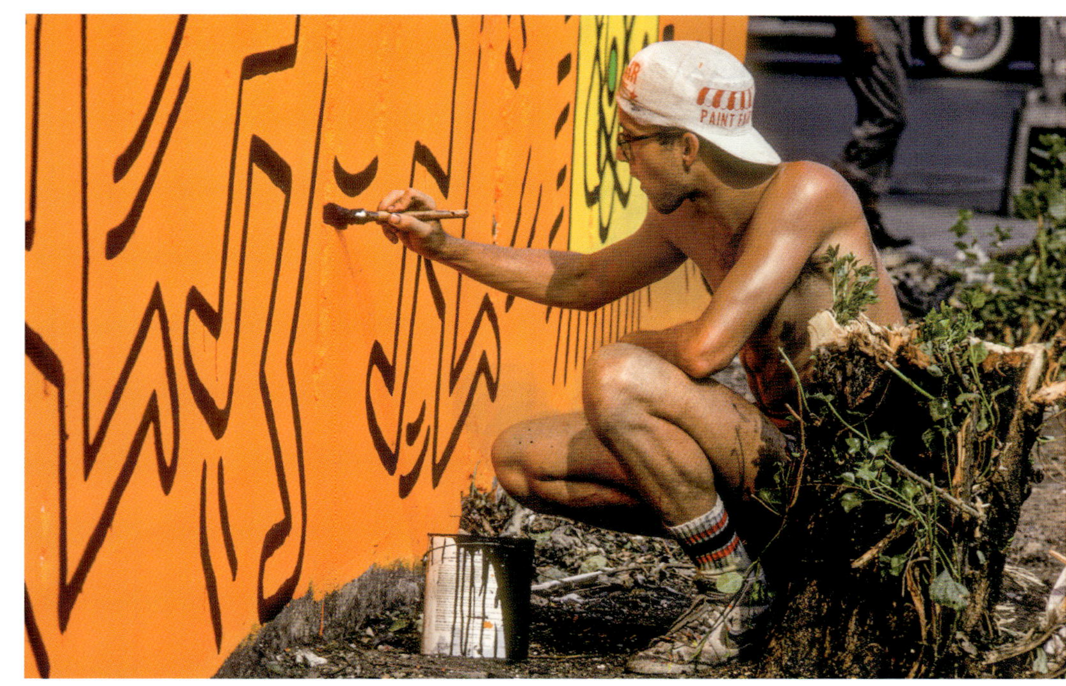

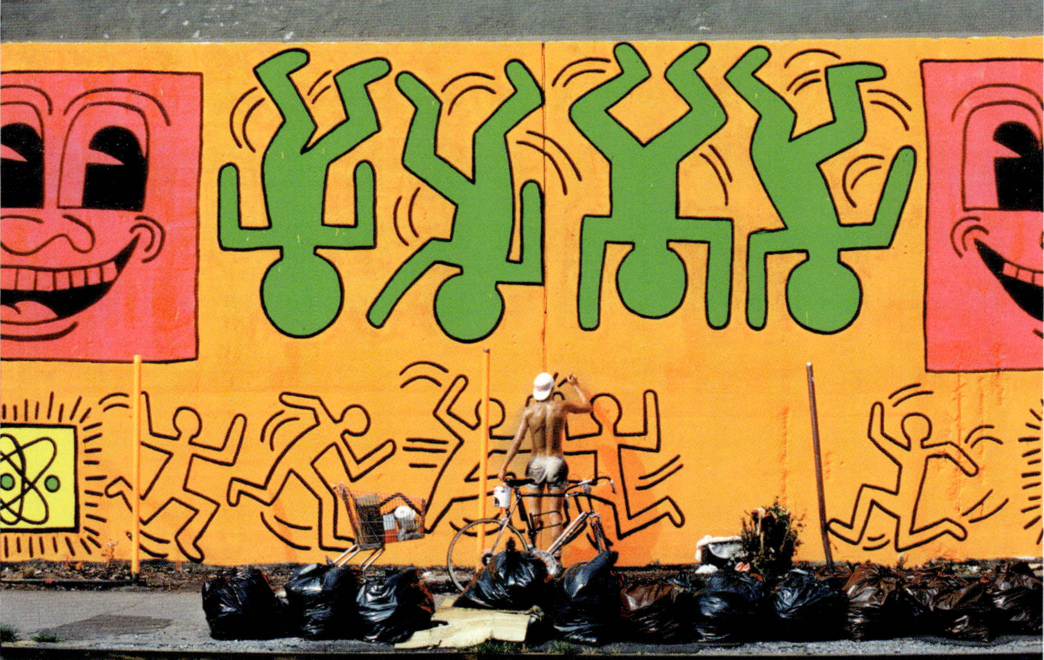

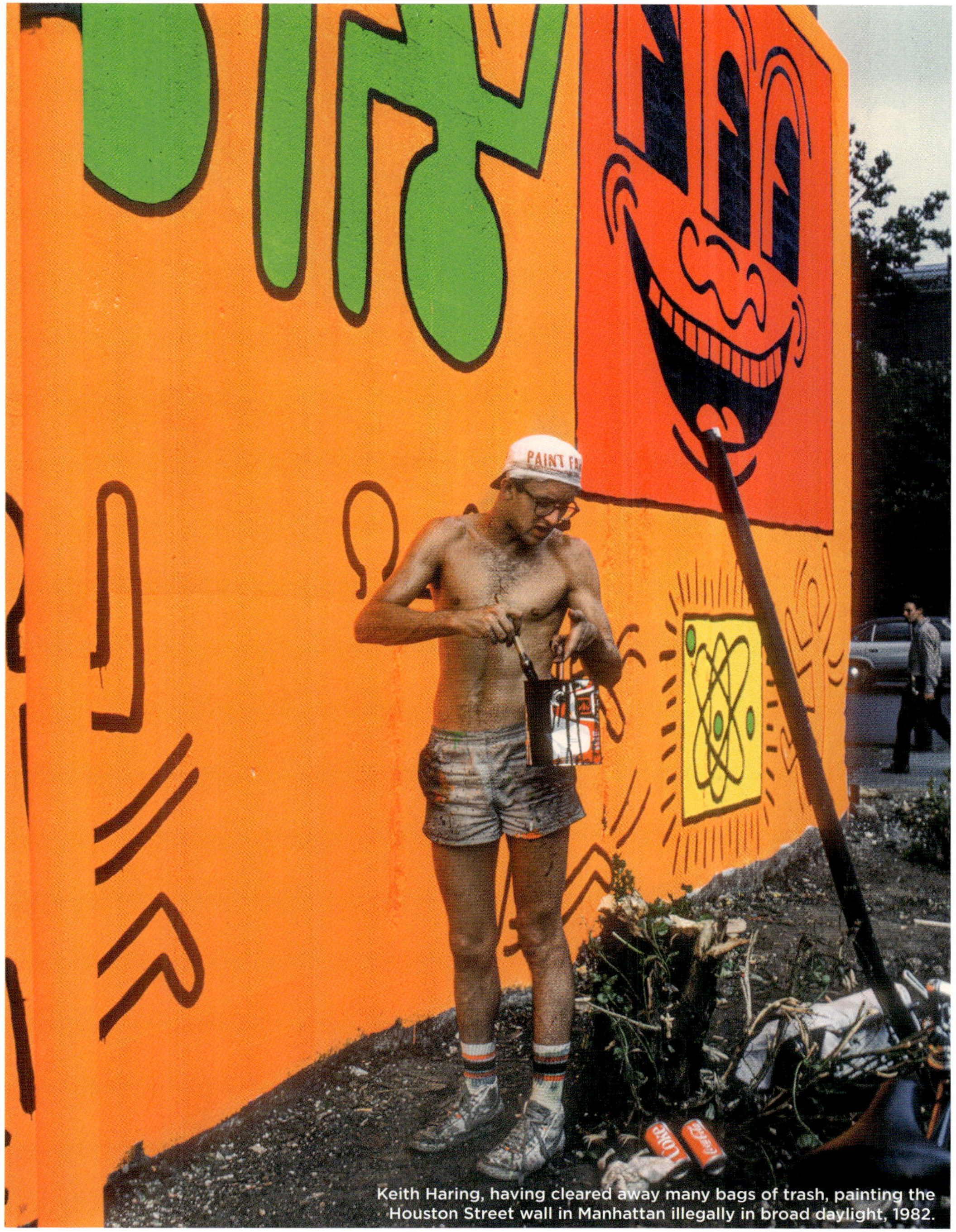

Keith Haring, having cleared away many bags of trash, painting the Houston Street wall in Manhattan illegally in broad daylight, 1982.

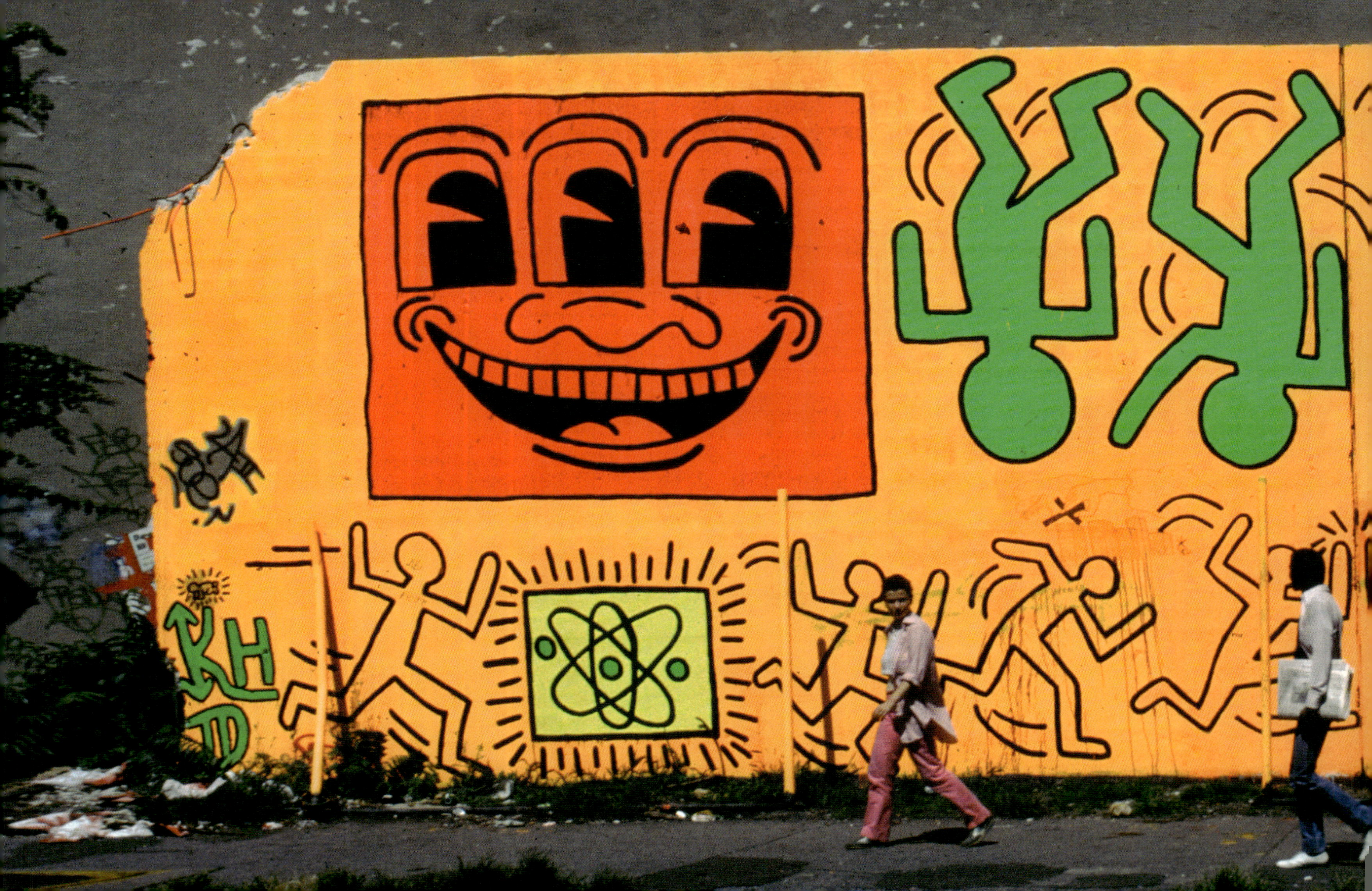

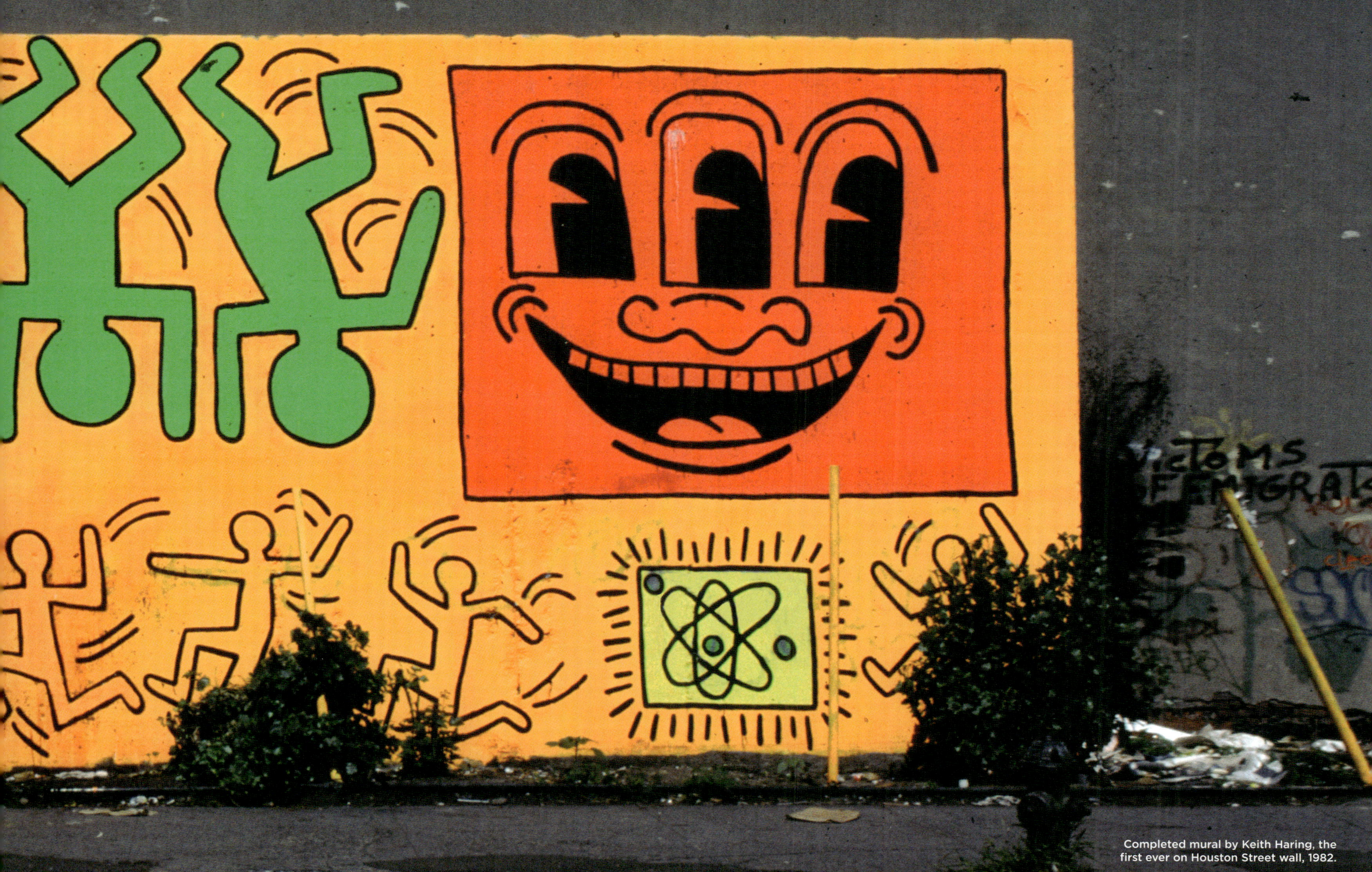

Completed mural by Keith Haring, the first ever on Houston Street wall, 1982.

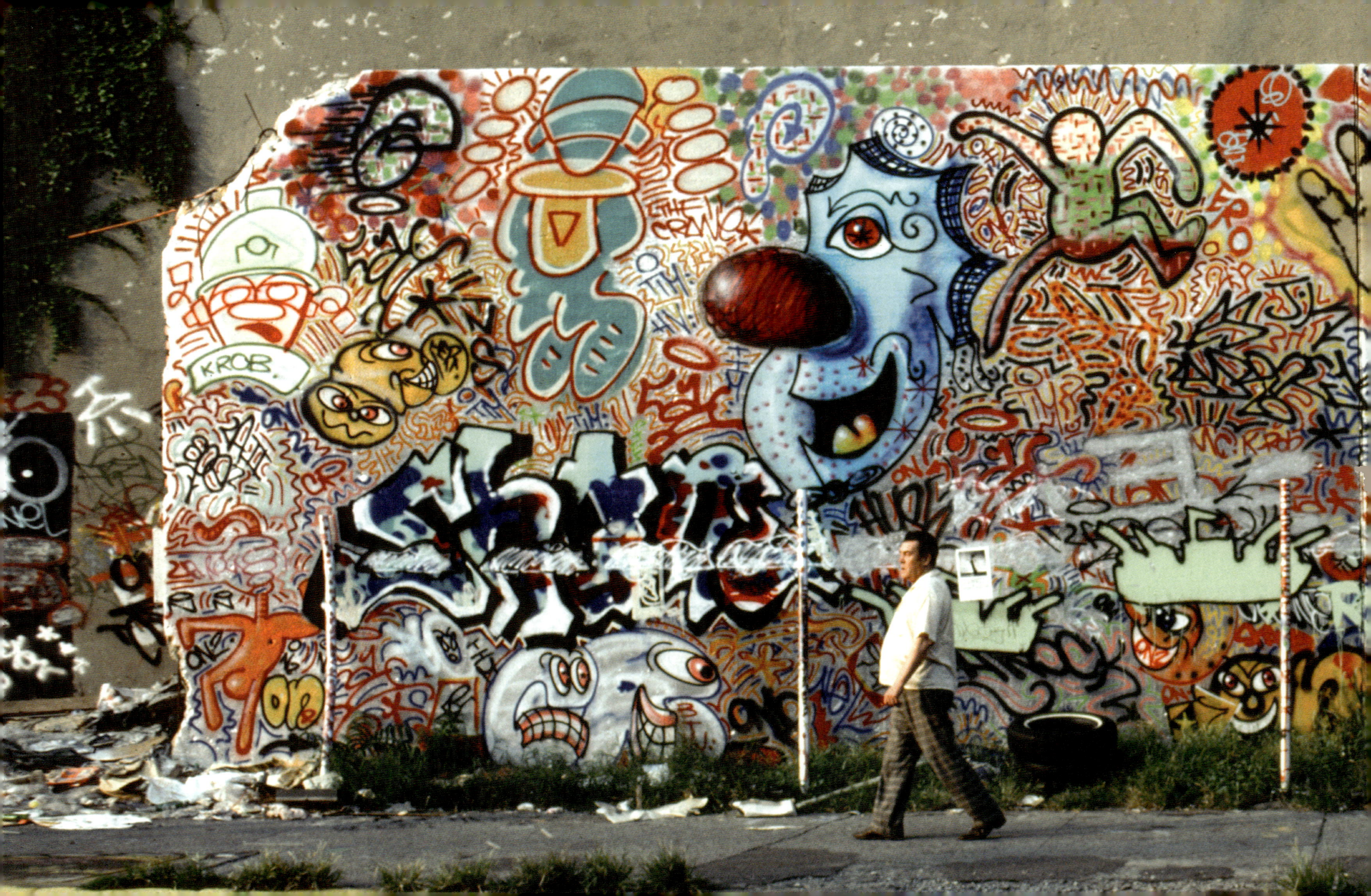

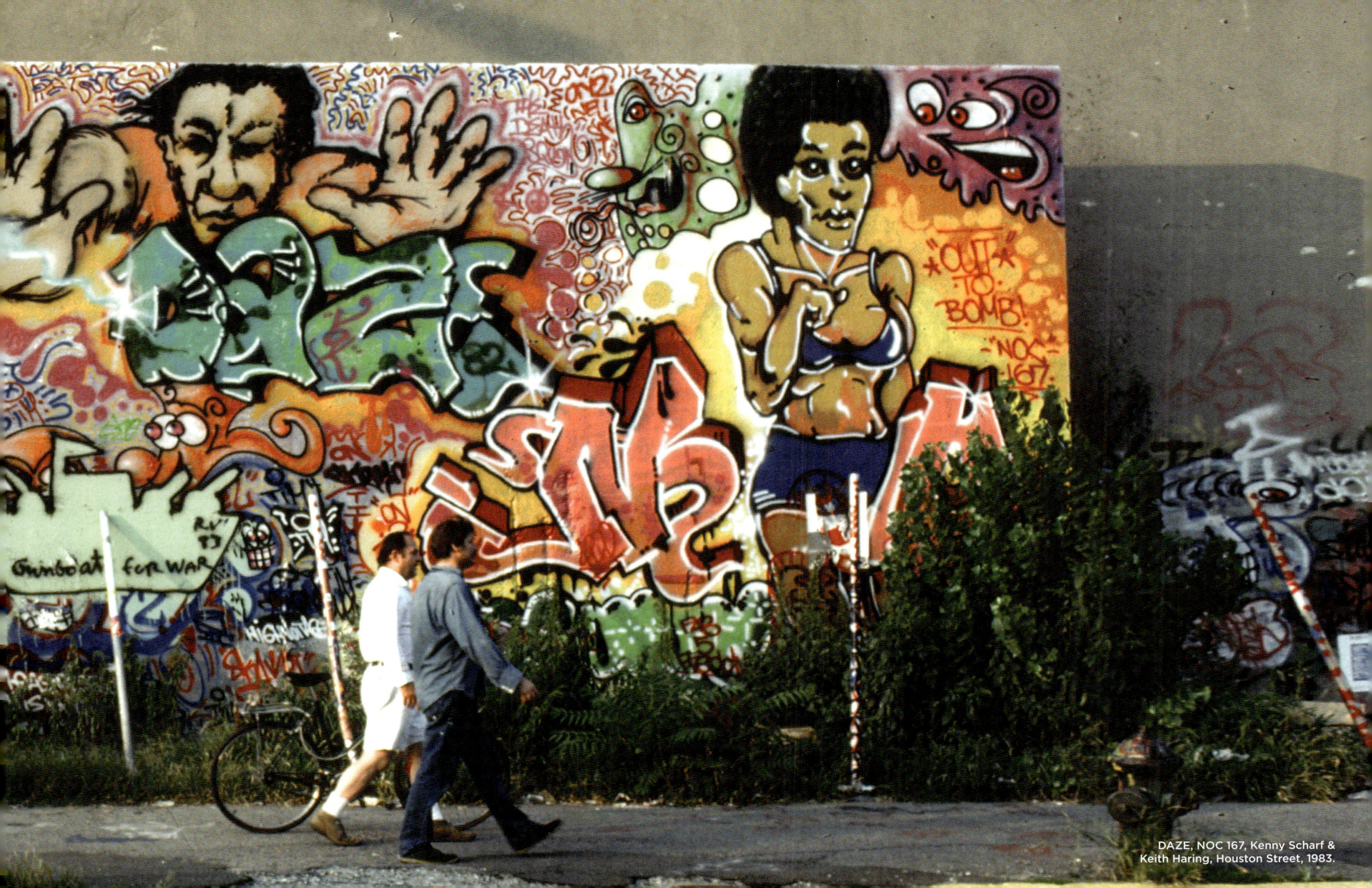

DAZE, NOC 167, Kenny Scharf &
Keith Haring, Houston Street, 1983.

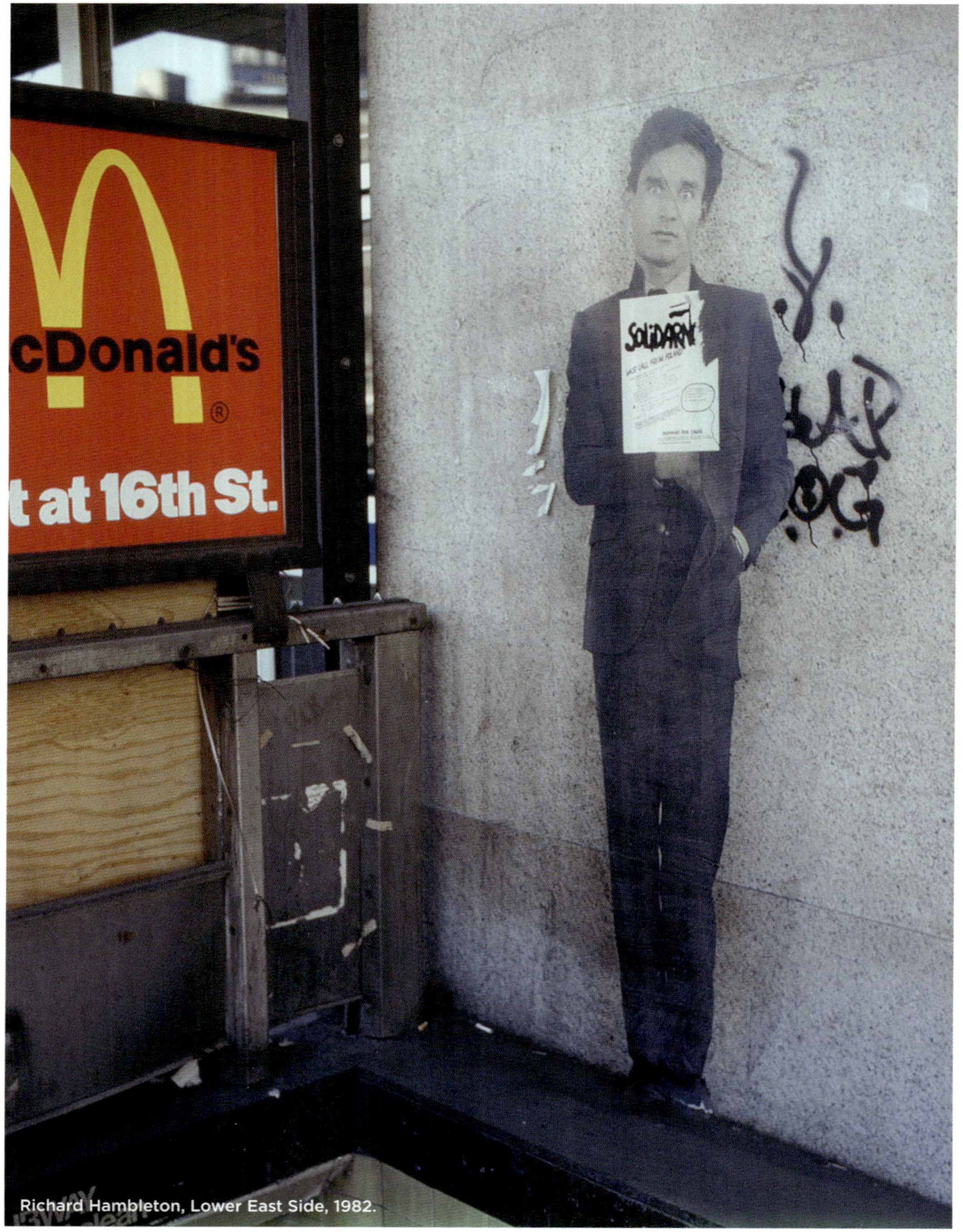

McDonald's

at 16th St.

SOLIDARN

Richard Hambleton, Lower East Side, 1982.

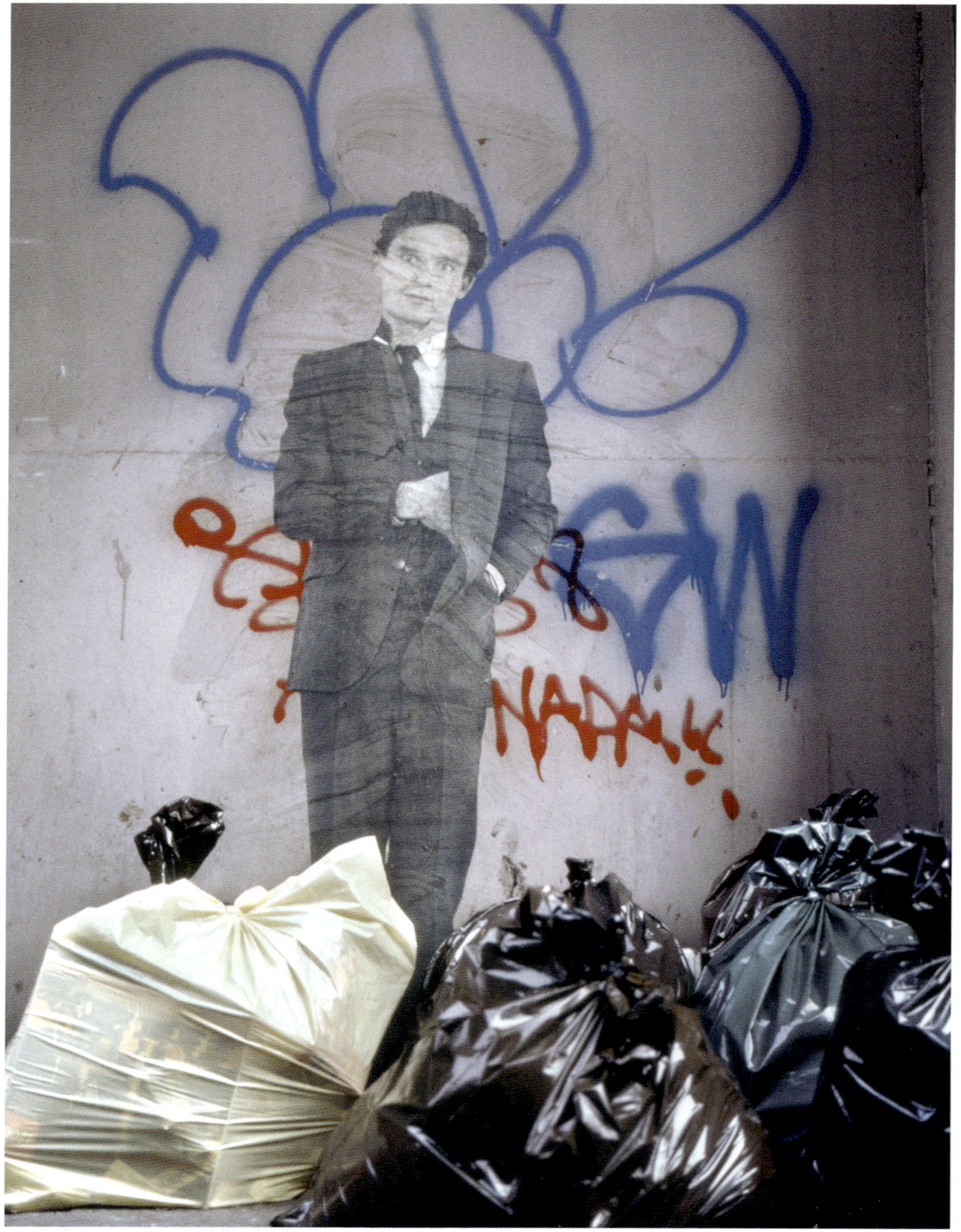

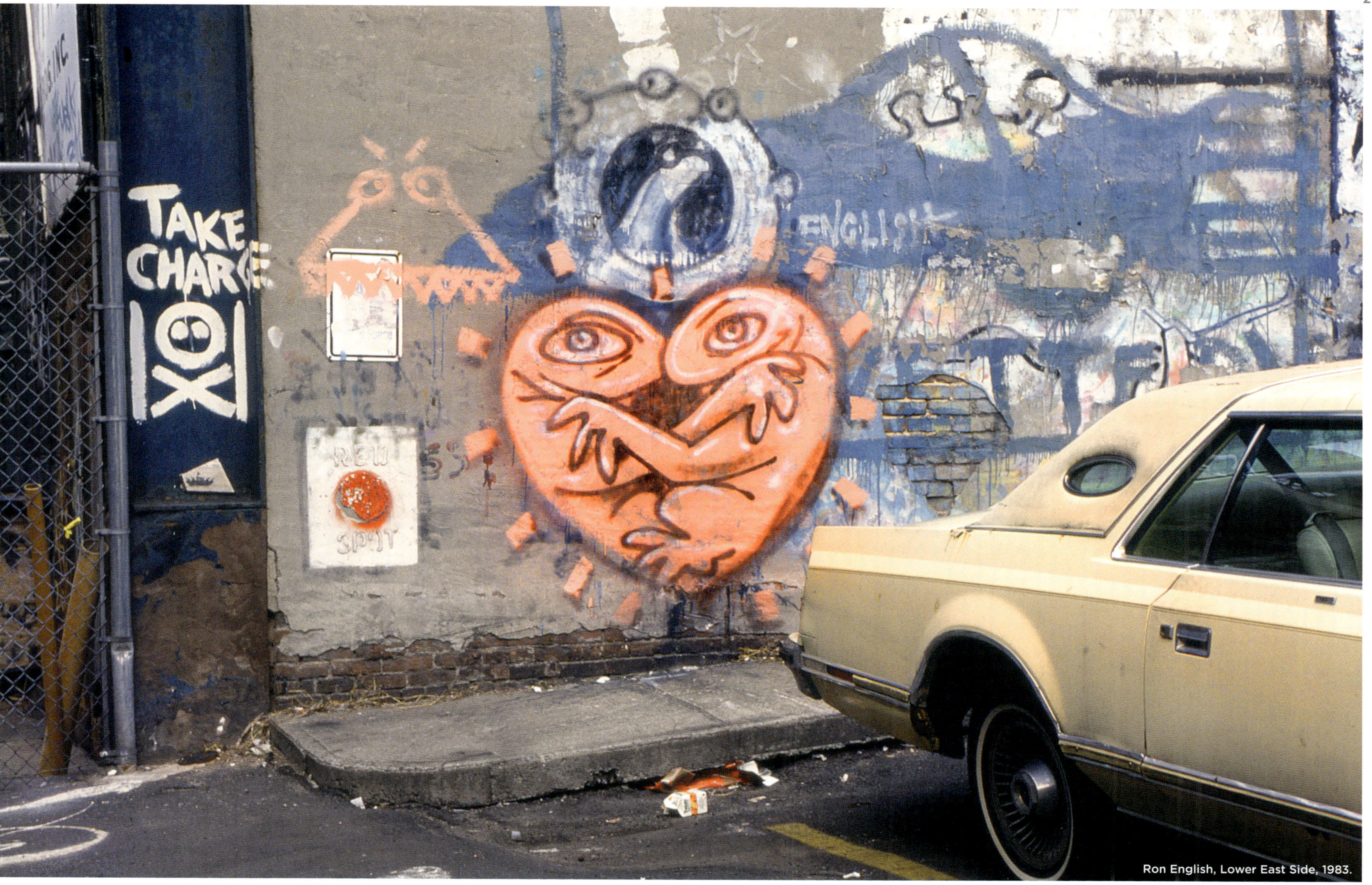

Ron English, Lower East Side, 1983.

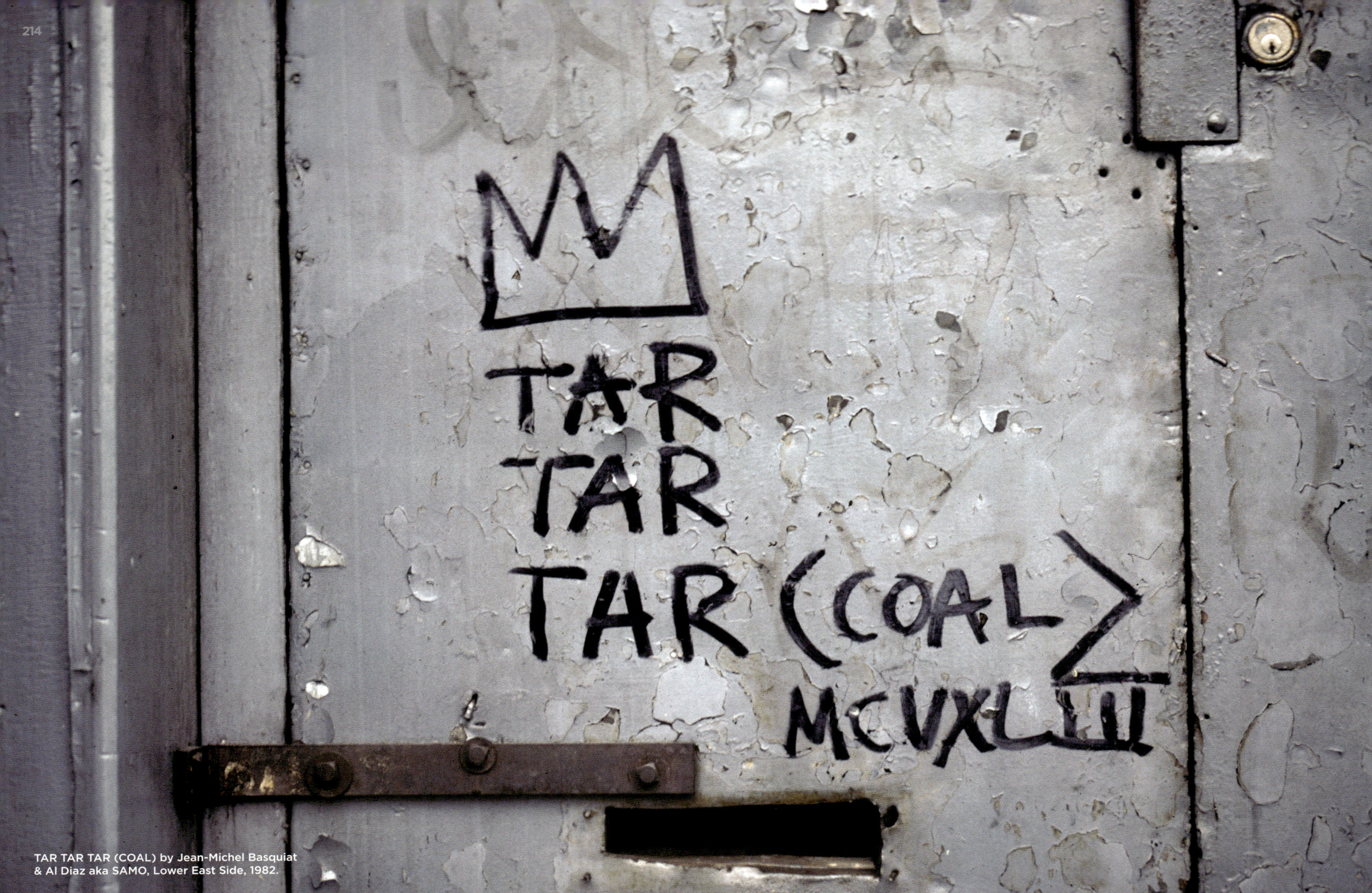

TAR TAR TAR (COAL) by Jean-Michel Basquiat & Al Diaz aka SAMO, Lower East Side, 1982.

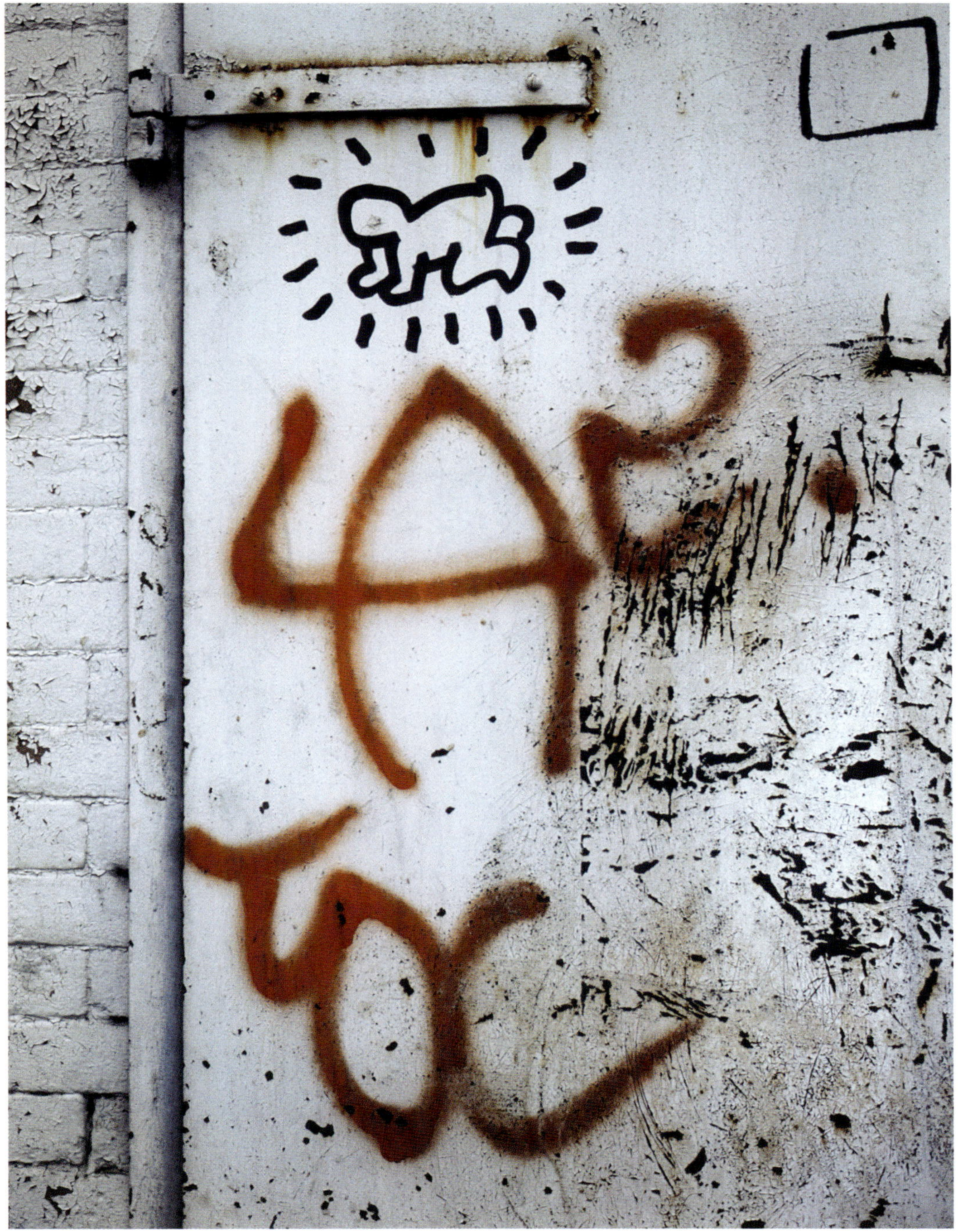

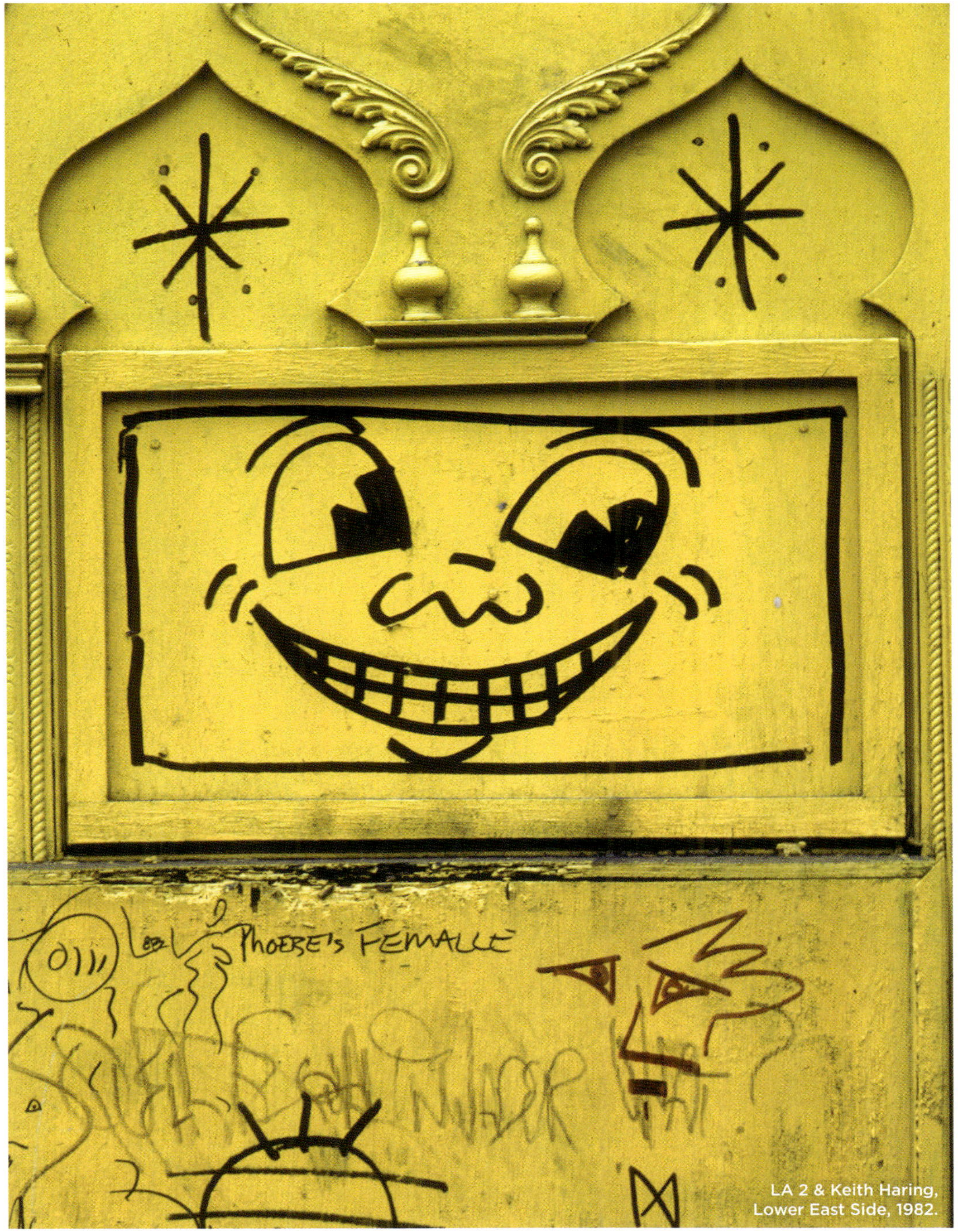

LA 2 & Keith Haring,
Lower East Side, 1982.

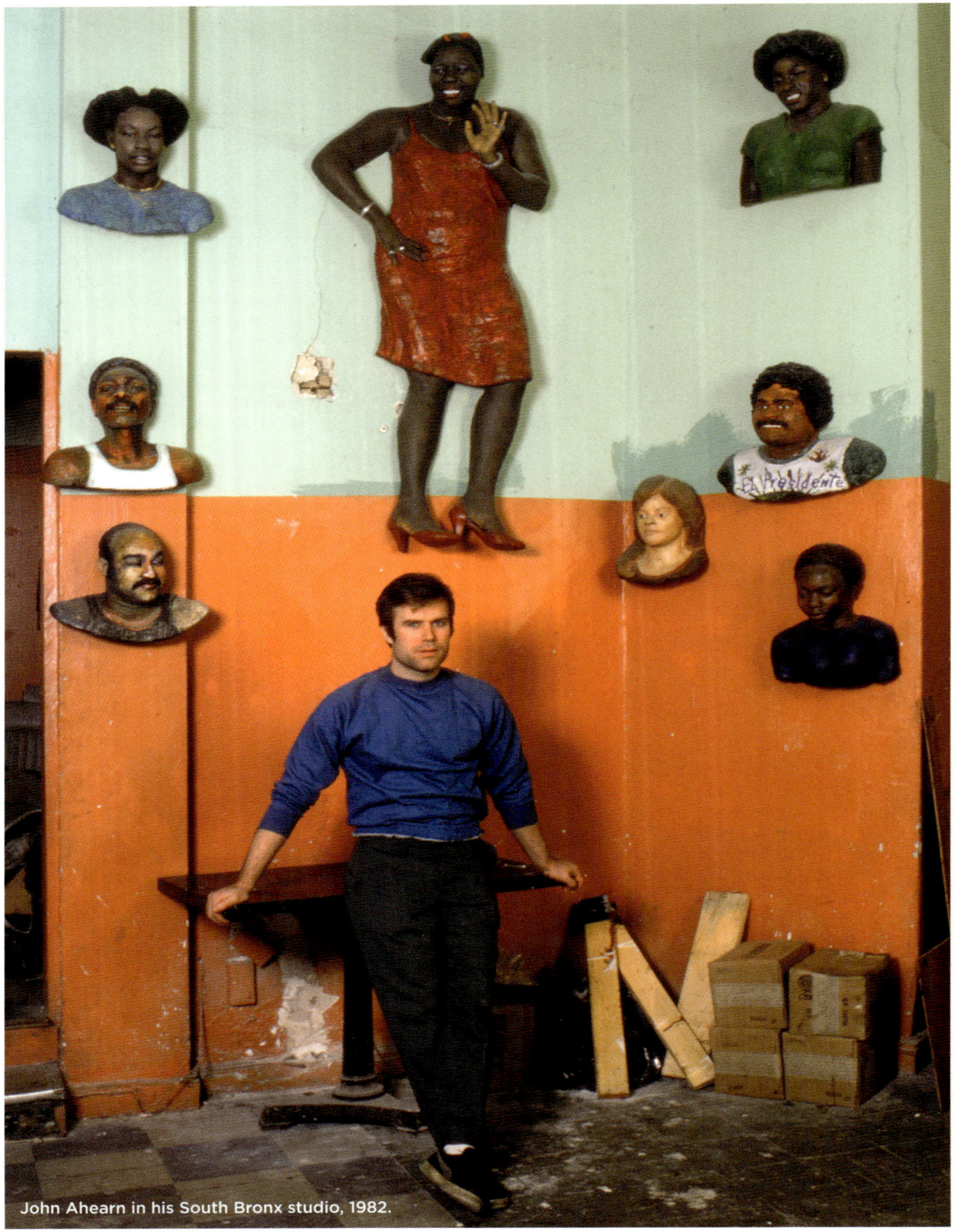

John Ahearn in his South Bronx studio, 1982.

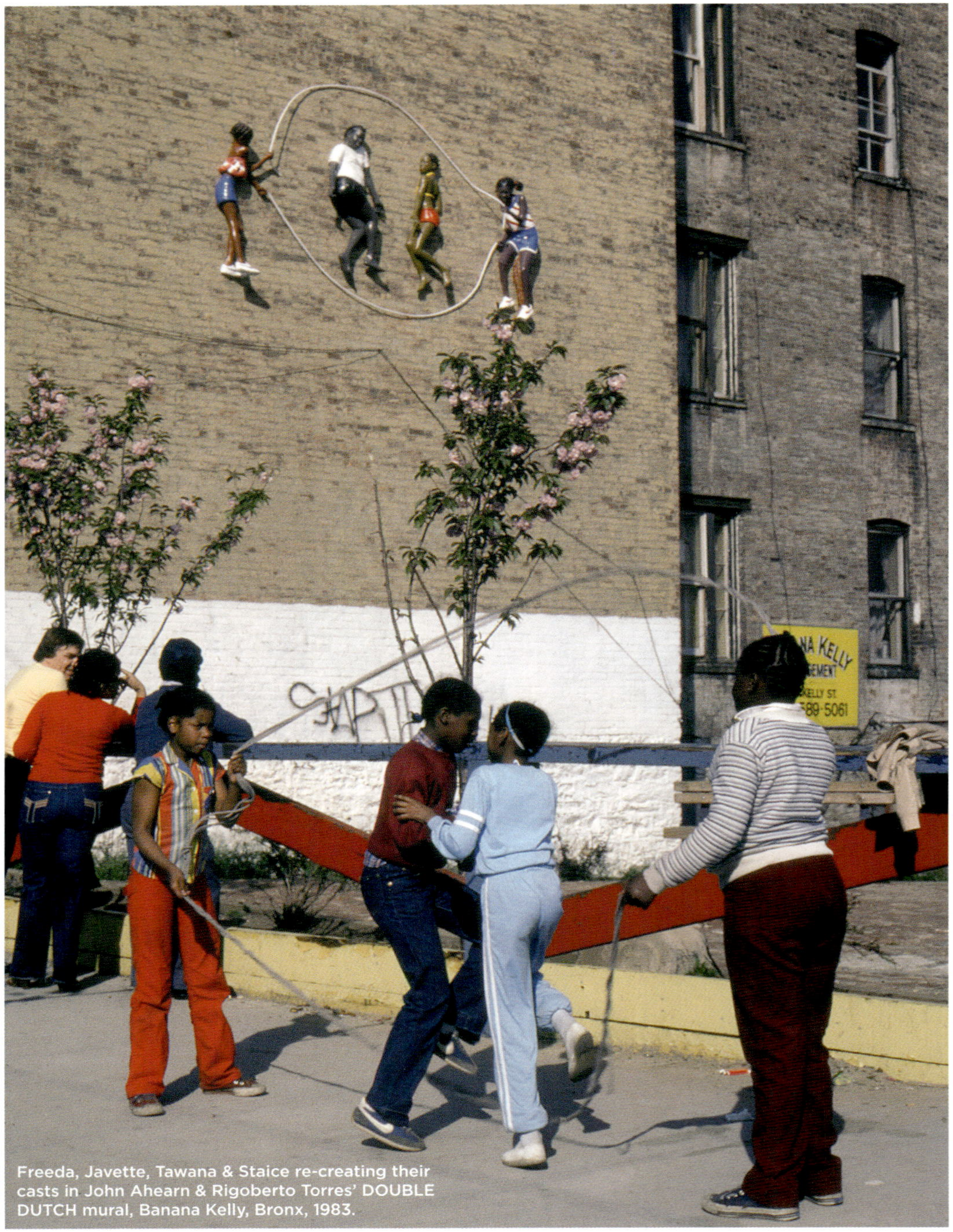

Freeda, Javette, Tawana & Staice re-creating their casts in John Ahearn & Rigoberto Torres' DOUBLE DUTCH mural, Banana Kelly, Bronx, 1983.

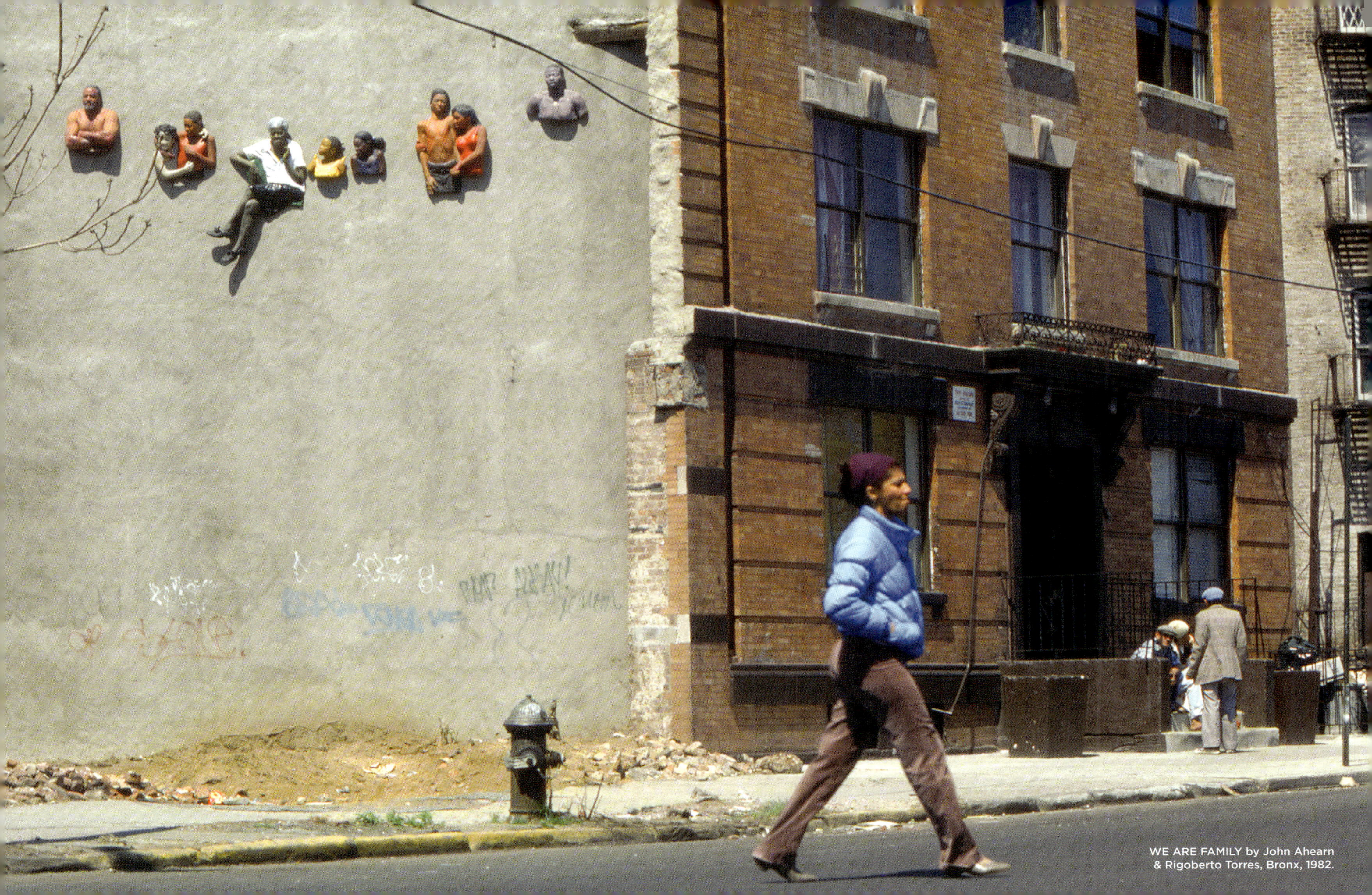

WE ARE FAMILY by John Ahearn
& Rigoberto Torres, Bronx, 1982.

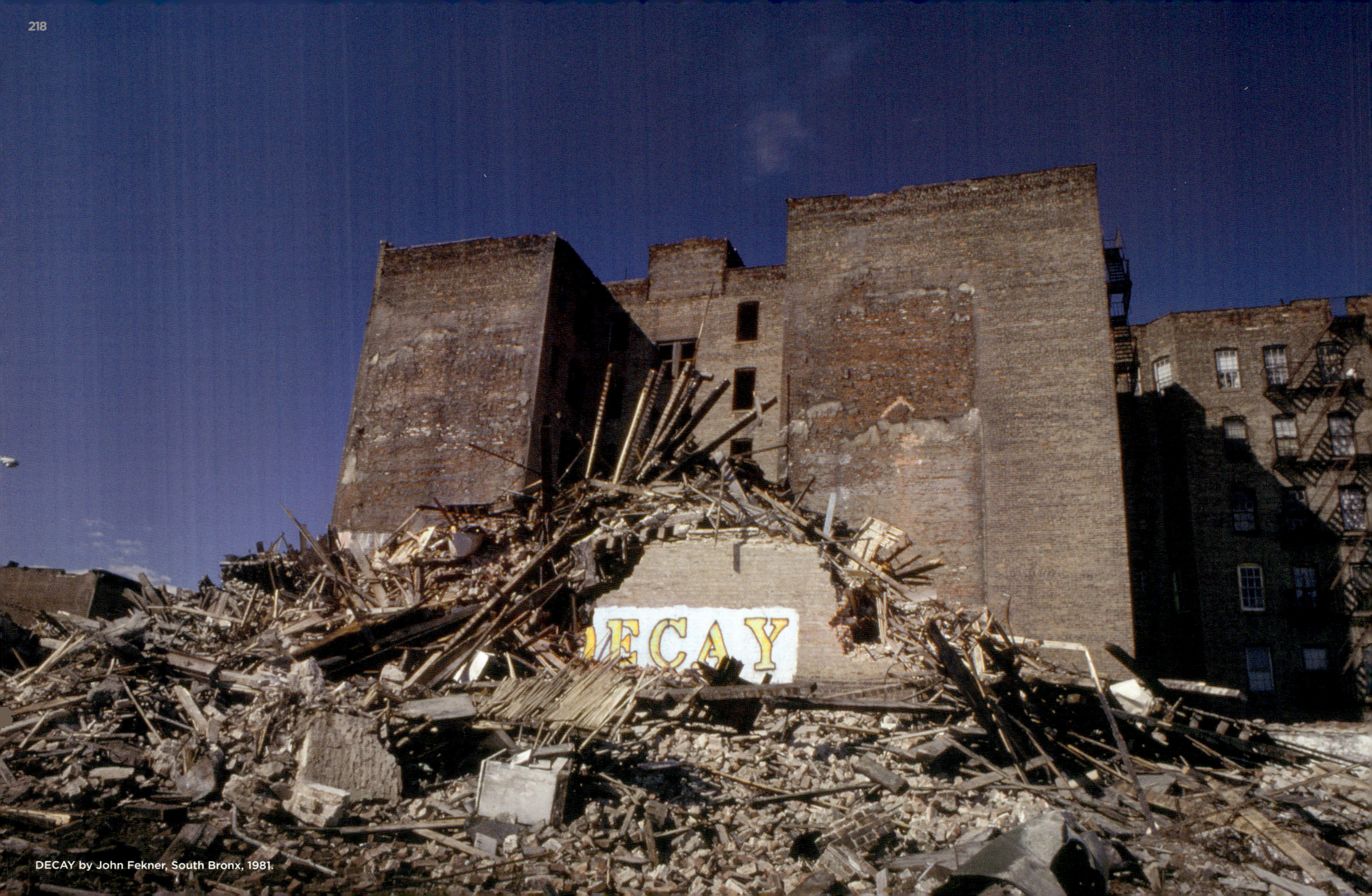

DECAY by John Fekner, South Bronx, 1981.

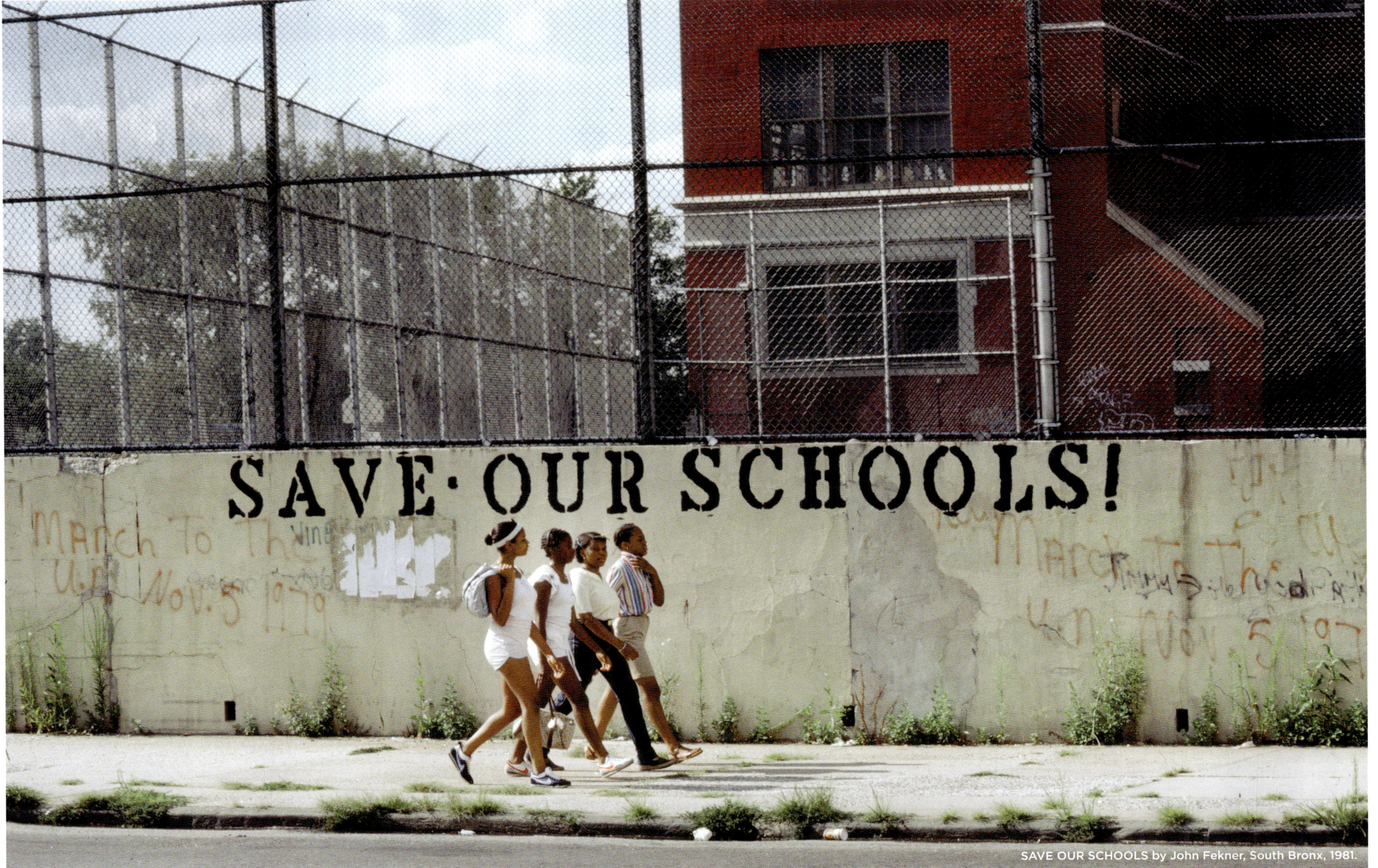

SAVE OUR SCHOOLS by John Fekner, South Bronx, 1981.

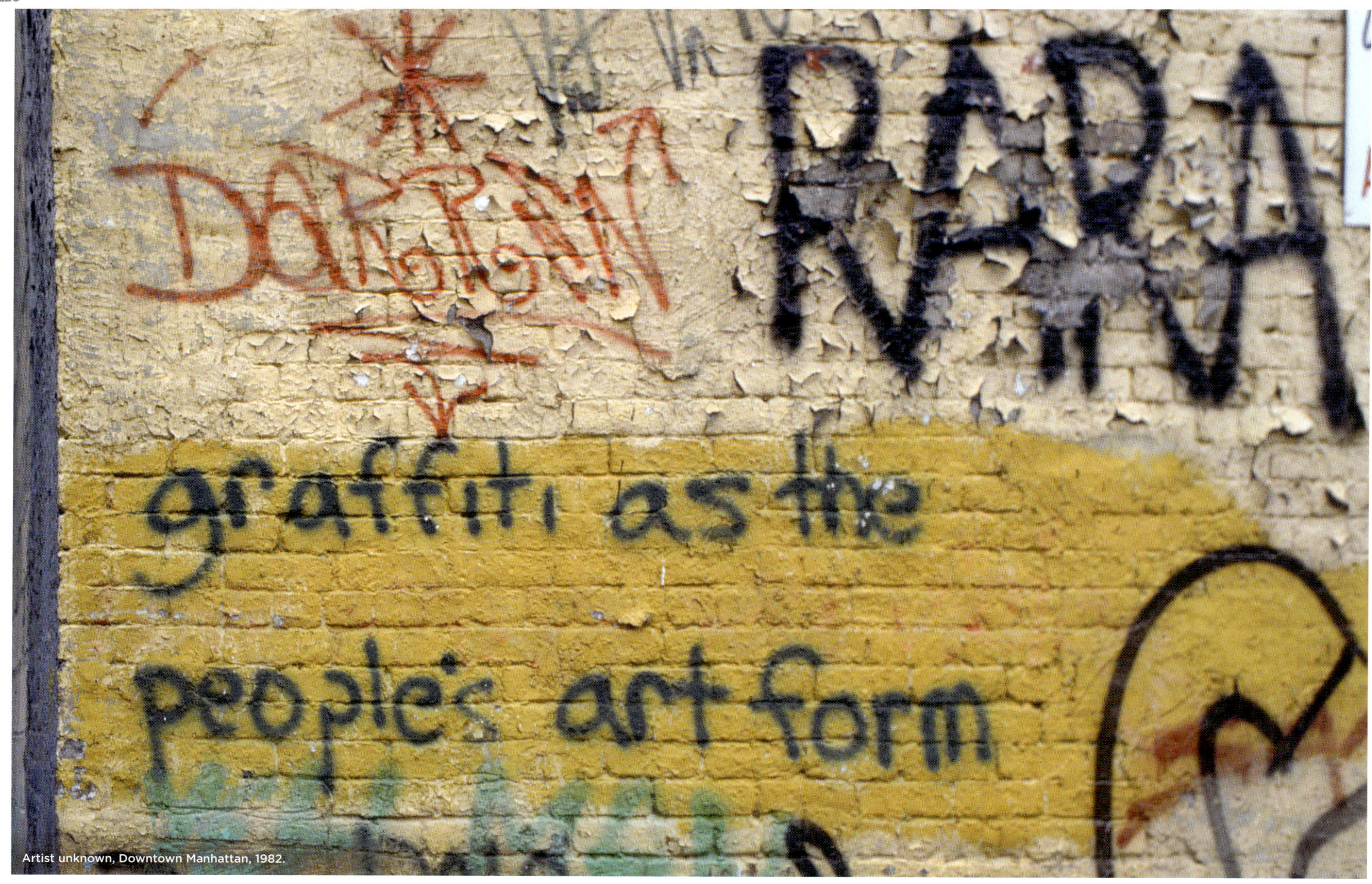

Artist unknown, Downtown Manhattan, 1982.

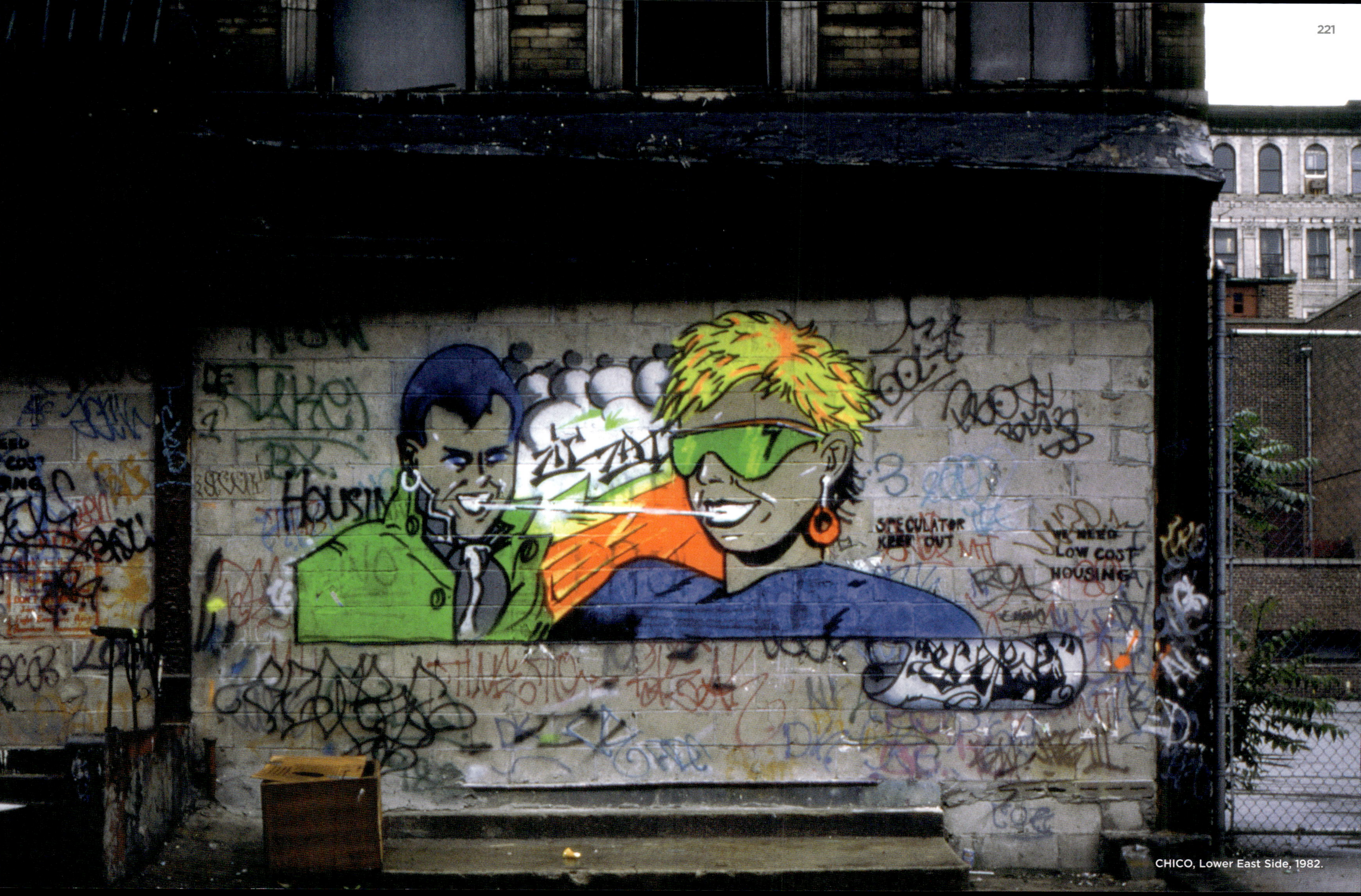

CHICO, Lower East Side, 1982.

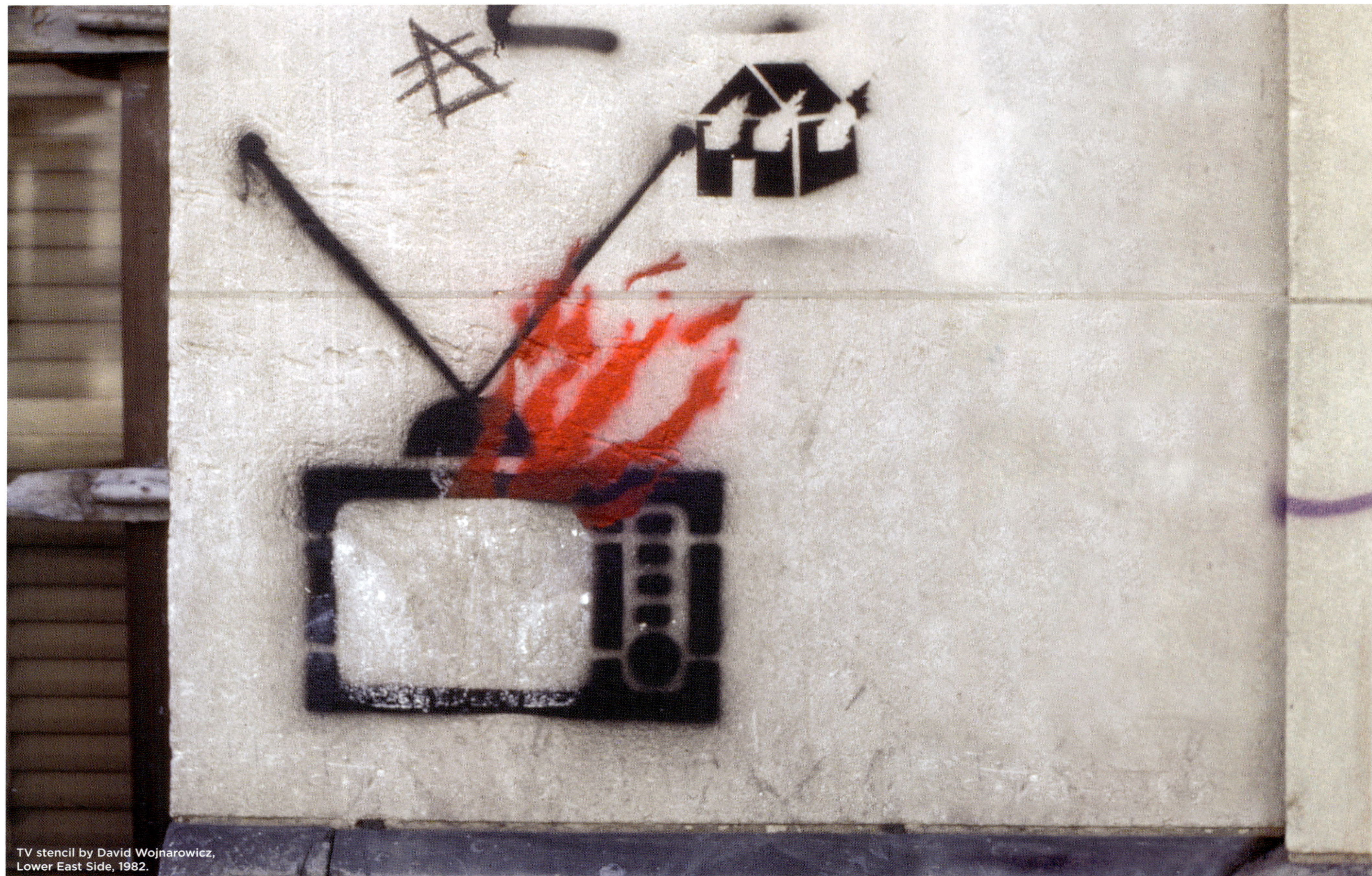

TV stencil by David Wojnarowicz,
Lower East Side, 1982.

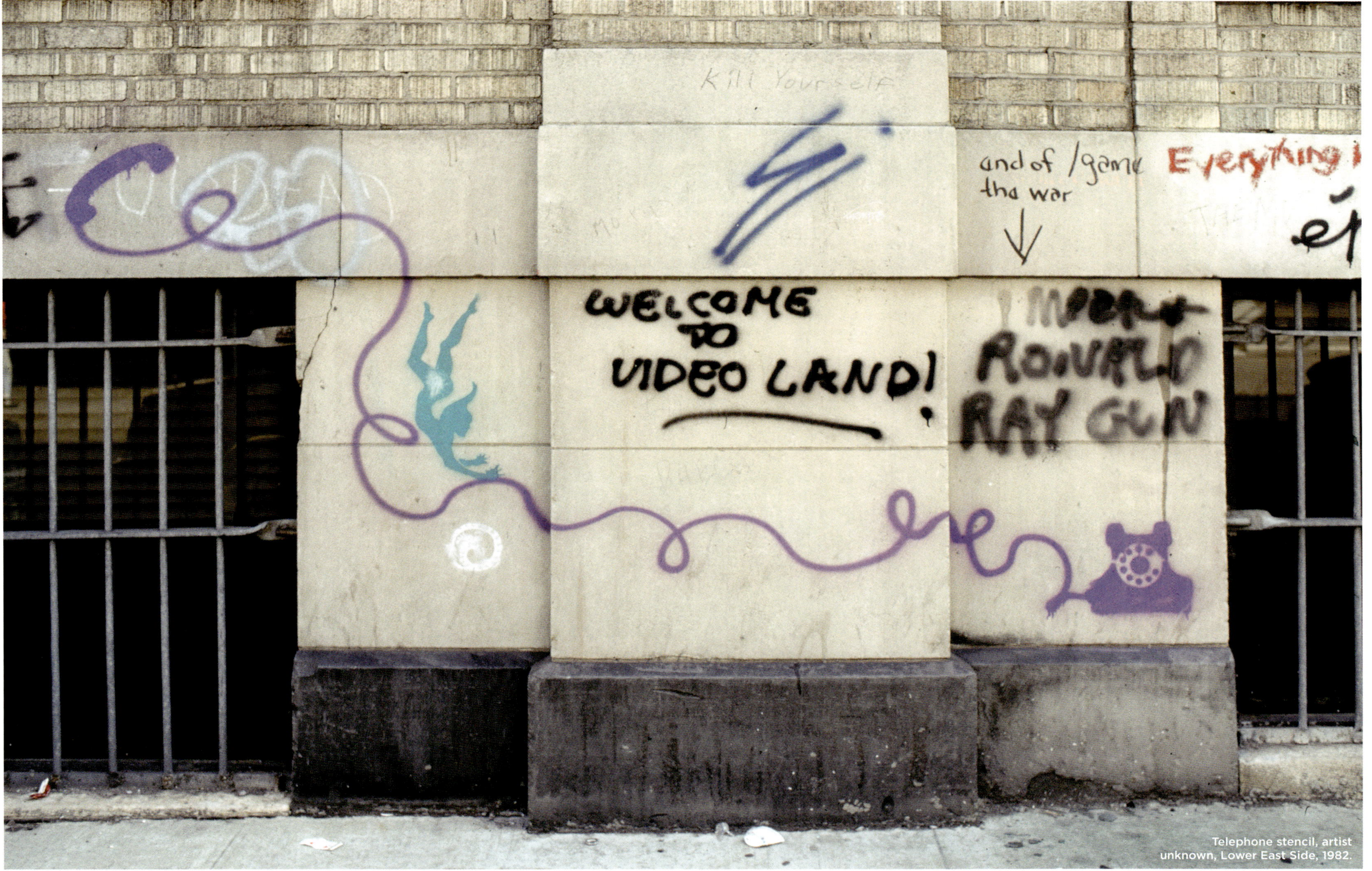

Telephone stencil, artist
unknown, Lower East Side, 1982.

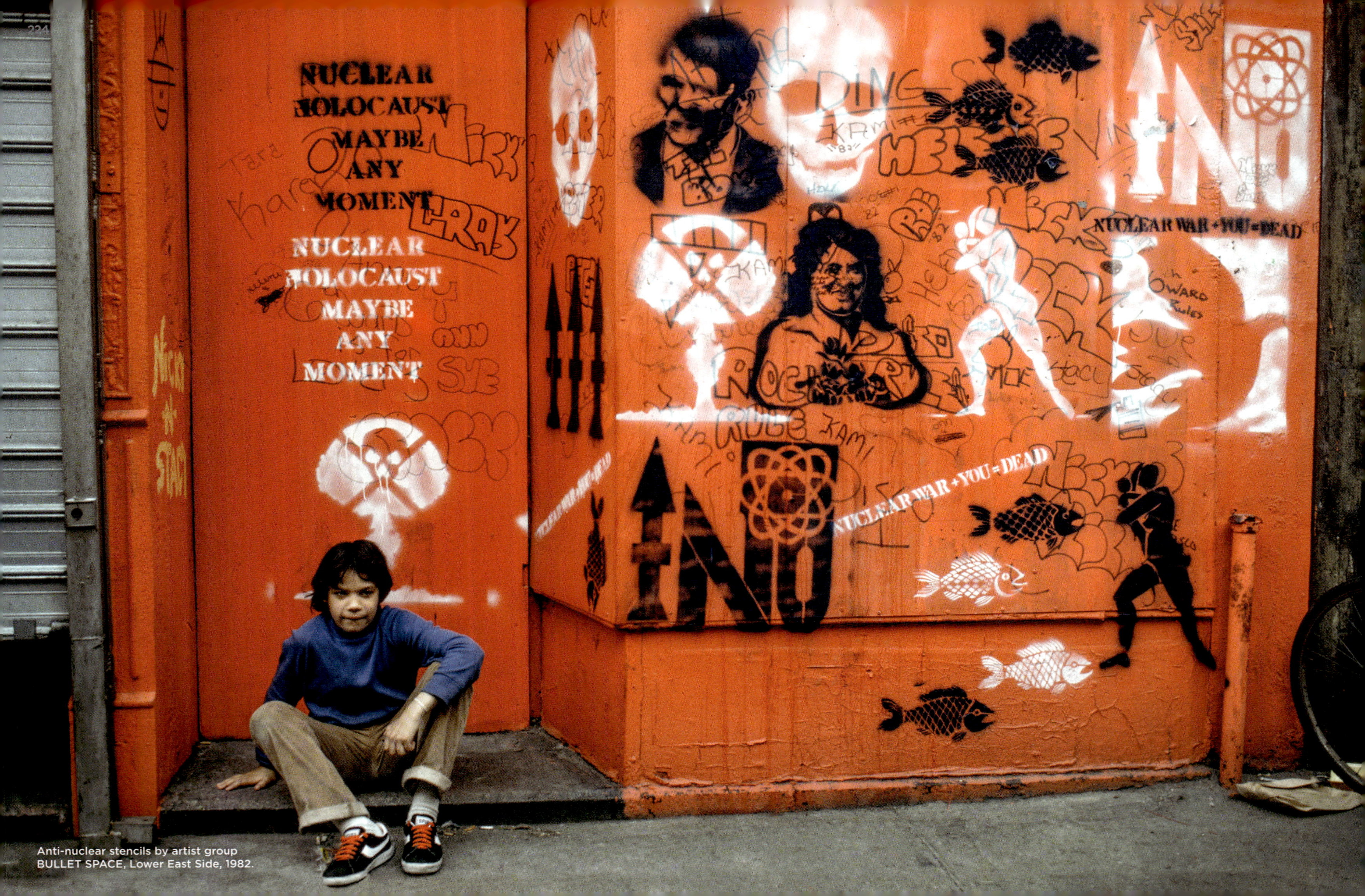

Anti-nuclear stencils by artist group
BULLET SPACE, Lower East Side, 1982.

Artists unknown, Lower East Side, 1982.

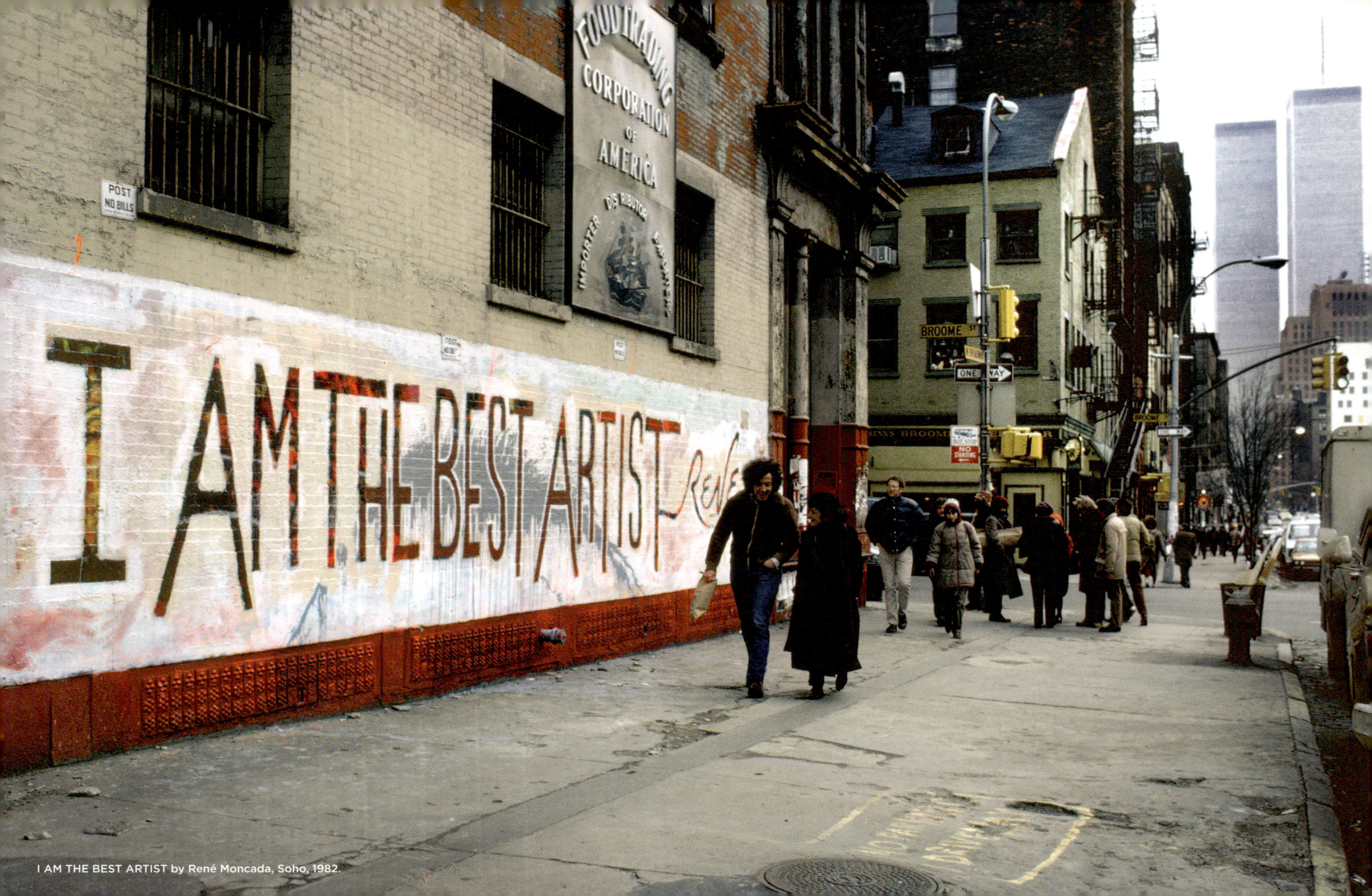

I AM THE BEST ARTIST by René Moncada, Soho, 1982.

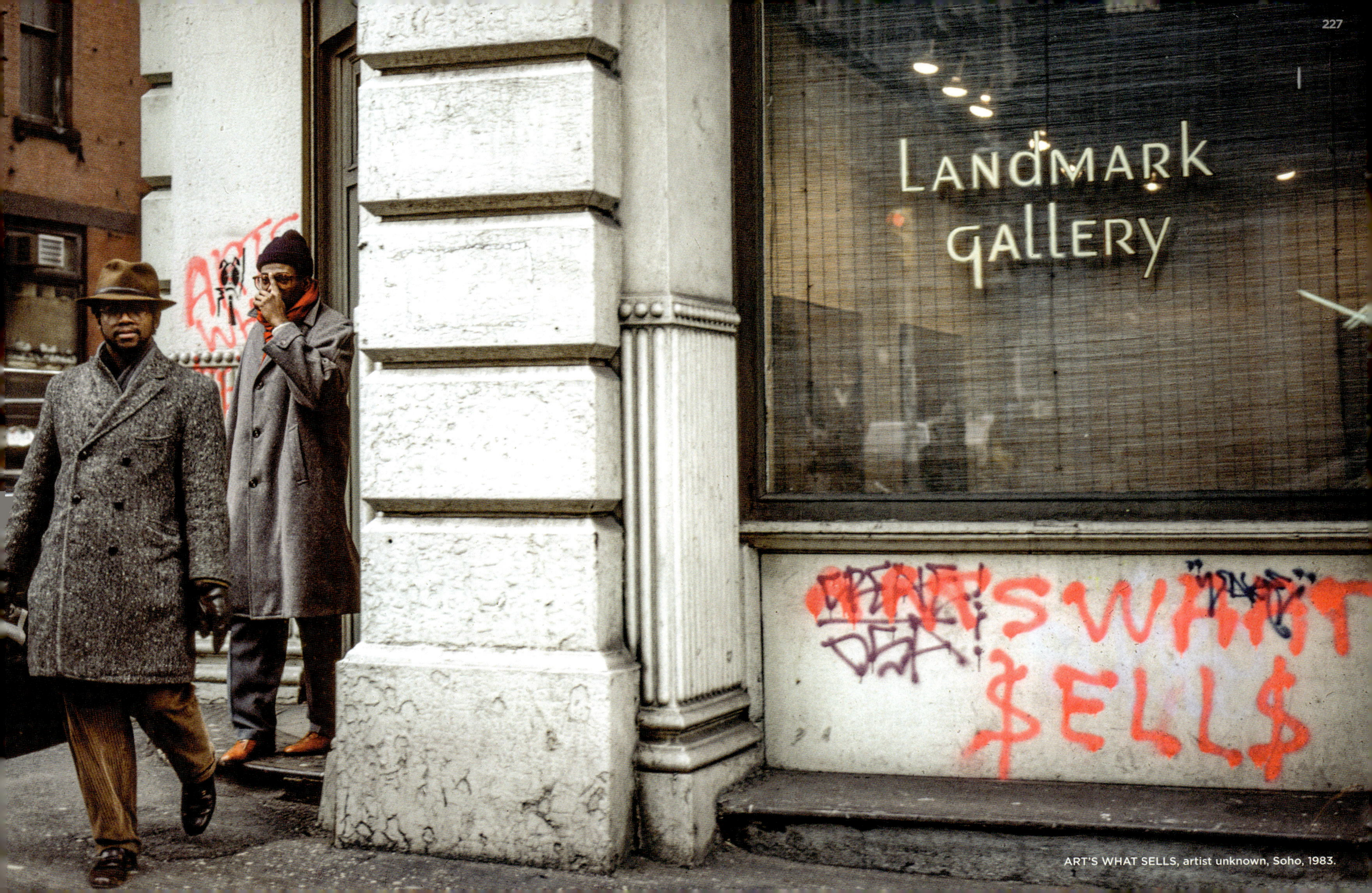

ART'S WHAT SELLS, artist unknown, Soho, 1983.

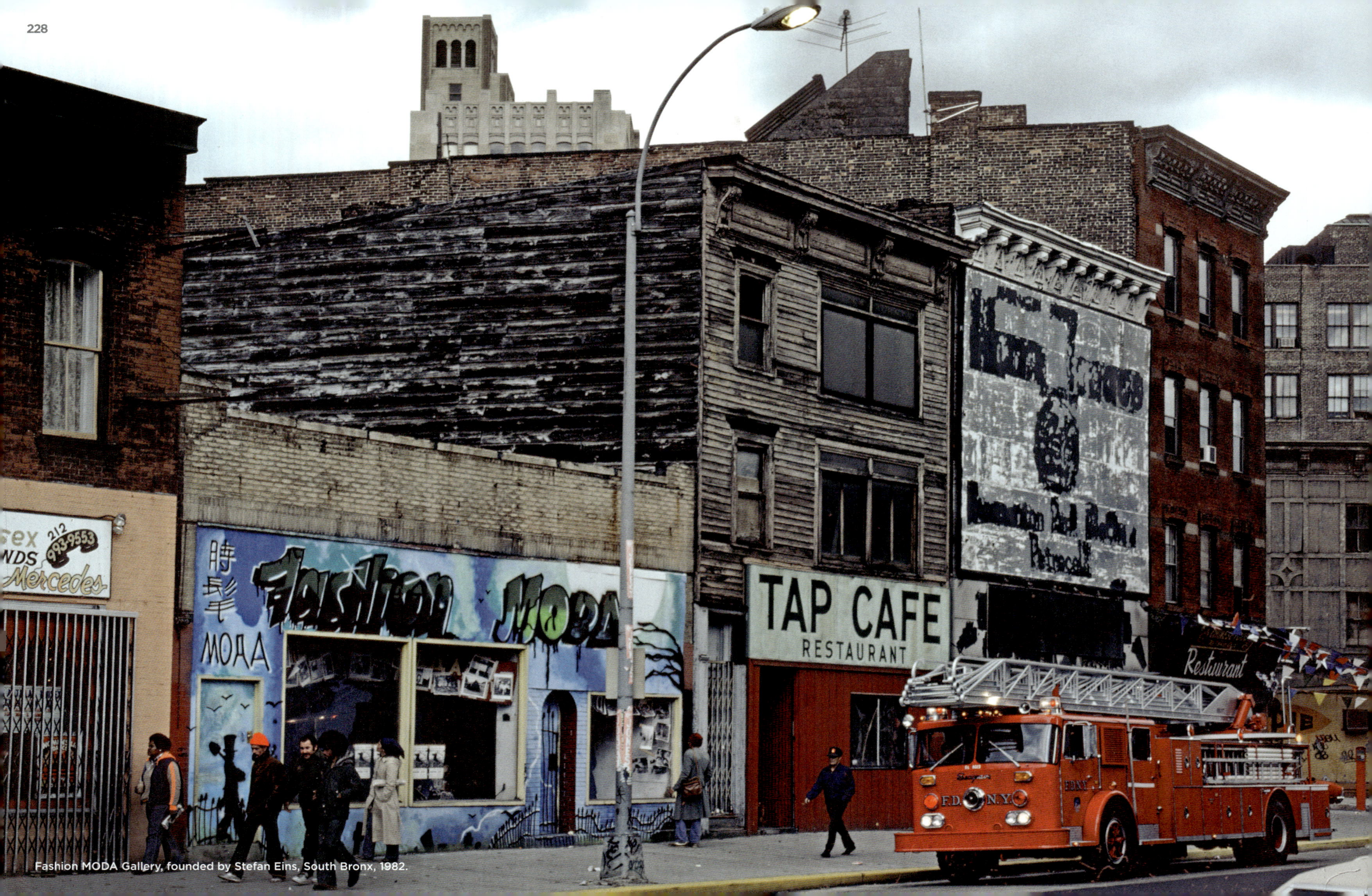

Fashion MODA Gallery, founded by Stefan Eins, South Bronx, 1982.

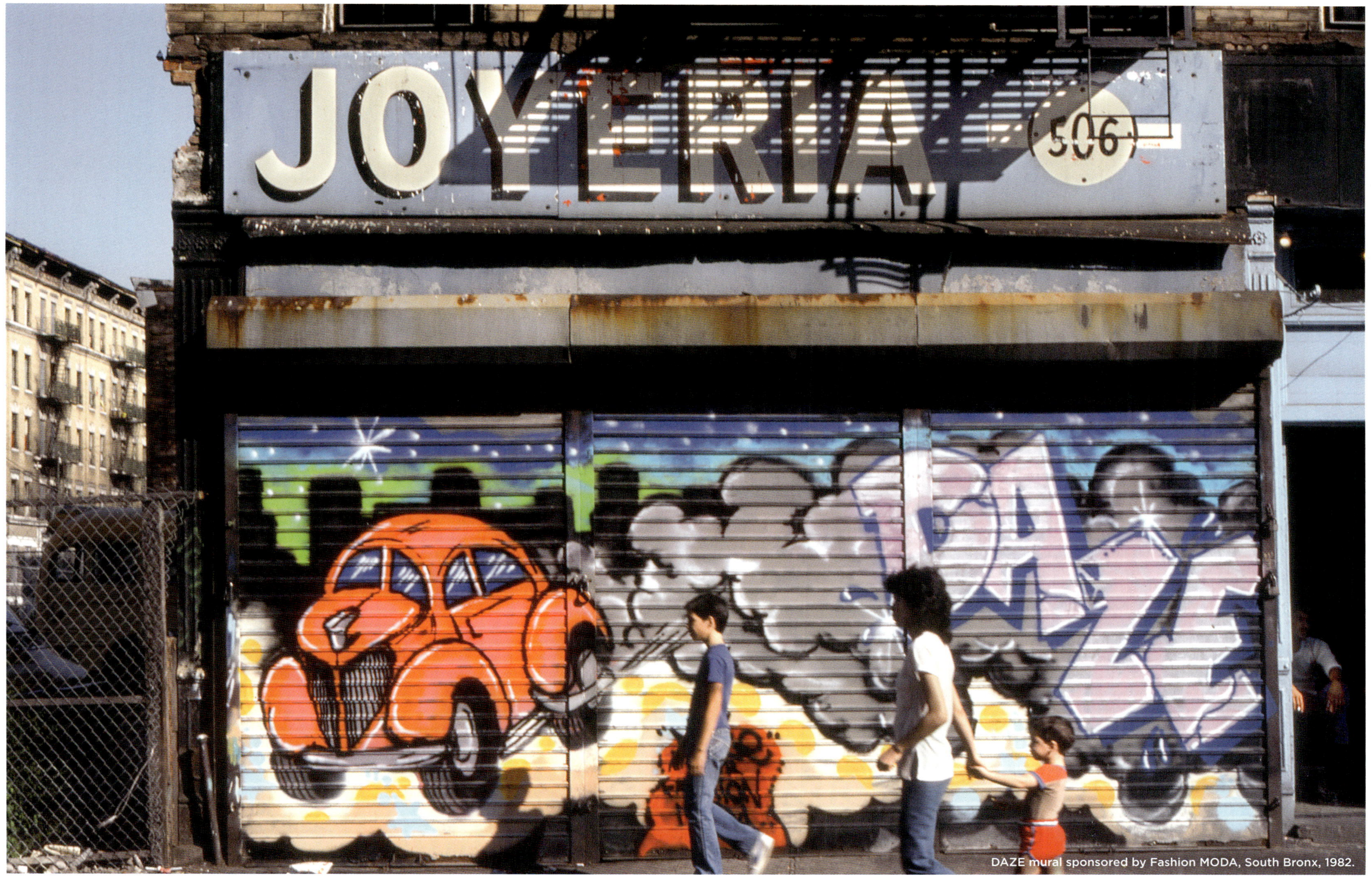

DAZE mural sponsored by Fashion MODA, South Bronx, 1982.

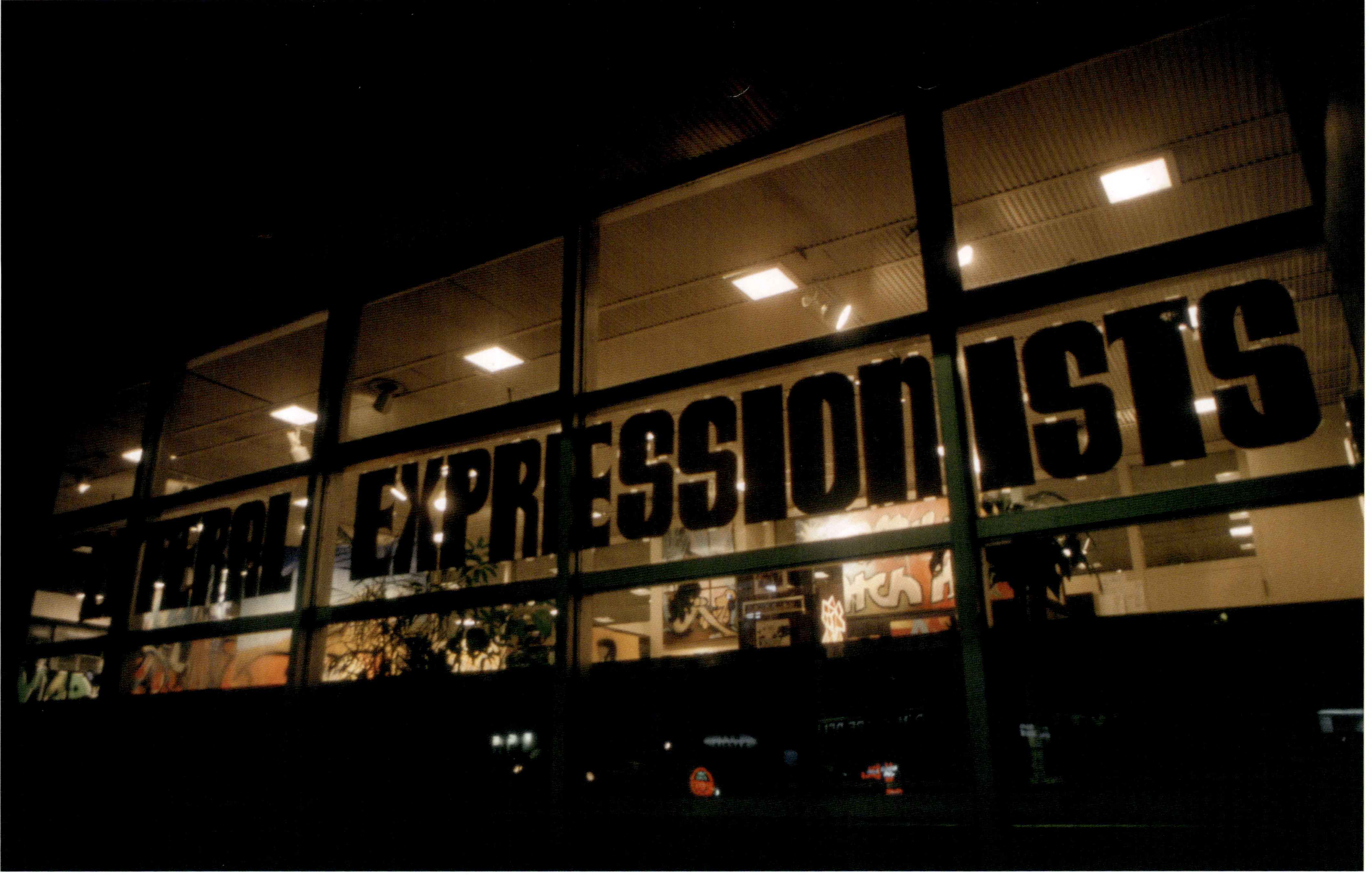
FERAL EXPRESSIONISTS

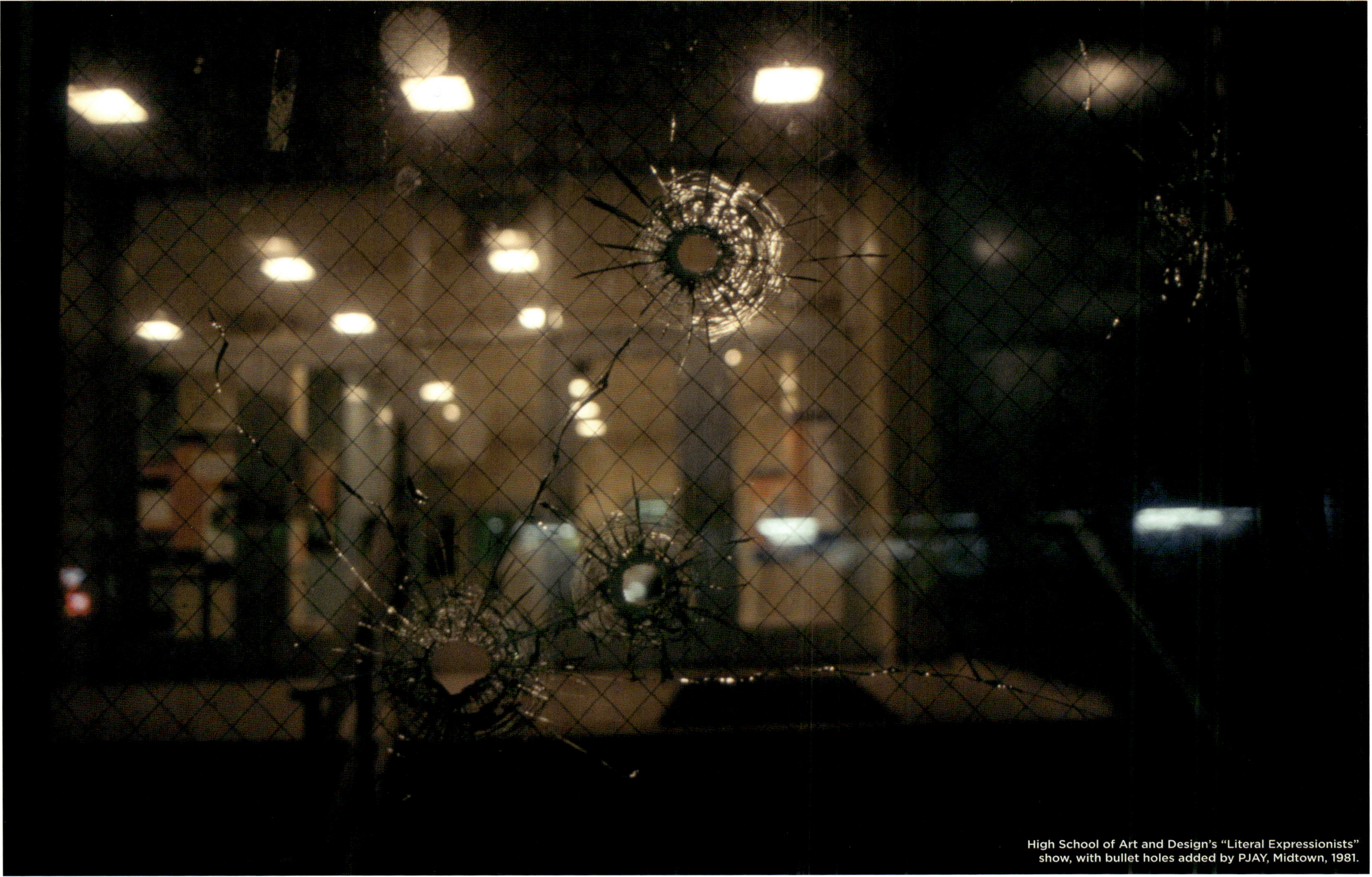

High School of Art and Design's "Literal Expressionists"
show, with bullet holes added by PJAY, Midtown, 1981.

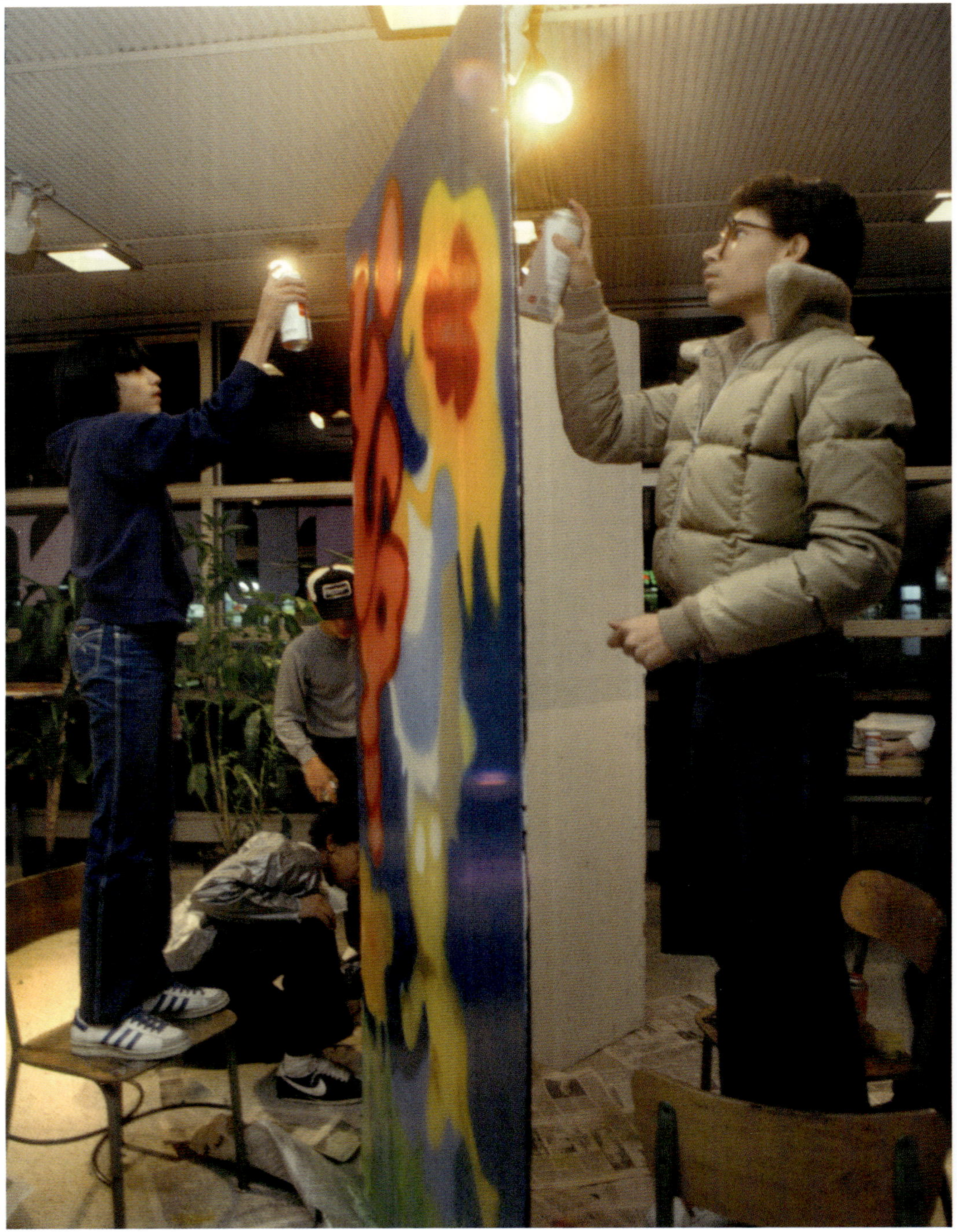

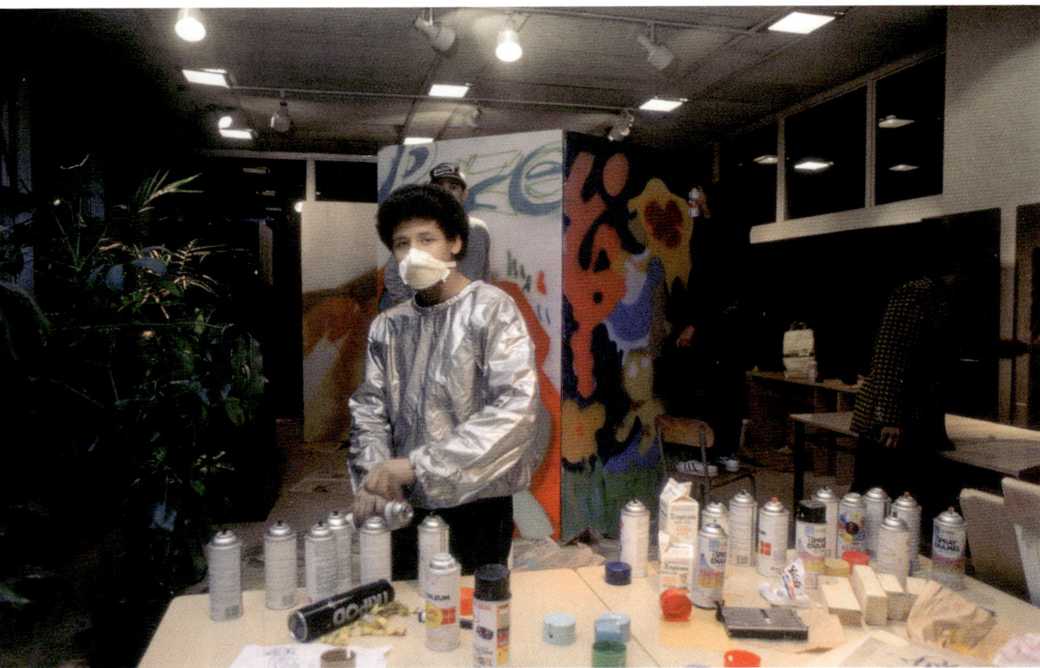
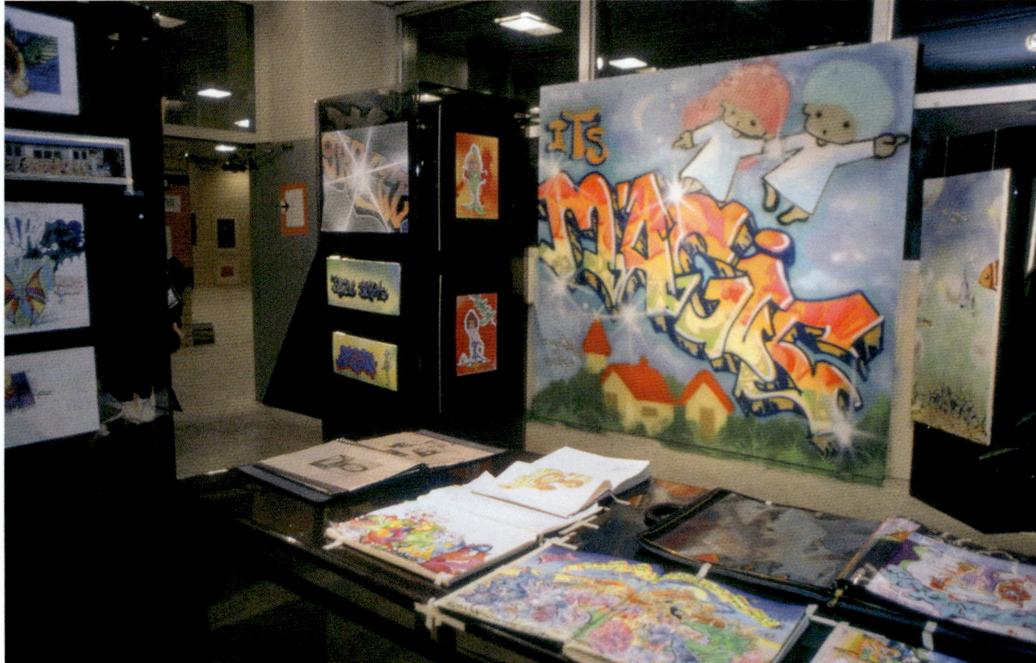

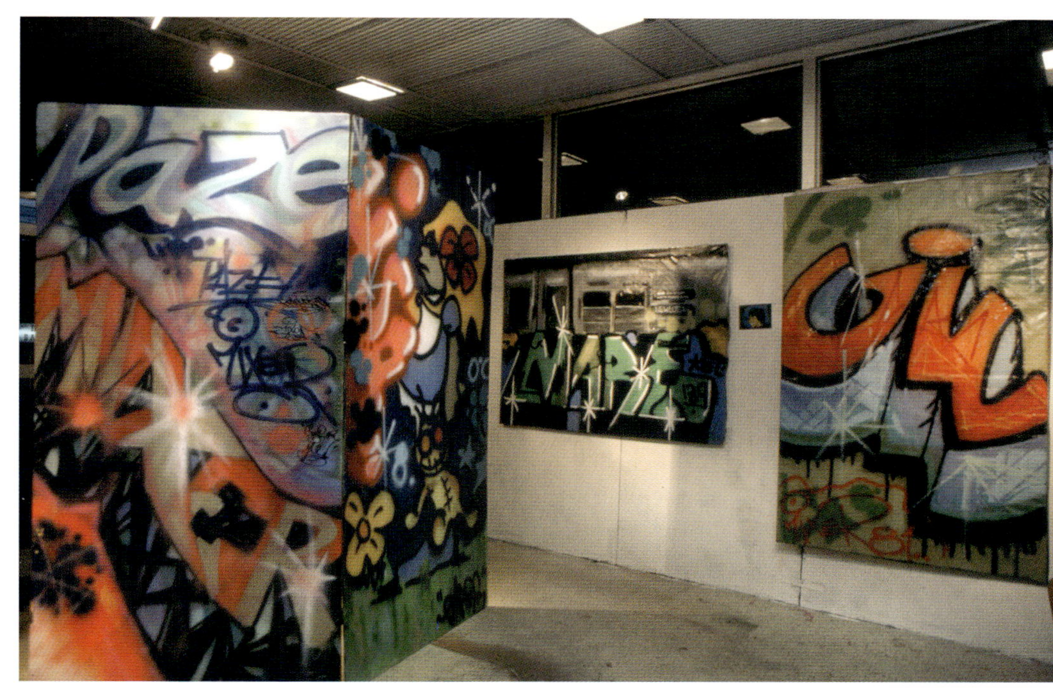

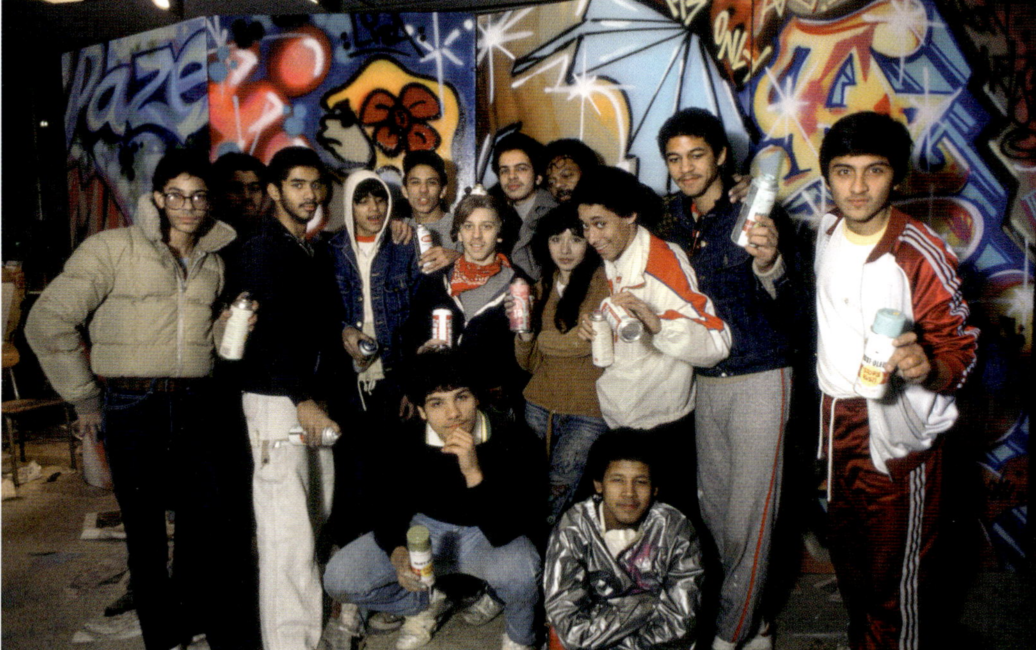

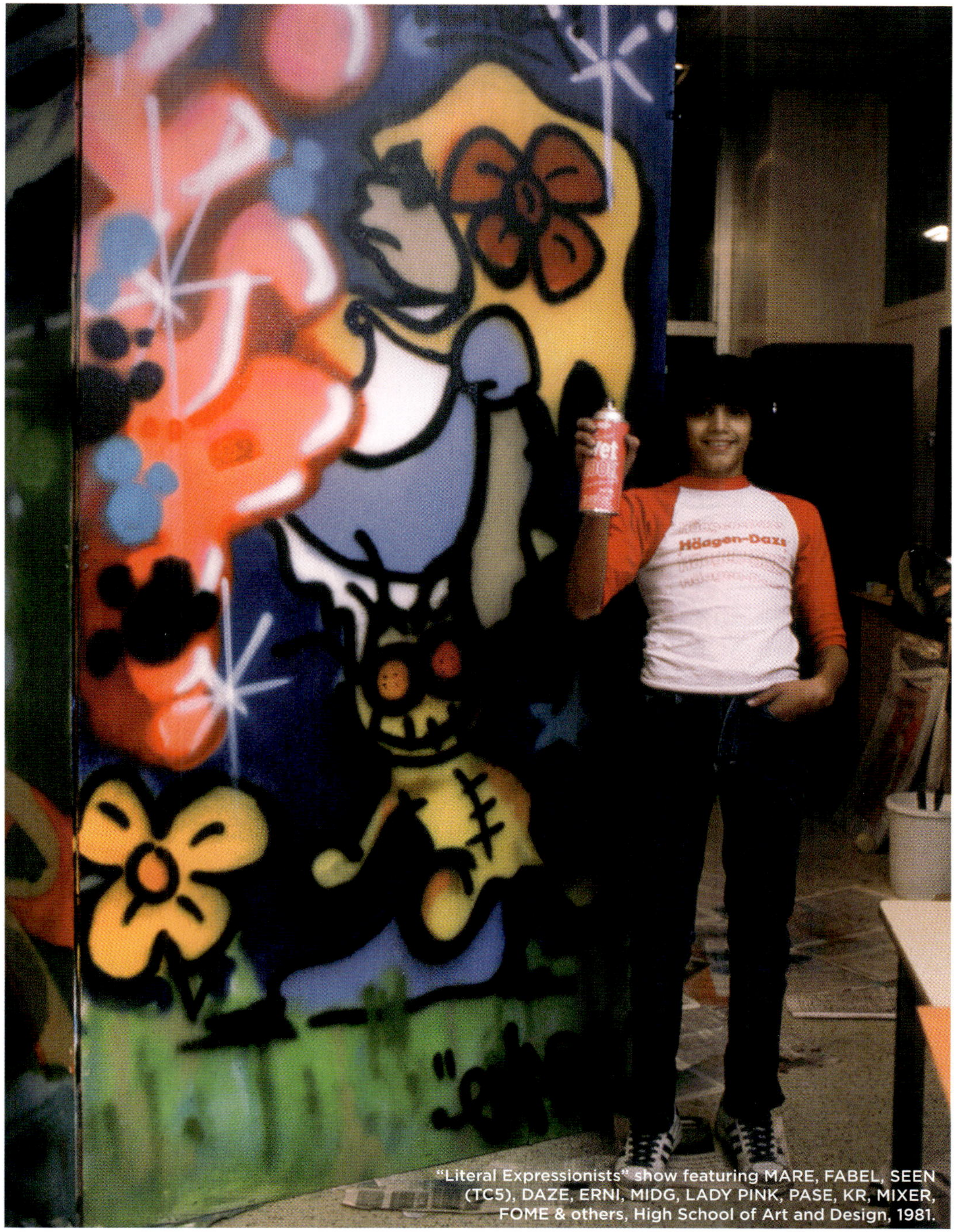

"Literal Expressionists" show featuring MARE, FABEL, SEEN (TC5), DAZE, ERNI, MIDG, LADY PINK, PASE, KR, MIXER, FOME & others, High School of Art and Design, 1981.

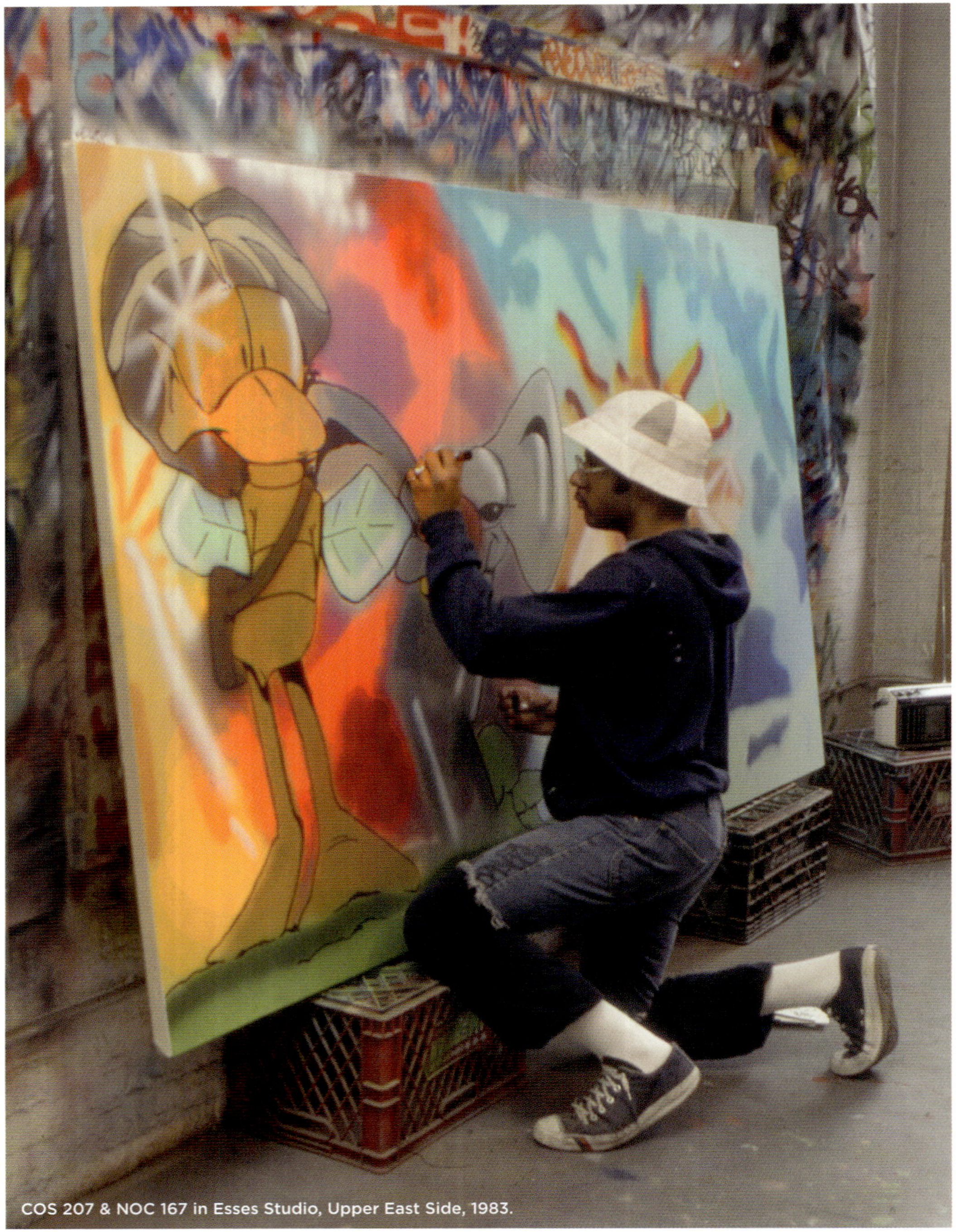

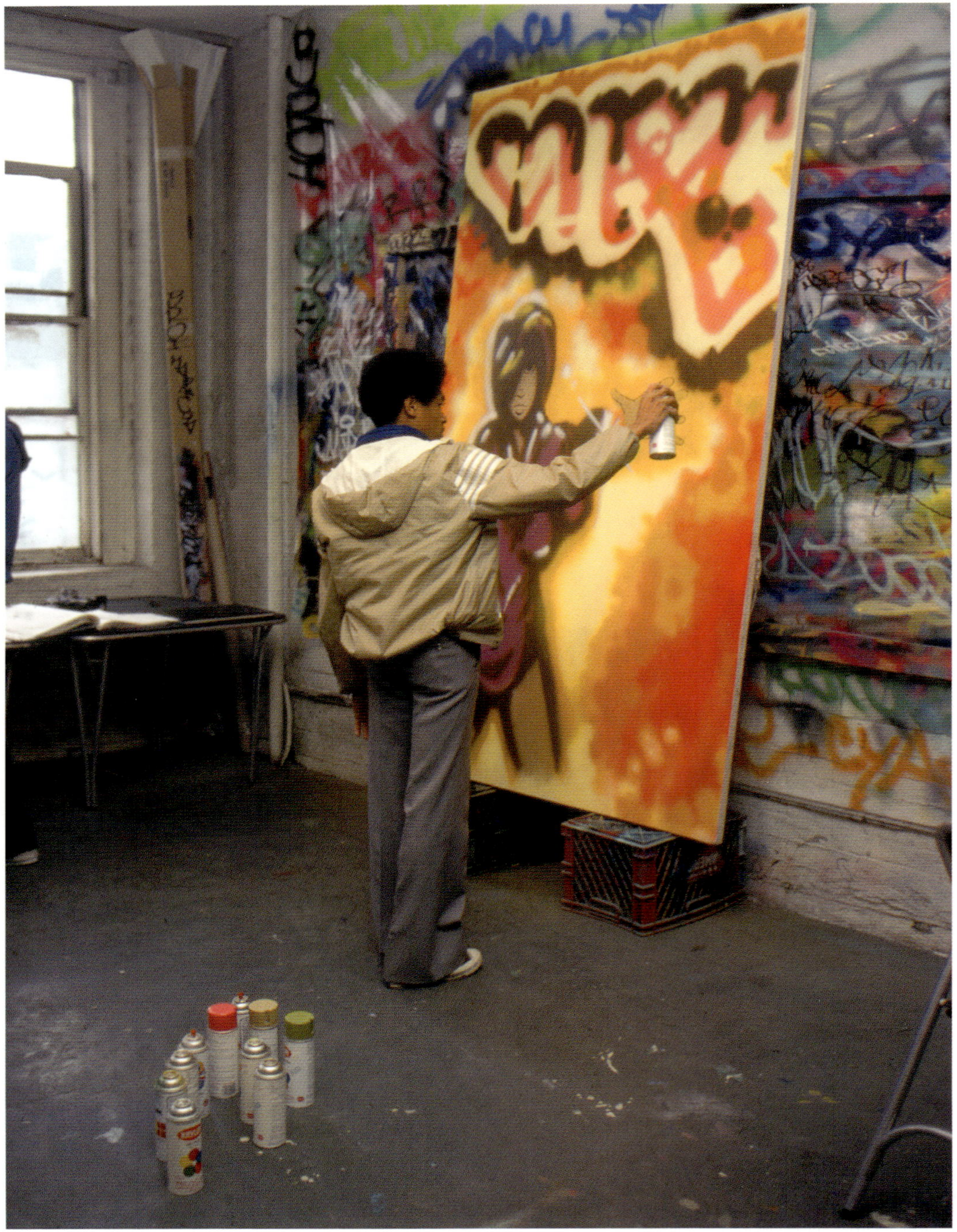

COS 207 & NOC 167 in Esses Studio, Upper East Side, 1983.

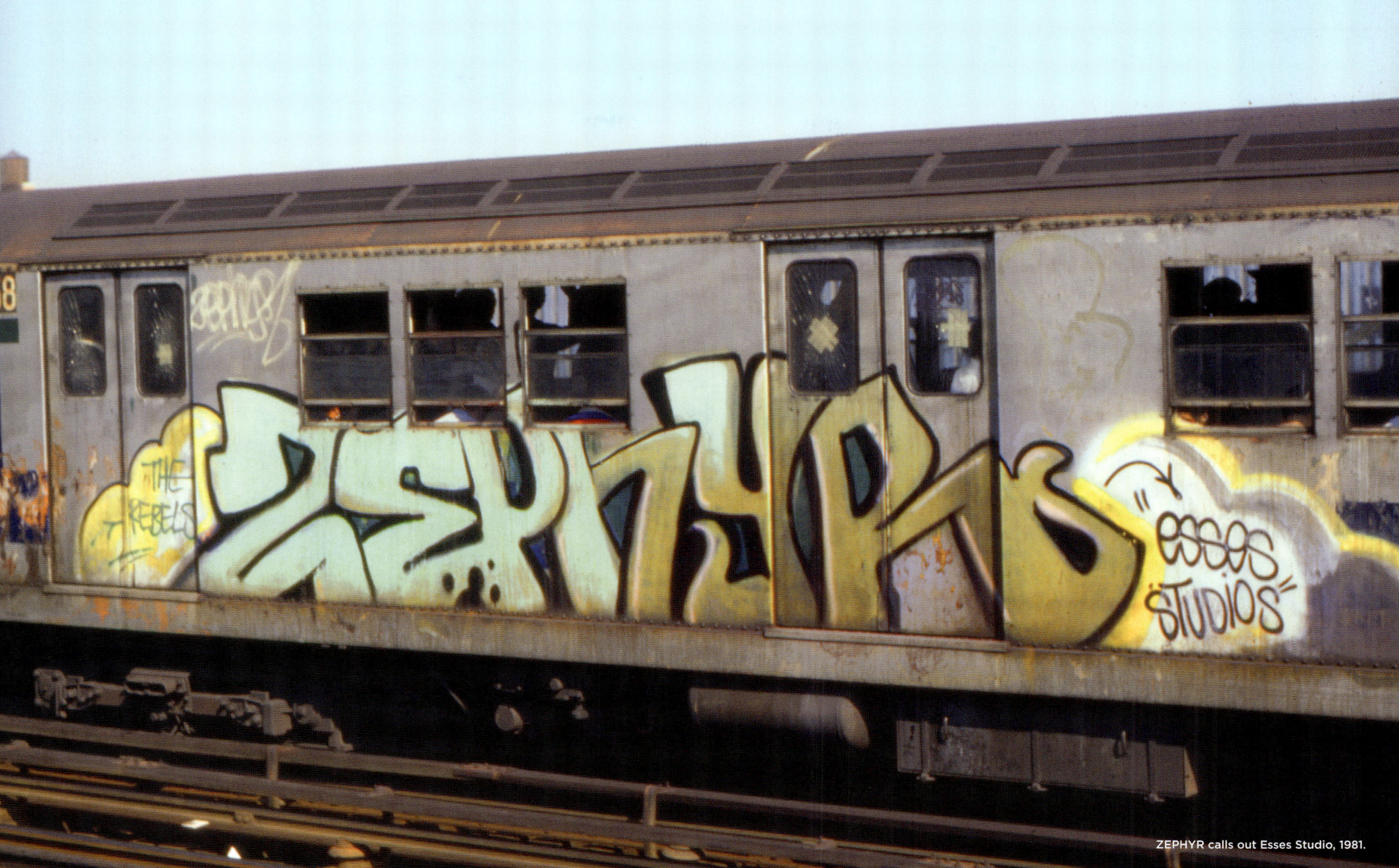

ZEPHYR calls out Esses Studio, 1981.

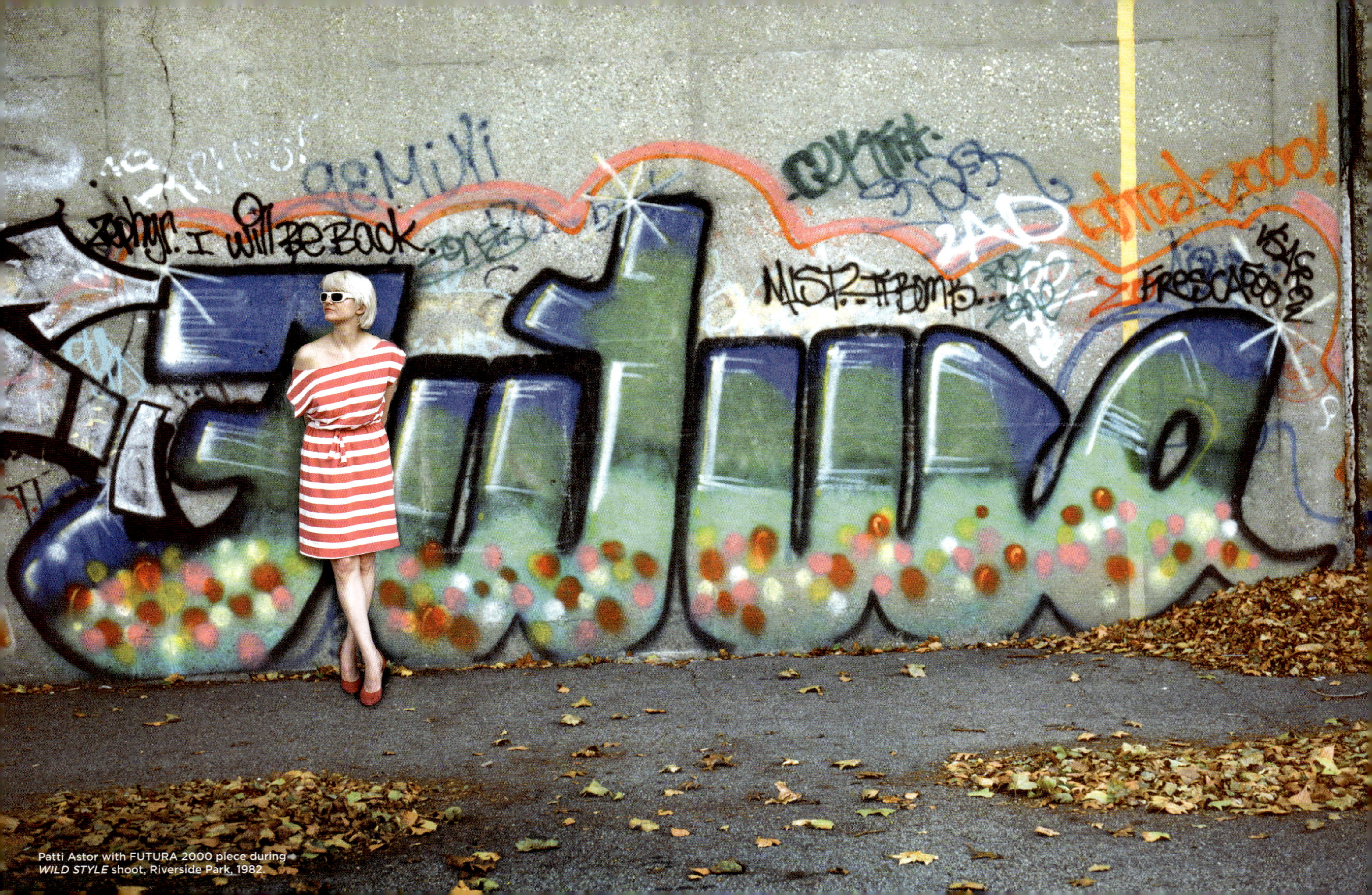

Patti Astor with FUTURA 2000 piece during
WILD STYLE shoot, Riverside Park, 1982.

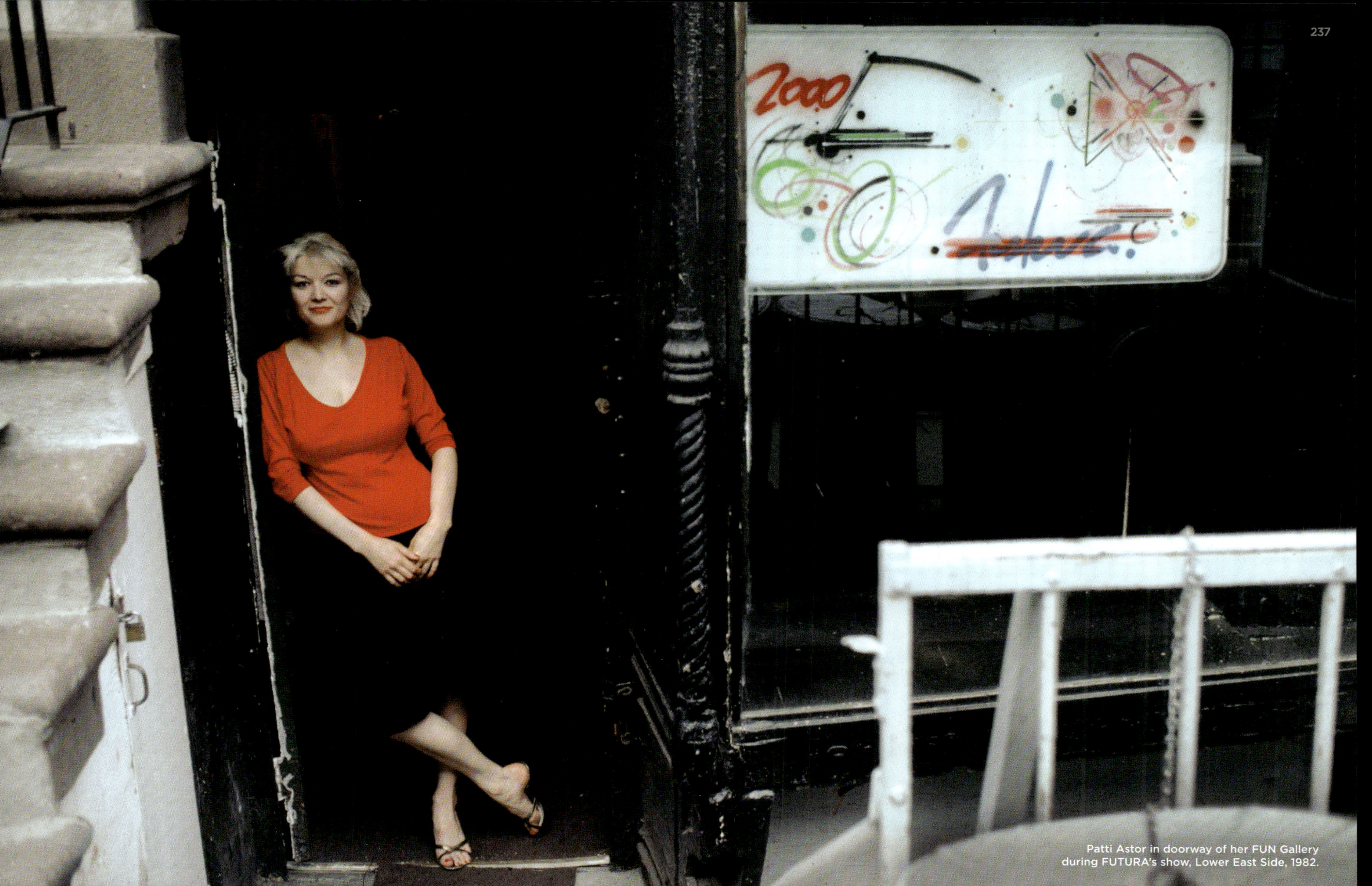

Patti Astor in doorway of her FUN Gallery
during FUTURA's show, Lower East Side, 1982.

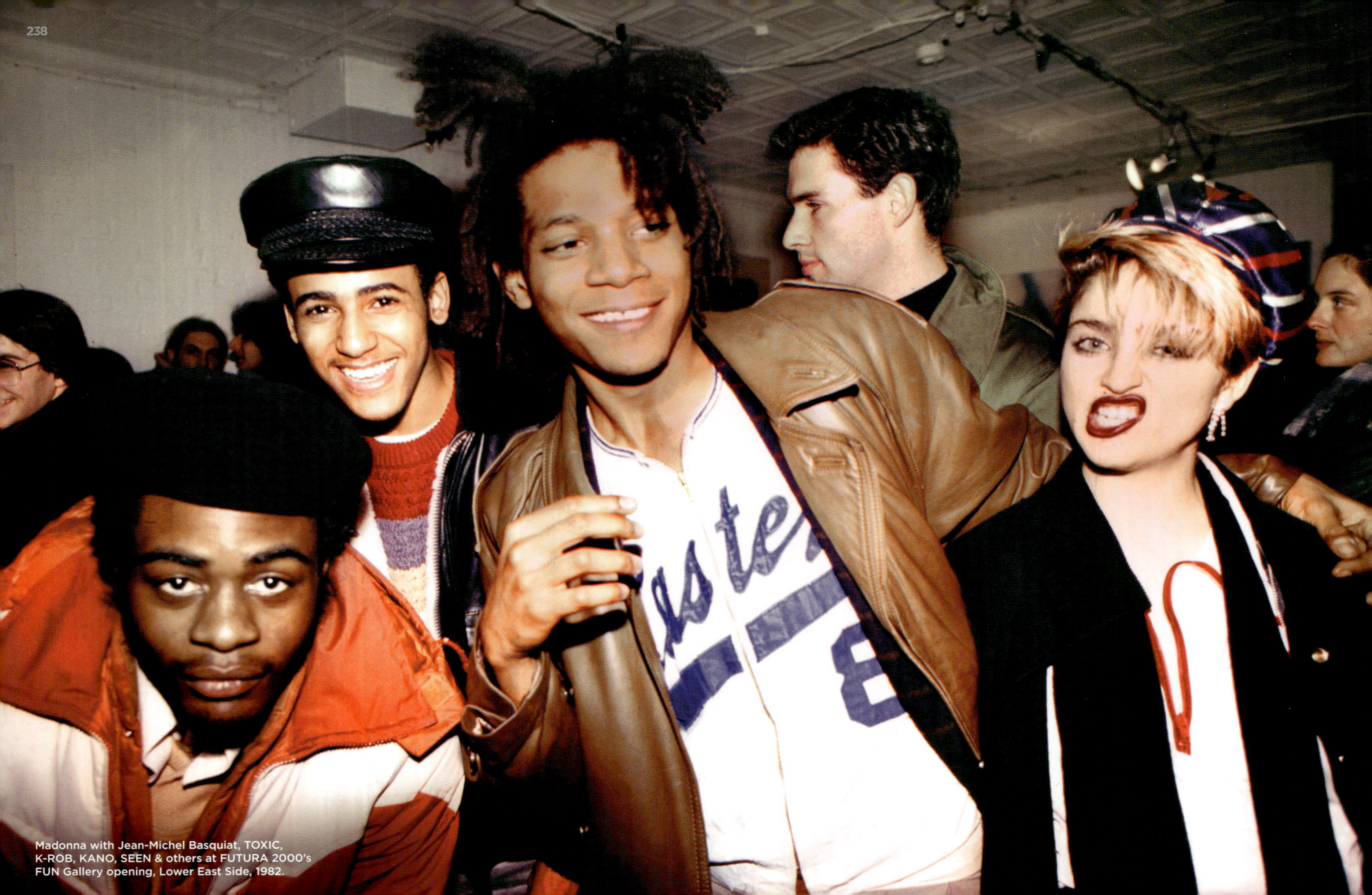

Madonna with Jean-Michel Basquiat, TOXIC,
K-ROB, KANO, SEEN & others at FUTURA 2000's
FUN Gallery opening, Lower East Side, 1982.

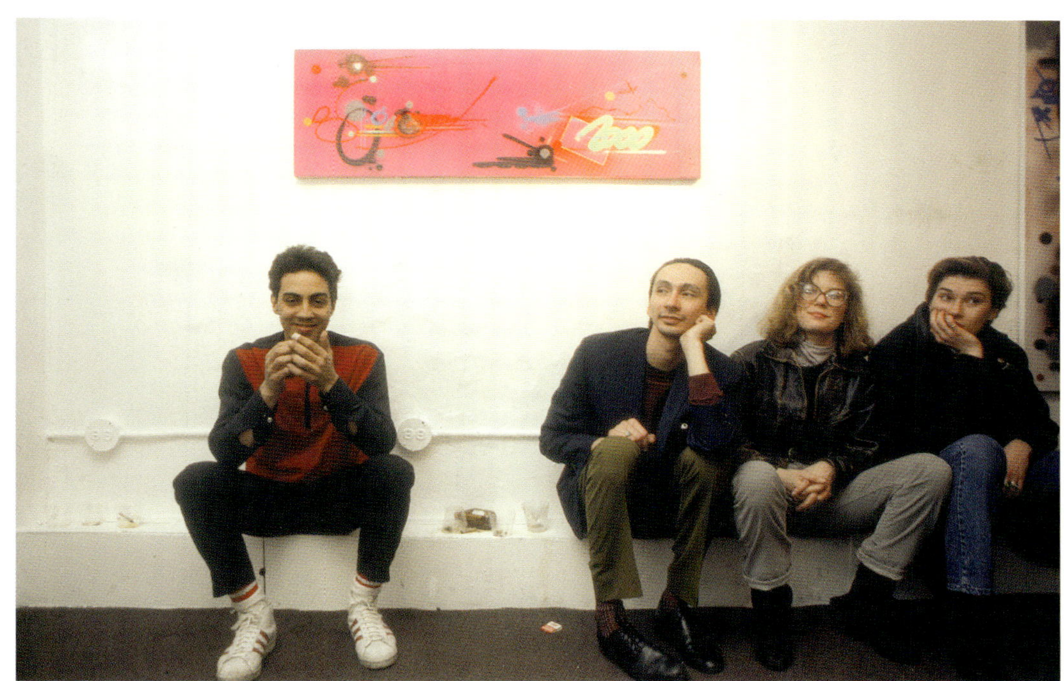
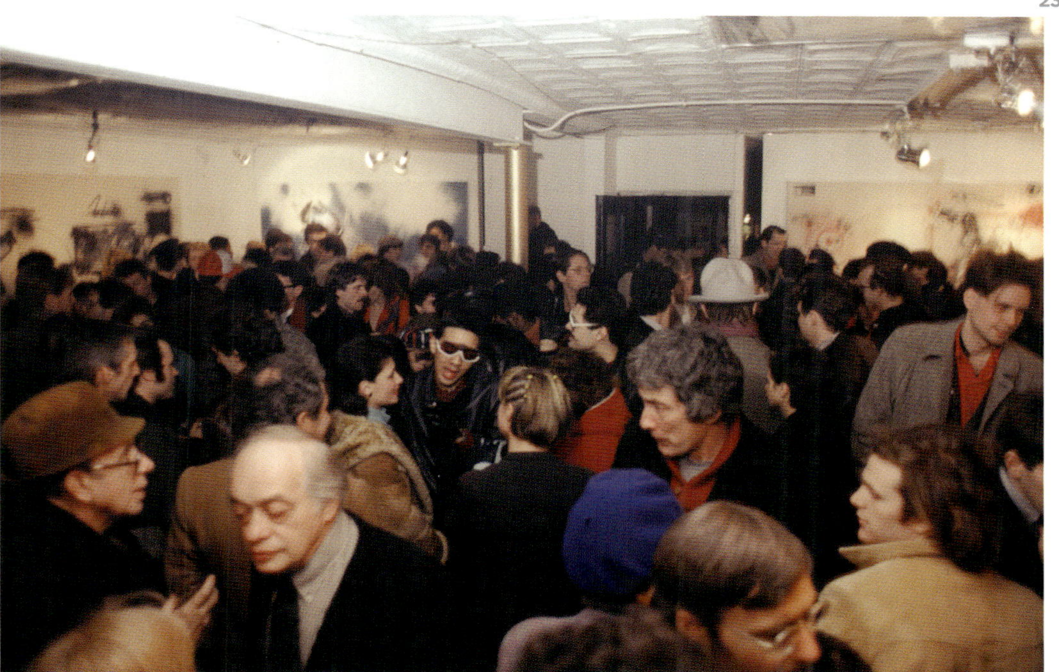
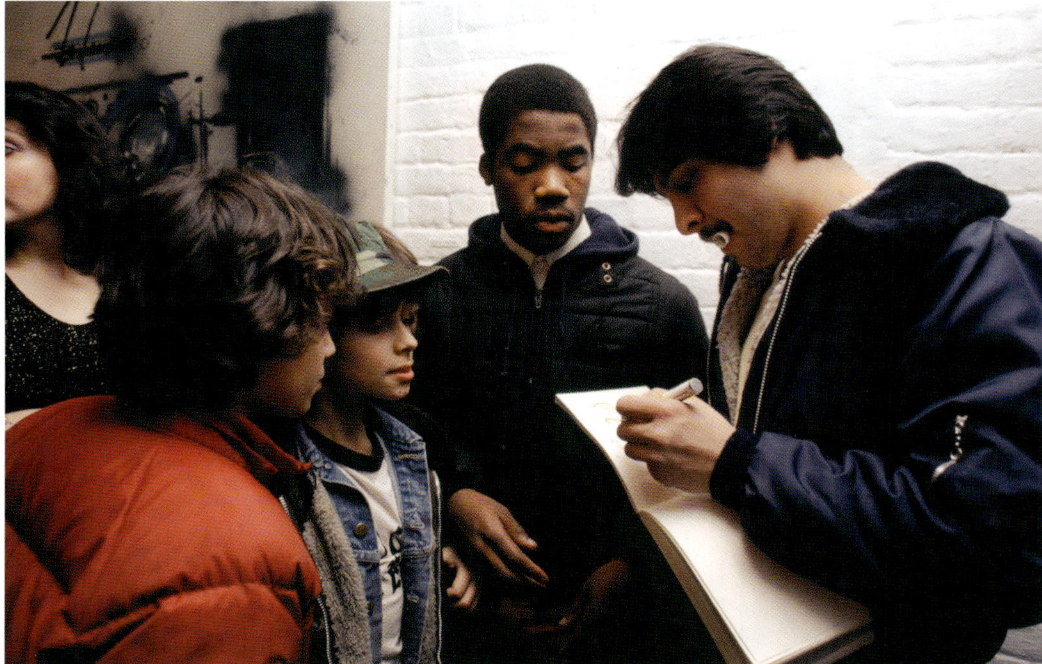
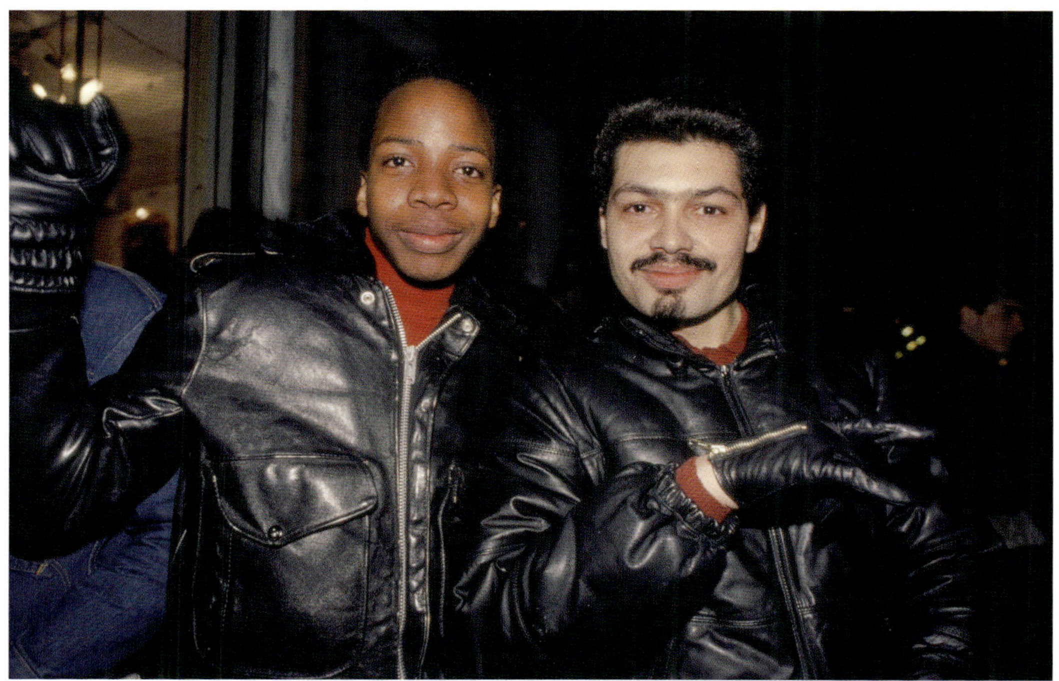

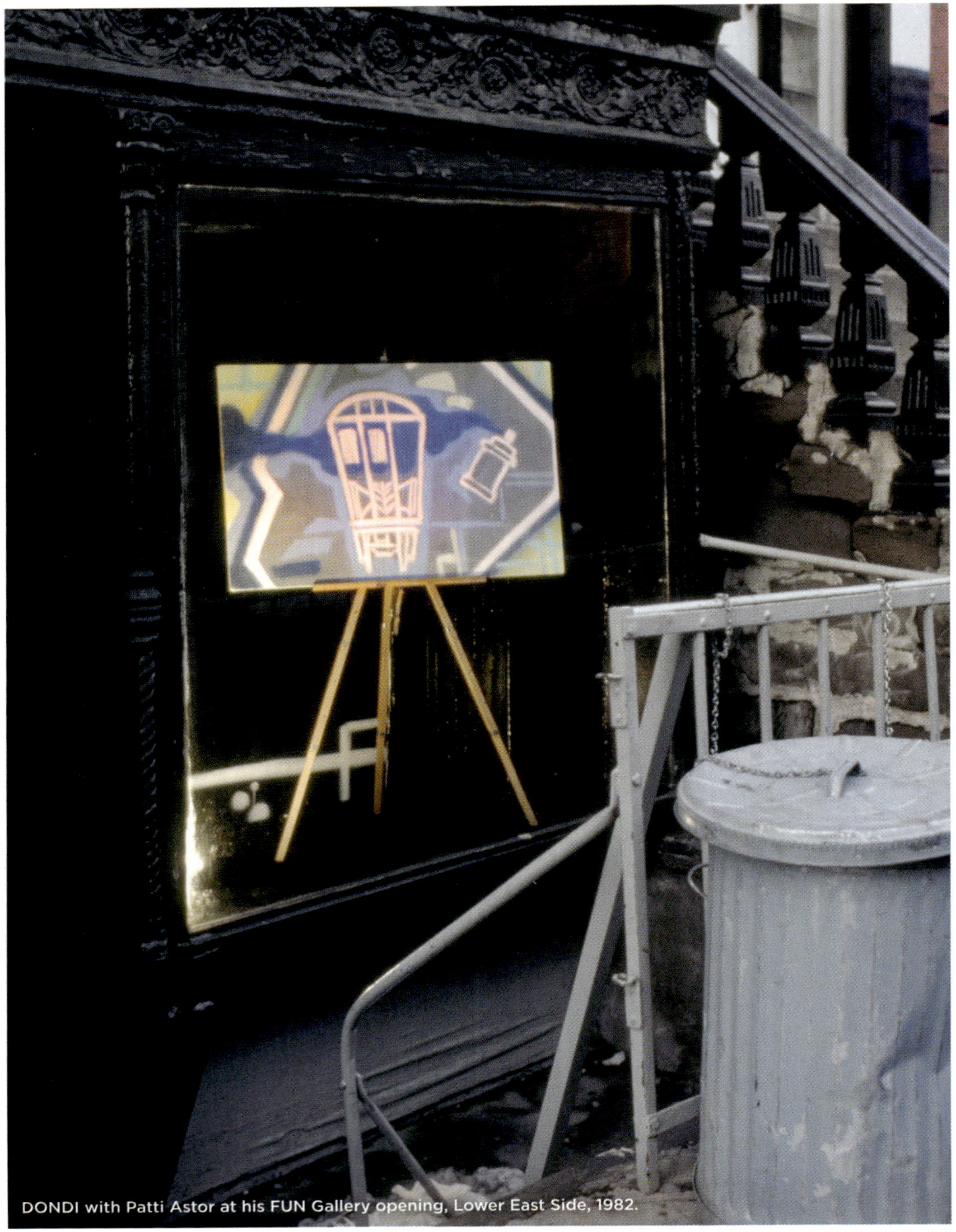

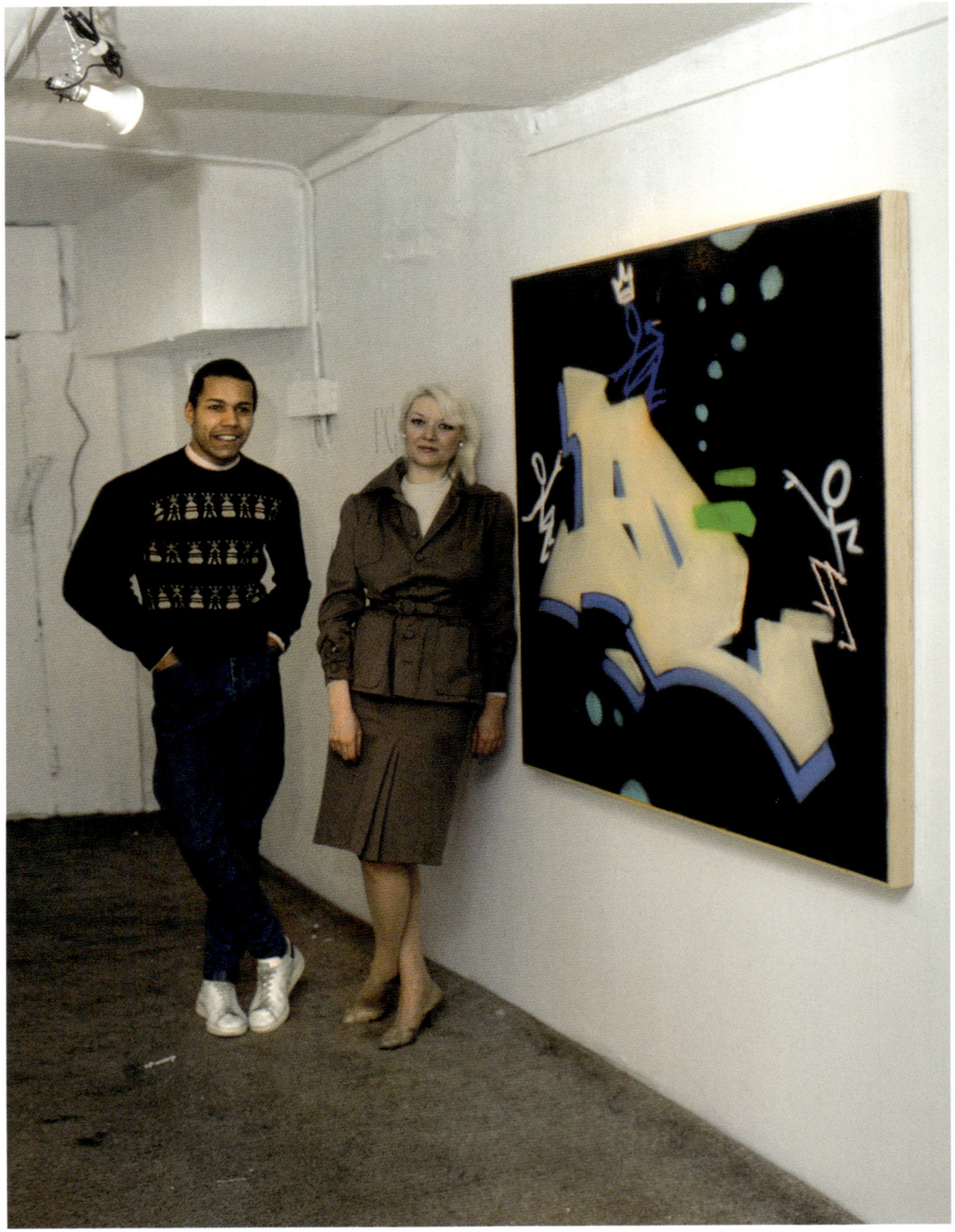

DONDI with Patti Astor at his FUN Gallery opening, Lower East Side, 1982.

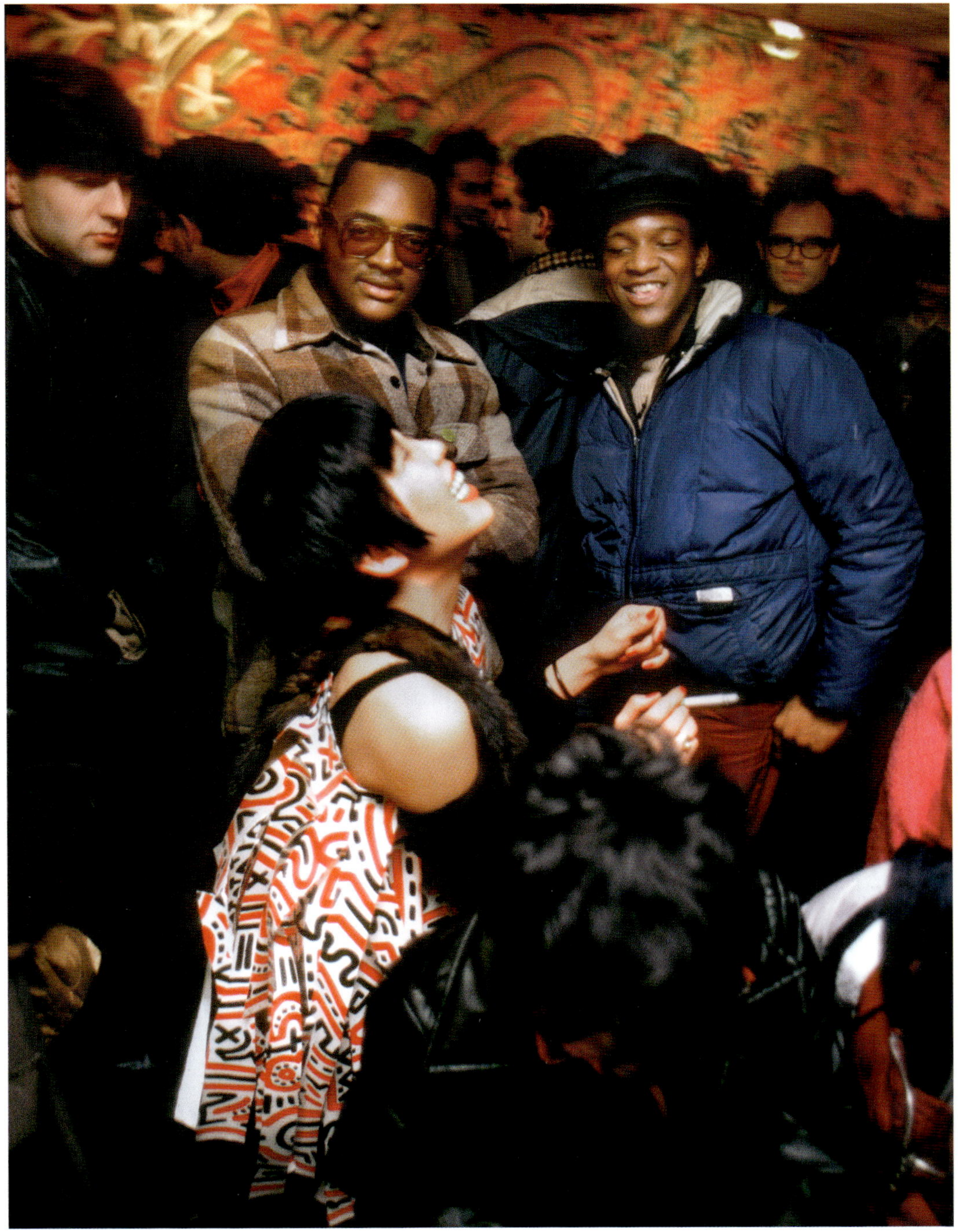

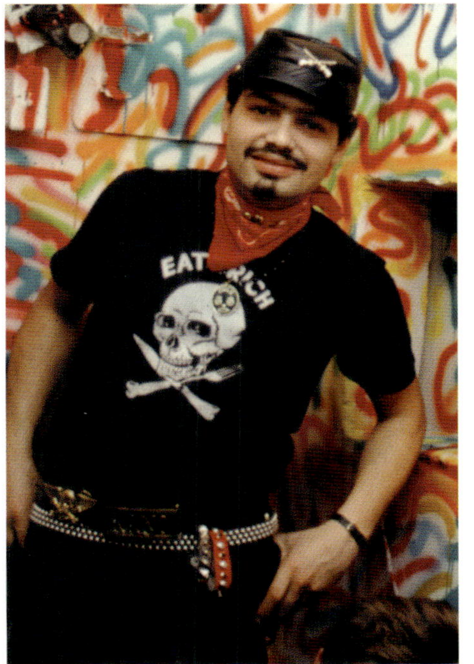

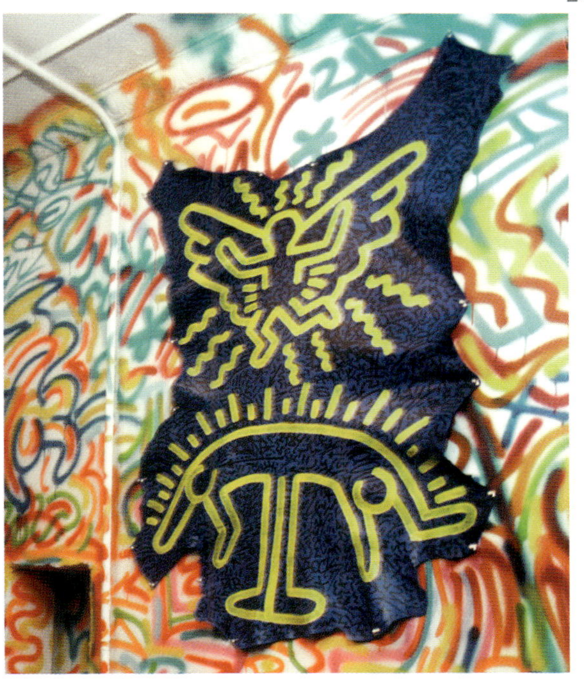

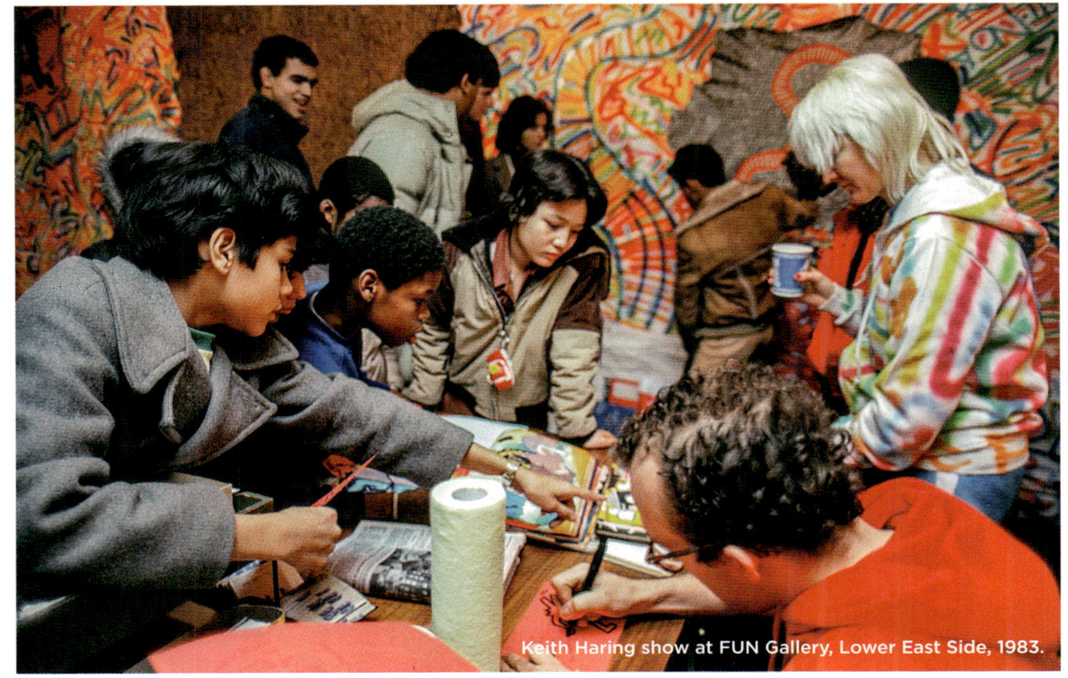

Keith Haring show at FUN Gallery, Lower East Side, 1983.

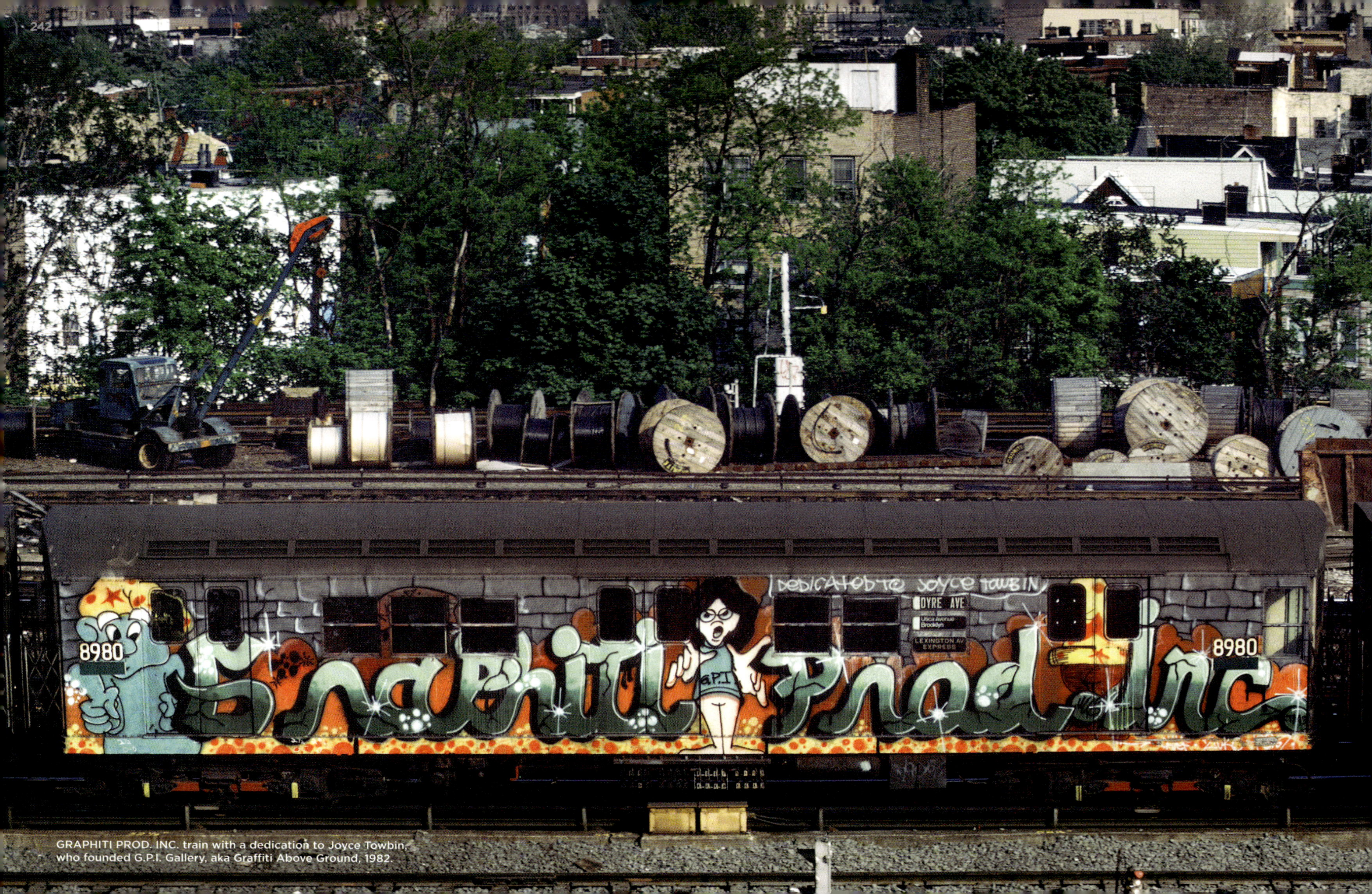

GRAPHITI PROD. INC. train with a dedication to Joyce Towbin, who founded G.P.I. Gallery, aka Graffiti Above Ground, 1982.

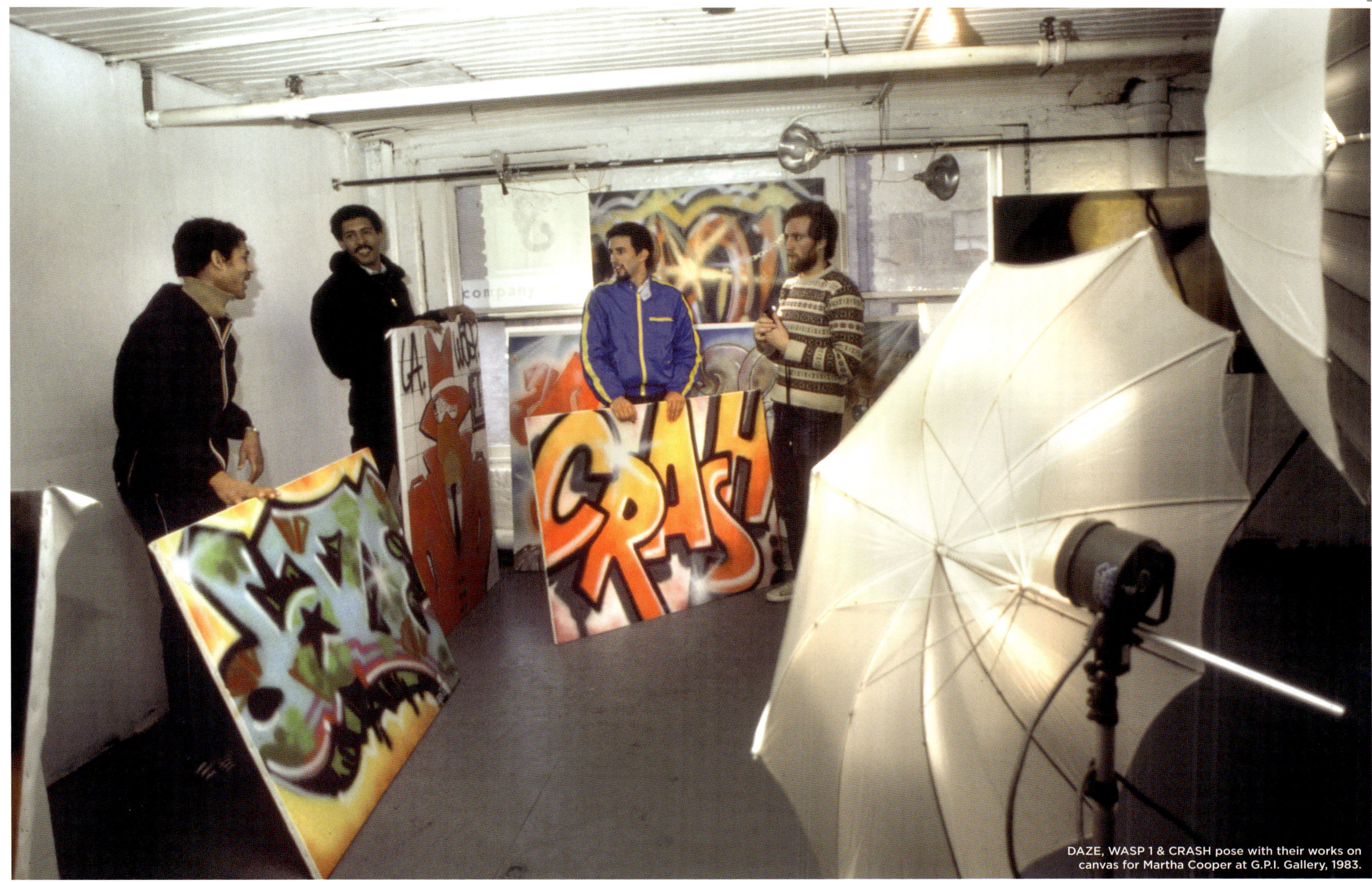

DAZE, WASP 1 & CRASH pose with their works on
canvas for Martha Cooper at G.P.I. Gallery, 1983.

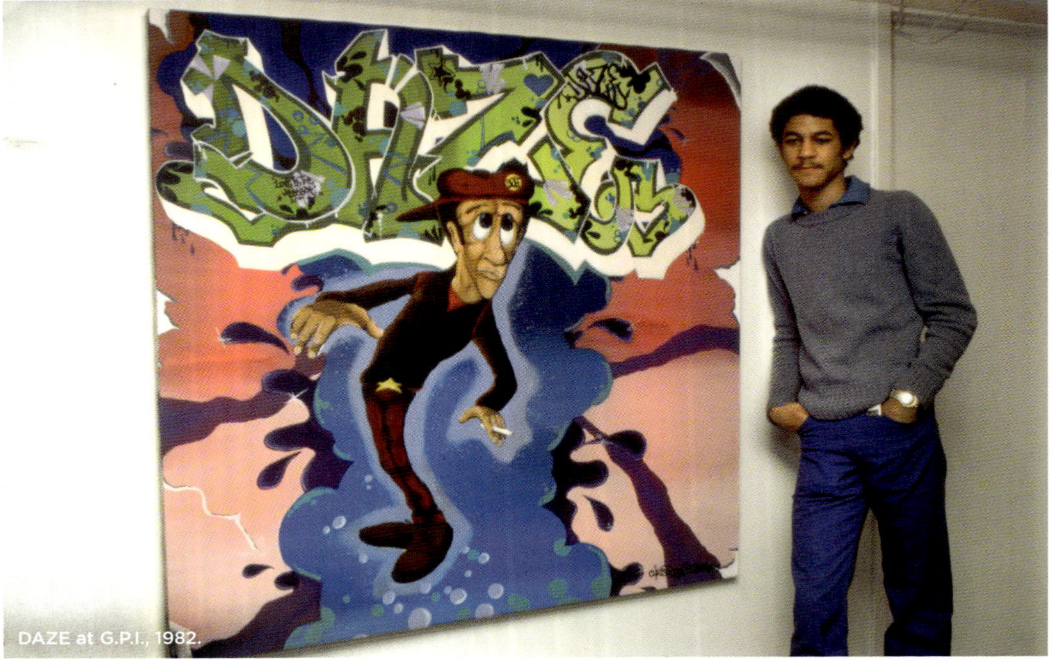

DAZE at G.P.I., 1982.

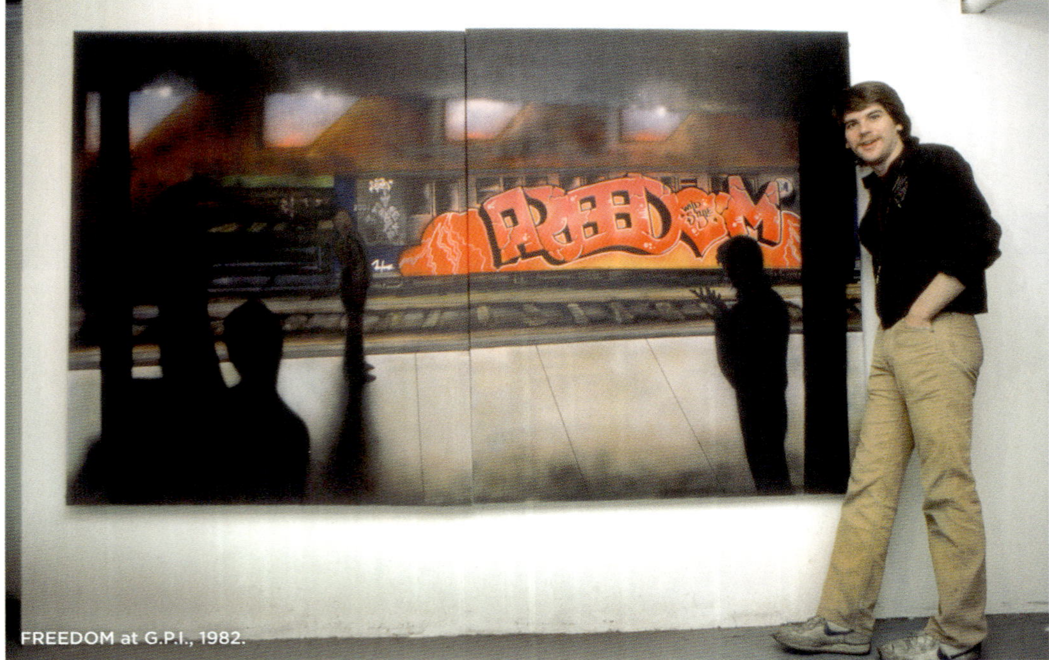

FREEDOM at G.P.I., 1982.

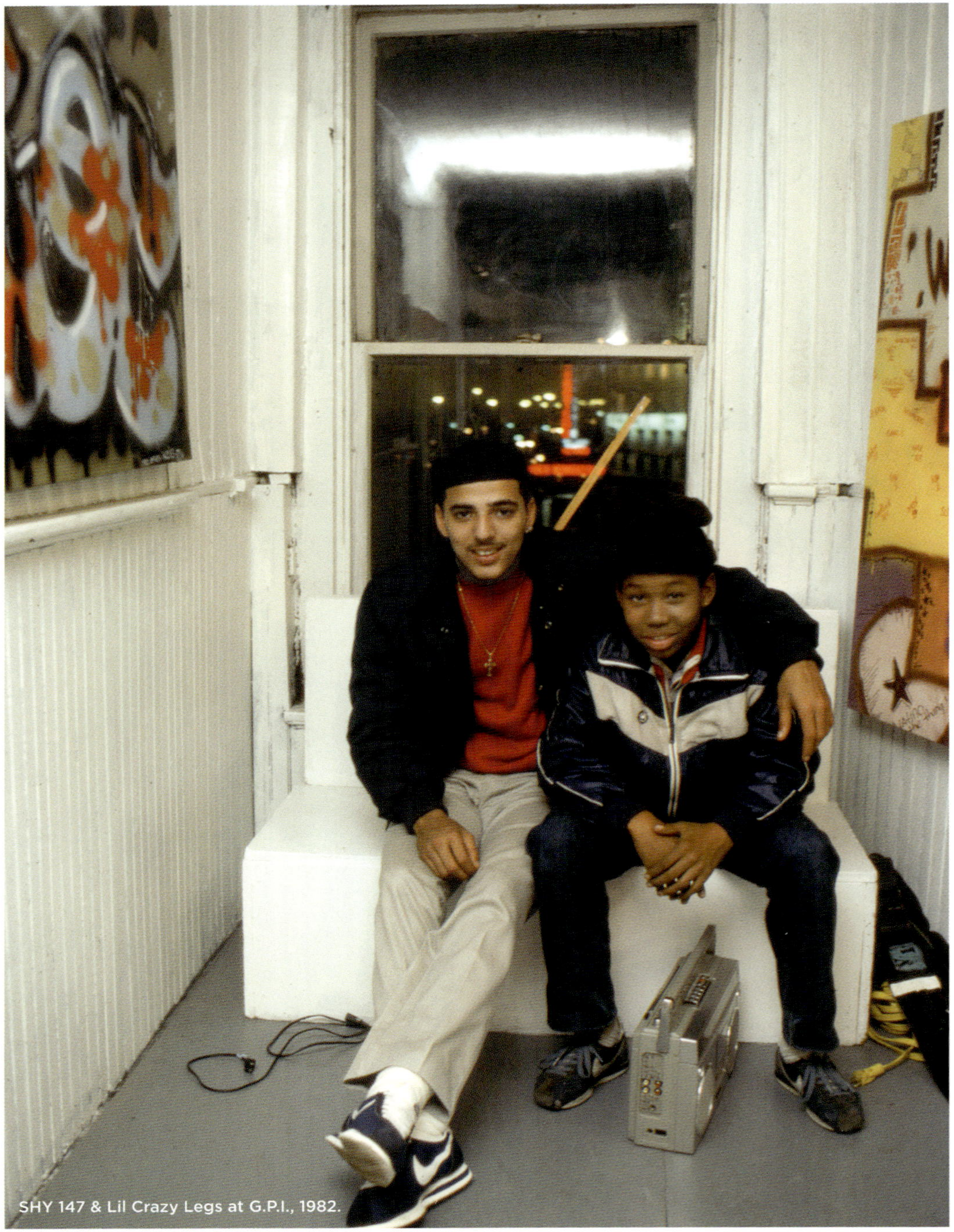

SHY 147 & Lil Crazy Legs at G.P.I., 1982.

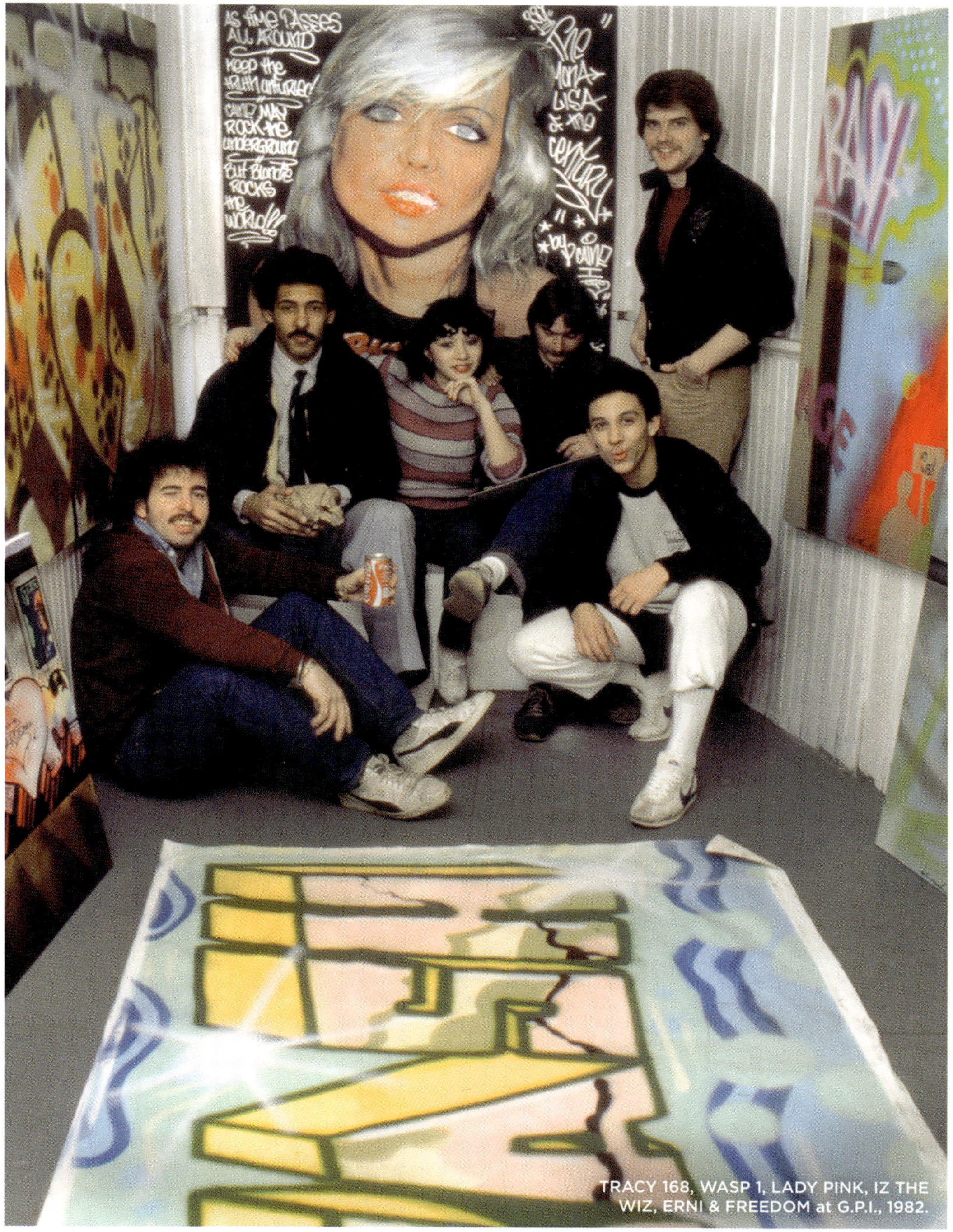

As time passes all around keep the faith unfurled. Can't may rock the underground. But Blondie rocks the world!! The Mona Lisa of the century" by Dean H.

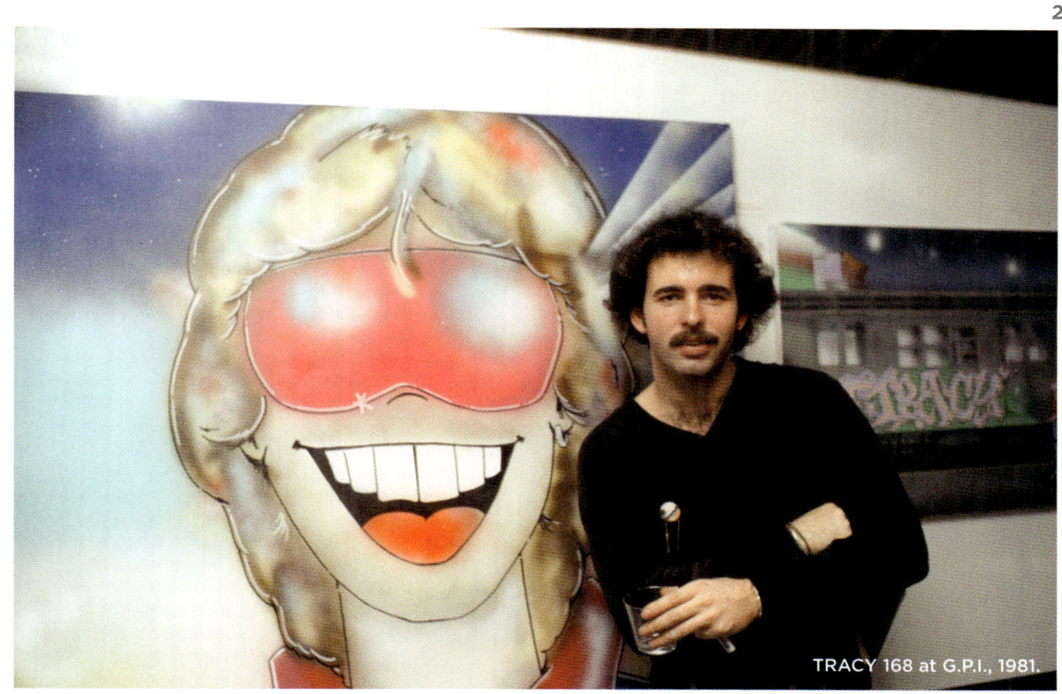

TRACY 168 at G.P.I., 1981.

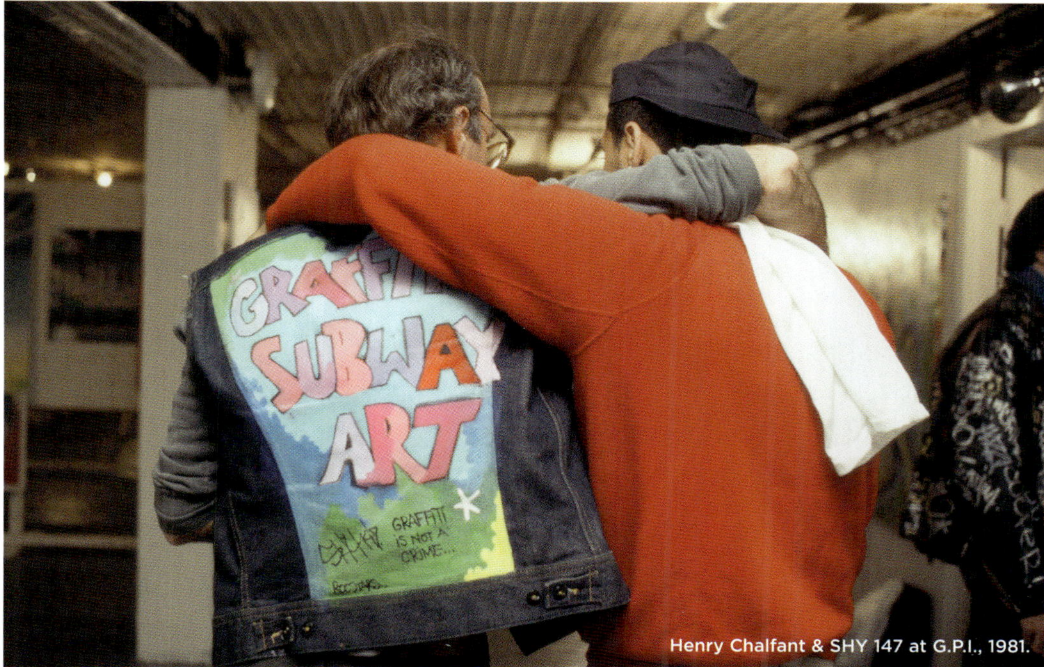

Henry Chalfant & SHY 147 at G.P.I., 1981.

TRACY 168, WASP 1, LADY PINK, IZ THE WIZ, ERNI & FREEDOM at G.P.I., 1982.

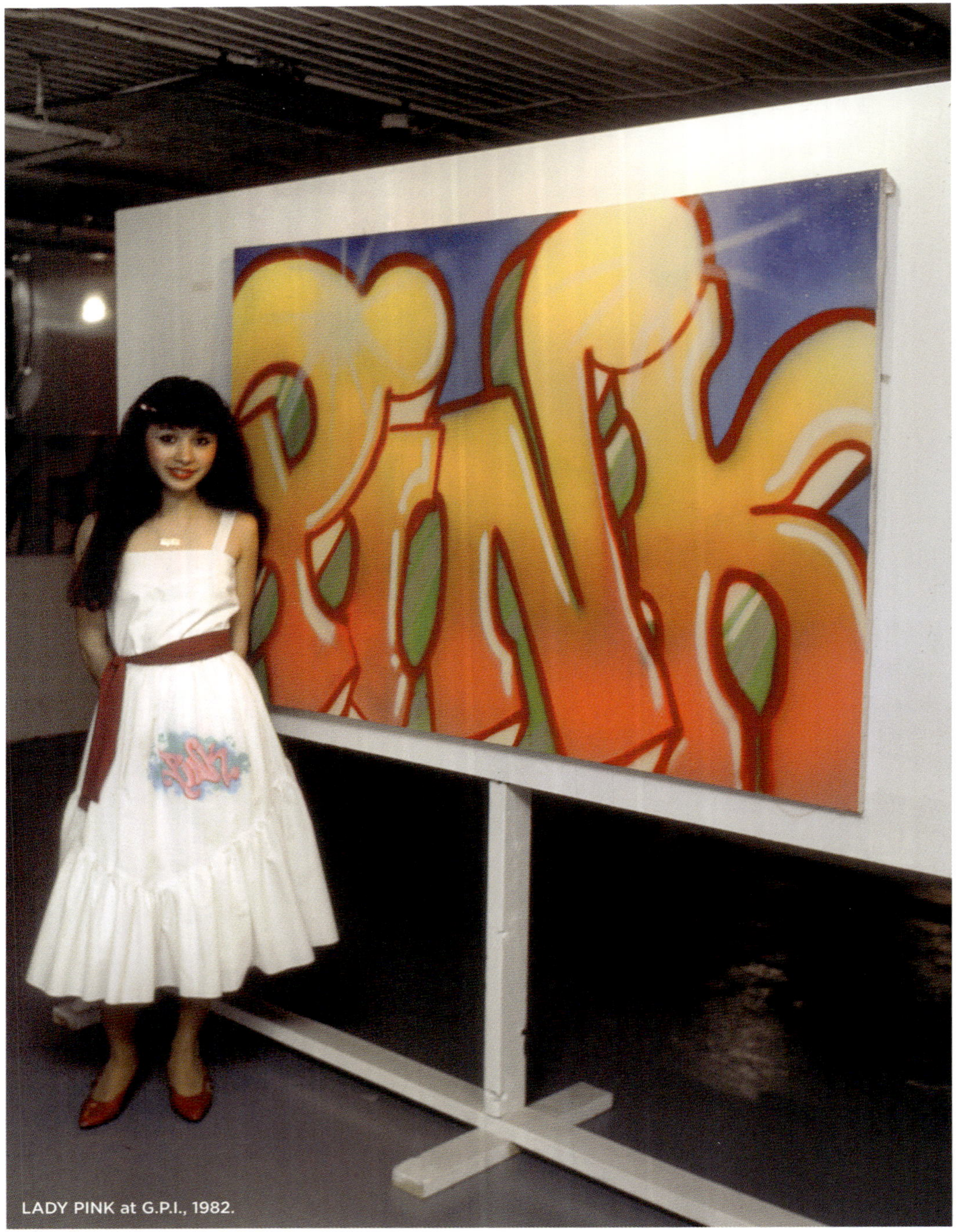

LADY PINK at G.P.I., 1982.

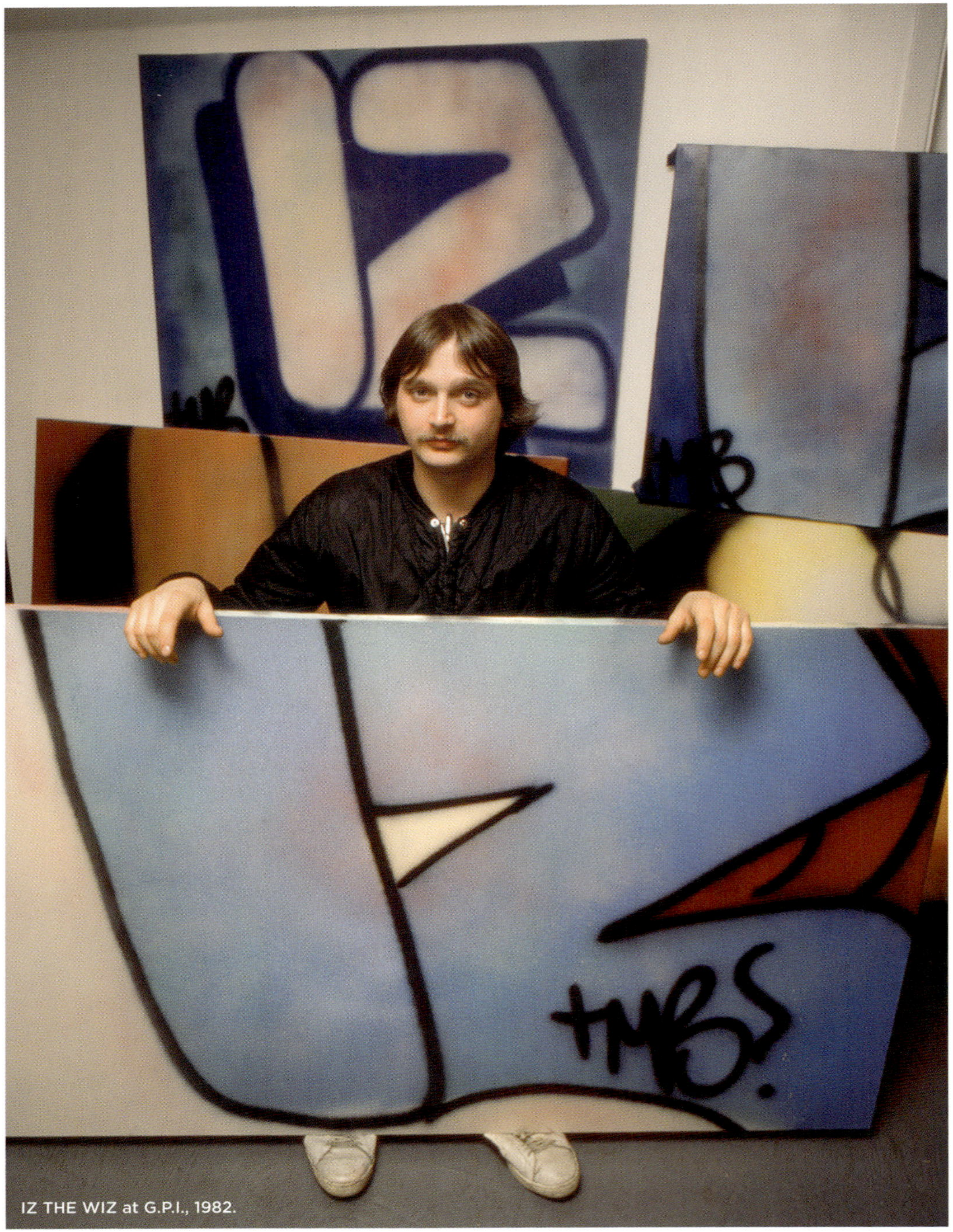

IZ THE WIZ at G.P.I., 1982.

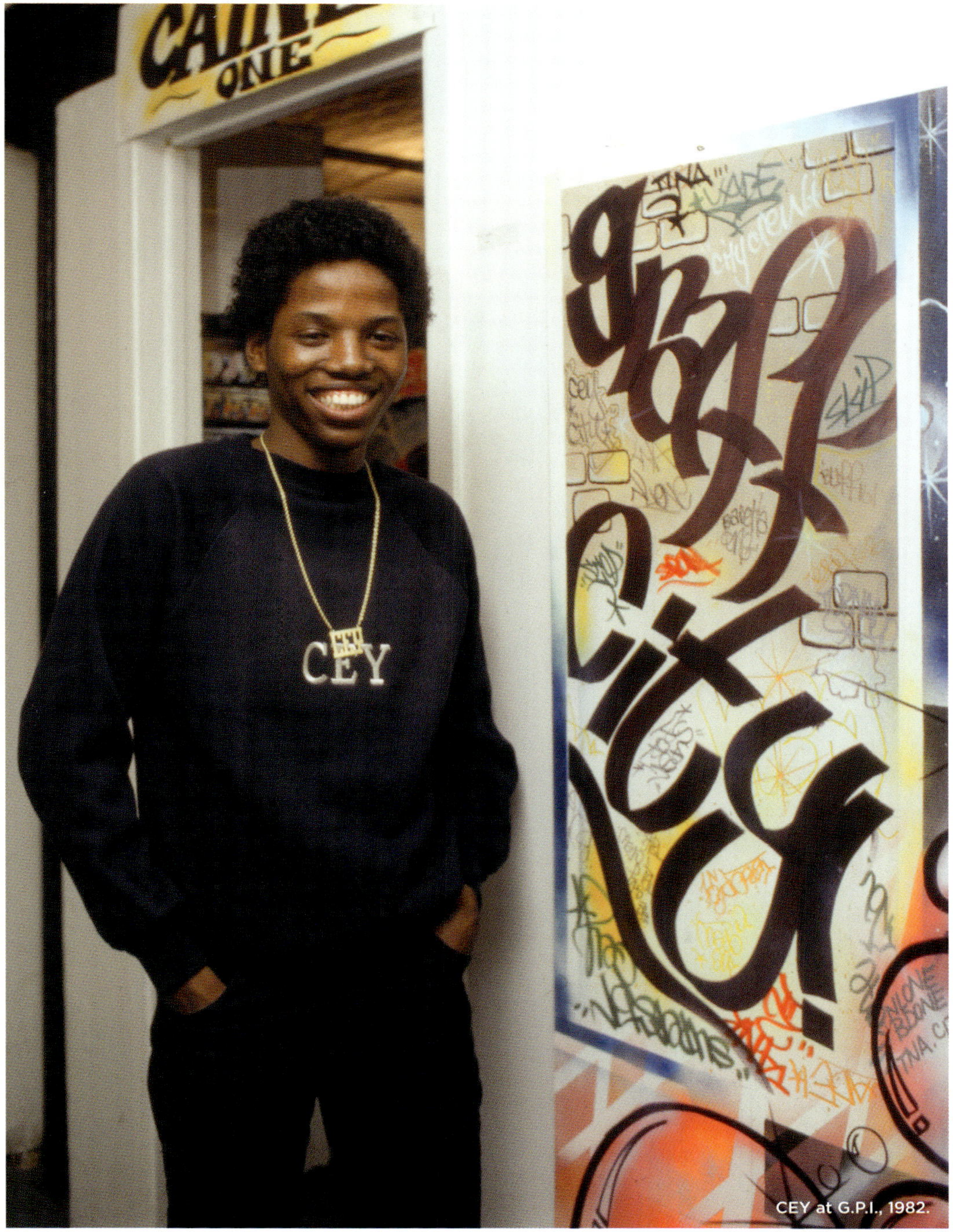

CEY at G.P.I., 1982.

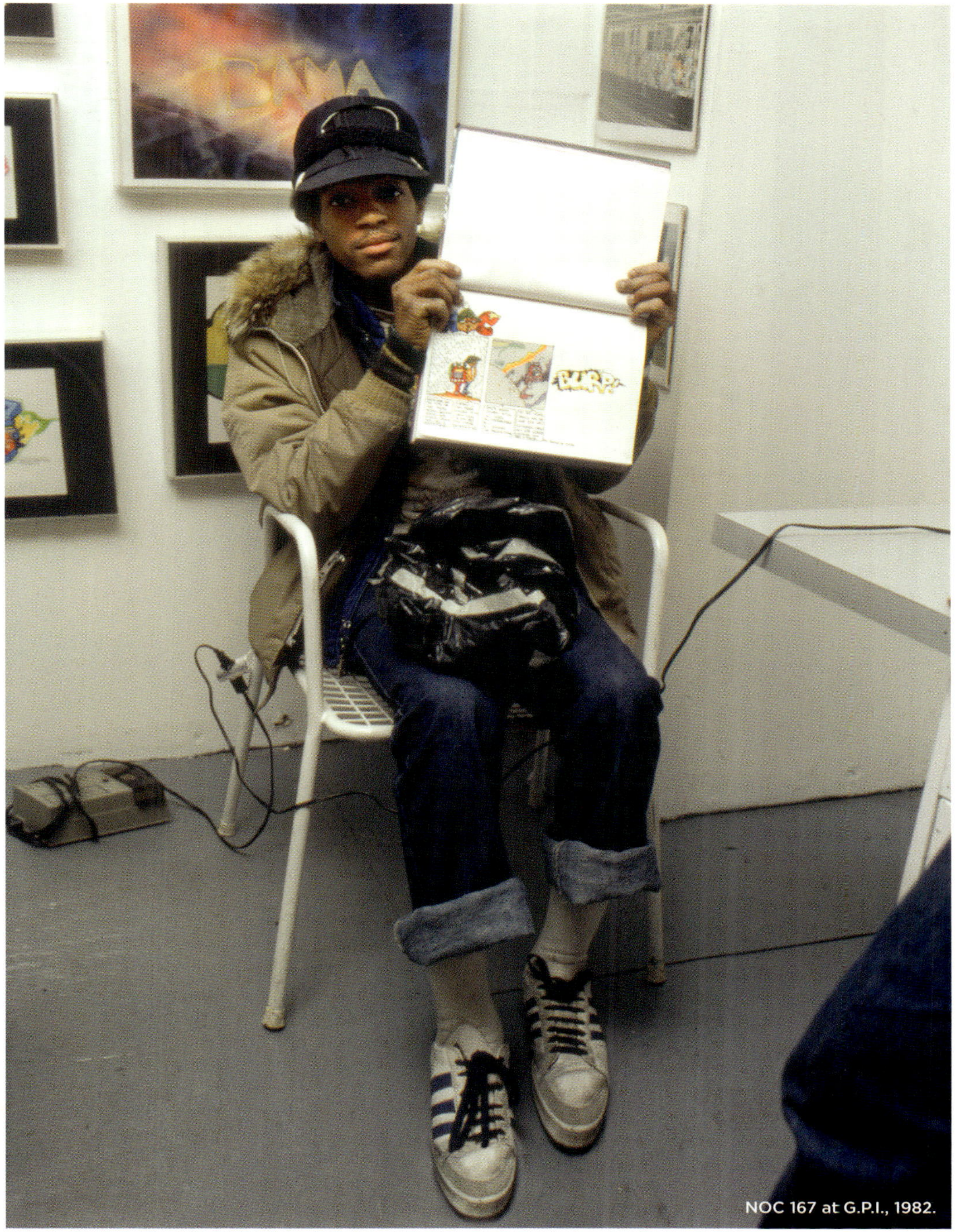

NOC 167 at G.P.I., 1982.

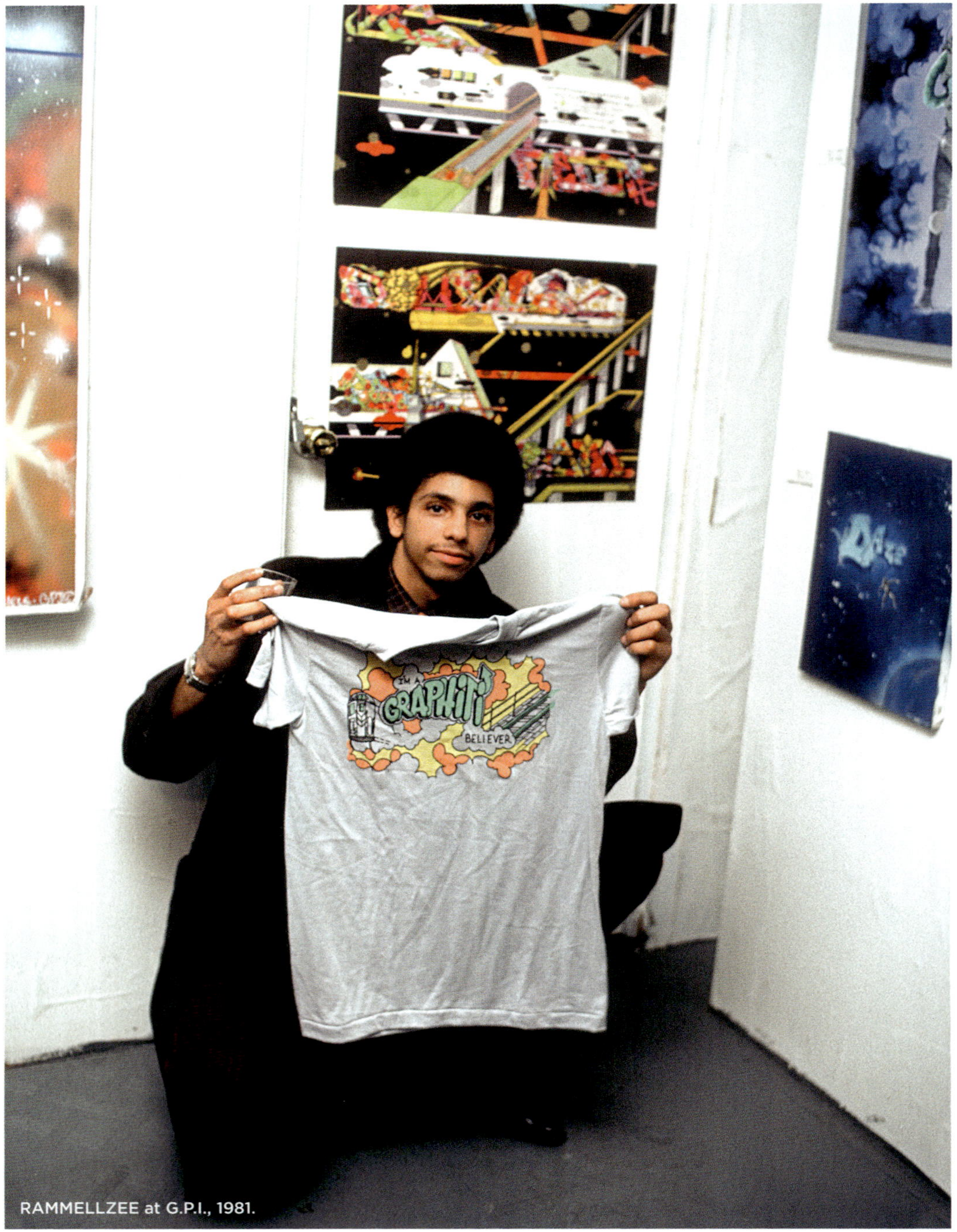

RAMMELLZEE at G.P.I., 1981.

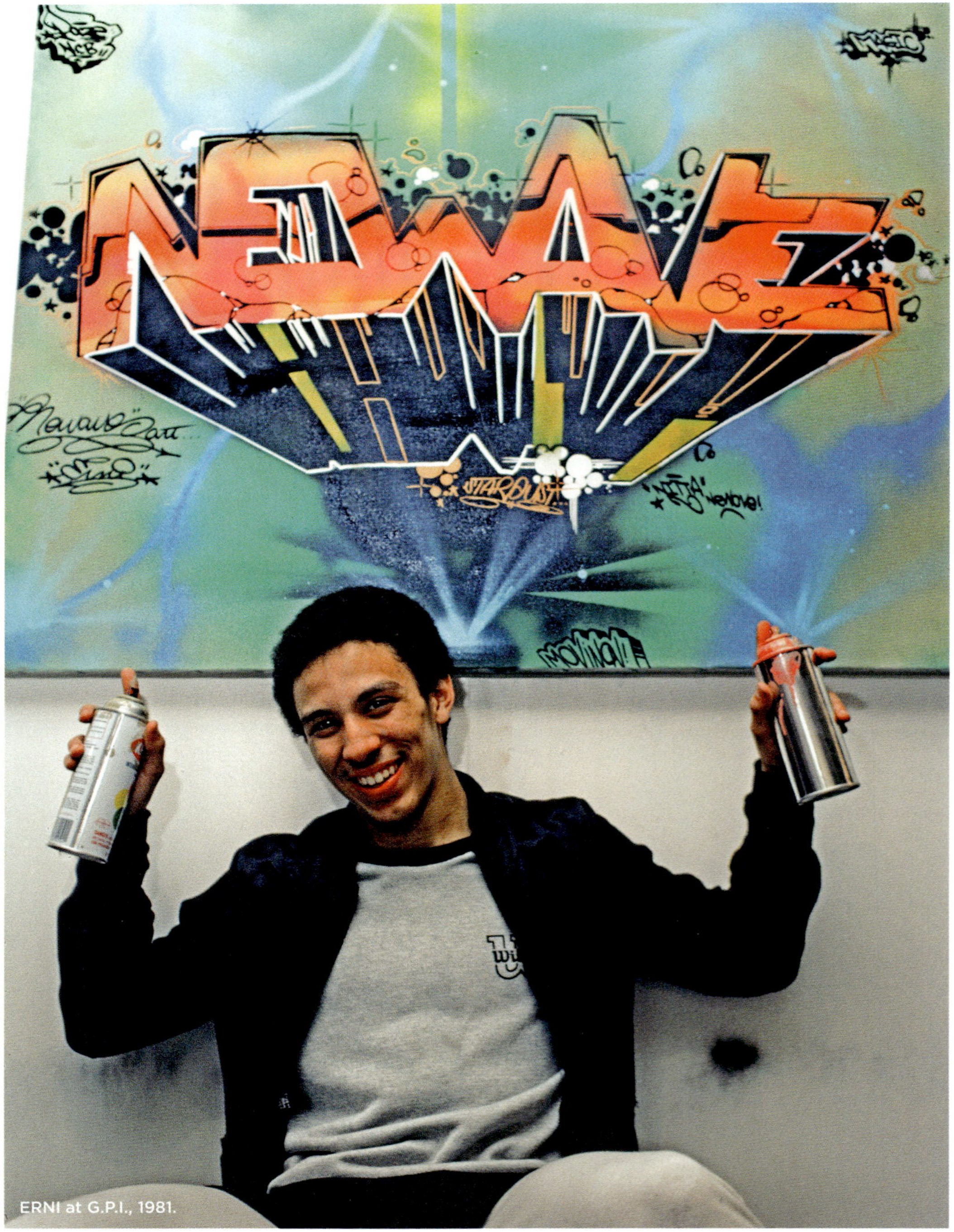

ERNI at G.P.I., 1981.

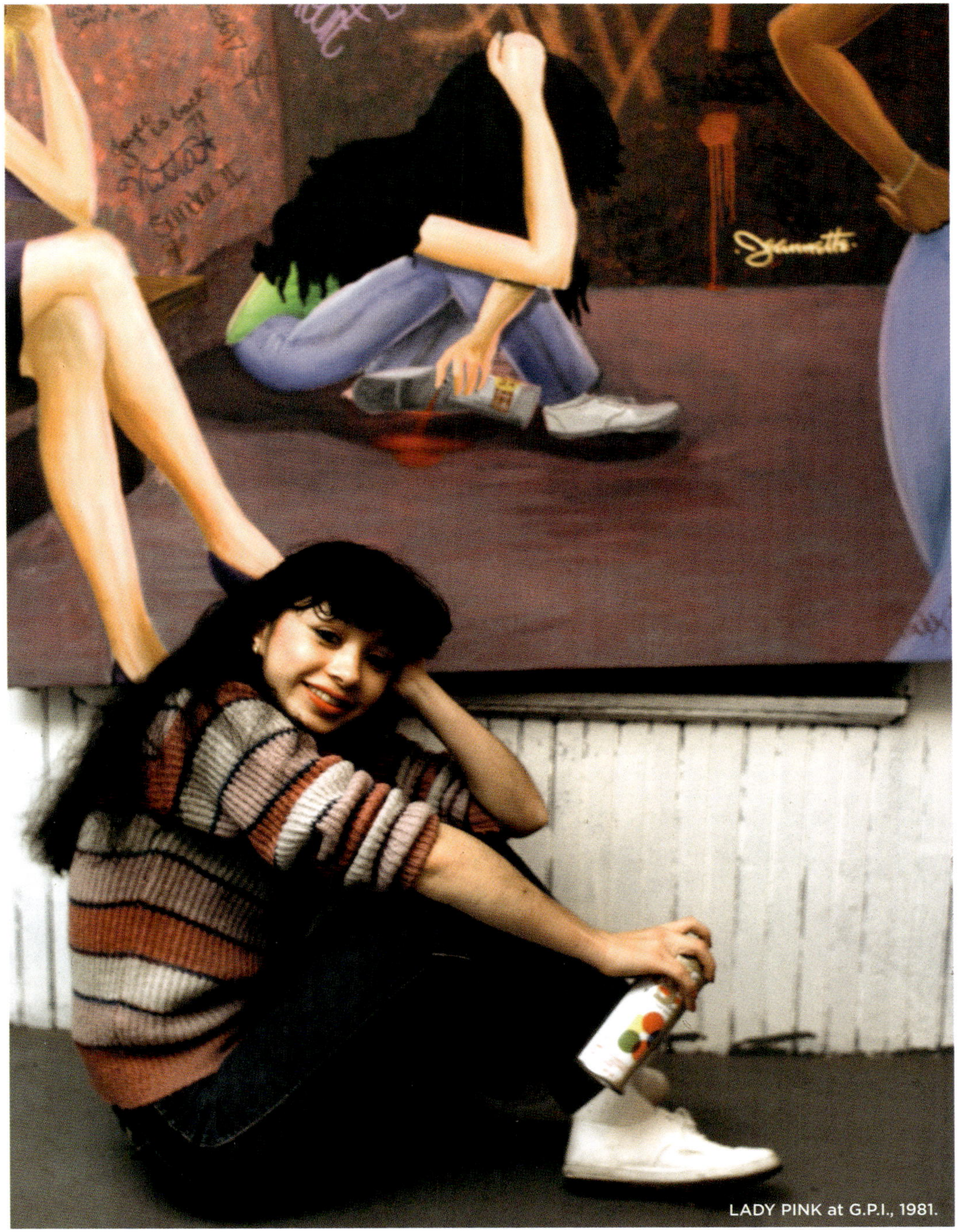

LADY PINK at G.P.I., 1981.

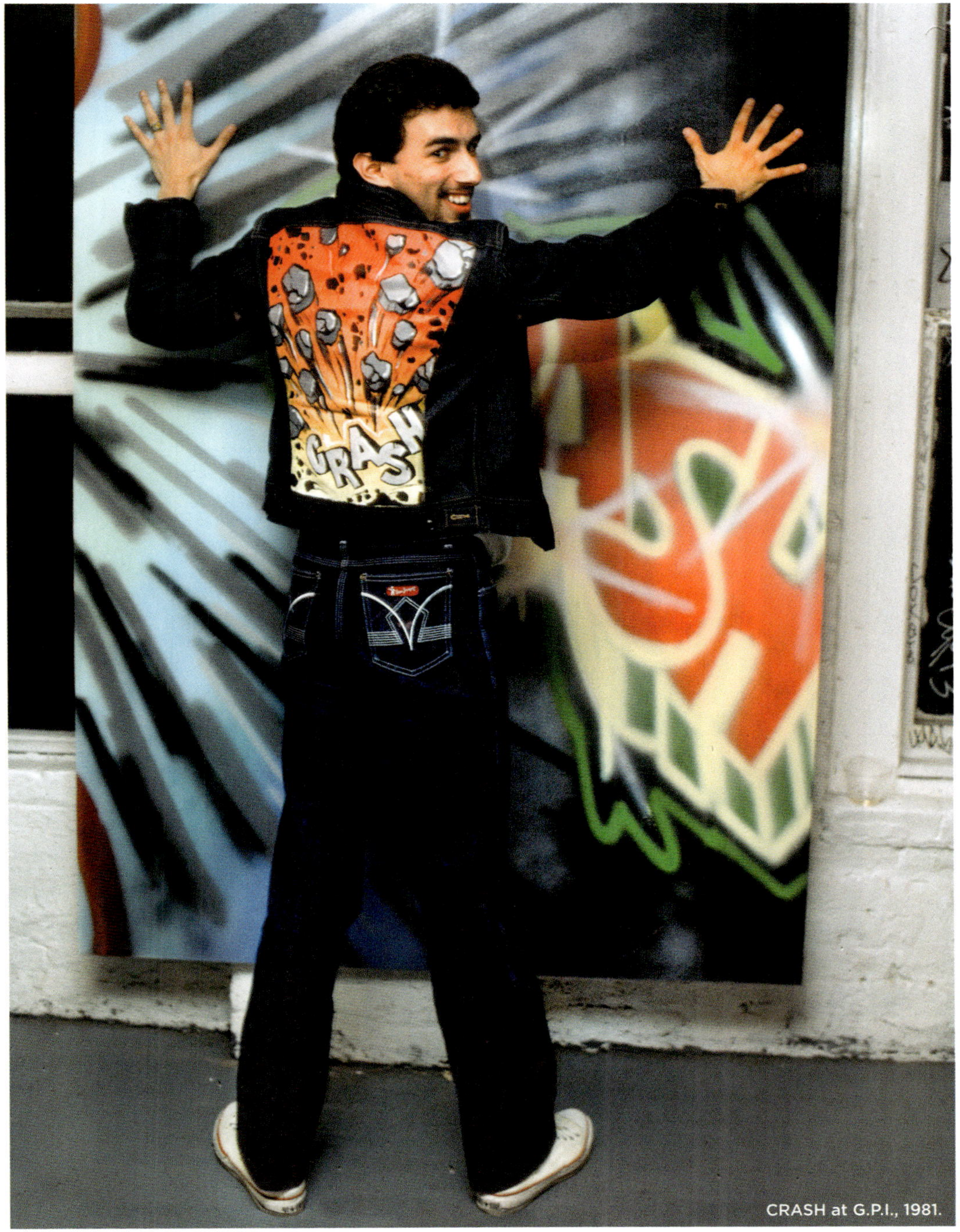

CRASH at G.P.I., 1981.

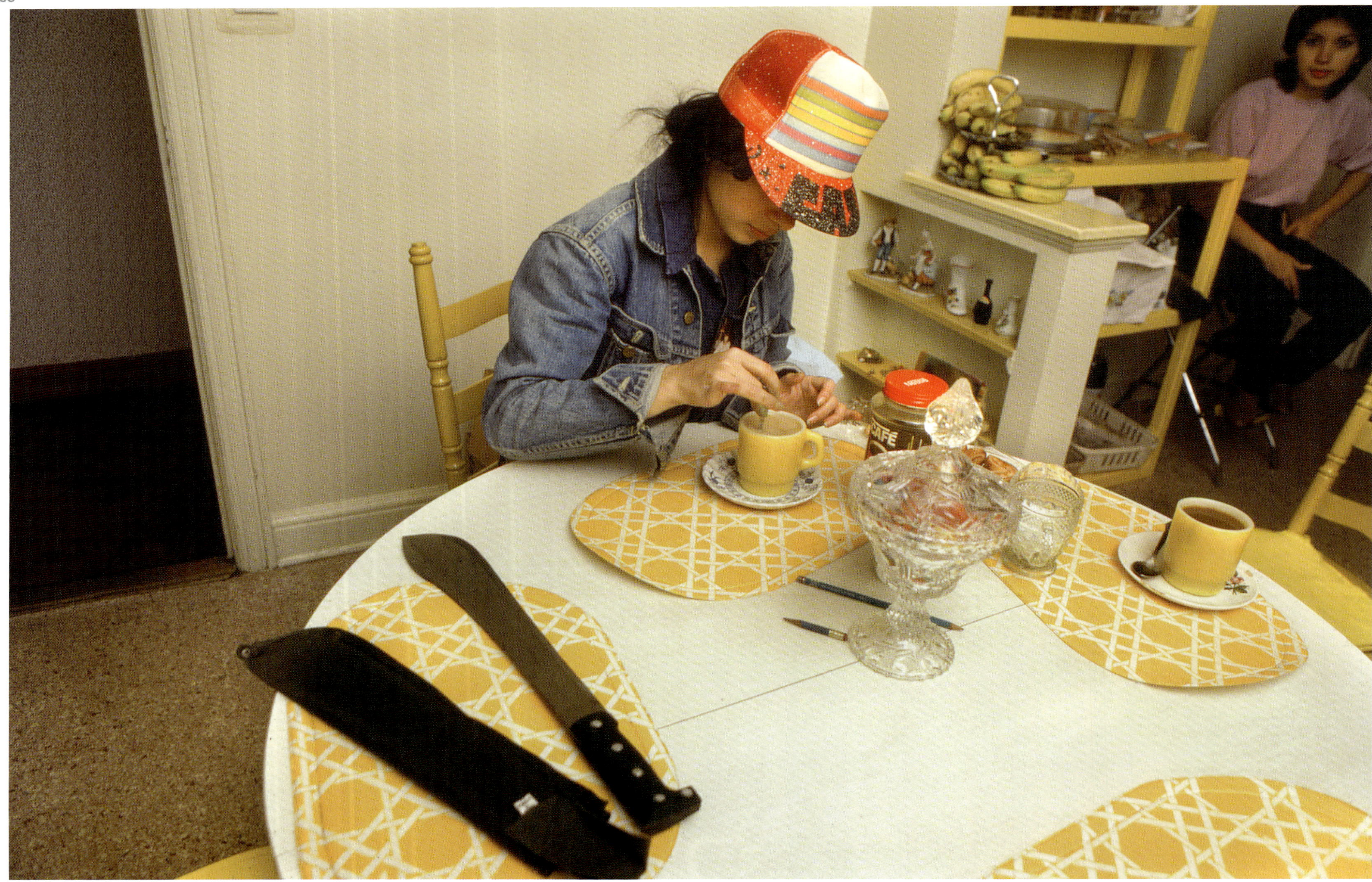

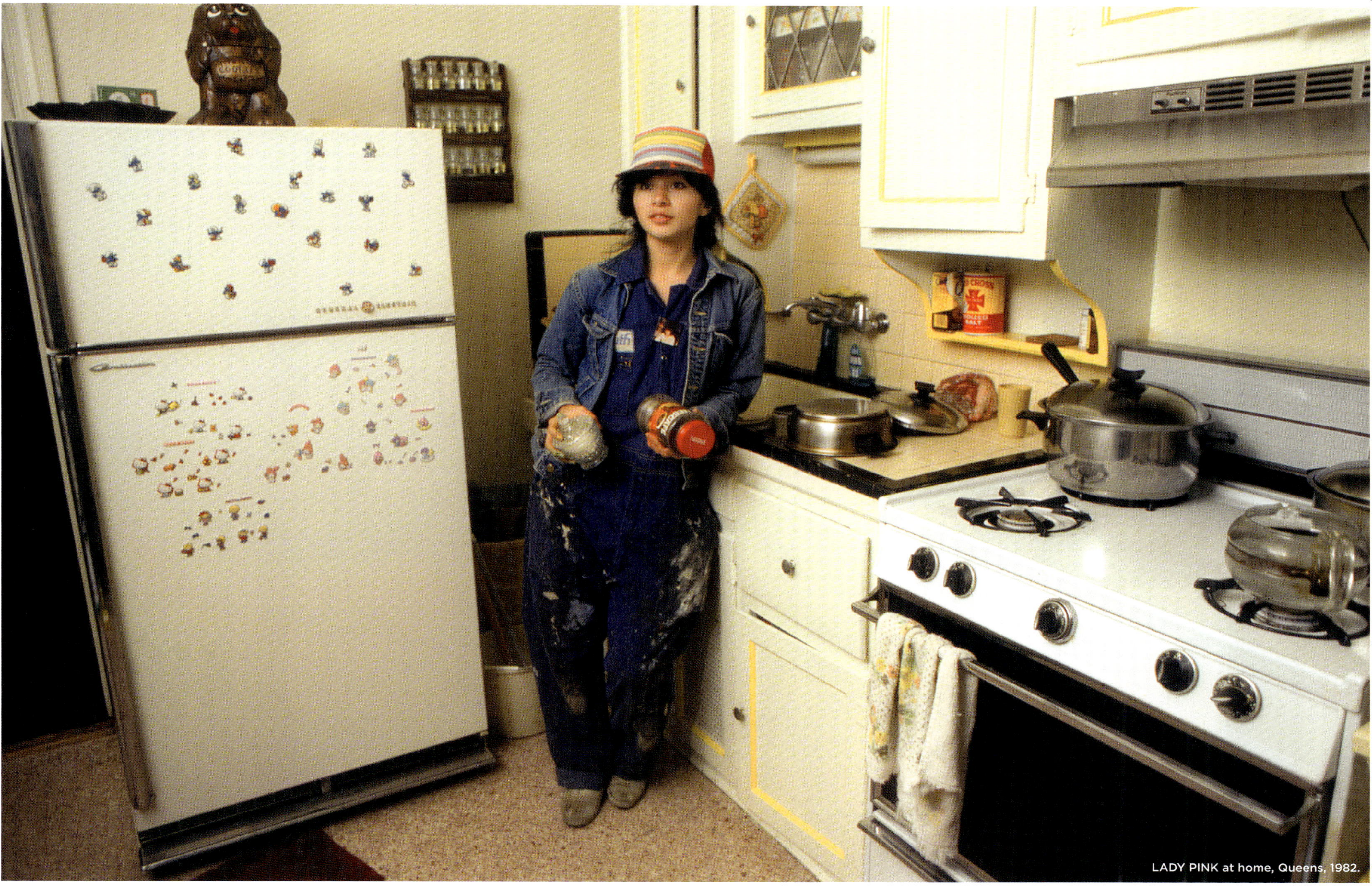

LADY PINK at home, Queens, 1982.

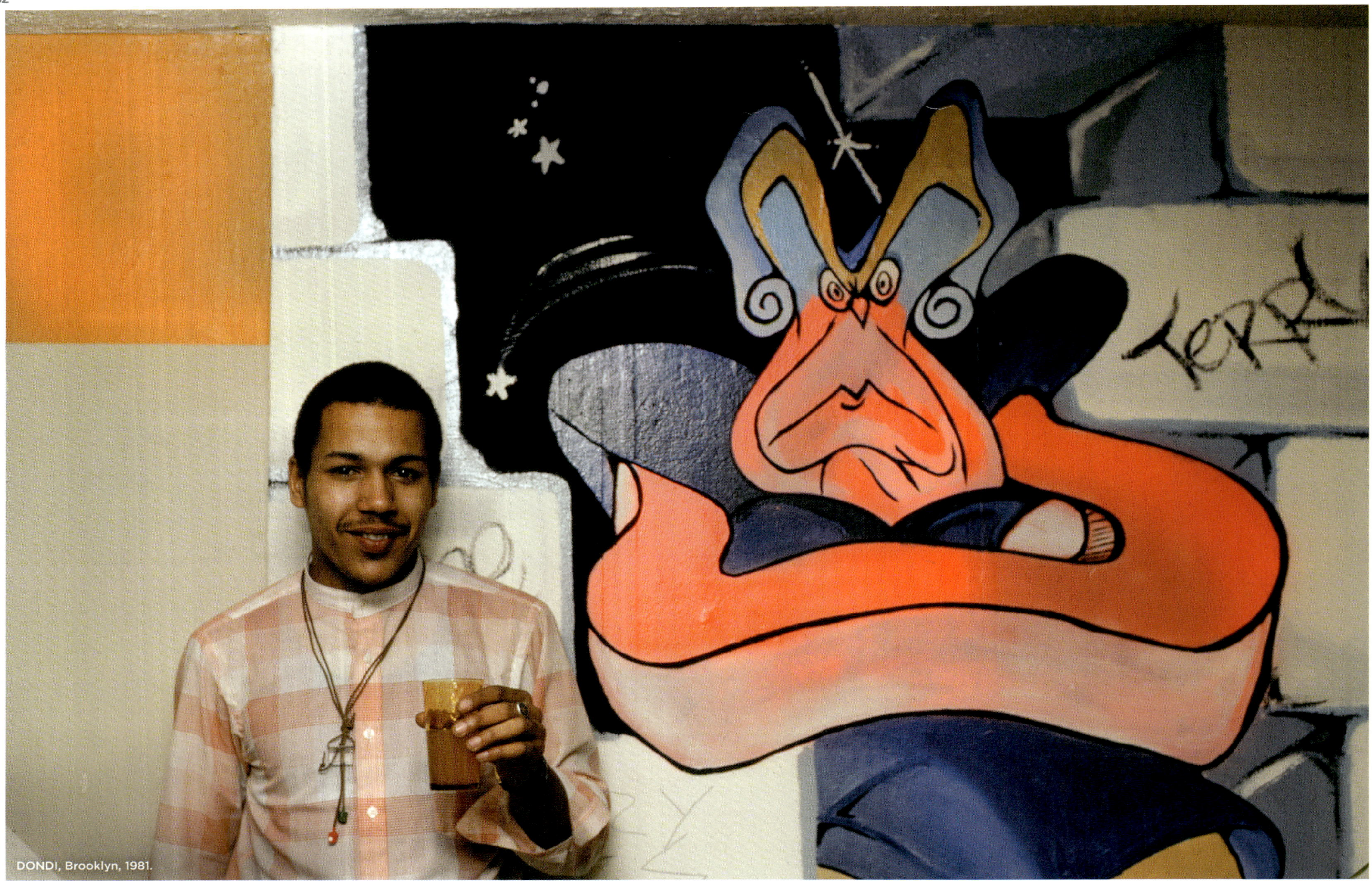

DONDI, Brooklyn, 1981.

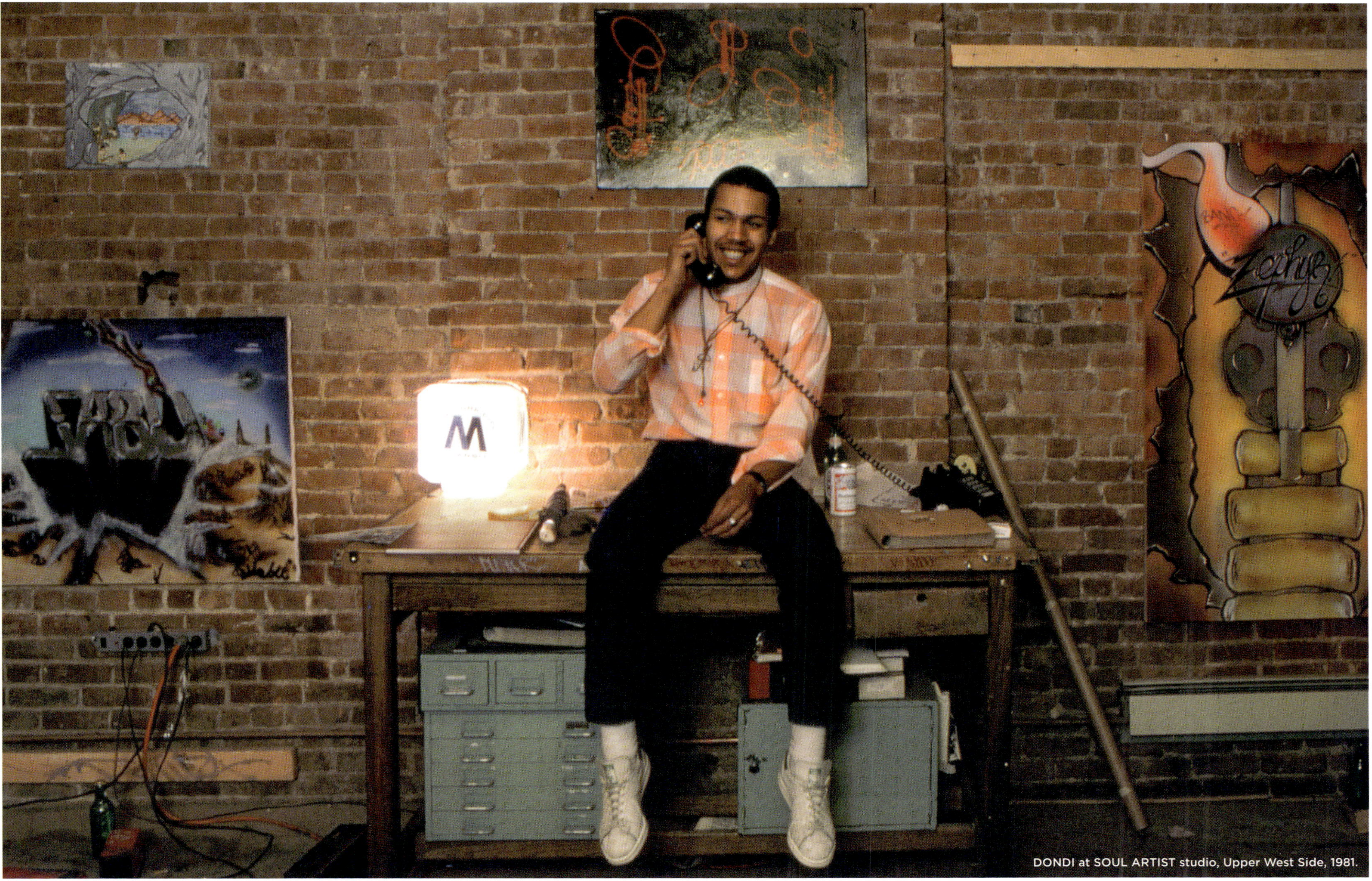

DONDI at SOUL ARTIST studio, Upper West Side, 1981.

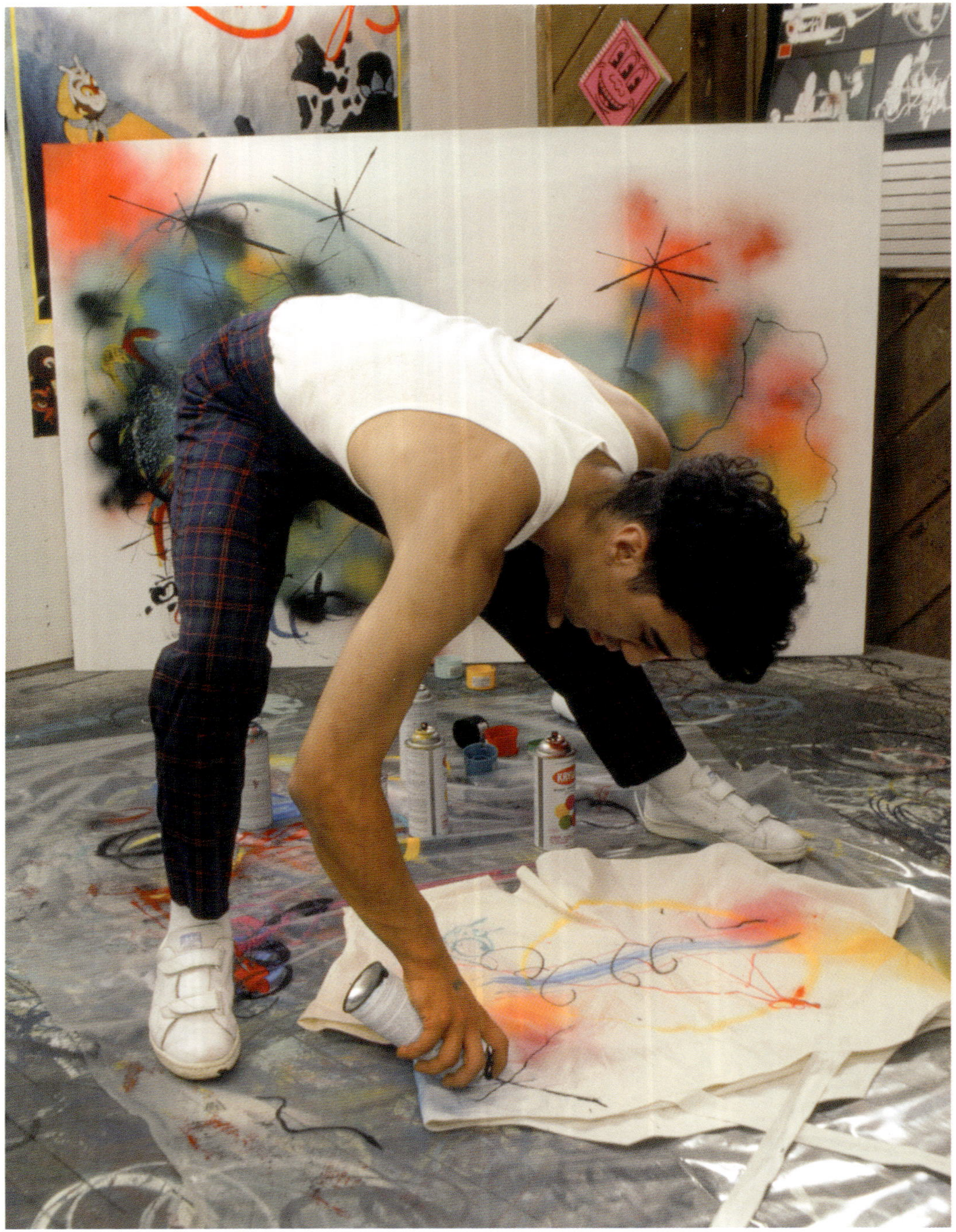

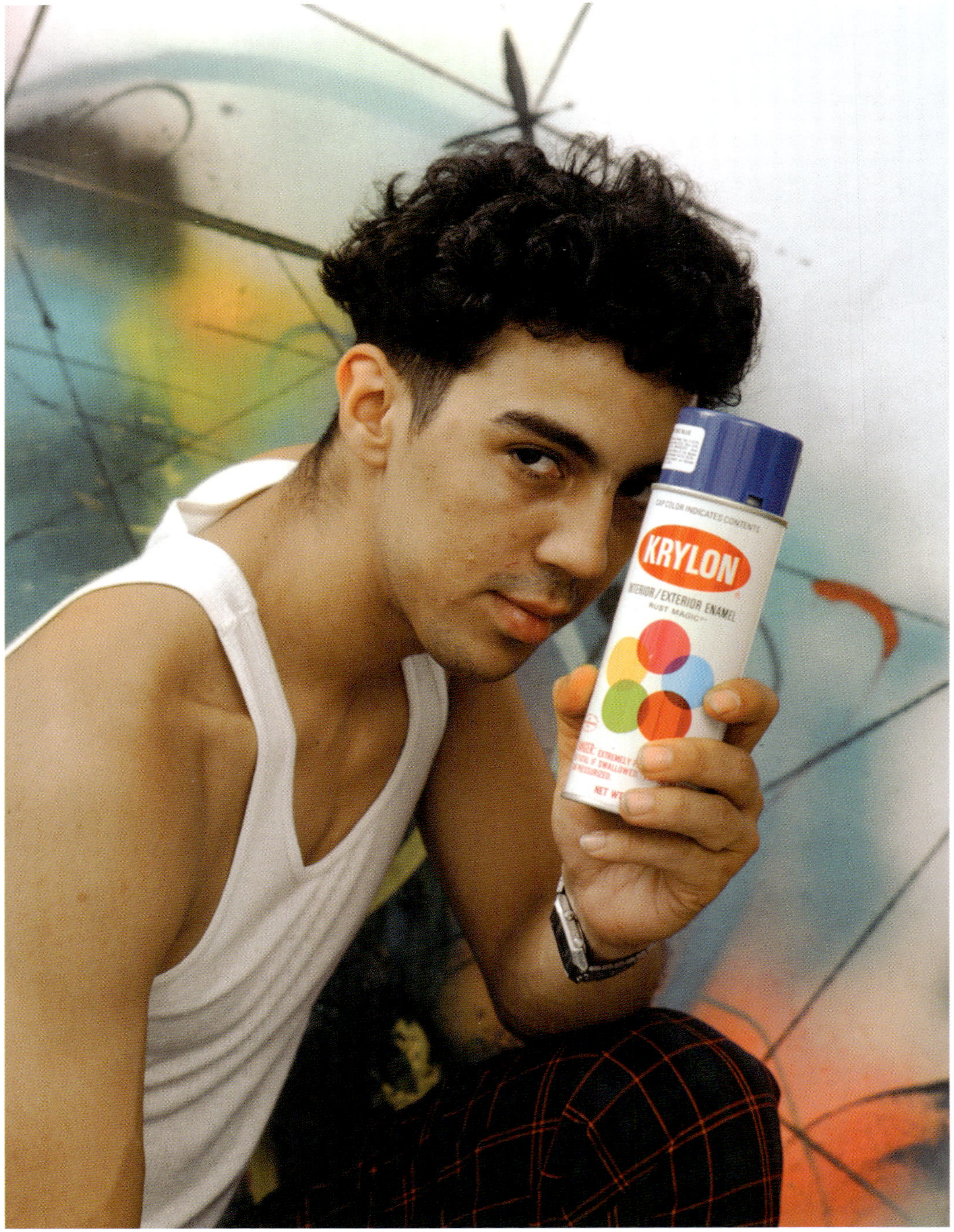

KRYLON
INTERIOR / EXTERIOR ENAMEL
RUST MAGIC

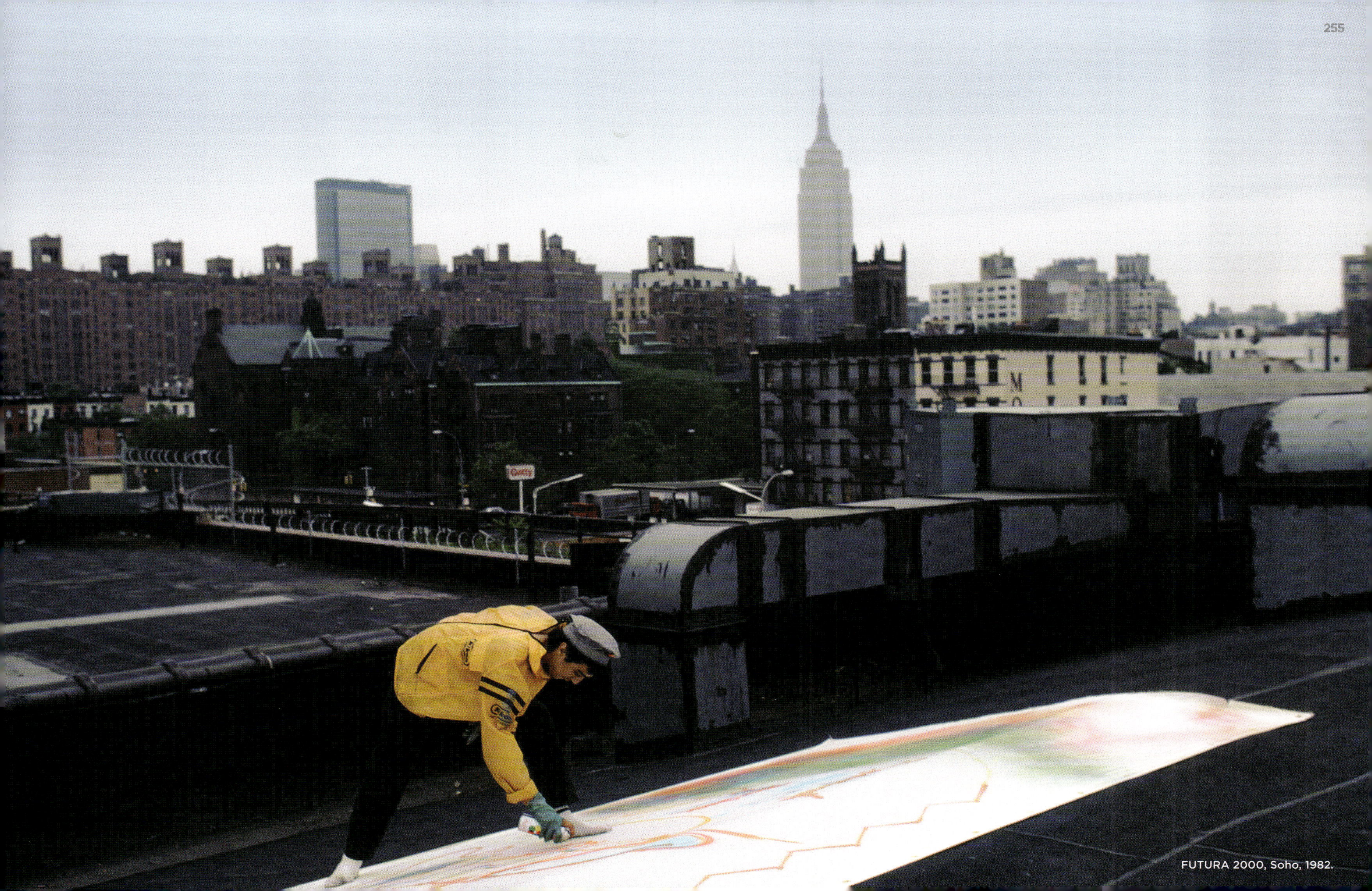

FUTURA 2000, Soho, 1982.

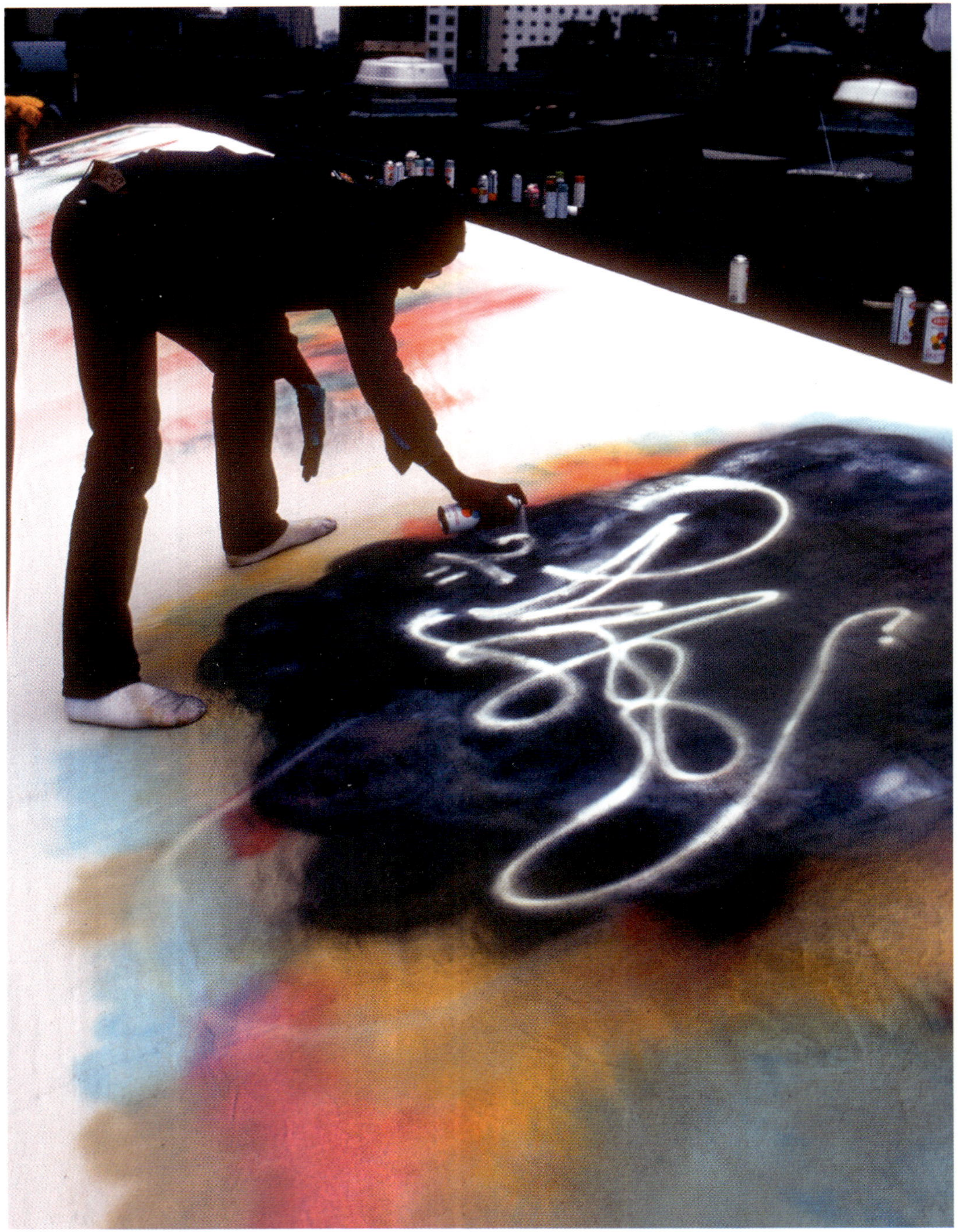

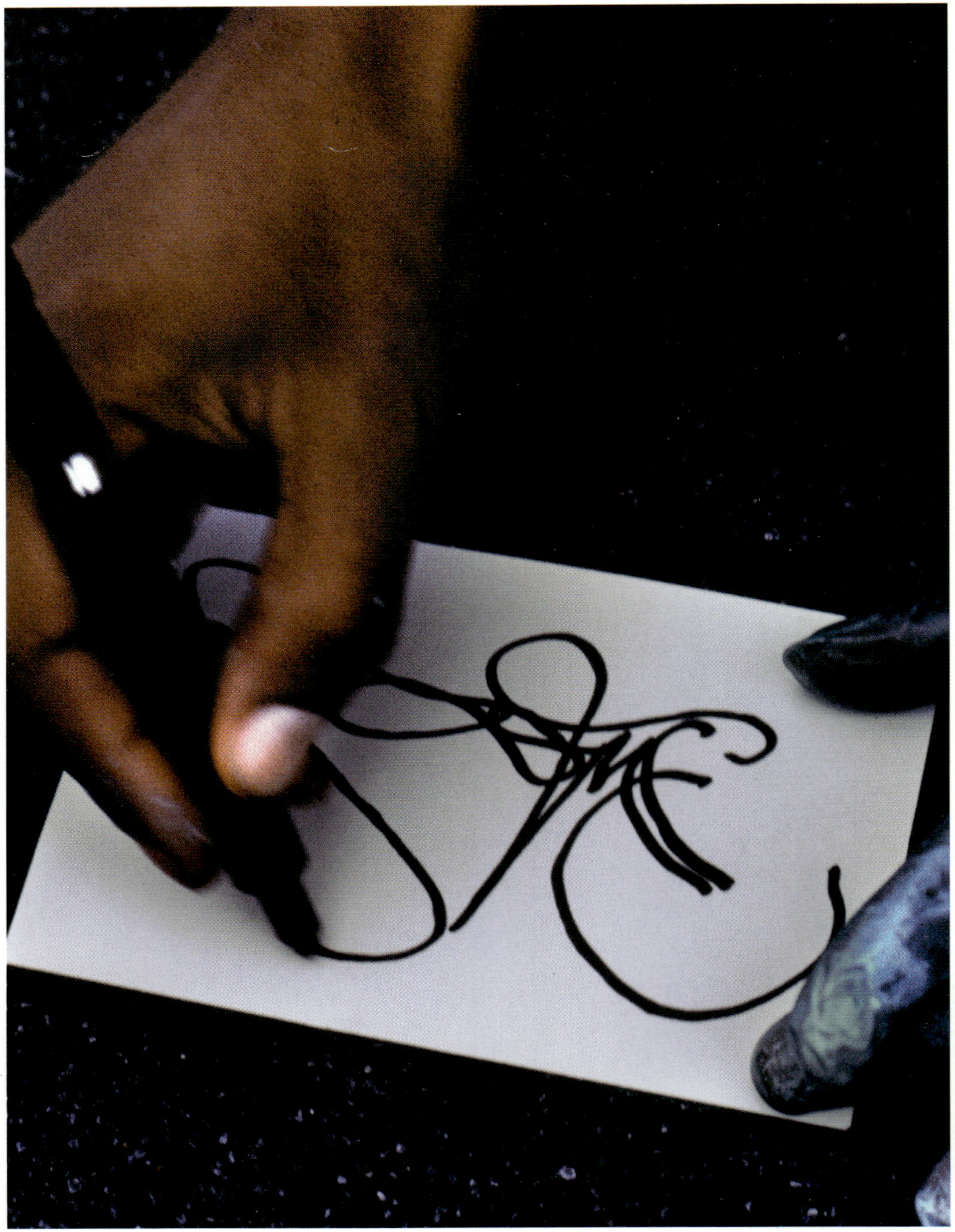

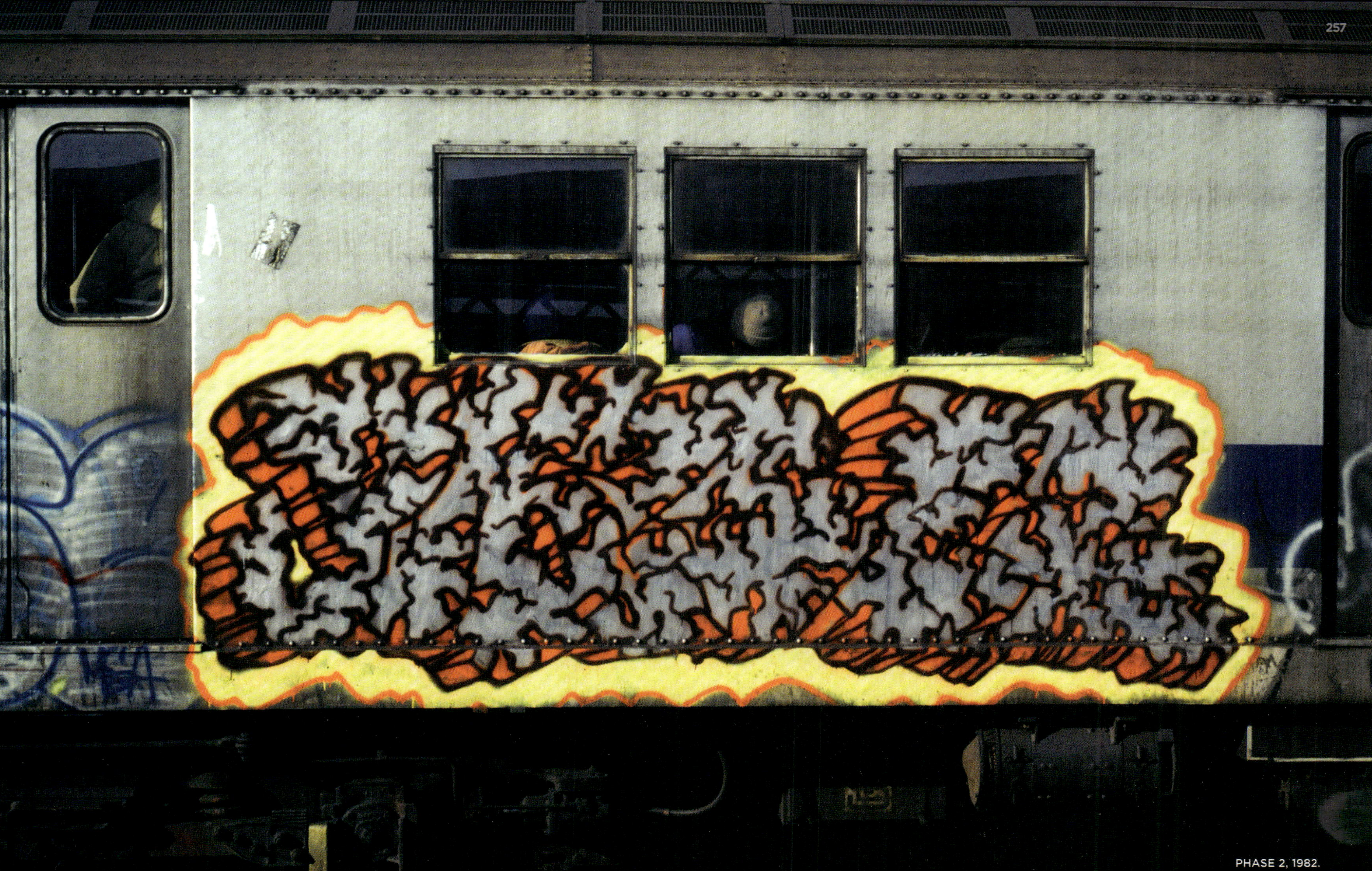

PHASE 2, 1982.

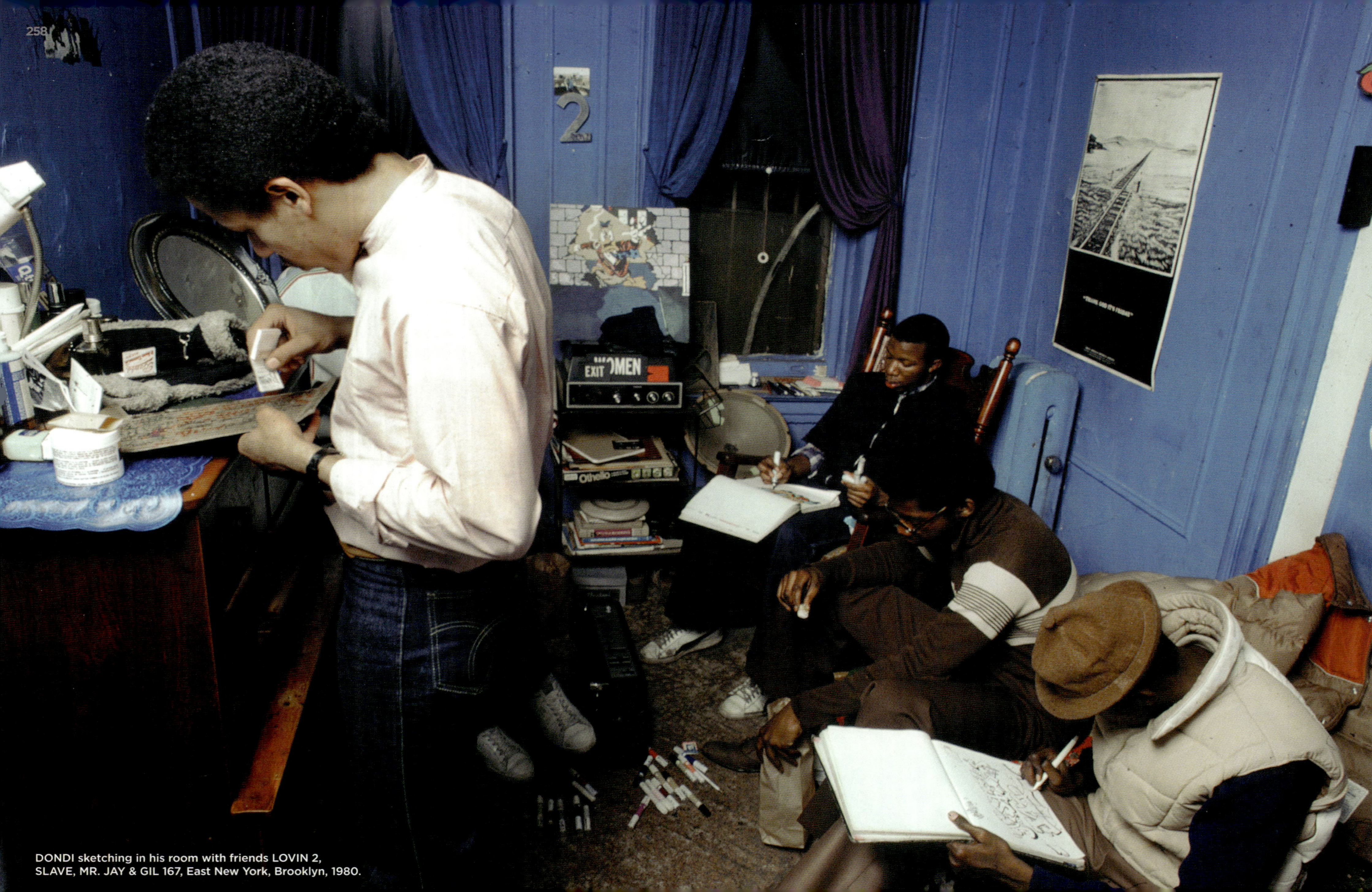

DONDI sketching in his room with friends LOVIN 2,
SLAVE, MR. JAY & GIL 167, East New York, Brooklyn, 1980.

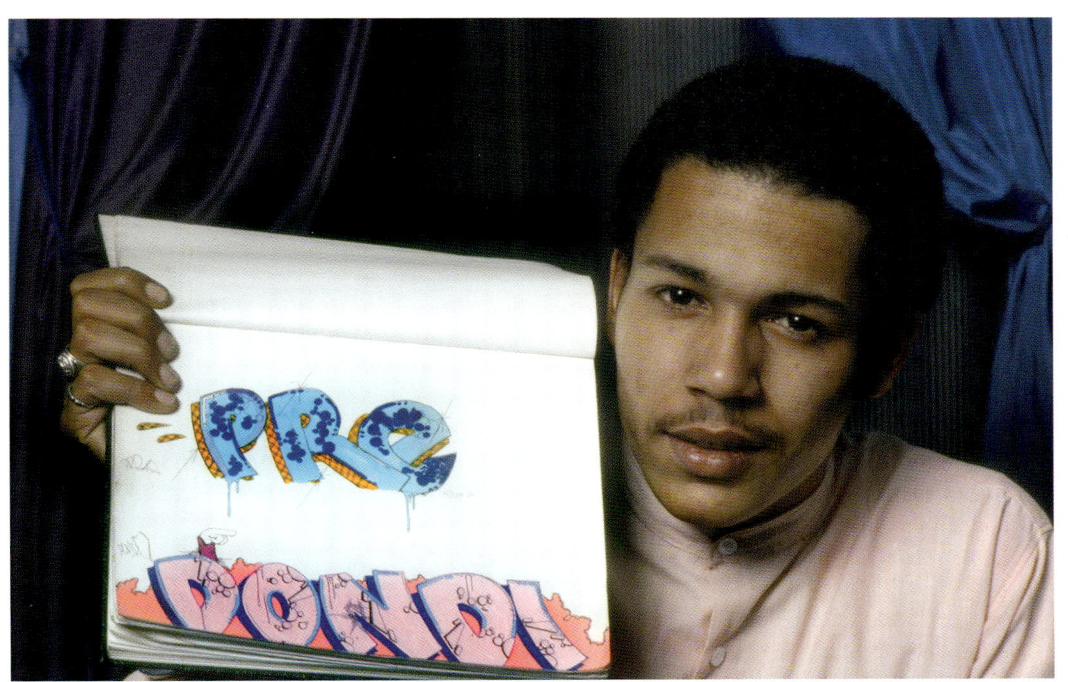

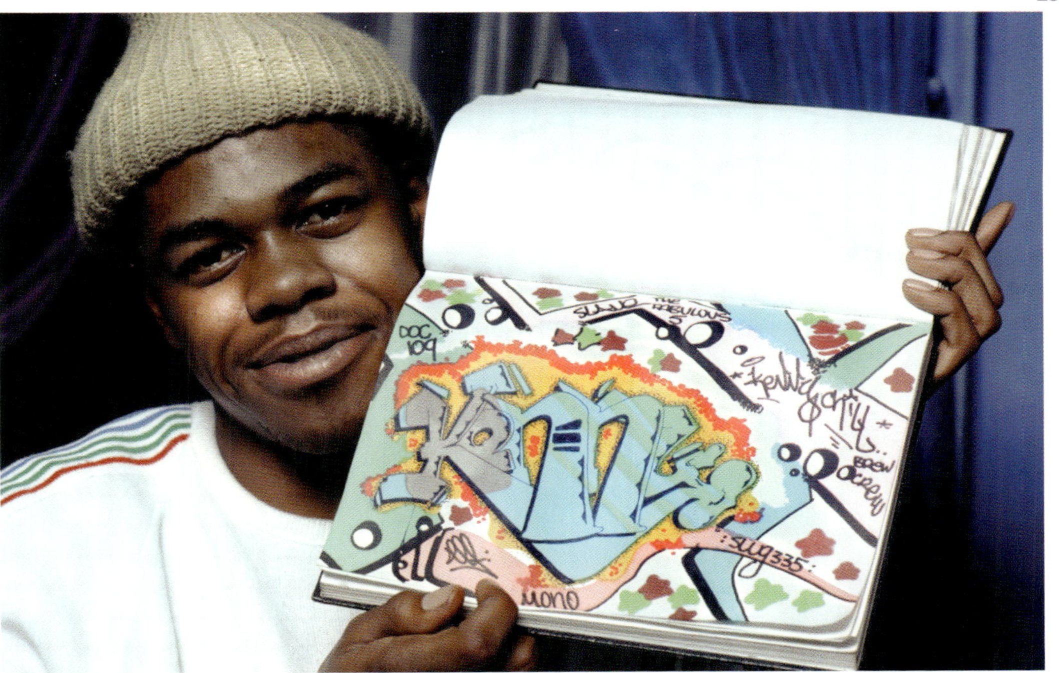

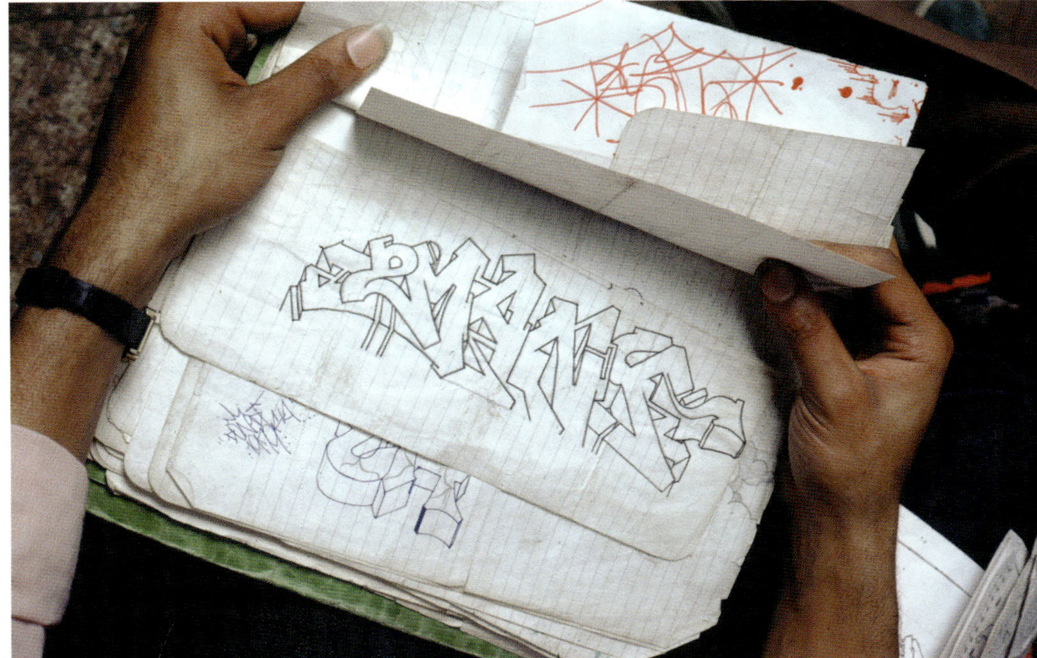

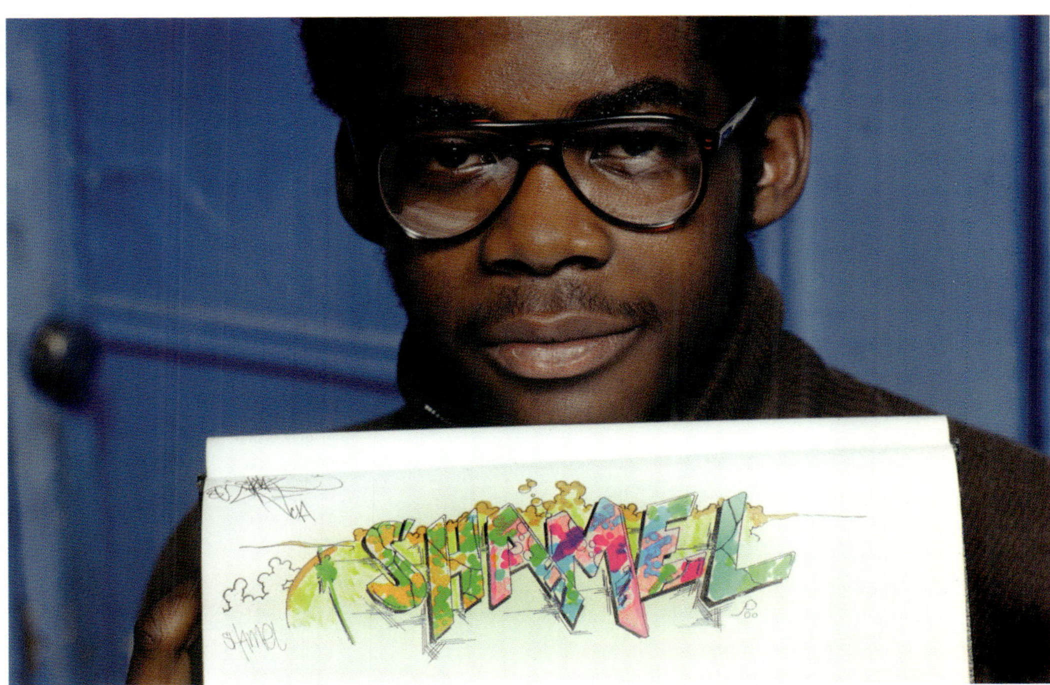

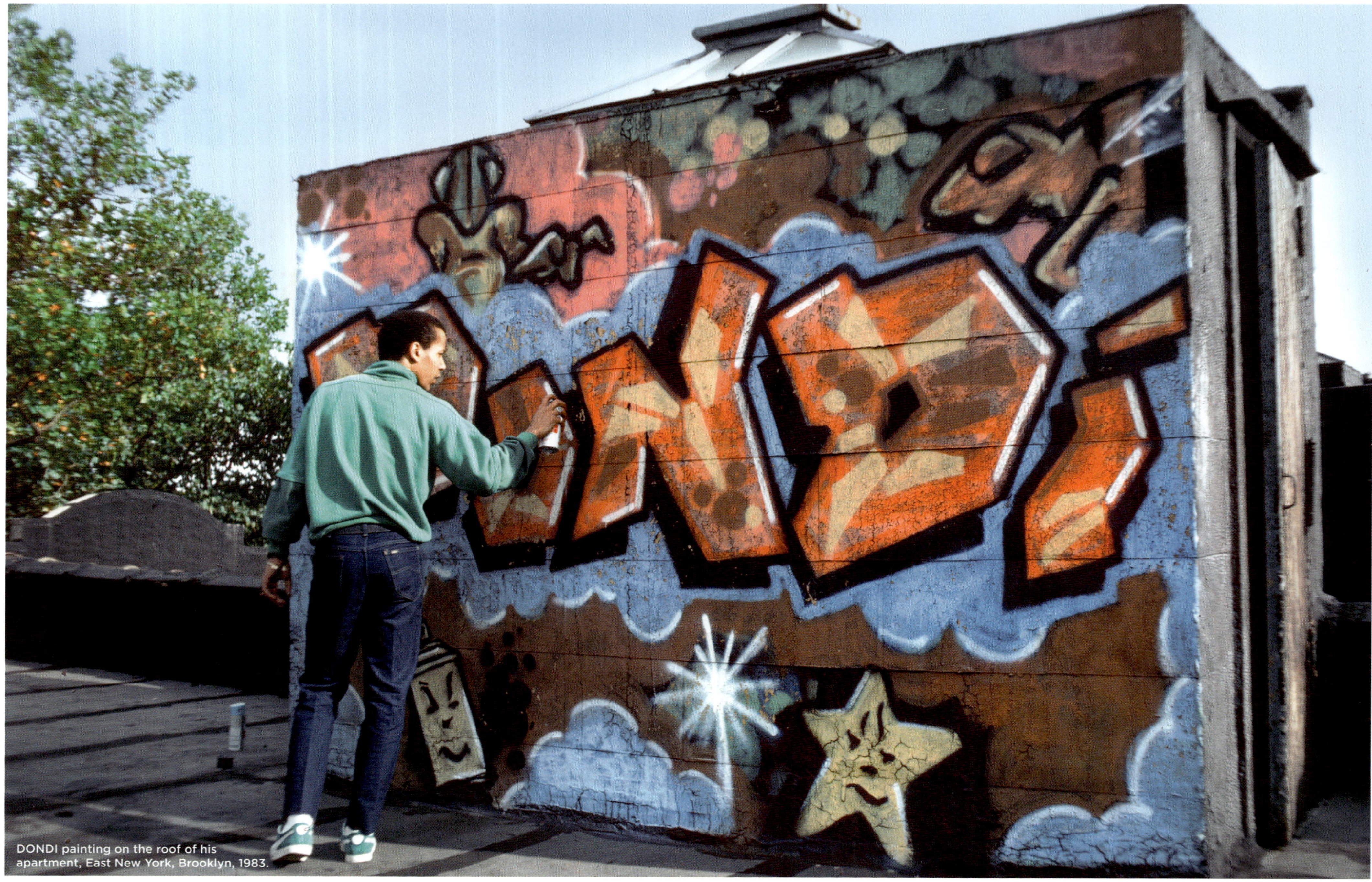

DONDI painting on the roof of his apartment, East New York, Brooklyn, 1983.

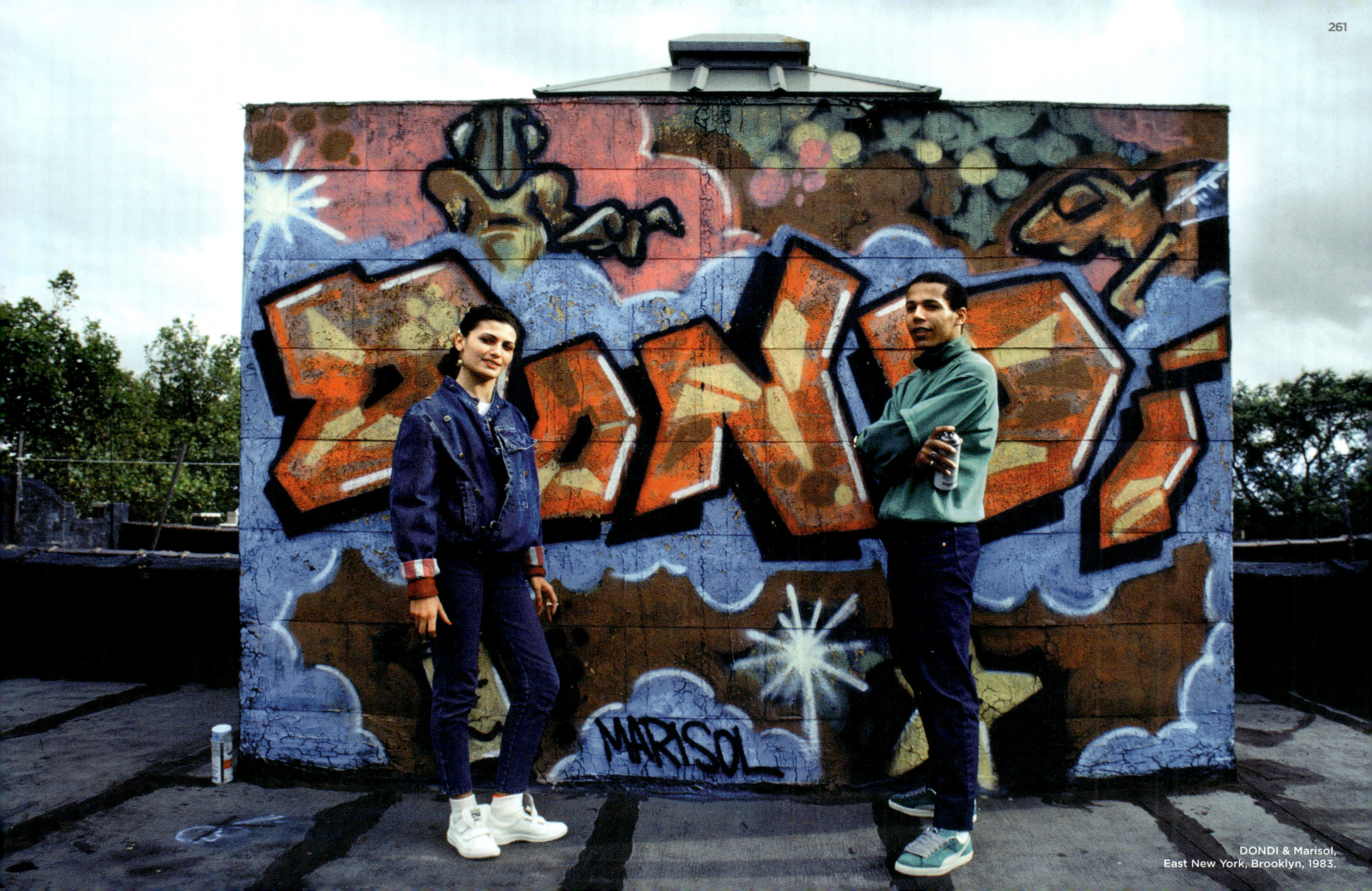

DONDI & Marisol,
East New York, Brooklyn, 1983.

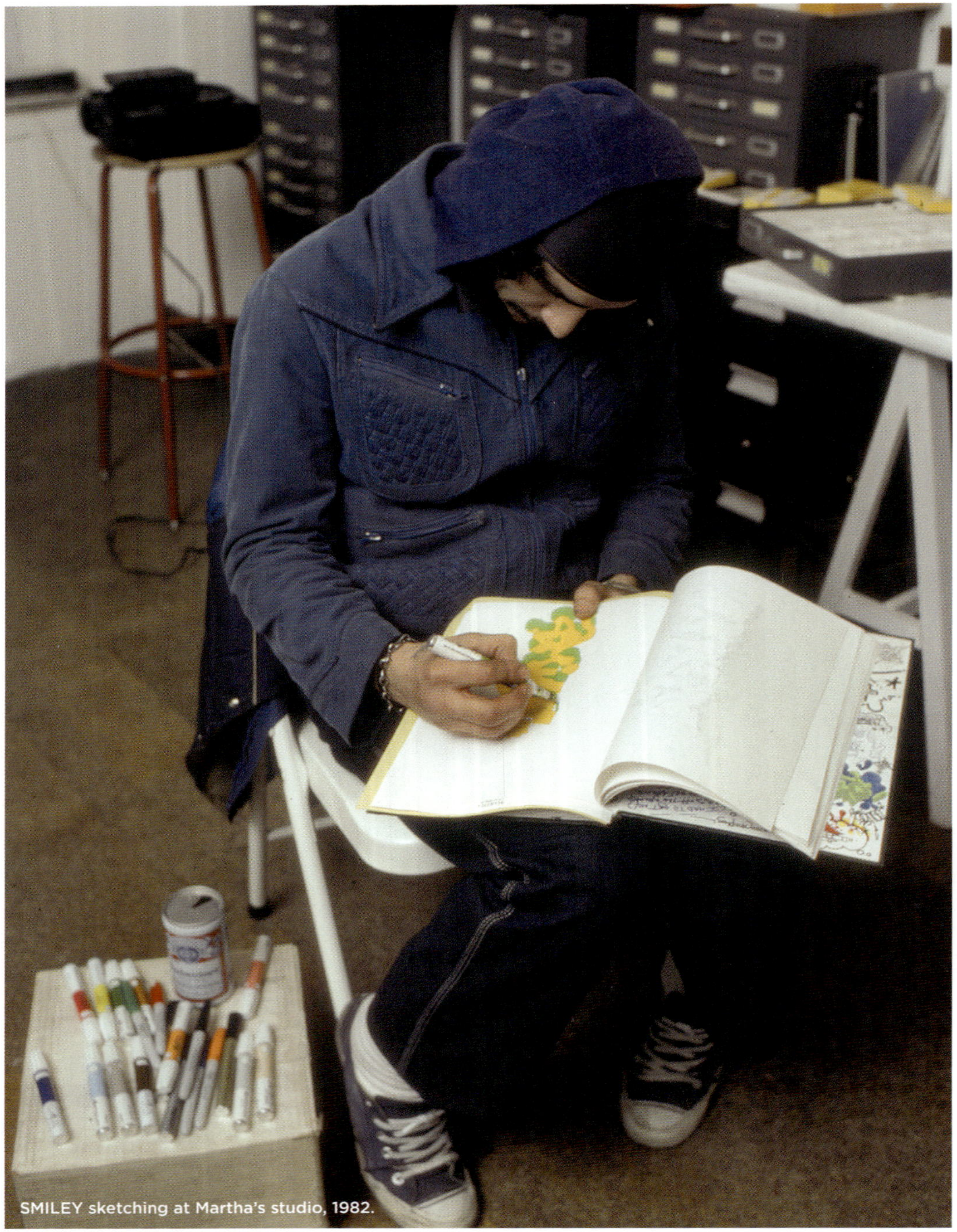

SMILEY sketching at Martha's studio, 1982.

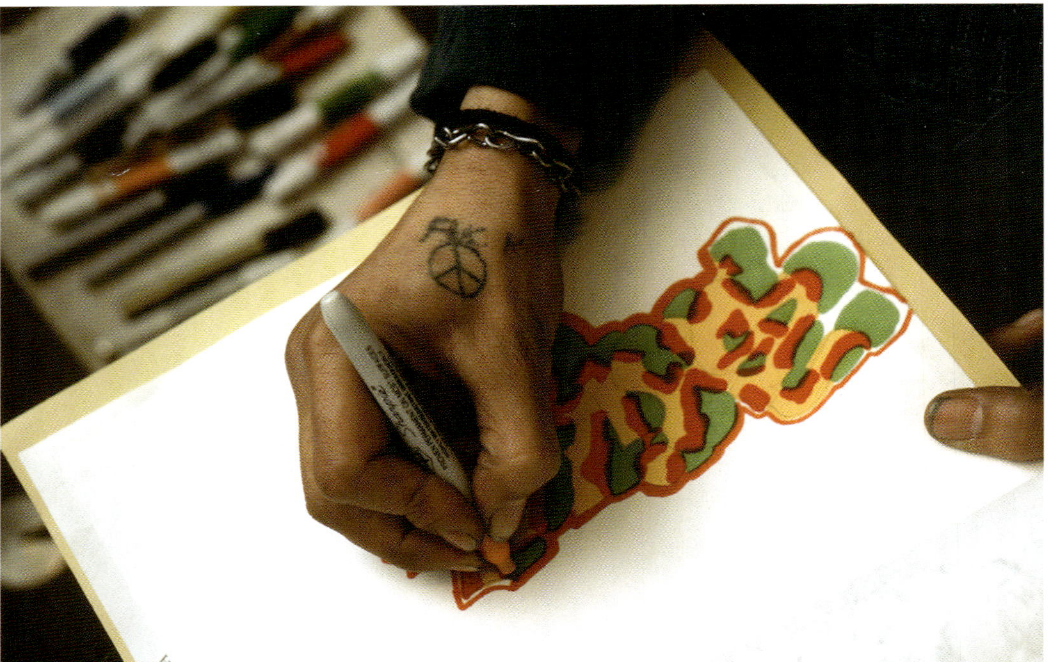

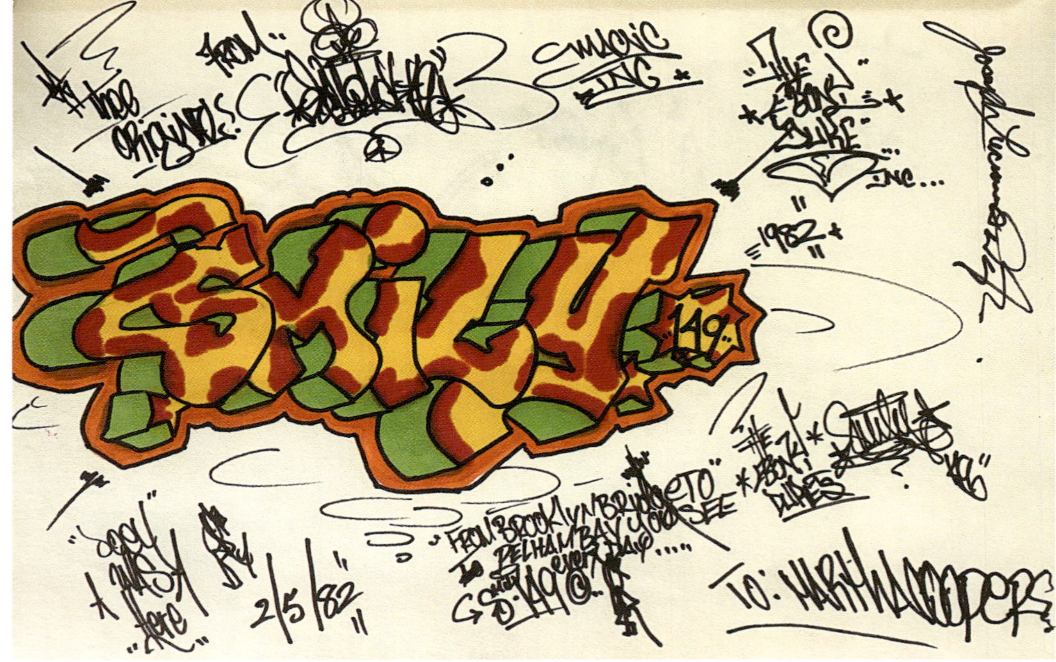

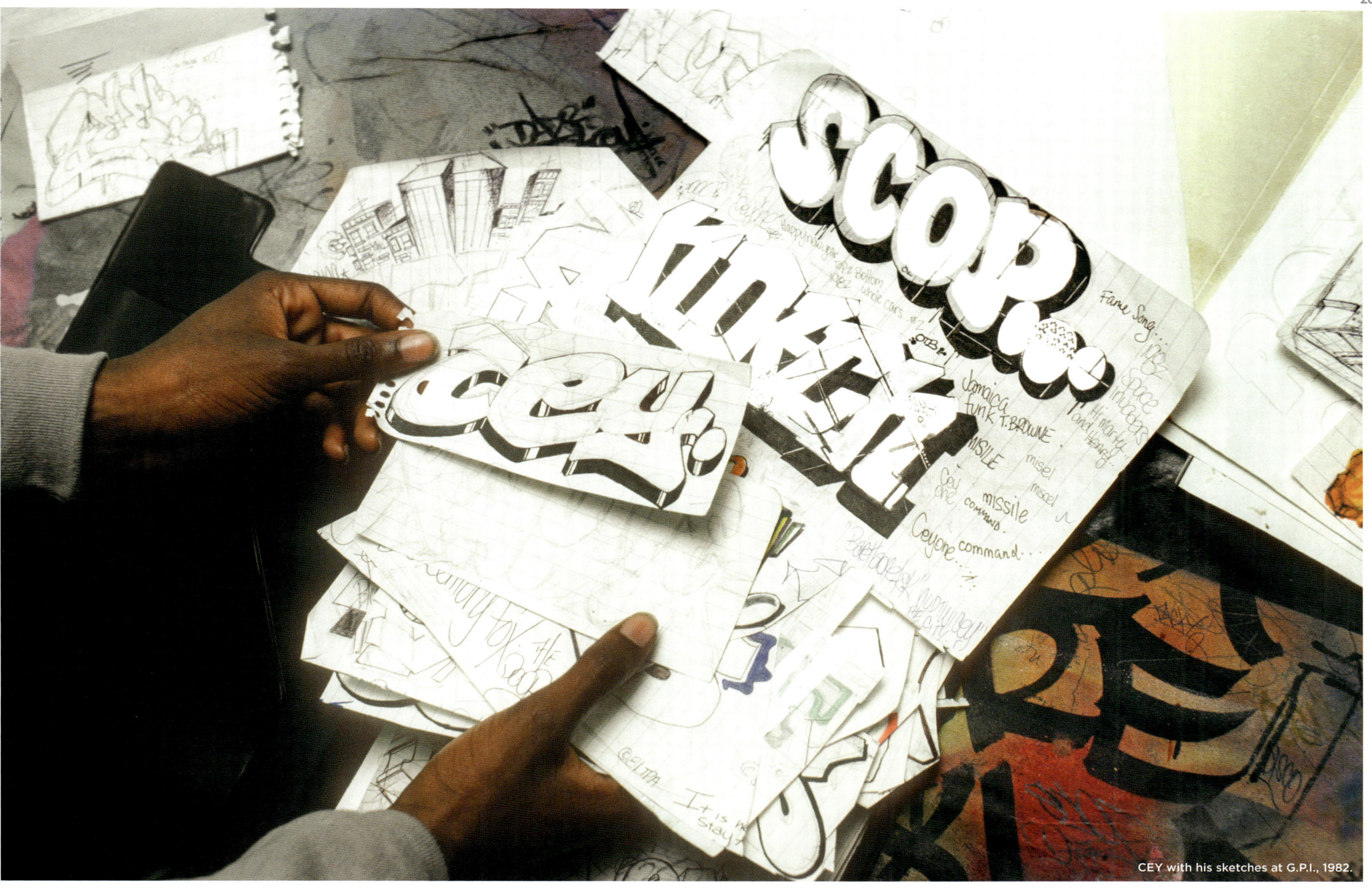

CEY with his sketches at G.P.I., 1982.

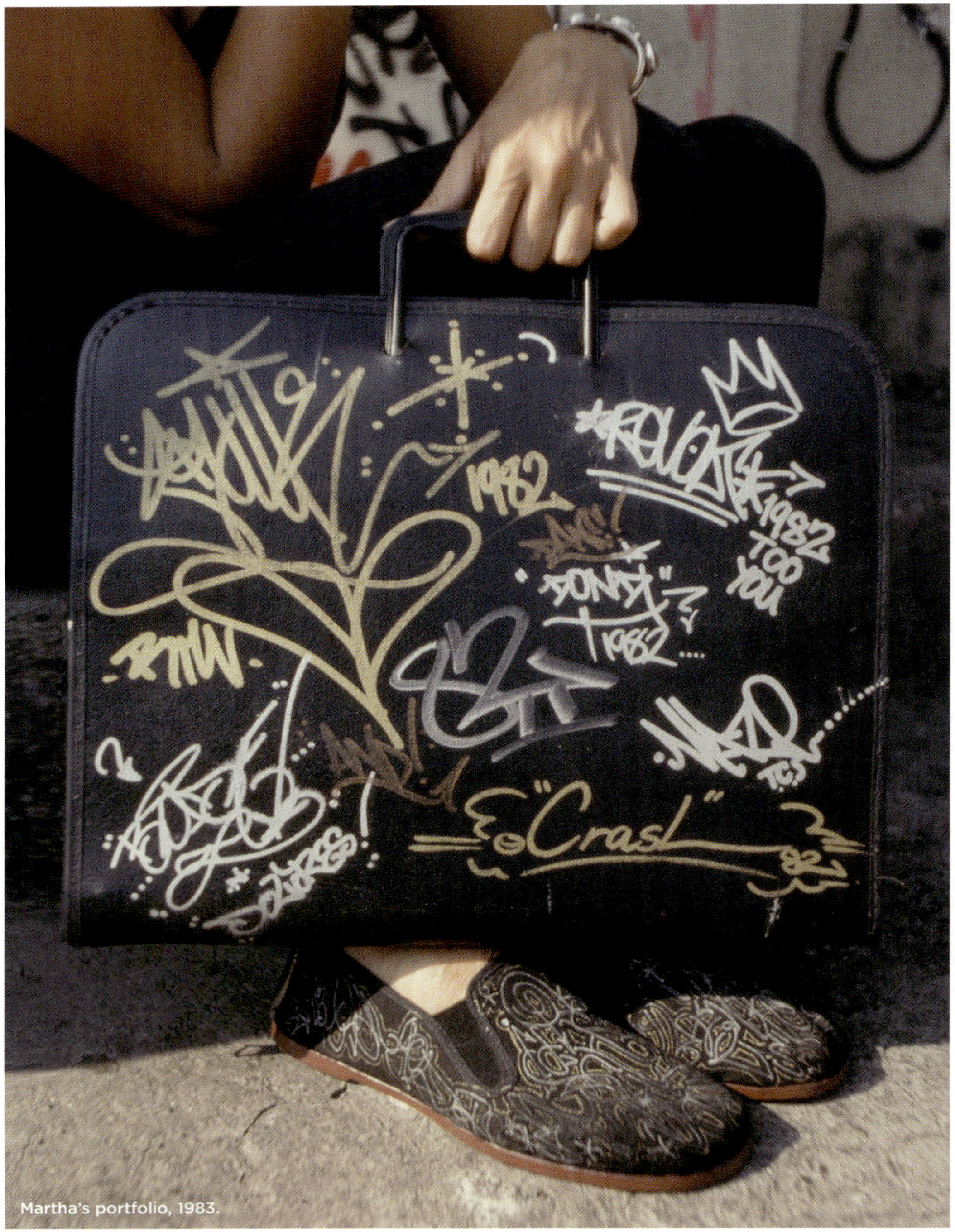

Martha's portfolio, 1983.

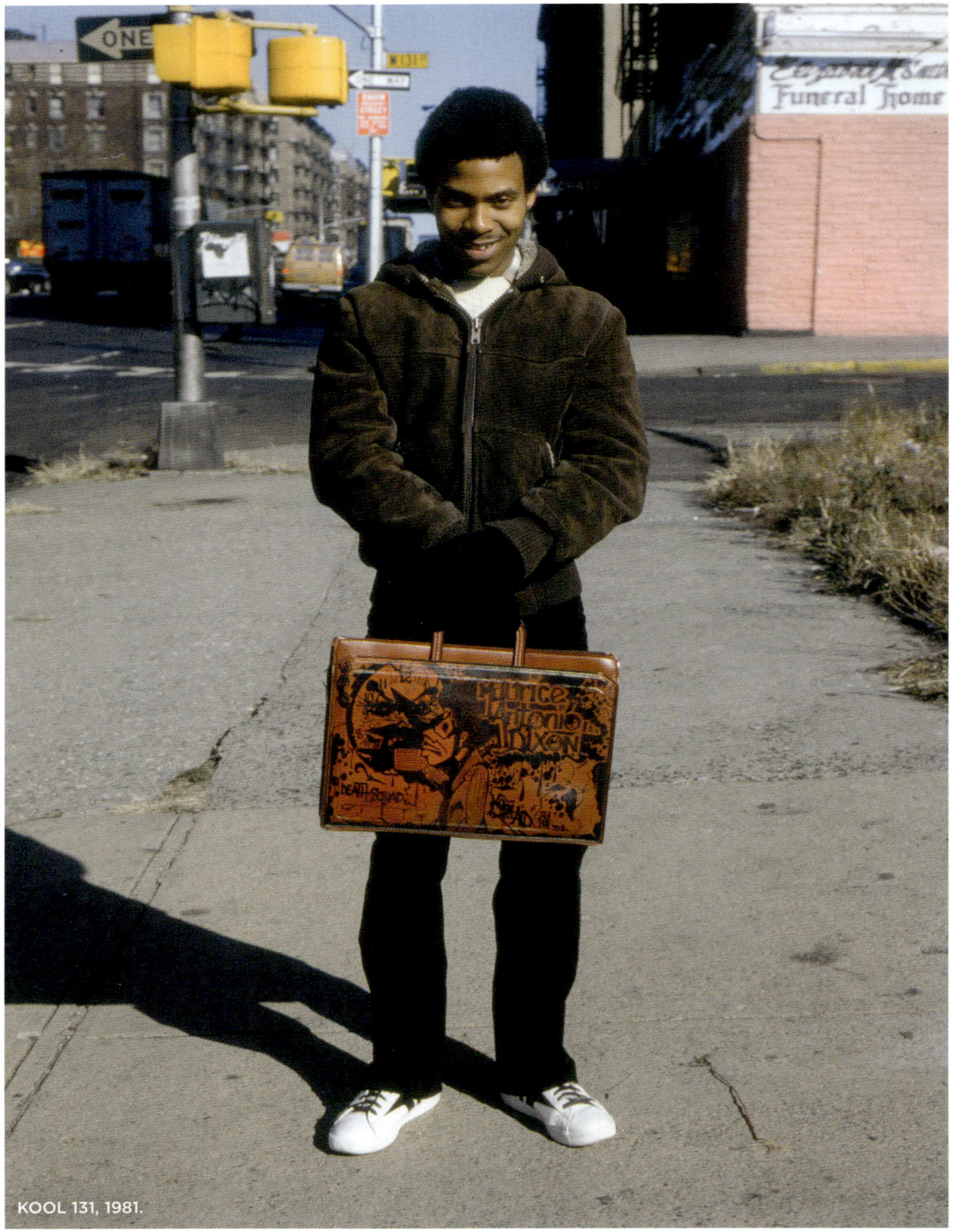

KOOL 131, 1981.

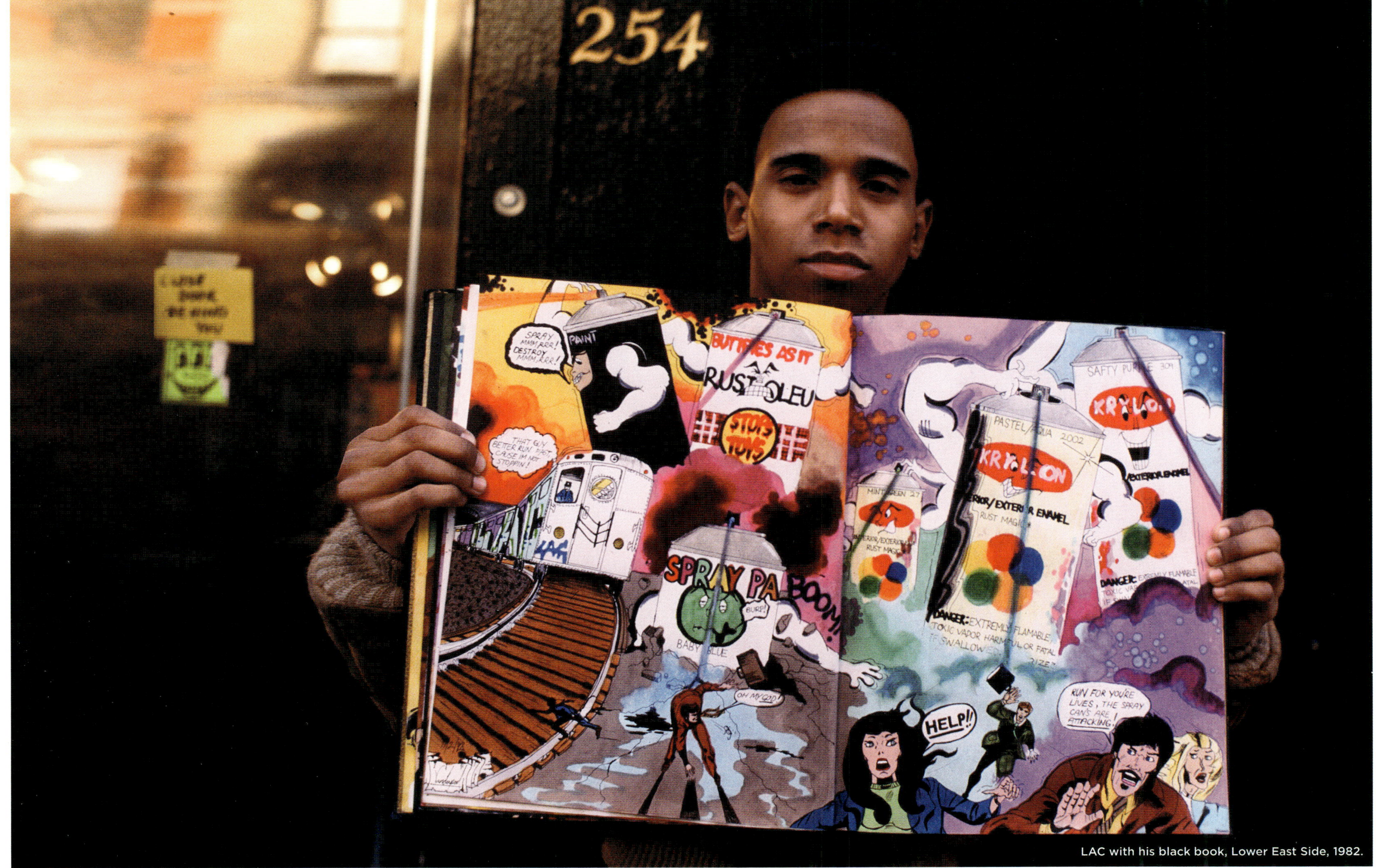

LAC with his black book, Lower East Side, 1982.

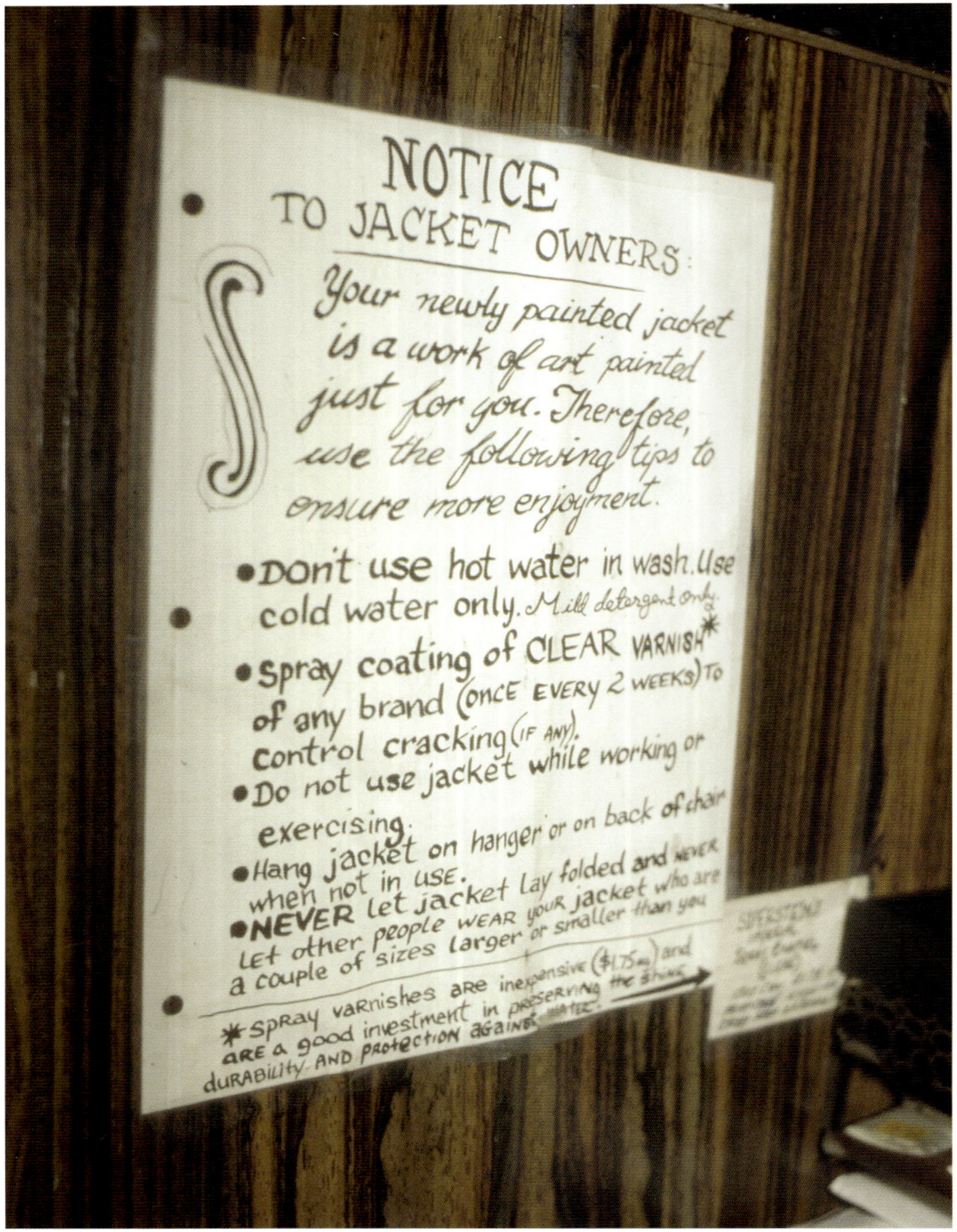

NOTICE
TO JACKET OWNERS:

Your newly painted jacket is a work of art painted just for you. Therefore, use the following tips to ensure more enjoyment.

- Don't use hot water in wash. Use cold water only. Mild detergent only.
- Spray coating of CLEAR VARNISH* of any brand (once every 2 weeks) to control cracking (if any).
- Do not use jacket while working or exercising.
- Hang jacket on hanger or on back of chair when not in use.
- NEVER let jacket lay folded and never let other people wear your jacket who are a couple of sizes larger or smaller than you

* Spray varnishes are inexpensive ($1.75 ea.) and are a good investment in preserving the shine, durability and protection against water.

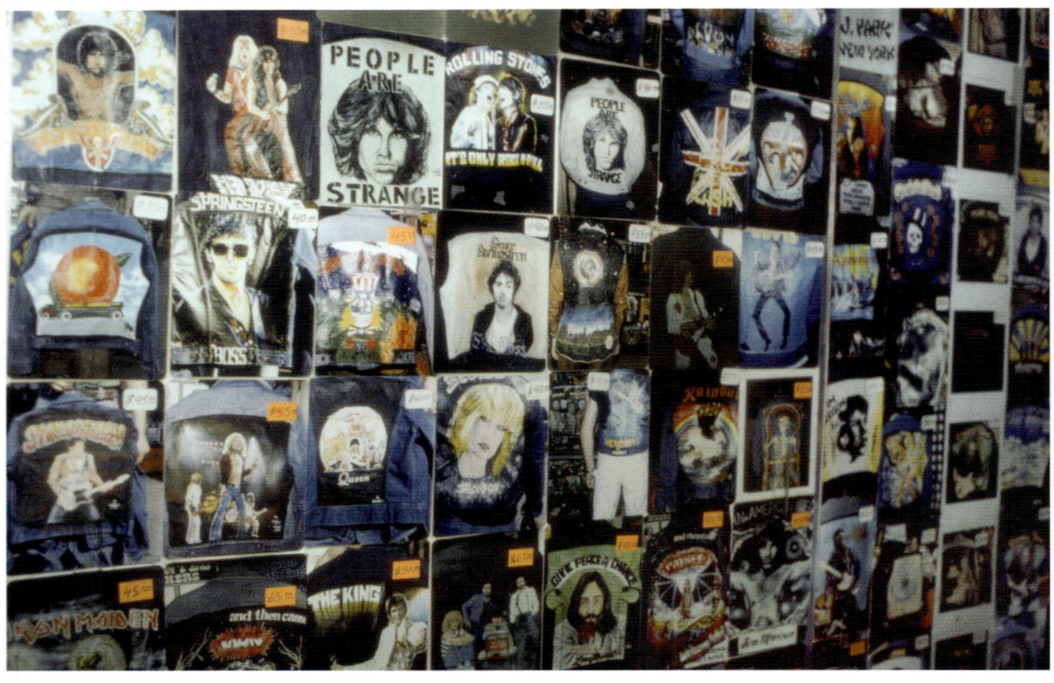

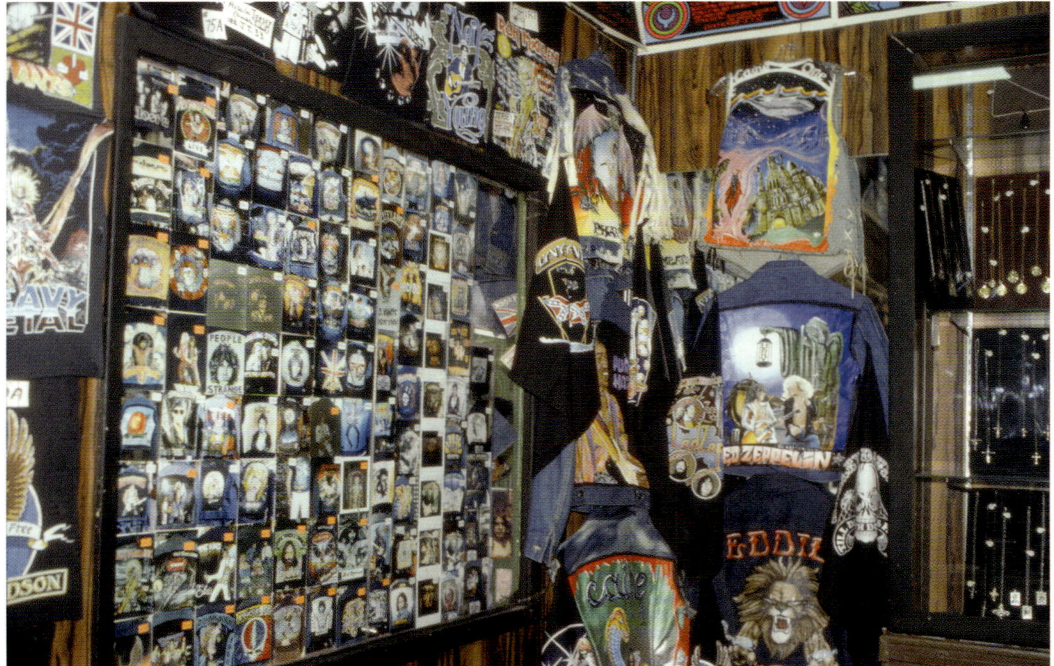

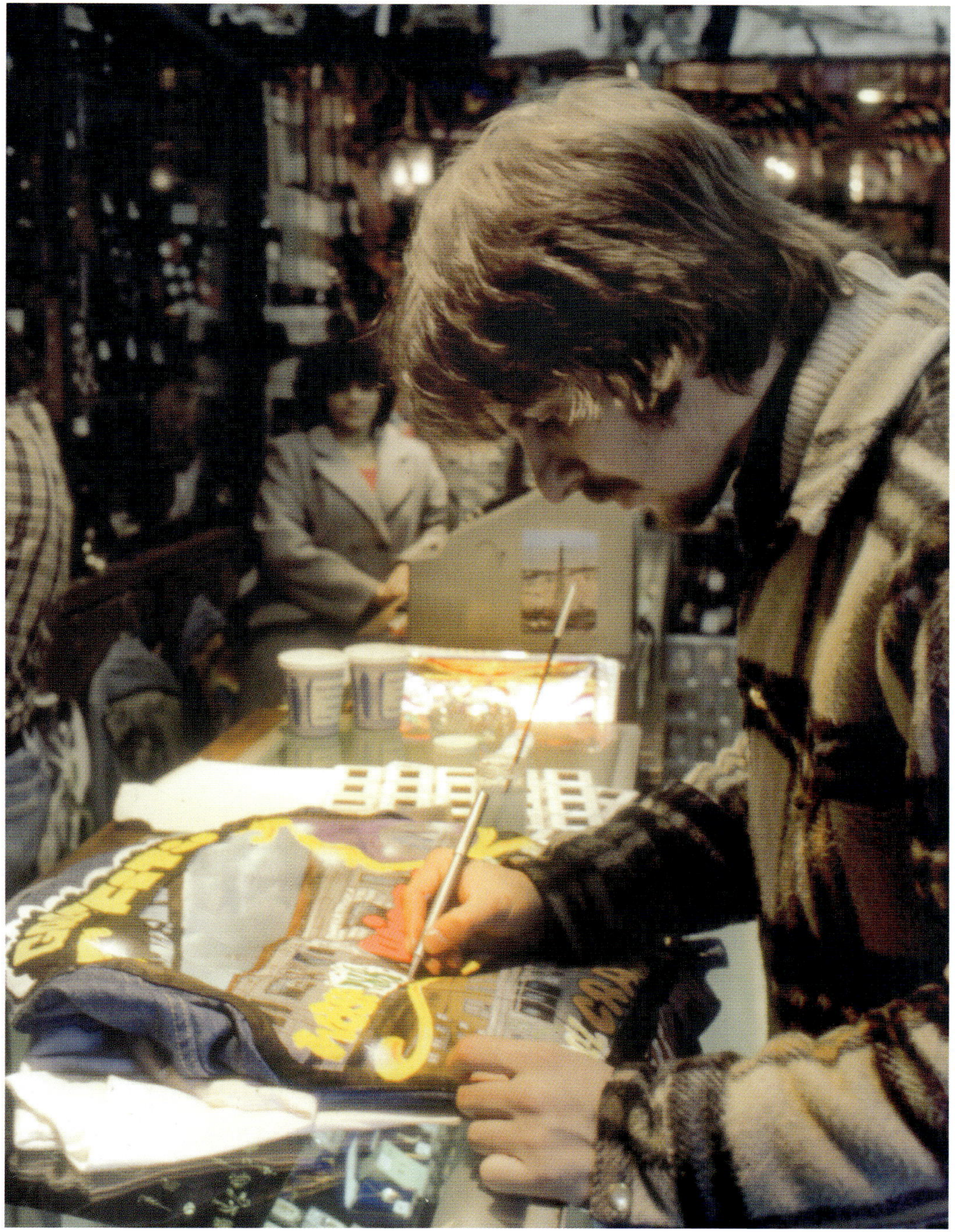

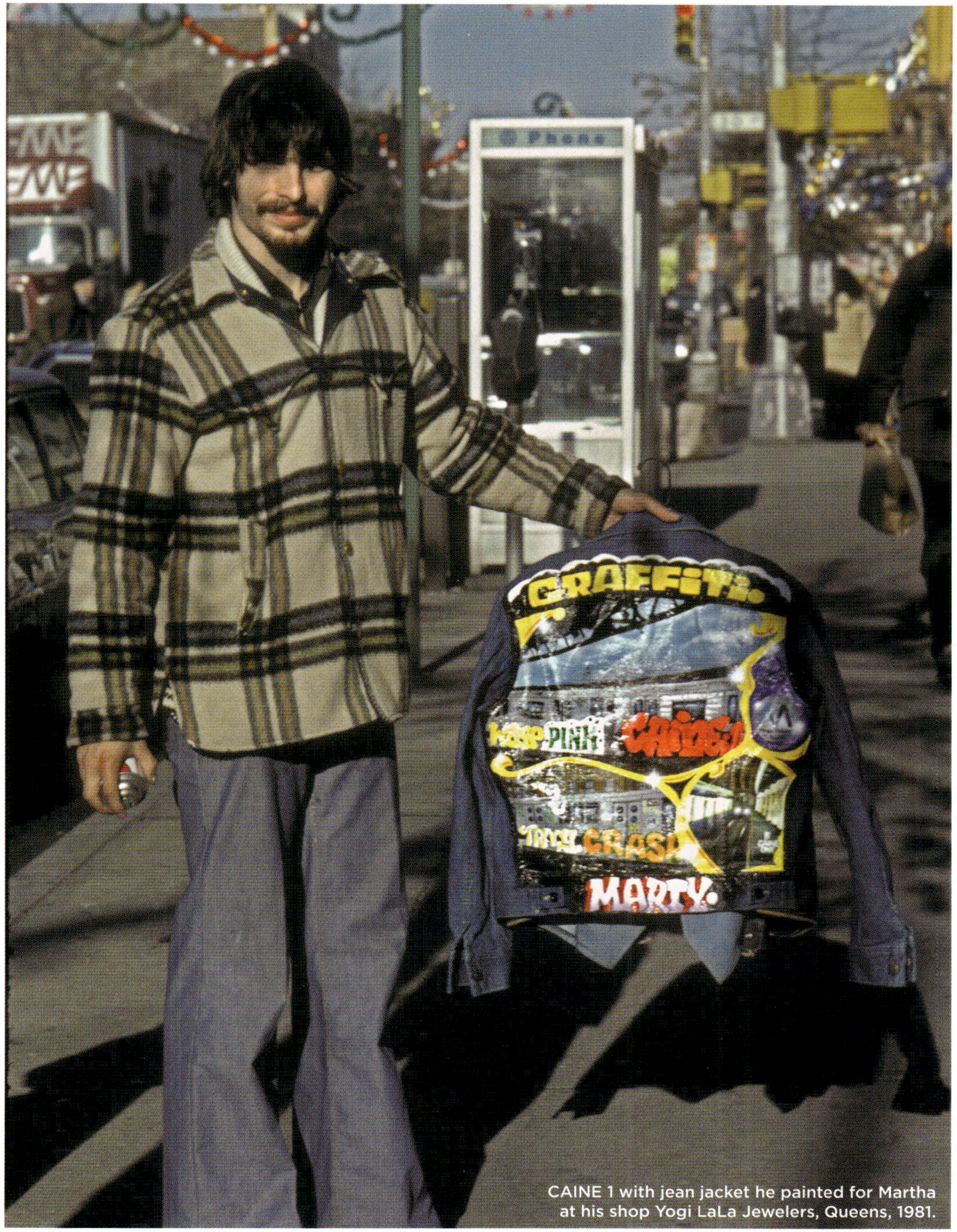

CAINE 1 with jean jacket he painted for Martha
at his shop Yogi LaLa Jewelers, Queens, 1981.

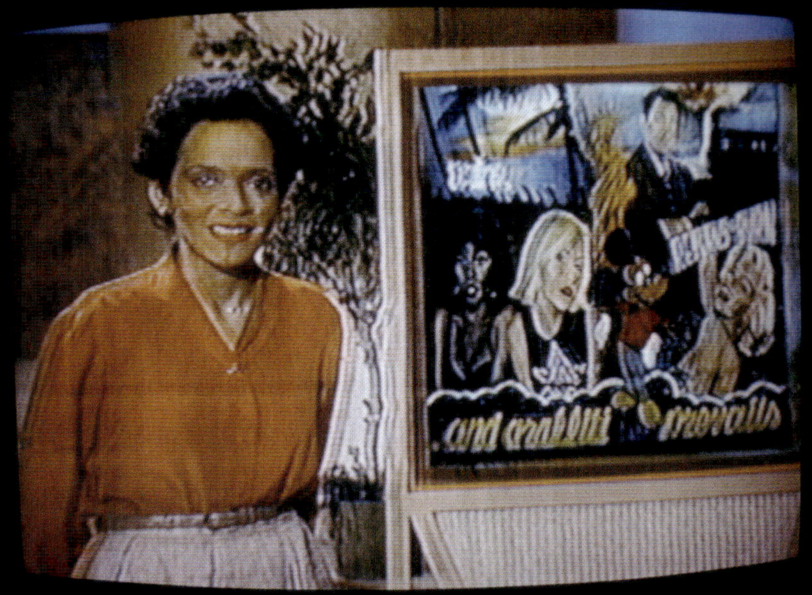

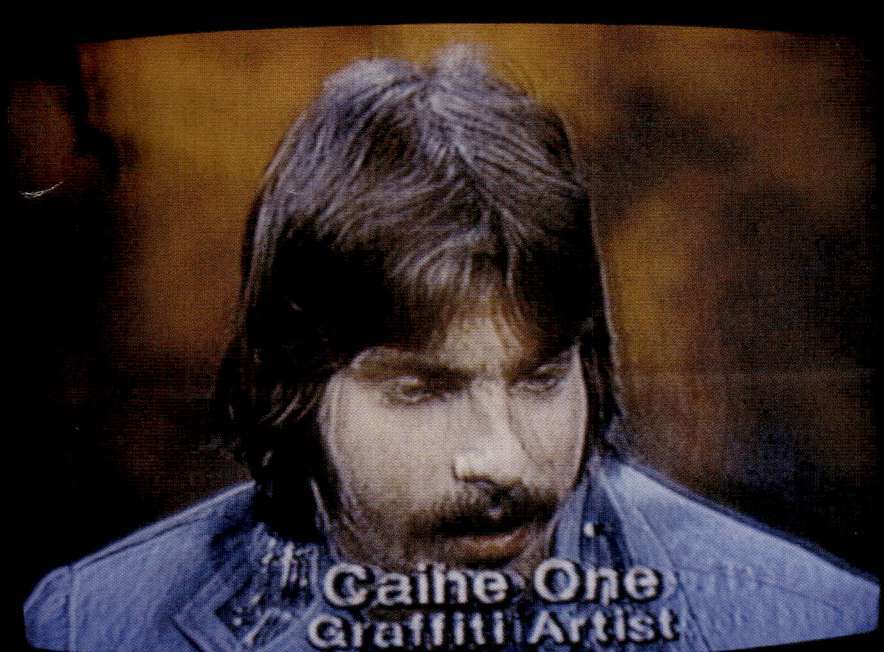

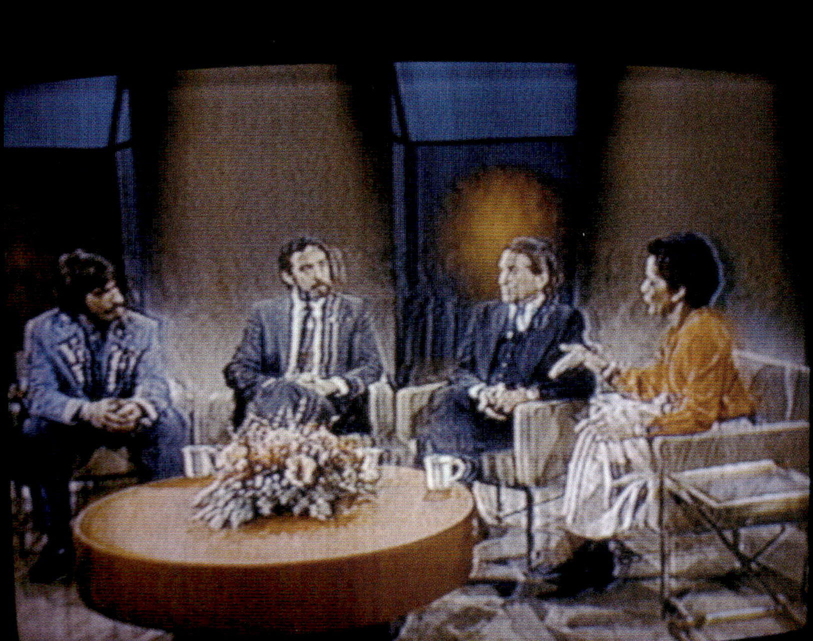

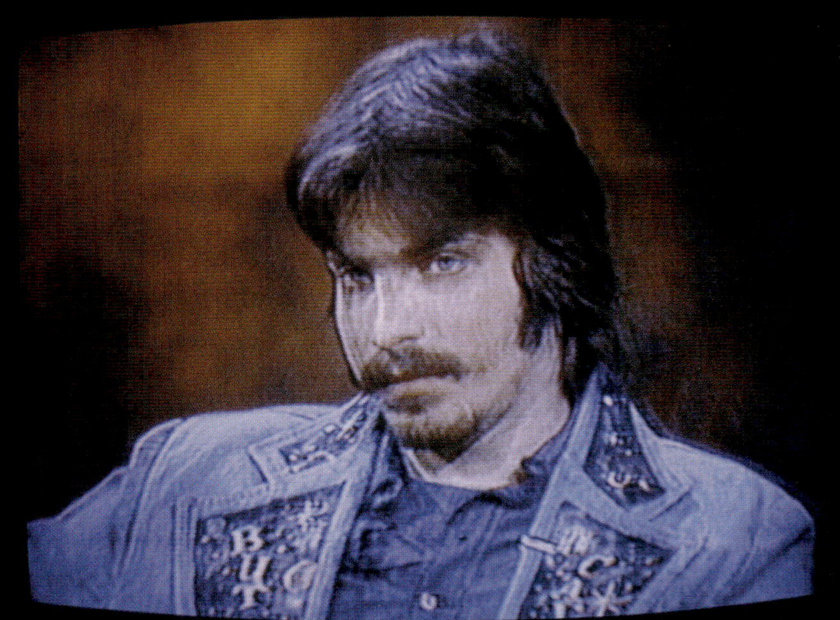

G.P.I. co-founder Mel Neulander and CAINE 1 discuss graffiti as art on TV just days before CAINE 1 was shot to death, 1982.

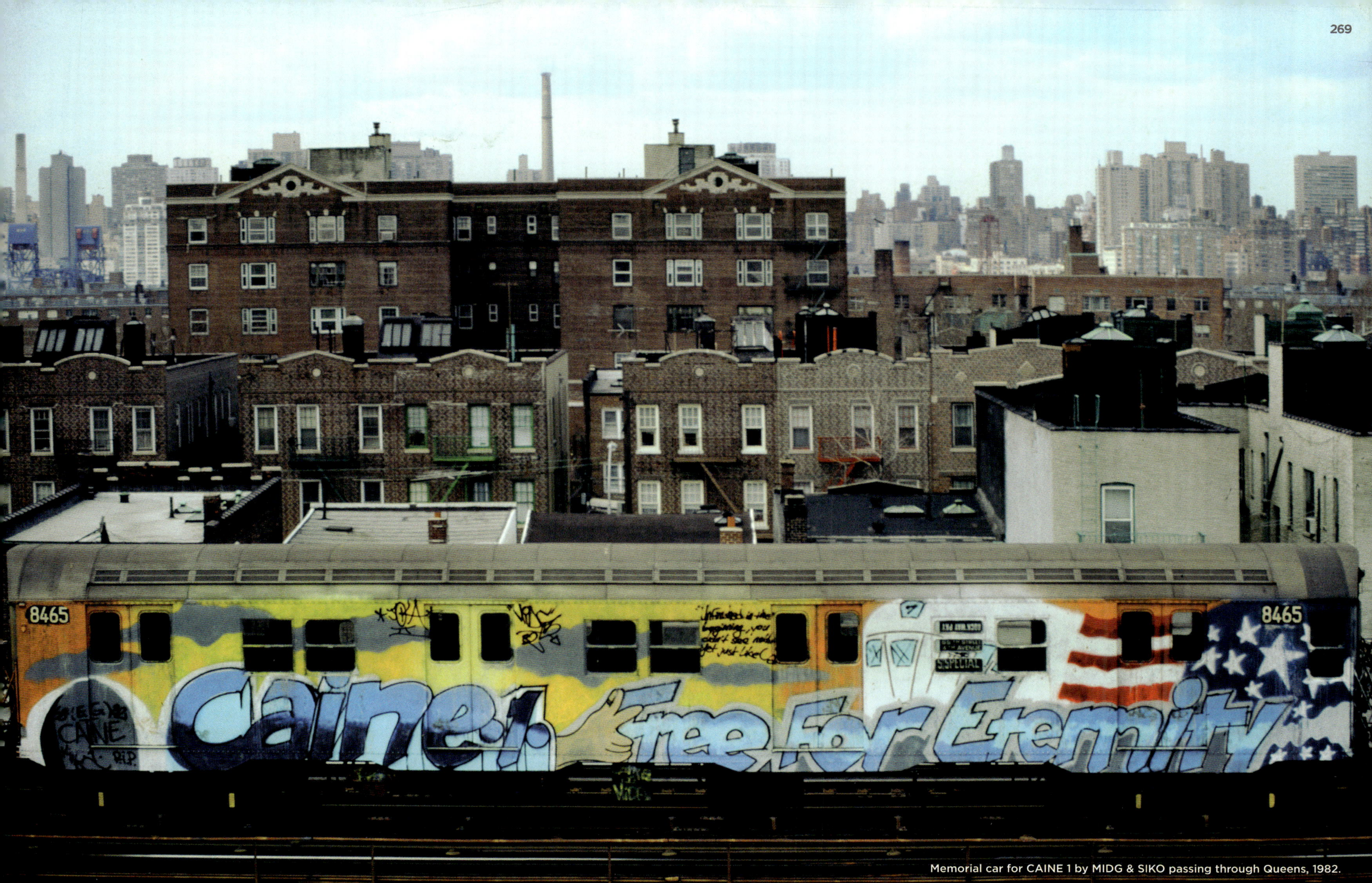

Memorial car for CAINE 1 by MIDG & SIKO passing through Queens, 1982.

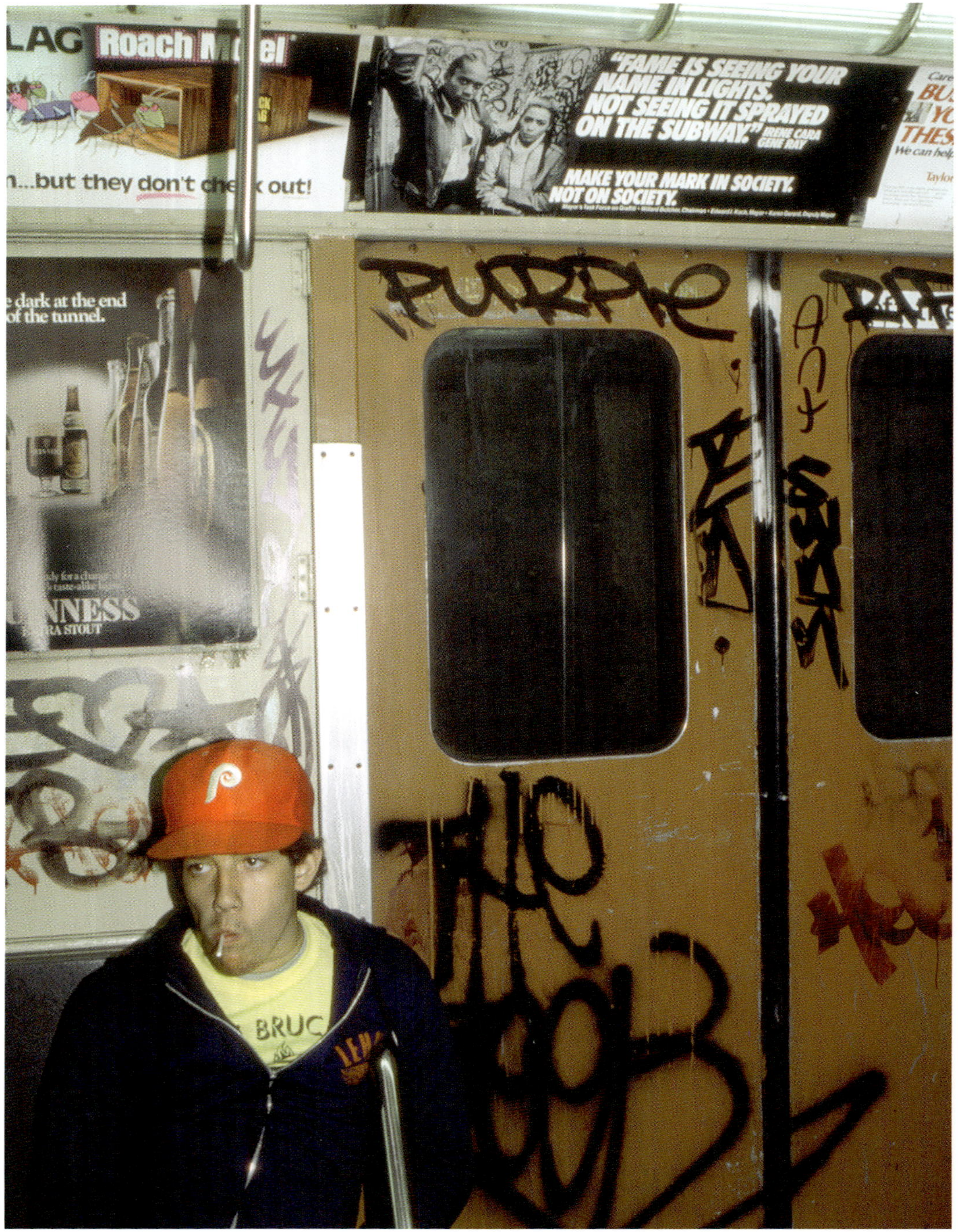

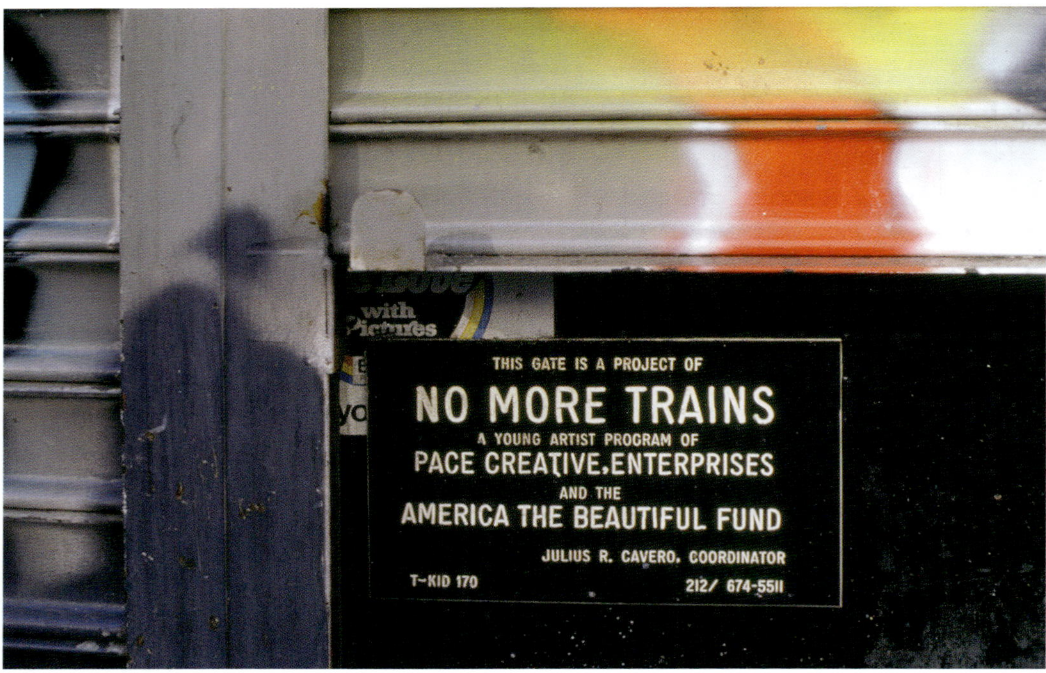
THIS GATE IS A PROJECT OF
NO MORE TRAINS
A YOUNG ARTIST PROGRAM OF
PACE CREATIVE.ENTERPRISES
AND THE
AMERICA THE BEAUTIFUL FUND
JULIUS R. CAVERO, COORDINATOR
T-KID 170   212/ 674-5511

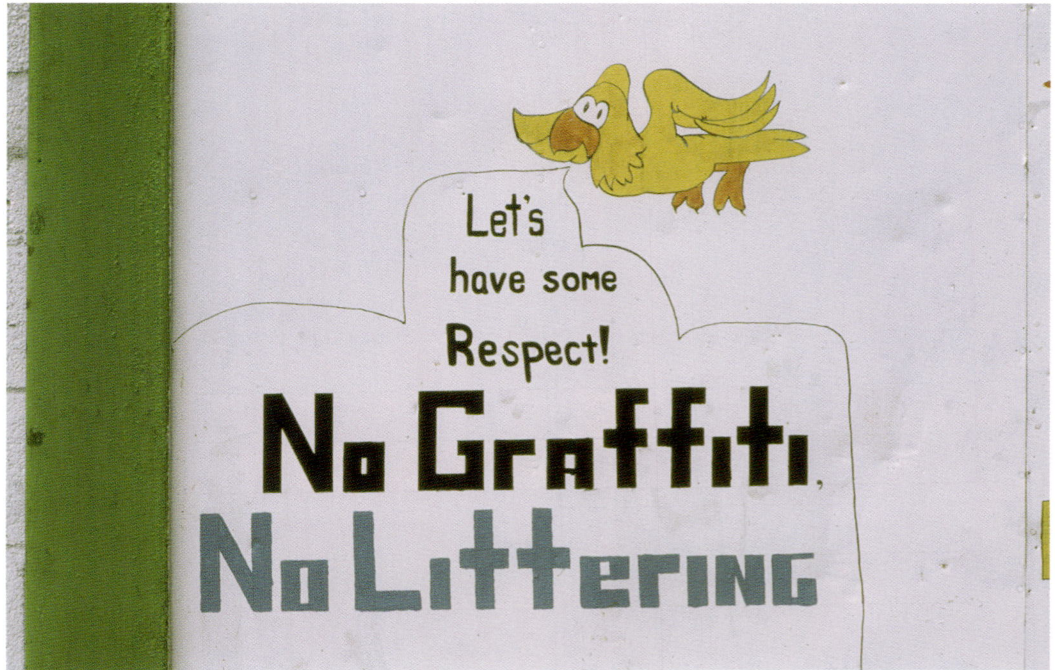
Let's
have some
Respect!
No Graffiti,
No Littering

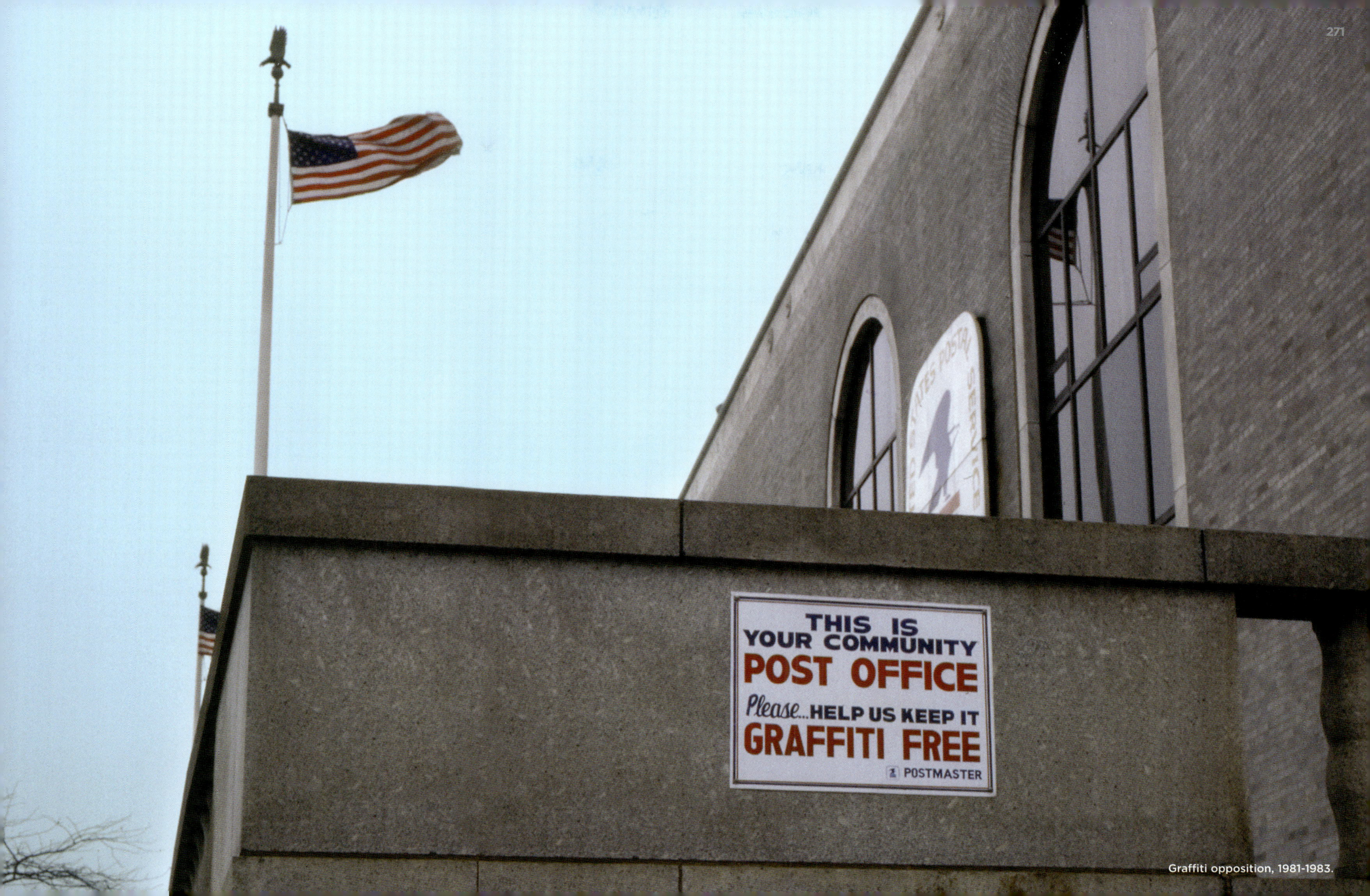

Graffiti opposition, 1981-1983.

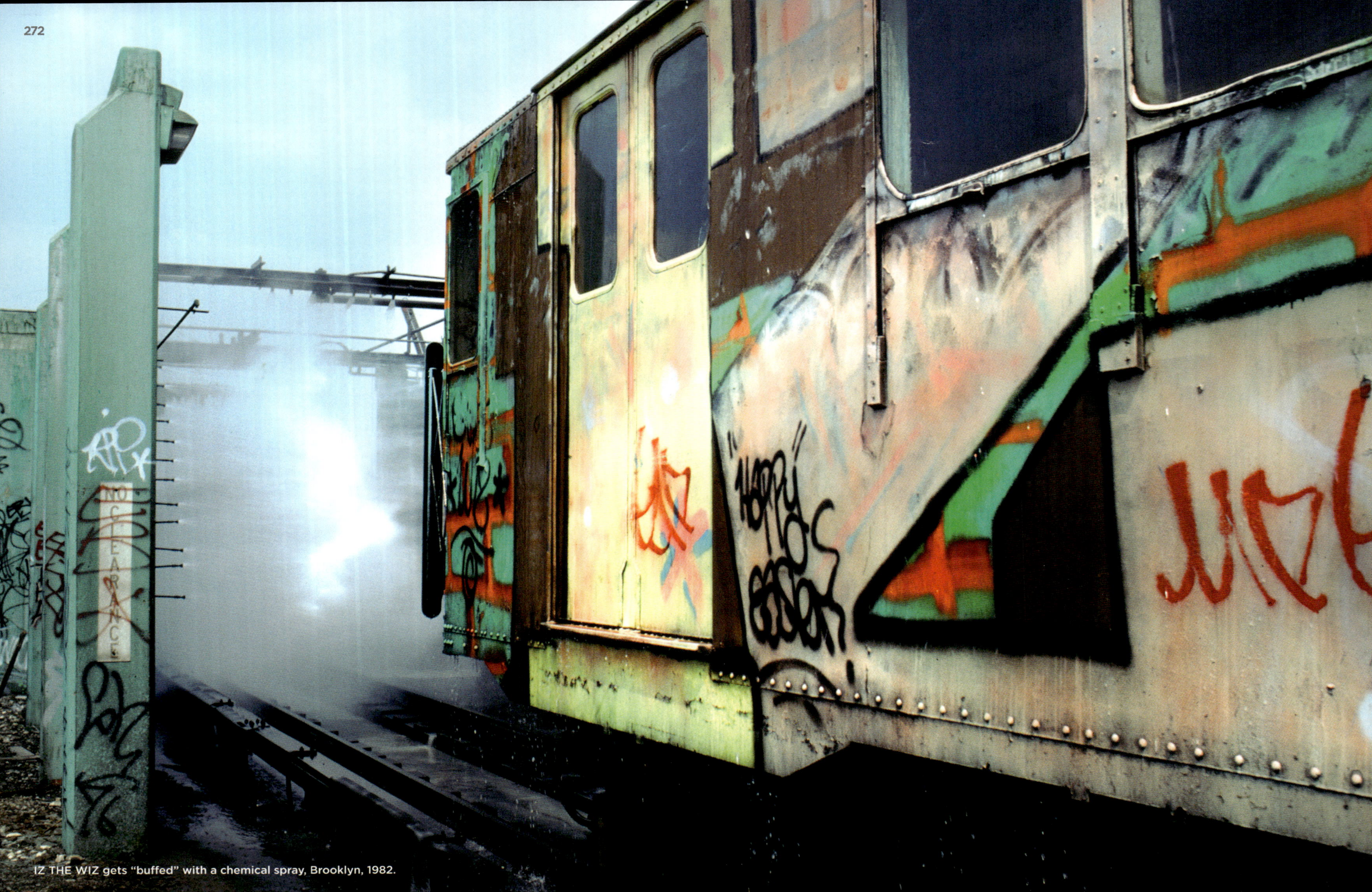

IZ THE WIZ gets "buffed" with a chemical spray, Brooklyn, 1982.

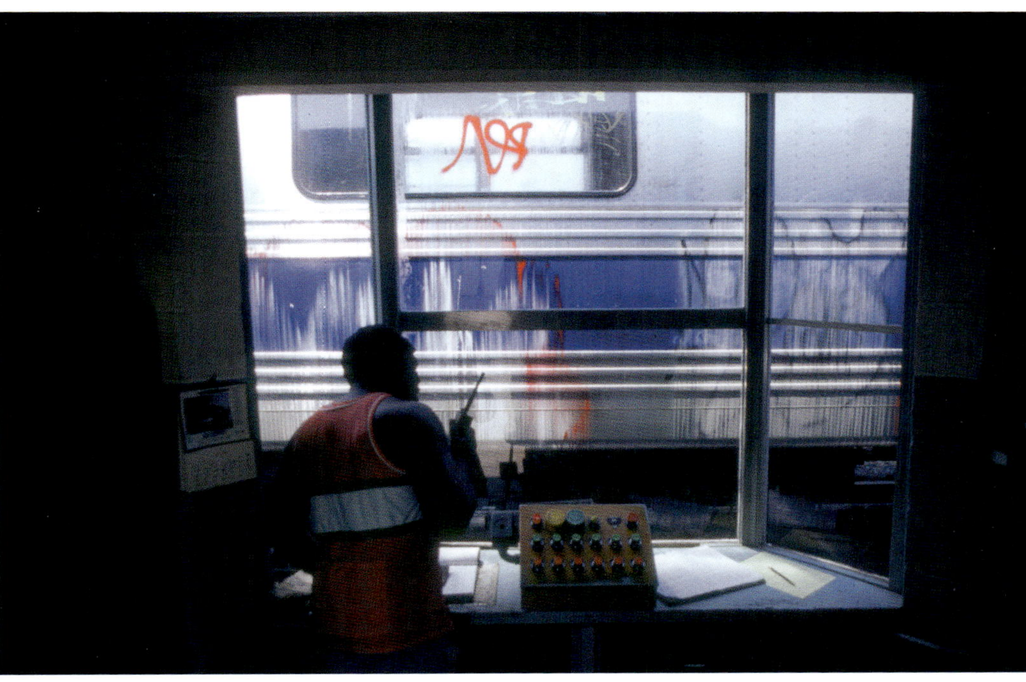

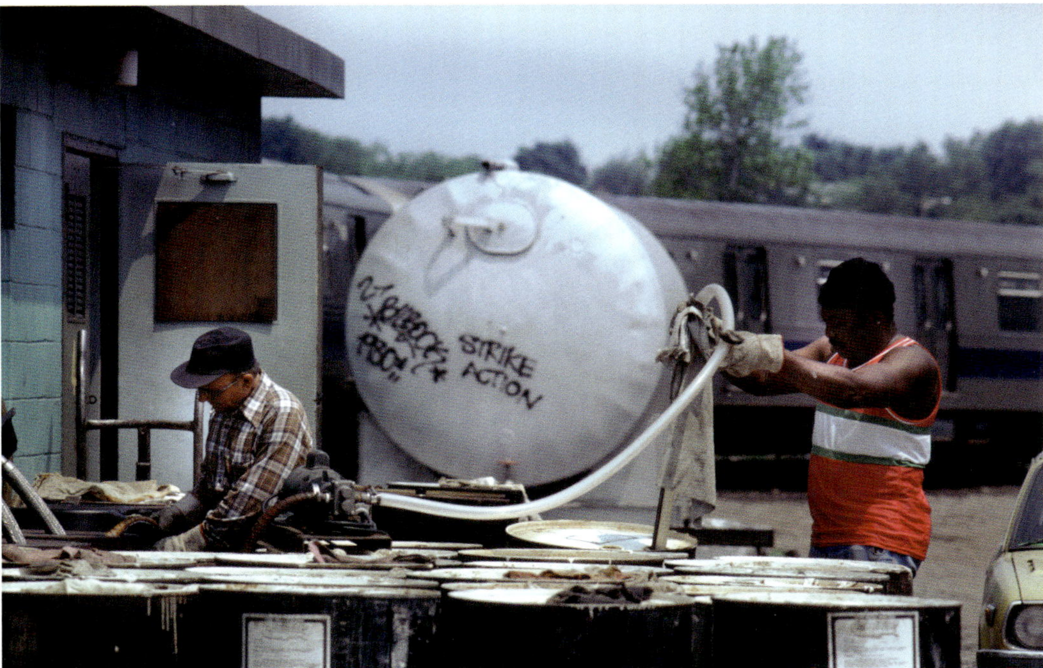

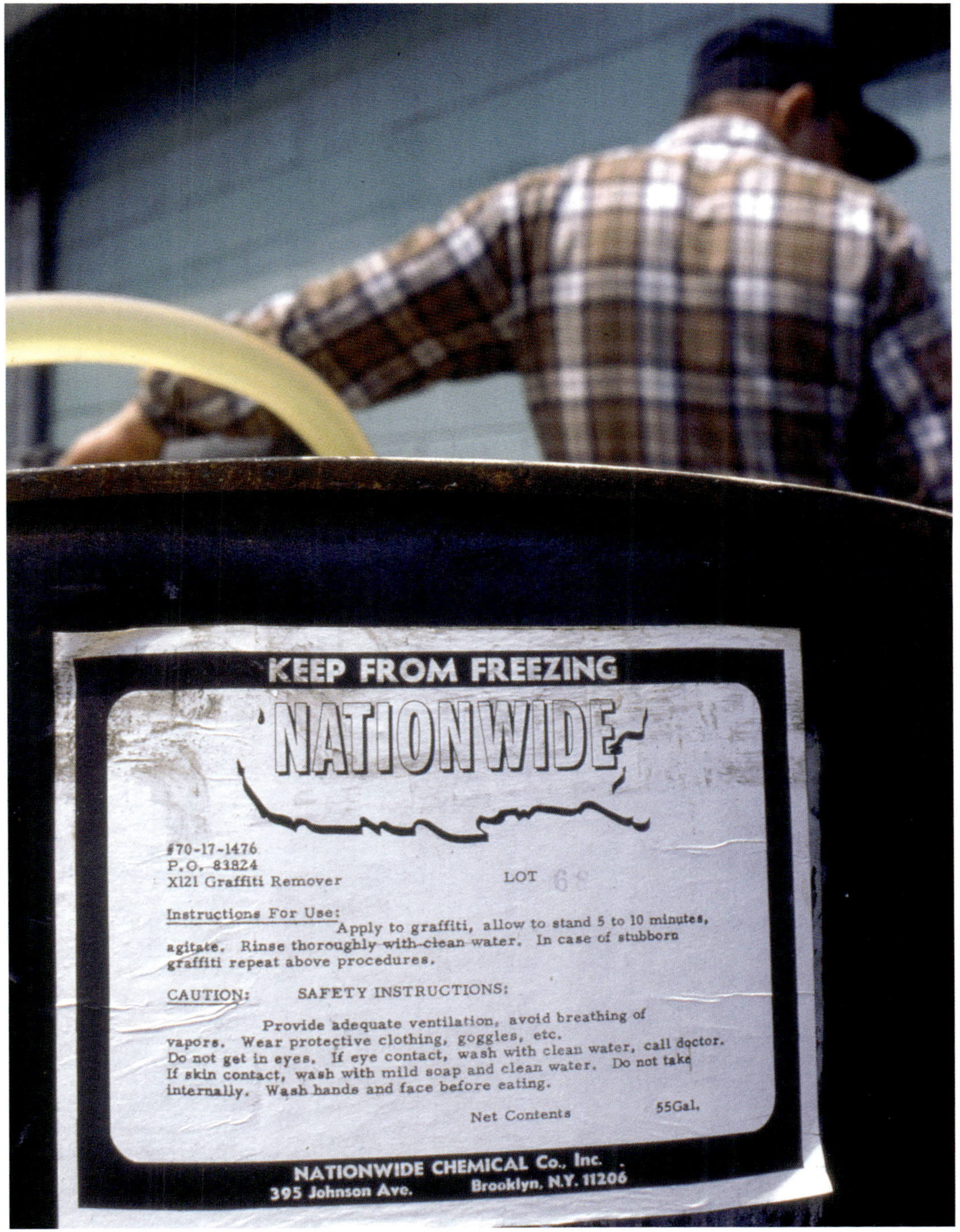

KEEP FROM FREEZING
NATIONWIDE
#70-17-1476
P.O. 83824
X121 Graffiti Remover   LOT 6
Instructions For Use:
          Apply to graffiti, allow to stand 5 to 10 minutes,
agitate. Rinse thoroughly with clean water. In case of stubborn
graffiti repeat above procedures.
CAUTION: SAFETY INSTRUCTIONS:
          Provide adequate ventilation, avoid breathing of
vapors. Wear protective clothing, goggles, etc.
Do not get in eyes. If eye contact, wash with clean water, call doctor.
If skin contact, wash with mild soap and clean water. Do not take
internally. Wash hands and face before eating.
          Net Contents   55Gal.
NATIONWIDE CHEMICAL Co., Inc.
395 Johnson Ave.   Brooklyn, N.Y. 11206

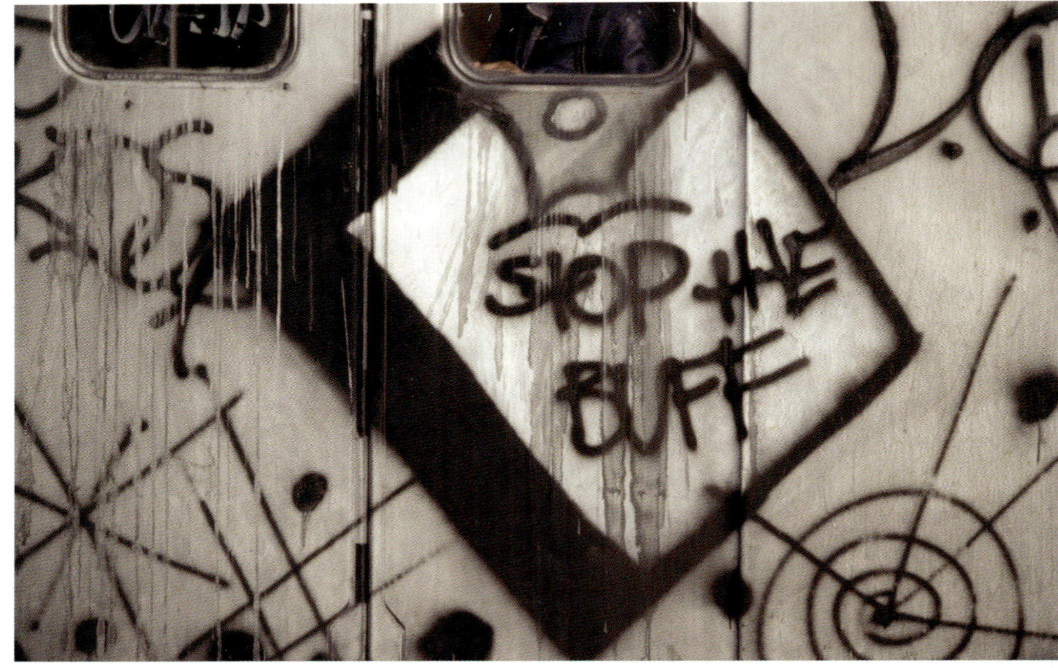

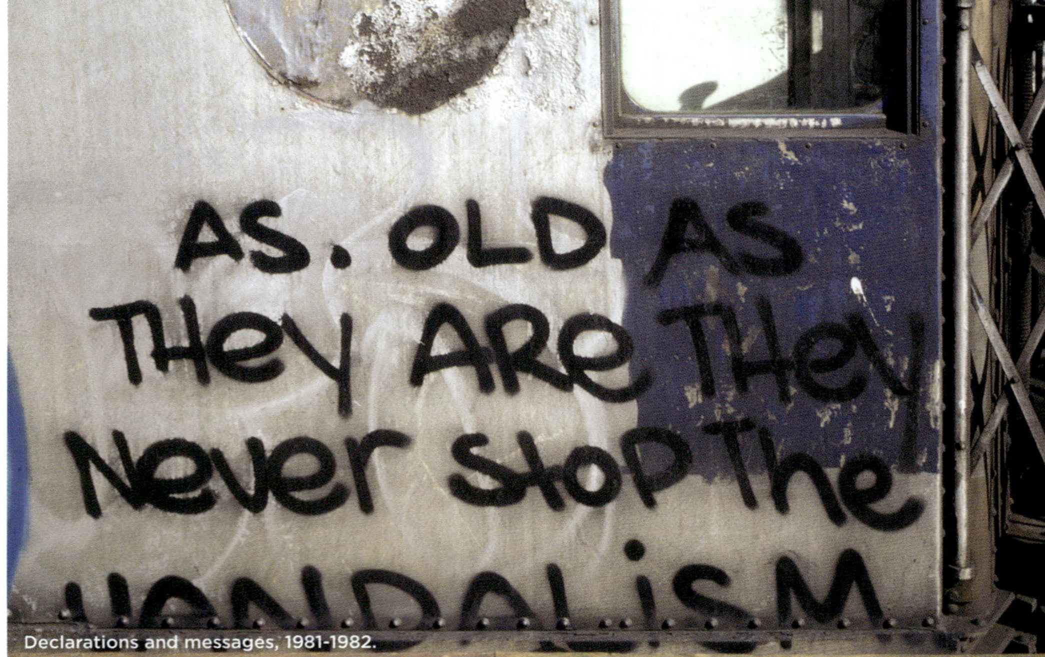

Declarations and messages, 1981-1982.

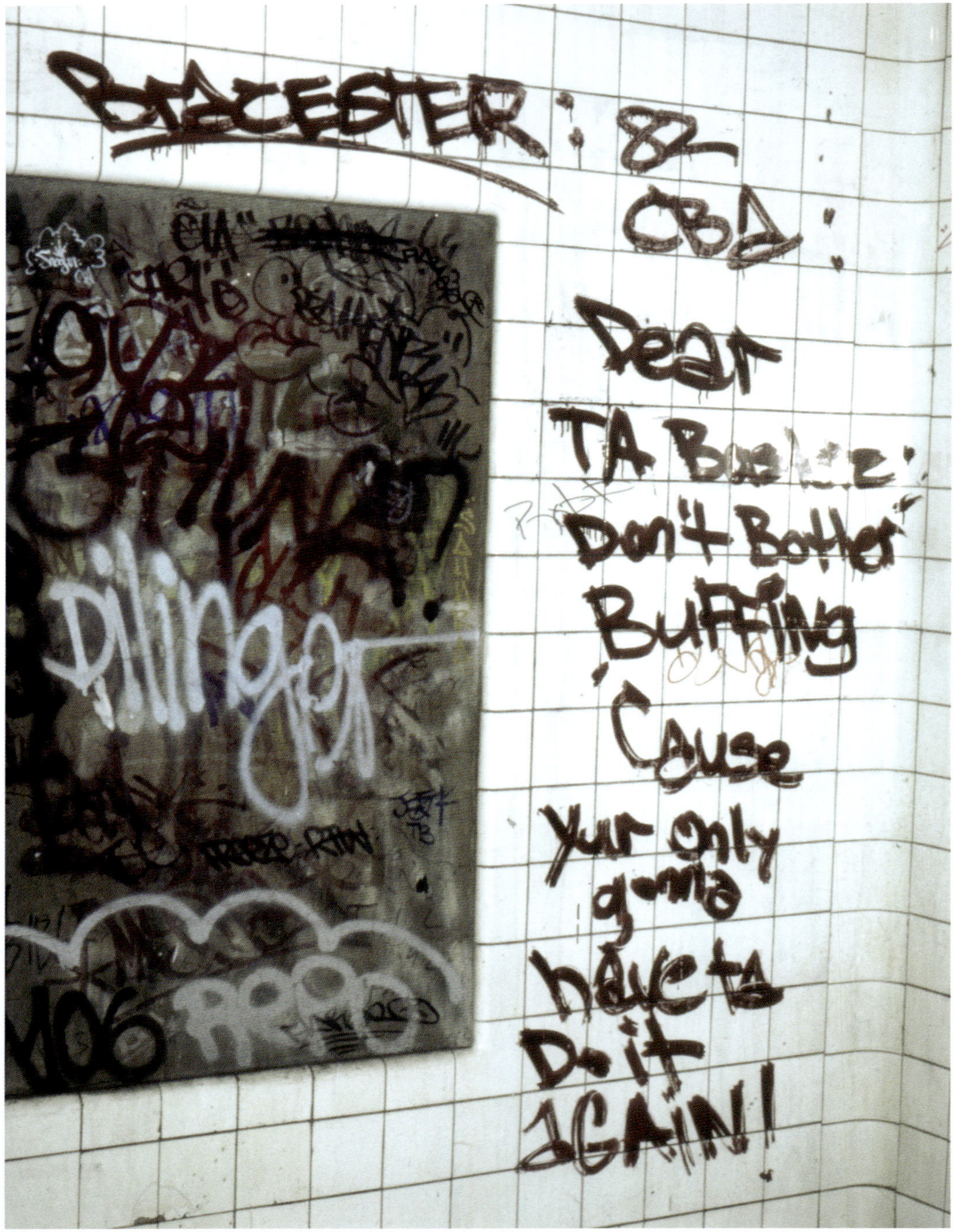

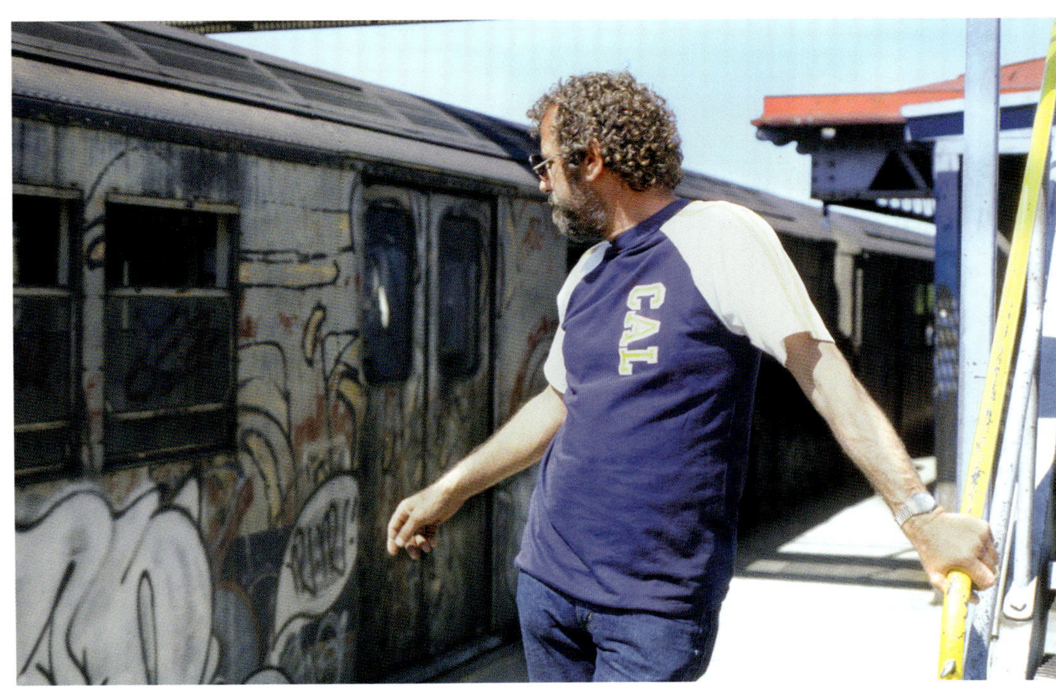

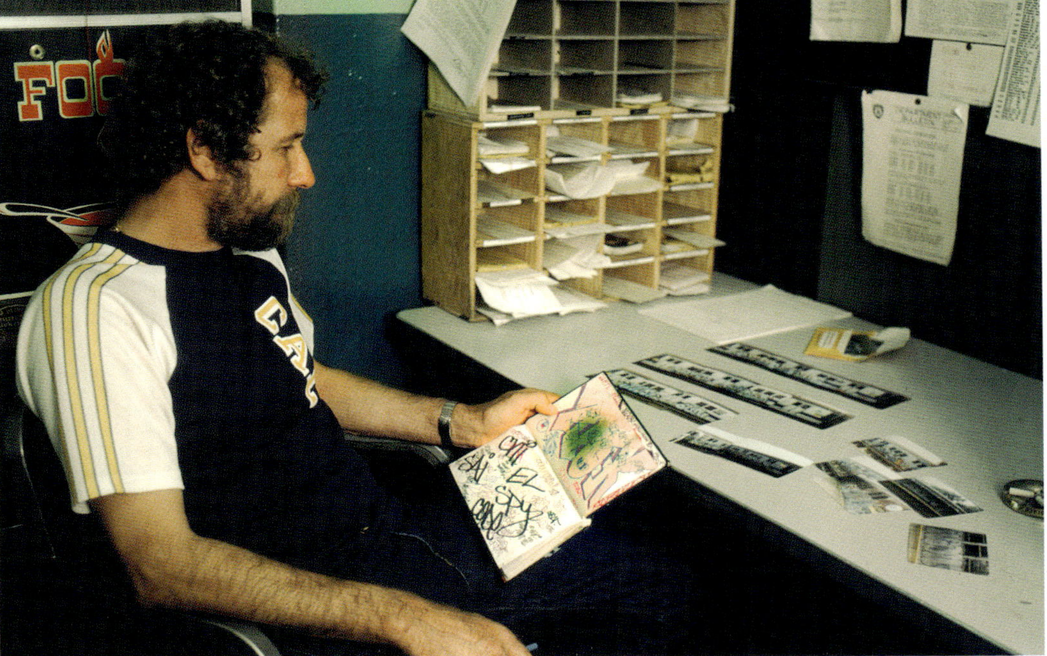

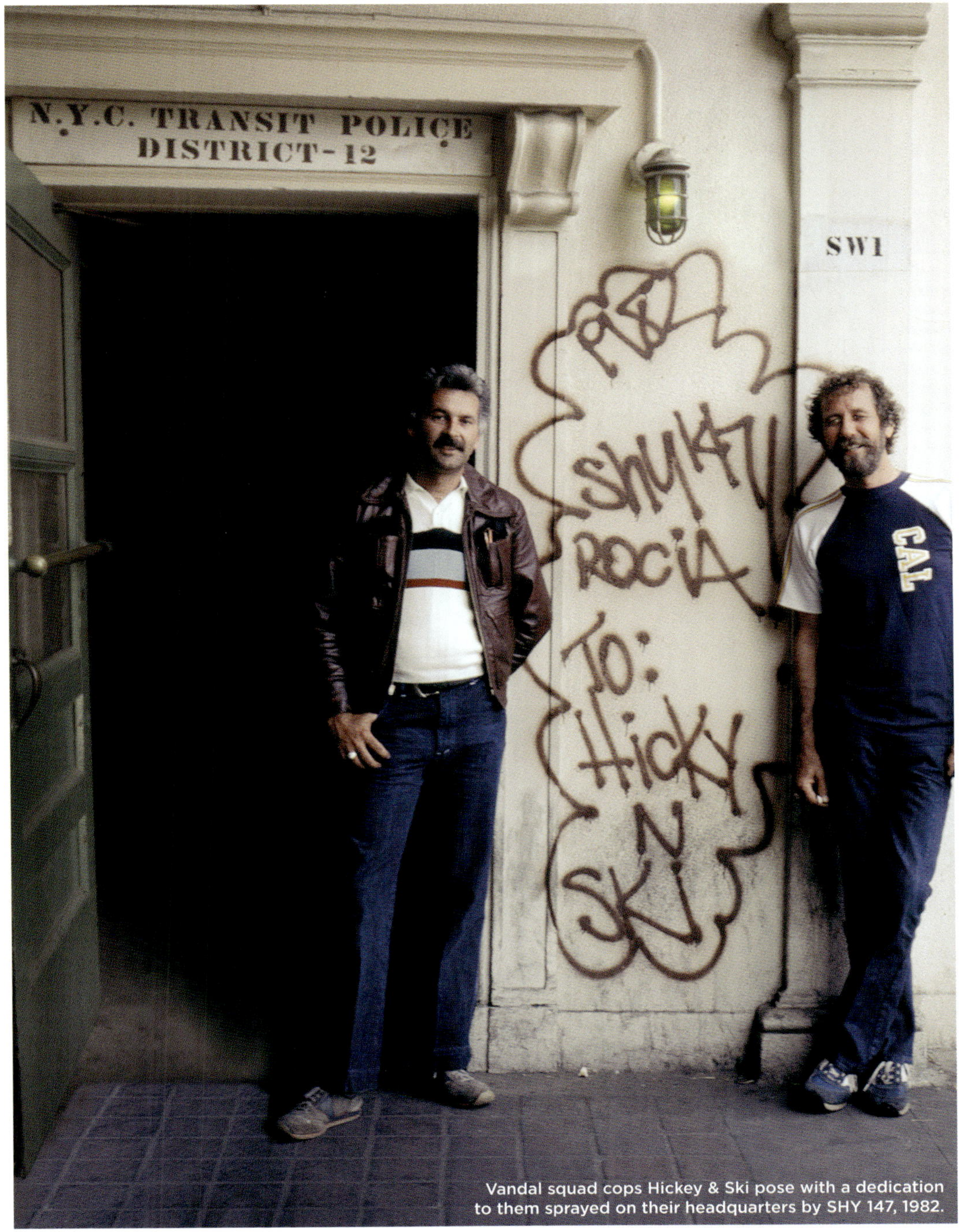

Vandal squad cops Hickey & Ski pose with a dedication to them sprayed on their headquarters by SHY 147, 1982.

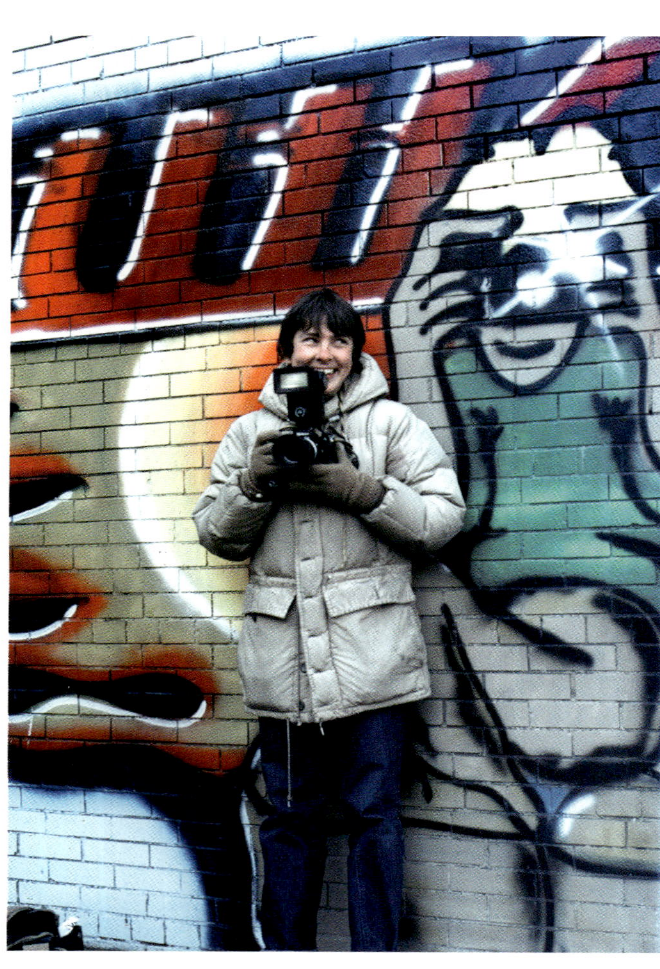

© Prestel Verlag, Munich · London · New York, 2022
Reprinted 2023
A member of Penguin Random House
Verlagsgruppe GmbH
Neumarkter Strasse 28 · 81673 Munich

Front cover: POD by DOZE, 2NEAR & SUB, 1980.
Back cover: Women on train, 1981.
This page: Martha Cooper poses in front of Foto Quik in the Bronx, 1981.

Martha Cooper's Special Thanks: All of the artists who are captured in my photographs; Roger Gastman for the herculean efforts of going through the archives; Leon Gonzalez for perseverance and countless hours of production; Amanda Bessette for cat toys; and Chris Pape and David Villorente for helping to ID many of the images.

All years listed refer to when the photo was taken. Much of the work seen in the images was completed before.

Best efforts were made to identify and credit all artists. Corrections and updates will be considered for any future editions.

In respect to links in this book, Penguin Random House Verlagsgruppe expressly notes that no illegal content was discernible on the linked sites at the time the links were created. The Publisher has no influence at all over the current and future design, content or authorship of the linked sites. For this reason Penguin Random House Verlagsgruppe expressly disassociates itself from all content on linked sites that has been altered since the link was created and assumes no liability for such content.

Library of Congress Control Number: 2021944318

A CIP catalogue record for this book is available from the British Library.

Creative direction/compiled and edited by: Roger Gastman

Design and layout: Leon Gonzalez

Production management: Steffen Zimmerman, Munich

Separations: Reproline Mediateam, Munich

Printing and binding: TBB, a.s.

Paper: Profisilk FSC

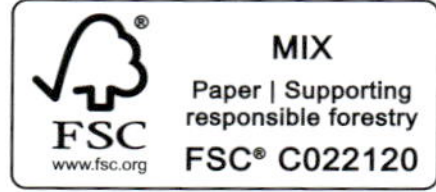

Penguin Random House Verlagsgruppe FSC® N001967

Printed in Slovakia

ISBN 978-3-7913-8874-8

www.prestel.com

www.BEYONDTHESTREETS.com

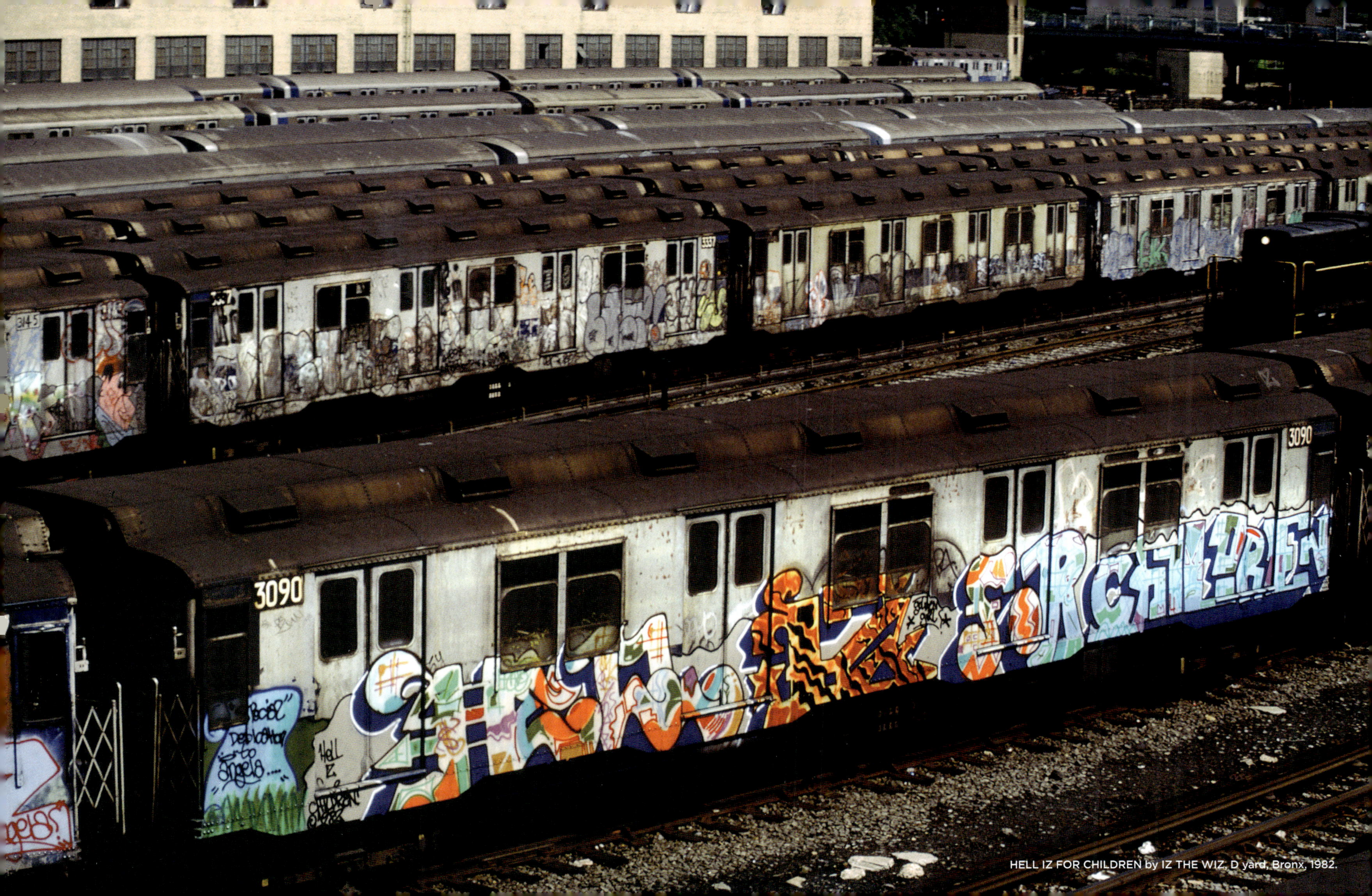

HELL IZ FOR CHILDREN by IZ THE WIZ, D yard, Bronx, 1982.

INDEX

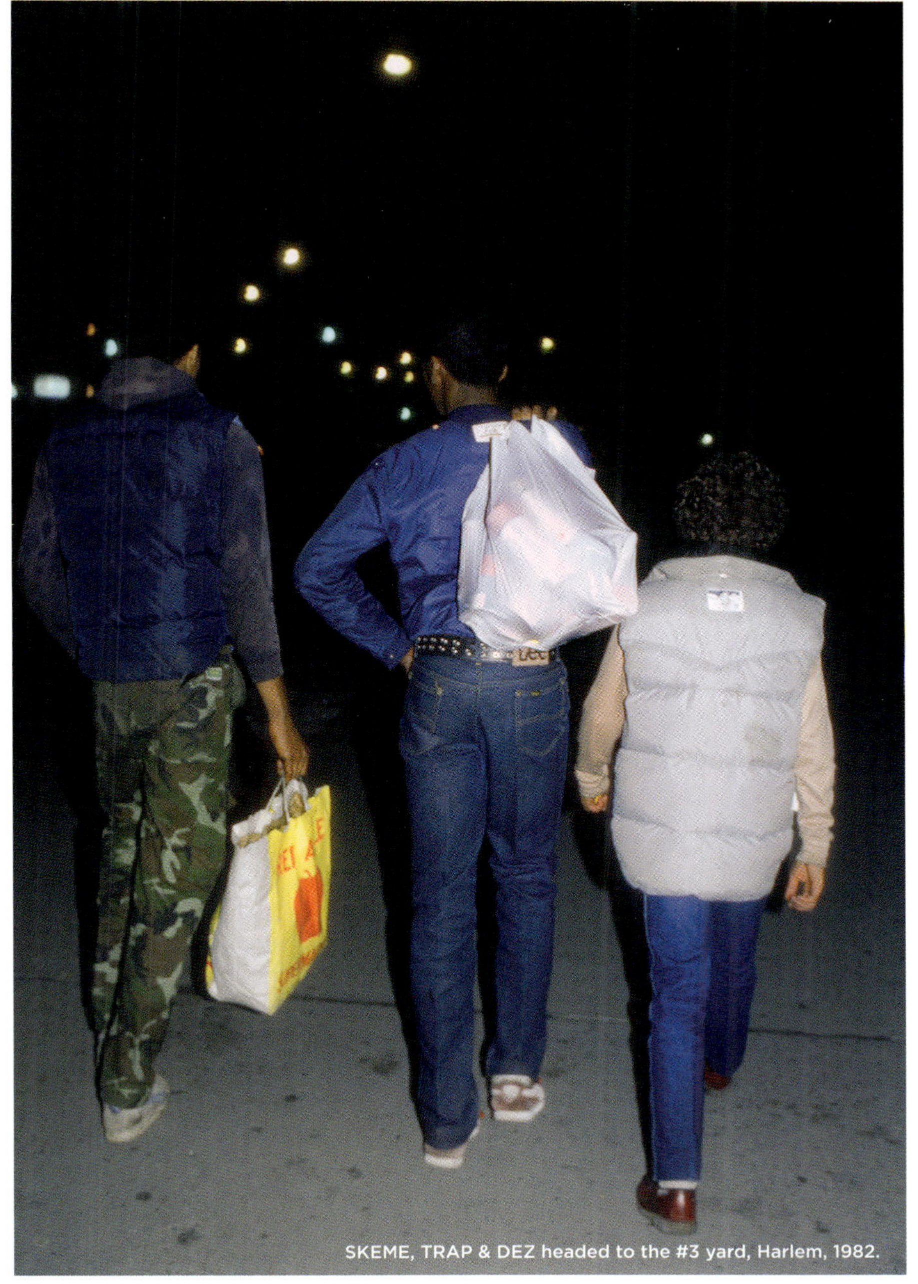

SKEME, TRAP & DEZ headed to the #3 yard, Harlem, 1982.

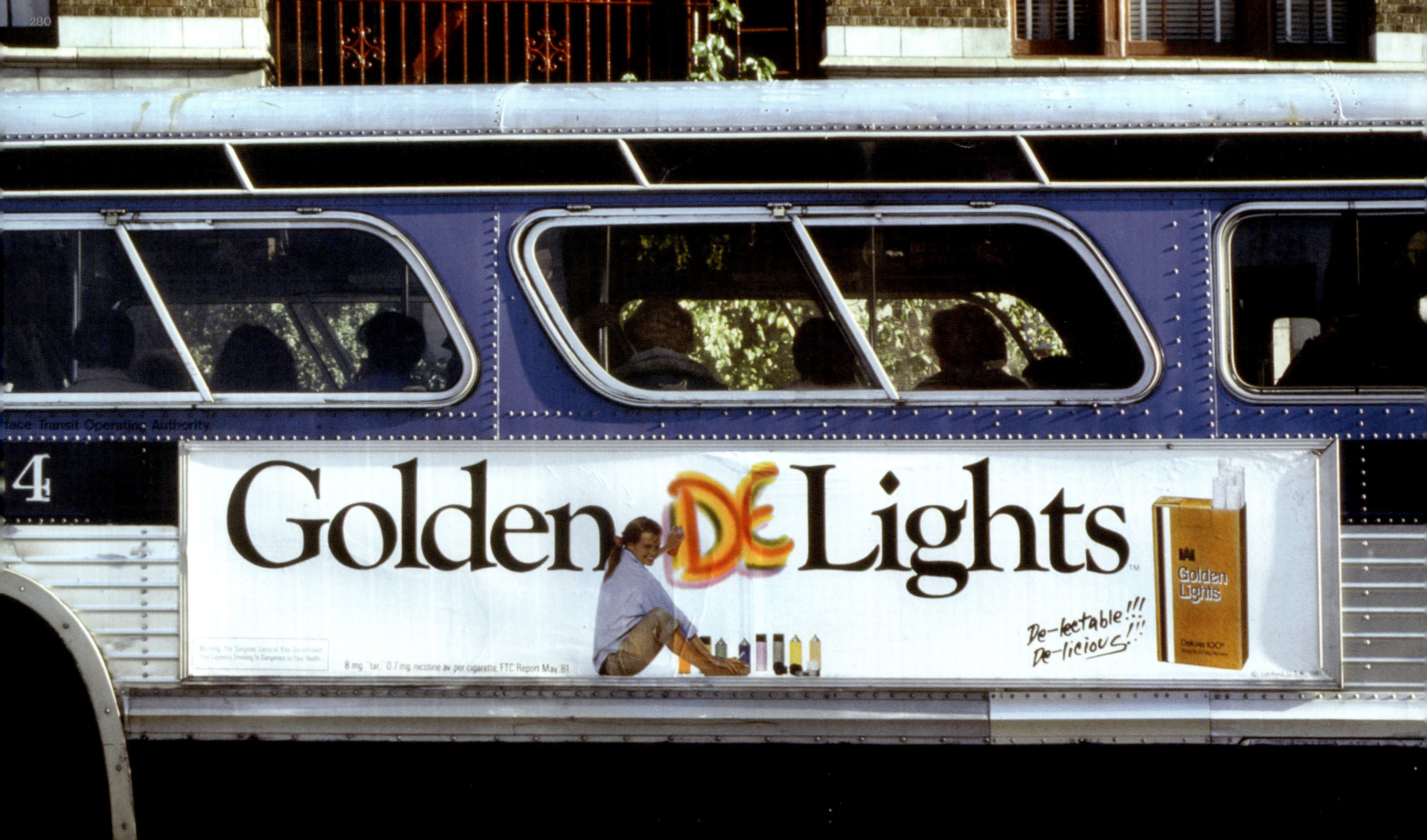
280
Surface Transit Operating Authority
4
Golden DE Lights
De-lectable!!!
De-licious!!!
Golden Lights
8 mg. "tar", 0.7 mg. nicotine av. per cigarette, FTC Report May '81

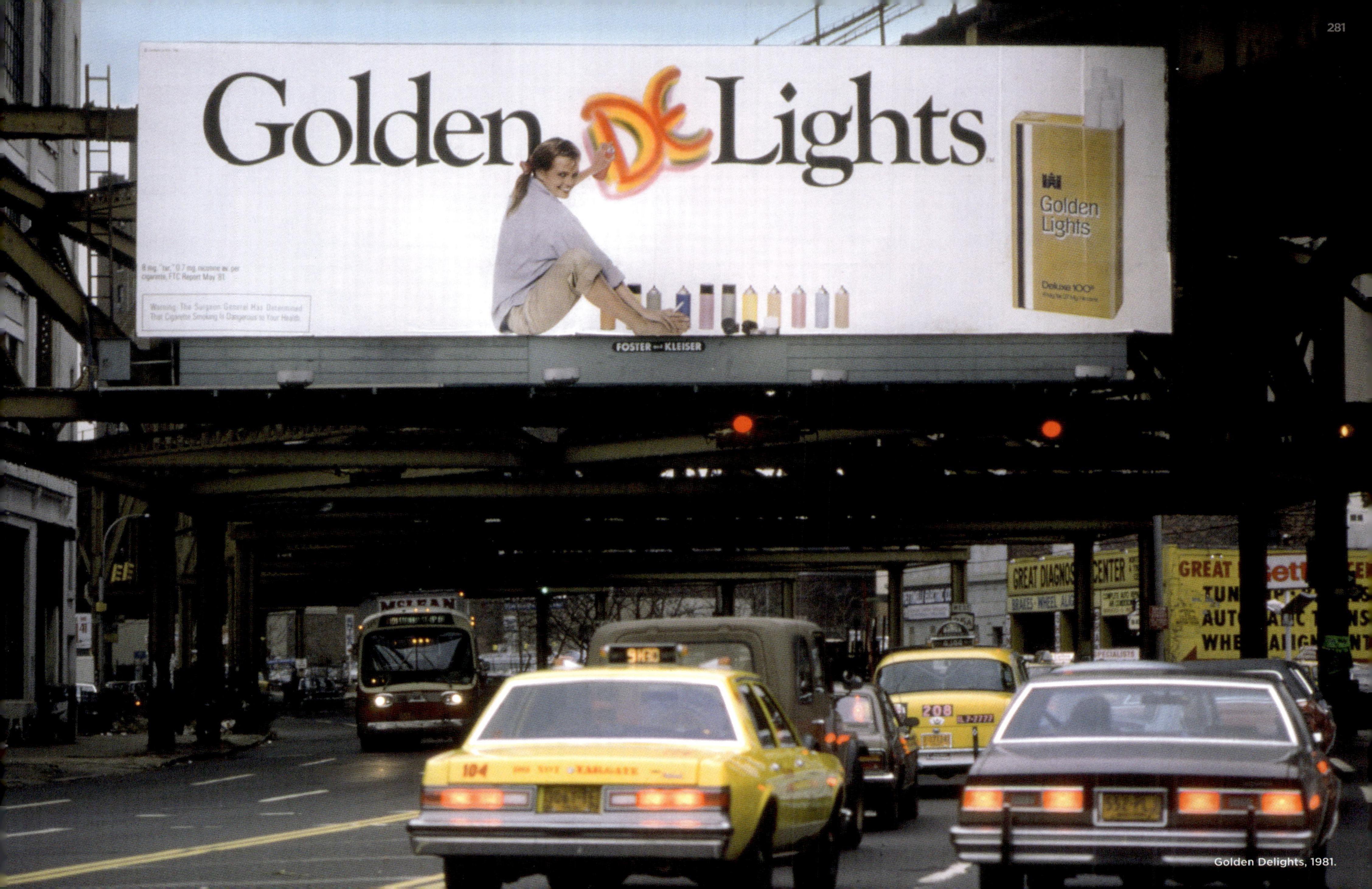

Golden Delights, 1981.

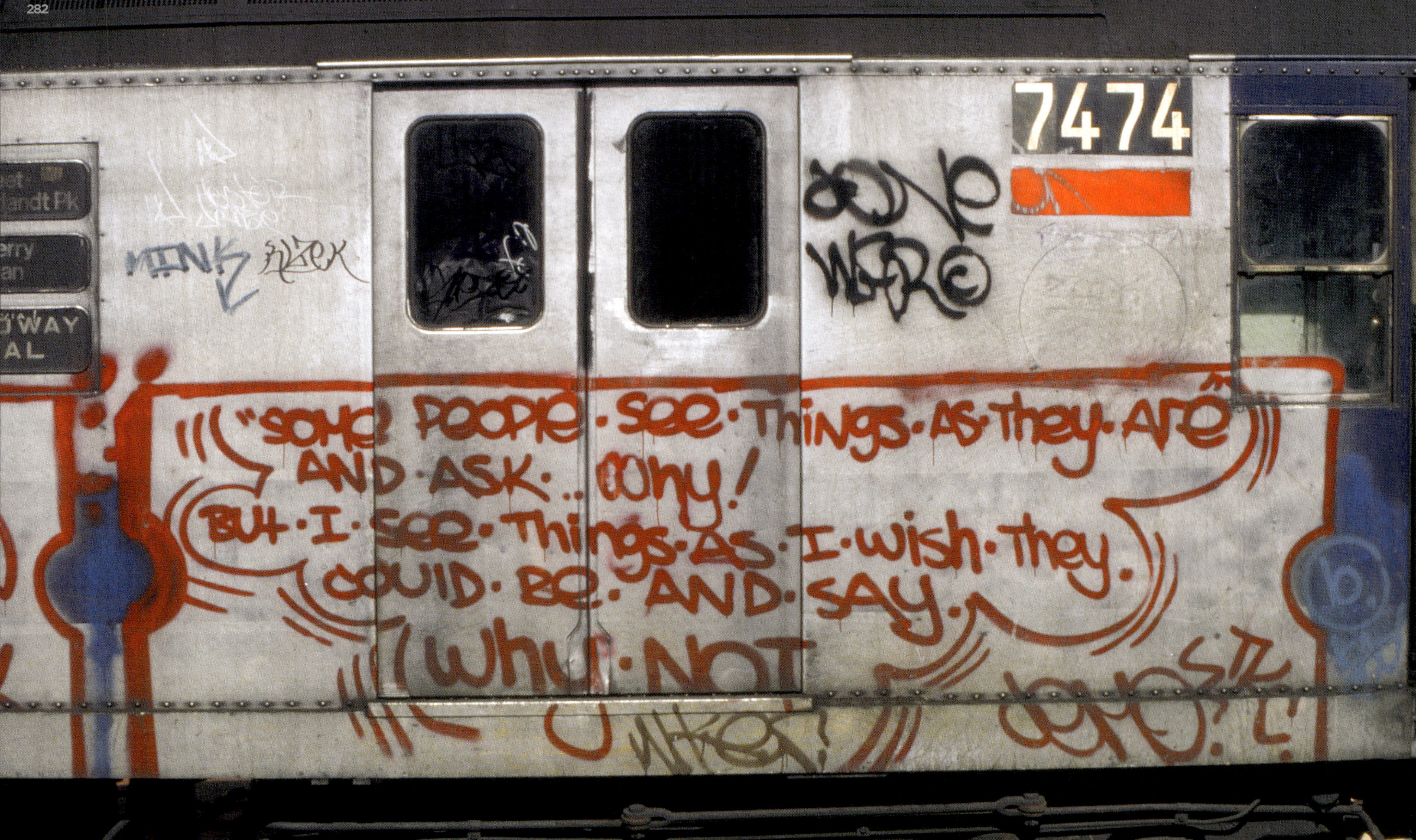
7474
"SOME PEOPLE SEE THINGS AS THEY ARE"
AND ASK ...WHY!
BUT I SEE THINGS AS I WISH THEY
COULD BE AND SAY
WHY NOT

DEMO, 1982.

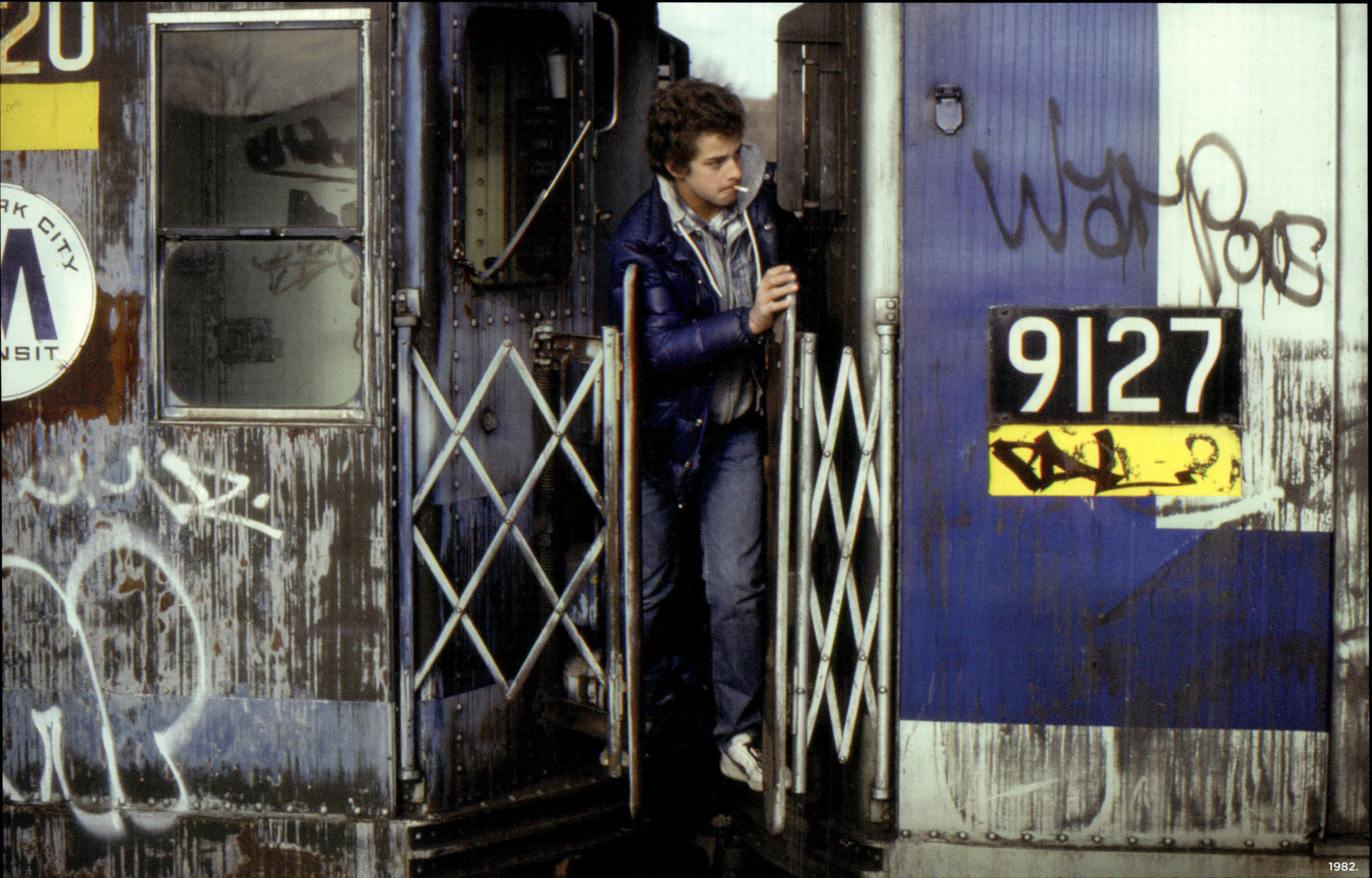

1982.

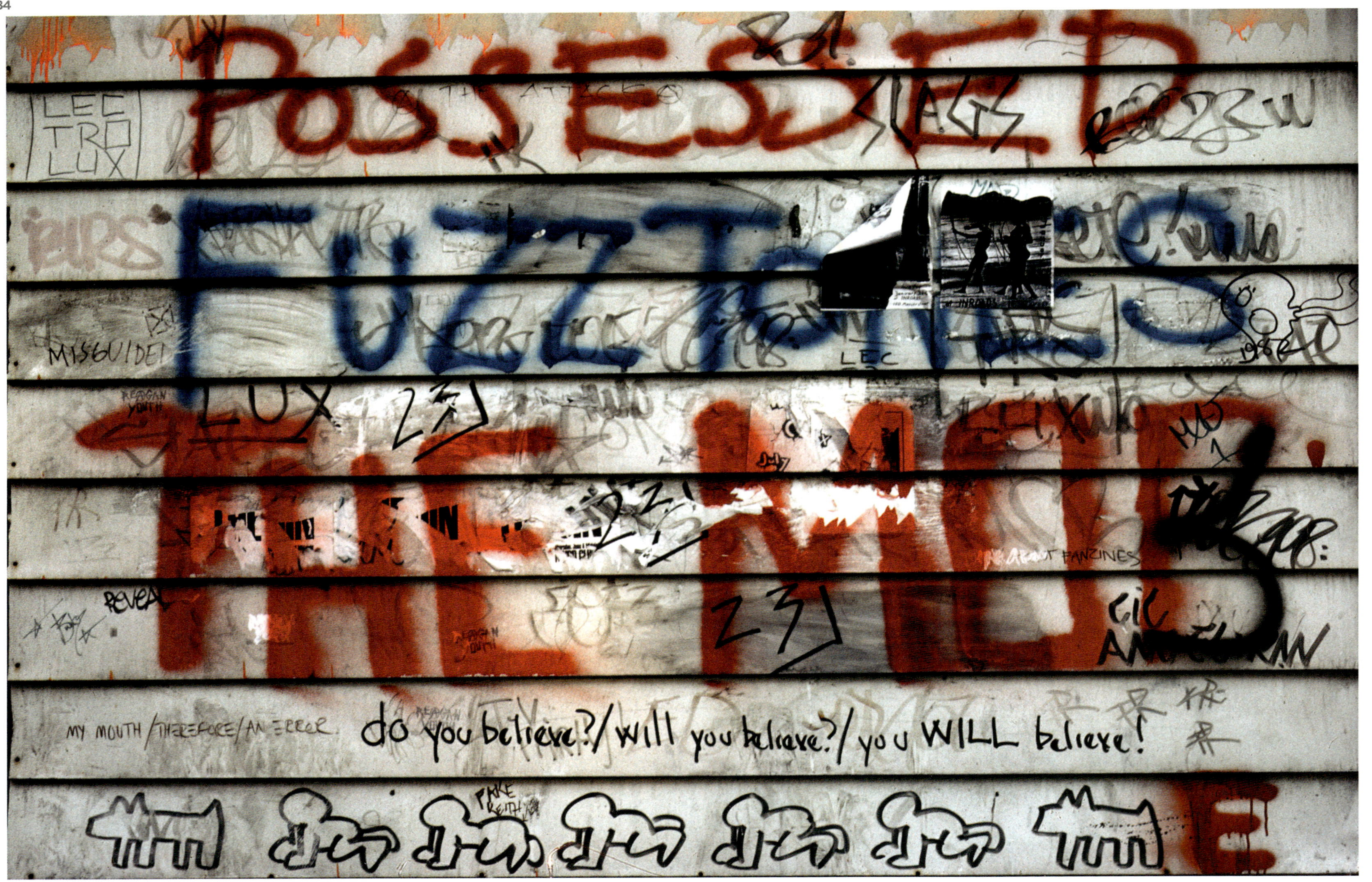
POSSESSED
FUZZTONES
LEC TRO LUX
MISGUIDED
LUX
REVEAL
MY MOUTH / THEREFORE / AN ERROR   do you believe? / will you believe? / you WILL believe!

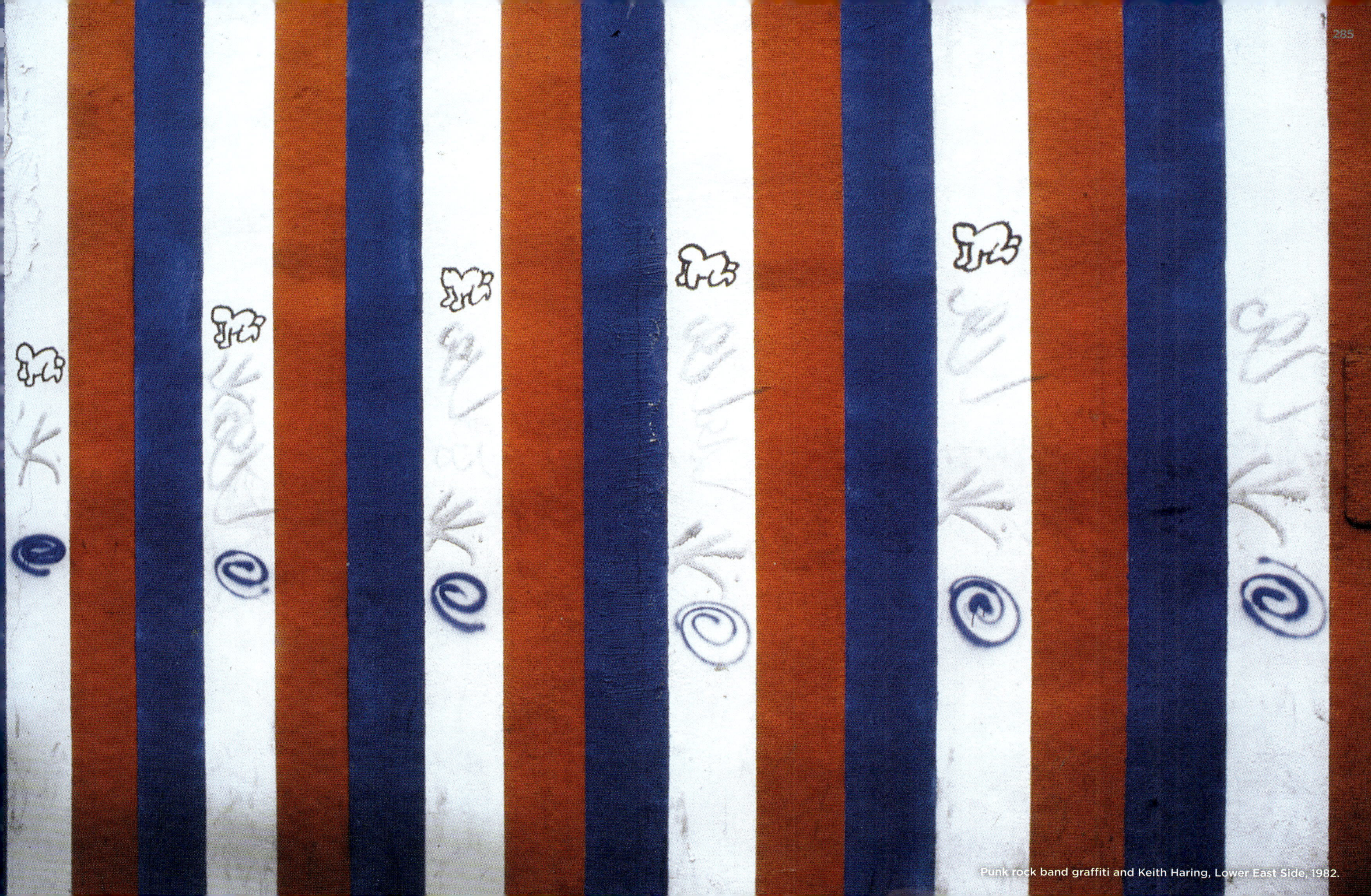

Punk rock band graffiti and Keith Haring, Lower East Side, 1982.

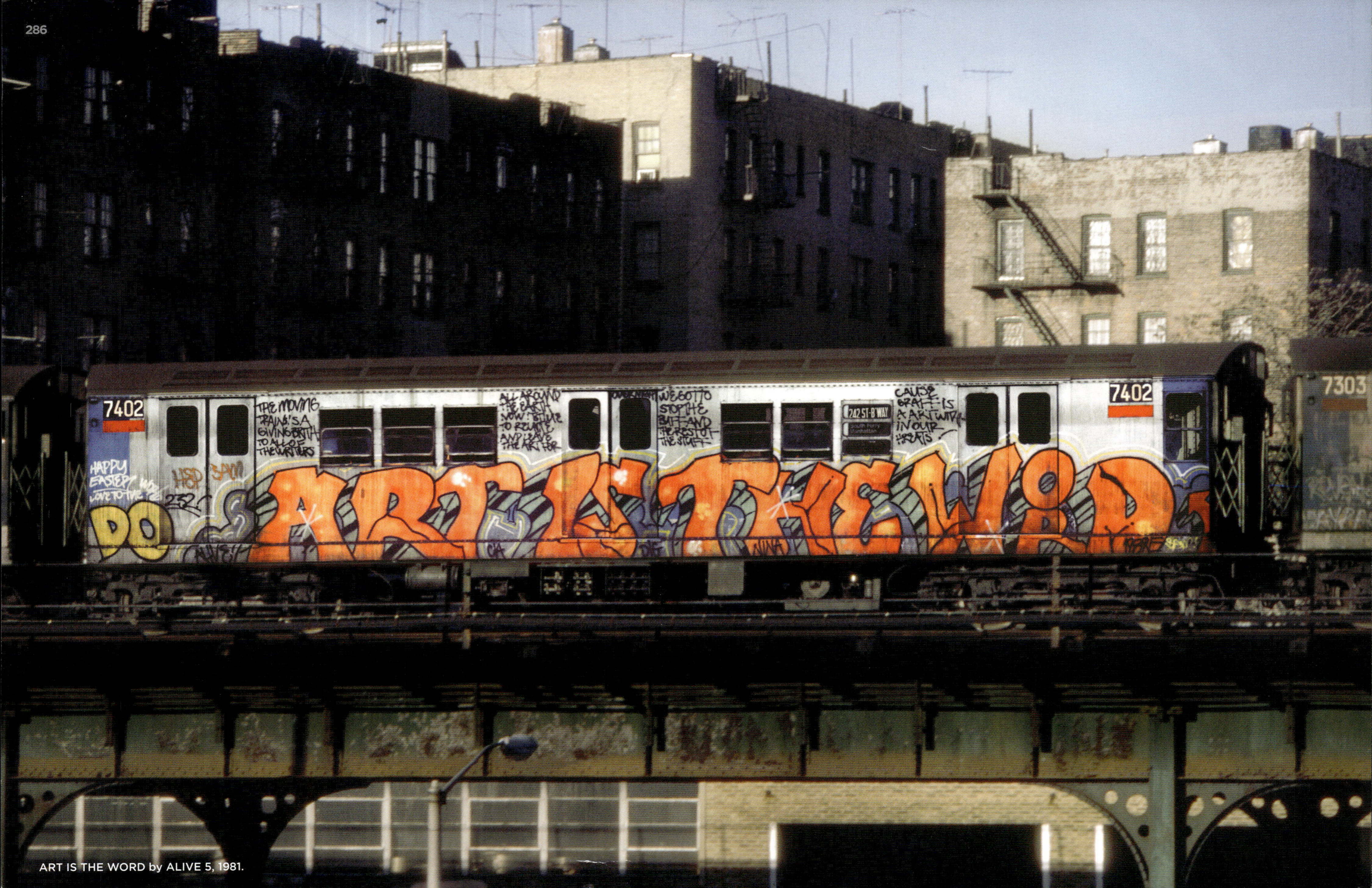

ART IS THE WORD by ALIVE 5, 1981.

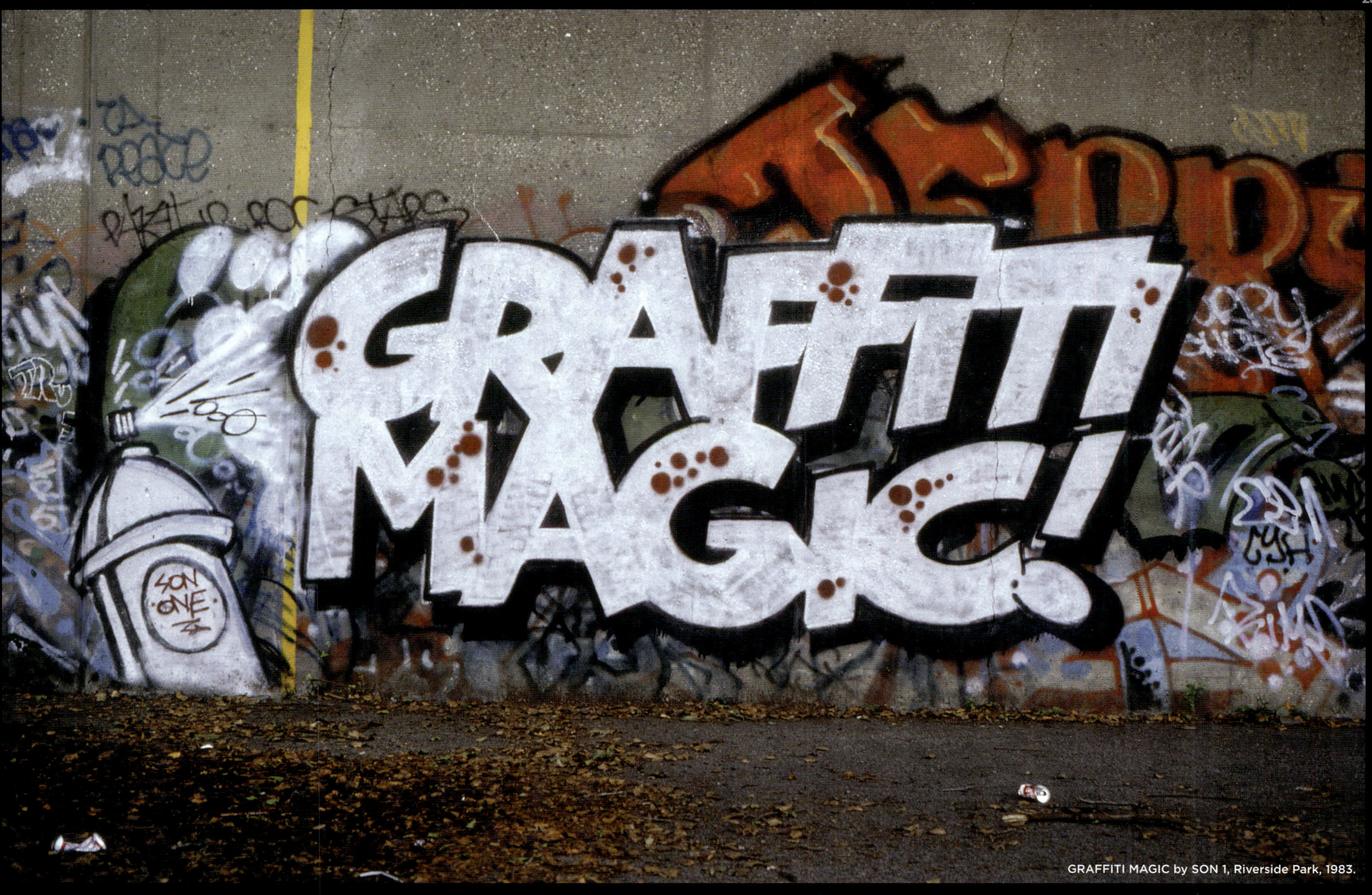

GRAFFITI MAGIC by SON 1, Riverside Park, 1983.

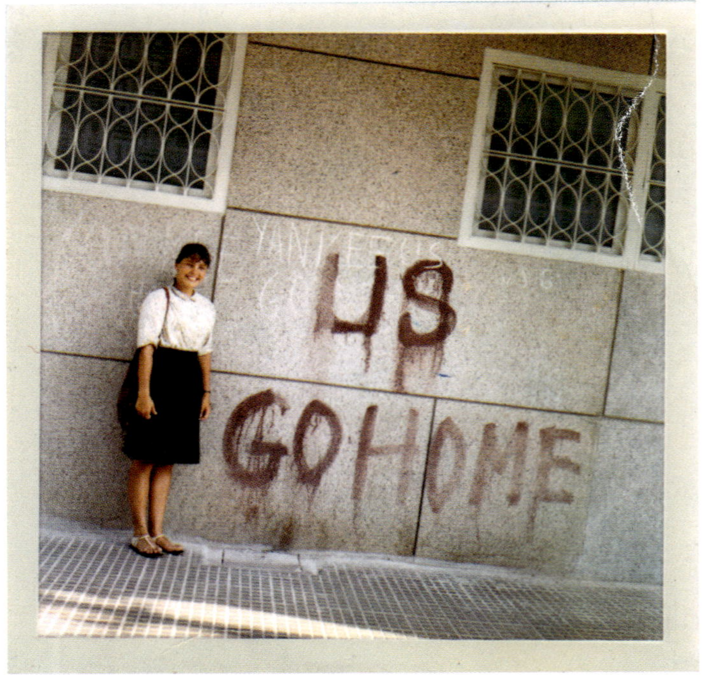

Martha Cooper traveling in Cambodia, 1964.

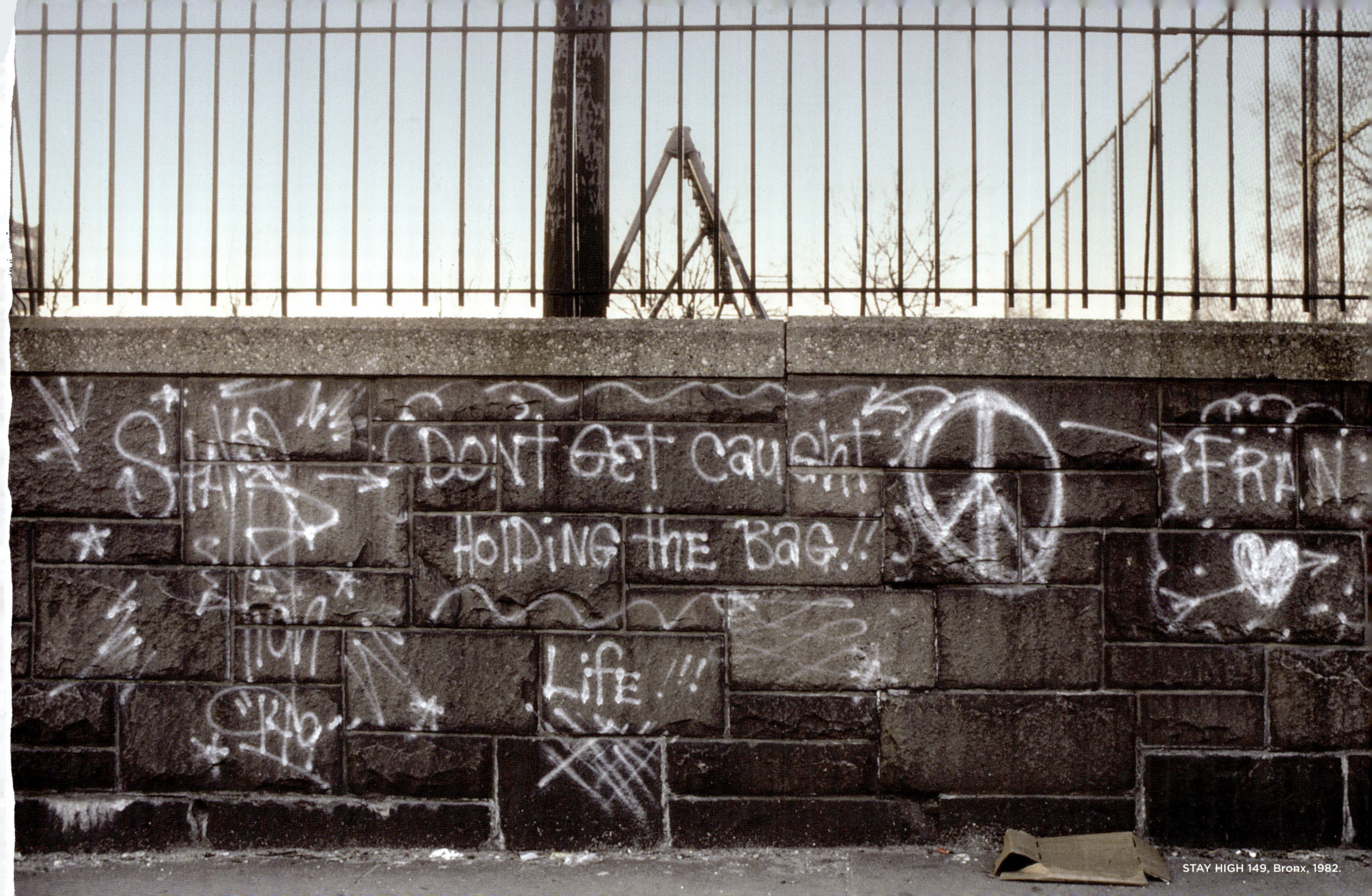

STAY HIGH 149, Bronx, 1982.